4th edition

The Office

PROCEDURES AND TECHNOLOGY

Mary Ellen Oliverio
Graduate Program
Lubin School of Business
Pace University
New York, New York

William R. Pasewark
Professor Emeritus
Texas Tech University
Office Management Consultant
Lubbock, Texas

Bonnie R. White
Professor
College of Education
Auburn University
Auburn, Alabama

THOMSON
SOUTH-WESTERN

Australia · Canada · Mexico · Singapore · Spain · United Kingdom · United States

THOMSON

SOUTH-WESTERN

The Office: Procedures and Technology, 4th Edition

Mary Ellen Oliverio, William R. Pasewark, Bonnie R. White

Editor-in-Chief:
Jack Calhoun

Vice President/Executive Publisher:
Dave Shaut

Team Leader:
Karen Schmohe

Acquisitions Editor:
Joseph Vocca

Director of Marketing:
Carol Volz

Senior Marketing Manager:
Nancy Long

Marketing Manager:
Mike Cloran

Marketing Coordinator:
Cira Brown

Consulting Developmental Editor:
Dianne S. Rankin

Editor:
Kim Kusnerak

Production Manager:
Tricia Boies

Manufacturing Coordinator:
Charlene Taylor

Copy Editor:
Denise McIntyre

Compositor:
D&G Limited, LLC

Printer:
Quebecor World
Versailles, KY

Design Project Manager:
Stacy Jenkins Shirley

Cover/Internal Designer:
Grannan Graphic Design

Cover Photos:
Courtesy of © Getty Images/
PhotoDisc, Inc. and Digital Stock

Photography Manager:
Feldman & Associates, Inc.

Photo Researcher:
Cary Benbow

Permissions Editor:
Linda Ellis

For more information, contact
South-Western
5191 Natorp Boulevard
Mason, Ohio 45040.
Or you can visit our Internet site at:
http://www.swep.com

For permission to use material from this text or
product, contact us by
Phone: 1-800-730-2214
Fax: 1-800-730-2215
http://www.thomsonrights.com

Table of Contents

Part 2

Managing Information to Enhance Productivity . . 65

TABLE OF CONTENTS

To the Student

You will enter a world of work that is being transformed. This world will be a challenging and demanding one because of the rate and nature of change. Many of the changes taking place in the workplace relate to the technology, while others relate to the changing needs of businesses and their employees. The workplace is not necessarily at a specific location. For example, four individuals in four different countries may be employed by the same multi-national corporation with each working from a home office. Yet, the four have virtually instant communication—via telecommunications—to develop plans and make decisions.

More and more, executives, managers, engineers, accountants, and administrative assistants—among others—are accessing databases, preparing electronic spreadsheets, and creating presentations. No longer are information processing tasks primarily the responsibility of secretaries and administrative assistants. All workers are expected to communicate effectively; access, analyze, and share information; make decisions; and use technology to improve productivity.

The Office, Procedures and Technology, Fourth Edition is designed to help you develop skills that will be important in your career in a professional or business position. The content you study will help prepare you to enter the workforce now and to face the inevitable changes you will encounter in the future.

Objectives for the Course

The critical concern for productivity throughout the workforce imposes on *all* workers the need to handle information management, problem-solving, and communication tasks both effectively and efficiently. These tasks must be performed skillfully for employees to achieve high productivity levels. As a student, you face a twofold challenge: to prepare for the initial demands of full-time employment and to acquire the skills to learn on the job and adapt to new procedures and technologies. This challenge is reflected in this comprehensive instructional package. *The Office, Procedures and Technology, Fourth Edition* has been designed to help you:

- Develop information management, technology, and communication skills that are valuable for all types of workers
- Develop an awareness of how to learn as new technology, processes, and procedures are introduced in an organization
- Develop a comprehensive view of time management and productivity
- Reinforce and extend basic skills involving math, language, decision making, critical thinking, and teamwork

- Develop understanding of basic qualities and attitudes that are critical in the work environment
- Develop awareness of your interests, strengths, and weaknesses related to the demands of a work environment

Features of the Textbook

The Office, Procedures and Technology, Fourth Edition is organized into 5 parts and 14 chapters. Each chapter is subdivided into two or three segments called topics. The text contains features designed to help you learn the skills and concepts presented.

Part and Topic Objectives	Part and topic objectives focus on key concepts that serve as guides in becoming familiar with the content.
Workplace Connections	These feature boxes give examples and place content discussed in a workplace context.
Focus On...	These feature boxes highlight key topics such as disaster recovery, ecommerce, and confidentiality of business information that relate to the chapter content.
Professional Development Resources	These feature boxes provide names of organizations, source references for articles from periodicals or online sources, and search terms related to content in the chapter. This information can be used for developing a professional reading file, researching topics for reports, or broadening the scope of the chapter.
Vocabulary Reinforcement	Terms of special importance or those that may be unfamiliar to some students are defined in the margin of the page on which the term is first introduced.
Activities	Activities to reinforce the major concepts and procedures and to provide realistic experience in working independently and in groups are included in each topic and at the end of each chapter.
Chapter Summary	Key points covered in the chapter are reviewed in this feature.

| **Key Terms** | Key terms that students should understand after studying the chapter are listed at the end of each chapter. |
| **Glossary** | Selected terms introduced in the text are listed and defined in the glossary. |

Student Activities and Projects Workbook

The *Student Activities and Projects* workbook designed to accompany the student textbook includes review activities for each chapter. Three workplace simulations, complete with company descriptions, instructions, documents and other materials, are provided. These simulations correspond to Parts 2, 3, and 4 of the student text. A note at the end of each of these parts reminds you when to complete the simulation for that part. A *Reference Guide* is included in the workbook and provides information helpful for completing the textbook and workbook activities. The *Reference Guide* includes the following sections:

- Section A, Proofreaders' Marks
- Section B, Punctuation
- Section C, Capitalization
- Section D, Math
- Section E, Two-Letter State Abbreviations
- Section F, Alphabetic Indexing Rules
- Section G, Sample Documents

Data Files

Data files for student use in completing activities in the textbook and the *Student Activities and Projects* workbook are provided on the *Instructor's Resource CD-ROM*. Your instructor will need to make these files available to you on disk or on your local area network. Some data files are in word processing or spreadsheet format and are to be revised or completed by the student. Other files are in Portable Document Format and are to be printed and used as source documents or reference material. In the textbook, a data disc icon identifies applications that require a data file.

 Data Disc Icon.

For the Instructor

The Office, Procedures and Technology, Fourth Edition is appropriate for any student preparing for a career that involves office skills. The textbook and related student workbook may be adapted for completion in one semester or two semesters by selecting an appropriate mix of activities from the textbook and student workbook.

PREFACE

Students should be comfortable with the basic features of their word processing, spreadsheet, database, presentation, e-mail, and browser software. Students will build skills with these programs as they complete the activities in the textbook and student workbook. Students should understand how to organize and manage the files they create during this course. You may wish to direct students regarding this issue early in the course.

Electronic Test Package

Instructors can purchase a flexible, easy-to-use test bank and test generation software program that contains objective questions for each test. Test bank questions are included for 14 chapter tests and a final exam. The *ExamView®* *Pro* software enables instructors to modify questions from the test bank or add instructor-written questions to create customized tests.

The chapter tests and a final exam are also available on the *Instructor's Resource CD-ROM* in Portable Document Format. These tests may be printed and given to students. Answers to these tests are also provided on the *Instructor's Resource CD-ROM*.

Instructor's Resource Guide

The *Instructor's Resource Guide* is available to instructors who adopt the textbook for class use. The guide is a comprehensive source for practical ideas in course planning and enrichment. The guide includes teaching and grading suggestions; solutions for chapter activities, workbook review activities, and simulations; and transparency masters.

Instructor's Resource CD-ROM

An *Instructor's Resource CD-ROM* is available to instructors who adopt the textbook for class use. The CD-ROM includes:

- Data files for use by students in completing activities for the textbook and student workbook
- Reference materials for use by students in completing exercises
- Lesson plans for the instructor
- Sample solution files for selected student activities
- Electronic slides (in Microsoft PowerPoint format) for each chapter for use during class discussions
- Transparency masters for use in class discussions
- Tests and solutions (in Portable Document Format)

Annotated Instructor's Edition

An *Annotated Instructor's Edition* (AIE) is available for instructors who adopt the textbook for class use. The AIE contains the student textbook pages in a reduced size along with annotations to assist the instructor in presenting material and facilitating student learning. The annotations provide information for:

- Challenge Option
- Expand the Concept
- For Discussion
- Getting Started
- Points to Emphasize
- Supplementary Activity
- Teaching Tips
- Thinking Critically

A Commitment by the Authors

The Office, Procedures and Technology, Fourth Edition continues a long tradition of providing training for many types of workers who function, at least in part, in an office environment. Both industry surveys and research by private and governmental organizations make clear the need for information, technology, and teamwork skills that are emphasized in this text. We believe that students with a wide range of occupational goals can profitably study together. We are committed to providing quality learning materials that will help students develop highly portable skills relevant to today's work environment.

Mary Ellen Oliverio

William R. Pasewark

Bonnie Roe White

Expect More From South-Western...

... And Get It!

Business Skills Exercises 3E provides realistic experiences for improving the skills required for entry-level business employment. Coverage includes spelling, vocabulary, filing, telephoning, and completing forms.

Text: **0-538-69481-5**

Alphabetic Indexing 6E features exercises and applications using ARMA filing standards, with an introduction to subject, numeric, and geographic filing methods.

Text: **0-538-66926-8**

Business Records Control 8E introduces the comprehensive field of records management, with emphasis on ARMA alphabetic indexing rules and procedures.

Text: **0-538-69340-1**

Office Filing Procedures 8E is an envelope simulation with 15 business record control jobs that provide hands-on activities to prepare for the world of work.

Envelope Simulation: **0-538-69330-4**

Simplifile 5E is a self-contained box simulation that can be used to provide additional filing experience using realistic source documents.

Box Simulation: **0-538-69327-4**

Calculators—Printing and Display 3E is designed to teach the ten-key touch method of operating print, display-print, or display calculators.

Text: **0-538-68247-7**

Calculator Simulation 5E is an envelope simulation that covers a variety of practical uses for an electronic display calculator, printing calculator, or combination display/printing calculator.

Envelope Simulation Complete Course: **0-538-68946-3**
Envelope Simulation Short Course: **0-538-68948-X**

Calculator Applications for Business 3E teaches how to manage time, become familiar with business forms, develop accuracy in machine operation, expand and refine math skills, and explore career opportunities. *Text:* **0-538-69799-7**

Internet Office Projects is a project-based approach to teaching about the Internet as a research tool. Each project requires students to use the Internet to accomplish realistic tasks such as searching for jobs, planning vacation and business travel, retrieving investment and financial information, marketing a business, and designing Web pages.

Text: **0-538-72186-3**

Coasters, Etc. is a beginning integrated office application simulation. Students work with Internet, e-mail, electronic scheduling, and presentation graphics utilizing word processing, spreadsheet, database, and desktop publishing software. *Simulation:* **0-538-67929-8**; *Data Disk (required):* **0-538-68262-0**

CyberStopMedia.com is a non-software-specific integrated applications simulation. As employees of a cyber business that sells CDs and DVDs, students use intermediate to advanced word processing, voice technology, spreadsheet, database, desktop publishing, and telecommunications skills to complete their tasks. *Text/CD Package (data files on CD are Windows only):* **0-538-72439-0**

Join us on the Internet at www.swep.com

Part 1

The Office in the Business World

Millions of Americans spend much of each workday in offices. Many changes in technology have occurred during the last decade. These changes have created a widespread need for knowledge and skills that are commonly referred to as office competencies. Whatever their fields of specialization or careers, workers share a need to know how to perform efficiently and effectively in offices. *The Office in the Business World* introduces you to the office as a workplace.

OBJECTIVES

- Describe the relationship of the office to the overall organization
- Describe typical goals and structures of businesses
- Identify the types of office competencies workers need
- Explain employer expectations and factors related to developing office competencies

The Office in a Changing Business World

The office is changing. Many workers now perform office tasks. The recruiter in a human resources department, the technician in a chemical laboratory, the curator in a museum, the buyer in a department store, and the CPA in a public accounting firm all perform a range of office tasks during a typical workweek. All office workers, regardless of their responsibilities, must understand the significance of office functions in relation to their work and to the total organization.

In Chapter 1, you will learn about various types of offices and office workers. You will also gain an understanding of typical goals and structures of businesses, not-for-profit entities, and governmental units.

The Office Today

OBJECTIVES

- Describe various types of offices
- Describe types of workers who use office skills
- Explain how technology influences office practices
- Identify common information-related office tasks

The term *office* is used in a variety of ways. An **office** is a place in which the affairs of a business, professional person, or organization are carried out. For example, you may have heard a lawyer say, "I will be out of the office during the afternoon," or an instructor say, "Come by my office." The office is a place of work for many categories of workers. Accountants, marketing managers, systems analysts, human resource directors, as well as secretaries, records clerks, administrative assistants, and many others work in offices. Although each of these employees has varying responsibilities, all of them must be knowledgeable about many office practices.

The office as discussed in this textbook reflects a focus on the many workers who need to understand office practices and use a variety of office skills. Regardless of what you plan for your life's work, you will benefit from studying the topics in this book and from the competencies you will develop.

office: a place in which the affairs of a business, professional person, or organization are carried out

WORKPLACE CONNECTIONS

Carole Federman is an internal auditor for an international bank with headquarters in Philadelphia. Her work requires traveling to branches throughout the United States and to such cities as Paris, Milan, and Tokyo. She must write many reports communicating her conclusions and recommendations. Carol composes her reports at her laptop computer, usually completing the reports with no assistance from office support staff.

© LARRY LAWFER/INDEX STOCK IMAGERY

Figure 1-1.1

This executive prepares reports using her laptop computer.

Offices Are Information Driven

information: data or facts that have been summarized or organized into a meaningful form

Information is made up of data or facts that have been summarized or organized into a meaningful form. Information is at the core of all office activities. Office workers use information in many ways. Some illustrations include:

- Creating information: A manager writing the policy for sales returns
- Searching for information: A securities broker accessing a database for the current price of a company's stock
- Processing information: A sales clerk entering details of a customer's order at a computer
- Communicating information: A customer service representative responding by telephone to an inquiry about procedures for installing a new piece of electronic equipment

Workers need to understand thoroughly the business or organization in which they are employed. Each task is related to the organization's purposes and goals. For example, a purchasing agent often makes telephone calls to place an order for materials or supplies. To answer questions that the **vendor** may ask, the employee needs to know the details about what is being ordered. The employee also needs to know when the item is needed, what the company believes the cost to be, and similar details.

vendor: a seller of goods or services

Office Functions Are Varied

In some offices, every employee does a wide variety of tasks. In other offices, each employee's work is more specialized or focused on a few tasks. Even within the field of administrative support services, some employees perform a limited number of tasks while others have varied tasks. Note some common information-related office tasks performed in the workplace in Figure 1-1.2. Can you identify two activities that might be completed by a manager? Can you identify two that might be performed by an office assistant? Think of a particular office career and identify two activities that might be performed by someone in that career.

WORKPLACE CONNECTIONS

Helen Serreno works as an office assistant to the director of a relatively new art gallery in Santa Fe, New Mexico. Helen talked about her job in these words:

*I never know what a day will be like. I handle all the office tasks for the director, the art assistant, and the manager of exhibits. I do some tasks every day such as open and organize the mail and write notes about the correspondence to assist the director in responding as quickly as possible. I have a **state-of-the-art** personal computer, a photocopier, a fax machine, e-mail and Internet access, and a wide range of software programs that I use daily. I'm responsible for maintaining all the equipment, too.*

state-of-the-art: using the latest technology

You might wonder why some offices are specialized while others are not. Offices that process large volumes of the same type of transaction tend to be specialized. For example, a large manufacturing company that buys 500 different raw materials is likely to have a specialized buying office. In a company that uses only a dozen raw materials, the buying may be done in an office where various other tasks are also performed.

Figure 1-1.2

KEY OFFICE ACTIVITIES

Creating/Analyzing Information
- Composing memorandums, letters, and reports
- Organizing, summarizing, and interpreting data
- Creating presentations
- Making decisions and recommendations based on information studied

Searching for Information
- Accessing databases, the Internet, and company intranets
- Inquiring of persons within the company
- Inquiring of persons outside the company
- Using reference manuals and books

Processing Information
- Editing and proofreading
- Keyboarding
- Opening and reviewing incoming communications
- Entering data in databases
- Photocopying
- Preparing outgoing communications
- Preparing checks, orders, and invoices
- Preparing spreadsheets

Communicating Information
- Answering telephones
- Greeting callers
- Responding to persons within and outside the organization
- Providing instruction to colleagues
- Preparing and delivering presentations

Managing Information
- Maintaining calendars
- Maintaining databases and files
- Maintaining financial records

Even though many employees handle office tasks, some individuals, as well as entire departments, devote full time to administrative support services. These tasks are also referred to as office support services. Some organizations, for example, have a word processing center where reports, letters, and other documents are prepared. Specialized office functions are often necessary for achieving the goals of the company.

The president of a midsize bank in Columbia, South Carolina, talked about the role of administrative support services in these words:

*From the communication of our **mission statement**, which provides the overall inspiration for all our employees, to the timely payment of wages and salaries, we are completely dependent on the large staff of dedicated office employees. There would be chaos throughout this company without our efficient and effective office personnel. We value them and provide them with state-of-the-art technology.*

mission statement: the goals, priorities, and beliefs of a company

Figure 1-1.3

The assistant manager in a small company is instructing a new staff member.

Technology in Modern Offices

The use of technology is common in today's offices. The architect that designs and constructs buildings works at a computer. An executive uses the World Wide Web to find a schedule for travel to London and Madrid. Sales people from several states communicate with the regional manager at headquarters in Philadelphia using a company **intranet**.

intranet: communications network within an organization that is meant for the use of its employees or members

Many companies use up-to-date technology in their offices to help employees be highly productive. Because the technology available is changing, the way work is accomplished is also changing. Workers may expect their responsibilities, as well as the way they work, to change markedly from time to time. The pressure for high productivity and quality performance means that all workers must be willing to participate in change. Furthermore, office workers must be skillful learners—on their own and in more formal training and educational settings.

Marie Ann describes what she is doing today that she was not doing just three years earlier:

Three years ago, we were a domestic company. Today we do business in 60 countries. I regularly send e-mail messages to China, Singapore, Hong Kong, Prague, and Moscow, and other places around the world. I used to prepare printed letters, place hard copies of correspondence in a file drawer, and conduct research by telephone. Now I send e-mail messages instead of letters in many cases, use databases and electronic files to store information, and access the Internet to research and communicate information.

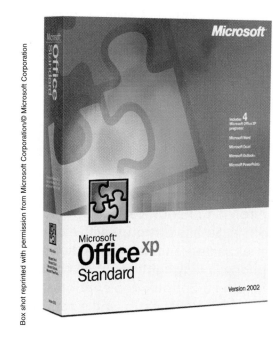

Box shot reprinted with permission from Microsoft Corporation© Microsoft Corporation

Figure 1-1.4

Many companies upgrade their software regularly to help employees be more productive.

Alternative Offices

Where is the office? The office may be at headquarters, in a carrying bag, or at home. It may be a temporarily assigned workspace. No longer is the office always a particular space used for the same purpose day after day.

The typical office from earlier days is referred to as the traditional office. A traditional office is permanent and located where the company does business. In such an office, employees travel daily to a central location. They spend the working day at the same desk or in the same workspace and generally report directly to a supervisor or manager. Many businesses still use traditional offices; however, other types of work arrangements are being used more frequently.

The practice of working and communicating with others from a home office or other remote location is called telecommuting. A worker who **telecommutes** shares information with clients or coworkers using the **Internet** or intranet connections and equipment such as a computer, telephone, and fax machine. These workers may work in virtual offices, mobile offices, or home offices.

telecommute: the practice of working and communicating with others from a remote location

Internet: a public, worldwide computer network made up of smaller, interconnected networks that spans the globe

7

Topic 1-1: *The Office Today*

Professional Development Resources

— International Association of Virtual Office Assistants (IAVOA)
Rt. 1 Box 275
Red Oak, OK 74563
www.iavoa.com

— Mary Campbell. "Introducing Virtual Assistants." ABCNews.com. Online. Available: http://abcnews.go.com/sections/business/dailynews/sbb_va980520/. October 30, 2001.

— Morgan Luciana Danne. "Changing Spaces in Workplaces." *Building Design & Construction.* May, 2001.

— Search terms:
home office
mobile office
office competencies
office technology
telecommute

virtual office: the capability to perform work activities away from a traditional office setting

mobile office: an office temporarily located at a particular site or one that can move from place to place

nonterritorial workspace: area not assigned to a specific person or task

hoteling: assigning temporary office workspace to workers as needed

Virtual Office

The term *virtual* describes something that has a conceptual form but no physical form that you can see or touch. For example, you are acquainted with your local library, a physical building that contains shelves of books you can use to get information. A virtual library might be a computer station capable of providing you access to many libraries from your school or home. Although the virtual library has no physical form, it allows you to gather information just as a physical library does. The **virtual office**, therefore, has no physical form but allows you to perform work activities as you would in a traditional office setting.

Just as some office workers use virtual offices, some offices use virtual workers. A virtual assistant is a worker with office skills who performs tasks normally handled by an on-site secretary or administrative assistant. This growing field provides advantages to both the company and the virtual assistant. A virtual assistant can work from a home office, set her or his own work schedule, and work only as many hours per week as desired. Virtual assistants do not require on-site office space and are usually paid only for the hours they work. This means cost savings for the company, which can be especially important for small businesses.

WORKPLACE **CONNECTIONS**

Susan Gray is a successful interior designer in St. Louis. Although Susan refers to her office as the portable office, it is really a virtual office. Susan visits prospective clients as well as clients for whom projects are under way. In her bag she can carry a cellular phone, a very lightweight computer with fax and e-mail capabilities, and a portable copier/printer. Susan can provide plans for a room, cost estimates, and a contract right in the client's living room.

Mobile Office

Mobile offices are very much like traditional offices, but they are temporary. Offices set up at construction sites and manned by office staff are one type of mobile office. Another type of mobile office is the **nonterritorial workspace**. Nonterritorial workspaces are available on an assignment basis. They are not assigned to anyone permanently. This type of workspace is often found in professional organizations. For example, an accounting firm or law firm may have many staff members who work away from the company a great deal of the time. Because such personnel do not need a permanent office, they can request an office on their arrival at headquarters.

The use of nonterritorial workspace is sometimes referred to as **hoteling**. The assignment process is similar to that of a hotel assigning a room to a guest. Computer software makes maintaining information and assigning

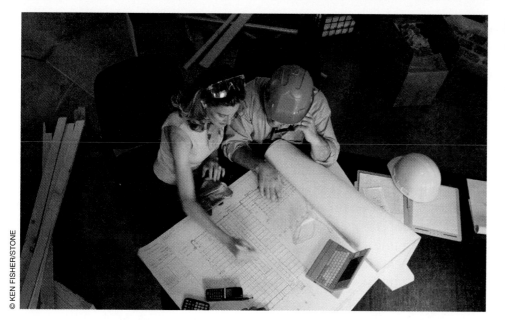

Figure 1-1.5

Two architects review building plans in a mobile office.

space prompt and effective. Employees who generally work from a home office, for example, may be assigned office space on those infrequent occasions when they do work at the company office.

Home Office

A space within a person's home that is organized for the efficient performance of office tasks on a full- or part-time basis is referred to as a **home office**. In many home offices, workers can communicate easily with others using e-mail, the Internet, an intranet, fax, and the telephone. Some people who work at home are able to participate in teleconferencing with persons at headquarters as well as at other locations in any part of the world.

Many people who work in home offices are self-employed. Such persons are often called **freelancers**. Freelancers may occasionally meet with customers or clients in person. However, they may communicate primarily by e-mail, telephone, and mail.

home office: space within a person's home that is organized for the efficient performance of office tasks

freelancer: independent contractors who work for others, usually on a project-by-project basis

Figure 1-1.6

Freelancers often work from home offices.

Ingrid Thomason owns and manages an accounting service business as a freelancer, working from her home. Having worked in the accounting department of a large company, she is knowledgeable about accounting systems. She decided that she would prefer to live in a small rural town and believed there were many small businesses that would find her service appealing. She was successful in finding as many clients as she could handle. Her state-of-the-art computer and software programs allow clients to transmit financial information to her for processing and organizing. Her clients have online access to their financial statements on a timely basis. Ingrid notes that she has a number of clients that she has never seen in person!

Predictions Are for Further Change

The current era is considered one of rapid change. However, all organizations do not apply change at the same rate or in the same way. Some companies monitor changes in technology and introduce the newest equipment and software related to their work as quickly as possible. Such organizations see the value in updating their operations. At the same time, other companies decide that no changes are needed.

A company with the latest ideas and technology, though, may not necessarily be as effective and efficient as a company that continues to use more traditional ideas and technology. New technology may be an aid to high productivity, but it does not ensure that high productivity will take place. For example, dedicated workers may be able to complete more work with older equipment than indifferent workers are able to complete with the latest equipment. Over time, however, highly successful technology tends to be accepted by most organizations.

Reviewing the Topic

1. List five information-related office tasks.

2. What kinds of employees need office competencies?

3. As you consider the office functions in Figure 1-1.2, identify at least three that you believe would require skill in using equipment.

4. As you consider the office functions in Figure 1-1.2, identify at least two that you believe at this point you could handle. Explain why.

5. Why might an organization have specialized offices? Give an illustration of such an office.

6. How does a traditional office differ from a virtual office, a mobile office, and a home office?

7. What makes telecommuting a feasible way of handling office work?

8. The offices in Company A are state-of-the-art, while those in Company B are traditional. Explain the difficulty of determining which offices are most effective.

Making Decisions

Assume that you have completed your studies and are seeking your first full-time position. You have been interviewed by personnel recruiters in two companies. Each company has offered you a position. You like both companies as far as the nature of the work, the salary, and the employee benefits. But there is a difference in where you will work.

In Company A, you would be expected to come to headquarters each day. The company has excellent computer facilities, and the supervisor seems very helpful and friendly. In Company B, you would be telecommuting. Company B would provide you with all the equipment and furniture for your workstation at home. You would have access to the supervisor via telecommunications. From time to time—possibly no more than once in three weeks—you would be expected to attend a training session or a team meeting at headquarters. Which position would you accept?

1. Make a list of the factors you would consider in making a decision.

2. Write a brief paragraph in which you discuss your decision and the basis for it.

Reinforcing English Skills

For a group of words to be a complete sentence, they must contain both a subject and a verb. In this exercise, you will identify complete and incomplete sentences. You will change incomplete sentences into complete sentences, choosing words that make sense to you.

1. Open the data file **Sentence**. Read the paragraphs, noting which sentences are complete and which are incomplete.
2. For all incomplete sentences, add a word or words to make complete sentences.
3. Save your edited sentences.

Note: Save all documents created for exercises in this textbook using meaningful file names. Print documents or e-mail them to your instructor as your instructor directs. Keep all files for possible use in other exercises.

COMPOSITION
INTEGRATED DOCUMENT
RESEARCH
SPREADSHEET
TEAMWORK
WORD PROCESSING

Topic 1-1   ACTIVITY 1

Getting Acquainted with Local Offices

In this activity, you will become familiar with the types of offices in your own community. Work in a team with three other class members to complete this activity.

1. Develop a list of four or five major employers in your area.
2. Find answers to the following questions through inquiry or observation.
   • What is the primary product(s) or service(s) of the business or organization?
   • What percentage of the employees work in offices at this location?
   • How many workers telecommute? If there are workers who telecommute, how many of them are considered office workers?
   • What technology is being used in preparing letters and memorandums? for telecommunications? for records management?
   • In general, determine if the technology in use is state-of-the-art, somewhat up-to-date, or primarily a noncomputerized type.
3. Prepare a written report of one to two pages in which you present the information you gathered. Use spreadsheet software to prepare a pie chart showing office use of technology that is current, somewhat current, and not current. Incorporate this pie chart in your report.
4. Participate in a discussion that summarizes what offices are like in your community.

12

Topic 1-1   ACTIVITY 2

Qualifying as a Home Office

In the United States, a person who works in a home office may be able to deduct costs related to the home office from federal income taxes. The home office and its use must meet certain requirements, however. You will learn about those requirements in this activity.

1. Open the data file **Qualifying** and read the excerpt from IRS Publication 587, Business Use of Your Home.

2. Briefly describe the requirements a home office must meet to qualify for a business tax deduction.

3. A freelance writer uses a portion of her den for a home office. The den is also used as a family gathering place for watching TV and playing games. Does this home office qualify for a business tax deduction? Why or why not?

4. Publication 587 was published for use in preparing year 2000 tax returns. Have the regulations changed for the current year? Access the IRS Web site at www.irs.gov. Search the site using the term *home office* to find current regulations. Explain how current regulations differ from those in Publication 587.

5. Prepare a one-page flyer that summarizes the requirements for a home office to qualify for a business tax deduction. Use the current information you found on the IRS Web site or the information from Publication 587 to prepare the flyer. Include a source note on the flyer similar to the one shown in the file **Qualifying**. Use different font sizes, bullets, graphics, or other design elements to create an attractive, easy-to-read flyer.

13

OBJECTIVES

- Explain how employees develop understanding of organizations in which they work
- Describe common types of organizations
- Identify goals for different types of organizations
- Explain a common structure for personnel
- Describe the role of office employees within an organization

Office tasks are related to the work of others in the organization. Completing tasks often requires judgment and making decisions. Understanding the organization will help you make sound decisions in completing your work.

Understanding the Organization

Office activities are basically related to information. Through creating, processing, communicating, and maintaining information, you learn much about your organization. Such learning, however, is not automatic. You must make an effort to learn about the company. Tasks become more interesting and employees become more valuable when they give attention to understanding their organizations.

Learning from Your Work

confidential: private or secret in nature

The information you handle is related to your organization. You should be alert to opportunities to learn from the content of your work. Of course, you must realize at all times the information you handle may be **confidential**.

WORKPLACE CONNECTIONS

acquisitions: that which is purchased

Linda Jansen works for a senior vice president, Mr. Roberts, in a large advertising company. Mr. Roberts is involved in buying several small advertising agencies. Linda knows that much information about possible **acquisitions** is confidential. She notes for her own use, however, information from reports and other documents. She finds that her understanding of the specific deadlines, for example, can help her prioritize her work.

Learning from Resources Available

Many organizations encourage employees to become well acquainted with the total company's work. Annual reports contain much valuable information about the company's achievements. These reports are sometimes provided to all employees. Employees find such reports helpful, for example, in understanding the company's mission as well as its goals for the coming fiscal year. Company newsletters and other communications are also valuable sources for employees.

Figure 1-2.1

Reading trade magazines is a good way to learn about trends in your field.

© JOHN A. RIZZO/PHOTODISC

Noting articles in local newspapers or periodicals about your organization is a worthwhile practice. Employees frequently have access to publications or Web sites that deal with the industry in which the company operates. These sources also provide information for increasing understanding of the company's business. Workers who understand the company know whom to call when they need information related to their work or to answer an inquiry from someone else.

Types of Organizations

In the United States, organizations are categorized as businesses, not-for-profit entities (but not governmental), or governmental units. The goals of these organizations vary, as well as their methods of operation.

Businesses

Businesses are organizations that seek to make a **profit**. For the most part, businesses in the United States are organized as single proprietorships, partnerships, or corporations. Additionally, some variations within the type of organization exist. Single proprietorships and partnerships can be organized without approval by any governmental body. Corporations, on the other hand, are required to secure **charters** from the states in which they incorporate. All businesses, regardless of form, must adhere to the laws and regulations governing business activity.

profit: monetary gain; advantage

charter: written grant of rights from a government

Single Proprietorship

A business owned by one individual is a **single proprietorship**. Such a business may or may not also be managed by the owner. Single proprietorships may be of any size, but many of them are small. Welsh Internal Access is an example of a small business. This small company with about 1,000 customers provides Internet access for companies as well as consulting services for those who want to build intranets.

single proprietorship: a business owned by one individual, also called sole proprietorship

Figure 1-2.2

These attorneys have formed a partnership.

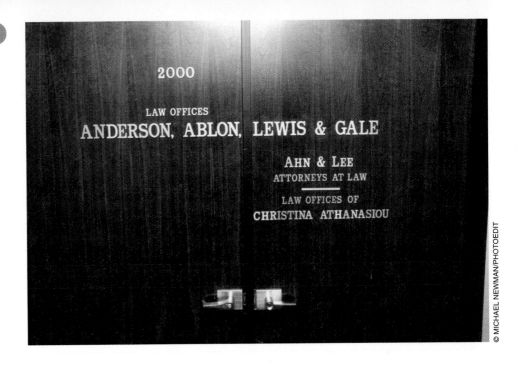

Partnership

partnership: a business that is not incorporated and has two or more owners

A business that is not incorporated and has two or more owners is known as a **partnership**. Different types of partners may participate in a partnership. Some partners may provide funds for the business but not participate in managing it. Other partners may actively lead and manage the business. Partnerships, too, may be of any size; many are small, however.

Ramos & Saunders Graphics is an example of a partnership owned and operated by Bill Ramos and Sally Saunders. The business provides a wide range of artistic services to a variety of clients.

Corporation

corporation: a business organized under the laws of a particular state for which a charter was secured

A business organized under the laws of a particular state for which a charter was secured is a **corporation**. Corporations may be privately or publicly owned. Owners have shares of ownership, which are represented by stock certificates. Owners are called stockholders or shareholders. The corporation is considered a legal unit, separate from its shareholders. Most large companies in the United States are corporations. Publicly owned corporations are required to report to shareholders on a timely basis. Such reports become available to many others besides the stockholders.

S. C. Johnson and Son, Inc. is an example of a privately owned corporation. The company develops and sells software systems to individuals, companies, and government agencies.

Professional Service Organizations

Professional service organizations are considered businesses, too. Professionals such as lawyers, physicians, dentists, and accountants operate their businesses as single proprietorships, partnerships, or corporations. The laws and regulations governing a company of professional persons, such as physicians, however, are different from those that apply to other businesses.

Shareholders in a corporation, for example, are generally not held responsible for the behavior of managers of the business. If the business has debts that it cannot pay, shareholders cannot be forced to pay those debts. Members of a professional service organization, however, may be **liable** for each other's actions as well as for the debts of the company. For example, suppose one accountant in a firm is sued for **negligence** in managing a client's affairs and found guilty. All members of the firm can be forced to help pay the damages awarded to the client. If the firm does not have enough money to pay the damages, members can be forced to use their personal money to pay the debt.

liable: responsible, legally bound or obligated

negligence: failure to use a reasonable amount of care resulting in damage

A professional company may choose to organize as a limited liability company (LLC) or a limited liability partnership (LLP). Both these forms offer some personal liability protection to members of the company. For example, in an LLC a member generally cannot be forced to use personal money to pay for debts of the company. Note, however, that an LLC does not protect a member from liability created by his or her own negligence or criminal activity.

Not-for-Profit Entities

Many organizations in the United States provide services without the intent of making profits. Among these organizations are associations that sponsor programs for young people, such as 4-H clubs, Girl Scouts, Boy Scouts, and the Future Business Leaders of America. Other common not-for-profit groups include centers for performing arts, museums, libraries, hospitals, and private colleges and universities. Many hospitals and schools, however, do operate as businesses and do seek to be profitable.

© RUDI VON BRIEL/INDEX STOCK IMAGERY

Figure 1-2.3

This museum is a not-for-profit entity.

Topic 1-2: *The Office in Relation to the Total Organization*

Not-for-profit organizations secure funds from a variety of sources. Many depend on contributions from individuals and groups. They also receive money from dues and fees paid by participants. In some instances, funds are provided to not-for-profit entities by government agencies at the local, state, or federal level. For example, the Metropolitan Museum of Art in New York City is a not-for-profit institution that gets some funding from the local government. Increasingly, not-for-profit entities operate in what is referred to as a businesslike manner. This means that resources are carefully budgeted as though the entity were a profit-making business.

Governmental Units

Governmental units at the local, state, and national levels play a critical role in society. These units are called by different names such as agency, commission, bureau, department, and board. Each unit has specific responsibilities for services considered important for the citizens served. Examples include:

National	Department of the Treasury, Bureau of Labor Statistics, Environmental Protection Agency
State or Province	Department of Commerce, Occupational Safety & Health Division
Local	Marriage License Bureau, Board of Education

Figure 1-2.4

The EPA's mission is to protect human health and to safeguard the natural environment.

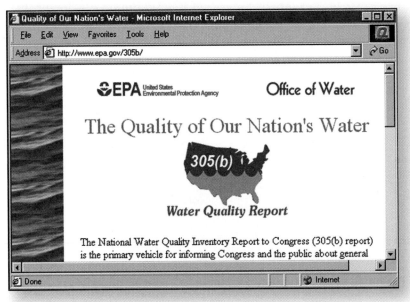

Source: U.S. Environmental Protection Agency. Online. Available: http://www.epa.gov. November 5, 2001.

Goals of Organizations

Each of the three major types of organizations has different overall goals. Businesses, including professional companies, seek to make a profit. On the other hand, not-for-profit entities and governmental units do not seek to earn profits. They have overall goals, however, that relate to the services they provide. These goals influence the work of organization employees.

Goals of Businesses

You may have heard a comment such as, "It's the bottom line that counts." Prior to the comment, a discussion may have taken place about what a business should choose to do. Various strategies for increasing profits may have been discussed. In general, strategies that will provide the most profit are selected. This increases "the bottom line"—the amount of profit shown on the bottom line of the company's profit and loss statement. Profits allow a business to expand through investment in new facilities and new equipment. Profits also provide the means to make payments (called dividends) to shareholders in a corporation.

WORKPLACE CONNECTIONS

Many tasks that workers perform relate to helping to meet the profit goals of the business.

Hans Welenz works in the customer service department for a large personal computer manufacturing company. The company sells computers nationwide, primarily to businesses. Hans's main task is to understand exactly a complaint or question from a customer. He gives the information to the person in the company who can help the customer. Hans and other staff members try to answer all complaints or questions within 24 hours. Hans knows that his work aids the company in meeting profit goals. A satisfied customer will be likely to buy more computers in the future. A dissatisfied customer is likely to make future purchases from another company.

A profit and loss statement may also be called an income statement. An income statement details the results of business operations for a certain period of time. It answers the question, "How successful was the business during the time period?" The income statement lists the amounts and sources of **revenues**, as well as **expenses**, and the income (profit) or loss of a business for the reporting period. A net income results if revenues are greater than expenses. A net loss results if expenses are greater than revenues. Dandy's Delights' (a single proprietorship) income statement for the recently ended fiscal year is shown in Figure 1-2.5 on page 20.

revenue: income, money, or other gain received

expense: financial cost; fee; charge

assets: goods and property owned

liabilities: debts

owner's equity: owner's share of the worth of a firm; capital

A balance sheet is a report that presents the financial condition of a company as of a specific date. The balance sheet reports the **assets, liabilities,** and **owner's equity** or capital. The assets of a company include all the goods and property owned by the firm as well as the amounts due the company from others. Liabilities are the debts of the company—what the company owes. The owner's equity or capital is the owner's share of the worth of the firm—the difference between assets and liabilities. On every balance sheet, the total assets must equal the total liabilities plus the owner's equity. This accounting formula applies to every balance sheet, whether the balance sheet is for a large corporation or a small, individually owned business.

Topic 1-2: *The Office in Relation to the Total Organization*

Figure 1-2.5

An income statement shows a company's profit or loss for a specific period of time.

DANDY'S DELIGHTS
INCOME STATEMENT
For the Year Ended December 31, 20--

			% of Sales
Sales		$200,000	
Cost of Goods Sold	100,000		
Gross Profit on Sales		$100,000	50%
Operating Expenses			
Advertising Expense	500		
Delivery Expense	1,000		
Office Supplies Expense	800		
Payroll Taxes Expense	4,500		
Salaries Expense	58,200		
Utilities Expense	3,500		
Miscellaneous Expense	500		
Total Operating Expense		69,000	
Net Income from Operations		$31,000	16%
Other Income and Expenses			
Interest Expense		2,000	
Net Income Before Income Tax		$29,000	15%
Less Income Tax		8,200	
Net Income After Tax		$20,800	10%

Goals of Not-for-Profit Entities

Not-for-profit organizations, as the title states, do not seek to make a profit. The chief goal of such organizations is to provide valuable services to those who can benefit from them. Museums strive to provide interesting exhibitions of various types of art. Social agencies provide food and cleaning services for the elderly. Such organizations try to make sure all who need their services actually receive them.

WORKPLACE CONNECTIONS

Workers in not-for-profit entities perform many office tasks. Here is just one example:

Elvira Sidney works as a counselor in a not-for-profit outreach program in Apopka, Florida. Much of her time is spent helping those who come to enroll in literacy and job skills programs. Elvira realizes that many of her clients are shy and unfamiliar with offices. She is friendly, helpful, and sensitive to the need for encouragement. The outreach organization is aware of the numbers of people in the community who could benefit from the programs offered. They strive each year to increase the enrollment in their programs, which are free.

Figure 1-2.6

A balance sheet shows a company's financial condition on a specific date.

DANDY'S DELIGHTS
BALANCE SHEET
As of December 31, 20--

Assets

Current Assets		
Cash	$12,000	
Accounts Receivable	3,500	
Baking Supplies Inventory	2,000	
Office Supplies	500	
Total Current Assets		$18,000
Fixed Assets		
Delivery Van	$7,000	
Baking Equipment	5,000	
Building and Land	95,000	
Total Fixed Assets		107,000
Total Assets		$125,000

Liabilities

Current Liabilities		
Notes Payable	$1,500	
Accounts Payable	1,000	
Salary and Wages Payable	200	
Total Current Liabilities		$2,700
Fixed Liabilities		
Long-term Note Payable	$5,000	
Mortgage Payable	35,000	
Total Fixed Liabilities		40,000
Total Liabilities		$42,700

Owner's Equity

Dan Burts, Capital			
Beginning Balance		$63,500	
Net Income for 20--	$20,800		
Less Withdrawals	2,000	18,800	
Dan Burts, Capital			
Ending Balance		82,300	
Total Liabilities and Owner's Equity		$125,000	

Goals of Governmental Units

Governmental units, like not-for-profit entities, do not seek to make a profit. These units are supported primarily by tax receipts. The overall goals of governmental units are related to providing services that citizens desire or need. For example, the government maintains a federal highway system, which ensures ease of travel throughout the country. Such a system is an aid to commerce and to the quality of life that citizens enjoy. Many workers in government are required to handle the tasks required to meet the needs of citizens.

This brief description of the duties of one worker in a federal office will provide an idea of what is done in one governmental office:

Judy Chen works as an assistant at the Federal Deposit Insurance Corporation. This federal agency regulates most insured banks in the United States. Judy's office is responsible for assigning staff to examine banks and receiving reports. Attention to details and to prompt updating of all records is critical in Judy's position. She finds her work challenging and interesting. She believes she is learning much about the total banking system in the United States through her interaction with examiners and their reports.

Structure of Organizations

Organizations require many different types of employees at various levels of the organization. Because these employees work together, they must understand who is responsible for each activity. They must also understand what authority each person has. Office workers, especially, find it helpful to understand the responsibilities and authority of those with whom they work.

hierarchical: in order of rank or authority

Knowing how an organization is structured will give you a better understanding of how it operates. Many organizations prepare an organization chart that shows positions in **hierarchical** order. As you can imagine, the organization chart for a large company will have many pages. Figure 1-2.7 shows a partial organization chart for a small company. Note the levels of responsibility and the different titles.

Board of Directors

Many large corporations have boards of directors. Publicly owned corporations must have such boards. Owners elect members of the board of directors. The board establishes the policies that guide senior management in directing the company. Generally, some senior managers of the company are members of the board. The board has a number of committees that may meet more frequently than does the full board. Some members of boards of directors are not employees of the company. These directors are expected to provide guidance and to make decisions that will serve the best interests of the company. Such outside directors receive a payment for their services, which are limited to a number of meetings each year. Generally, the full board of directors may meet no more than four to five times each year.

Not-for-profit entities also have a board of directors (sometimes called a board of trustees) whose responsibilities are similar to those of a corporation's board.

Senior Management

Those persons who provide direction in carrying out the policies of the board of directors are identified as senior management, or top management, in both businesses and not-for-profit entities. The chief executive officer (CEO), the president, the chief operating officer (COO), and the chief financial officer (CFO) are generally included in this group. The CEO and president have overall responsibility for everything that happens in the company. In some companies, one person holds both of these positions, and even additional ones.

Large companies and not-for-profit entities are often subdivided into units in some manner that is appropriate for the work of the organization. Often the units are called divisions or strategic business units. Divisions are usually managed by vice presidents.

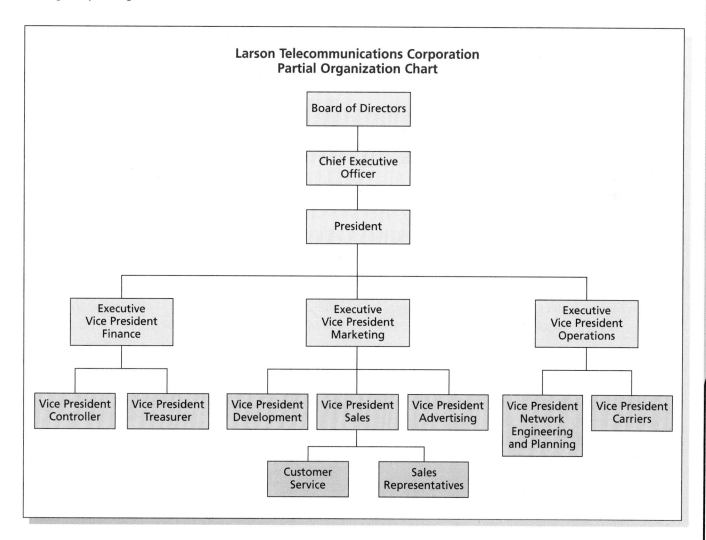

Figure 1-2.7

An organization chart shows the structure of a company.

Topic 1-2: *The Office in Relation to the Total Organization*

Employee Empowerment

Our employees are empowered. We couldn't function in this fast-paced world without every employee responding wisely to the changes that surround us. We rely on the common sense and wise judgment of every employee.

The president of a bank in a large North Carolina city who spoke these words is not alone in his belief in empowering all 300 of the bank's employees. He understands the value of empowerment, which is the privilege to make decisions or changes in what you do without having to get approval.

Empowerment requires that you understand your company. You read earlier in Chapter 1 that "Workers need to understand thoroughly the business or organization in which they are employed." By understanding your organization, you will find every aspect of your job of greater interest. You will better understand what you are doing, and you will be able to use the privilege of empowerment successfully. Consider this example of employee empowerment.

Melissa works in a large consulting company that believes in employee empowerment. She is a new receptionist on the fourth floor, which serves as a center for meetings and conferences for employees and clients. Every day, three, four, or even more individuals would come to her desk asking: "Where is the meeting for _____?" She would have to get the name of the person responsible for the meeting, call that person's office, and get the needed information. In the meantime, others were waiting to know where they should go. Melissa realized that a problem existed due to lack of information and clear communications.

Melissa had not been told that she would need to guide individuals to the right room. When she realized this task would be a routine part of her job, however, she began to think about how she could resolve the problem. Melissa knew that conference rooms were reserved and that those assistants making arrangements submitted the details of the meeting via e-mail. She called the office that handled room assignments and asked: "Could you add my name to your list for a copy of your confirmation for a room? I will be able to direct visitors to the right room with this information." The staff member was cooperative and responded: "Melissa, that is no problem at all. We'll also keep you informed of changes in plans." In addition, Melissa decided to post a schedule for the day inside the entrance so visitors could check the time and location of the day's meetings.

Melissa remembered her orientation to the company and how she and other new employees were informed of the functions of each department of the company. She realized how that information was now helping her as she thought of better ways to handle her assignments. She enjoyed being *empowered*!

Middle Management

Managers and supervisors who direct day-to-day activities of the organization are referred to as middle management. Increasingly, American companies have fewer middle managers. You may have heard references to a flatter organization. Such an organization has fewer layers or levels of managers. Increasingly, workers are given authority to make decisions without review by one or more higher-level managers. This concept is sometimes called **employee empowerment.**

employee empowerment: enabling employees to make decisions

Computers have helped in processing and managing information in new ways that enable companies to reduce the ranks of middle management. A movement toward working in teams with all members participating in decision making also reduces the need for middle managers.

Department Employees

The nature of a company's activities determines the types of workers that will be employed. Each type of employee has certain duties. Working together, they are expected to meet the goals of the organization. In most medium- and large-sized companies, employees are organized in departments or teams that relate to the functions of the company. These functions may include finance and accounting, communications, sales and marketing, information technology, legal services, and human resources. Office workers can be found in all these areas.

Production workers are found in manufacturing companies. These workers make the products the company sells such as cars, computers, or furniture. A manufacturing company will also have employees in departments such as research and development, inventory control, and shipping. Many organizations sell or provide services rather than products. Employees such as financial counselors, legal assistants, and real estate agents who provide these services are needed in these organizations.

The size of a company influences the types of workers needed. In a small company, a single person may, as is commonly stated, wear many hats. For example, one manager may determine how the funds will be spent, authorize all expenditures, sign all payments for goods and services, and be present to oversee the business on a daily basis. You can imagine that an office assistant in such a company would be likely to do tasks related to communications, records management, and purchasing, for example, in the course of a single day. In a large corporation, one person would probably not have the range of responsibility and authority that is common in a small organization.

As you have learned, employees in an organization work at various levels and in many different departments. With few exceptions, you will find office workers in all areas of an organization. Even in departments such as production, office workers are needed to process information.

Topic 1-2: *The Office in Relation to the Total Organization*

Reviewing the Topic

1. Why is it valuable for a worker to understand the business of the organization in which he or she is employed?

2. In what ways can workers learn about the organizations in which they are employed?

3. What are common forms of businesses?

4. How does a corporation, in general, differ from a single proprietorship or a partnership?

5. What do not-for-profit entities provide?

6. What kinds of services do governmental units provide?

7. Contrast the overall goal of businesses with that of not-for-profit entities and governmental units.

8. What are common titles for persons who are in top management, and what is the general nature of their responsibilities?

9. How does an organization chart aid in understanding a company?

10. At which levels in a large organization are you likely to find office workers?

Interacting with Others

You were standing at a desk of a coworker when her telephone rang. This is what you heard her say:

Who do you want?

A Mr. Ted Wells? Are you sure he works for this company?

Gee, I really don't know who the executives are. I don't work for any of them. I work for the diretor of catering services.

Oh, you work for Johnson Corporation. Well, you know how hard it is to know your own job, let alone know what is going on in the company.

You say our operator gave you this extension? Possibly, the operator doesn't know much more about the company than I do.

If I knew the extension for the president's office, I'd transfer you because I'd guess the president's secretary knows where everyone is—but, I don't know the number offhand, and I could never find my directory on this messy desk . . . Let me transfer you back to the operator. Is that okay? I so wish I could be helpful.

Just hold on. But, first where are you calling from? Why don't you call when you aren't busy, and we can have a chat. Do you have my number? It's 513-555-0192, extension 344.

Hold on. Good luck in finding Mr. Wells. Goodbye.

1. Describe the impression you think the caller has of your coworker's knowledge of the company and of her way of working.
2. Identify what you believe the coworker said that reflects positive attitudes toward others.
3. If your coworker maintained an orderly desk, what would she have done as soon as it was clear that the caller had the wrong extension? What might she have said instead of the comments shown here?

Reinforcing Math Skills

As you learned in this chapter, the goal of a business is to make a profit. To judge the extent to which the profit goal is being met, businesses analyze their sales on a regular basis. Assume that you are working for a technology development company. The director has given you sales figures related to a new style of wireless communications. You have actual figures for four years and projections for three. Create a spreadsheet or table and use formulas to analyze the sales as follows:

1. Calculate the total yearly sales by adding the U.S. and international sales.
2. Calculate the percentage U.S. sales are of the total yearly sales. Show no decimal places for all percents.
3. Calculate the percentage international sales are of the total yearly sales.
4. For U.S. sales for each year, calculate the percentage increase over 1999 sales.
5. For international sales for each year, calculate the percentage increase over 1999 sales.
6. For total sales for each year, calculate the percentage increase over 1999 sales.
7. Use appropriate column heads and format the information attractively. Add a comment below the data giving your impression of the rate of growth for this technology.

	ACTUAL AND PROJECTED SALES	
	($ in Millions)	
Year	U.S. Sales	International Sales
1999	70	30
2000	100	40
2001	150	50
2002	200	50
2003	240	80
2004	300	100
2005	350	170

Organization Chart

An organization chart is often used to show the structure of an organization. Prepare an organization chart showing the management team for the World Wide Sales and Service Division of a multinational company. Refer to Figure 1-2.7 on page 23 for a sample chart.

1. Begin with the company name, GLOBAL MANUFACTURING, followed by the division name, centered at the top as the chart title.

2. Place Thomas McEwen's name and title, CEO, in the top block of the chart.

3. Insert a block for Paul B. Kalis, Sr. Vice President, who is head of the division and reports to Thomas McEwen.

4. Insert blocks for the following vice presidents who report to Paul B. Kalis:

   Marco Ortiz, Vice President, Latin America

   Akira Komuro, Vice President, Asia, Pacific

   Rachel J. Kohnstamm, Vice President, Europe, Middle East, Africa

5. Insert a block for James E. Phelps, Assistant Vice President, Europe, who reports to Rachel J. Kohnstamm.

6. Insert blocks for Jean L. Lucent, Manager, France, and Howard A. Toole, Manager, Denmark, who both report to James E. Phelps.

Income Statement

The goal of a business is to make a profit. Financial statements such as income statements and balance sheets report how successful a business has been in achieving this goal.

1. Use spreadsheet software to create an income statement for Holly's Crafts using the data shown below step 8. Format the income statement similar to the one shown in Figure 1-2.5 on page 20. Use appropriate number formats and rules under numbers as shown in Figure 1-2.5.

2. Enter the appropriate headings and date the income statement for the year ended December 31 of the current year.

3. Enter a formula to subtract the cost of goods sold from sales to find the gross profit on sales.

4. Enter a formula to subtract the total operating expenses from the gross profit on sales to find the net income from operations.

5. Enter a formula to subtract other expenses or add other income to find net income before income tax.

6. Enter a formula to subtract income tax to find net income after income tax.

7. Enter formulas to calculate the percentage of sales for gross profit on sales, net income from operations, net income before tax, and net income after tax. (Divide each number by sales.)

8. One goal of Holly's Crafts is to have net income that is 25 percent of sales or higher. Assuming Holly's Crafts sells the same amount of merchandise and expenses and taxes remain the same, how much would the company have to increase prices to meet this goal?

Data for an income statement for the year ended December 31 of the current year:

Sales	$325,000
Cost of Goods Sold	175,000
Operating Expenses	
Advertising Expense	1,000
Delivery Expense	2,000
Office Supplies Expense	500
Payroll Taxes Expense	5,000
Salaries Expense	58,000
Utilities Expense	3,000
Miscellaneous Expense	400
Other Expense	
Interest	2,500
Income Tax	11,500

Summary

During your study of Chapter 1, you learned about the role of the office in today's organization, types of organizations and their goals, as well as their structure. Also, you have become acquainted with the varied personnel required by organizations. Consider the points listed below as you reinforce your understanding of the topics in this chapter.

- Offices are found in almost all types of organizations, and many workers in today's workplace must perform office tasks.

- Offices are information driven.

- Modern offices are subject to rapid change as new technology is introduced.

- The office is not necessarily a place at the organization's official location. Technology makes the virtual office or mobile office an appealing alternative.

- An understanding of the total organization increases an employee's ability to handle office activities effectively.

- Organizations are categorized as businesses, not-for-profit entities, or governmental units.

- Organizations, beyond the very small, require varying types of employees to be ensured of meeting the goals established by those who lead the organization.

- While many employees perform office activities, the responsibilities of administrative support services employees relate fully to office activities.

Key Terms

acquisitions	hoteling	office
assets	information	owner's equity
charter	Internet	partnership
confidential	intranet	profit
corporation	liabilities	revenue
employee	liable	single
empowerment	mission statement	proprietorship
expense	mobile office	state-of-the-art
freelancer	negligence	telecommute
hierarchical	nonterritorial	vendor
home office	workspace	virtual office

COMPOSITION
DATABASE
RESEARCH
TEAMWORK
WORD PROCESSING

Organizations in Your Community

Learn more about the organizations in your community by developing a database of the organizations. Work with two classmates to complete this activity.

1. Develop a list of local organizations in your community (businesses, not-for-profit entities, and governmental units).

2. Each team member, select a different type of entity. For at least three organizations in this type of entity, obtain the information shown in step 4.

3. After obtaining the information, work as a group to design a database to record the information. Enter the data in the database. Sort the data by type of entity. If possible, post the database in a location where the information can be viewed by all members of the class·

4. Each team member, select one of the organizations from the database that you would like to consider as a place of employment. Write a brief essay in which you identify your choice. Give reasons why you think you would like to work for this type of organization.

   Information about each organization:

   • Type of entity
   • Complete name and address of the main office
   • General telephone number
   • World Wide Web site address(es), if any
   • Brief description of the main activity, product, or service of the organization

      For businesses, include the form of organization

      For not-for-profit entities, include the major sources of funds

      For governmental units, include the level—local, state, or national

   • Brief description of types of workers employed

Balance Sheet

You are the assistant to Holly Cooper, the owner of Holly's Crafts. Holly has asked you to create a balance sheet for Holly's Crafts.

1. Open the data file **Balance**. The data is in rough format. Format the balance sheet similar to the one shown in Figure 1-2.6 on page 21. Use appropriate number formats and rules under numbers as shown in Figure 1-2.6.

2. Enter the appropriate headings and date the balance sheet as of December 31 of the current year.

3. Assets: Enter a formula to add the current assets to find the total current assets. Enter a formula to add the fixed assets to find the total fixed assets. Enter a formula to add the total current assets and the total fixed assets to find the total assets.

4. Liabilities: Enter a formula to add the current liabilities to find the total current liabilities. Enter a formula to add the fixed liabilities to find the total fixed liabilities. Enter a formula to add the total current liabilities and the total fixed liabilities to find the total liabilities.

5. Owner's Equity: Enter the net income after taxes figure from the Holly's Crafts Income Statement you created earlier in this chapter as the net income. Enter a formula to subtract Holly Cooper's withdrawals from the net income. Enter a formula to add the remaining income to the capital beginning balance.

6. Enter a formula to add the total liabilities and the capital ending balance to find total liabilities and owner's equity. This number should equal the total assets.

Office Competencies

As you learned in Chapter 1, office competencies are a requirement for many workers in performing their jobs. Whether or not you know what you want to do as a worker, you will find the content of this textbook valuable. You will develop skills and understandings that have application to all types of careers and will be useful preparation for work of any kind.

....

In the first topic of this chapter, you will find a brief overview of overall occupational projections to the year 2008. Next, you will be introduced to basic office competencies. These competencies are discussed in relation to basic skills and job opportunities. The second topic of the chapter focuses on overall goals of organizations and the contribution expected of employees. A discussion of how you can plan your strategy for developing office competencies follows.

OBJECTIVES

- Discuss the need for workers through the year 2008
- Identify office competencies
- Explain future prospects for employment where office competencies are valuable

The business office has changed a great deal. Before the personal computer became common in business offices, companies often employed two office workers to support each executive or manager. Today, executives and managers are not likely to have the services of office support staff as full-time assistants. **Projections** to 2008 show a strong demand for executives, managers, professionals, and technicians. Yet, administrative support services jobs are not expected to increase at as high a rate as total jobs.

Many persons entering the workforce are expected to have basic office skills or competencies. These skills can be acquired through your studies while you are still a student gaining your basic education.

projection: estimates or guesses about the future based on known data

Much information is available about types of jobs in the United States. The federal government, through the Department of Labor, monitors the total workforce and provides information about the current employment situation. Also, the Department of Labor undertakes research to predict the need for workers in the future. Such information is valuable to individuals as they plan for their future careers. Schools and universities, too, use such predictions to plan courses that prepare students for jobs.

Figure 2-1.1

A purchasing manager of a large chemical company uses office skills daily.

© CORBIS/STOCK MARKET

National Overview of Employment

online: available in electronic format such as on the Internet or an intranet

The U.S. Department of Labor publishes and provides **online** *The Occupational Outlook Handbook*, which discusses the major occupations in the country. From this book, you can learn about job prospects in a wide range of fields. The 2000–01 issue has projections to 2008. The monthly magazine *Monthly Labor Review* updates projections and provides additional information about job opportunities.

Employment by Major Occupational Group
(1998 and Projected 2008)

Occupational Group	Employment Number (Thousands of Jobs)		% Change
	1998	2008	1998–2008
Total, All Occupations	140,514	160,795	14.4%
Executive, administrative, and managerial	14,770	17,196	16.4%
Professional specialty	19,802	25,145	27.0%
Technicians and related support	4,949	6,048	22.2%
Marketing and sales	15,341	17,627	14.9%
Administrative support, including clerical	24,461	26,659	9.0%
Service	22,548	26,401	17.1%
Agriculture, forestry, fishing, and related	4,435	4,506	1.6%
Precision production, craft, and repair	15,619	16,871	8.0%
Operators, fabricators, and laborers	18,588	20,314	9.3%

Source: U.S. Department of Labor, Bureau of Labor Statistics. Online. Available: http://stats.bls.gov/news,release/ecopro.t02.htm. November 6, 2001.

Figure 2-1.2

In projecting employment to 2008, the government's economists judged rate of increase. The overall projected rate of increase in jobs was 14 percent. Professional specialty occupations are expected to increase by 27 percent from 1998 to 2008. Administrative support occupations, which are also referred to as office support services, are expected to increase by 9 percent during the same period. Note the percentage of change (growth rate) projected for other occupational groups in Figure 2-1.2.

Figure 2-1.3 shows the ten occupations that are projected to grow the most in number of jobs from 1998 to 2008. Note that office competencies are needed in most of these occupations.

Outlook for Employment of Office Workers

Automation will continue to have an effect on many administrative and clerical support occupations. This effect is shown in the low rate of growth projected to 2008. However, many jobs will be available in this area because many persons in this group will need to be replaced. Some workers will leave the field to enter new jobs or to retire. For example, approximately 3.2 million persons work as secretaries and nearly 2 million work as information clerks. These are among the largest of all the job groups in the United States workforce.

Topic 2-1: *Office Competencies Needed for Employment*

10 Occupations with the Largest Job Growth
(1998 and Projected 2008)

Occupation	Employment (Thousands of Jobs)		% Change
	1998	2008	1998–2008
Systems analysts	617	1,194	94%
Retail salespersons	4,056	4,620	14%
Cashiers	3,198	3,754	17%
General managers and top executives	3,362	3,913	16%
Truck drivers, light and heavy	2,970	3,463	17%
Office clerks, general	3,021	3,484	15%
Registered nurses	2,079	2,530	22%
Computer support specialists	429	869	102%
Personal care and home health aides	746	1,179	58%
Teacher assistants	1,192	1,567	31%

Source: U.S. Department of Labor, Bureau of Labor Statistics. Online. Available: http://stats.bls.gov/news.release/ecopro.t07.htm. November 5, 2001.

Figure 2-1.3

WORKPLACE CONNECTIONS

Toula Ahara was hired nine months ago as a receptionist in a travel agency. She acquired office skills in high school. She completed a liberal arts program at a community college before she accepted the job. Toula loves to travel. She had taken many trips while a student. Soon after her job began, the manager asked her to assist clients. Toula enjoyed this part of her job. Just a short while ago, Toula was promoted to travel agent. She said this about her new job: "My love of travel is one key to my promotion. The other key is my skill with the personal computer—from word processing to database management."

Workers Face Expanded Job Responsibilities

global marketplace: buying and selling of goods or services throughout the world

innovation: new method or idea

Office activity is increasing because of the growth of business throughout the **global marketplace**. A change has taken place, however, in who handles office tasks. Far more workers are performing office tasks than in the past. Modern technology is responsible for the shift. All types of workers can handle office tasks because of the technology available. If no **innovations** in technology had occurred during the last 20 years, about six times as many office support employees as are now employed would be needed to handle the volume of activity. Remember, though, many office support workers will continue to be employed in businesses.

CHAPTER 2: OFFICE COMPETENCIES

Many managers now do much of their own office work. Donna Komari is a product manager in the international division of a home appliance company. She spends much time traveling. Donna works for hours during a flight from Newark to London. Using her notebook computer she writes letters, accesses databases, and creates a spreadsheet. When she reaches London, she has completed a day's work. Donna commented about her way of working: "Before we had today's technology, I would have needed a full-time secretary to do what I did alone while on the flight from Newark to London."

Figure 2-1.4

Executives accomplish much work while traveling.

© JACK HOLLINGSWORTH/CORBIS

An Overview of Office Competencies

A wide range of activities make up office competencies. However, four major groups based on primary skills reflect the overall nature of office work. These are:

- Word processing
- Data processing
- Information management and transmission
- General managing and communicating

You will now become acquainted with each of these categories. Pay attention to the basic skills needed for doing tasks effectively and efficiently.

Word Processing

Communicating information effectively is important in all types of organizations. Much information is communicated using written documents. **Word processing** is the producing of written documents such as letters or reports by using software programs and computers. Usually these documents are shared in printed form. Increasingly, however, written documents are shared and read online. Electronic mail messages, for example, are often used to

word processing: producing written documents such as letters or reports

HTML: hypertext markup language, authoring language used for World Wide Web and intranet documents

desktop publishing: producing documents that include both text and graphics

communicate within a company. Some word processing programs allow the user to save documents in **HTML** format. These documents can be posted on the company intranet, for example, and viewed in browser software.

Desktop publishing is closely related to word processing and requires many of the same skills. **Desktop publishing** is the producing of documents that include both text and graphics. Examples of these documents include newsletters, brochures, and forms. Basic desktop publishing can be done using word processing software such as Microsoft Word. Desktop publishing software programs, such as Adobe PageMaker, are used for advanced desktop publishing.

Basic Competencies

The proper and efficient use of a personal computer in composing, revising, and preparing many types of documents is the goal of skill development in this category. The essential skills include:

- Keyboarding with speed and accuracy
- Knowledge and skill in use of software programs
- Skill in formatting and proofreading documents
- A large vocabulary

proficiency: ability to perform at a satisfactory level

- **Proficiency** with grammar, punctuation, and spelling
- Ability to learn special vocabularies
- Ability to follow instructions
- Skill in preparing copy from audio recordings, if employed as a transcriptionist

speech recognition software: computer programs that allow the user to input text and commands by speaking into a microphone

- Skill in dictating text and commands if using **speech recognition software**

Workers Who Need These Competencies

Word processing skills are needed by many workers. Executives and managers, both general and technical, spend much time composing written communications. Technical personnel, such as engineers, advertising designers,

Figure 2-1.5

This software program is used to do word processing.

Box shot reprinted with permission from Microsoft Corporation/© Microsoft Corporation

architects, and public relations specialists, are employees likely to use word processing and basic desktop publishing skills in their work.

Opportunities in Office Support Services

Some office support staff provide full-time assistance handling word processing and basic desktop publishing activities. Among the positions observed in organizations in this category are typist, word processor, and transcriptionist. Such workers prepare drafts as well as final copies of letters, memorandums, and reports. They may assist one other worker or several. Some word processing workers assist an entire department.

Such office support workers are considered for promotions to jobs in the same category that require more advanced skills. For example, workers who quickly learn new software programs and can explain the details to other employees may be promoted to a supervisory or training job. Workers with good writing skills may become administrative assistants.

WORKPLACE **CONNECTIONS**

Bob Wells is a transcriptionist in a large financial services company. At the moment, Bob is transcribing from a tape of a speech given to a group of employees. After Bob keys the speech, the draft will be sent to the speaker for review. When the document is considered complete, Bob will prepare multiple copies. He will also save the file in HTML format. The file will be posted on the company's intranet so employees who missed the speech can access it easily.

Data Processing

Data processing is the collecting, organizing, analyzing, and summarizing of data, generally in numeric form. Many positions require competency in such skills. This type of activity is usually done at a computer, using spreadsheet and statistical software programs. Though we think of data processing as primarily dealing with numerical data and word processing as dealing with text, the two processes often blend with one another. This blending process is made easier by the integration capabilities of software programs. Data processing and word processing are often collectively referred to as information processing. Many workers do this type of office activity.

data processing: collecting, organizing, analyzing, and summarizing of data

Basic Competencies

Among the skills important for workers who handle data processing activities are the following:

- Proficiency with spreadsheet, database, and related software programs
- Knowledge of arithmetic processes and statistical methods
- Ability to be consistently accurate
- Knowledge of methods of organizing and analyzing data
- Ability to interpret data
- Ability to prepare reports that communicate information in a meaningful way
- Ability to maintain an organized workstation

Topic 2-1: *Office Competencies Needed for Employment*

Figure 2-1.6

Data processing is a basic office competency for many workers.

Workers Who Need These Competencies

Accountants, budget analysts, brokers, insurance salespersons, and many other types of personnel found in all kinds of organizations deal with data and prepare reports. As new software programs make processing data faster and easier, these workers must continually learn to use new programs and methods in their work.

WORKPLACE **CONNECTIONS**

Cathy Leitman is a budget analyst in a large company. She works at her computer much of the time. Cathy accesses information from various departments of the company. For example, she finds data about the number of product defects in some of the company's factories. She then analyzes the data and prepares reports and tables to present to the executives who must make decisions using the information. Cathy studied economics in college. When asked what prepared her for her job, Cathy said: "My college studies were of great value for what I do. The basic skills I learned in my high school office procedures class are also critical to my work every day."

Opportunities in Office Support Services

Many workers continue to be employed in the data processing category. They include specialized clerks, such as accounts payable clerk, billing clerk, order clerk, payroll clerk, and shipping clerk. Such clerks prepare and process sales, purchases, invoices, payrolls, and other types of transactions. Their work is vital to the whole organization.

Office support employees in this category have offers for promotion. Companies need workers who can oversee increasingly more automated systems for processing data. Consequently, beginners who have an **aptitude** for understanding the total operation and have learned their jobs thoroughly are good candidates for promotions.

aptitude: a natural ability or talent

WORKPLACE CONNECTIONS

The experience of one entry-level data processing worker reflects the opportunity for advancement. Gail began working as an order clerk in a manufacturing company when she graduated from high school. After six months, she was transferred to the controller's office where she did tasks such as enter data from invoices and create reports. The controller noted that she learned quickly and talked with Gail about her future plans. He suggested that Gail consider enrolling in a college program to study accounting. Gail liked the idea. She began night studies at a local college. She realizes that she will not complete her college studies in four years. She likes working full-time and studying part-time. Gail's long-term goal is to complete a college program and become an accountant.

Information Management and Transmission

Information management refers to the organizing, maintaining, and accessing of data. Transmission refers to the communicating of information both within and outside the organization.

information management: organizing, maintaining, and accessing records or data

Basic Competencies

The skills considered basic in this category include considerable variety:

- Identification of information needed in the situation
- Ability to maintain or develop an information system
- Ability to give attention to details
- Ability to use established procedures
- Knowledge of records management principles and basic filing rules
- Good keyboarding skills
- Proficiency in working with databases
- Ability to meet deadlines and solve problems
- Ability to work with others

Workers Who Need These Skills

A wide range of workers is likely to need the skills for information management and transmission. Personnel such as buyers, real estate brokers, and property managers must have well-organized information systems. The details they need to make decisions often require them to design their own systems. Often their information must be available to others, too. Following a well-designed system is the key to easy use of information.

Opportunities in Office Support Services

People who find gathering and organizing data interesting will enjoy work in this category. This category consists of updating information on a timely basis and transmitting information promptly. Among common jobs in this category are hotel and motel desk clerk, mailroom clerk, records clerk,

Topic 2-1: *Office Competencies Needed for Employment*

Figure 2-1.7

Information management is a vital function for most businesses.

© ANTONIO MO/PHOTODISC

reprographics clerk, travel clerk, and communications center operator. Alert beginning employees in this category learn much about the organization. Such knowledge is a key to gaining promotions.

General Managing and Communicating

general managing: handling work time and tasks efficiently, creating and monitoring schedules, and tracking and reporting the progress of tasks or projects

General managing and communicating are broad areas that involve handling work time and tasks efficiently and interacting with other employees and customers. Setting up schedules, meeting deadlines, and tracking the progress of tasks are aspects of general managing. Communicating with customers and coworkers is a common activity for many types of workers in a company. Reporting on the progress of tasks, projects, or budgets are also aspects of general managing. Often, these reports are given orally and delivered with the use of a multimedia presentation.

Basic Competencies

The skills and knowledge needed to handle the activities in this category are varied. In general, they include the ability to:

priorities: a listing of items in order of importance

- Establish **priorities**
- Establish schedules and meet deadlines
- Work in teams
- Motivate others to complete work
- Use a personal computer and manage files
- Handle telephone calls effectively
- Give attention to several tasks at the same time
- Determine the time required for completion of tasks
- Communicate effectively both orally and in writing
- Interact with many types of people at all levels of an organization or outside the organization

CHAPTER 2: OFFICE COMPETENCIES

The marketing manager of a packaged goods company commented about his work in these words:

Our staff of ten is hardworking. I set the pace. We have just developed a database to record far more information about product sales. We have achieved our goal: The supermarket's bar code reader and our PCs are connected. We have staff members working on various ways to connect with our customers in an interactive fashion. As I think of our progress, I realize that basic managing skills, including establishing priorities, and communicating clearly what has to be done are critical.

interactive: involving the user or receiver, exchanging information

Workers Who Need These Competencies

General management and communication skills are critical for a wide range of employees, from executives to salespeople to office support staff. Office employees must be good managers of their own time. In addition, they must be skillful in guiding the work of any employees who report to them. They must be able to establish priorities and follow schedules for the completion of tasks. They must communicate clearly and effectively to coworkers and customers.

Opportunities in Office Support Services

Many office support staff provide the services of this category. The most common jobs include administrative assistant, secretary, customer service clerk, receptionist, and general office assistant.

Some positions in this category require specialized skills. The position of secretary, for example, may require high-level information processing skills. Receptionists must be at ease in meeting and talking with all types of people, both inside and outside the company. General assistants learn the special responsibilities of the offices in which they work. Then they take the **initiative** in completing tasks in the proper manner. For example, office assistants in travel agencies answer questions about advance payments required for tours, penalties for canceling tours, and documents required for travel to other countries. Office assistants in a governmental office, such as immigration services, understand the rules and procedures for processing an application for admission to the country.

initiative: ability to act or think without prompting or guidance

Higher-level jobs are available to those who perform their initial tasks with success. There are many jobs in companies for those who have the ability to:

- Complete tasks with little or no supervision
- Use oral and written communication skills effectively
- Meet deadlines
- Organize tasks and work independently
- Evaluate their own performance **objectively**

objectively: in a detached manner without bias or prejudice

Topic 2-1: *Office Competencies Needed for Employment*

Figure 2-1.8

Effective communication skills are essential for office workers.

© LISETTE LE BON/SUPERSTOCK INTERNATIONAL

Your Future Prospects

Your education, including your study of business subjects, provides you with a background of value in many occupations. You can enter some jobs after your high school graduation. Others require further education.

Some openings for high school graduates will continue to be available. Increasingly, however, jobs require skills and knowledge beyond those acquired through high school studies. Many organizations have on-the-job training and formal courses to prepare employees for new tasks or new ways of performing their jobs. Additionally, postsecondary schools that provide specialized training, such as business schools, community colleges, four-year colleges, and universities, have degree programs and continuing education programs. Continuing your education will add to your competencies for jobs that interest you.

Reviewing the Topic

1. In what way has the computer changed the nature of employment in companies?

2. What kind of information is provided in *The Occupational Outlook Handbook*?

3. By what percentage is the entire workforce expected to increase by 2008?

4. Explain why job responsibilities are expanding because of technological innovations.

5. Identify skills needed to handle word processing tasks.

6. What kind of workers need data processing competencies?

7. What are the critical skills and understandings needed to effectively perform information management and transmission tasks?

8. What are examples of good managing skills?

9. What qualifications do office support workers in entry-level positions need to be promoted?

10. What types of educational opportunities are available after graduation from secondary school?

Making Decisions

Craig is soon to be a high school senior. He needs very few courses in order to graduate at the end of the school year. He has asked you and a couple of other friends to give him your opinions about what he should do about his school program. He has listed on a sheet of paper what he believes are his options. His list has these options, which are not in order of preference:

- Take only the courses required in the mornings. Relax in the afternoon until my friends are free.

- Take some extra courses, such as accounting, business law, or office procedures. Because I think I want to work in the business world or become a lawyer after college, these courses might be helpful.

- Get a part-time job at one of the local fast-food places.

- Really learn all about the new computer at home.

1. With a group of three or four other students, discuss the alternatives Craig has outlined. Select the alternative your group believes is best for Craig.

2. As a group, write a paragraph or two that identifies the alternative you think Craig should choose. Support your choice with reasons, and be prepared to share your ideas with the class.

Reinforcing English Skills

The following description of the job outlook for general office clerks is taken from *The Occupational Outlook Handbook* online. No spelling errors were in the original copy. However, misspelled words have been introduced.

1. Key the paragraph, correcting the spelling errors.
2. Use the spell check feature of your word processor to check for additional errors. If you are not sure about a word, check a dictionary. Remember to check for forms of words that are not used correctly such as "to" for "too."

Job Outlook

Employmnet of general office clerks if expected too grow about ash fast at the average for awl occupatinos through 2008. The employment outlook for office clerks will bee afficted by the increasing use of computers, expamding office automstion, and the consoledation of clerical tasks. Automatoin has led to productivity gains, allowing a wide variety of duties two be preformed by few office workers. However, atomation all so has led to a consoledation of clerical staffs and a diversification of job responsibilityes. This cansolidation increases the demand for general office clerks, because they preform a variety of clerical tasks. It will become increasingly common within small busines to find a single general office clerk in charge of all clerecal work.

Source: U.S. Department of Labor, Bureau of Labor Statistics. Online. Available: http://stats.bls.gov/oco/ocos130.htm. November 6, 2001.

COMPOSITION
RESEARCH
TEAMWORK
WORD PROCESSING

Topic 2-1 ACTIVITY 1

Jobs in Your Community

In this activity, you will become acquainted with jobs in the ten occupations that are projected to grow the most in number of jobs from 1998 to 2008 as shown in Figure 2-1.3. Work in a group with two or three classmates to complete this activity.

1. Choose occupations from the list in Figure 2-1.3 that you would like to investigate in your own community. Choose twice as many occupations as there are members of the group.
2. Decide who will investigate each of the occupations listed. You may choose to work in groups of two investigating the same four occupations, or each member of the group may select two occupations to investigate.
3. Through group discussion, determine the places in the community where you are most likely to get information about the occupation.

(There may be a local association of persons in an occupational field, for example.) Find answers to these questions:

- In what local organizations do you find workers in this occupation?
- What are the basic educational qualifications for these workers?
- What are the key duties of persons in this occupation?
- To what extent are workers responsible for office tasks?
- What promotional opportunities exist for persons in this occupation?

4. Review the information gathered by all group members and prepare a table that presents the information. (Hint: Column headings can be the occupations. Each row can deal with the response to a question.)

5. Participate in a class discussion of job opportunities in the community for these occupations.

COMPOSITION
INTERNET
RESEARCH
WORD PROCESSING

Topic 2-1 ACTIVITY 2

Study an Occupational Field

For this activity, choose an occupational field that interests you. You may choose an occupation that you explored in Activity 1 or any other occupation. Do some research to become acquainted with this field.

1. Use the Internet or the resources of your school or local community library to get information about your occupation. A reference that is likely to be helpful is *The Occupational Outlook Handbook*, which was described briefly in this chapter. Find the following information for the occupation:

- Educational requirements
- General responsibilities
- Employment opportunities
- Promotional opportunities

2. Interview a person working in this occupational field. In your interview, seek answers to these questions:

- What are the primary duties of a beginner in this occupation?
- What do you consider your primary duties?
- For each primary duty, would you consider education, on-the-job experience, or training the best source of preparation?
- To what extent do you use a personal computer in completing your job tasks?
- What office skills do you find most valuable in your work?
- What advice would you give a student who is thinking of preparing for your field?

3. Create a report that summarizes the information you gathered. The final paragraph of your report should be your current opinion about the appeal of the occupational field as a career for you.

OBJECTIVES

- Describe issues that affect achieving company goals
- Explain the general expectations for workers
- Prepare a strategy for developing office competencies

Organizations seek to hire the qualified workers who will be highly productive. In this topic, issues that affect achieving company goals will be introduced. All personnel are expected to help achieve company goals. Then the general expectations for employees will be described. Finally, a strategy for you to consider as you develop office competencies commonly needed at work will be presented.

Goals Influence Expectations for All Employees

Fortune 500 companies: largest companies listed in *Fortune* magazine

If you were to read a dozen annual reports of **Fortune 500 companies**, you would find information about company achievements during the past year. You would also read about goals for the future. In some instances, goals are simply expressed as a long-term vision statement. For example, the head of one computer company declared that the company's vision was to have a computer on every workplace desk and in every home. Others make predictions about level of earnings, new markets, new products, or improved customer service. The goals set by the company affect the work of all employees.

reliable: dependable, trustworthy

cooperative: willing to act or work with others for a common purpose

Issues such as quality management, customer satisfaction, and teamwork affect how successful the organization is in achieving its goals. These issues must be the concerns of all employees. The company expects all employees to be **reliable** and **cooperative** in efforts to increase productivity and meet company goals.

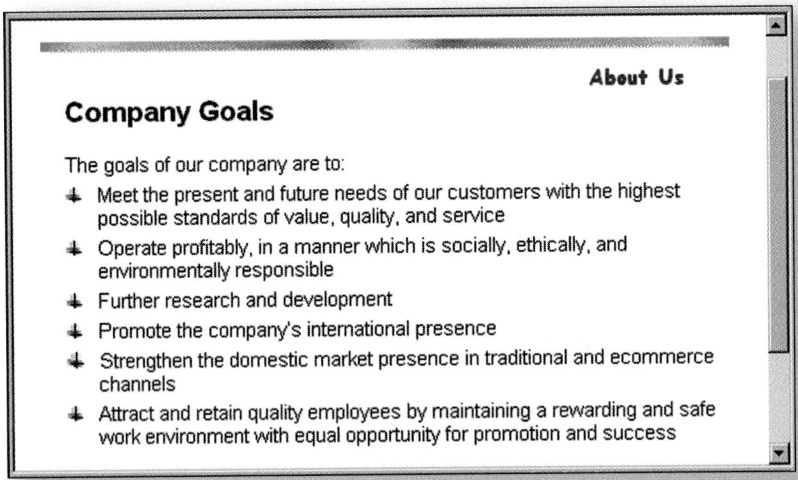

Figure 2-2.1

Some companies post their goals on their company Web sites.

About Us

Company Goals

The goals of our company are to:
- Meet the present and future needs of our customers with the highest possible standards of value, quality, and service
- Operate profitably, in a manner which is socially, ethically, and environmentally responsible
- Further research and development
- Promote the company's international presence
- Strengthen the domestic market presence in traditional and ecommerce channels
- Attract and retain quality employees by maintaining a rewarding and safe work environment with equal opportunity for promotion and success

Total Quality Management

total quality management: establishing and maintaining high standards in how work is done

The primary goal of all businesses is to make profits. In an effort to increase profits, many companies have adopted **total quality management** (TQM) plans. TQM means establishing and maintaining high standards in how work is done and in the creation and delivery of goods and services. All personnel, from the president to staff in the mailroom, are asked to view their work with an awareness of TQM.

The thrust of TQM is that managing quality is everyone's business. Quality standards apply throughout the organization. For example, in one company, all office support workers were asked to keep track of the errors in their work. Two common errors were omitting an attachment with a letter and failing to answer questions of callers. After recording such errors, the next step was to establish a new way of working so the errors would not recur.

In some companies, an executive is assigned to lead the company's efforts to improve quality. This executive works with groups of employees to find out what will improve performance or products. Many companies have developed slogans such as "Quality is everybody's business" or "We want to be the best in all we do" to highlight their quality goals.

Continuous Improvement

Over time, the policies and procedures used by a company may become outdated or inefficient. Companies seek to avoid this problem by applying the concept of continuous improvement.

Continuous improvement means being alert at all times to ways of working more productively. Continuous improvement is a concept that overlaps the principles of TQM. All employees are encouraged to participate in continuous improvement efforts.

Because of new technology, companies are finding that many aspects of their work require changes. Continuous improvement begins with looking at the work that is done and how it is being done. Improvements are often possible. The attitude reflected in the question "Could this be done in a better way?" helps workers think creatively about improvements.

continuous improvement: being alert at all times to ways of working more productively

Topic 2-2: *Developing Office Competencies*

O ne office assistant found that continuous improvement helps her be more productive:

I must telephone many people to get specific information. Frequently the person I need is out, and I leave a message, which states: "Please call Sally at . . ." Often when the person calls back I am out, so I find a message on my voice mail. When I considered how I handled such calls, I thought: Why not leave a message asking for the information I need? Then the caller could leave an answer at my voice mail if I am away from my desk. This is a timesaving way of handling my calls. When I get to my office after lunch or after a meeting, I now find answers to my questions. I do not need to make a follow-up call.

Customer Satisfaction

"We are here to serve customers" is a message that all kinds of organizations send to employees. Thinking through what you do in relation to what it will mean to customers is a key focus in many organizations. Many people believe that attention to customers is very important for long-term success.

T he staff of an organization is involved in a variety of ways in meeting the goal of customer satisfaction. One begining worker, for example, described his experiences in these words:

I serve as an assistant in our Customer Hotline office, which is open seven days a week, 24 hours a day. Among the team are members who speak English, Spanish, French, Chinese, and Japanese. Together, we are able to provide customers around the world with information about our produts. We can quickly put a customer in touch with a technical person, if additional assistance is needed.

Companies often conduct surveys to see if they are consistently delivering the value demanded by customers. They study the results of such surveys and then make changes to improve customer satisfaction.

Ethical Standards

Ethical standards require honesty, fairness, and justice in all business dealings. These qualities provide the foundation of trust. Leaders of organizations are responsible for making clear their attitude toward standards of ethical behavior. Companies want to be considered trustworthy by their employees, their customers, companies with which they deal, and the public.

code of ethics: moral standards or values and related behavior; also called code of conduct

Companies have developed standards of conduct for their employees, called **codes of ethics** or codes of conduct. Such codes are communicated to all workers. Employees are generally informed about the code of conduct when they first join the organization.

Figure 2-2.2

Companies conduct surveys to assess customer satisfaction.

CUSTOMER SATISFACTION SURVEY

Understanding and serving your needs is our goal. Please help us improve our customer service by completing this survey.

Check the box by your response.

1. How would you rate the overall service you have received from our company?
   - ☐ Excellent
   - ☐ Good
   - ☐ Average
   - ☐ Poor

2. How quickly did you receive a response to your most recent question or problem?
   - ☐ The same day
   - ☐ 1–2 days
   - ☐ 3–4 days

3. Was your most recent question or problem resolved to your satisfaction?
   - ☐ Yes
   - ☐ Somewhat
   - ☐ No

From time to time, employees are called together to discuss what the code means in relation to specific behavior and actions. For example, all staff involved with purchasing—from directors to office staff—may attend a meeting dealing with a new conflict of interest statement. This staff interacts with many vendors who are eager to sell their products. The new statement makes clear that no employee is to accept gifts of any value, including trips to attractive vacation spots, from any vendor.

Figure 2-2.3

A portion of a company's code of conduct.

Employee Handbook

Confidentiality Policy

During your course of employment, you will handle information sensitive to our company, partner companies, and clients. All information, both written and verbal, with which you come in contact in the scope of your duties, is confidential. Please respect this trust, which our clients and customers have given us. Confidentiality is critical; communication of confidential matters may be grounds for corrective action up to and including immediate dismissal.

Companies also have procedures for handling violations of ethical standards. Employees found guilty of violating the code of ethics may be subject to disciplinary action. Continued or very serious violations may lead to immediate dismissal of an employee.

Topic 2-2: *Developing Office Competencies*

Teamwork

One common question asked of prospective employees is: "How willing are you to participate in teamwork?" Interviewers are asking this question because today's business world is complex. Many of the tasks performed in any department require the skills and knowledge of several staff members who can cooperatively assess what is to be done, how it is to be done, and who will accept responsibility for parts of the task.

Working as a team, employees bring varying experiences, observations, insights, and knowledge to determining what action should be taken and following through with those actions. A team, thinking critically, is often far more successful than an individual working alone. This belief is commonly held in successful organizations and by many successful employees.

You have probably had experience as a team member—possibly as a member of a sports team, in a science laboratory, or in an after-school club. You may enjoy teamwork, or you may feel that you would rather work alone. If you have a positive view of teamwork, you will be a valuable employee. If you have a negative view of teamwork, reconsider your attitude. As an office worker, you will be expected to work in teams, and you will want to be successful in this aspect of your job. Consider these guidelines for working effectively in teams:

- Set clear goals for the team and create an action plan for achieving the goals.

- Define the responsibilities of each team member in achieving team goals.

- Identify how success will be measured. How will the team know when its goals have been accomplished?

- Identify obstacles to achieving the team's goals and discuss ways to overcome the obstacles.

- Communicate clearly and often with all team members, and be open to all feedback and ideas. Schedule regular meetings or reports to track the progress toward achieving team goals.

- Discuss how differences will be resolved. Understand that all members of a team may not have the same level of authority.

- Build on the strengths of individual members. Encourage all members of the team to participate in making decisions and contributing ideas. Each team member has different skills and ideas that can be valuable to the team.

- Recognize accomplishments of team members and the team as a whole.

- As an individual team member, develop your colleagues' trust by fulfilling your responsibilities, acting in a professional manner, and maintaining a positive attitude when discussing team activities.

Responsible Teamwork

Some people work alone at the company offices or at home. Frequently, however, employees must work in teams to complete tasks. Teamwork involves combining the efforts of two or more people to accomplish a task or achieve a goal. For a team to function effectively, each team member must understand the purpose or goals of the team. Each member of the team must accept responsibility for completing his or her duties and communicate clearly with other team members. For remote teams, in which team members may be located around the world rather than down the hall, communication is especially important.

Team members often are not from a single department. For example, customer collections were a problem in a relatively small shoe manufacturing company. The controller realized that those involved worked in the order entry, shipping, and billing departments. A team composed of several members of these departments was assigned the task of reviewing the policies and procedures involved. Through teamwork, the group recommended a new policy and related procedures. Soon thereafter, the problem was resolved to everyone's satisfaction.

Global Marketplace

The area in which a company does business is called its marketplace. In the past, many U.S. companies sold their goods or services only in the domestic marketplace, meaning within the United States. Many of these companies now produce and/or sell their products in countries around the world. Some companies have moved into the global marketplace using only traditional sales channels, such as retail stores. Other companies have expanded using **ecommerce** to enter the global marketplace. These companies, sometimes called e-companies or dotcoms, sell goods and services online using a company site on the **World Wide Web**.

Whatever their sales strategy, moving to the global marketplace has affected activities in these companies. Employees must travel beyond the United States to other countries. Company personnel who live in other countries visit headquarters in the United States. Communications, too, must be international. Information for Web sites, advertising materials, and product instructions must be available in many languages. All personnel must be sensitive to variations in culture as they communicate with people of other nations. Employees must be acquainted with varying time zones, sources for information about travel, and places for travelers to stay and work in other countries.

ecommerce: business conducted electronically, as in making purchases or selling products via the World Wide Web

World Wide Web: computers on the Internet that use and transmit HTML documents

© CORBIS/STOCK MARKET

Figure 2-2.4

Many employees travel to foreign countries as businesses operate in a global marketplace.

Topic 2-2: *Developing Office Competencies*

Diversity

diversity: reflected in a workforce with people from a wide range of ethnic and cultural backgrounds

Diversity, as it relates to organizations, means having a workforce with people from a wide range of ethnic and cultural backgrounds. Many companies seek to have diversity at all levels of the organization. In some companies, a diversity coordinator collects data about the company's hiring and promotion policies. This person also tracks the progress of the company in achieving its diversity goals. Employees are expected to respect coworkers and customers from all backgrounds. Diversity training programs are conducted to help employees become aware of issues related to diversity.

Figure 2-2.5

Employees with different backgrounds and new perspectives help businesses meet the needs of diverse customers.

© GUY CALI/CORBIS

WORKPLACE **CONNECTIONS**

Meg works in the human resources department where diversity is getting attention. She is one of the staff members planning diversity seminars. She was especially interested in comments from the managers who participated in the seminars. They described how their evaluations of employees are now influenced by what was learned in the seminar. Her company has an awards program honoring individuals who demonstrate a respect for diversity in their work.

General Expectations for Employees

A company expects the same basic work qualities in all employees. The way these qualities are shown, however, will vary depending on the nature of the employee's work. Reliability, productivity, cooperativeness, and independence in learning are important qualities for all employees.

Reliability

Companies expect employees to be reliable. Reliable means dependable and trustworthy. Employers rely on employees to report to work on time and to devote their time on the job to completing their work. They expect to be able to trust employees to keep company business confidential and to protect the assets of the company.

WORKPLACE CONNECTIONS

A director of administrative services in a large bank commented on employee reliability:

Employees who have to be watched every minute in order to keep them doing what they should do are worthless in our bank. We must have reliable employees. One of the most common reasons for dismissal in our bank is unreliability. For example, one new employee failed to be at the office at eight o'clock on the mornings she was scheduled to open the office. The office was unattended. She didn't call to explain her lateness; she just arrived two hours later. This pattern continued for a month. At that point, we had to dismiss her. We cannot function with such indifference to schedules.

Productivity

Productivity is demonstrated by completing an appropriate amount of work on time and according to instructions. Organizations are cost conscious, meaning that they are aware of how they spend their money. Employee wages is one of the major expenses in many organizations. Employers expect employees to produce a reasonable amount of work and contribute toward achieving company goals. Often specific, measurable standards for a day's work are not practical. Supervisors and managers, however, have some level of output that they believe is reasonable for an employee. Following a schedule that ensures you will complete the amount of work expected of you is important.

Valuable workers are aware of what they are accomplishing each day. They are able to evaluate their own work and make changes as needed. Some managers discuss productivity with their workers in informal ways from time to time. Other managers expect workers to decide on their own what changes are needed to improve productivity.

Managers and executives identify the following barriers to high productivity among employees:

- Talking with friends by telephone
- Chatting with coworkers for long periods of time

Topic 2-2: Developing Office Competencies

Figure 2-2.6

A disorganized
workstation limits
productivity.

© PHOTODISC, INC.

- Failing to maintain an organized workstation
- Failing to set priorities
- Moving from task to task before any one is completed

Cooperativeness

Most office employees work with others daily. Information must be shared, and tasks often require more than a single worker. Being cooperative is an important quality for all employees. Employees must be prepared to learn new skills and handle new tasks as circumstances change. Most office workers have job descriptions, but seldom do such descriptions fully describe everything the employee will do on the job. Employees who believe they need to do only what is outlined in their job descriptions are not effective workers.

WORKPLACE **CONNECTIONS**

One manager described an employee who was not cooperative in these words:

As long as Betty was not interrupted, she was a good worker. When I asked her to spend the next day at a conference center at midtown, however, she said she didn't understand that she would have to work in another location. She said she was hired to work in the office. Even though nothing was stated about where she would work, she was right in assuming that she would be located at headquarters. From her own observations, however, she should have realized that employees travel out of town and many employees work at conference sites. After this encounter, I became more aware of Betty's attitude, which was reflected in small ways as she worked with others. At the end of the year, Betty's performance was assessed. Her level of cooperativeness was listed as an area for improvement. She was not added to the list of persons to be considered for promotion.

Independence in Learning

As you undoubtedly realize, all you need to know to be an employee—in any field—will not be learned while you are a student. One of the characteristics of modern life is that learning must be a lifelong activity. Professional workers, such as lawyers, doctors, and accountants, for example, must have continuing education experiences each year in order to maintain their professional credentials. Although some continuing education can be in formal programs, much of it is self-directed. Workers are in an environment where they can learn much from what they do and what they observe. Furthermore, organizations have resources such as databases and libraries that are available to employees. Companies expect their employees to learn how to use new equipment, software, and methods for completing tasks on an ongoing basis.

Maintaining a professional reading file is one example of how an employee can continue to learn. Magazines, newspapers, journals, and **ezines** contain many articles and reports related to office work. Many professions and industries have associations that seek to provide current information to members. For example, the International Association of Administrative Professionals is an organization for the office administration profession. Many of these associations have magazines or journals and Web sites devoted to topics related to the profession. Many also have yearly conferences or more frequent seminars that members can attend to learn about current developments, new equipment or methods, and issues of concern.

The *Professional Development Resources* feature boxes in this textbook provide the names of some associations that may be of interest to office workers. Articles from a wide variety of magazines and Web sites are also listed. Access and read these articles to learn more about topics related to the chapter content. If the articles listed are not available, or to find more current articles, search the Internet or library databases using the search terms provided.

Professional Development Resources

- International Association of Administrative Professionals (IAAP)
  10502 NW Ambassador Drive
  P.O. Box 20404
  Kansas City, MO 64195-0404
  www.iaap-hq.org

- Barbara Feinberg. "Where Is Your Career Going?" *OfficePro*. October, 2001.

- Sherwood Ross. "Lack of Face-to-Face Connection Hurts Teamwork." *Chicago Tribune*. November 7, 2001.

- Search terms:
  employment outlook
  global marketplace
  information processing
  productivity
  teamwork
  total quality management

ezine: electronic magazine available on the World Wide Web

Strategy for Developing Office Competencies

You are a student. What you have experienced as a student is of great value to whatever you choose as your career. You are evaluated when you submit assignments, complete quizzes, and take examinations. You have some idea of what you are able to do, what you would like to learn, and, possibly, how you can learn. You will develop many competencies as you study and participate in the activities provided in this textbook. You can develop general and specific competencies for becoming an effective worker. These competencies will be valuable in a wide variety of jobs and careers.

Consider the competencies you have now. What skills and understandings do you have today that would be of value to an employer? You may have work experience, either paid or volunteer. This gives you an introduction to what work is like. Think about what those experiences required and the extent to which you were comfortable in doing the work.

Topic 2-2: *Developing Office Competencies*

Figure 2-2.7

Which of these competencies can you improve during this course?

COMPETENCIES FOR THE OFFICE

- Composing letters and reports
- Creating spreadsheets and charts
- Formatting memos, letters, and reports
- Keeping workstation organized
- Keyboarding accurately
- Learning software programs
- Listening and following instructions
- Maintaining records and files
- Managing time wisely
- Meeting deadlines
- Prioritizing tasks
- Proofreading
- Speaking appropriately by telephone
- Using references such as the Internet, databases, and reference books
- Working in teams effectively

Your education has been focused on developing basic competencies that are critical for gaining the most value from your life. Those basics included reading, writing, arithmetic, speaking, and listening. You have also studied math, literature, history, social studies, physical sciences, languages, and other subjects. Think of your educational experience. Identify your key competencies that you believe will have value at work. Competencies commonly developed in elementary and secondary school are valuable competencies for the office. Note those listed in Figure 2-2.7.

Set goals for improving or developing new competencies. What do you want to accomplish this year? What skills do you want to improve? What new skills do you want to learn? Only you can make such plans. Only you can make a commitment to developing your office competencies.

Reviewing the Topic

1. What information are you likely to find in a company's annual report?
2. What does a company hope to achieve with a total quality management program?
3. Who is expected to participate in a program for continuous improvement?
4. Why do companies value customer satisfaction?
5. To what do ethical standards relate?
6. Why is teamwork considered important in today's world of work?
7. What changes are likely to be made in a company that shifts from being a domestic company to being a global one?
8. Why is a company interested in diversity?
9. Describe what you might observe to conclude that a worker is reliable.
10. "If it isn't in my job description, I will not do it." What does this comment imply about cooperativeness?

Interacting with Others

Tanya, a manager in an advertising agency, called a meeting for three members of the staff, Jill, Dave, and Donna. Tanya explained that she had just received a telephone call about an exciting offer to submit a proposal for a new account. Tanya told them the project will require an intensive period of work because a proposal must be submitted within two weeks.

The project is complex. Tanya believes, though, that the three of them can do the job. They will be given some help from the departmental secretary. They must research the types of advertising campaigns used in the industry. They must also gain information about what the client's goals are and what its present image is in the marketplace. After they have gathered the information, they must develop what they believe are promising campaigns. Tanya told them that they can decide among themselves how to divide the work to be done.

Jill, Dave, and Donna met immediately after leaving the supervisor's desk. Jill said: "Look, I feel rather tired and I just don't want to start work on this right away. Could I just beg off the research? Then I'll be happy to help you develop some plans for a campaign. I think I'm better in the creative part of such a project. I know that there will have to be many overtime hours during this first week of work. I just do not want to change my plans."

1. In a group with two or three other students, discuss what you would say to Jill if you were Dave or Donna.
2. Prepare notes on your response for use for a class discussion.

Reinforcing Math Skills

In planning for next year's budget for the accounts payable department, a study was done of how the work could be improved and costs reduced. The conclusion was that the office should operate with a supervisor and only two clerks, rather than the four clerks employed in the department last year. State-of-the-art equipment was purchased to help two clerks do the work formerly done by four clerks. This new equipment will increase the depreciation charge, however.

	Last Year's Expenses	Proposed Budget
Salaries	$133,000	$96,000
Supplies	4,000	3,800
Repairs and Maintenance	5,000	2,500
Depreciation	3,000	6,000
Telephone	3,500	3,900

1. Calculate the total expenses for the department using last year's figures.
2. Using last year's figures, calculate the percentage of total expenses each of the expenses items represents. Round percentages to one decimal place.
3. Using last year's figures, calculate the cost per invoice processed if 144,500 invoices were handled during the year.
4. Determine the difference in total expenses between last year's figures and the proposed budget.
5. Calculate the percentage decrease in total expenses if the proposed budget is used.

COMPOSITION
INTERNET
RESEARCH
TEAMWORK
WORD PROCESSING

Topic 2-2 **ACTIVITY 1**

Checklist for Evaluating Team Projects

For this activity, work in a group of three or four students to develop a checklist for evaluating team project participation.

1. Search the Internet or other reference sources to find at least two articles about effective teamwork. Make a list of the main points of each article and share this list with the group.

2. As a group, prepare a list of factors to be included on an evaluation checklist. For example, one factor might be: Completed work on time. Decide on a system to use in rating how well a student does on each factor on your list. (Hint: Should there be A, B, C grading? or 1, 2, 3, 4, 5? or Excellent, Good, Poor?)

3. Prepare a final copy of the checklist with the factors and rating scale. Use an appropriate title and format the document so that it will be easy to read and use.

4. Participate in a class discussion and share the factors your team used on the checklist.

DATABASE
INTERNET

Topic 2-2 **ACTIVITY 2**

Professional Reading File

Develop a database to record the source of newspaper, magazine, or online articles that will help you increase your knowledge of office work and related issues. Many articles that are published in hard copy newspapers and magazines can also be found online. Use your favorite search engine or sites such as Find Articles.com (www.findarticles.com) to look for articles online. Many major newspapers also have online sites (www.ChicagoTribune.com, for example) where you can find some of their articles.

1. Create a new database file to store information about articles for professional development.

2. Include the following fields in the database:

Field Name	Description
Title	Title of the article
Subject	Subject of the article (Sometimes the title may not clearly suggest the subject of the article.)
Author	Author name
Publication	Name of magazine, newspaper, or Web site
Date	Date of the publication or the date you accessed the article online
Web Address	For articles accessed online
Notes	A place to record your brief notes about the article

3. Format the data table or design a form to make entering the data convenient.

4. Begin your reading file using the articles in the *Professional Development Resources* feature boxes from Chapters 1 and 2 on pages 8 and 57. Enter the data for these four articles in your database.

5. Search the Internet or use hard copy publications to find two additional articles related to topics studied in Chapters 1 and 2. Read these articles and enter them in your database.

6. As you study each remaining chapter in this textbook, find at least one article related to topics studied in the chapter. Read the article and update your database.

Chapter Review

Summary

Chapter 2 gave you an overview of the workforce as provided by the U.S. Department of Labor in *The Occupational Outlook Handbook*. You also learned about key categories of office competencies needed by many workers in today's workforce, employer expectations, and a strategy for developing office competencies. Consider the points listed below as you reinforce your understanding of the topics in this chapter.

- The information provided by the U.S. Department of Labor is useful in learning about occupations. Projections for workers are given through the year 2008.

- Although there will continue to be job opportunities in office occupations, the rate of increase is lower than that for some other occupational groups.

- In many occupations, workers are expected to have office competencies. Therefore, your study of this subject is valuable for your future, regardless of your career interests.

- Office competencies are considered in four categories: word processing, data processing, information management and transmission, and general managing and communicating.

- Goals of companies influence their expectations for all employees.

- Organizations focus attention on concerns including total quality management, continuous improvement, customer satisfaction, ethical standards, responsible teamwork, global outreach, and diversity.

- Qualities considered important for employees are reliability, productivity, cooperativeness, and independence in learning.

- Planning a strategy for developing office competencies will be valuable to you no matter what you choose for your life's work.

Key Terms

aptitude	general managing	projection
code of ethics	global marketplace	reliable
continuous	HTML	speech recognition
improvement	information	software
cooperative	management	total quality
data processing	initiative	management
desktop publishing	interactive	word processing
diversity	online	World Wide Web
ecommerce	priorities	
ezine	proficiency	

Expectations of Employers

Become acquainted with workers' opinions regarding basic expectations employers have for employees.

1. Working with one other student, interview someone about his or her work. The purpose of the interview is to learn opinions about the importance of basic expectations in specific situations. Collect the following information:

   • Name and current position of the employee

   • The employee's opinion of how important each of the following qualities is to his or her employer: reliability, productivity, cooperativeness, independence in learning

   • A specific example that shows the importance of each of the qualities listed above

   Ask the employee to respond using these evaluation ratings:

   > Very Important, Somewhat Important, Of Limited Importance, Of Little or No Importance

2. Key a report of your findings.

3. Discuss the findings in class, noting similarities and differences in responses.

INTEGRATED DOCUMENT
INTERNET
RESEARCH
SPREADSHEET
WORD PROCESSING

Chapter 2 ACTIVITY 2

Employment Projections

Research current employment projections. Then key a report highlighting the information.

1. Open and print the data file **Projections.pdf**, which contains the report. Follow the formatting instructions written on the document. Correct any spelling or word usage errors you find in the document.

2. Use the current edition of *The Occupational Outlook Handbook* to find current employment projections. You can access the *Handbook* online at the Bureau of Labor Statistics Web site (http://stats.bls.gov). If you do not have access to the current edition of the *Handbook*, use the information provided in the Chapter 2 text and figures.

3. Create a column chart using your spreadsheet software to show the three occupational groups with the largest percentage increase. Then copy the chart into the report.

4. Proofread carefully and correct all errors before printing the report.

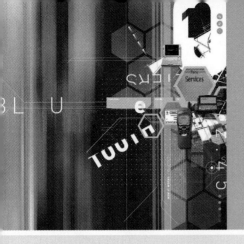

Part 2

Managing Information to Enhance Productivity

Information is critical to all organizations. Effectively managed information helps an organization serve its customers better and operate more efficiently. Business employees need accurate information for use in making decisions. This information must be communicated in both visual and oral forms. In *Managing Information to Enhance Productivity*, you are introduced to common business information systems and resources. You will have an opportunity to improve your communication and information processing skills.

OBJECTIVES

- Explain the vital role that information plays in operating a business
- Describe common business information systems
- Communicate effectively in written form and in oral form
- Plan, prepare, and deliver business presentations
- Explain the purpose of common financial reports and aid in their preparation
- Process financial information such as payments, receipts, and bank reconciliations

Information: A Vital Business Resource

To prosper and grow, an organization must make sound business decisions. To do this, the organization needs accurate, up-to-date information. Information is simply facts that are organized in a meaningful and usable form. Information is a vital resource that helps an organization serve its customers and operate efficiently.

As an office worker, you will help maintain the flow of information in your organization. You will find your work more interesting and more meaningful when you understand how it relates to the total information system of the organization. As you study this chapter, you will become acquainted with common information systems and resources found in businesses. You will also develop an understanding of how technology can enhance the effectiveness of the information system.

PHOTO © PHOTODISC, INC.

Information Processing

OBJECTIVES

- Define information
- Explain how businesses use information
- Describe information processing activities
- Explain how information technologies enhance information systems
- Describe local area networks and wide area networks
- List security measures for information systems

Businesses use many resources in their daily operations—raw materials and equipment for manufacturing, workers to process orders and build products, investment money for expansion and improvements, and computers and other technology for communication. The specific resources used will vary from business to business. Regardless of the nature of the business, however, information is an essential resource that affects how other resources are used and the overall success of the business.

How Businesses Use Information

Most of the work performed in offices involves the processing of information. Information starts as basic facts or raw data made up of numbers, symbols, and letters. This raw data becomes information when it is organized in a meaningful way. Consider these examples:

- A payroll manager prepares the weekly payroll checks. The raw data used includes hours worked, rates of pay, and payroll deductions. When such data is arranged for individual employees, it becomes information to use in preparing the payroll.

- An office worker in a shipping department answers a customer's inquiry about a shipping date. The basic facts used are the customer's name, the invoice number, and the shipping date. Locating the specific invoice gives the office worker the information to answer the customer's question.

- A sales associate in a real estate office prepares for a business trip. The basic facts used are travel dates, destinations, and flight numbers and times. When the sales associate arranges the facts into a meaningful form, an itinerary is created.

The most common forms of information are identified in Figure 3-1.1. These individual forms of information are often used together. Using information effectively is increasingly important in achieving success.

Figure 3-1.1

Common Forms of Information

numbers	amounts, quantities, sizes, weights, capacities, ages organized to convey meaning, as in a table or listing
text	words organized to convey meaning, as in letters or reports
image	charts, graphs, photographs
voice	messages conveyed in person; messages conveyed by telephone

Topic 3-1: *Information Processing*

Information enables businesses to answer some of their most important questions:

- What do our customers want?
- How can we improve our product and deliver it faster?
- Who are our most productive employees?
- How much can we increase prices before we lose revenue?
- Where can we reduce costs?

Many businesses gather data to use in making business decisions. Consider the questions listed below and the decisions that may be affected by information answering these questions.

Information Needed	Decisions Affected
What do our customers think of us?	Image to be built or points stressed through advertising
	Improvements to product quality or customer service
Who are our best customers and where are they located?	Placement of new branch locations
	Warehousing of goods to be shipped
	Areas or Web sites targeted for advertising
What are our best-selling products? Why are these products successful?	Products to keep and products to discontinue
	Changes for less successful products to make them more popular
Who are our best dealers? Where are our most productive sales channels?	Reward plans for dealers
	Strategies for improving sales in other channels—retail stores, catalog sales, Web sites
Who are our biggest competitors? What do they offer customers that we do not?	Points stressed through advertising
	Improvements to product quality, product features, customer service

sales channel: method of marketing products such as through retail stores or catalogs

Managing Information

The amount of data processed daily by a business can become unmanageable without procedures and technology designed to handle the data efficiently. The complexity of running a business, the volume of **transactions** processed, and the need for accurate and up-to-date information make effective management of information essential.

transaction: business deal or agreement, exchange of data, or sale

Complexity of Business

Operating even a small business can be quite complex. In a very small business, the owner may take care of all office activities. In many small businesses, a few office workers handle all the daily business operations.

CHAPTER 3: INFORMATION: A VITAL BUSINESS RESOURCE

Figure 3-1.2

To be successful, a small business must manage information efficiently.

Typically, all the information needed to operate the business is in one central location, usually the business office. For a small-business owner, efficient organization of information is necessary to maintain a competitive edge.

Efficient organization of information is even more important in large organizations with many employees. Several workers may need to use the same information to process work or make decisions. Effective organization of information meets the needs of workers in all areas of the company.

Volume of Transactions

Some organizations must deal with thousands of transactions each day. Effective management of information allows these organizations to run smoothly. Consider the following examples:

- Banks process thousands of checks, receive thousands of deposits, and pay out thousands of dollars in cash each day.
- Manufacturing companies complete the production of thousands of products, ship thousands of orders, and receive payments from thousands of customers each day.
- Insurance companies receive thousands of payments, issue thousands of new policies, and send out notices to thousands of customers each day.

Think of the problems that would occur if these organizations did not manage information effectively. The volume of transactions would be overwhelming. The access and retrieval of information would be slow and tedious.

Current and Accurate Information

For information to be valuable, it must be current and accurate. Outdated or incorrect information can be useless. Even worse, outdated information can cost the organization money because poor decisions are made based on the incorrect information. Coworkers and customers expect to receive information quickly, and they expect it to be accurate and up-to-date.

Figure 3-1.3

Manufacturing companies ship thousands of products each day.

With the growth of ecommerce, customers' expectations for current information have risen. For example, when buying from a traditional catalog order company, a customer completes an order form and mails it to the company. The customer has no assurance that the item ordered is currently in stock or when the item will be shipped. For customers buying online, the Web site often indicates whether an item is in stock and when the item will be shipped. Many ecommerce sites provide order tracking where a customer can see the progress his or her order is making on the way to its destination.

WORKPLACE **CONNECTIONS**

Consider the value of current and accurate information in the following examples:

Major airlines are able to provide an international network of service because current information is available. Travelers can request a reservation for a flight between two cities anywhere in the world. They immediately receive information about the number of seats available on the flight. Customers making reservations are not willing to wait days for a response.

A manager keeps detailed information about the company's cash-flow needs. The manager knows exactly how much cash is on hand. Cash not needed immediately is transferred to short-term investments that earn money. The company benefits because accurate information is kept.

Obstacles to Managing Information

Information has unlimited potential for helping organizations operate effectively. Yet, information can be difficult to manage. Data can be hard to organize, easy to lose, easy to alter, hard to locate, and even incorrect. Obstacles to using information efficiently in an organization include:

- Uncoordinated procedures and files
- Duplication of information
- **Incompatible** databases
- Outdated or inaccurate information
- Missing information
- Limited access to information

incompatible: unable to work together

| WORKPLACE **CONNECTIONS** |

Using incompatible databases can make sharing data difficult and may increase errors. Janis works in customer service for a small company. She handles calls about the status of customer orders as well as product questions or complaints. Before answering product questions, Janis must verify that the product was purchased from her company and when. This information is entered into a database by an employee in another department when the product is sold. Information related to product complaints or questions is stored in a different database. Because the two databases are not compatible, Janis must also enter the customer's name, product, and purchase date when the customer calls with a question or complaint. This means that helping each customer takes longer and entering the data twice doubles the chances for errors.

The office worker is often the company's first line of defense against these obstacles. The office worker is frequently the person gathering or processing the information. Therefore, he or she is often the person who first recognizes that databases are incorrect or that critical information is missing.

If you experience difficulties in using information or technology efficiently, follow your company procedures for reporting the difficulties. If no procedures exist, inform your supervisor. Include a description of the problem in your report. If a company can move quickly to correct problems with its information resources, the negative effects of these problems can be reduced.

Information Processing Activities

Information processing is putting facts or numbers into a meaningful and useful form. Five types of activities or operations are typically involved: input, processing, output, distribution, and storage. These operations are summarized in Figure 3-1.4.

information processing: putting facts or numbers into a meaningful and useful form

As you perform your duties, you will often proceed directly through the input, processing, output, distribution, and storage operations. For example, you may enter numbers into a spreadsheet program, perform calculations and create a chart, print ten copies of the chart, distribute it to members of your department, and store the file and printed copy. At other times, you

Figure 3-1.4

Information Processing

Operation	Example
Input: Entering data into the information system	Taking orders by phone and keying them into an order entry system to generate shipment and billing for the order Entering data about a new employee to activate payroll and benefits Writing product features and benefits for an advertising brochure
Processing: Handling data to create meaningful information	Formatting and arranging text and graphics to create a newsletter Generating a report from a database Calculating and sorting data in a spreadsheet
Output: Retrieving information from the system	Viewing a list of out-of-stock items from an inventory database Printing labels and brochures for a customer mailing
Distribution: Sending information to the appropriate people	Faxing product updates to sales representatives Mailing price quotes to customers Sending a report to a coworker as an e-mail attachment Posting a survey on the company Web site
Storage: Saving information for future use	Filling paper documents Saving computer files

may complete only some of the operations. For example, you may receive a request from a coworker for another chart using some of the figures in the spreadsheet. You can proceed to the processing operation because the data has already been input earlier. Information can be stored and retrieved at any point.

Information Technologies

The information processing efforts of a business are aided by the information technologies it uses. Information technology refers to the equipment and software that allow the user to create, store, and retrieve information.

The information processing methods found in businesses vary according to how technology is used. The telephone is the most common piece of equipment that is found in almost all offices. Photocopiers, fax machines, and computers are becoming almost as common. Usually only small offices requiring few transactions rely heavily on manual processing methods. Using information technology increases the speed at which communications are processed. Technology allows for rapid processing of a huge quantity and variety of information. Some firms have enjoyed a competitive advantage by being the first to use a new technology within their industry.

Citibank, a leader in the banking industry, was the first bank to use automated teller machines (ATMs) throughout its organization. Citibank tripled its market share within the first few years after introducing ATMs. What advantages did Citibank gain? Citibank increased its number of banking transactions and earned ATM fees. It also attracted many new customers from other banks. At the same time, Citibank reduced the number of tellers and increased the accuracy and timely handling of information. Citibank held its competitive edge by using this new information to analyze customers' needs. As a result, it offered additional services based on those needs and explored new markets.

Information technologies can be used to improve communication among the staff and between companies and their suppliers and customers. Examples of common information technologies used in offices include:

- Computers connected to networks, the Internet, and online services—providing access to a wide range of resources
- **Electronic imaging** and transmission of documents—reducing paperwork, saving valuable time, and increasing customer satisfaction
- Electronic mail, instant messaging, online databases, and two-way video—increasing the flow of information and speed of responses
- **Interactive voice response** systems—reducing manual processes for obtaining data and/or providing information
- Interactive CD-ROM reference media—making retrieval of data quick and easy
- Multimedia employee training programs—enhancing training effectiveness

Businesses must handle large amounts of information in increasingly shorter time spans. To be successful, they must respond more quickly and with more accurate and flexible approaches to customer needs and wants. Effective use of information and technologies helps businesses meet these challenges.

electronic imaging: converting paper documents to pictures stored and displayed via computer

interactive voice response: recorded messages accessed and directed by the user to provide or record information

Understanding Databases

Prepared by Kaoru Takase

This seminar is designed to teach you the basics of databases and help you understand the importance of Corporate View's incident report database system. After completing this seminar, you will be able to contribute to more powerful and helpful database systems in the future. Click on the first topic, Database Elements, to begin the seminar.

SEMINAR TOPICS
- Database Elements
- Creating A Database File
- Entering Data
- Adding Fields and Modifying Forms

SEMINARS
REGULAR FEATURES
INTRANET HOME

Figure 3-1.5

Many companies provide training seminars on the company intranet.

Computerized Processing

Computer-based systems are common in today's offices. Computerized processing relies heavily on equipment (the computer) and related software to turn data into meaningful and timely information.

Hardware

hardware: the physical parts of a computer or related equipment

Hardware refers to the physical parts of a computer or related equipment. Although we often speak of "the computer," many variations exist. Computers can be classified by their size, speed, and processing capabilities. With continued advancement in technology, however, the differences among computer categories have become more difficult to identify. Three major categories of computers are used in business: mainframe computers, minicomputers, and microcomputers.

Mainframe computers are large, multipurpose machines with very high processing speeds. Mainframes can handle many users and store large quantities of data. Mainframe computers use sophisticated programs to control their operation and require specially trained employees to operate the system. The mainframe computer has traditionally done tasks such as payroll, accounting, and personnel record keeping for large organizations.

Minicomputers are midsized computers capable of supporting a number of users. They are less powerful than mainframe computers but can perform a wide variety of processing tasks.

Microcomputers, also called personal computers, are the small, desktop variety. The system is made up of several components such as the central processing unit, a keyboard, mouse, and monitor. Microcomputers are designed for individual use and are used by people at all levels of business organizations. Laptop and notebook computers are other forms of microcomputers. As these computers can be battery powered, they are especially helpful to employees who must work on the road or at locations where desktop systems are not practical. Companies may have several types of computers to meet their processing needs.

Figure 3-1.6

Laptop and notebook computers are forms of microcomputers.

© LAWRENCE MANNING/CORBIS

Data from business transactions frequently consist of handwritten, keyed, or printed facts. Before these data can be processed, however, they must be entered into the computer system. Workers use input devices to enter data into computers. An input device is hardware that allows the computer to accept the data for processing. Common input devices that you probably use regularly include the keyboard and mouse. Other input devices include touch screens, light pens, and scanners. Touch screens and light pens are used to give commands, draw, or write input directly on the screen. Scanners are used to input text, graphics, and photos by "reading" printed documents. Speech recognition is also a form of input for voice-activated systems.

A computer system must have at least one output device. An output device prints, displays, speaks, or records information from the computer. The most common output devices are monitors and printers. Other output forms include speakers, floppy disks, tape drives, laser discs, and microfilm.

Because the amount of primary storage in a computer is limited, additional external storage is often needed to store data. Storage devices such as optical discs and magnetic disks and tapes allow large volumes of data to be stored and retrieved easily.

Software

Thousands of **software** programs are available to meet information processing needs. Software may be divided into three broad categories: operating system software, application software, and utility software.

software: programs containing instructions for a computer

Operating system software contains programs that control the operation of the computer and provide the means for communicating with devices connected to it, such as a printer. Windows XP is an example of a popular operating system software with multitasking features that enable the user to run two or more applications at the same time.

Application software directs the computer to carry out specific tasks. The application software may perform a single function, such as word processing. Other single-function software applications include inventory control and database management. Software that shares information (such as word processing, database management, spreadsheet, and presentation) between applications is known as integrated software. When these applications are packaged as one, they are commonly called a suite.

Application software can be quite powerful and can provide numerous advantages for a business by improving the accuracy and efficiency with which it processes information. Software manufacturers continue to upgrade their products and add new features. As new applications are created, they become easier to learn and use with features such as onscreen help, tutorials, and templates or "wizards" that automate common tasks. With the wide selection of application software available, the use of computers in offices continues to grow. Figure 3-1.7 lists common types of software you are likely to encounter in an office.

Utility software carries out "housekeeping" duties, such as formatting a disk, making copies of data, deleting and organizing files, and protecting or recovering data. Many of the utilities you will use are included with the operating system software. Many more features are available by purchasing utility software packages. As the use of computers has grown, utility software has become essential in preventing data loss.

Figure 3-1.7

modem: device that allows computer data to be transmitted via the telephone system

Common Types of Software

Software Category	Software Function
Browsers	Display HTML files such as Internet pages
Communications	**Modem** connections; fax; voice, electronic, and Internet mail; file transfers
Database Management	Records creation and maintenance, records updating and editing, data querying, report creation
Desktop Publishing	Page composition, use of features such as type style and fonts to produce high-quality documents that contain text and graphics
Development	Tools for creating interactive applications including animations and pages for the Internet
Graphics and Design	Clipart images, photos, line art, and drawing and design tools for use in desktop publishing documents as well as computer-aided design
Finance	Checkbook, online banking, accounts receivable/payable, billing, financial reports, financial forecasting, tax planning, inventory, and job costing
Operating System	Controls the operation of the computer and communicates with devices such as printers
Network	Server performance for networks, security, management, directory services, intranets
Presentation	Multimedia shows with graphics, sound, text, and animation
Project Management	Timeline schedules, calendars, appointment reminders, travel guides, address books, prioritizing and task management, and employee performance evaluations
Specialized	Software developed for specialized needs such as medical, law, and real estate offices
Spreadsheet	Number calculations using formulas, sorting, charts, "what-if" analyses
Utility	Scan and disable viruses, compress files, boost performance, recover lost files, repair disks, troubleshoot, protect, and backup data
Word Processing	Document creation and editing; spelling and grammar checking; merging of text, data, and graphics into integrated documents

Virus protection programs are also utility software. This software identifies and clears files of **computer viruses**, which if undetected could result in loss of data and computer operations. Virus protection software is generally updated regularly to keep up with the new viruses.

computer virus: a destructive program loaded onto a computer and run without the user's knowledge

Networks

A computer network links two or more computers so they can share information. Networks are used in organizations to link computers as well as many other types of electronic hardware. Two types of networks, local area networks (LANs) and wide area networks (WANs), help workers complete their daily tasks and share information. Today's technology, however, does not limit our communications just to internal networking within the organization. Growth and creativity in the ways in which the Internet and the World Wide Web are being used to conduct business are affecting workers in surprising and exciting ways.

WORKPLACE **CONNECTIONS**

Cal-Giftorama is a national catalog-order company specializing in unique, handcrafted items imported from all over the world. The company has recently expanded its ecommerce activities. A B2B (business-to-business) network makes it possible to place orders with exporters located in Europe and Asia, as well as to conduct everyday business within the United States.

Thanks to its information network, the company ships 98 percent of all incoming customer orders within 24 hours. When a customer places an order over the telephone, an employee is able to access the inventory database to see immediately whether the ordered item is available. Within minutes, the order is processed, and a packing list is printed at the distribution center. Soon the order is on its way to the customer. Without the network, it could take five or more days to process the order.

Cal-Giftorama has recently launched a company Web site for B2C (business-to-consumer) transactions. The site offers audio files and a live camera in the catalog showroom. Visitors to the site can view and order items from the online catalog. The company believes that selling in the virtual marketplace will help the company stay competitive in the import business.

To use a network efficiently, workers must first be trained to perform networking tasks such as logging on and off, exchanging files, setting password security, sending and receiving messages, managing files, and viewing network printer queues. New workers may be introduced to networks in a variety of ways. Some organizations provide hands-on training by support staff; others assign an experienced coworker to train the new user. Still others may give the user a network procedures manual to follow.

Local Area Networks

A network used to link computers that are close to each other—usually within several hundred feet—is a **local area network** (LAN). With a LAN, several computer users can share data files, software, and equipment such as printers or scanners. LANs are set up as peer-to-peer networks or server-based networks.

local area network: a group of connected computers that are close to each other

In a peer-to-peer network, computers are connected with cables to each other and operate as equals in the network. A computer in this type of network can access software and data stored on the hard drives of all the connected computers. Individual users and the organization determine which data or software files will be made public for other network users to access. All that is needed to set up a peer-to-peer network using most current computers is cabling and special software.

In a server-based network, one computer fills requests for data and program files from network users. The central computer that performs this service is called a file server because of its primary task of supplying or "serving" files to computers on the network. In this type of network, every computer to be connected must be cabled and have special software and hardware for networking.

The term *transmission carrier* refers to the cables or other equipment used to link computers in a LAN. Three types of cable that are commonly used to link computers and other equipment are twisted-pair, coaxial, and fiber-optic cables. When setting up networks, many organizations use a variety of transmission carriers to connect devices. They must consider cost, speed, efficiency, and reliability when choosing cables for use in the network.

Figure 3-1.8

Transmission Carriers

Twisted-pair cable	Similar to widely used, older telephone wiring
	Inexpensive
	Prone to interference from other electrical devices
Coaxial cable	Widely used by cable television companies
	Faster and more reliable over longer distances than twisted-pair
	More expensive than twisted wire
	Interference is much less
Fiber-optic cable	Made from thin glass strands
	Transmits laser light pulses efficiently at very high speeds over long distances
	Not affected by electrical interference

Wireless communication (without cables) for LANs is possible using infrared light waves or radio waves. Infrared light waves transmit information in a straight line and require a clear path between objects. Wireless communication via infrared light waves is usually limited to computers, keyboards, monitors, and peripherals that are only a short distance from each other with no obstructions to block the signals. Wireless communication using radio waves is more versatile because the radio waves do not

CHAPTER 3: INFORMATION: A VITAL BUSINESS RESOURCE

Figure 3-1.9

Fiber-optic cable is made from thin glass strands.

© PHOTODISC, INC.

travel in a straight line. Radio waves can be used to transmit data between equipment in a larger area such as several rooms or a whole building.

Wide Area Networks

A **wide area network** (WAN) links computers that are separated by long distances. A WAN for a small company may cover several cities or states. WANs for a large, multinational company may cover several countries. Wide area networks, like LANs, are used for file access, data exchange, and e-mail. Electronic data interchange (EDI) allows the exchange of data between companies that may or may not have compatible computer or network systems.

wide area network: links computers that are separated by long distances

WORKPLACE **CONNECTIONS**

The use of wide area networks and electronic data interchange speeds business transactions. Consider this example:

A clothing manufacturer in Atlanta needs silk fabric from a supplier in Hong Kong. A purchase order is sent from a computer at the factory in Atlanta to a computer in the warehouse in Hong Kong. The order is filled, the fabric is shipped, and an electronic invoice is sent to the computer at the factory in Atlanta. No paper has been exchanged. It would take weeks for the order to be received, filled, and invoiced without use of electronic data interchange.

As you have learned, in a LAN data travels over cables called transmission carriers. In a WAN, use of data transmission lines is purchased from a communications business that specializes in providing these services. When setting up a wide area network, organizations choose a type of transmission

Topic 3-1: *Information Processing*

connection that will best meet their needs. A dedicated line, also called a leased line, remains connected and ready for use at all times. A dial-up line provides connections only when needed. Both provide a relatively secure, clear transmission from one computer to another.

microwave transmission: radio waves that carry data

Microwave transmissions play an important role in data transmission in a WAN. Microwave dishes and microwave towers relay signals to each other directly. You have probably noticed imposing microwave towers on hillsides. The higher the dish or tower, the further the message can be sent. Obstructions between the two relay stations will interfere with the signal. In a WAN, electronic data travels by fiber-optic cable or telephone lines to the nearest microwave carrier. The data travels from carrier to carrier until it reaches the one nearest its final destination. From the last microwave carrier, the data is then transmitted over cables to the receiving computer.

satellite: man-made object placed in orbit around the Earth containing electronic devices for relaying communications data

In international communications, **satellites** may play a major role in transmission of the data. Signals are sent from your computer to a satellite relay station. The satellite relay station transmits the signal to an orbiting satellite that will bounce the electronic message to a receiving station on earth. From there, the signal travels over cable to a modem and computer.

The use of wireless devices to connect to the Internet and then to other networks is growing. Currently, the coverage areas for wireless connections in the United States are limited. The small screen size and limited memory and processing power of wireless devices such as personal digital assistants make them impractical for many business applications. In the future, as these obstacles are overcome, however, wireless computing may make the entire range of a company's software and data available to any employee at any remote location.

Figure 3-1.10

WANs may use fiber-optic cables or microwaves to transmit data.

CHAPTER 3: INFORMATION: A VITAL BUSINESS RESOURCE

Marcie is a broker for a large real estate company. On entering a home that is about to be listed for sale, she counts rooms, measures windows and doors, and notes special features of the house. She also takes some photographs. All her notes are entered on a laptop computer. The pictures are taken with a digital camera and loaded on the laptop also. Using a high-speed wireless modem in her laptop, Marcie sends all the information, including the photographs, to online databases. The new listing can be viewed online by potential buyers within a few minutes after Marcie tours the house.

Although WANs can be worldwide, difficulties sometimes occur when establishing connections to computers in foreign lands. Some international standards have been established; however, usage taxes are determined by each individual nation. Because of the demands placed on countries to be a part of a global economy, many are building communications systems to attract electronic visitors to their lands.

The variety of technology available for worldwide, long-distance transmission of all types of data—voice, image, text, and video—makes it necessary for organizations to evaluate their needs and spend their dollars wisely. One thing is certain: The need for global communications links will continue to increase as organizations strive to remain competitive. This hunger for easily accessible international communications is reflected in the amazing growth of the best-known wide area network of all—the Internet. Getting connected to the Internet is discussed next. The Internet as an information resource is discussed in Topic 3-2.

Getting Connected to the Internet

Many government facilities, educational institutions, and organizations have direct Internet access through their local or wide area networks. Workers can easily gain access to the Internet if their LAN or WAN is connected to it.

Direct access is not the only way to get online. **Internet service providers** (ISPs) sell entry to the Internet, usually based on a monthly fee and the number of hours spent online during that month. Accessing the Internet through an ISP requires a computer with a modem, telecommunications software, and a phone line. With a dial-up access account, your computer contacts the ISP each time you want to go online. The ISP then provides you with a connection to the Internet. With a DSL (direct service line) account, your computer remains online, and you can access the Internet at any time. Dial-up access is widely available. DSL service is not yet available in many areas. Both types of service are inexpensive and easy to set up. When selecting an ISP, evaluate the cost of the service; the company's reliability, security, and overall performance; user satisfaction; restrictions; types of services provided; and quality of customer assistance.

Internet service provider:
a company that sells users access to the Internet

Maintenance and Security

Office workers are expected to be responsible users of information processing technology. They must be concerned with maintenance, security, and ethics related to information processing systems and software.

Whether a business uses complex and diverse computer networks or simply stand-alone computers, managing the maintenance, security, and controls of the system is important. With the increased dependence on technology, disaster planning is essential for uninterrupted computer service. The responsibilities can be so demanding that some companies hire security administrators and disaster recovery coordinators who handle plans for safeguarding the system and recovering quickly if data is lost or destroyed. Read more about disaster recovery on page 374.

Maintenance

Computer systems are relied on daily and are often used extensively. Yet, a surprising number of businesses neglect to conduct proper maintenance on the systems. For efficient operation and best performance levels, the systems must be serviced and maintained on a regular basis. Failure to maintain the equipment could result in lost data and even lost business.

WORKPLACE **CONNECTIONS**

Jan received a phone call from a new customer requesting a rush delivery on an important order. She checked the inventory system and found that the needed items were in stock and could be delivered the same day. Little did Jan know that the computer had been shut down for unscheduled repairs early that morning, preventing some shipments from being entered and deducted from the inventory count. The needed items were not really in the warehouse. Jan's company lost a customer because accurate inventory information was not available when needed.

When you use a computer, follow proper maintenance procedures. Read and follow equipment operation instructions so that you do not accidentally harm the equipment. Many companies instruct employees in preventive maintenance procedures. If you are responsible for the maintenance of your computer, be sure you understand the procedures you are to follow.

Security

Businesses handle sensitive information daily and depend on their computer networks to process orders and provide needed information. As a result, security is a critical issue. Security for computer information systems involves protecting against loss of data, theft or unauthorized access and use of information or computers, and loss of service.

Figure 3-1.11

Regular cleaning is an important part of computer maintenance.

Loss of data can occur when a computer or network does not work properly because of hardware or software problems. To protect against loss of data, backup copies of the data are made and stored in another location. Data can also be lost through errors made by employees, such as deleting a file or incorrectly updating a customer database. Companies try to avoid losses of this nature through employee training.

Companies must be careful to protect their confidential data and the data gathered from their customers and business partners. Unauthorized users, called hackers, may be able to access and misuse or steal the information if proper safeguards are not in place. Companies use software and equipment called **firewalls** in an effort to prevent unauthorized users from accessing their computer networks. Many companies use data encryption during transmission of data. This encryption process helps protect data, such as a customer's credit card number or a business partner's new product design, from being intercepted during transmission.

A computer virus is a destructive program loaded onto a computer and run without the user's knowledge. Viruses are dangerous because they can quickly make copies of themselves and cause a computer to stop working because all available memory is used by the virus. Some viruses can travel across networks and sneak past security systems. Antivirus software is used to help prevent data loss from computer viruses.

Computer viruses called Trojan horses may be used in creating distributed denial of service (DDOS) attacks. In a DDOS, hackers flood a system with so many requests for connections that the system cannot operate properly or at all. For an ecommerce site, this could mean lost sales while the site is not operating. A loss of customer confidence in using the site can also lead to lost sales in the future. DDOS attacks are illegal, but finding the person who launched the attack is very difficult. Companies can use filtering methods and adjust networks setting to help protect against DDOS.

Professional Development Resources

— Computer Security Institute
600 Harrison St.
San Francisco, CA 94107
www.gocsi.com

— Randy Myers. "Ecommerce, Unplugged" (Wireless access). *eCFO*. Summer, 2001.

— Cade Metz. "What They Know" (Privacy issues). *PC Magazine*. November 13, 2001.

— Search terms:
information technology
privacy or security
relational database
intranet
extranet

firewall: software and hardware designed to prevent unauthorized users from gaining access to a computer or network

Topic 3-1: *Information Processing*

Figure 3-1.12

CyberNotes provides computer security professionals with a current summary of security-related topics and issues.

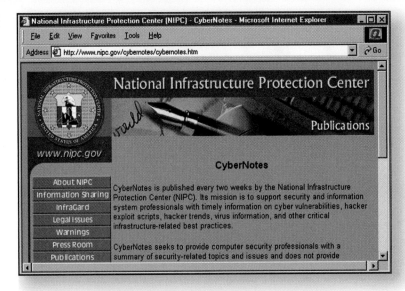

Source: National Infrastructure Protection Center. Online. Available: http://www.nipc.gov/cybernotes. November 15, 2001.

Government agencies and private organizations seek to promote awareness and prevention of computer crimes. The National Infrastructure Protection Center (NIPC) was established in 1998. The NIPC publishes CyberNotes online every two weeks. CyberNotes provides current information on computer viruses, hackers, and related security issues.

Not all security threats come from outside the company. Employee theft of **proprietary information**, such as product designs, can be costly. The Computer Security Institute (CSI) regularly surveys large corporations and government agencies regarding computer crime and information security breaches. The CSI surveys report that large financial losses result from theft of proprietary information.

proprietary information:
privately owned information, such as a design or formula; also called intellectual property

Security risks are handled in a variety of ways depending on the complexity of the system and the risk involved. Figure 3-1.13 shows a list and description of typical security measures. All personnel should be trained in security procedures and should fully understand security policies. Adequate policies, procedures, and precautions help safeguard valuable information. In spite of security measures, however, companies lose millions of dollars each year to cyber crimes. Because theft and misuse of information and loss of service cannot be totally prevented, some companies purchase special insurance policies. These policies help pay for losses that result from cyber crimes or losses and lawsuits arising from Internet operations.

Figure 3-1.13

Typical Security Measures

Security Measure	Purpose
Access Control	Employees limited to access information within their job responsibilities
	Outsiders prevented from accessing company networks
Identification and Authentication	Use of passwords or other identification to check for authorized users
	Use of digital signatures to ensure a transmitted document has not been altered
Accuracy Checks	Guard against errors and unauthorized changes
Data Scans	Search for computer viruses or other software problems
Data Encryption	Seeks to secure transmissions of data
Accountability	Links all activities to the user's identity
Audit Trails	Maintains a log of all attempts to gain access to the system, all activity, unusual activity, and variations from established procedures

Reviewing the Topic

1. Define information.
2. What are the most common forms of information?
3. What effect might use of outdated or incorrect information have on a business?
4. List five obstacles to using information efficiently.
5. Describe the five operations involved in information processing.
6. Describe five common information technologies.
7. Name three general categories of software and describe each one.
8. Explain the difference between a peer-to-peer LAN and a server-based LAN.
9. List three types of transmission carriers used in LANs.
10. How does a WAN differ from a LAN?
11. Explain the difference between a dedicated line and a dial-up line for WAN transmissions.
12. Why should computer systems be serviced and maintained on a regular basis?
13. List three major security concerns for computer information systems.
14. List three security measures businesses can use to help safeguard information stored in their computer systems.

Interacting with Others

Kristin and Tyler work together in a small office. One of Tyler's main responsibilities is updating customer account records. He enjoys completing the paperwork, but really dislikes filing. He is very prompt about updating customer account information, but not about filing the completed paperwork in the customer files. Kristin's main responsibility is customer service. When responding to customer concerns, she pulls the customer file to access the information. Kristin did not have up-to-date information available when she responded to three different customer calls because Tyler had not yet filed the paperwork he completed two weeks ago.

1. Explain why it is important for Kristin to have up-to-date information when she responds to customer calls.
2. If you were Kristin, what would you say to Tyler about this issue?

CHAPTER 3: INFORMATION: A VITAL BUSINESS RESOURCE

You work for Craig-Weston Mansion, a small inn in Nova Scotia, located on a bluff above Pandora's Harbor. A member of your work team has asked you to proofread and edit some copy that is to be added to your organization's Web site. These statements contain grammar, spelling, word usage, and punctuation errors that will give a very poor impression of the organization.

Key a copy of the statements, correcting all errors.

Welcome, to the beautifuly restored Craig-Weston Mansion. Overlooking Pandoras' Harbor in Nova Scotia the mansion becons you to visit. Fourteen well appointed bedrooms with private baths are furnished in antiques. A full hearty breakfast awaits you after a good nights sleep in your own king size feather-bed.

As your day begins chose from walks by the sea or horseback riding on our 5 miles of trails. Enjoy teatime with homemaid treat's galore. Nestle by the fireside, and read your favorite book by it's warm glow. Diner will be prepared by our chef and desert will be served in the parlor. Conversation, and parlor games will make you forget your hurried life back home.

You will I am sure never forget your stay at Craig Weston Mansion.

DATABASE

RESEARCH

Topic 3-1 ACTIVITY 1

Equipment Inventory

Office workers are often responsible for keeping an inventory of the computers, software, and other equipment used in the office. Because theft is a serious problem in some companies, having an accurate record of items purchased and assigned to the office is important. Equipment inventories are also used in scheduling equipment maintenance and upgrades. In this activity, you will complete the five operations involved in information processing as you create and update an inventory record. Because you probably do not currently work in an office, you will create an inventory of the hardware, software, furniture, and other equipment found in your classroom.

1. **Input.** Create a new database file. Each record in the database should have the following fields:

FIELD	DESCRIPTION
Item	Enter the type of item, such as computer, software, desk, or display screen.
Description	Briefly describe the item, such as "Microsoft Office XP," "desk chair on rollers," or "Lexmark inkjet printer."
	If there is more than one brand or type of item (printer, computer, word processing software, desk) in the classroom, list each separately.
Category	Enter data in this field only for software items. List the type of software (word processing, utility, communications). List items in a suite separately.
Quantity	Enter the number of the items.
Condition	In this memo field, briefly describe the condition of the item, for example "Good," "Unusable," or "Top paper tray is broken."

   Enter data to create a record for each item (hardware, software, furniture, and other equipment) found in your classroom. Other equipment might include items such as paper cutters, bulletin boards, or display stands.

2. **Processing.** Generate a report from the data to include only the Item and Quantity fields. Sort the data in the report in ascending order by the Item field. Create a query to find only records with "printer" in the Item field.

3. **Output.** Print the report and the results of the query created in step 2.

4. **Distribution.** Give the report and the query results created in step 2 to your instructor.

5. **Storage.** Save the database file using a meaningful file name.

Topic 3-1 **ACTIVITY 2**

Local Area Networks

Learn about the local area network used in your school or in a local business. Find answers to the questions listed below regarding the LAN in your school. If your school does not have a LAN or if your instructor so directs, interview someone from a local business that uses a LAN. Create a short report that gives the name of the organization you are researching and summarizes your findings.

- What physical area does the LAN cover?
- Does the LAN use peer-to-peer or server-based networking?
- What types of cabling does the LAN use (twisted-pair coaxial, fiber-optic)?
- Are any wireless connections used on the LAN? If yes, describe.
- What types of equipment (computers, printers, scanners, etc.) are connected to the LAN?
- Approximately how many computers are connected to the LAN?
- Approximately how many people use the LAN?
- Are users required to enter a password to log on to the LAN?
- What other types of security measures are used with the LAN?
- Can users access the Internet through the LAN? If yes, is firewall software used?
- What are the primary uses of the LAN (storing data files, providing users with access to programs, etc.)?

You learned in Topic 3-1 that information technology refers to the computer equipment and software used to process information. Technology is only one part of managing information. Managing information effectively also includes people who follow procedures to run the information technology efficiently. An information system is composed of people, the information technology and resources, and procedures used to process information.

Typical Information Systems

Information systems help workers perform business operations efficiently. The information systems found in business relate to typical business operations such as accounting or manufacturing. Three typical information systems are described in the following paragraphs to help you understand how businesses use information systems. In reality, all the internal information systems of a particular business would probably be interrelated.

Accounting Information Systems

An accounting information system enables a business to record business transactions and report financial information. Information processed in an accounting system provides a variety of reports. These reports give information about many aspects of the business such as expenses, accounts receivable, and income. The following list describes how employees in a small business would use this information to make decisions or process work.

- A billing clerk prepares invoices and computes amounts due.
- The credit department manager approves credit for an established customer.
- The **controller** prepares the annual budget and recommends ways to increase profits.

controller: employee who oversees company finances

Marketing Information Systems

A marketing information system helps the business keep track of the customer from an initial contact, to the point of the sale or service, to a customer satisfaction follow-up. The data provided by marketing information systems identifies whether or not:

- A particular marketing approach is successful
- A customer is satisfied with the product or service
- A customer intends to make future purchases from the company

Figure 3-2.1

Businesses must maintain accurate accounting information.

© DIGITAL STOCK

Product Information Systems

If a business manufactures a product, the business must determine the cost of the goods it sells. The activities that take place within the business to create the product are recorded in the information system. This system contains the cost of materials, labor, and **overhead**. The information stored in this system is essential in helping determine the cost of the product. The following examples illustrate how different people access the information system in a manufacturing firm.

overhead: business costs not directly related to a product or service sold

- A stock control clerk checks the inventory of raw materials and processes a purchase order to replenish stock.
- A receiving clerk scans bar code labels on incoming shipments to create a record of goods received.
- A production supervisor accesses purchase order data for goods used to determine production costs.
- A production worker completes an assembly operation, scans part-number information, and enters the quantity of completed products.
- An accounts payable clerk verifies invoices and receipt of goods before approving payment for purchases.
- A department manager uses prior months' financial data in creating a budget.

Topic 3-2: *Information Systems and Resources*

Figure 3-2.2

Bar code labels are used in creating a record of goods received.

Traditional Resources

Companies can get information from numerous resources. Much of the information a business uses comes from within the company. You have already learned about some typical internal information systems. Business can also get information through external resources. Some of these resources are described in the following paragraphs.

Marketing Research Firms

Marketing research firms make data available in a variety of forms for business needs. They focus on the customer and the market. Marketing research firms use questionnaires and interviews to gather information about consumer behaviors and attitudes. They also look at marketing trends and collect valuable **demographic data**. Computer technology makes it possible for researchers to collect a variety of data, analyze huge amounts of information, and forecast market conditions.

demographic data: statistics that describe a population, such as age or race

Organizations, both large and small, often rely on the information provided by these marketing research firms. Conducting market research might be too expensive for a small-business owner. Even though a large corporation might be able to afford the investment for such research, the company could save valuable time by using the information already gathered by the research firm.

Trade Publications and Associations

Many organizations look to trade publications, books, and journals for facts and forecasts about their industry. These publications include information about trade associations and provide good sources of information for the particular products, service area, or industry in which the business specializes. Trade associations often conduct or sponsor research related to the industry. Association meetings and workshops provide an opportunity to network—meaning to interact and share information with others who have similar interests or concerns. Conventions or trade shows provide an opportunity to view new products and services designed for the industry.

Government Agencies and Libraries

Information from government agencies is useful to many organizations. Government publications often include forecasts and results from research studies. The Small Business Administration and the U.S. Census Bureau are examples of sources that provide demographics, statistics, and other data useful in making business decisions.

WORKPLACE **CONNECTIONS**

A toy manufacturer is interested in the demographics of a particular region. By acquiring information about the number of individuals within a certain age range, the company can decide whether to advertise its products in that region. If the demographics indicate a large population under the age of twelve, then toys could probably be marketed successfully. On the other hand, if the population under the age of twelve is small, the advertising money might be better spent in another region.

University libraries are an excellent information resource. Many offer research services as well as specialized publications not readily available elsewhere. Some companies also have libraries—an estimated 6,000 nationwide. Many of these libraries also specialize in research.

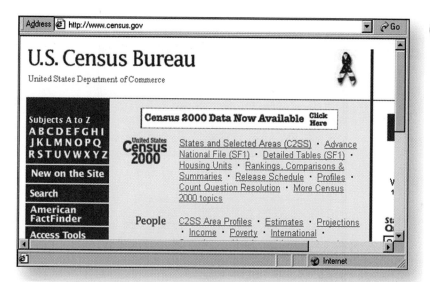

Figure 3-2.3

The U.S. Census Bureau provides demographic data for the United States.

Source: U.S. Census Bureau, U.S. Department of Commerce. Online. Available: http://www.ensus.gov. November 26, 2001.

Topic 3-2: *Information Systems and Resources*

Electronic Resources

With advancements in information technology come new sources of information and new ways to access the information. Electronic resources, often called online resources, are those available via the computer. Online resources are becoming more popular because of the wide range of available information and the instant access to and timeliness of the information.

Electronic Databases

A database is a collection of related information. Use of electronic databases has grown rapidly in the past few years. Electronic databases are available on CD-ROM, the Internet, and online services such as CompuServe. These databases provide information on many topics useful to businesses. Most electronic databases have powerful search features that allow the user to find information quickly and easily.

Some databases support natural language searches. This means that the user simply enters a question in everyday terms and the database search feature interprets and answers the question. No special searching techniques or rules are needed.

relational database: software program that allows the user to link data from a number of database files or tables to find information or generate reports

Companies often maintain relational databases as part of their internal information system. **Relational databases** allow the user to link data from a number of database files or tables to find information or generate reports. This linking capability means that data can be stored in relatively small files that are easy to work with. Data updated in one file can be used to update other files easily.

data mining: process in which software program searches for significant patterns in data

Data mining is a process that helps businesses analyze the wealth of information contained in databases. With automated data mining, the program searches for interesting and significant patterns of information in the database without detailed questions posed by the user. The information is then presented in graphs, reports, and so forth. The user can look at the data

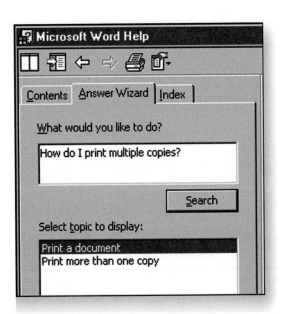

Figure 3-2.4

The Microsoft Word help database supports natural language searches.

CHAPTER 3: INFORMATION: A VITAL BUSINESS RESOURCE

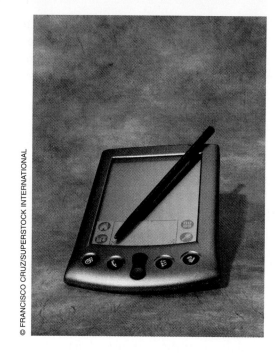

Figure 3-2.5

PDAs are used to store and access information.

from several viewpoints, and the results may reveal perceptions the user never considered. Data mining can be used to help a business target consumers and predict market trends.

Personal Digital Assistants

The personal digital assistant (PDA) provides another means for retrieving information. PDAs are handheld computers. They can be used to store a variety of data, from a personal diary of schedules and appointments to a reference text.

WORKPLACE **CONNECTIONS**

Consider this example of how healthcare workers use PDAs:

Healthcare workers need to access not only clinical data, but also educational resources, decision aids, and other professional information. PDA technology stores several medical reference texts and clinical data. All this information is stored on a memory card about the size of a credit card. A medical calculator is also included for standard calculations. The healthcare workers have immediate access to reference material where and when they need it.

Intranets

Intranets are internal information networks based on Internet technologies and standards. The intranet may reside on a company's local area network or be part of a wide area network, depending on its intended uses. An intranet

Topic 3-2: *Information Systems and Resources*

is designed for users within an organization and is protected by a firewall. A firewall works two ways: first, to block outsiders from entering the company's intranet and, second, to allow company intranet users to access the Internet. Only those individuals who have registered and/or received passwords are given access to an intranet.

Intranets save time and money for businesses by allowing employees to communicate quickly and easily. Employees use the intranet to access information to help them make better decisions, serve customers more effectively, and be better informed of the company's products, procedures, and activities. Intranets have many applications within organizations, such as:

- Centralized information source—providing immediate access to product information (catalogs, price lists, product manuals, shipping information), employee information (telephone directories, organizational charts, job descriptions), and organizational information (calendars, press releases, public relations activities)

- Inventory control—tracking parts and new materials, resulting in less waste and reduced inventory costs

- Production scheduling—providing instant access to scheduling information that can change frequently

- Employee handbook—providing updated personnel policies while saving printing and distribution costs

- Employee benefits information—providing employees an opportunity to review and enroll in benefit plans

- Employee recruitment—allowing internal posting and matching of job openings and employee resumes

- Expense reports—reducing errors, paperwork, and cost by submitting electronic forms

Figure 3-2.6

Employees can access the company intranet for current, accurate information.

© CORBIS

The U.S. workforce is increasingly mobile. More workers than ever are on the road on a regular basis or work from home offices. With a laptop computer and modem, these workers can easily access the company intranet and interact with coworkers. Consider these examples of intranet use.

CHAPTER 3: INFORMATION: A VITAL BUSINESS RESOURCE

- Using an intranet a distribution company sends sales information daily that was previously sent by overnight mail to 400 sales people world-wide.
- An import firm with offices around the world sends data on product availability to the home office via the intranet.
- A technology firm links research efforts by engineers in Europe, Asia, and the United States via the company intranet.
- Employees access computer-based training programs and find answers to frequently asked questions while away from the office via the intranet.

WORKPLACE CONNECTIONS

The use of intranets has helped businesses achieve better results by making up-to-date information readily available. Prior to using an intranet, a national sales firm had problems with customer satisfaction. Price quotes to customers often were outdated. Items promised for immediate delivery were often not available to be shipped right away. Sales personnel spent hours on the phone with headquarters to get current price quotes. They had to wait for faxes or returned e-mails about their customers' orders. Sales were declining.

In an effort to solve these problems, the company installed an intranet. The intranet provides a central database of information for all sales associates regardless of their locations or the time of day. Now, the sales associates have immediate access to the company's intranet for real-time price quotes, stock inventory, delivery schedules, and product details. Sales are increasing.

The company also places product demonstrations on the intranet. Sales people can download these high-quality sales presentations and share them with customers. The company is now developing online training programs to update and improve the skills and product knowledge of their sales force. Sales associates report that they not only feel more satisfied in their jobs, but that they also have time to make more sales contacts.

The development of corporate intranets is a growing trend. As the technology needed to develop an intranet continues to grow less expensive and easier to use, more and more companies will make an intranet part of their information system.

The Internet

The Internet, a giant network of computers and smaller networks that spans the globe, is the world's largest information resource. Using the Internet, businesses can connect with other people, businesses, organizations, and information resources around the world quickly and easily. The Internet is used for research, transferring files, exchanging messages, promoting organizations, advertising products and services, and buying and selling products.

Topic 3-2: *Information Systems and Resources*

extranet: an information network like an intranet, but it is partially available to select outside users

Intranets to Extranets

Many individuals are comfortable using the Internet for personal or business activities. Similarly, businesses and large organizations are increasingly using intranets to provide accurate and current information to employees. Some businesses use a combination of intranet and extranet technologies to meet customer and employee needs. An **extranet** is an information network like an intranet, but it is partially available to select outside users. An extranet uses a firewall to provide limited access to information to users outside the organization.

Many extranets have evolved from the successful use of a company's intranet. For example, Federal Express began tracking the receipt, in-transit location, and delivery of packages years ago through its mainframe system. Operators would key information to locate a package while customers waited on the telephone. Now, Federal Express has developed an extranet for users to track their own packages via the Internet. Users enter their package identification number to retrieve the tracking information quickly themselves.

Banks, insurance companies, investment firms, and universities are frequent users of extranets. In these instances, outside users seek information specific to themselves. They gain access to the extranet with some form of identification, such as passwords or ID numbers. The extranet can also link business partners with one another by linking their corporate intranets. Kodak, for example, provides access to engineers from partner firms to collaborate on design projects, such as digital camera designs.

By skillfully using the Internet, intranets, and extranets, businesses can provide timely and consistent information to employees and customers. Updating a centralized source allows businesses to respond to change quickly. Costs are lowered by reducing the printing and distribution of paper documents to employees and business partners. The use of intranets and extranets helps to keep both employees and customers better informed and satisfied.

The following examples describe a few ways that businesses use the Internet.

- Through electronic mail, coworkers are able to communicate with each other. Workers can send and receive messages through computers used in the office, laptop computers used by employees working outside the office, and computers used by employees working at home.
- A sales representative plans an out-of-state trip, making the airline reservations using a travel service on the Internet.
- An investment broker accesses information on the Internet to get up-to-the-minute stock quotes.
- A small-business owner uses a site on the Internet to sell sports memorabilia such as baseball trading cards, league pennants, autographed products, T-shirts, and sports items.
- A civic organization uses a Web site to provide information about the organization, list upcoming events, and post public service announcements.
- A clothing manufacturer provides product information on a company Web site. Customers can order products and track the progress of orders that have been placed.

Finding and Sharing Information

The Internet is loaded with information about many topics. Finding the specific information you need among the large amount of data available may be a challenge. Programs are available to help you search for information on the Internet. Printed directories containing popular or interesting Internet addresses may be purchased.

Web Browsers

Knowing where and how to look for information is basic to using electronic resources. With the increased use of the Internet, browser software programs have become very popular. Browsers provide navigation and search tools to help you find topics and locations on the World Wide Web.

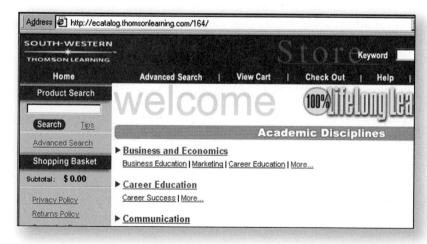

Figure 3-2.7

This textbook publisher makes shopping online easy.

Source: South-Western Thomson Learning. Online. Available: http://ecatalog. thomsonlearning.com/164/. November 26, 2001.

URLs (Uniform Resource Locators) are Internet addresses that can be understood by any Web Browser as it searches for **hypertext** documents on computers around the world. URL addresses start with *http://*, which stands for HyperText Transfer Protocol. This is a set of instructions telling computers how to send and receive hypertext data and documents. The *www* in the URL stands for World Wide Web. Periods in the URL are separators and are pronounced "dot." Three letters in the URL represent the domain name. Some common domain names are *edu* for education, *org* for organization, *com* for commercial, and *gov* for government. Other parts of the URL identify sections or levels within the Web site.

When an organization is outside your country, a two-letter country code is used at the end of the address. Every country has its own unique geographic domain code. For example, *.uk* is used for the United Kingdom and *.mx* is used for Mexico. If there is no geographic code in a name, then the domain is located within your own country. Some examples of URL addresses are shown below. Can you guess the information you might find at these addresses?

- http://www.harvard.edu/admissions (Harvard University)
- http://www.redcross.org (The American Red Cross)
- http://www.delta.com (Delta Airlines)
- http://www.dol.gov (U.S. Department of Labor)
- http://canada.gc.ca (Government of Canada, official site)

When you want to visit a location on the Internet, you may do so by entering the URL address in your browser. Pay close attention to spelling, punctuation, symbols, and capitalization when entering the address. URLs are sensitive to the use of upper- and lowercase letters. You may also move to a different location on the Internet by clicking a hypertext link. When you use hypertext links, the associated URLs are often invisible. You merely click on the hypertext entry, and your browser takes you to the Internet address (URL) that is associated with that hypertext.

Browsers enable you to customize searches and help you locate information from several information sources. Though the programs vary in appearance and terminology, they offer many of the same capabilities and features. Examples of browsers include Netscape and Microsoft Internet Explorer. Internet Explorer is shown in Figure 3-2.8. The lines of text shown in blue and underlined in Figure 3-2.8 are hyperlinks.

Search Tools

If you are looking for information about job opportunities, doing research for work or hobbies, or planning a trip, you might need help finding Internet sites that relate to these activities. Many search tools, often referred to as search engines, can help you locate sites. You may be familiar with some widely used search engines such as AltaVista, Lycos, WebCrawler, or Yahoo!. Once you find a Web site, you can use the site's search tool to find information on the site.

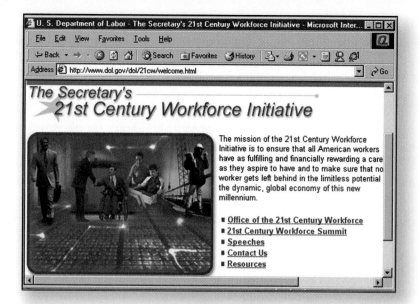

Figure 3-2.8

The U.S. Department of Labor Web site provides information related to employment.

Source: U.S. Department of Labor. Online. Available: http://www.dol.gov/dol/21cw/welcome.html. November 26, 2001.

To perform a search on most Web sites, simply identify and type two or three keywords related to the topic and then click the search button. The search tool will locate sites/documents, called "matches" or "hits," that contain these keywords. Your search may result in no matches, several matches, or thousands of matches. If your search results in a large number of matches, you may want to use more specific keywords to locate the information. On the other hand, if you receive only a few hits, you may have to broaden your search by using more general keywords. You may need to use several search tools to perform a thorough search because not all search tools look at every site that may contain the information you need.

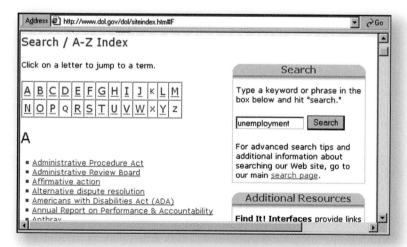

Figure 3-2.9

The U.S. Department of Labor Web site provides various ways to search for information.

Source: U.S. Department of Labor. Online. Available: http://www.dol.gov/dol/siteindex.htm. November 26, 2001.

Transferring Files

Millions of files are available on the Internet—research papers and data, software, pictures, sounds, and more. Perhaps a software vendor is offering a free update or "patch" to correct a problem for a software product. The publisher of your textbook may have a site offering student data files or special software tutorials. You may have to research a particular topic at work. You search for information about the topic with Yahoo!, Gopher, or other search tools. When you find sites with data you would like to use, what do you do? You can transfer or download many of these files from a distant computer to your computer by using something called file transfer protocol.

file transfer protocol: tool that allows files to be uploaded to or downloaded from a remote computer

File transfer protocol (FTP) is a powerful tool that allows a copy of the file you request from a remote computer to be copied to your computer. There are two types of FTP transfers—private and anonymous. In a private FTP transfer, you must have permission to access and download files. A private user name or account number and password are needed before you can download files (copy from) or upload files (copy to) to the remote computer. In an anonymous FTP transfer, the site can be accessed easily without privately issued user names or passwords. Thousands of anonymous sites are open to everyone.

E-mail, Mailing Lists, and Newsgroups

E-mail, mailing lists, and newsgroups all provide means for communicating and sharing information via the Internet.

E-mail

e-mail: the electronic transfer of messages using computers and software

One popular use of the Internet is electronic mail, or **e-mail**. E-mail is the electronic transfer of messages. LANs and WANs offer e-mail to all computers that are connected, whether they are in the same office or in different countries. Users are limited to sending and receiving messages only to and from those on their network unless their network is connected to the Internet. If they are connected to the Internet, they can send and receive messages all over the world.

E-mail messages may contain not only text, but also audio and graphics. Files containing information such as research findings, corporate financial statements, or client databases may be attached to the e-mail message. When an e-mail file is received, it is automatically stored in a user's electronic mailbox. An e-mail mailbox is an online computer storage space designated to hold electronic messages. These messages are stored for the owner of the mailbox and may be read, saved for later reference, printed, or deleted. E-mail is inexpensive, fast, and easy to use for workers at all levels in organizations. You will learn more about using e-mail in Chapter 4.

Mailing Lists

mailing list: directory of Internet user addresses

A **mailing list** is a directory of Internet user addresses of people who want to have information about a topic delivered regularly to their addresses. Some mailing lists are maintained by businesses while other lists are private. The user subscribes to the mailing list to receive messages.

Figure 3-2.10

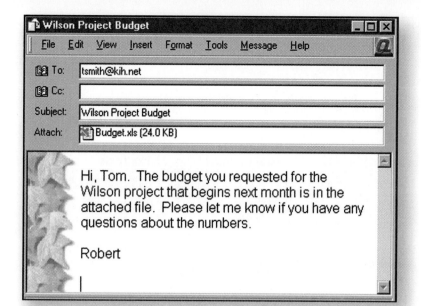

This e-mail has a file attachment.

Newsgroups

When people want to share ideas and information with others on the Internet, they can do so via Usenet. Usenet, which stands for User's Network, is a collection of topically organized newsgroups. **Newsgroups** publish online articles and messages related to a huge number of topics. Users participate in public discussions about a topic by sending messages that all participants in the newsgroup can read. Newsgroups are available for thousands of topics.

newsgroup: publication of online articles and messages related to a certain topic

Promoting Organizations

Many organizations are going online for promotion purposes. For example, many colleges and universities maintain sites with information about their programs. Potential students visit the sites and are able to compare curricula, costs, and other aspects of campus life to help them choose a school. What about the colleges that are not on the Internet? They are missing the opportunity to inform many potential students about their programs.

Many states and cities have Web sites to promote tourism and industry in the area. These sites typically include general information about the area, a calendar of events, attractions and sites of special interest, and links to area hotels, restaurants, and other businesses.

Civic and charitable organizations maintain Web sites to provide information about the mission and goals of the organization, to advertise special events, and to encourage contributing to the organization.

Figure 3-2.11

The state of Colorado promotes its scenic byways on its Web site.

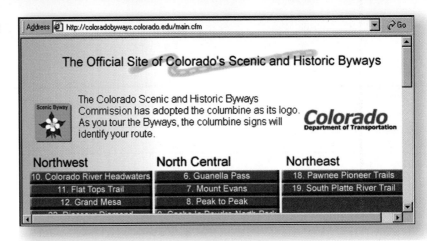

Source: Colorado Department of Transportation. Online. Available: http://coloradobyways.colorado.edu/main.cfm. November 27, 2001.

Many companies promote themselves and their products on company Web sites. If the company does not sell products directly to consumers, the Web site usually gives a list of retail stores where the products may be purchased. The site may also show information such as the company's mission and goals, the history of the company, the structure of the company, and charitable or civic causes supported by the company.

Ecommerce—Buying and Selling Online

Responding to the amazing growth of the Internet over the past decade, businesses are changing the ways they acquire, use, and share information. For example, customers who buy online typically provide information about themselves to the company. This information is called a customer profile. Companies may also build their store of information about online customers by using cookies. Cookies are messages exchanged by the user's Web browser and the Web server being visited. They can be used to track the user's identity and online behavior.

The information acquired from online customers allows the business to analyze customer buying habits. The company can then suggest related products that may be of interest to a customer. Amazon.com, one of the most successful e-commerce companies, uses this technique. When you purchase a book or movie from the company's Web site, the site suggests other titles that may be of interest to you.

Businesses can use information gathered from many customers to customize advertising on appropriate Web sites or television channels likely to be viewed by its customers. Using customer information to target advertising helps the company increase sales.

Consumer trust in the company is very important in ecommerce. Companies seek to increase customer trust and loyalty by building long-term relationships with customers. They offer services such as on-line customer support, order shipment tracking, and online newsletters or discussion groups about their products or related topics. By using the Internet to share information with customers, they strengthen their relationships with customers.

Privacy of customer data is an area of concern related to ecommerce. Will the company share information such as customer name, e-mail address, and buying habits with other organizations that the customer might not want to have this data? Many companies have privacy statements on their Web sites that state how customer information will be used. Such statements reassure customers about how their data will be used and help build customer trust.

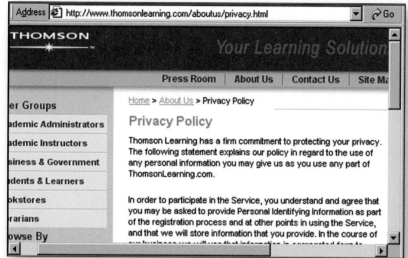

Figure 3-2.12

Figure 3-2.12

A Web site's privacy policy discusses how customer data will be used.

Source: Thomson Learning. Online. Available: http://www.thomsonlearning.com/aboutus/privacy.html. November 27, 2001.

E-commerce has created a lack of geographic boundaries for many businesses. This brings new challenges in communicating and sharing information with people of many countries and cultures. Web sites must be designed to be attractive and easy to use for all customers. Product instructions, warranties, and customer support may be needed in several languages. Marketing personnel may need to study the cultures of their new customers to learn how to create appealing advertisements.

Just a few aspects of information related to ecommerce have been described in this section. As Internet use and ecommerce continue to grow, companies will need to adapt to new ways of acquiring, using, and sharing information.

Topic 3-2: *Information Systems and Resources*

Reviewing the Topic

1. What kinds of information does an accounting information system provide?

2. Give two examples of how people access information from a product information system.

3. List and briefly describe three traditional external resources where companies get information.

4. Describe how relational databases differ from nonrelational databases.

5. What is data mining?

6. How is an intranet similar to the Internet? How is it different from the Internet?

7. List four activities for which businesses use the Internet.

8. Describe the purpose of Internet browser software programs.

9. What is hypertext, and how do hypertext links work?

10. What is a URL?

11. How does a Web browser differ from a search engine?

12. What is file transfer protocol?

13. Give two examples of how organizations promote themselves using Web sites.

14. Give two examples of how an ecommerce business can use information to build consumer trust.

15. Describe how the Internet affects the way businesses acquire, use, and share information.

Interacting with Others

While completing some tasks to meet a deadline, you noticed that a member of your sales team, Jeremy, was using the computer at his workstation to download copyrighted clipart. You observed him pasting the clipart into the department's online newsletter and posting it on the company's Web site. When you asked Jeremy about his activities, he shrugged and said that no one should mind because the chances of his getting caught were very slim. And besides, he was not really hurting anyone.

What should you do?

- Let the matter drop and ignore his illegal actions.
- Inform your supervisor about Jeremy's use of the Internet.
- Send an e-mail message to Jeremy condemning him for his actions.
- Talk with Jeremy again and list reasons why you think his behavior is inappropriate.

CHAPTER 3: INFORMATION: A VITAL BUSINESS RESOURCE

1. Prepare a written response to each of the four suggested actions.
2. If you feel there is a fifth alternative that would be more effective, describe and discuss the action.

Reinforcing Math Skills

Assume that you are an office worker for a professional organization that sponsors training seminars for various information technologies. Recently, the company completed a series of seminars in five cities throughout the United States. The fee for each participant at three of the seminars was $1,000. At two of the seminars (Update on Virtual Meetings and Using PDAs) the fee for each participant was $500. You were given the task of e-mailing the manager of each seminar site and getting enrollment figures for the courses. The details you recorded are shown below.

1. Record the title of each of the five seminars on a separate line. Calculate and record the following:
   - The total number of participants for each seminar
   - The grand total number of participants for all seminars
   - The total revenue earned from each seminar
   - The grand total of all revenue received
   - The total number of participants in each city
2. Identify the seminar with the largest total number of participants and the seminar producing the largest total revenue.

PARTICIPANTS

Seminar and Date	Boston	New York	Washington	Chicago	San Francisco
Data Mining January 6 – 10	125	245	110	117	97
Managing Databases February 15 – 18	105	325	175	130	110
Security for the Internet March 1 – 4	78	110	45	72	70
Virtual Meetings March 19 – 22	170	295	140	110	115
Using PDAs April 1 – 2	210	410	175	102	117

Topic Review

Topic 3-2   ACTIVITY 1

Internet Use Report

Research current Internet use numbers. Then key a report highlighting the information.

1. Open and print the data file **Internet.pdf**, which contains the report. Follow the formatting instructions written on the document. Correct any spelling or word usage errors you find in the document.

2. Search the Internet to find current Internet use numbers. Update the reference at the end of the report to reflect your source of information. (If you do not have access to the Internet, use the numbers provided in the report.)

3. Create a pie chart using your spreadsheet software to show Internet use by language groups. Then copy the chart into the report.

Topic 3-2   ACTIVITY 2

Update Equipment Inventory

Update the equipment inventory database you created in Topic 3-1 Activity 1.

1. Assume the following equipment changes have been made in your classroom:
   • Two new Lexmark inkjet printers in good condition have been added.
   • Three desks have been removed.

2. Update the inventory using this information.

3. Print a new report showing the Item and Quantity fields for all records.

4. Create a query to find only records with "desk" in the Item field. Print the query results.

5. Save the database file and give the updated report and the query results to your instructor.

Chapter Review

Summary

Information is critical to every organization regardless of its size or purpose. Because organizations use information to make decisions, they give a great deal of attention to managing information effectively and to using technology for processing it efficiently. Managing information effectively, however, means more than using current technologies. To perform operations efficiently, businesses depend on information systems composed of people, information technology and resources, and procedures for processing the information. Key points in this chapter include:

- The common types of information found in businesses are numbers, text, image, and voice. The way office workers process this information varies depending on the nature of the business.

- When information is managed effectively, organizations can operate efficiently, regardless of the complexity of the business or the volume of transactions. If information is not current or not accurate, a business may make poor decisions that could prove costly.

- Incompatible databases, duplicate or missing information, or limited access to information are examples of obstacles to using information efficiently.

- The information processing workflow consists of five operations: input, processing, output, distribution, and storage.

- Information technologies improve the workflow and communication in companies both internally and externally, and technology can even give a company a competitive edge.

- Computerized processing relies heavily on hardware and related software to turn data into meaningful and timely information.

- Software may be divided into three broad categories: operating system software, application software, and utility software.

- Local area networks (LANs) and wide area networks (WANs) help workers complete their daily tasks and share information.

- Office workers must be concerned with maintenance, security, and ethics related to information processing systems and software.

- Information systems found in business relate to typical business operations such as accounting or manufacturing.

- A company's success may depend on its sources of information. Traditional resources include marketing research firms, trade publications and associations, and government agencies.

- Advancements in information technology provide new sources of information and new ways to access the information, including electronic databases, personal digital assistants, the Internet, intranets, and extranets.

- Using the Internet, businesses can connect quickly and easily with other people, businesses, organizations, and information resources around the world.

- Tools such as Web browsers, search engines, file transfer protocol, e-mail, mailing lists, and newsgroups help workers find and share information.

- Many organizations maintain Web sites to promote the organization or sell products or services online. As Internet use and ecommerce continue to grow, companies will need to adapt to new ways of acquiring, using, and sharing information.

Key Terms

computer virus	hypertext	modem
controller	incompatible	newsgroup
data mining	information	overhead
demographic data	processing	proprietary
ecommerce	interactive voice	information
electronic imaging	response	relational database
e-mail	Internet service	sales channel
extranet	provider	satellite
file transfer	local area network	software
protocol	mailing list	transaction
firewall	microwave	wide area network
hardware	transmission	

COMPOSITION
INTERNET
RESEARCH
TEAMWORK
WORD PROCESSING

Chapter 3   ACTIVITY 1

Privacy Policies

Privacy of customer data is a concern for many consumers. Most well-established online companies post a privacy policy on the company Web site. This policy tells the user what the company will do with consumer data. Work with a classmate to explore the privacy policies of major online companies.

1. Each student, surf the Web and locate at least two companies that sell products online. Find and print the privacy policy for each company Web site. Read the privacy policy and highlight or underline key points in the policy.

2. As a team, discuss the key points identified by each student. Write a short report that lists the companies for which the team found privacy statements and summarizes the key points identified in the statements. In the report, discuss how the policies are similar and how they are different. List the companies to which you would be comfortable giving personal data and the ones to which you would not want to give information about yourself. Explain the reasons for your choice.

Computer Security Tips

The National Infrastructure Protection Center (NIPC) publishes articles online related to computer security. Key a document containing computer security tips as a bulleted list that can be posted on a bulletin board or Web site.

1. Open and print the data file **Security.pdf**, which contains the rough draft document.

2. Key the document with a 1.5-inch top margin and 1-inch side margins. Center and bold the title lines in all caps. Quadruple space (QS) after the title. Key the paragraphs and then apply bullets to create bulleted paragraphs. Apply bold to the first sentence of each bullet paragraph for emphasis. Correct errors in spelling or word usage as you key the document. Proofread carefully and correct all errors before printing the document.

Communicating in Written Form

This chapter focuses on reading and preparing written communications at work. Many business communications are in written form, and their preparation is a time-consuming task that requires many competent employees. The ability to read and understand written documents is a basic yet vital skill for all types of office workers.

In this chapter, you will examine the importance of reading skills and learn some strategies for improving your reading skills. You will also learn to develop and process effective business documents. You will become acquainted with the procedures to prepare effective business letters, memos, reports, and related documents.

Reading and Writing at Work

OBJECTIVES

- Describe the kinds of reading common at work
- Identify critical components of reading skills
- Explain common techniques for improving reading skills
- Describe the nature of writing tasks common at work
- Describe the characteristics of effective written messages
- Describe an effective procedure for managing a writing task

Most jobs in today's business world require reading and writing. Talking with people in a wide range of jobs reveals considerable differences in their responsibilities. A reasonable conclusion is that those who work must have adequate reading and writing skills.

The Value of Reading Skills

Regardless of your career choice, you will find that you will spend a considerable amount of time reading. A major study titled, *What Work Requires of Schools: A SCANS Report for America 2000*, includes the following comment:

> *. . . First, all employees will have to read well enough to understand and interpret diagrams, directories, correspondence, manuals, records, charts, graphs, tables and specifications. Without the ability to read a diverse set of materials, workers cannot locate the descriptive and quantitative information needed to make decisions or to recommend courses of action. What do these reading requirements mean on the job? They might involve*
>
> - *dealing with letters and written policy on complaints*
> - *reading the text of technical manuals from equipment vendors**

Reading at Work

On many occasions you will need to read on the job. You will find that reading is vital to understanding the total company in which you work. You will also need to read to complete your work tasks.

Learning About Your Company

Employees who want to understand how their work relates to the total company will do much voluntary reading of information about the company that is available in memos, internal newsletters, and other documents.

WORKPLACE CONNECTIONS

A new receptionist describes how reading helped her learn about her company:

I knew little about this company when I came here to work six months ago as a receptionist/clerk. How could I be able to answer questions of callers if I was completely uninformed about the company? We were introduced to the company and received some brochures

(continued)

---

*U.S. Department of Labor, The Secretary's Commission on Achieving Necessary Skills. *What Work Requires of Schools: A SCANS Report for America 2000.* June, 1991. Washington, D.C.: U.S. Government Printing Office.

Many policies and procedures related to your job will be available in written form. A manager may explain how a particular task is to be done or what policies are to be followed. You will find it helpful, though, to read the written version of what was presented. You read to have a thorough understanding of what you are to do. From time to time, memos related to ways of doing tasks or changes in policies are sent to employees. Such correspondence should be read and filed for easy reference later.

Understanding Instructions for Equipment

Employees are frequently provided new equipment that requires them to learn new methods of work. Sometimes demonstrations of the equipment are provided. Workers generally find, however, that they must read and understand the written instructions for the equipment. For example, an employee who works for a company that does surveys was asked to accompany one of the researchers in the field and to use a portable tape recorder. The employee was expected to read and follow the written instructions for using an external microphone as shown in Figure 4-1.2.

Following Instructions on Forms

Businesses develop forms to simplify the task of collecting appropriate and complete information. You will find forms for such tasks as recording telephone messages, requesting supplies and equipment, ordering goods, reporting travel expenses, and submitting time reports. Reading all instructions on

Figure 4-1.1

An informed employee works more effectively.

© IMAGE 100/ROYALTY FREE/CORBIS

CHAPTER 4: COMMUNICATING IN WRITTEN FORM

Recording from Various Sound Sources

MIC PLUG IN
POWER

Recording with an External Microphone

Connect a microphone to the MIC jack. There is a small projection to show the position of the MIC jack near the jack. Use a microphone of low impedance (less than 3 kilohms) such as ECM-T10 (not supplied).

When using a plug-in power system microphone, the power to the microphone is supplied from this unit.

Note

• When recording with an external microphone, the VOR system may not work properly because of the difference in sensitivity.

Recording from Another Equipment

Connect another equipment to the MIC jack using the RK-G64HG connecting cord (not supplied).

Figure 4-1.2

Written instructions for using an external microphone

forms and providing all information requested is very important. If some item of information is not needed in a particular instance or is not available, a comment should be added to indicate that. Note Figure 4-1.3, which shows a telephone message recorded on a form. What information did the person who recorded the message fail to add?

To _Gil Swartz_

Date _11/7_   Time _9 15_   A.M. ☐ / P.M. ☐

WHILE YOU WERE OUT

M _s. Carol Radice_

of _Central Bank_

Phone _(212) 316-4211_

Area Code   Number   Extension

TELEPHONED	✓	PLEASE CALL	✓
CALLED TO SEE YOU		WILL CALL AGAIN	
WANTS TO SEE YOU		**URGENT**	
RETURNED YOUR CALL			

Message _Needs additional details_

Operator

Figure 4-1.3

A message should include all necessary information to respond to the call.

Topic 4-1: *Reading and Writing at Work*

Responding to Inquiries

Many employees must respond to inquiries from other departments and from customers or clients. The subject of inquiries varies considerably. Employees are not expected to know every requested detail from memory. Knowing the sources of information in company-developed databases is critical to responding promptly. Once the appropriate source is accessed, the worker needs to read quickly and accurately the information sought by the caller or visitor.

WORKPLACE CONNECTIONS

Linda works in customer services for a mail-order company that sells a variety of items related to books, such as bookcases, lamps, and reading tables. Linda often receives specific questions, such as: "I have a bookcase that is not the exact size as the one you advertise. I need a bookcase to place on top of the one I have, so I need to know what your bookcase's exact dimensions are. Can you help me?" Linda is able to access her database quickly and provide the caller with the correct information.

Using Written References/Databases

Office workers frequently use a variety of references. References commonly found in many offices are dictionaries, atlases, telephone directories, and policy and procedures manuals. Your organization may maintain information

Figure 4-1.4

Sample Currency Exchange Rates

Base Currency	Exchange Rates for Converting to:					
	U.S. Dollars	Euro	Canadian Dollars	Australian Dollars	Great Britain Pounds	Japanese Yen
U.S. Dollars	-	1.1316	1.5942	1.9141	0.7065	123.8995
Euro	0.8837	-	1.4088	1.6915	0.6243	109.4900
Canadian Dollars	0.6273	0.7098	-	1.2007	0.4431	77.7186
Australian Dollars	0.5224	0.5912	0.8329	-	0.3691	64.7295
Great Britain Pounds	1.4155	1.6018	2.2566	2.7094	-	175.3804
Japanese Yen	0.0081	0.0091	0.0129	0.0154	0.0057	-

CHAPTER 4: COMMUNICATING IN WRITTEN FORM

in databases or other formats or subscribe to online information services. You will be expected to become familiar with all sources available, so that you will know where to search when requests are made. You will also want to develop references to aid you in your specific responsibilities.

For example, an office assistant who helps executives prepare for overseas trips might need to know about the exchange rate for currencies of a number of countries. This information can be accessed online. Figure 4-1.4 shows a typical currency exchange table.

Improving Reading Skills

High-level reading skills aid productivity in your work. For this reason, adopt a positive attitude toward improving your reading skills. Strive for reading skills that are so natural that you need not give detailed, deliberate attention to the reading task itself. Instead, you can focus on the content of what you are reading. Critical skills for high-level reading are comprehension, vocabulary, and speed.

Comprehension

Comprehension is the ability to understand what you have read. To comprehend is "to know." Comprehension involves a transfer of information from the printed page or the computer screen to your memory. A simple example of comprehending is keeping in mind a number that you have just found in the telephone directory. A more complex example is reading about a supplier's new product and being able to determine whether the product appears superior to the brand your company is currently using. Some techniques that you may find helpful as you strive to increase reading comprehension are listed below.

comprehension: ability to understand concepts or material that has been read

1. *Focus:* Put aside anything else on your mind when you begin to read.

2. *Identify purpose:* Before you begin, ask: "What do I want to know when I have completed this reading?"

3. *Scan:* Get an overview of the page, the chapter, or the entire article or book so you can anticipate what you will encounter as you read carefully.

4. *Summarize:* Mentally summarize as you move from one paragraph to another, particularly if you are reading to gain information for handling a task.

5. *Sequence:* After reading several paragraphs, try to think of the ideas in an appropriate order.

sequence: order

6. *Draw a mental picture:* Attempt to imagine what it is that is being discussed, especially if your reading is about a matter that is unfamiliar to you.

7. *Checkup:* Determine, through a fast review process of recalling key points, whether you have learned what you believe you should have learned.

8. *Reread:* Begin anew to read what you have just read if you are not satisfied with your checkup process.

Figure 4-1.5

Practice techniques
to improve reading
comprehension and speed.

© SUPERSTOCK INTERNATIONAL

Vocabulary

vocabulary: collection of words

Your **vocabulary** is groups of words you know and understand how to use. Having an extensive vocabulary means that you know the definitions of a large number of words. Words that are unfamiliar to you are a barrier to your reading. Certain techniques can expand your vocabulary and help you to be an effective reader. Consider using some of these as you study the content of this book:

1. When you read an unfamiliar word, try to determine its meaning from the way it is used in the sentence. After you have a meaning you think is correct, check the dictionary. If you were right, you will now be more confident as you consider what unfamiliar words might mean.

2. When you read an unfamiliar word, try separating the word into parts to see if you can guess a meaning for one or more of the parts. You read, for example, the word *rearrange*. You know from earlier experience that *rekey* means that you must key again. You know the meaning of *arrange*. You then guess that *rearrange* means to put in a new or different order. You check the dictionary and find that your guess is right.

3. While reading, have at hand a notepad and pencil to record words you don't know. Write down your best guess of what the word might mean. Also, record the page on which the uncertain word appears.

When you pause to reflect on what you have read, check the words on your list in a dictionary. As you read a definition, compare what you thought the meaning was with the dictionary's definition. You may want to refer to the place where the word occurred. Reread the passage and assure yourself that you understand what is being said. If there is more than one definition provided, be sure to select the definition that is appropriate in the context in which the word appeared. Context refers to the parts of a sentence or paragraph around a word that can help you with meaning. You may find it useful to collect new words and review your list from time to time. Try using new words in your conversations as a way of reinforcing your new knowledge.

You may find a specialized vocabulary required in your work. You will want to be alert to such terms. You may have available a specialized dictionary or other reference that will help you master new words.

Figure 4-1.6

Definitions of words are provided in this online reference on a company intranet.

ShopTalk

Choose a Letter: / A / B / C / D / E / F / G / H / I / J / K / L / M / N / O / P / Q / R / S / T / U / V / W / X / Y / Z

Acceptable Use Policy (AUP): Policies first published by universities that hosted the early Internet. They state the appropriate and inappropriate uses for the Internet and how it should be managed.

Accounts Payable: The department responsible for paying a company's bills, including payments to outside contractors, and tracking amounts owed by the company.

Speed

Another aspect of reading skill relates to speed or the time required for reading a passage. Problems with comprehension and/or vocabulary can slow the rate at which you read. The rate at which you read can merely be a habit. You probably can learn to read more quickly. Some strategies that can be useful in increasing reading speed include:

1. Focus your attention on a whole paragraph at one time. Tell yourself, "I want to read this paragraph as a single thought, and I want to know what it says." By doing so, you are forcing yourself to break a common habit of deliberately pausing at each word or each sentence as you read. When you have finished reading the paragraph, try to summarize it in a sentence or two. If you realize that you have not grasped the meaning, read it once again as quickly as possible. Again, attempt to summarize it. You are likely to improve on your second attempt.

2. Time your reading. Set a goal such as: "I will read this page, which has approximately 350 words, in three minutes." Check to see if you reached your goal. If you did, try the same passage with a reduced time allowance.

3. Deliberately force yourself ahead as you read. Do not set a specific time goal. Note the extent to which you return to your slower way of reading. Determine why you do not continue reading quickly.

Reading as a Single Process

The critical areas of comprehension, vocabulary, and reading speed have been highlighted separately. When you are actually reading, however, these areas interact. In some cases, a weakness in one area may be compensated for by strength in another. For example, you may comprehend well what you read. If you encounter an unfamiliar word, you figure out its meaning from your understanding of the rest of the sentence or paragraph. Or, you may read rapidly, but your comprehension is limited. By reading rapidly, you have time to reread the material to improve your comprehension. Ultimately, you want high skill levels in all three components.

As you consider the variety of reading tasks you may handle at work, you will come to realize how much good skills are worth. As you complete the varied assignments in your study of office procedures, regularly assess your reading skills and think of ways to improve them.

Writing at Work

The extent and nature of your writing responsibilities are related to the nature of your job, the extent to which writing tasks are assigned to you, and your own interest and willingness to assume such tasks. All office workers need strong writing skills. Among the common writing tasks are these:

- Summarizing written messages and meetings
- Revising others' writing and making changes
- Preparing communications for others to review
- Composing communications and revising them before they are distributed

Like most activity in business, business writing is purpose driven. A practical reason exists for all writing activity at work. Some of the most common purposes are:

- Communicating policies and procedures—People must be informed about the company and their work. Many written messages relate to the policies and procedures in an organization.

- Communicating plans in progress—Businesses know that planning for the future is important for success. Numerous meetings are held within businesses to think carefully about what lies ahead. Written reports are valuable for informing everyone of plans or the progress of various projects.

- Seeking or providing specific information—Specific information is often required to make a business decision. Information is needed from outsiders as well as others in the company. Often messages are exchanged for the purpose of seeking or providing such information.

Figure 4-1.7

Written reports are valuable for communicating plans or progress of projects.

© CORBIS

CHAPTER 4: COMMUNICATING IN WRITTEN FORM

- Sending messages to customers—Communications are a means of encouraging greater demand for the products and services of businesses. Letters, brochures, flyers, catalogs, and World Wide Web sites all require well-chosen words to communicate effectively. Correspondence is also required to remind customers with overdue bills of the actions that will be taken if payment is not made. Efforts to get payment are done in a friendly manner so that the customer will continue to buy from the company.

- Following up oral discussions—Much of the interaction among businesspeople is oral. Discussions may be in group meetings, person-to-person, by telephone, or by teleconferences. A written record of what was discussed is often required for those who participated and others who did not. Such a report serves as a summary of what happened and as a preview for further discussions.

WORKPLACE **CONNECTIONS**

A team of five managers met to consider quality management as it applies to their five departments. These five departments have the most interaction with the public. The purpose of the meeting was to review problems with telephone calls. Customers calling the company's customer support department had to wait on hold too long before their calls were answered. One of the engineers in the group acted as recorder, keeping notes and preparing a report shortly after each meeting. The report was forwarded to the five people on the committee to serve as a record of what had been decided and to state where the group would begin at the next session.

Effective summarizing is a valuable skill. To do it well, you should:

- Understand what is at issue or what is critical to those who are to read the summary
- Listen and/or read attentively
- Identify the critical points
- Write a summary as concisely as possible
- Review the summary to see if it actually reflects the written communication or the meeting

Reviewing the Writing of Others

Rewriting is often required for the preparation of an effective message. Administrative assistants are frequently asked to review the written communications of others. Some executives expect their assistants to act as editors. An **editor** is a person who reviews what has been written to suggest changes in wording, organization, and content. Workers with editorial responsibility are expected to:

- Identify precisely what the writer's intent is
- Focus on the purpose of the task—to ensure that the message is meeting all requirements for effectiveness

editor: person who reviews what has been written to suggest changes in wording, organization, and content

- Be candid in making suggestions
- Review their own suggestions in an objective manner

Read the message prepared by a human resources manager shown in Figure 4-1.8. Note the suggested changes made by a colleague. Consider the changes proposed. Do you think they improve the message?

Figure 4-1.8

A paragraph marked for revision using Microsoft Word's Track Changes feature

EXCESSIVE USE OF PHOTOCOPYING SERVICES

~~We are spending too much on p~~Photocopying ~~in this Company. The~~ costs <u>exceed our</u> ~~are far beyond what we have~~ budgeted. <u>Your help is needed.</u> ~~As you know, we should not be wasting resources. Have you thought carefully about how many documents really deserve to be photocopied? Have you thought carefully about how many copies you need?~~ Will you reconsider what you are submitting to be photocopied? <u>We appreciate your help.</u> ~~Something has to be done.~~

Composing Messages

Communications may reflect the point of view of a department or the company. Often, one person is assigned to prepare a **draft**, which is then reviewed by others. Staff at all levels may participate in writing tasks.

draft: a rough or preliminary version of a written message

WORKPLACE **CONNECTIONS**

The staff of the human resources department met to discuss the company's move to a new location 2,000 miles away. A staff member, noted for her writing skills, was assigned the task of drafting a message to be sent by e-mail to all employees. The staff member listened carefully to what had to be communicated. Many employees would be disappointed with the news, so an honest, carefully worded message was needed.

Administrative assistants and secretaries contribute to the efficiency of their managers by their help with incoming messages. In some offices, administrative assistants and secretaries prepare drafts of responses to messages received. Then the executive reads the incoming messages and the suggested response at one time. Often executives are satisfied with their assistants' suggestions. Little editing is needed. Final copies are prepared quickly. Recipients will have responses within a relatively brief period of time.

You may have complete responsibility for certain writing tasks. You will want to be at ease when you write messages on your own. Little time may be available to get reviews from others and rewrite what you want to communicate. You will want to develop the skill of writing a message appropriately the first time so little revision is needed. When you are doing the entire job of composing and signing memos and letters, you must be your own editor. If you are candid and objective, you will be a good editor of your own work.

Characteristics of Effective Writing

Writing in the business world is expected to reflect basic concerns for efficiency and effectiveness. Unlike a poem, for example, where meaning can be obscure, business writing is expected to be direct and meaningful to all who read it. Common characteristics of good business writing are listed below.

- Clear—A clear message is logically arranged when the information is in an order that is natural for the recipient to follow. To prepare a clear message, you must know why you want to communicate, what you want to communicate, and who your recipient will be. A clear message eliminates the need for requests for additional comment.

- Concise—A concise message states what you want to communicate in the fewest and most direct words possible. The recipient will waste no time in reading words and thoughts that add nothing to understanding the message.

- Courteous—Written communications are courteous when they conform to the expected polite, considerate behavior of the business world. Expressions such as "thank you," "please," and "you are welcome" are commonly used in business correspondence. The so-called *you* approach is commonly recommended for the tone of messages.

- Complete—A complete message provides all the information needed. Think of the recipient by asking yourself: "Does this answer all the questions the recipient might raise about this matter?"

- Correct—A correct message is accurate and up-to-date. Details provided in messages should be verified before the final copy is prepared.

Figure 4-1.9

Examples of Clear and Unclear Writing

Unclear	Tell everybody on the team that we'll meet on Friday morning to discuss plans for the new project.
Clear	All members of the accounting department will meet on Friday, November 10, at 10 a.m. in Conference Room C. We will discuss plans for updating our Accounts Payable system.

Changes are common in business, and any message must carry current information to be of value to the recipient. Incorrect information causes many problems in business. Further correspondence often is required, and the goodwill of customers can be lost.

Part of Kathy's job was to answer inquiries about availability of products for future delivery. A customer wanted to know whether a certain product could be shipped at four dates throughout the year. Kathy knew that the company maintained good inventories, so she responded by e-mail that there would be no problem in meeting the customer's order. Only after the customer sent the order with the dates for delivery did Kathy make an inquiry. At that point, she learned that the company was discontinuing the manufacture of the item within the next two months.

English Skills for Business Writing

Effective business writing reveals good command of the English language. To create effective messages, follow these guidelines.

- Check sentence structure and be sure all sentences are complete.
- Use proper grammar. Check grammar references as needed and use the grammar check feature of your word processing software.
- Follow rules of punctuation and capitalization. Check reference sources as needed.
- Spell words correctly. Use the spell check feature of your software and have a dictionary at hand. Remember that a spell check program does not find misused words such as "to" for "two" as shown in Figure 4-1.10.

Management of Writing Tasks

Writing tasks must be managed wisely if they are to be completed successfully and on schedule. The management of writing tasks has two aspects. One relates to the actual writing task itself; the other relates to scheduling the task properly to meet deadlines.

Figure 4-1.10

A spell check program often does not find misused words.

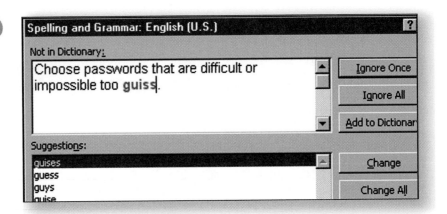

CHAPTER 4: COMMUNICATING IN WRITTEN FORM

Managing the Task of Writing

The following steps will prove useful to you in completing a writing assignment.

1. Identify the reason for the written communication.

2. Secure all the information required for the message.

3. Compose a draft of your message. Prepare an outline of what you plan to say if the message is long. Key your message directly at your computer using your outline as a guide.

4. Review your message; make corrections if needed.

5. If required, submit your draft to a colleague or manager for review and approval.

6. Prepare a revised copy of your communication.

7. Proofread carefully.

8. Sign and prepare the final communication for distribution.

Managing the Schedule for Writing Tasks

In most instances, you will have a deadline for the completion of a writing task. This means that when you accept a writing task, you must review how much time is required for each aspect of the work you must do.

One strategy is to review the steps in the preceding section, noting just how much time is needed to do the task well. For example, having required information at hand in a letter eliminates the need for time to search for information. A schedule may be needed for a major writing task to ensure that you work within the time period allowed. The time available must be scheduled so that each aspect of the task can be done properly.

You will have many occasions during your study of office procedures to develop your writing skills. Remember that all written communications do not need to be of the same quality. For example, a message to the manager of the stockroom, whom you know personally, might be written informally and e-mailed without editing. On the other hand, a letter to thousands of customers might be rewritten several times, with others reviewing drafts to make sure the letter will attract customer attention.

With practice, you will improve your skill in preparing simple messages the first time you try. Also, you will gain a sense of what a good message should be and how to prepare one. With practice, you will develop skill in evaluating and improving your writing.

Reviewing the Topic

1. Identify several situations that require reading at work.
2. How can you determine the meaning of an unfamiliar word that you find while you are reading?
3. What are the key components of reading skill?
4. Describe a procedure to increase your comprehension of what you read?
5. What might you do to build your vocabulary through reading?
6. In what ways might the speed of reading be increased?
7. List four common business writing tasks.
8. What are important skills for a person who is summarizing written messages or meetings?
9. What should a person keep in mind while reviewing a draft of a written communication?
10. Describe a situation where you would prepare a written communication to seek information.
11. For what purpose are written communications prepared after oral discussions?
12. Identify five characteristics of good business writing.

Interacting with Others

Brad works as an assistant manager in the office of a warehouse facility where he interacts with a number of employees. The office is a busy place because an inventory of over 11,000 items is maintained. On several occasions, Charles, a part-time employee, asked Brad to help him with instructions for incoming merchandise. Brad began to realize that Charles, who was still in high school, did not understand instructions. Then Brad began to wonder if Charles was having problems with reading. One evening after work, Brad and Charles were leaving at the same time. The two began to talk. Charles said to Brad: "I think I should give up this job; it is too hard for me. I guess I don't really want to work."

If you were Brad, what would you say to Charles? Write or key your response.

The following sentences have errors in noun and verb agreement. Key the sentences correcting the errors.

Simple rules of writing applies to e-mail. This type of writing seem informal, but it is still business communications. Experts points out that brisk and brief writing are fine. Considering this type of communication impersonal is not wise. Insensitive and discourteous statements should not be in your messages. The ease in corresponding via e-mail have led to many unclear and confusing messages. Reviews of e-mail has discovered all types of inappropriate and irrelevant material that are really clutter.

COMPOSITION
RESEARCH
WORD PROCESSING

Topic 4-1 ACTIVITY 1

Reading to Answer Inquiries

Assume that you are an agent in the customer service department of a major bank. You spend a lot of time talking with customers by telephone. One area where questions are frequent is early withdrawal costs. The bank's rules regarding early withdrawals can be accessed on the company intranet.

1. Open the data file **Rules.pdf**, which shows a portion of the company intranet that contains your bank's rules regarding withdrawal costs. Read this document carefully.

2. Assume that you respond to calls in which the following questions are raised. Prepare a written response to each of the customers using information you learned from reading the bank's rules.

Customer A: *I have an account that has a term of 30 months, which I opened four months ago. I would like to withdraw about half of that money now. What will it cost me to do this?*

Customer B: *My one-year deposit will mature in eight months. Could I withdraw the money next month?*

Customer C: *I have an 18-month account that matures in six months. What penalty do I face if I withdraw all the money now?*

Customer D: *I would like to make an additional deposit to my account that I opened a year ago. May I do this?*

127

Topic Review

COMPOSITION

TEAMWORK

WORD PROCESSING

Writing Procedures for a Task

Office workers must follow procedures for tasks such as operating equipment and using software. These procedures may need to be documented for the worker's own reference or for use in training others. Practice writing procedures for a common office task—changing a printer cartridge.

1. Write procedures for changing the printer cartridge on a printer used in your classroom. (Your instructor may need to demonstrate this process.) Title your document "Procedure for Changing Printer Cartridge."

2. Begin the document by giving the brand name, model number, and type of printer (inkjet, laser, etc.). Give the part or item number that identifies the cartridge and tell whether it is a black or color cartridge.

3. Next, include step-by-step directions for changing the printer cartridge. Review the steps to be sure they are clear, complete, and correct.

4. (Ask for your instructor's approval before completing this step.) Give your procedure to a classmate. The classmate should attempt to change the printer cartridge following your procedures. The classmate should perform only the actions in your procedures and only in the order you have listed them. Revise your procedures, if needed, using your observations of how successfully your classmate was able to complete the task following your procedures.

Business Correspondence

OBJECTIVES

- Identify the characteristics of effective business letters, memos, and e-mail messages
- Prepare effective business correspondence
- Explain the function of business letters, memos, and e-mail messages
- Identify and use appropriately the parts of business letters, memos, and e-mail messages
- Choose appropriate formats for business letters
- List and apply guidelines for preparing documents using desktop publishing

Employees often compose business letters and memos. These documents may be prepared for a supervisor or coworker or written for the employee's own signature. The ability to compose and prepare effective business letters and memos will make you a more valuable employee. As you study this topic, take time to review the document parts and standard formats thoroughly. By doing so, you will reduce the number of occasions when you must check references to determine how to format a document.

Preparing Effective Documents

As you learned in Topic 4-1, effective business documents are clear, concise, courteous, complete, and correct. These characteristics are known as the five Cs of business writing. They are your guidelines to preparing business documents. You can quickly check the effectiveness of your documents by considering these factors.

An effective document is planned well and prepared carefully. The three stages of preparing effective documents are drafting the document, revising and editing the document, and proofreading the document for final presentation.

Drafting

Your first draft of a document will probably not be your final or finished version; it is considered a rough draft. Your goal in preparing the rough draft is to record your ideas. Do not try to make each sentence perfect. You will refine your document during the editing and proofreading stages.

To help focus your writing as you develop your document, ask yourself these questions:

1. What is your purpose in writing?
2. What is your message?
3. Who and where is your audience?
4. What response do you want from the reader?

Purpose

Fix the purpose of the document clearly in your mind before you begin writing. Business documents are often written to inform. For example, you may want the reader to know about a new product or a new procedure. Business documents are also written to persuade or describe. Although these purposes may overlap, you need to have a clear understanding of why you are writing the document before you attempt your first draft.

Message

Determine the points you need to make. What do you need to say to get your message across? What information do you need to include to build support for your position?

Figure 4-2.1

This employee is creating the first draft of a letter.

tone: style, manner of writing or speaking that shows a certain attitude

The **tone** of your message can be as important as the content. Keep these points in mind as you draft your message:

- Prepare an outline of the document, particularly for longer documents. An outline will help you prepare the message in a logical sequence. The better you organize your points, the easier it will be for you to write the message and for your reader to understand your message.

- Focus on the reader as you write. Avoid using too many "I" and "we" words. Instead, use "you" and "your" frequently. This technique is called the *you* approach.

- Give your message a positive tone. Avoid using negative words or a negative tone. Always be courteous. Make an effort in your writing to be helpful to the reader.

Figure 4-2.2

This employee is focusing on the reader as he drafts a letter.

CHAPTER 4: COMMUNICATING IN WRITTEN FORM

Maria, an administrative assistant at a travel agency, wrote this draft:

We are happy to announce that The Traveler's Agency will now offer a full range of travel services. In addition to our regular travel services, we are now promoting three travel discount packages that we designed for the business traveler. Please contact our offices for more information.

Maria's supervisor reviewed the draft and had these comments: "This draft includes all the needed information, Maria, but the approach isn't quite right. Please revise the draft using a reader-focused approach." Maria's revision met with the supervisor's approval.

All your travel needs can now be met through The Traveler's Agency's full range of travel services. As a frequent business traveler, you are eligible for special travel discount packages. Three such discount packages have been designed for you, the frequent business traveler. Please return the enclosed postage-paid card to receive more information about these money-saving packages.

Audience

Knowing certain characteristics about your reader(s) is important to how you develop your document. Is the reader already familiar with the topic? The reader's familiarity with the topic will help you determine how much information to include. Is your document going to one reader or to many? Is the document for external or internal distribution? These factors may influence how formal your writing needs to be, whether confidential topics may be mentioned, or how responses may be requested.

Response

How will the reader use this document? To make a decision? To gain information? If you want a response from the reader, let the reader know the specific action you want. Make it easy for the reader to respond by stating your message and the desired response clearly.

Revising and Editing

Many business documents are changed one or more times between the rough draft and the final document. This process of making changes to refine the document is known as editing or revising.

The primary purpose of editing is to make certain the message is accurate and conveys what the writer intends. In the editing stage of preparing your document, focus on the details of your writing. Read your draft carefully and consider the five Cs of effective documents. Editing is your chance to polish your writing by making changes in response to these questions:

- Can you improve your word choice?
- Are your transitions smooth, flowing logically from one topic to another?

Topic 4-2: *Business Correspondence*

- Should the order of your points be changed?
- Are there inconsistencies in your writing that need to be corrected?

To make editing changes that can be understood easily by others, writers often use standard proofreaders' marks, as shown in Figure 4-2.3, when editing on printed copy. Reviewing features of popular word processing programs allows you to edit and make comments in a document file. Once the changes are identified and marked, you can make the changes quickly using the editing features of your word processing software.

WORKPLACE **CONNECTIONS**

Steve works as an assistant to an engineer who prepares many reports. He has been instructed to prepare rough drafts of all reports. The engineer makes comments and indicates revisions in the document file. After the engineer gives Steve the reviewed file, Steve makes all text and formatting changes indicated. The engineer may revise complex reports several times. Steve's knowledge of word processing features allows him to make changes easily.

Proofreading

proofreading: checking a document carefully for errors or omissions

Proofreading, the third phase of preparing a document, is your careful, overall check of the document. During this process, verify that the changes you marked in the editing phase have been made correctly. Check all numbers and unusual spellings against original documents. Use a spell checker and a grammar checker if available with your software. Then complete a detailed manual proofreading. Remember that the spelling feature of your software is limited in the errors it can identify. For example, errors such as "there" for "their" will not be detected.

Figure 4-2.3

Proofreaders' marks are used in editing printed documents.

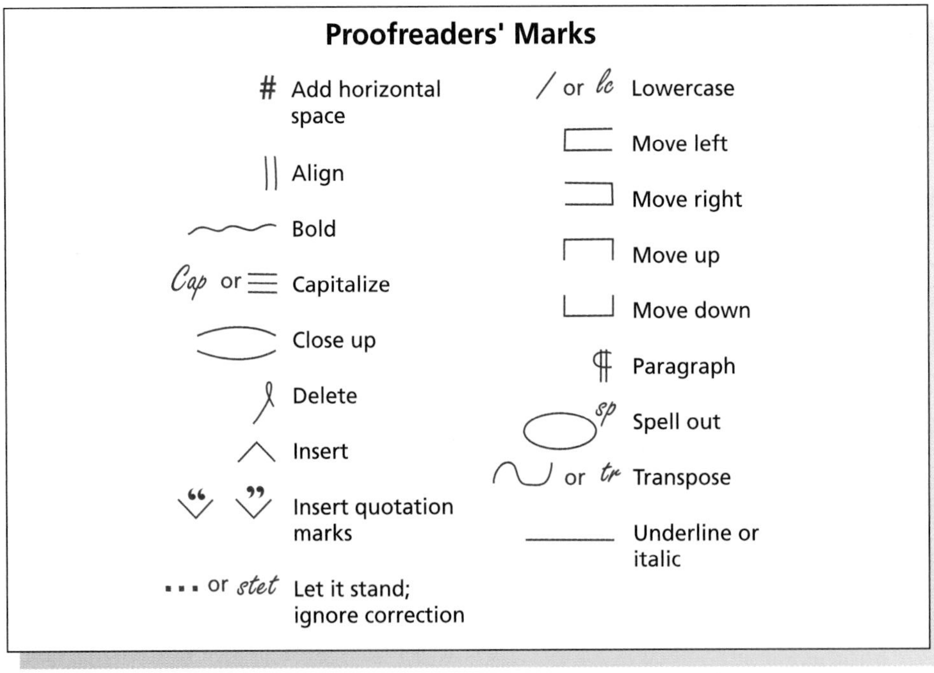

Proofreaders' Marks

Mark	Meaning	Mark	Meaning
#	Add horizontal space	/ or *lc*	Lowercase
‖	Align	⊏	Move left
~	Bold	⊐	Move right
Cap or ≡	Capitalize	⌐	Move up
⌣	Close up	⌊	Move down
ℓ	Delete	⧦	Paragraph
⋀	Insert	*sp* ◯	Spell out
⌄⌄	Insert quotation marks	⌣ or *tr*	Transpose
··· or *stet*	Let it stand; ignore correction	___	Underline or italic

CHAPTER 4: COMMUNICATING IN WRITTEN FORM

Proofreading requires your complete attention to produce error-free documents. Depending on the importance and complexity of the document, you may edit and proofread the document several times before it is final.

Message Types

Three message types are common in business correspondence: positive or neutral messages, negative messages, and persuasive messages. Each group of messages has unique characteristics that should be considered as you prepare documents. To determine which type of message your letter contains, consider the effect the message will have on the receiver.

Positive or Neutral Messages

The reader is not going to be disappointed with a **positive** or **neutral message**. The strategy for writing a positive or neutral message, therefore, is built on giving good news or neutral information to the reader in a straightforward way early in the document. Examples of positive or neutral messages include:

- Placing or acknowledging an order
- Placing or filling a request for information
- Filling or extending a request for credit
- Making, approving, or adjusting routine claims

To prepare good news or neutral messages, use the direct approach. Go directly to the main point of the message and give specific, complete information. Note how the message in Figure 4-2.4 follows these general guidelines.

positive message: communication of good news or agreement

neutral message: communication that simply relays facts; neither positive or negative

Figure 4-2.4

Use a direct approach to prepare a positive message.

Dear Mrs. Racine

Congratulations! Your request for a car loan was approved by our loan officers this morning.

Your loan for $10,000 is now being processed and will be available for your use within 24 hours. Please contact our loan officer, Jan Truong, at 555-0121 for an appointment to sign the final papers and to discuss your monthly payments.

Thank you for your business. We are pleased to serve you.

Negative Messages

Negative messages typically involve a refusal or other news that the reader will find disappointing or upsetting. The strategy for preparing negative messages is based on having the reader understand why a request is being refused or other action is being taken while keeping the reader's **goodwill**. Examples of negative messages include:

negative message: communication that will be disappointing to the recipient

goodwill: a friendly feeling or attitude

Figure 4-2.5

Use an indirect approach to prepare a negative message.

Dear Mr. Roberts

Thank you for considering the Trust Bank for your car loan. Our loan officers met this morning to consider your loan application.

After a careful review of your application, they determined that your monthly income must be higher to support a loan of $10,000 with your current debt liability. Therefore, we cannot approve your loan at this time. Please consider resubmitting your loan application once your monthly payments of $250 on your existing loan are finished at the end of the year.

Your patronage is important to us, Mr. Roberts. We at Trust Bank hope you will continue to consider us for your future banking needs.

Sincerely

- Refusing a request for an adjustment, a credit, or a favor
- Canceling a service
- Reporting unfavorable results

Negative messages require the writer to take considerable care in preparing the response. Use the indirect approach. Begin the message with a neutral statement that lets the reader know the message is your response to the request or to a situation that has arisen. Build your position by stating the reasons for your decision. State the refusal or other negative news. Close on a positive note and suggest alternatives if appropriate. Figure 4-2.5 gives an example of a negative message.

Persuasive Messages

persuasive message:
communication designed to convince the recipient

In preparing a **persuasive message**, the writer wants to influence the reader to take a desired action. Sales letters, collection letters, and solicitation letters are all examples of persuasive messages. When you write a sales letter, for example, you want to influence the reader to buy your product or service. The basic steps to preparing a sales letter are as follows:

- Gain the reader's attention
- Stimulate the reader's interest and desire
- Give the reader an opportunity to act

When you write a collection letter, you are trying to persuade the reader to pay his or her bill. Collection letters are typically a series of letters that move through different stages of persuasion: reminder stage, strong reminder stage, inquiry stage, and urgency stage. If collection messages are used at your job, you will probably have sample letters available for each phase of the collection writing process.

Business Letters

A business letter is a written communication to a person(s) or an organization. Letters are usually written to someone outside the organization. As the writer of a business letter, you are your company's representative. Your letter helps the reader form an opinion about your organization.

Letters provide a long-lasting record of your message. Unlike oral communications, a business letter can be read and reread many times and can serve different purposes. Reasons for writing business letters include:

- Requesting information or an action
- Giving information or fulfilling a request
- Being courteous or maintaining goodwill (congratulation and thank-you notes)
- Explaining or stating a position or persuading the reader
- Selling goods or services

Presentation of Business Letters

The primary purpose of a business letter is to convey a message. However, even before the message is read, the recipient makes a judgment about the letter and its sender. An attractively presented letter on quality paper will encourage the recipient to read the message with care. On the other hand, a carelessly presented letter on smudged paper may fail to get close attention.

A letter makes a good first impression if it has the following characteristics:

- The margins, indentions, and spacing are pleasing to the eye.
- Each letter part is correctly placed within the letter.
- Appropriate stationery is used.
- There are no obvious errors.
- The print is neat and clear.
- There are no smudges or fingerprints.

Make your letters as attractive as possible. If the appearance of the letter is pleasing to the eye, the receiver will be encouraged to read what you have written.

Letter Parts

Business letters represent a form of communication within the business world that follows a standard **protocol**. That is, those who receive business letters expect to see them written using designated letter parts. In Figure 4-2.6 on page 136, you will find all the parts that could be included in a business letter. Of course, few letters will include all these parts. Some parts are included in most letters, whereas other parts are included only when needed. The standard letter parts that should be included in most business letters, as well as optional parts, are listed below.

protocol: generally accepted customs or rules

Standard Letter Parts	**Optional Letter Parts**
Printed letterhead	Mailing notations
Date	Attention line
Letter address	Subject line
Salutation	Enclosure notation
Body	Separate cover notation
Complimentary close	Copy notation
Signature, printed name, and title	Postscript
	Reference initials
	Multiple-page heading

Topic 4-2: *Business Correspondence*

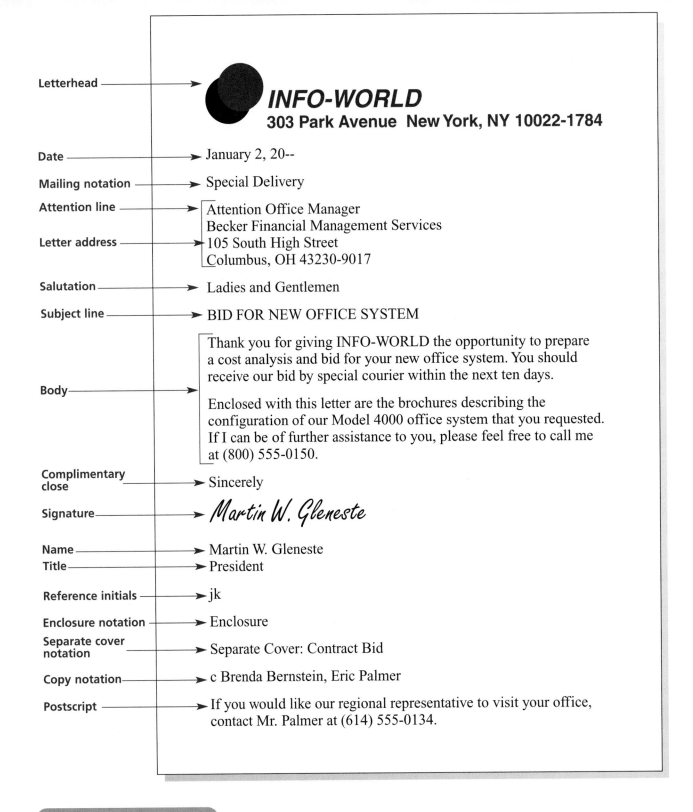

Letterhead	**INFO-WORLD** **303 Park Avenue New York, NY 10022-1784**
Date	January 2, 20--
Mailing notation	Special Delivery
Attention line	Attention Office Manager
	Becker Financial Management Services
Letter address	105 South High Street
	Columbus, OH 43230-9017
Salutation	Ladies and Gentlemen
Subject line	BID FOR NEW OFFICE SYSTEM
Body	Thank you for giving INFO-WORLD the opportunity to prepare a cost analysis and bid for your new office system. You should receive our bid by special courier within the next ten days.
	Enclosed with this letter are the brochures describing the configuration of our Model 4000 office system that you requested. If I can be of further assistance to you, please feel free to call me at (800) 555-0150.
Complimentary close	Sincerely
Signature	*Martin W. Gleneste*
Name	Martin W. Gleneste
Title	President
Reference initials	jk
Enclosure notation	Enclosure
Separate cover notation	Separate Cover: Contract Bid
Copy notation	c Brenda Bernstein, Eric Palmer
Postscript	If you would like our regional representative to visit your office, contact Mr. Palmer at (614) 555-0134.

Figure 4-2.6

Business letter in block format with open punctuation

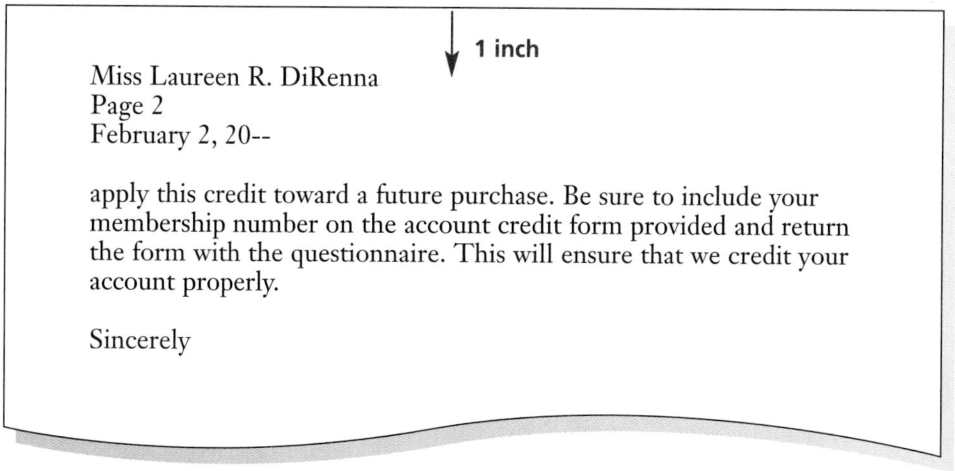

Figure 4-2.7

Multipage letter heading

↓ 1 inch

Miss Laureen R. DiRenna
Page 2
February 2, 20--

apply this credit toward a future purchase. Be sure to include your
membership number on the account credit form provided and return
the form with the questionnaire. This will ensure that we credit your
account properly.

Sincerely

Occasionally, a letter will require more than one page. In such instances, a
multiple-page heading is prepared to identify each page. As shown in Figure
4-2.7, the heading includes the name of the addressee, the word *Page* and a
page number, and the letter date.

Business Letter Formats

The arrangement of the letter text on the page is referred to as its **format**.
Using a standard format for letters increases efficiency for both the writer
and the recipient. For the writer, extra time is not needed to decide how to
arrange the letter. For the recipient, the task of reading and comprehending
is simplified because the format of information is familiar.

format: arrangement or layout,
as of text on a page

Many companies have procedures manuals that contain standard format
instructions and examples for frequently prepared documents. If examples
are not available, you will be expected to make format decisions. These
decisions should reflect your desire to produce attractive, easy-to-read
documents.

Writers most frequently use the block and modified block letter formats.
In the block format, all lines begin at the left margin; paragraphs and other
letter parts are not indented. The letter in Figure 4-2.6 is in block format.
Block format is highly efficient because it saves time in moving from one
part of the letter to another.

In modified block format, the date, complimentary close, and signature
block (writer's signature, typed name, and title) begin at the horizontal
center of the page rather than at the left margin. The first line of each
paragraph may be indented one-half inch. The letter in Figure 4-2.8 is
in modified block format.

The two punctuation styles typically used in the special lines of business letters are open punctuation and mixed punctuation. In open punctuation style,
no punctuation marks are used after the salutation and the complimentary
close. See Figure 4-2.6. In mixed punctuation style, a colon is placed after
the salutation and a comma after the complimentary close. See Figure 4-2.8.
Either punctuation style may be used with a block or modified block letter
format.

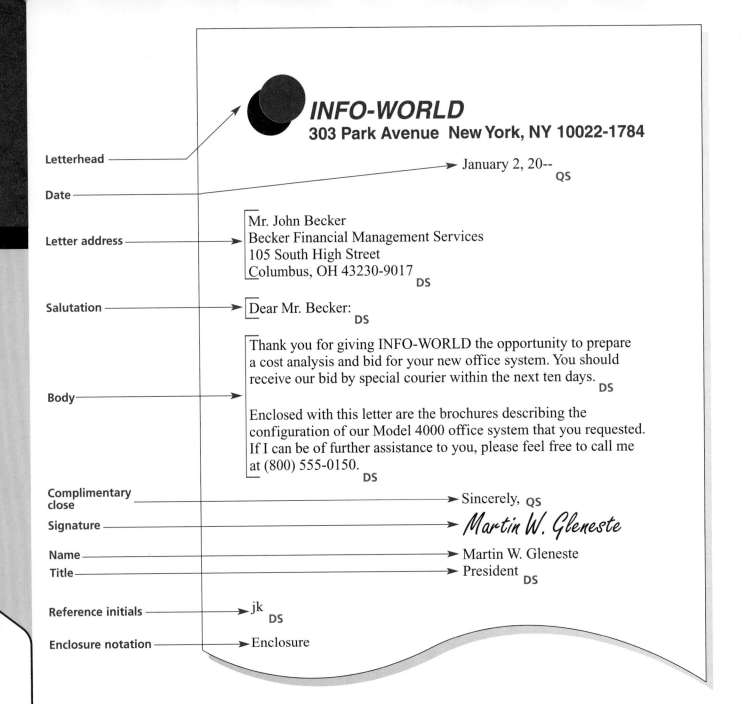

INFO-WORLD
303 Park Avenue New York, NY 10022-1784

Letterhead

Date
January 2, 20--
QS

Letter address
Mr. John Becker
Becker Financial Management Services
105 South High Street
Columbus, OH 43230-9017
DS

Salutation
Dear Mr. Becker:
DS

Body
Thank you for giving INFO-WORLD the opportunity to prepare a cost analysis and bid for your new office system. You should receive our bid by special courier within the next ten days.
DS

Enclosed with this letter are the brochures describing the configuration of our Model 4000 office system that you requested. If I can be of further assistance to you, please feel free to call me at (800) 555-0150.
DS

Complimentary close
Sincerely, QS

Signature
Martin W. Gleneste

Name
Martin W. Gleneste

Title
President
DS

Reference initials
jk
DS

Enclosure notation
Enclosure

Figure 4-2.8

Business letter in modified block format with mixed punctuation

Repetitive Letters

Writing in the office often involves preparing the same message or similar messages that are used again and again. Businesses often individualize letters even though similar letters may be sent to hundreds of people. If your responsibilities include preparing such documents, you may want to use form letters or paragraphs and features of your software to speed preparation.

Standard text, sometimes called boilerplate text, can be combined with other data to form a finished document. The writer assembles the document by combining custom text, often called variables (the individual's name and address), with selected standard sentences and paragraphs. Once the document is assembled, it is printed and saved in the same manner as other documents. A special feature of your word processing software, often called merge, may allow you to combine standard text and variables auto-matically. The variable data may be stored in a database file such as a customer address file.

Marian often prepares mailings for groups of customers. The customer name and address information is stored in a database file. Marian sorts the data or creates a query to find just the customers she needs, such as those in a particular city or ZIP code. She then uses the merge feature of her word processing software to create a personalized letter for each customer on the list. Using the merge feature saves a great deal of time and ensures that the customer addresses are accurate because the addresses do not have to be rekeyed. The merge feature is also used to create an envelope for each customer.

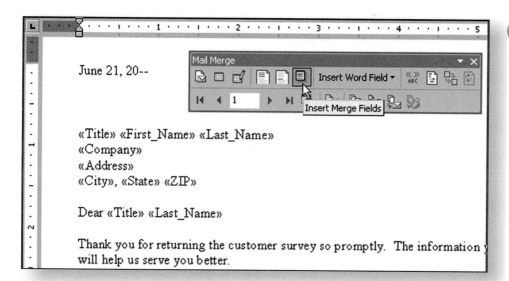

Figure 4-2.9

Field names from a database are entered as variables. The main document is merged with the database to create personalized letters.

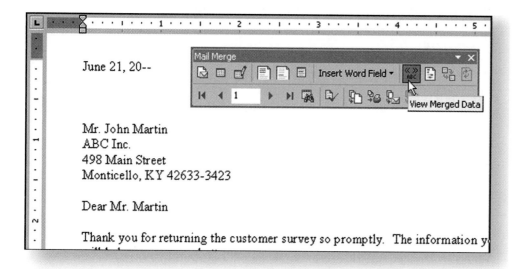

Envelopes

Most business letters are written to individuals outside the company and require an envelope for mailing. Because the receiver begins forming an opinion of the document when he or she views the envelope, the same care should be used in preparing envelopes as in preparing letters. The letterhead stationery and the envelope stationery should be of the same quality and color. The print should be clear, and the envelope should be free of smudges.

Figure 4-2.10

Recommended envelope format

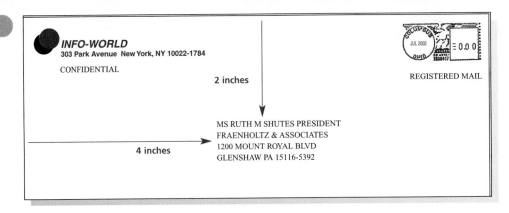

INFO-WORLD
303 Park Avenue New York, NY 10022-1784

CONFIDENTIAL

2 inches

REGISTERED MAIL

MS RUTH M SHUTES PRESIDENT
FRAENHOLTZ & ASSOCIATES
1200 MOUNT ROYAL BLVD
GLENSHAW PA 15116-5392

4 inches

In addition to making a good impression on the recipient, the envelope must be of a proper size and material acceptable to the United States Postal Service (USPS). To ensure prompt delivery, envelopes should include the following information:

- The recipient's name and address
- The sender's return address
- Special addressee notation, if any
- Special mailing notation, if any

The USPS recommends using all capital letters in the address with no punctuation marks except the hyphen in the ZIP code. Nonaddress data, such as a customer number or attention lines, should appear at the top of the address. Place special mailing notations that affect the cost of mailing, such as REGISTERED MAIL or SPECIAL DELIVERY, below the stamp area, as shown in Figure 4-2.10. Place special addressee notations that do not affect the cost of mailing, such as CONFIDENTIAL or HOLD FOR ARRIVAL, just below the return address. If you have questions about addressing mail, contact your nearest Postal Business Center or find help online by accessing the USPS Web site at www.usps.gov.

Memos

A memo (more formally called a memorandum) is a streamlined business document used to communicate with an individual or a group within an organization. Memos are useful for giving identical information to several people. They can be used effectively to give instructions, explain or clarify policy and procedures, or make announcements. Personnel directors, for example, send memos to inform employees of vacation and holiday schedules. Payroll department managers send memos to tell employees about new social security rates or income taxes. Credit managers send memos to sales representatives describing new terms for extending credit to customers.

Each memo you write makes an impression on the receiver whether the receiver is your coworker, your staff, or your supervisor. If the memo is prepared well, the reader forms a positive image of you as an employee. When preparing a memo, follow the five Cs of effective writing and use a positive tone. Notice how the following message that is written in a positive tone sounds courteous while the message written in a negative tone does not.

Positive tone:

> *In the future, please communicate with your supervisor immediately if you see a delay developing. Early reporting of potential delays will give us time to contact an alternative supply source.*

Negative tone:

> *In the future, try not to wait so long to bring these delays to the attention of your supervisor. It is impossible to correct a situation if you cannot communicate with your supervisor in a timely fashion.*

A memo may be prepared on preprinted memo stationery or printed on plain paper with the company name and headings printed as part of the document. Memo stationery or headings with a special slogan or campaign logo may be used to provide updates on special events sponsored by the company.

The headings and body are the standard parts of a memo. Other parts, such as copy or enclosure notations, are optional. When a memo is sent to a large group of people, do not list all the recipients after the To heading. Instead, enter *Distribution List* after the To heading and list the recipients at the end of the memo under the heading *Distribution List*.

If the person receiving a printed memo is located nearby, the memo may be placed in the person's in-basket or mailbox. In this case, an envelope may not be needed. If the receiver is in a different location, however, the memo typically is sent in an interoffice envelope. A confidential document should always be placed in an envelope marked *Confidential*.

Figure 4-2.11

Memo parts

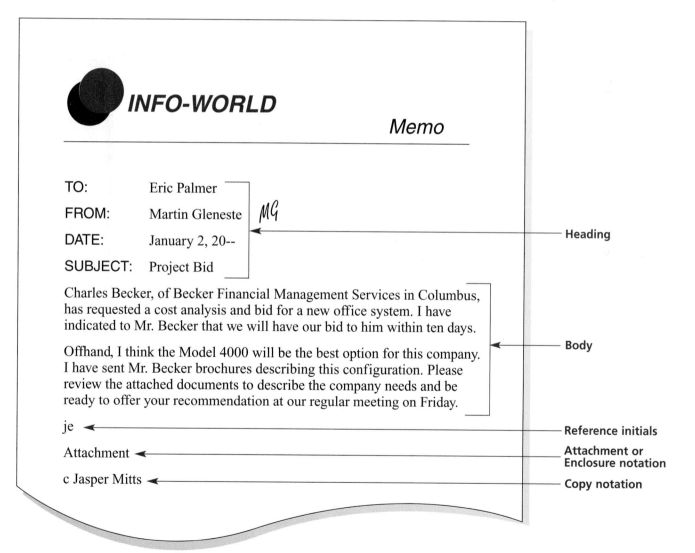

Topic 4-2: *Business Correspondence*

E-Mail

E-mail is the electronic transfer of messages. Local and wide area networks usually offer e-mail to all computers that are connected, whether they are in the same office or in different countries. If users are connected to the Internet, they can send and receive messages all over the world. Workers use e-mail for routine correspondence within the organization and with customers, colleagues, and others outside the organization.

E-mail is appropriate for quick, informal written correspondence. Longer files containing information such as research findings or client databases may be attached to an e-mail. E-mail is inexpensive, fast, and easy to use for workers at all levels in organizations. Remember, however, that e-mail messages are recorded and may be viewed by people other than the person to whom you wrote. Your e-mail may be read by your employer or by coworkers. At work, never write an e-mail message that you would not want other employees or your supervisor to read.

WORKPLACE **CONNECTIONS**

Jon is a human resources associate for a large manufacturing company. He has access to a great deal of confidential information about employees such as salary data. Jon uses e-mail to communicate with various managers in the company. He takes for granted that his e-mail messages will be read only by his intended recipient. Ellen Wilson, a company employee, was considered for a promotion and more job responsibility. Ellen's manager, who was new to the company, sent an e-mail message to Jon asking for Ellen's current rate of pay and the date of her last salary increase. Jon replied by e-mail giving Ellen's manager the requested information. Ellen's manager accidentally forwarded Jon's message to all the employees in his department, including Ellen. Jon was called to his supervisor's office and **reprimanded** for sending confidential employee information via e-mail.

reprimand: discipline, scold, rebuke

E-Mail Addresses

Before you can send and receive e-mail, you must have a unique e-mail address. E-mail addresses begin with a user id, which is a unique identifier such as *dsmith* (for David Smith). The user id is followed by the @ sign, which serves merely as a separator, and the domain name. To understand a domain name, read from right to left. The highest level of the domain appears at the right and identifies the type of organization. When you read the address *dsmith@eng.unlv.edu*, starting at the right, the *edu* identifies that this address is located at an educational institution. The next section, *unlv*,

CHAPTER 4: COMMUNICATING IN WRITTEN FORM

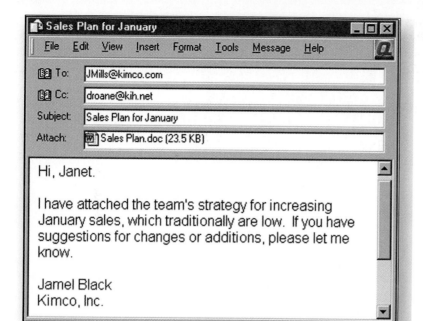

Figure 4-2.12

E-mail makes communicating fast and easy.

identifies the specific educational institution, such as University of Nevada, Las Vegas. The *eng* identifies the department, such as English or Engineering, and the last section, *dsmith* identifies an individual.

When you pronounce the e-mail address *Djones@cmu.com*, you would say, "d jones at c m u dot com" rather than spell out each letter. Be careful when recording an e-mail address. Addresses are often case sensitive. If you key an address incorrectly, your message will not be delivered to the intended address.

E-Mail Features

E-mail software varies somewhat in look and feel from one package to another; however, certain features are found in most e-mail packages. E-mail messages contain headings and a section for the body of the message. E-mail programs allow the user to read mail, check for new messages, compose and reply to messages, delete messages, attach files to messages, and send new mail.

An e-mail address book is provided to store the user's most frequently used addresses. The Inbox collects incoming messages. A user alert, such as a tone or flashing icon, often accompanies the receipt of new mail. The Outbox holds e-mail messages to be sent to others. It may also hold messages that have already been sent, or these messages may be stored in a separate Sent box or folder. Because these messages are actually stored on your hard drive, you should frequently delete messages that are no longer needed. Most mail programs will allow you to **prioritize** an e-mail message, that is, to rank it in importance, usually from urgent or high to low.

prioritize: rank in order of importance

Improving Communications in Organizations

How workers communicate with others in the organization influences how effectively the organization operates. Following the proper procedures for preparing and sending messages will help improve the communications in

Topic 4-2: *Business Correspondence*

Figure 4-2.13

This employee is careful to communicate effectively even when working under pressure.

© CORBIS/STOCK MARKET

an organization. Begin by choosing the appropriate type of message. Letters are usually used for formal communications with individuals and organizations outside the company. Letters should be used sparingly within the organization. For example, a worker might prepare an application letter to apply for a different position within the company. Serious issues, such as making an harassment complaint, might also be addressed in a formal letter.

Reports are useful for sharing information with coworkers and managers. When you must prepare a report, consider the purpose and the audience when deciding how formal and detailed the report should be. You will learn more about reports in Topic 4-3.

Memos and e-mail are the most commonly used written communications within an organization. Memos should be used to communicate confidential information or for routine messages to workers who do not have access to e-mail such as factory production workers. E-mail is appropriate for most other short in-house written communications. You should follow the same proper writing techniques for memos and e-mail as you do for your other communications.

An effective memo or e-mail must be written clearly and concisely. Often the message must be written under considerable time pressure because of the need for prompt decisions or sharing of information. Exercise care to prepare an accurate, well-written message even though it is created quickly and the tone of the message is less formal than in a letter.

Consider these guidelines for improving in-house communications:

- Give the writing your best effort. Consider in-house communications as important as correspondence to outside readers.
- Follow a logical sequence in presenting the information.
- Be tactful when expressing personal opinions in your writing.

- Handle sensitive situations positively. Avoid using negative words; write using a positive tone.
- Follow the same strategies as you would for a business letter to deliver positive, neutral, negative, or persuasive messages.
- Use a descriptive subject line so the recipient can see immediately the topic of your message.
- Create a single-subject message using words that are clear and concise.
- Keep the message short. Attach a report to the message if more details are needed.
- Carefully read your message checking for application of the five Cs. Is the message clear, concise, complete, correct, and courteous? Use the spell check feature of your software and proofread carefully. When communicating online, observe proper **netiquette**.
- Check for messages regularly and reply to your messages promptly. Do not, however, send a message quickly in frustration or anger that you may regret later.
- When using e-mail, enter the address of the recipient carefully.
- Reading messages uses an employee's valuable time. Send the message only to people who really need to read the message. When replying to a message, reply only to the sender—not to everyone who received the message—unless everyone needs your answer.
- Take steps to safeguard confidential information. Never send confidential information in an e-mail; prepare a memo or printed report instead. Place the document in an envelope and mark it *Confidential*. Do not leave confidential memos or reports that you receive lying on your desk where anyone might read them.
- Make the tone of your message professional. Limit or avoid the use of emoticons, which are pictures of faces showing emotions: happy :-) sad :-(.
- Consider carefully before forwarding messages you receive to others. Honor others' rights of privacy. Never forward chain messages or send **spam**.
- Delete unneeded message files regularly to free space on the network server.
- Use caution when opening messages or attachments from someone you do not know. Use virus protection software to detect computer viruses in file attachments.

netiquette: guidelines for proper behavior when communicating online, derived from *network* and *etiquette*

spam: electronic junk mail, advertisements, or other messages not requested by the recipient and often sent in a mass mailing

Desktop Publishing

Not all business correspondence follows standard formats as letters do. Product brochures, newsletters, and flyers may each use a unique format and design. These documents often contain graphics (clipart, photos, or other images) as well as text. They may use fancy **fonts** or banner headings to draw the reader's attention. **Desktop publishing** software is used to create these documents.

Desktop publishing programs, such as Quark Xpress and Adobe PageMaker, contain page layout features for creating complex documents containing text and images. These programs allow the user to control type characteristics such as **kerning** and allow full-color output. The text and images appear on your computer screen exactly as they will when printed. The images are often

font: style or design for a set of type characters

desktop publishing: using a computer and software to create high-quality and often complex printed documents

kerning: adjusting the space between characters

Topic 4-2: *Business Correspondence*

Figure 4-2.14

This software program is used in desktop publishing.

created or edited with programs such as Adobe Illustrator, CorelDraw, and PhotoShop and then placed in the document using the page layout program. Word processing programs usually have basic desktop publishing features. Programs such as Microsoft Word may be used to create simple publications for in-house or informal use.

Resolution

resolution: the number of dots per inch (dpi) in printed text or images

True desktop publishing results in high-resolution printed documents. **Resolution** is the number of dots per inch (dpi) the printer creates when printing a document. The greater the dpi, the higher the resolution and the sharper the printed image. Professional printers use around 2400 dpi for many documents. Because many businesses do not have high-resolution printers, the document files may be created in-house and sent to an outside company for printing. For in-house or informal communications, 600 dpi is considered acceptable, and many businesses have printers that can produce this resolution.

Desktop Publishing Guidelines

When creating messages for documents to be desktop published, follow the five Cs of effective writing as you would for other business correspondence. Consider the purpose of the document—to inform, to persuade, to request information—and the audience for the document. Determine whether in-house (probably low resolution) printing is acceptable or whether a professional printer should be used.

Your goal is to create a document that makes a good impression, is visually attractive, and delivers your message effectively. Consider these guidelines for creating desktop published documents.

- Use consistency in the design. For example, format all heads of the same level in the same way. If the company logo appears on each page, place it in the same location on every page.

- Use ample **white space** to rest the eye and identify the beginning and end of sections. Effective use of white space keeps the text and images from looking cramped on the page.

white space: area of a printed page that is empty, having no text or images

- Create a pleasing balance of elements (headings, body text, and images) on the page. Documents balanced symmetrically, with roughly the same amount of material on each side of the page, have a formal, traditional look. Documents with asymmetrical balance have a more informal look.

- Create contrast in the design by placing different objects next to each other. A graphic placed next to text, for example, creates contrast on the page.

- Include artwork or photos that are relevant to the message and place them near the text to which they relate. Use decorations or other artwork that are appropriate for the document. Take special care in very formal or serious documents that any artwork used is in keeping with the formal tone of the document.

- Use fonts that are easy to read and limit the number of fonts in the document to two or three. Use bold, italic, and different sizes to vary the font appearance. Do not use font sizes that are too small to read easily.

- Use all capitals sparingly because text in all caps is hard to read.

- Avoid widow lines. Adjust the spacing or rewrite the sentence if necessary to prevent widow lines.

- Use printer's curves for apostrophes and quotes (' and " rather than ' and ").

- Avoid large horizontal spaces between words, which look unattractive. Using a ragged right margin and hyphenating words helps avoid this problem.

- Use copyrighted text or images in your publications only with proper permission from the copyright holder.

- If the document will be printed by a professional printer, obtain detailed information from the printer about how the file must be created to print successfully.

The height of characters is measured in *points*. Each point is approximately 1/72 inch. The width measurement is called *pitch*, which refers to how many characters can fit in an inch. Common pitch values are 10 and 12. If the character widths vary depending on the shape of the character, the font is called a *proportional font*.

Figure 4-2.15

Avoid large horizontal spaces between words, which look unattractive.

Topic 4-2: *Business Correspondence*

Reviewing the Topic

1. Describe the five characteristics of an effective document.

2. When creating the first or draft copy of a document, what four factors should you consider to help focus your writing?

3. Describe the three categories of messages common in business correspondence.

4. How can a writer use a reader-based approach in writing?

5. What reader characteristics are important for the writer to know?

6. Contrast the strategies used in preparing positive messages and negative messages.

7. What letter parts should be included in every business letter?

8. Identify the characteristics of a letter that make a good first impression.

9. Why do businesses use standard formats for their business letters and memos?

10. What is the purpose of a memo? How does it differ from a letter?

11. For what purposes are e-mail messages used?

12. List four guidelines that you think are the most important ones for improving written communications within an organization.

13. Define desktop publishing.

14. What is print resolution? How does it relate to clarity of printed material?

15. List five guidelines to follow when creating desktop published documents.

Interacting with Others

You are working on a special research project with Larry Moore (whose e-mail address is LMoore@trophe.com). He was supposed to e-mail you a lengthy attachment vital to your completion of the project. He promised to transmit it to you by noon yesterday. At 4:30 p.m., you have not heard from Larry. You are becoming very concerned because the deadline for the project is only one week away. You must study Larry's material carefully before you can complete your part of the project. By your estimate, it will take you approximately nine hours to review Larry's data.

1. Compose and key an e-mail message to Larry that is appropriate for the situation described above. If you do not have e-mail software, key the message in your word processing software. Include the proper heading information for To (Larry's e-mail address) and Subject. (The Date and From information would be added automatically by the e-mail program.) (If using e-mail software, save and print the message. Do not actually send the e-mail.)

2. Follow proper guidelines for preparing e-mail communications as you compose your message. Make the tone of the message positive while stating your concerns and the action that you want Larry to take.

Reinforcing English Skills

An excerpt from a draft of a letter from Computer Corner Furniture is shown below. Notice the negative tone of this response to a customer who was having difficulty assembling a computer workstation.

1. Key and revise the excerpt, making changes to give the message a more positive tone.

2. Spell check, proofread, and correct all errors before printing the message.

> You obviously did not read the instructions that accompanied the computer desk, Model 122, which you purchased from our company. In case you misplaced or lost your instructions, I have enclosed another copy for you.
>
> The instructions clearly state that you must assemble the base of the desk first, then the electrical wiring is inserted through the left front leg of the desk and through the slot in the top of the table. Obviously, it's too late to insert the electrical wiring once you have assembled the entire desk. You'll have to take the desk apart and start all over. This time, follow the instructions.
>
> If you have any more problems with this desk, we do have a branch office in Independence. Please contact them; you should have sent your complaint to that office in the first place.

DATABASE
WORD PROCESSING

Topic 4-2   ACTIVITY 1

Form Letters

The form letter that appears below has several errors in spelling, capitalization, and word usage. These errors must be identified and corrected before the form letter can be used to prepare responses to routine inquires for employment.

1. Key the standard text for the form letter shown below step 4. Assume the letter will be printed on company letterhead. Use the current date, modified block letter format, and mixed punctuation. Add an appropriate salutation and closing. Correct errors as you key, then spell check and proofread the message.

2. Create a database containing the following fields: *Title, First Name, Last Name, Address, City, State, ZIP Code,* and *Position.* Enter data for the five customers as shown below in the database.

Mr. Toma Roberts, 298 Apple Lane, Springfield, MO 65804-1189, administrative assistant

Ms. Alice Lamson, 19 Talley Street, Englewood, CO 80111-7825, accounts payable specialist

Mrs. Mabel Jones, 339 Hogan Street, Topeka, KS 66612-1045, order entry associate

Mr. Ken Hinrichs, 809 Northsky Square, Cupertino, CA 95014-0692, customer service representative

Mrs. Joyce Jennings, 56 Barrow Road, Westerville, OH 43081-2243, secretary

3. Enter fields from the database for variables in the standard letter. Merge the letter with the customer information from the database file to create personalized letters. View the merged letters and make corrections, if needed, before printing the letters.

4. Enter fields from the database for variables in a standard envelope. Merge the envelope with the customer information from the database file to create personalized envelopes. View the merged envelopes and make corrections, if needed, before printing. (Use paper cut to envelope size if envelopes are not available.)

Thank You for your inquiry concerning a position with our company as a(n) (position name). We do hve opeings available for this position from titme too time.

please complete and return the enclosed application from. The form will be keept on file and reviewed when an opening occurs.If you decide to persue a position with our Company, you will find that we have very attractive workin conditins and an excellent promotion policy.

Tom Ryan,

Human Resources Director

Enclosure

COMPOSITION
WORD PROCESSING

Standard Letter Format

Assume that you work for Western Security Systems. After several meetings, the support staff has recommended that a block style letter with open punctuation be adopted as the company standard for all business letters. You have been asked to provide a sample of the block letter format. You decide to use the body of the letter to describe the block format and open punctuation style so that everyone will understand how to prepare letters using this standard format.

1. Compose and key a sample block letter with open punctuation. Use the following information for the address and supply an appropriate salutation. The letter is from you, and your title is Administrative Assistant.

Address:

Customer's Name

Street Address

City, State ZIP

2. Create a memo form for Western Security Systems to include the company name and heading lines to print on plain paper. Prepare a cover memo to all employees asking them to begin using block format for all letters. State in your memo that you are enclosing a sample letter using block format with open punctuation as an example.

OBJECTIVES

- Identify the characteristics of business reports
- Prepare reports in formal and informal formats
- Create visual aids used in reports
- Use software features effectively in creating and editing reports

analytical: involving detailed study

A business report is a presentation of organized information that will be used by the reader for a specific business purpose. Reports are an important method of communication for a business. How often you prepare business reports will depend on the size and type of your organization and on your job duties. In many organizations, office workers write, edit, assemble, and distribute business reports.

In this topic, you will be introduced to two forms of business reports: the informational or procedural report and the **analytical** or persuasive report. These reports may be presented in formal or informal formats. In addition, you will explore special features of reports such as tables and graphs. Your ability to gather, organize, write, and present information in a standard report format will allow you to adapt easily to specific reports you may encounter on the job. You will also study some guidelines for using desktop publishing to prepare documents such as newsletters or flyers.

Informational Reports

Informational reports are typically based on data gathered within the normal operations of the company. Some reports are made so frequently that standard report forms, such as the one shown in Figure 4-3.1, are developed. The company relies on employees to complete the forms accurately and neatly. Using printed forms saves time and ensures that data is collected uniformly across the company.

WORKPLACE **CONNECTIONS**

Louisa works as an administrative assistant in a small insurance company. One of Louisa's responsibilities is keeping track of the office supplies, which are stored in a central location. Every month she prepares a report for her supervisor giving a summary of the supplies used and those ordered as replacements. Employees who remove supplies from storage are supposed to let Louisa know what materials have been taken. Some employees leave a note on Louisa's desk, others send her an e-mail or voice mail message, and yet others leave a note in the supply cabinet. The messages are often incomplete, leaving out the quantity or a clear description of the supplies removed. Louisa realized she was spending a lot of time contacting employees for complete details about the supplies removed as she prepared her report each month. "This system just isn't working. There has to be a better way," Louisa thought.

Louisa created a form with spaces for an employee to record his or her name, the current date, code numbers for the supplies removed, and the quantity of the supplies removed. The forms are kept in the supplies closet. Each employee who removes supplies now completes a form and leaves it in a specially marked tray on Louisa's nearby desk. Using the information from the supplies forms, Louisa can now create the monthly report quickly.

Figure 4-3.1

Informational reports are often prepared from data collected using forms.

Cory's Copier Services

Person Reporting Problem _Leslie_

Date _1/11_   Time _9:15_   am ✔ pm

Customer Name _Amy's Hair Salon_

Address _1538 South Elm_

Riverton

Copier Model _C-248_   Number of Copies _235,687_

Problem Reported _Lines across bottom of page_

Action Needed _New Drum_

Action Taken _Drum on order_

Repair Person _Ryan Barnes_

Every organization requires some reports on a regular basis. Indeed, most businesses establish procedures for gathering data needed to write these routine reports. In the example shown in Figure 4-3.1, a completed copier repair form is submitted to the supervisor each week. The supervisor uses the weekly reports to write a repair summary report. One of the purposes of this report is to spot high maintenance trends and to anticipate when major maintenance will be needed on a copier. The supervisor uses the data to write a two-page **memo report**. The memo follows the same format each week. The similar data is summarized for each report using designated headings. The supervisor then adds comments and **interpretations** at the end of the report.

memo report: information represented in a memo format rather than a more formal report format

interpretation: explanation or view

Many companies use handheld computer devices to gather data that is later used to create reports. For example, utility company workers use handheld computer devices to read meters that monitor the use of electricity. The data gathered is downloaded to a computer. Office workers use the data in creating reports and generating customer bills.

In writing an informational report, follow the same guidelines used for direct correspondence. State your purpose early and clearly. For example, use the subject line in a memo report or the title in a formal report to help focus the reader to your purpose. Consider the audience in determining the level of formality needed and the appropriate use of technical terms or confidential information. Make certain that the reader knows why the report is being written and what response or action is required. Provide complete and correct supporting information. Write the report in a positive and courteous tone.

Organize your report by outlining the points you need to make. If you are expected to follow a standard format, your organization is already

Topic 4-3: *Business Reports and Related Documents*

determined. If, however, you can develop your own reporting format, organize your thoughts around a logical pattern or sequence.

Present only relevant data; do not clutter the report with unnecessary information. If you are expected to add your own comments or interpretations to the data, identify these comments clearly. Writers often use headings such as *Comments*, *Recommendations*, or *Implications* for their analysis and interpretation of the data.

Give attention to the formatting and final presentation of the report. As with letters and memos, the report represents you or your company and can make a positive or negative first impression affecting how the content of the report will be received.

Analytical Reports

The analytical report is generally a longer, more complex report than the informational report. Such a report is normally prepared as a formal business report and often requires considerable research and information gathering. An analytical report takes more time to write and may require in-depth analysis of situations to persuade the reader.

The information and analysis presented in the analytical report is often used to make important company decisions. Typically, an employee or group of employees is asked to research a specific problem or situation. The employees gather data related to the problem. Then they write their report presenting the data they have collected along with their interpretations. They are often expected to draw conclusions and make recommendations.

Gathering Data

Reports are often completed under the pressure of deadlines. Employees are expected to gather data quickly and accurately to be incorporated into reports in a timely fashion. You may be asked to contribute to a formal business report. These guidelines will help you gather and process data quickly, accurately, and with attention to detail.

- Record complete source details for all data you locate (title of publication or Web site and address, author, publisher, date, and page).
- If information must be keyed during the data-gathering stage, key it as it is collected.
- If information must be recorded manually, use note cards to allow for ease in rearranging the data while writing the report.
- Use a scanner with **optical character recognition** (OCR) software, if available, to reduce the amount of time needed to enter large quantities of previously keyed data or technical material into the report. If scanning is not possible, photocopy the material (such as tables) to be sure that the details are accurate. Photocopying is faster and more accurate than copying the material by hand.
- If your duties include creating many reports or other text-heavy documents, consider using **speech recognition software** to speed data entry. A typical office worker might enter text using the keyboard at 50 words per minute (wpm). After a little practice using speech recognition software, the same worker could probably dictate text at 130 wpm.

optical character recognition: reading text printed on paper and translating the images into words that can be saved in a computer file and edited

speech recognition software: computer programs that allow voice input, also called voice recognition

Figure 4-3.2

Scanning text and graphics can save valuable time when creating reports.

© SIEDE PREIS/PHOTODISC

The worker's productivity would more than double using speech recognition software. If a document has sections that are often repeated, even more time can be saved by using boilerplate text and **macros**. With a voice command, such as "Insert Section 1," an entire passage could be included in the document with one command.

macro: a list of computer commands, actions, or keystrokes that can be executed with a single command

- Use handheld computer devices to collect data as an alternative to keying data. These devices allow the user to handwrite notes on a touch screen or scan bar codes. The handwriting can be converted to text and downloaded to a desktop computer. This process can be much faster than recording data manually on note cards or forms and then keying the data.

WORKPLACE **CONNECTIONS**

Stan Bridge works for a package delivery service. He uses a handheld computer device to gather data. When each package is delivered, Stan scans the package bar code label that identifies the package and the delivery location. The customer signs for the package entering his or her signature on the touch screen of the computer device. At the end of each day, Stan places the handheld device in a unit that allows the data to be downloaded to a computer. The data is used to create a report that shows the number of deliveries Stan made that day, the number of pounds the packages weighed, and the types of items (overnight letters, small packages, large boxes) delivered.

The data collected by several drivers is also used to create analytical reports. These reports address issues such as how long a route various drivers should be assigned, how large a truck each driver needs, how long each driver might need to complete the day's deliveries, and the number of drivers needed in a particular delivery area.

Voice Recognition Systems

Voice recognition systems, also called speech recognition, convert the human voice into digital form for processing by computers. As the user speaks into a microphone, the spoken words appear on the computer screen. As an input device, voice recognition systems rely on software to translate the user's spoken words into keystrokes. The software uses *continuous speech recognition* technology, which is designed to decode speech. Current software versions allow the user to speak up to 160 words per minute with 95–98 percent accuracy.

In the office environment, voice recognition systems are particularly useful for repetitive tasks. For example, custom macro commands allow the user to insert boilerplate text with just a spoken command. Recent improvements in these software programs have helped make voice recognition systems a practical alternative to keyboarding.

Voice recognition systems increase office productivity through:

- Prevention and easing of repetitive strain injuries, such as carpal tunnel syndrome

- Less use of mouse clicking through voice commands

- Shorter time for work to be transcribed, particularly in professional offices

- Elimination or reduction in the need for outside transcription service

- Use of handheld digital recorders when away from the computer for later transcription

- Use of prewritten codes or macros as building blocks for documents and applications

- Searching documents, databases, or the Internet using voice commands

In the future, more applications for voice technology will be developed for portable and wireless computer devices. Small, handheld units will allow users to communicate with any computer. Wearable units now in development will bring flexibility to many business applications. Such upgrades will provide greater freedom and higher productivity for users in the workplace.

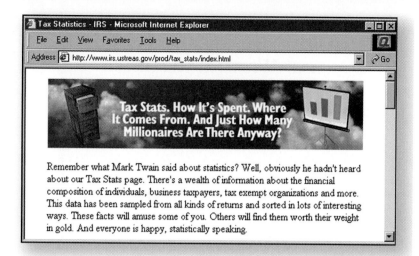

Figure 4-3.3

Tax statistics can be researched online at the IRS Web site.

Researching Information Online

Using the many sources available on the Internet or private information services provides access to accurate and timely data that otherwise may not be available to a business. Many of the sources available on the Internet are free for all users. Private information services, however, usually charge a connect fee and then bill according to time used or the number of searches made. Many businesses find an external information service is less costly than maintaining expensive journal subscriptions and more efficient than using staff time to search for information.

By using the Internet or an information service, volumes of information can be searched quickly. Company financial profiles, investment advice, text of magazines and journals, U.S. Census data, and government regulations are a few examples.

Writing the Report

When the report data has been gathered, organized, and analyzed, you are ready to begin writing the report. Use the general guidelines presented in Figure 4-3.4 to begin creating the report. If several drafts of the report are required, cycle through step 4 as often as revisions are required. These steps are common to all business reports.

As a writer, you will need to consider and use an appropriate tone and a degree of formality in the report. If the report is for limited distribution to your coworkers, an informal style may be acceptable:

> *Jason, this report contains the information on the delivery routes and schedules you requested. You're right, two of the delivery schedules overlap, leaving the third route only partially covered on Tuesdays and Thursdays. No wonder we have had complaints from our customers on the third route. I'm taking immediate steps to correct this schedule.*

Figure 4-3.4

Focus report preparations by using these guidelines.

GUIDELINES FOR ORGANIZING AND WRITING REPORTS

1. Focus the report.

- Know why you are writing.
- Identify your readers.
- Know why readers want to read the report.
- Identify data needed for the report.
- Identify information sources.

2. Plan the writing.

- Identify the main topics and subtopics.
- Prepare an outline of the report.
- Identify potential visuals/graphics.

3. Write the first draft.

- Write a draft of the text.
- Develop related visuals/graphics.

4. Revise your first draft.

- Revise the outline if necessary.
- Edit/revise text of the first draft.
- Verify and document sources used.
- Finalize visuals/graphics.

5. Present your report.

- Use standard formats.
- Check headings/subheadings.
- Prepare preliminary report pages.
- Proofread the final copy.

If the report is to be distributed to a broad audience or outside the company, however, your writing style should also be more formal:

> *On July 8, 20--, the Board of Directors authorized a study to determine the effect of downsizing on the production capability of the Houston plant. Several additional factors were determined to contribute to the 20 percent overall production drop.*

Using a more formal style is appropriate when the report will be read by a larger number of people or when the topic is complicated or critical. To achieve the formal style in the second example, note that the writer

CHAPTER 4: COMMUNICATING IN WRITTEN FORM

- Did not use first names (*the Board of Directors* vs. *Jason*)
- Did not use contractions (for example, *you're* or *I'm*)
- Used **passive voice** (*were determined* vs. *report contains*)

Business Report Formats

Several acceptable formats are available for presentation of business reports. Your company, however, may have a preferred format that you can determine from previous reports or from the company procedures manual. Two common business report formats are the unbound and leftbound formats.

The unbound report is fastened together (generally in the upper left-hand corner) with a fastening device such as a paper clip or staple. No extra space is provided in the margin of the unbound report for fastening the report together. Writers have found this format to be particularly useful for short informal reports that will be distributed internally.

The leftbound report format moves the left margin one-half inch to the right of the margin for the unbound report. The extra space allows for binding the report at the left. All other margins are the same as those of the unbound report. Writers use this format for longer, more complicated reports. Leftbound format is also useful for reports that require a formal presentation or are being sent outside the company.

The formats presented to you in this topic represent acceptable business report formats. Refer to Figure 4-3.5 for a summary of report formatting guidelines.

Formal Business Reports

A formal business report includes standard parts that readers find valuable in helping them understand and interpret the report. A formal report generally contains an explanation of the reason for the report, presentation of data, explanation of the meaning of the data, and conclusions and/or recommendations. The writer also documents the types and sources of information used to write the report. As such, a formal business report may contain all or some of the common report parts.

Figure 4-3.5

Report format guidelines

Business Reports

Format	Top Margin	Bottom Margin	Left Margin	Right Margin
Unbound				
First page	2 inches	1 inch	1 inch	1 inch
Other pages	1 inch	1 inch	1 inch	1 inch
Leftbound				
First page	2 inches	1 inch	1.5 inches	1 inch
Other pages	1 inch	1 inch	1.5 inches	1 inch

Body of the report is usually double-spaced, but may be single-spaced.

Topic 4-3: *Business Reports and Related Documents*

Typical report parts used in a formal business report include:

- Title page
- Table of contents
- Summary
- Body
- References
- Appendices

Title Page

The title page contains the report title, the writer's name, the name of the organization, and the report date as shown in Figure 4-3.6 on page 161. In addition to the writer's name, the writer's title and company address may be appropriate.

Pages coming before the body of the report are numbered with lowercase Roman numerals. Although the title page is considered the first of the report **preliminary pages**, it is never numbered.

Table of Contents

The table of contents presents an overview of the material covered in the report by listing the report headings and their corresponding page numbers. (Refer to Figure 4-3.6.)

Writers prepare the final copy of the table of contents after the entire report has been completed. This procedure permits titles and page numbers to be verified, particularly if any last-minute changes were made in the report. The word processing software used to create the report may have a feature that can be used to create the table of contents from headings marked in the body of the report.

Summary

The summary is a brief description that gives the reader an overview of the report. In a business office, you may hear the summary called by a variety of names, including *executive summary* or *abstract*. An executive summary highlights the report's findings, conclusions, and recommendations. An abstract, however, is shorter and simply states the report's contents.

Body

The body is the text or message of the report. Basically, the body of the report is used by the writer to define the purpose and scope of the report, present and evaluate alternatives, draw conclusions, and make recommendations. In long reports, the body will be divided into chapters or sections. The body may be double-spaced or single-spaced with a blank line between paragraphs.

The main heading is the title of your report. Use the heading to introduce your reader to the report's topic. Give the heading a prominent position in your report by using capital letters, bold type, a slightly larger type size, or a different complimentary font style. The secondary heading provides additional, clarifying information. If a secondary heading is used, give it less prominence in your report than the main heading. Capitalize only the first letter of key words. Use the same font style, perhaps in a smaller size, as used for the main heading. Use

preliminary pages: report pages that come before the body of the report, such as a title page or table of contents

CHAPTER 4: COMMUNICATING IN WRITTEN FORM

Teleconference Feasibility Study

Sandra K. Marshall
Office Communications Consultants

February 16, 20--

SECTION 1
TELECONFERENCING FACTORS

The factors involved in the decision to implement a teleconferencing or videoconferencing network at National Enterprises, Incorporated, are presented in this section. The factors include equipment, facilities, personnel, management, supplies, and overhead.

Equipment
The success of a teleconferencing network is dependent in large part on the equipment the company uses. Most experts recommend a mix of teleconferencing and videoconferencing equipment that is designed for the individual company. According to Rhodes (2001, 1):

Thanks to recent technological advancements and the dynamics of a fiercely competitive telecommunications market, there are hundreds of powerful, cost-effective video communications solutions and services to choose from. There are also many vendors—ranging from system manufacturers and integrators to network service providers and consultants—all eager to provide you with the "perfect" solution.

2

especially suited for the participant who needs to conduct long telephone conversations while referring to papers, files, online information, or other materials. The speakerphone can be effective for the small-group, two-location meeting.

TABLE OF CONTENTS

REFERENCES

Rhodes, John D. Videoconferencing for the Real World. Woburn, MA: Focal Press, 2001.

Wilcox, James R. Videoconferencing: The Whole Picture. Gilroy, CA: Telecom Books, 2000.

Figure 4-3.6

Unbound report format examples

Topic 4-3: *Business Reports and Related Documents*

side headings to divide your main topic into subdivisions. Key side headings in capital and lowercase letters on a separate line beginning at the left margin. Insert a blank line before each side heading. Use underscore, bold, or the different font style used for the main and secondary headings for emphasis.

As you prepare a report, you may need to include quotes from the sources of information used. **Quotations**, which are excerpts from other sources, are identified in the body of the report. A quotation of more than three lines is set off from the rest of the text, as shown in Figure 4-3.6.

quotation: excerpt from a different source

Giving credit to the sources of information you used in a report is called **documentation**. Two common methods of documentation in addition to quotations are endnotes and textual citations. When the endnote method is used, a superior (raised) reference figure is placed at the appropriate point in the copy. The matching numbered reference is then listed at the end of the report with a separate page titled *ENDNOTES*.

documentation: identification or list of the sources of information used

> *When writing the report, credit must be given for material quoted either directly or indirectly from other sources.[1]*

When the textual citations method is used, the source information is placed in parentheses within the text. This information includes author(s), date of publication, and page number(s).

> *When writing the report, credit must be given for material from other sources (Tilton, Jackson, and Rigby, 1996, 398).*

If the source is identified by name within the report copy, only the publication date and page number are used.

> *According to Tilton, Jackson, and Rigby, credit must be given for material from other sources (1996, 398).*

References

references: sources of information, used in preparing a report

The **references** section follows the body of the report and identifies the sources used in preparing the report. Include the sources for direct quotes, paraphrased sources, and sources used to obtain ideas or background information. This section may be titled *REFERENCES*, *BIBLIOGRAPHY*, or *WORKS CITED*.

Appendices

appendix: section of a report that provides detailed or supplementary data

An **appendix** provides more detailed data (usually in the form of a chart, graph, table, or text) to support the body of the report. The appendix (or appendices if several are included) is placed at the end of the report for the benefit of interested readers. If more than one appendix is included, number or letter each in sequence.

Informal Business Reports

Like a formal business report, an informal report is written to convey information in a clear, concise manner. Informal reports, however, often do not have as many parts as formal reports. How you organize an informal report will be based on the purpose of the report. In presenting the informal report, you may wish to follow samples of previous reports found in the company files.

The presentation formats discussed here are for informal, unbound reports of no more than five to six pages. For longer reports, you may wish to consider the formal report presentation format. Figure 4-3.7 shows part of the first page of an informal, unbound report. The unbound report may fit on one sheet of plain paper or it may require several pages. Unbound reports do not allow extra margin space for fastening the pages together.

Informal reports include both a main heading (or title) and text, or body of the report. Informal, brief reports also may include the following parts:

- Secondary heading
- Reference list (or bibliography)
- Side headings
- Title page
- Reference citations
- Abstract

The number of additional parts a writer includes in an informal report will depend on the nature of the report and the subject matter covered. Essentially, reports are organized to communicate information quickly and clearly.

Short informal reports are often prepared in memo format. The subject heading is used to identify the topic of the report just as the main heading is used for an unbound report. Side headings, like those used for unbound report format, may be used to identify sections of the report.

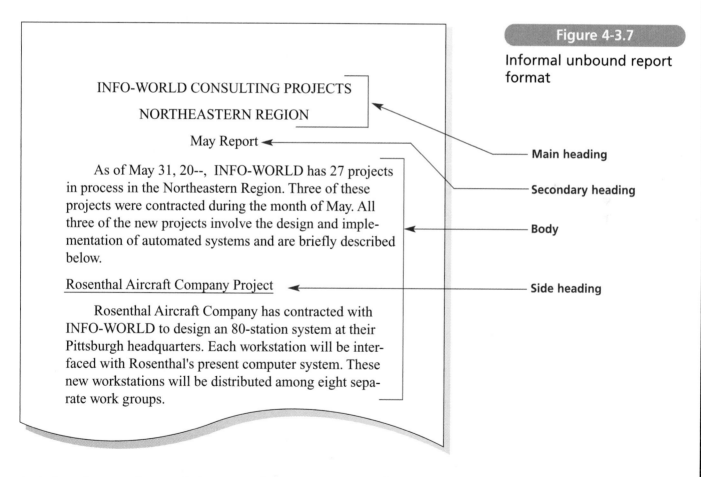

Figure 4-3.7

Informal unbound report format

An informal report frequently has more than one page. In such instances, number each page except the first. If a heading is used on the second and succeeding pages, the page number is part of that heading, as shown in Figure 4-3.8. Use the header feature of your word processing software to automatically print the page number and/or heading at the top of succeeding pages.

Topic 4-3: *Business Reports and Related Documents*

Figure 4-3.8

Headings for second and
succeeding report pages

↓ 1 inch

INFO-WORLD CONSULTING PROJECTS
NORTHEASTERN REGION
Page 2

three northeastern regional offices. This $260,000 project will
enable Baltimore Recreational Enterprises to interface with their
branch offices around the country.

↓ 1 inch

INFO-WORLD CONSULTING PROJECTS
NORTHEASTERN REGION   2

three northeastern regional offices. This $260,000 project will
enable Baltimore Recreational Enterprises to interface with their
branch offices around the country.

Visual Aids

Visual aids consist of the tables, graphs, and other illustrations, such as maps,
which are used to present data in an appealing and efficient manner. The
purpose of using visual aids is to help make the report easy to understand.
They may also reduce the amount of text needed, presenting the data in a
chart or table instead.

Tables

A table is a systematic arrangement of facts, figures, and other information.
Tables can be used to summarize information and to make comparisons.
When developing a table to be used in a report, be certain that it relates
directly to your report. The table should have a clearly defined purpose and
should focus the reader's attention on a specific aspect of your report.

A report table should be self-explanatory. That is, the reader should not have
to refer to text that may accompany the table to understand the table contents. Look at the table in Figure 4-3.9. Is it self-explanatory? Which
employee received the highest commission? How much were his or her
total sales for the first quarter? Which employee received the lowest commission? How much were his or her total sales for the first quarter?

Figure 4-3.9 displays the standard parts of a table. Some simplified tables
will not include all these parts. More complex tables will include other parts
such as a source note indicating the source of the data, ruled lines to separate the data visually, and dot leaders to aid in reading across the table from
one column to the next.

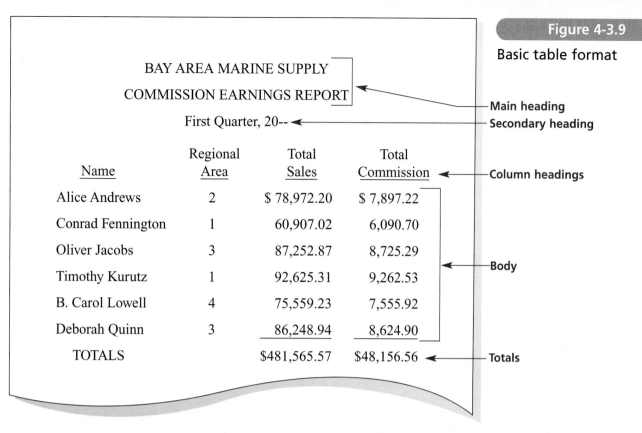

Figure 4-3.9

Basic table format

BAY AREA MARINE SUPPLY
COMMISSION EARNINGS REPORT ← Main heading
First Quarter, 20-- ← Secondary heading

Name	Regional Area	Total Sales	Total Commission
Alice Andrews	2	$ 78,972.20	$ 7,897.22
Conrad Fennington	1	60,907.02	6,090.70
Oliver Jacobs	3	87,252.87	8,725.29
Timothy Kurutz	1	92,625.31	9,262.53
B. Carol Lowell	4	75,559.23	7,555.92
Deborah Quinn	3	86,248.94	8,624.90
TOTALS		$481,565.57	$48,156.56

Column headings ← (Total Commission)
Body ←
Totals ←

Most word processing software packages have a table-generating feature that automatically determines column spacing and prepares the table layout. You may wish to start with the table layout that is generated automatically and then make adjustments as needed. Your goal is to create a table that is easy to read and highlights the appropriate information.

Main Heading

The main heading is the title of the table and describes its overall content. A carefully written table title helps the reader focus on the table content. The main heading of a table is treated in the same manner as the main heading of an informal report. The heading is usually centered horizontally over the table data and keyed in all capitals.

Secondary Heading

Some tables require a secondary heading such as the one shown in Figure 4-3.9. A secondary heading gives the reader more specific information about the table contents.

Column Headings

Column headings identify the information provided in the columns. A column heading may be centered above the longest line in that column or left-aligned even with the column data. Alignment of column headings may be mixed within the table as appropriate for the column data. For example, when using a spreadsheet program to create a table, the heading for a text column is often left-aligned while the headings for number columns are right-aligned to match the data alignment. Underscore column heads or use a bold or alternate type to set them off from the table body.

Body

The body contains data indicated by the column headings and may be single- or double-spaced. Tables are often double-spaced for improved readability. When the table is placed within the text of a report, use the space available on the page to determine how you will space the table body. The table width should not exceed the left and right margins of the report body.

Summary Lines

Data in a table is often summarized or calculated with the results shown at the end of the table. *Total*, *Average*, *Maximum*, and *Minimum* are common summary lines included on tables. The last entry in a column is often underscored to separate the table data from the summary lines. The summary line is typically labeled. For example, by using the word *Total*, the writer indicates that the figures in the column have been added.

Graphs

graph: pictorial representation of data

A **graph** is a pictorial representation of data. Graphs make a report more interesting and informative. In many cases, data is easier to interpret in a graph than when shown in columns of figures or blocks of text. Graphs, therefore, are used frequently in reports to display supporting information.

Figure 4-3.10

Pie charts show the relationship of a part to a whole.

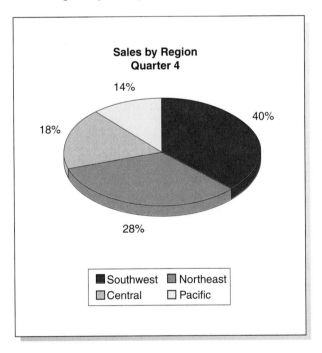

As you prepare business reports containing graphs, study previous reports from the company to determine style preferences. If the graph is half of a page or less in size, include it in the body of the text. Leave enough space before and after the graph to separate it visually from the text. Position the graph as near as possible to the portion of the text in which it is mentioned, ideally on the same page. If the graph is larger than half a page, place it on a separate page and include a reference to the graph's page number.

Three graphs commonly used in business reports are the circle graph or pie chart, the bar graph, and the line graph, shown in Figures 4-3.10, 11, and 12. Spreadsheet or charting programs are commonly used to convert numbers into percentages and prepare pie charts, bar graphs, and line graphs.

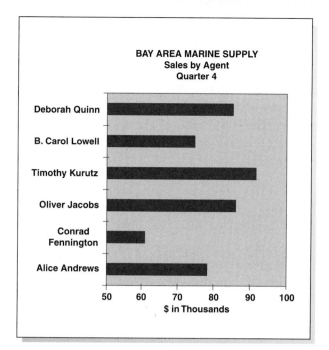

Figure 4-3.11

Bar graphs are used to show comparisons between items.

A **pie chart** (so called because the graph wedges look like pieces of a pie) is a display of how a part contributes to the whole. The whole circle represents 100 percent, and each wedge represents a portion of the whole. Each wedge should be identified with an appropriate label, color, or pattern.

pie chart: graph showing how a part contributes to the whole

A **bar graph** is used to show comparisons, as seen in Figure 4-3.11. Use bars of equal width and space the bars equally across the graph. If more than one set of data is included in the graph, use different colors or patterns to identify the sets of data. Stacked bars, three-dimensional bars, and gridlines may be used to make the data easier to read or understand. The number scale should be adjusted to show an appropriate range. For example, if the numbers graphed range from 75 to 103, the graph scale might begin at 70 rather than at 0. Consider carefully the point you intend to make with the

bar graph: chart used to show comparisons

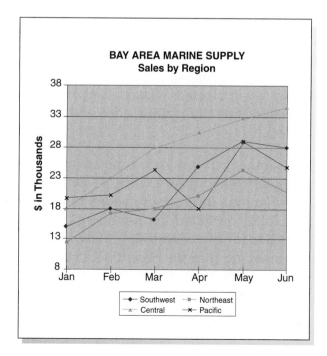

Figure 4-3.12

Lines graphs are used to show changes over a period of time.

Topic 4-3: *Business Reports and Related Documents*

graph. Adjusting the graph scale can make differences in the data appear smaller or larger.

line graph: chart used to display trends that emerge over a period of time

A **line graph**, as shown in Figure 4-3.12, is used to display trends that emerge over a period of time. Monthly sales, for example, are frequently represented in line graph form. In preparing such a graph, place the time categories across the horizontal axis and the amounts along the vertical axis. If more than one set of data is shown on the graph, use different-colored lines to distinguish each set.

Spreadsheets

Many writers use spreadsheet software to perform calculations and analyze the data they use in tables. Tables, graphs, and charts used in business reports may be created easily using spreadsheet software. The documents can be integrated directly into the report or printed separately as attachments to the report.

Spreadsheets are commonly used to record and report current data (an income statement, for example) or create projections (of costs or sales, for example) and test alternatives. Calculations representing various scenarios can be made quickly and the results analyzed. Conclusions or recommendations for reports can then be made based on the projections. For example, an executive might use a spreadsheet program to forecast income based on different sales forecasts.

WORKPLACE **CONNECTIONS**

Todd works in the accounting department of a small company. Mr. Jackson, the department manager, asked Todd to compare the costs of renting or buying a new copier for department use. Todd created a spreadsheet to include the costs of renting and the costs of buying a copier. If the copier is rented, the regular maintenance and any needed repairs will be handled by the copier rental company. Todd's company must pay only a flat monthly fee. If a copier is purchased, however, the long-term costs will include the maintenance and any repair costs for the copier.

Todd used his spreadsheet to test various possible scenarios including only regular copier maintenance, a low instance of needed repairs, and a high instance of needed repairs over the life of the copier. Todd concluded that renting a copier would be more cost-effective for the department. He wrote an informal report recommending that the department rent a copier and included data from his spreadsheet to support his recommendation.

Multi-page Report Preparation

Preparing lengthy reports often involves extensive editing as the document goes through several revisions. Sections of the report may be revised, deleted, or rearranged. Data to be included in tables or charts may change. Use your word processing and spreadsheet software effectively to save time in making these changes. Linking data in a spreadsheet to the report can save time when revisions are needed. Data that is updated in the spreadsheet file can be updated automatically in the report if the files are linked properly.

Pagination

Pagination is the process of dividing a document into individual pages for printing. Page breaks are determined by the software inserting an automatic page ending as the page is filled or the user entering the command for a forced page ending. Use the automatic page numbering feature of the software to accurately record each page number. When revisions change the page endings, the repagination feature will adjust the text automatically and renumber the pages.

Headers and Footers

A **header** is used to place the same information above the text at the top of pages of a document. Page numbers and abbreviated report titles are frequently used as headers. A **footer** is used to place information below the text at the bottom of the document pages. Page numbers or the report date are commonly included in footers. Once activated, header and footer text will appear on every page of the document unless instructions are given to suppress (prevent) its printing on a specific page. If changes are needed in the header or footer, you need only make the change once to correct all headers or footers in a section of the document.

Widows and Orphans

Because the pagination feature of your software merely counts lines before dividing a page, some paragraphs may be divided inappropriately. Paragraphs divided between pages should contain at least two lines on each page. A first line of a paragraph printed by itself at the bottom of a page is a widow line. The last line of a paragraph printed by itself at the top of a page is an orphan line. Avoid widows and orphans by reviewing the page breaks in the report and adjusting them as needed. Your word processing software may allow you to set options that automatically prevent widows and orphans.

Footnotes or Endnotes

Use the footnote feature of your software to automatically place footnotes at the bottom of the proper page or endnotes in order at the end of the report. If a text segment that has a related footnote is moved to another part of the document, the footnote will also be placed on the new page and renumbered automatically. If the moved text contains an endnote reference, the endnotes will be renumbered appropriately. Footnote and endnote numbers will also be adjusted when new footnotes or endnotes are inserted.

Professional Development Resources

— Association for Business Communication
Baruch College/Communication Studies/Box B8-240
One Bernard Baruch Way
New York, NY 10010
www.theabc.org

— Business Editors. "A First in Higher Education, Drexel University Distributes Speech Recognition Software Free to Students." *Business Wire*. September 19, 2000.

— Doug Harper. "How's Your Netiquette?" *Industrial Distribution*. November, 1999.

— Search terms:
speech recognition or voice recognition
merge documents
netiquette
e-mail
business communication

pagination: the process of dividing a document into individual pages for printing

header: information that appears above the body text on pages of a document

footer: information that appears below the body text at the bottom of document pages

Topic 4-3: *Business Reports and Related Documents*

Reviewing the Topic

1. What is a business report? What do all business reports have in common?

2. How does an analytical report differ from an informational report?

3. What guidelines should a writer of an informational report follow?

4. Describe three methods or technologies an office worker could use to input data for a report rather than keying the data.

5. What are the advantages of researching information online or using information services?

6. When is a formal writing style appropriate for reports?

7. How do unbound and leftbound reports differ?

8. How does the informal report differ from the formal report? What are the common parts of a formal business report?

9. Identify visual aids commonly used in business reports. Why are visual aids useful?

10. Describe the best uses of pie charts, bar graphs, and line graphs.

Interacting with Others

Beth is the new office assistant to Mr. Hope, supervisor of the customer service division. This morning Mr. Hope called Beth into his office and asked her to arrange for dinner reservations for him and two clients at a local restaurant. When Beth returned from Mr. Hope's office, she looked upset. "I don't think I was hired to be a social secretary," she said. "I guess rank has all the privileges. Don't you agree?"

1. Prepare a brief response to Beth's question.

2. What is Beth's professional responsibility in this situation?

Reinforcing Math Skills

You work in the accounting department of Black's Computers, a small retail computer store. Your supervisor, Mrs. Lowell, has sent you a file containing part of the data needed for a report and asks you to complete the spreadsheet. "We'll need this information to fill in the figures for the revised quarterly earnings report," Mrs. Lowell says.

1. Open the data file **Earnings**, which contains the report data.

2. Enter the column headings *Total Sales*, *Cost of Units Sold*, and *Gross Profit* in columns F, G, and H.

3. Enter formulas to calculate the total sales for each product.

4. Enter formulas to calculate the cost of units sold for each product. (Multiply units sold by the wholesale price.)

5. Enter formulas to calculate the gross profit for each product. (The gross profit is the difference between the total sales and the cost of units sold.) Add the gross profit column to determine the total gross profit figure.

6. Refer to your figures to determine the information Mrs. Lowell needs to complete the portion of her draft report. Include the completed statement at the bottom of your page. Save your work; you will use it in another activity.

COMPOSITION
INTEGRATED DOCUMENT
SPREADSHEET
WORD PROCESSING

Topic 4-3   ACTIVITY 1

Table and Memo Report

Refer to the Reinforcing Math Skills activity for this topic. You previously calculated the total sales, cost of units sold, and gross profit of several products for your supervisor, Mrs. Lowell. The two of you have been working on a quarterly report. She has asked you to prepare a table using your computations to include with the short memo report. "Please include the Product Description, Units Sold, Total Sales, and Gross Profit columns," Mrs. Lowell said. "We also need a secondary heading to identify the reporting period. I suggest you use *Reporting Period January 1–March 31*."

1. Refer to the spreadsheet you completed earlier. (If you did not complete the math exercise before, do so now.) Prepare an appropriately formatted table using the columns Mrs. Lowell requested.

2. Create a memo form for Black's Computers. Prepare a short memo report for Mrs. Lowell's review. Address the memo to Carlos Morales, Vice President of Sales. The memo should be from Virginia Lowell. Use an appropriate subject heading.

3. Begin the body of your memo report with the lines of the completed handwritten draft (below). Next, inform Mr. Morales that you are including a complete product sales breakdown in the table. Place a copy of the table in the report.

Several factors have affected our profits for this quarter. Due to the weakened economy, sales are slightly below our goals. In spite of strong competition in the market, however, we have retained our market share. The introduction of our new x15 computer system boosted sales in the home-user market.

Our gross profit for this period was $_____. The three products (by product numbers) that produced the highest total sales were _____ ($_____), _____ ($_____), and _____ ($_____). The three products (by product numbers) that produced the highest gross profit for the store during the period were _____ ($_____), _____ ($_____), and _____ ($_____).

COMPOSITION
INTEGRATED DOCUMENT
SPREADSHEET
WORD PROCESSING

Topic 4-3 ACTIVITY 2

Graphs

Mrs. Lowell has asked that you prepare charts using data from the spreadsheet you created earlier. She requests a pie chart showing total sales dollars for each product and a bar chart that compares wholesale and retail prices for monitors, keyboards, and disk drives.

1. Use the data in the spreadsheet you created in Activity 1.
2. Create a pie chart showing the total sales dollars for each product as a percentage of the total sales for all products. Include a chart legend to identify the products. Use the chart titles:

BLACK'S COMPUTERS

Product Sales

CHAPTER 4: COMMUNICATING IN WRITTEN FORM

3. Create a bar chart to show bars for wholesale prices and retail (selling) prices for monitors, keyboards, and disk drives. Include a chart legend to identify the products. Adjust the chart scale for appropriate minimum and maximum dollar figures. Use the chart titles:

BLACK'S COMPUTERS

Wholesale vs. Retail

4. Add a paragraph to the memo report you created in Activity 1. Introduce and explain what is shown in the pie chart. Insert the pie chart into the report.

5. Add another paragraph to the memo report to introduce the bar chart. Insert the bar chart into the memo report. Print the updated report.

Chapter Review

Summary

Because much of the communication in business is in written form, reading and writing skills are essential for all types of office workers. People who work in offices are often responsible for preparing written communications such as letters, memos, reports, tables, and graphs. In this chapter, you were introduced to guidelines for planning, preparing, and presenting written business documents. From your study of this chapter, you should be able to discuss the following points.

- Employees read at work to learn about the company, understand instructions, use reference sources, complete forms, and respond to inquiries.

- Critical areas for high-level reading are comprehension, vocabulary, and speed. All three areas can be improved with practice.

- All office workers need strong writing skills. Among the common writing tasks at work are summarizing messages and meetings, revising writing done by others, and preparing communications in various forms.

- Effective documents are well planned. They are clear, concise, courteous, complete, and correct. These characteristics apply to all documents.

- Proper application of English skills, such as spelling, punctuation, and correct grammar, are important for writing at work.

- Managing the schedule for writing tasks is important for meeting writing deadlines.

- The three stages of planning effective documents are creating or drafting the document, revising or editing it, and proofreading it for final presentation.

- When writing a document, know your purpose, your message, your audience, and the response you want from your audience.

- Several categories of messages are common in business correspondence: positive or neutral, negative, and persuasive messages.

- Business letters are generally written to people outside the organization. Memos are generally written to people inside the organization. E-mail messages are written to people both inside and outside the company.

- Business documents have standard formats, or protocol, that are commonly used in business communications. Using standard formats provides greater efficiency for both the writer and reader of business documents.

- Writing in the business office often involves preparing the same message or similar messages that are used again and again. Businesses often individualize letters even though similar letters may be sent to hundreds of people.

- Memos and e-mail are the most commonly used written communications within an organization. Memos should be used to communicate confidential information or for routine messages to workers who do not have access to e-mail such as factory production workers. E-mail is appropriate for most other short in-house written communications.

- How workers communicate with others in the organization influences how effectively the organization operates. Following the proper procedures for preparing and sending messages will help improve the communications in an organization.

- Desktop publishing is used to create high-quality printed documents. These documents usually contain text and images and often have complex formats.

- Business reports are a source of information for making business decisions. They are basically either analytical or informational in nature and may follow either a formal or an informal format and presentation.

- Visual aids are commonly used in business reports to make the report more understandable. They add interest to the report and may reduce the text needed to explain the information.

- Electronic resources are helpful aids to the business report writer. Preparing long business reports often involves extensive research and many revisions. Electronic-based aids can be used in different phases of report preparation, such as conducting data searches, using spreadsheets to calculate and graph data, and using pagination aids to revise multi-page documents with ease.

Key Terms

analytical report	header	positive message
appendix	negative message	quotation
comprehension	netiquette	references
desktop publishing	neutral message	speech/voice
documentation	optical character	recognition
draft	recognition	software
footer	pagination	tone
graph	persuasive message	vocabulary

Press Release

Assume that you are an assistant manager in the public information department of your company, Laughlin & Mead Corporation, headquartered in Asheville, North Carolina. The Board of Directors met yesterday and elected Mr. T. W. Gomez to the company's new position of vice president for technology. The public information director has asked you to prepare a draft of a press release to be sent to local newspapers as well as to business periodicals.

1. Open the data file **Press Release.pdf**, which contains a sample press release. Read the document to learn about writing and formatting a press release.

2. Compose and key a draft of a press release for review by the department manager. Use the current date, your name as the contact person, and the details given below step 5.

3. Work with a classmate. Act as the department manager and review your classmate's press release. Use proofreaders' marks or the editing feature of your word processing software to add comments and corrections to the document.

4. After your classmate has reviewed your document, make corrections and print a final copy of the press release.

5. If your software allows, save the document in HTML format appropriate for posting online. View the document in your browser software. Make corrections to the format as needed for an attractive online document. Save and print the HTML version of the press release.

   • The company address is 289 Westlake Avenue, Asheville, NC 28803-0956; Telephone: 704-555-0101. Your e-mail address is <u>pidassistant@laughlinmead.com</u>.

   • Mr. T. W. Gomez was elected by the Board of Directors at its meeting yesterday to fill the newly created position of vice president for technology.

   • Mr. Gomez has had ten years of experience in transforming the way work is done at Treadway Corporation in Boston, where he most recently served as assistant vice president for technology.

   • Mr. Gomez is a graduate of Midwest University, where he earned a B.A. degree in mathematics and an M.B.A. in computer science.

   • Our company sees the need to introduce state-of-the-art technology throughout our facilities in the 12 countries where we have operations.

   • Mr. Gomez will assume his new responsibilities on the first of next month.

   • When Mr. Gomez accepted the position, he said: "I like the challenge of this large company that has a vision of what it can become. I want to be a part of that vision. I look forward to working with the fine group of people who lead the company."

Chapter 4   ACTIVITY 2

Netiquette Flyer

Guidelines for communicating courteously and effectively online are called *netiquette* (derived from *network* and *etiquette*). Prepare a flyer on netiquette related to e-mail to distribute to coworkers.

1. Search the Internet or other reference sources for several articles or Web sites that provide information about netiquette. For each article or Web site, record the source information including the author for articles, the article or Web page name, the publication or Web site name and address, and the date of the publication or the date you view the Web site.

2. After reading about netiquette, write in your own words a list of eight to ten netiquette rules that relate to e-mail.

3. Create a one-page flyer to communicate your netiquette rules. Follow the design guidelines found in this chapter for creating effective documents.

4. List the source information for three articles or Web sites you reviewed as sources of additional information on netiquette.

Chapter 4   ACTIVITY 3

Formal Report

You are employed by East Coast Office Consultants. You have been writing a report on legal documents for a client to distribute to the legal secretaries in her firm. You have finished your first draft. You now need to edit your draft and prepare your final copy. Once you are satisfied with the copy, you need to prepare the preliminary and reference pages. The assembled report and a letter of transmittal will be sent to your client.

1. Open the data file **Legal**. Edit the report and format it as a leftbound report. Although you are a careful writer, you know your first draft is never your final draft. Improve the wording or make the document easier for the readers to understand. Side heads are indicated by an underscore. You may wish to format the headings using styles in your word processing program.

2. Prepare these additional report pages:
    *   Title page that gives (a) the title of the report, LEGAL DOCUMENTS; (b) your name; (c) the name of your company; and (d) the current date
    *   Table of contents, generated by your word processing software if possible

177

- Abstract of the report no longer than 100 words to give a brief description of the information provided in the report
- Reference page. The source you referred to in Chapter 1 is:

  Rita Sloan Tilton, J. Howard Jackson, and Sue Chappell Rigby. *The Electronic Office: Procedures and Administration*. Cincinnati: South-Western Educational Publishing, 1999, p. 603.

3. Prepare a short cover letter to your client, Ms. Hilda Treanor of Treanor Legal Assistance, 3435 Adelphia Blvd., Hastings, NE 68901-6884. Assume the letter will be printed on company letterhead. This is the first work you have done for Ms. Treanor, and you hope she will use your services again. Your title is writing consultant.

Communicating Orally

You will need to express yourself clearly in your oral communications at work so others will understand you. This is true whether you are talking with a coworker, addressing meeting participants, or giving a presentation. In most cases, you will speak either to motivate and influence or to inform and educate. You will also need to listen effectively so you can give appropriate feedback, answer questions, or carry out instructions.

....

This chapter focuses on oral communication skills and their importance to your success at work.

In this chapter, you will learn how to improve your listening and speaking skills for both communicating with coworkers and giving formal presentations.

OBJECTIVES

- Describe the importance of listening
- Explain techniques that aid in active listening
- Describe what an effective speaker achieves
- Explain the factors considered in speaking

modulated: adjusted to a proper level

Regardless of the career you choose, you will want to be confident about your listening and speaking skills. These oral communication skills will play a role in many aspects of your responsibilities.

The Importance of Listening

Imagine you are walking along a hall in a high-rise office building downtown. You notice that many conversations are under way. You cannot hear what is being said because voices are **modulated** so that only persons nearby hear the actual words. You would undoubtedly observe persons talking by telephone and others in conference with other people. In every instance, listeners are taking part in the communication process.

You will need to listen at work countless times. When you listen effectively, you will be able to:

- Follow through on oral instructions correctly
- Consider the additional information as you continue your work and make decisions
- Use time productively

Figure 5-1.1

Effective listening skills are vital to every office worker.

© NASI SAKURA/SUPERSTOCK INTERNATIONAL

Helena, an assistant manager, wasn't sure what the manager told her about a task she was about to begin. She had not taken notes during their discussion of the task. When she got back to her desk, she realized she did not understand when certain information was needed from the Hong Kong and Tokyo offices. Did she have enough time to send e-mail messages or should she telephone instead? She decided that she would not bother the manager but would just send e-mail messages and trust that the information would be forwarded in time for the manager's schedule. Unfortunately, the manager called early the next morning wanting the information. Can you imagine what happened in the conversation at this point?

Later, as Helena thought about this incident, she realized what had happened. She realized her mind was elsewhere when the manager turned to her after a telephone call, which had interrupted their discussion. Helena's mind did not return to the matter at hand; however, she continued thinking about something else. Helena made a promise to herself to be a more attentive listener.

Effective Listening Strategy

Listening is required to gain an understanding of what is being said. Conversations, meetings, lectures, answering machines, and voice mail will be meaningless if you fail to listen. Listening involves a mental process as well as the physical aspects of hearing. You may hear a speaker but not actively listen to the speaker by giving your full attention to what is being said. Mental participation is the critical part of listening. The listener must think about what is being discussed. When you listen, your mind processes the information you hear through reshaping what is already known about the topic and storing the information for future use.

Figure 5-1.2

This worker is not listening effectively.

© DTF PRODUCTIONS/IMAGE BANK

Ineffective listening may occur for a number of reasons. Some common reasons are

- A feeling of insecurity in the presence of the person who is attempting to explain something; the listener is so fearful that it is difficult to pay attention to what is being said
- An attitude on the part of the listener that what is being said is something already known
- An immediate judgment that there is no value to what is about to be said

Carefully assess your immediate mental response when someone begins to talk with you. Notice what **prejudgments** or attitudes are influencing your own listening. The following attitudes will help you improve your listening skills.

- An attitude of openness—wanting to learn—is critical to being an effective listener. If you think you can learn from others, you are likely to listen with a sincere wish to know what the other person or persons think. You are likely to follow up comments made by others with a closely related question or further comment.
- An attitude that others deserve your respect is important for effective listening. Remember that no two persons have had exactly the same experiences. Respecting the unique backgrounds of others will help you communicate with attention and awareness.
- An attitude that you can contribute to moving communications forward will help you listen attentively. "We can all gain from this communication" is the unspoken thought of an individual who is listening attentively.

Focus Attention

Have you ever heard someone—a parent, a good friend, or an instructor—say: "Please pay attention!" If you have, you may recall that the person was encouraging you to listen. Possibly, during a conversation you were asking again and again, "What did you say?" In such a situation, you were not really listening attentively to what was being said. After the plea to pay attention, you may have sharpened your focus and put aside mental **distractions**. Your willingness to respond aided your listening. Making an effort to think about what is being said can improve your **comprehension** of what you hear.

prejudgments: coming to conclusions before having full information

distractions: things that draw away attention

comprehension: understanding

WORKPLACE **CONNECTIONS**

Harold worked in a busy office as an industrial engineer. At times, he had to be on the factory floor. Often he would return from the factory to find a number of messages in his voice mailbox. He would retrieve the messages, but he found that even though he heard the messages, he wasn't listening. He had to replay the messages two or three times. He realized he was wasting valuable time because of his failure to listen effectively. He made a promise to himself: "I will listen carefully the first time, so I do not need to repeat messages." He listened to his own promise. He was surprised at his success.

CHAPTER 5: COMMUNICATING ORALLY

Figure 5-1.3

Take notes about instructions to reinforce your careful listening.

© EYEWIRE COLLECTION

Mentally Summarize and Review

If possible, anticipate what you will hear and prepare for listening by mentally creating an outline. For example, if you know that the manager often gives you assignments, you should set up a mental outline with the following sections: What is to be done? Why must it be done? What is the deadline? At what points does my manager want to know about my progress? With such a mental outline, you can listen to your supervisor and put what is said in its proper place. A quick review of your mental outline will assure you that you have all the information you need or help you identify what is missing.

Pause, even if momentarily, to review what you have heard. Assess whether you have clearly understood what you heard. Does it make sense? Do you have all the information you need? This review acts as a reinforcement of new information. Mentally reviewing a conversation and your notes assures you that you have gained what you needed to move ahead with your work or undertake a new assignment.

Take Notes and Ask Questions

Frequently, details are involved in talking with someone in person or by phone. Make a note of instructions, dates, figures, telephone numbers, and scheduling requirements to supplement your careful listening.

The person talking with you is interested in your understanding clearly what is being discussed. In most cases, he or she will welcome your questions. By listening carefully and raising questions, you can confirm that you understand the message. Your questions can also focus on points that were not clearly specified.

Speaking Effectively

The companion skill of listening is speaking. You will have many occasions when you must speak to coworkers or customers about your work and what is to be done. On such occasions, you will want to speak with ease and confidence.

To communicate your thoughts effectively, you must show your listeners that you are interested in what you are saying. Have you ever listened to a

Figure 5-1.4

A speaker who is interested in the topic will capture the audience's attention.

© SUSAN VAN ETTEN/PHOTOEDIT

speaker who seemed to be reading a speech with no understanding of the words? In such an instance, the speaker did seem to be interested in the content. If you have heard such a speaker, do you recall whether you enjoyed what you heard or did you learn much? You probably did not.

On the other hand, you may have heard someone who seemed very interested in what was being said. Your attention was captured because of the way the person spoke as well as by the content of the message. The interest of the speaker in communicating with the listeners **enhanced** the effectiveness of the communication.

enhanced: made greater, improved

WORKPLACE **CONNECTIONS**

Karen was the manager of special events and reported to the director of food services in a large manufacturing company's headquarters offices. The director praised Karen for her skill in working with so many different people who came to the office to arrange luncheons, dinners, and other special events in the company dining rooms. As the director noted: "Karen is happy to explain the alternative menus that are available, and she clearly conveys her interest in being helpful and giving people all the information needed to make choices."

Express Ideas Clearly

momentarily: briefly

Thinking must precede speaking, if only **momentarily** so. Try asking a mental question such as: "What do I really need to say to communicate my meaning?" Consider the purpose you are trying to accomplish with your communication. You are not likely to be misunderstood if you think about what you want to say before speaking.

WORKPLACE **CONNECTIONS**

The supervisor asked an assistant: "What do you still have to complete for the Thompson report I gave you on Monday?" Without a pause for thought, the assistant responded: "Not much."

If the assistant had given thought to the question, the response might have been: "I have to key the conclusions, the three short appendices, and the bibliography. Then I will print the entire document."

Which of the two responses is the supervisor likely to consider more satisfactory?

Speak Clearly in an Appropriate Tone

Your oral communication is worthless if the listener is unable to hear and understand your words. Speaking clearly requires that you say each word carefully. This is referred to as proper **enunciation**. When you enunciate words properly, your listener is more likely to hear them correctly. Two common problems for listeners occur when speakers run words together and when syllables are not sounded fully. Note the examples in Figure 5-1.5.

enunciation: pronouncing words clearly

Words and Phrases Commonly Enunciated Poorly

'preciate	for	appreciate
cam	for	calm
didya	for	did you
gimme	for	give me
gonna	for	going to
granite	for	granted
labatory	for	laboratory
libary	for	library
nothin'	for	nothing
'r	for	our
winda	for	window
winnin'	for	winning

Figure 5-1.5

Enunciate carefully to avoid these mispronunciations.

Topic 5-1: *Listening and Speaking*

Figure 5-1.6

People who learned English as a second language can easily understand people who use standard language.

© CORBIS

tone of voice: manner of speaking that expresses the speaker's attitude or feelings

Speaking at an appropriate volume level and using an appropriate **tone of voice** are important for clear communications. Consider the situation in which you are speaking and the distance your voice must carry. Regulate the volume level of your voice so listeners can hear you clearly, but so you do not disturb others who may be working nearby. Make the tone of your voice match the message you are trying to convey. Speak in a warm and friendly tone when complimenting a coworker on a job well done. Use a questioning tone when asking for information. When giving a warning, let your tone of voice convey caution or danger. Remember that the tone of voice and expression you use in speaking can be as important as the words you say in communicating your message.

Use Standard Language

Standard language is that language taught in English courses in elementary and secondary schools. This language is explained in current dictionaries. However, most dictionaries acknowledge common terms that are not standard language.

Oral communications at work should be done using standard language and correct grammar. Use of standard language helps ensure understanding. Global communications are increasingly important. Many people in the global community have learned English as a second language. For these people, knowledge and skill in speaking English are primarily related to standard language. They use the English language in an environment that may be very different from that in which people who speak English as a native language or as a second language learned in the United States. Imagine the difficulty people from other countries are likely to have when talking with people in the United States who use colloquialisms and slang in their conversations.

colloquialism: informal language used among a particular group

Colloquialisms are informal words and phrases used among people who know each other well or among people from a specific geographic area. Some colloquialisms are commonly used at work among employees who know each other well and tend to speak informally. A few of these are:

- finish off ... for ... *complete*
- get out of line ... for ... *fail to conform*
- head up ... for ... *serve as chairperson*
- touch bases ... for ... *discuss a matter*
- walk the talk ... for ... *carry through what you say*

Slang is informal language and has hard-to-discover meaning to those out-side the group in which such language is popular. Slang expressions are often short-lived. Most of the time, slang expressions are inappropriate when com-municating with others at work.

slang: informal language

Consider Your Audience

Audience is another term for listeners. Whether you are talking with one person, several people in a small conference room, or with a large group in an auditorium, you will want to consider the interests and needs of your audience, as well as your purpose for communicating. Talking with a single person or a small group usually permits you to be more informal than when you are speaking with a large group.

audience: listeners

You want to consider: (a) what your listeners want to know, (b) what they might already know, and (c) how what you are saying can be related to their experiences. You also want to be sensitive to how listeners are reacting to what you are saying. Are they looking away with lack of interest? Do they seem impatient with the length of your comments? Are they confused? Do they seem eager and attentive while you are talking? Do they seem ready to move on to another topic?

WORKPLACE CONNECTIONS

Leon was asked to instruct a new employee, Abby, in the use of a spreadsheet software program. Leon sat at the computer with Abby, beginning the explanation as though she knew nothing about the computer.

Leon did not inquire about Abby's experience at the computer and with spreadsheets. If he had, he would have learned that Abby had considerable experience with spreadsheets, even though she didn't know the one Leon was explaining.

Leon should have asked some **preliminary** questions. He then would have realized that Abby was not a beginner. He could have quickly moved to the explanation specific to the spread-sheet program that Abby needed to learn. Also, Abby would have a more positive impression of Leon if he had been consid-erate of what she already knew. Both of them would have saved valuable time if the explanation were focused on what needed to be learned.

preliminary: coming before the main consideration

Topic 5-1: Listening and Speaking

Body Language

You may have heard the saying, "Actions speak louder than words." This saying can be quite true in the case of nonverbal interpersonal communications, commonly called **body language**. Many studies have been done on communicating through nonverbal behavior. Interpretations of body language vary, so that such communications are not always as clear as words. Sensitivity to the possible meaning of nonverbal cues, however, can aid in understanding others and in communicating your messages more effectively.

Facial expressions are important nonverbal cues. A smile can convey understanding or support for what is being said. A frown, on the other hand, may indicate lack of understanding or disagreement. A smile at an inappropriate time, however, may convey smugness or insensitivity. Raised eyebrows may convey surprise or disapproval.

Eye movement can signal your attentiveness and openness. Making eye contact frequently shows your interest in what is being said and that you are being honest or open when speaking. Letting your eyes roam around and seldom making eye contact can signal that you are not paying attention when listening or that you are being evasive when speaking.

Posture and gestures are important elements of body language. Good posture when sitting or standing projects confidence and being at ease. Slouching or stooping indicates an indifferent attitude or lack of self-confidence. Leaning closer or nodding conveys interest, while leaning or turning your body away conveys discomfort or disagreement with what is being discussed. Crossed arms show a defensive or unwelcome attitude. Sitting calmly with hands folded in your lap conveys an openness to listen. Placing your hand to your cheek generally indicates that you are evaluating or considering, while placing your hand over your mouth generally indicates your disapproval.

Tapping fingers on the desk or fidgeting while talking or listening indicates a lack of concentration or nervousness. Constantly glancing out at the corridor or at a clock while speaking with a colleague can convey disinterest and may reduce the effectiveness of what your are saying.

When talking with coworkers or participating in meetings, observe the body language of the speaker and those around you. Paying attention to body language as well as words will help you understand better what others are trying to communicate. When communicating in person with coworkers or giving a formal presentation, be aware of your body language. Use your body language to reinforce the message you want to communicate.

body language: posture, body movements, gestures, and facial expressions that serve as nonverbal communication

CHAPTER 5: COMMUNICATING ORALLY

Be Aware of Nonverbal Communication

More than words are a part of communications when talking with coworkers in person or giving a presentation. Facial expressions, gestures of hands and arms, posture, and various other movements of the total body also communicate to listeners.

Nonverbal behavior is difficult to interpret accurately. For example, some people might think that glancing at a clock is considered evidence that a person is eager to get away as quickly as possible. However, perhaps the person wants to remain there to the last possible minute before going to a scheduled appointment elsewhere in the building. Making immediate eye contact with someone who comes to your workstation may indicate a **genuine** interest in being helpful, or it might merely reveal pleasure in having an excuse to interrupt some intensive work under way.

genuine: real

Be aware of the nonverbal behavior that accompanies what is said. Make sure it agrees with the **intent** of the words used. Nonverbal behavior should reinforce what is said, not distract from its meaning. Do not confuse your listener or listeners by saying one thing and having nonverbal behavior communicate something else.

intent: purpose

Be Interested in the Listener's Response

When speaking, allow time for interaction, if possible. Give listeners a chance to respond. One of the major advantages of oral communication is that there can be immediate feedback. When talking with others, be interested in getting questions, comments, and reactions to what is said. A skillful communicator is a good listener.

Reviewing the Topic

1. What are possible outcomes of listening effectively?
2. In what way is listening a mental process?
3. Why is listening necessary at work?
4. What are some reasons for ineffective listening?
5. How do you mentally summarize?
6. What does it mean to have an interest in communicating?
7. What is required to speak clearly?
8. What is standard language, and why is using standard language at work important?
9. Why should you take notes and ask questions when receiving instructions?
10. What factors should a speaker consider about the audience?

Interacting with Others

Three classmates were talking together after school one afternoon. One of them, Jack, said to the other two: "Listen, can I talk with you about my problem? I will confess to you that I don't want to give a talk in class next week. I'll just pretend that I am sick and not come to school for a few days. Sitting here and talking with you is fine. But I can't get up before the class. I have figured out a way to get out of doing this all through high school. I'll be honest with you. I remember having to stand before the class in the seventh grade to recite part of a poem. I was so scared that after the first two lines I couldn't remember a word. Oh, was I embarrassed. Aren't these assignments ridiculous? I'm not going to have to stand up before anyone and talk when I am out of school and earning a living. Do you agree with my scheme for next week?"

1. What would you say to Jack? What decision do you think would be best for him?
2. What tips can you give Jack to help him overcome his fear of public speaking?

You overhear the following conversation between two colleagues who are standing at the photocopying machine. Both of your colleagues have made a number of errors in their use of pronouns.

1. Key a copy of the conversation between Melissa and Steve, changing all pronouns used incorrectly.

2. Underscore all the pronouns you substituted for those in error.

> **Melissa:** "Do you plan to take the continuing education class for we staff people that Ms. Galson discussed at the meeting yesterday? Do you think she means for us to attend?"
>
> **Steve:** "I don't know if I'll go. Both me and Earl wonder if we would be better off taking a course later in the year. The topics are interesting though, aren't it?"
>
> **Melissa:** "Well, between you and I, I think there are likely to be some good courses later; but Betsy and me have pretty much decided we will go. We believe Ms. Galson would like we to go."
>
> **Steve:** "Melissa, if you go, will you tell us what them said at the meeting?"
>
> **Melissa:** "Of course. The instructor will be good, I guess. I won't be as good as her, but I'll do my best."

COMPOSITION
TEAMWORK
WORD PROCESSING

Topic 5-1   ACTIVITY 1

Speaking and Listening in a Meeting

Office workers must often present ideas or plans at small group meetings. Practice organizing your ideas and presenting them at a meeting in this activity.

1. Work with two classmates to complete this activity. (Read all the instructions for the activity before you begin completing the steps. You will repeat some of the steps so that each student will be a speaker, listener, and observer.)

2. As a team, create a form or checklist to use in recording observations about the effectiveness of communications during a meeting. Review Topic 5-1 and list important points for listening and speaking on the form. Also include a place to comment on the body language of both the speaker and listener.

3. As the speaker, choose a topic from the following list to develop into a three- to five-minute talk. List the main points you want to convey and then place the points in logical order. Be specific and give examples or supporting information as appropriate. Present your talk to the listener as if the two of you were in a meeting. Answer your listener's questions.

Topics

- Why you need new equipment or software
- How you want to change a procedure and why
- Why your company should sell a new product or service
- Instructions for a work project the listener is to complete

4. As the listener, pay careful attention to the speaker. Using two or three minutes after the speaker finishes, note the main points of the talk. Then ask relevant questions related to the information presented.

5. As the observer, pay careful attention as your classmates role-play the meeting. Then note your observations on the form. Discuss your observations with your classmates.

6. Repeat steps 3 – 5 so each person plays each role—speaker, listener, and observer. Give your instructor a copy of your notes for the talk as a speaker, notes and questions as a listener, and the observation form you completed as an observer.

COMPOSITION

WORD PROCESSING

Topic 5-1   ACTIVITY 2

Summarize Meeting Proceedings

The ability to listen attentively and summarize what you have heard is a key skill for office workers. Practice your listening and composition skills by summarizing meeting proceedings.

1. Identify a meeting that you can attend or view on television. Examples of organizations whose meetings you might attend include school clubs, civic organizations, your local school board, and your local city or county government. Local government meetings, such as a city council meeting, are often televised in the local area.

2. Attend the meeting or watch it on television. Remember that your role is that of a guest observer. Your purpose is not to participate in the meeting, but merely to listen and watch. Write brief notes about the proceedings during the meeting.

3. After the meeting, write a one-page summary of the meeting. Include the name of the organization, the meeting place and date, the approximate number of people attending, and the main points of the items discussed or decided.

Preparing a Presentation

OBJECTIVES

- Identify the purpose of your message
- Profile your listeners
- Address the interests of your listeners
- Develop ideas for your message and organize them in a storyboard
- Create effective visuals and handouts
- Organize team presentations

Regardless of your position, you will need to express yourself clearly to others at work. Even though presentations may not be a part of your daily work, occasionally you may need to present information to others, formally or informally. The situation may require you to speak to a small group of your peers or to a large audience. Regardless of the size of your audience and whether the presentation is formal or informal, you must keep your goals and your listeners' interests in mind as you develop your presentation.

Identify the Purpose of the Presentation

When you have an opportunity to prepare a presentation, it will likely be for one of two purposes. You will either want to motivate and influence your listeners, or you will want to inform and educate them. The message of your presentation will include the main ideas and supporting details you want to present. When you are speaking to motivate or influence, your message needs to be persuasive. Your purpose is to get your listeners to take a course of action. When you are speaking to inform, your message should be clear and concise. Your purpose is to communicate the information so your listeners can understand and use the information. Identifying the overall purpose of the presentation and the specific goals you want to accomplish is the first step in preparing a presentation.

Profile Your Listeners

Regardless of the purpose of your presentation, in order to hold your audience's attention, your message must be important to them. Developing a **profile** of your listeners and learning what is important to them is the next step in preparing a presentation. You must determine your listeners' interests or needs so you can relate your message to something they want to hear about.

profile: description, picture

To determine what is important to your listeners, you must first describe them in as much detail as possible. Put yourself in their shoes. Write down everything you know about them:

- What do the listeners like or dislike?
- What do the listeners need?
- What is the expertise of the listeners?
- What **biases** do the listeners have?
- What responsibilities do the listeners have?
- Are the listeners decision makers?

biases: prejudices

Developing a listener profile helps you identify the interests of your listeners. At first this may seem difficult, but if you try to think as they think, you should be able to do so.

Figure 5-2.1

Your message must be important to your listeners.

© CORBIS

WORKPLACE **CONNECTIONS**

Robert is planning a presentation for office personnel in his department. The purpose of his presentation is to inform the personnel about new office procedures that are to be used by the department. The new procedures have been adopted to increase productivity and efficiency within the department. However, Robert's message to the office staff must address their concerns and interests.

Robert knows that several office personnel are responsible for updating the customer database. As a result, some customer records are overlooked because one office employee assumes another employee made the updates. Office personnel are never sure customer records are accurate. More efficient procedures are needed for updating customer records. When Robert makes his presentation about new office procedures, he can discuss how the procedures will affect this situation that is of interest to his audience. He will explain how the new procedures will make their jobs easier.

Develop the Message

Your ideas, or the main message of your presentation, must accomplish the purpose of the presentation and relate to your listeners' needs or interests. With the purpose clearly in mind, create a list of major points or ideas you must include to accomplish your purpose. Consider how you can relate each major point or idea to the interests of your audience.

Organize Your Ideas

storyboarding: recording and organizing ideas, as for a presentation

After you have identified the ideas or main points to be included in the presentation, organize them in a logical way that your listener will understand. Sketching out and organizing your thoughts is called **storyboarding**.

Storyboarding involves brainstorming several ideas and then organizing them to create an outline and notes for your presentation. The notes can be just words or phrases, or they can be complete sentences.

To create a storyboard, you can complete a worksheet page for each element or idea for your presentation. Figure 5-2.2 shows a sample of a storyboard worksheet. The worksheet helps you organize your thoughts about a specific idea.

Notice in the figure that the worksheet page provides an opportunity to consider ways of explaining each idea. You begin by stating the purpose of the presentation. Next, you describe your main idea and provide information that supports your idea. Then you identify a listener interest. You also list listener advantages. Don't be concerned right now with the worksheet box labeled "Visual Element." You'll learn about that shortly.

To complete the storyboard, you fill out a worksheet for each idea in your presentation. Once all your ideas are written down, you can improve the flow by rearranging the pages. The storyboard provides the basic organization of the presentation. Through this planning process, you organize your key concepts and define the overall presentation.

An alternative to completing storyboard worksheets is using a software outline feature to create the storyboard pages. Create the main topics (or ideas) and then break down each main topic into subtopics. Once you key your ideas, you can edit and rearrange them quickly and easily. Be sure to include listener interests, support for your ideas, and listener advantages for each idea.

Storyboard Worksheet

Purpose	Motivate and influence sales staff to increase sales during the fall campaign
Main Idea	Commission and bonus opportunities will increase
Support for Idea	Commissions on sale items raised from 10% to 15%
	$500 bonus for top ten total sales
Listener Interest	Commissions and bonuses that may be earned during the campaign
Listener Advantage	More income for the staff member
Listener Objection	Large number of clients to be handled during the sale
	Counter: The extra effort required will be rewarded with higher income
Visual Element	Growing dollar sign

Figure 5-2.2

A storyboard worksheet helps you organize your presentation.

Include Supporting Details

credibility: confidence, integrity

Whenever possible, add **credibility** to your presentation by providing evidence or details that support your ideas. For example, you can state facts or offer statistics to back up a proposal. You can use examples and comparisons to confirm a need. You can use expert opinions to endorse a recommendation. You can relate a situation to personal experiences of your listeners or experiences of your own.

WORKPLACE CONNECTIONS

In a presentation on new office procedures, Robert will describe an embarrassing situation he experienced recently. He was talking with a customer on the phone, and the information in the database was not up to date. As a result, he was not able to handle the customer's inquiry satisfactorily. Robert's audience, the office staff, easily identifies with this problem.

Consider Listener Advantages and Objections

Once you have developed your ideas and your listeners' interests, list the advantages for your listeners if they accept your ideas. If possible, prioritize these advantages in order of importance to the listeners.

objections: reasons to disapprove or reject ideas

Consider all the **objections** your listeners may have regarding your ideas. When you anticipate the listeners' objections, you can decide how to address them. You may be able to offer solutions or alternatives to what the listeners see as a problem. Your goal is to minimize the objections so the listeners no longer see them as a problem.

Choose Visuals and Audio

visual aid: picture, chart, graphic

Images are very powerful. A **visual aid** stimulates the listener and keeps the listener's attention. Studies show that we remember about 10 percent of what we hear in a presentation and about 20 percent of what we see. However, we remember about 50 percent of what we both see and hear. Even in one-to-one communications, visuals are extremely effective. Not only will the visuals help you present your content, they will also make your listeners feel important because you took the time to create them.

Plan a visual for each main idea (each page in your storyboard). This will help provide direction for your presentation. Each visual you create should be designed for consistency and simplicity. Carry out the theme of the presentation in all visuals. The first visual should introduce the topic and set the tone for the presentation. All visuals should support the overall message and should address the interests and advantages of the listeners.

Choose the Media

media: materials or means used to communicate

The **media** you choose for your visuals will depend on your budget and the equipment you have available. Your audience and whether the presentation is formal or informal will also influence the media you use.

CHAPTER 5: COMMUNICATING ORALLY

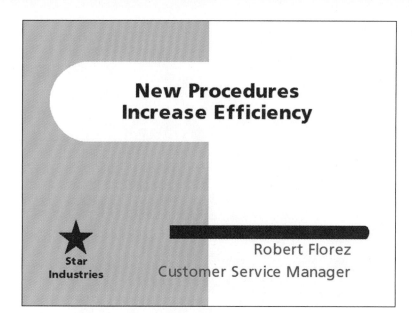

Figure 5-2.3

This visual introduces the topic and the speaker.

Figure 5-2.4

Flip charts are inexpensive and easy to use.

Flip charts are very effective for small, informal groups. They are inexpensive and easy to create and use. For one-to-one communications, desktop easels can be effective.

Overhead transparencies are effective for small or large groups and for formal and informal presentations. Overhead transparencies are inexpensive to create. They can be created in black and white or in color. If you have access to a copier that can handle transparency film, you can copy text, photos, and illustrations and turn them into transparencies quickly and easily. If the copier can produce color copies, you can create four-color transparencies inexpensively.

Topic 5-2: *Planning and Preparing a Presentation*

Figure 5-2.5

Overhead transparencies are effective for a variety of presentations.

© KEITH BROFSKY/PHOTODISC

sequence: order

Transparencies are easy to use. If you reorganize your presentation, you can quickly and easily rearrange the **sequence** of the transparencies. You can write on them and add to them during a presentation. You can overlay them to build a concept or to add special effects or emphasis.

Multimedia presentations are effective for both large and small groups, and they enhance formal presentations. With presentation software packages available, such as Microsoft PowerPoint, you can create professional electronic multimedia presentations quickly and easily. If a **multimedia projector** is available, you can display your presentation information directly through a computer. This is an economical and easy method for presenting your information.

multimedia projector: a device that shows video or images from a personal computer or videocassette recorder on a screen

Your needs may require you to create individual slides that are to be displayed through a slide projector. Perhaps you are adding slides to an existing set of slides, or you do not have other types of projection media available. You can have individual slides created commercially at photo centers. The slides can be produced from photos or illustrations, or they can be developed from the presentation you create using presentation software applications. The cost for creating these slides varies greatly depending on the media, turnaround time for development, and the company used.

Traditional presentations, such as those that use transparencies or individual slides, generally include static images. In other words, the images don't move. If you have access to more sophisticated software and equipment, you can add motion to your visuals. Most computers can display photographic-quality images and play high-fidelity sound. You can enhance your multimedia presentations by importing video, animation clips, and audio.

Create the Visual Elements

Think of your favorite book. Do you remember the story with visual elements or with words? Most of us mentally picture things we remember. When we recall previous experiences, we generally remember them visually.

Figure 5-2.6

Commercial software packages enable you to create professional slide shows.

You can remember graphics better than words. Whenever possible, use a graphic or picture instead of words or to reinforce words. Keep the graphics simple. Effective visuals help the presenter keep the listener's attention. In return, the listener can stay involved in the presentation and remember more of the message. Make sure the visual element you choose reinforces what you want to communicate. Do not use images that are unrelated to the content of the message. Use the storyboard worksheet to describe your visual element(s) as you plan and organize your presentation.

Computer technology provides us with a multitude of applications for using clipart, graphs, illustrations, and photographs. However, the graphics you incorporate in your presentations do not need to be elaborate. They can be simple creations that you draw or clipart that comes with your presentation software. For example, you can use an up arrow to represent "increase" or a clock to represent "time."

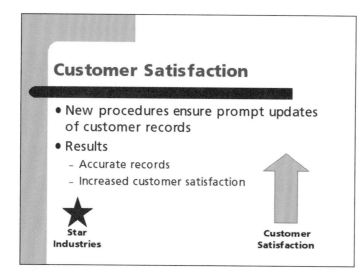

Figure 5-2.7

Simple graphics illustrate presentation ideas.

Topic 5-2: *Planning and Preparing a Presentation*

Design Strategies

white space: blank area, as on a document or slide

Limit your design to one main idea per visual, and use plenty of **white space**. Make the orientation of your visuals consistent throughout the presentation. Visuals in landscape orientation are wider than they are tall. Visuals in portrait orientation are taller than they are wide. Transparencies and slides (both individual slides and slides in an electronic multimedia presentation) are usually created in landscape orientation because that better utilizes the space. The visual in Figure 5-2.7 is in landscape orientation.

Keep the design of your visuals simple. Remember that the purpose of the visual is to help you maintain your listeners' attention and to help your listeners remember your message. Do not make your visuals too complicated or difficult to read or understand.

Text

Limit text on visuals. If the text on a visual is crowded, it results in a confusing appearance. If you have too much text, the audience becomes involved in reading the content of the visual instead of listening to what you are saying.

Limit the use of different text styles, sizes, and colors throughout to avoid a confusing appearance. For example, you might choose to use Arial, 24 point, blue text for main points or headings and Times Roman, 18 point, black text for subheads or supporting details. Lowercase text is easier to read than all caps. As a general rule, use all caps sparingly.

bullets: small graphics, such as circles or diamonds, used to draw attention to a line of text

Use **bullets** to help the audience follow the presentation. Bullets are effective for presenting important points and specific terminology. Indent bullets to establish a hierarchy of points or details. The visual in Figure 5-2.7 has two levels of bullets.

Make the wording on all visuals parallel in verb tense. Use strong, active verbs. Whenever possible, make the points short and concise.

Writing on the visual as you use it in your presentation is very effective. Not only does this draw the listeners' attention to the visual, but it also enables you to create a visual memory for your audience. For example, some presentation software programs allow you to underline or circle important information on a slide as you discuss the information.

Color

Use color effectively for maximum impact. Just because color is available does not mean it has to be used extensively. In fact, limiting the number of colors used is often best.

Consider the generally accepted associations of colors. For example, in business, red usually relates to cost and green usually relates to profit. In general, red draws the most attention and evokes excitement. Blues and greens are relaxing. Earth tones can be soothing but can also be dull or lack impact. A blending of colors or graduated colors instead of a solid background can help to guide the viewer's eyes to a focal point. Borders are effective for adding and using color wisely. They help to guide the viewer's attention and give the visual a professional look.

The colors you choose will depend on the media you are developing for the presentation. Overhead transparencies are most effective with dark text on a

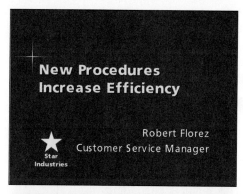

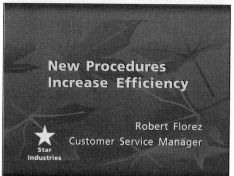

Figure 5-2.8

The same visual takes on different looks when different design templates are used.

light background. Computer slides and 35mm slides can be effective with a variety of background colors and textures. Choose your background color, text colors, and image colors to complement one another and to create a pleasing effect that will not distract your audience from the message. Some presentation software programs have design templates you can use to give your visual a professional look. Coordinating colors for background, text, bullets, and other design elements are part of the template design.

Use Motion

You can add motion to an electronic multimedia presentation in a variety of ways. Cascading bullets, transitions, video, and moving images can all be used to add interest to your electronic slides.

When creating electronic slides, bullet lines can be set to cascade or appear on screen one at a time at your command or after a certain period of time (usually seconds) that you specify. Using this technique is effective when you want to emphasize each point as you present it. Your listeners cannot read ahead to the next point you plan to discuss as they can when all bullets appear on screen at once. Your command (usually a mouse click or key stroke) that brings on the next bullet also signals to the audience that you are ready to move ahead to a new point.

Transitions in an electronic slide show are the motions used to move from one slide to the next. A variety of transition styles are available. You can make a slide appear to move in from one side of the screen and cover the slide that is already onscreen. You can have a variety of shapes, such as boxes, circles, or diamonds move across the screen as one slide disappears and another appears. Of course, you can simply have one slide disappear and another appear using no transition effect. Transition effects can be set to move slowly or quickly and can be accompanied by sound in some programs.

Figure 5-2.9

This slide uses cascading bullets.

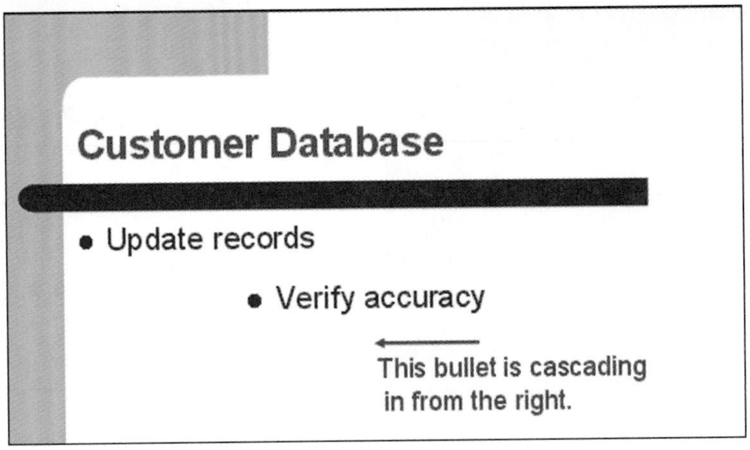

Customer Database

- Update records
  - Verify accuracy

⟵ This bullet is cascading
in from the right.

You can place links in your multimedia slide presentation to videos you want to play during the presentation. You might include a video of a company executive who could not attend the meeting in person, for instance. Or you might play a video that shows technical details or operation of a piece of equipment. You might want to include videos of customers commenting on a product. A video of a warm sunny beach with swaying palm trees can set the mood for a discussion of a winter sales meeting held in Florida. As with other images, be sure the video is appropriate for the content of the message and that it is fairly short so you do not lose the attention of the audience.

Use Audio Effectively

From soft music playing as your audience gathers to resounding applause to stress a job well done, audio can enhance your presentation. Like clipart and other graphics, audio collections are readily available and contain a wide variety of music, sound effects, and common phrases. If you require specific music or text, you may wish to record your own audio or have it prepared professionally.

If you add audio to your slide or multimedia presentation, make sure it is appropriate. The audio should enhance the presentation and not be over-bearing or distracting. Sound can be used effectively to introduce a topic, build excitement, or add special effects. If you decide to use sound, be sure you are not competing with it when you are talking. Like color, use sound wisely. Make sure it serves a purpose.

Create Handouts and Posters

handout: printed document used to summarize or provide details, as for a presentation

The audience will only remember a small portion of the content of your presentation. Provide **handouts** for your listeners so they can be used later for reference and as reminders of the key points in your presentation. The handouts need not be limited to text. Consider including some of the visual elements you've displayed in your presentation. Even if they are small, icon-like images, these visual elements will serve as reminders of the message you provided.

If you have several handouts to distribute during a presentation, consider printing them on paper of different colors. The colored pages will make it easy for you and your listeners to distinguish between the handouts.

Consider using a color copier to reproduce four-color handouts that will add impact to your presentation if the importance of the presentation justifies the added cost of color copies.

Purposes of Handouts

Handouts can be useful in guiding your listeners through the presentation. The intent of the handouts will determine how you design them and when you distribute them to the audience.

Sometimes handouts containing the outline of your presentation can be helpful. The outline will help your audience follow your presentation and stay involved. Throughout the presentation, the handout can be used for note taking.

Another reason to provide handouts is to supply your listeners with specific, detailed information that is too lengthy to provide on visuals. You may also want to provide additional information not contained in your presentation.

WORKPLACE **CONNECTIONS**

In his presentation on new office procedures, Robert provided a handout containing the outline of his presentation. He removed the details of the outline and replaced them with blank lines. As he presented the new office procedures, the staff members took notes to fill in the missing information.

One of the handouts Robert plans to provide during his presentation contains detailed descriptions of the new office procedures. The office staff will use this information later when they begin implementing the new procedures.

The information included in your handouts can also summarize the main points of your presentation. When creating this type of handout, use different words and examples in your summary handout so that the information does not simply duplicate your presentation. Obviously, you would not want to distribute a summary of your presentation until you have given the presentation.

Display Posters

Another way to reinforce the content of your presentation is to enlarge a slide, photo, or handout into a poster-size print. Display the poster to restate key points, introduce a new product, or review a visual element.

You can have posters created at photo centers. The cost will vary depending on the vendor, the poster size, and the turnaround time for development. Standard poster sizes include 16" × 20", 20" × 30", and 24" × 36". The positive impact a poster can have can justify the expense of creating it.

Figure 5-2.10

A poster can be effective for emphasizing important points in a presentation.

© STEVE NIEDORF PHOTOGRAPHY/IMAGE BANK

Plan Team Presentations

Office workers are often involved in giving team presentations. For a team presentation to be successful, each member of the team must be committed to accomplishing the task. When the individuals within the team work together to prepare the content and deliver the message, they can use the expertise of all the individuals involved. Not only can this expertise add credibility to the presentation, but it can also provide diversity and comprehensive coverage of a subject.

Figure 5-2.11

Individuals must work together to prepare a team presentation.

© KEITH BROFSKY/PHOTODISC

Determine Roles of Individuals

The first step in preparing a team presentation is to select a leader. The leader will ensure that the team stays focused on accomplishing its objectives.

CHAPTER 5: COMMUNICATING ORALLY

Each team member must have a valid role. All team members may not be involved in delivering the presentation, but each should make significant contributions. Those contributions can vary. For example, one or more team members may research and develop content for the presentation; another may create the visuals. One or more members may deliver the presentation.

Working as a Team

Once the team has been formed and each individual's role is established, all members of the team must agree on the purpose or objective of the presentation. All their contributions to the team presentation must be directed toward accomplishing this objective. Through sharing of ideas and brainstorming, the team can develop an outline of the presentation that will incorporate everyone's ideas.

Developing the content of the presentation takes some extra effort. Because several individuals have contributed, the team needs to make sure the tone and the terminology is consistent throughout the presentation. Furthermore, all the content must be presented from the listeners' point of view, and it must provide clear listener advantages.

The development of the visual aids must also be consistent in style and content. Using compatible media for visual aids can help to create a smooth transition from one presenter to another. For example, all presenters use the same template design for electronic slides.

Consider the effect of one presenter using an electronic slide show, a second presenter using flip charts, and a third presenter using overhead transparencies. The session would appear as three separate presentations. Following the first and second speakers, the presentation would halt with an equipment change as well as a change in lighting. The listeners would lose their train of thought, and the **continuity** of the presentation would be lost.

continuity: smoothness, flow

Once the content and visuals have been developed and organized, the team should review the entire presentation to make sure all the elements flow together well. The team can then determine time allowances and the content to be presented by each person and practice delivering the presentation as a group.

Topic 5-2: *Planning and Preparing a Presentation*

Reviewing the Topic

1. What are the two primary purposes of presentations?
2. What kind of information can you gather to profile your listeners?
3. Why should you consider listener advantages and objections in planning your presentation?
4. What kinds of evidence can you use to support your ideas?
5. Describe a storyboard and its purpose.
6. List two design strategies related to text and two design strategies related to color on visuals.
7. Give two examples of how motion may be used in visuals for a presentation.
8. Explain how audio may be used effectively in a presentation.
9. List three ways handouts may be used for a presentation.
10. What are the advantages of working in a team to prepare a presentation?

Thinking Critically

Assume that you are part of an office team assigned the task of improving the company-wide schedule for employee breaks and lunchtimes. The schedule was revised to eliminate overcrowding in the cafeteria at various times throughout the day. The team recently submitted a proposed schedule to management and has just received approval. The new schedule will be effective the first of next month.

You have been asked to present this new schedule to the personnel in your department. You have worked with the individuals in your department long enough to know that many of them are reluctant to accept change. You also realize that some of the employees in your department currently enjoy sharing their breaks and lunches with employees from other departments. Unfortunately, this may no longer be possible for some. Obviously, before you present the new schedule, you must be ready to address the concerns and needs of the personnel in your department.

1. Describe how you would introduce this new schedule with the listener in mind. What listener needs or interests would you address? What listener advantages would you present?
2. List some complaints and objections you might expect to hear from your colleagues in the department. Explain how you would attempt to minimize these objections.

Your colleague Elaine has asked you to review her ideas for a presentation she will give to train the new employees in using the company e-mail system. She plans to create electronic slides for her presentation. A partial list of her ideas is provided below step 3.

1. Restate Elaine's key ideas in short, concise phrases. Use strong, active verbs and limit the use of adjectives, adverbs, and prepositions.
2. Key the text to be contained on each slide. Use bullets to help organize the information.
3. Plan the flow of the presentation and place the material in logical order.

> This e-mail system offers many advantages that will improve your efficiency and reduce the amount of time you are online. For example, you have lots more options that you can preset. You can customize these settings for your particular needs. You get faster delivery times.
>
> The features include the following: You can upload and download files. You can automatically retrieve new incoming mail and send new outgoing mail. You can also get to the address book and retrieve data quickly and easily.
>
> Let's take a close look at the address book. You can store multiple e-mail addresses within an individual record. You can sort the records in the address book in alphabetical order. Or you can organize the address book to first display the addresses you use most frequently.

COMPOSITION
PRESENTATION
WORD PROCESSING

Topic 5-2 ACTIVITY 1

Plan and Organize a Presentation

In this activity, you will plan and organize a five-minute presentation to inform and educate your classmates on a topic of your choice. In later activities, you will prepare the visuals you plan here and give the presentation to your class.

1. Choose a hobby, sport, or activity that you really enjoy and about which you are knowledgeable and plan a presentation about this topic.
2. Create a storyboard worksheet for each main idea in your topic. See Figure 5-2.2 on page 195 for an example storyboard worksheet. Complete all parts of the storyboard worksheet, including ideas for the visual elements. (You will create the actual visuals in a later activity.)

Prepare Visuals and Practice a Presentation

In this activity, you will prepare visuals for the five-minute presentation you planned for Topic 5-2 Activity 1 and practice your presentation.

1. Choose the media you will use to create the visuals depending on the equipment and materials available for use in your classroom. Ask your instructor for the media options available to you.

2. Create a visual for each storyboard worksheet you prepared earlier.

3. After your visuals are complete, practice your presentation in front of a mirror. Or, if possible, videotape your practice session. Focus on using your visuals correctly so they help to emphasize the key points in your presentation. Notice your posture and gestures and concentrate on using a pleasant voice.

Delivering a Presentation

OBJECTIVES

- Apply methods for practicing and preparing for a presentation
- Describe appropriate personal appearance for making presentations
- Apply proper techniques for communicating with your audience
- Use visuals effectively
- Conduct question-and-answer sessions

Now that you have prepared your message, you are to put your ideas in motion. You may think that with all this preparation, you are ready to deliver the message. The content of your presentation may be right on target, but if you cannot communicate the content effectively, your efforts will not be rewarded. Several factors can help you communicate your message with confidence, enthusiasm, and professionalism.

Practice and Prepare

The more experienced you become in speaking to others, the less practice you will need. If you're new at making presentations, you will definitely want to practice. You can practice before friends or colleagues, or you can rehearse the presentation on your own.

Review each of your visuals and the notes you have created to accompany them. Rehearse out loud exactly what you plan to say. Make sure you state each idea from the listener's point of view. Also be sure to provide listener advantages.

For team presentations, each presenter must know the content he or she will present. Although each member should use his or her own style of speaking, everyone should reflect the overall theme. All team members should be present, even if some of them do not present. The team should practice the presentation as a group.

Prepare Notes

One of the best ways to ensure that you will make a successful presentation is to prepare well. The visuals you have prepared will guide you through the outline of the presentation. Use notes to remind you of the key points and the facts relevant to your presentation. You can use note cards or the notes feature of your presentation software to record details, ideas that each visual presents, content prompts, and reminders. If you've practiced at length, you'll probably find you no longer need to look at your notes because you are knowledgeable about the content and know what you plan to say. When you have done a thorough job of preparing your message, you can feel confident and remain calm during the presentation.

Videotape Your Presentation

Videotape your presentation so you can evaluate and critique yourself. Review your presentation and consider ways you can improve the delivery of your message. If necessary, practice and videotape yourself again and then reassess your presentation. Remember, you will most likely be much more critical of yourself than anyone in your audience will. Also, consider getting constructive criticism from friends and coworkers.

Figure 5-3.1

This speaker is using notes that contain detailed information.

Prepare the Meeting Room

There are many factors to consider regarding the meeting room. Make sure the seating arrangement is appropriate. A semicircular, or "U," arrangement is good for an audience that will focus on visuals at the front of the room. This arrangement also enables the presenter to control the focus of the group. If the presenter is standing before the audience, a rectangular seating arrangement also works well. A circular or oval arrangement is helpful to group discussions and shared communications but does not work well if the presenter will be standing to address the group.

Arrive early to set up equipment and support materials. Practice ahead of time with the specific equipment to be used in the presentation, such as a computer or projector. Even if you are familiar with operating a similar piece of equipment, make sure you practice on the one you plan to use. This will allow you to discover any differences or problems with the equipment. Test the audio equipment and get comfortable with the microphone. Know whom to call if you should need a technician.

Figure 5-3.2

Remember that the meeting room will grow warmer when filled with people and set the temperature accordingly.

CHAPTER 5: COMMUNICATING ORALLY

Check the lighting in the room and determine the best light level to use for the presentation. Even though your visuals may look good in a dark room, you want the lighting sufficient so your audience can clearly see you as you speak. Also, check the room temperature. Remember that bodies heat up a room. Setting the temperature to about 68 degrees will usually provide a comfortable environment when the room is filled with people.

Consider Your Appearance

Your appearance makes an impression on your audience and can influence how they receive your message. Dressing appropriately can help you gain their respect and hold their attention. When inappropriate, your appearance can distract your listeners or **detract** from your credibility.

detract: take away from

Good grooming is important. Be neat and clean in your appearance. Get a good night's rest before the presentation so you can look and be alert. For formal presentations, business suits are appropriate. For informal presentations, your attire can be more casual, depending on the audience. Dress comfortably but conservatively.

WORKPLACE **CONNECTIONS**

Pablo is inexperienced at giving presentations and is a bit nervous about addressing a group at next week's sales meeting. When deciding what he plans to wear for the presentation, Pablo considers the information he knows about the meeting. The sales team meets each winter in an area likely to be warm and sunny, such as Florida or southern California. The sales people enjoy this break in their normal routine of visiting clients and take the opportunity to dress in business casual attire at this company meeting rather than in business suits. Pablo considers dressing in business casual attire also. After further consideration, however, Pablo decides to wear a business suit. He believes the sales people will take his presentation more seriously if he dresses formally. He will wear business casual attire when he attends presentations given by others and wants to be seen as part of the group.

Present Opening Remarks

In a small- or large-group presentation, another person may introduce you to your audience. You should also introduce yourself. In your opening remarks, be sure to state your purpose. Your opening remarks help to set the tone for your presentation. You may choose to use a visual for this introduction.

Always remember that your remarks should be appropriate for the occasion. For example, some people like to begin with a joke or with a note of humor. This helps to break the ice and makes you more comfortable with your audience. Jokes should always be in good taste and appropriate for the audience. If the topic of your presentation is very serious in nature, however, a joke may not be appropriate.

Figure 5-3.3

Business attire is appropriate for formal presentations.

© AMY ETRA/PHOTOEDIT

Communicate with Your Audience

To deliver your message effectively, you must communicate with your audience. Although you will not be carrying on a two-way conversation with members of your audience, a sharing of ideas and information must take place. You will not be able to successfully communicate your message to your listeners until you have established a meeting of the minds. To do this, you must get your audience involved.

Your listeners will likely be involved in your presentation if you appear relaxed and comfortable. Being nervous is normal. Naturally, you want to do well, and you may experience some nervousness. Take deep breaths, concentrate on talking slowly, and think about what you're going to say next. You may think that you are talking too slowly, but that is generally not the case. The listeners will find you to be more credible because they can tell you are giving thought to what you are about to say. Maintain a positive self-image and an upbeat attitude. Remind yourself that you are well prepared and can deliver the message effectively.

Maintain Eye Contact

Making eye contact with one person in the audience helps all members of the audience feel like you are talking to them. Until you become experienced, you may find it difficult to make eye contact with your listeners. If this is a problem for you, try to maintain eye contact with one individual for at least five seconds before making eye contact with another person in the audience. Maintaining eye contact helps you involve your listeners and know whether your audience is following you. You can judge their reactions to what you are saying, and your listeners will feel more involved and important.

Avoid Non-Words

non-words: spoken sounds such as "uhh" and "ah"

Sounds or words that do not contribute to the meaning of the presentation are often called **non-words**. The use of non-words is a habit many of us need to break. Often we don't realize we say non-words such as "uhh" and

Figure 5-3.4

Establishing eye contact with someone in the audience makes all your listeners feel more involved.

© IMAGE 100/ROYALTY FREE/CORBIS

"ah." Review your videotape or have a friend help you identify non-words that you use. Count the number of non-words you say throughout your presentation. You may be surprised to find how frequently you use non-words.

Usually we say non-words because we are thinking about what we want to say next, and we do not want to allow a period of silence. Actually, a non-word does not fill up much time as we speak. Having quiet pauses between our statements is preferable to using non-words. The non-words can be much more annoying to listeners than a pause with silence.

If you know you use too many non-words, videotape your presentation a second time. This time, consciously pause instead of saying a non-word. Review your videotape and count the occurrences of non-words again. Hopefully, you were able to reduce them significantly. Don't be concerned if you cannot eliminate all non-words initially. Habits are difficult to break. Consciously work on avoiding non-words in your daily communications as well. You will soon see you can speak without them.

Non-Words	
ah	uh-huh
all right	well
and	yeah
and ah	you know
okay	you see

Figure 5-3.5

Avoid the use of non-words in your presentation.

Show Enthusiasm and Speak Convincingly

Speak with enthusiasm and conviction. A sure way to get your audience involved is to convince them that you are excited about the topic. If you believe in what you are saying, let your listeners know. Let your enthusiasm be genuine, however. Most listeners will know if you're not being honest, and that is a sure way to lose their attention.

Show a sincere interest in helping your listeners meet their needs. Use key-words that your listener wants to hear and to which they can relate. Describe experiences or examples with which your listeners can identify. In doing so, you can be very convincing as you share your ideas.

Control Your Posture and Gestures

Watching speakers who constantly pace back and forth or who shuffle their feet and shift weight from one leg to the other can be very distracting. Instead of becoming involved in your presentation, listeners start concentrating on your posture and gestures. You want them to think about your message, not your gestures.

Stand with your feet slightly apart and firmly planted, moving or shifting your weight only occasionally. Leave your hands at your sides until you use them for natural gestures that enhance your words. For example, if something is really big, show it by opening your arms really wide. If something is minor, use a gesture with your hands to show the problem is small. Make sure your gestures don't **contradict** your words. When your hands drop below your waist, your gestures are not effective.

contradict: deny, counter

Avoid other distracting gestures such as rubbing your hands together or crossing your arms. These forms of body language communicate nervousness. Your listeners will be watching your body language as they listen to you speak. Make sure your posture and gestures are not communicating something different than the message you want them to receive.

Figure 5-3.6

Gestures can enhance or detract from a speaker's words.

© IMAGE 100/ROYALTY FREE/CORBIS

Use Good Intonation

No one likes to listen to a person speaking in a monotone. As you review your videotape, close your eyes and listen to your voice. Do you use good **intonation**? Does your voice reflect enthusiasm? Is it easy to listen to? With practice, you can learn to speak with a pleasant voice that is neither too high nor too low. Your voice should sound relaxed and have an even tone.

Learning to relax can help you control your voice. If you are tense, your voice may sound shaky and high-pitched. Concentrate on speaking loudly enough without straining your voice or shouting. Vary your **inflection** to help you sound more interesting. Enunciate clearly and don't speak too quickly. If the meeting room and audience are large, use a microphone so you can speak normally and still be heard by everyone.

intonation: the rise and fall in voice pitch

inflection: tone of voice

Keep the Audience Focused

Watch the reactions of your audience. Make sure they are focused on what you are saying. If they seem confused or distracted, back up and rephrase your point. If you sense that you are losing their attention, try to focus again on listener interests and advantages.

Do not panic, however, if the audience does seem to lose focus. Keep in mind that this topic is something that you know and understand very well. Your listeners may need more time to think about the information and ideas you are presenting.

Use Visuals Effectively

If you've prepared well, you have some great visuals to help you communicate your ideas. These visuals, however, are not the key to your presentation. You are the key element. Begin by drawing the listeners' attention to yourself. Then, when appropriate, direct their attention to the visuals to make your message more powerful.

One way visuals can make your message more powerful is by creating anticipation. Do not reveal the visual too soon. Introduce or refer to the visual before you display it.

WORKPLACE **CONNECTIONS**

In a presentation about new procedures for reporting travel expenses, Melita Singh has a visual that summarizes data collected in a survey of staff members. To introduce the visual, Melita says, "You'll recall that last month we requested your input regarding our current travel expense reimbursement procedures. We received some interesting insights from many of you." Then Melita reveals the slide that summarizes the findings.

As you display your visuals, look at your listeners, not at your visuals. Continue to maintain eye contact. Stand to the left or right of the display of your visuals. Do not let the visuals replace you. Be sure your listeners can see you and the visuals.

Figure 5-3.7

The audience should be able to see the speaker and the visuals.

© V.C.L./FPG INTERNATIONAL

Pause to allow listeners time to view and think about your visuals. You've seen them and studied them, but your listeners have not. Also use pauses to allow for listener reaction. Allow listeners time to laugh if the visual is humorous, or give them an opportunity to read and evaluate a proposed solution displayed on a visual. During this pause you can study their reactions to your visual. For example, look for nods of agreement or expressions of disagreement. If appropriate, ask for their feedback before continuing.

Answer Questions

Allow your audience time to ask questions. Question-and-answer sessions are valuable to you as well as the audience. They provide you an opportunity to hear from your listeners as they share what they are thinking.

Anticipate Listener Questions

Many speakers become anxious about receiving questions from an audience. They are afraid they will not be able to answer the questions or that they will lose control of the situation. As with the overall presentation, the key to feeling calm and confident when receiving questions is preparation. Anticipate what your audience will ask you following your presentation. If you have prepared well, you have probably addressed many of their concerns in the content of your presentation. However, you may get questions about content you have already covered. This means that the listener either did not understand or did not retain that information.

Perhaps when you give your audience the opportunity to ask questions, no one will raise a question. This situation happens frequently. Initially, you may think the listeners are not interested in the topic and just want to leave. If you have been effective as a speaker, they have been listening and thinking about your ideas. You have been directing their train of thought. Perhaps they have not had time to think about their own ideas and questions to ask.

Curtis Babiak considers anticipating questions an important part of preparing for his presentation on reassignment of sales territories. He knows members of the sales team will have lots of questions about how the change will affect workloads, commissions, and follow-up on needs of customers in the territory previously assigned to a sales person. Curtis keys each question he thinks someone is likely to ask. Then he keys a complete and concise answer to the question. Curtis will use these notes for reference if needed during the question-and-answer portion of his presentation. Preparing questions and answers in advance helps Curtis feel confident that he will be able to answer most of the questions that arise.

Just in case no one in the audience asks a question, have some questions ready. This will help to fill the time you have allotted for questions and may help to **initiate** some questions from the audience.

initiate: begin, launch

Restate the Question

When you receive a question from the audience, the entire group needs to hear the question. Generally, the person asking directs the question to the speaker, and the entire audience does not hear the question. Restate the question for everyone to hear. Doing so gives you time to think about the answer and enables you to confirm to the listener that you understand his or her question.

© CORBIS

Figure 5-3.8

In question-and-answer sessions, the speaker should direct the focus of the discussion.

In one-to-one situations, you may wish to rephrase a question or incorporate part of the question in the beginning of your answer to let the listener know you understood it. Be careful, however, not to offend your listener by rephrasing all the questions. Instead, allow yourself time to think about the answer by making comments such as, "I can understand your concerns" and "I, too, have experienced that and this is what I've learned."

Respond to the Question

Respond to all questions in a courteous and sincere manner. Keep your answers brief to maintain the exchange between you and the audience. Direct your answer to the entire group, not just the person who asked the question. Maintain eye contact to keep the audience focused on the discussion. When appropriate, provide supporting details or evidence to back up your answer.

Be honest if you do not know the answer to a question. You will gain more credibility with your audience if you are honest than if you try to bluff your way through the answer. If appropriate, offer to find the answer and communicate it to the individual later.

dominate: command, take over

Professional Development Resources

Toastmasters International (A non-profit membership organization devoted to helping people learn the arts of speaking, listening, and thinking)
Toastmasters International
P.O. Box 9052
Mission Viejo, CA 92690
www.toastmasters.org

Anne Warfield. "Do You Speak Body Language?" *Training & Development.* April, 2001.

Yogi Schulz. "Are You Really Paying Attention?" (Effective listening). *Computing Canada.* August 24, 2001.

Ken Haseley. "Build Bridges to Make Your Q & A Session Successful." *Presentations.* November 1, 2001.

Search terms:
    presentation
    visual aid
    listening
    speaking
    presentation software
    multimedia projector

Do not become frustrated if the question relates to information already covered in your presentation. If one listener missed details or became confused, chances are that others did too. Provide the details or explain the point again briefly, perhaps using different words. Offer to provide more details on an individual basis later if appropriate.

Sometimes one individual will ask more than one question and begin to dominate the question-and-answer session. The other listeners often become aggravated when this happens, and they can begin to feel unimportant or unnoticed. If this happens, you can quickly lose the audience's attention. If one individual begins to **dominate** the questions, break eye contact with the individual before he or she has an opportunity to ask another question. When giving an answer to that individual's question, establish eye contact with another person and ask, "Does anyone else have a question to ask?"

In a team presentation, the team members should decide in advance how they will handle questions from the audience. For example, they may decide that one team member will direct the questions to the appropriate person for an answer. All presenters should be included in the question-and-answer session.

Present Closing Remarks

Following the question-and-answer session, you have one last chance to get your point across. Your closing remarks should be a concise review of the major points in your presentation, but be careful to word your closing so that you do not repeat exactly what you have already said. Restate the specific points. Then close the presentation, thanking your audience for listening.

Evaluate Your Presentation

After the presentation is completed, evaluate yourself. Consider the strong points of your presentation and what seemed to be effective. Think about what you could do to improve it. Did you forget to mention something?

CHAPTER 5: COMMUNICATING ORALLY

Could you have used more visuals, or did you use too many? What would you do differently the next time?

Ask your audience to evaluate the presentation also by providing an evaluation form. Evaluation forms are valuable tools that can help you improve your communication skills. To be effective, though, the evaluation form has to gather appropriate information from your listeners. Be specific about the feedback you want from the audience. Figure 5-3.9 shows a sample evaluation form. For example, ask listeners the following questions:

- Have you convinced them to take a course of action?
- Have they learned something from your presentation?
- Was the length of your presentation appropriate?
- Could they relate the content of your presentation to their personal experiences?

You will get the most accurate feedback if you ask your listeners to complete the evaluation immediately following your presentation. Their reactions are fresh, and their comments will be more specific.

Learn from the evaluation comments and use the information constructively to improve the content and/or the delivery of your message. Each time you speak before a group, you will grow in confidence and ability. If you have the opportunity to give the same presentation again, you can refine and improve it using the feedback you receive.

Figure 5-3.9

Evaluation forms provide valuable feedback.

PRESENTATION EVALUATION FORM

Topic: _____   Speaker: _____

Date: _____

Please check one of the choices at the right for each of the statements below. Place your completed form on the table by the door on your way out. Thank you for your feedback.

	Very Much	Somewhat	Not at All
The coverage of the topic met my expectations.	☐	☐	☐
The topic was of interest to me.	☐	☐	☐
The length of the presentation was appropriate.	☐	☐	☐
The presenter addressed the topic effectively.	☐	☐	☐
The concepts were presented clearly.	☐	☐	☐
The presenter related the information to my experiences.	☐	☐	☐
The information presented will be useful to me.	☐	☐	☐
The visuals used were helpful and appropriate.	☐	☐	☐

Comments:

_____

_____

_____

Topic 5-3: *Delivering a Presentation*

Reviewing the Topic

1. What types of information would you include in notes for a presentation, and how should you use these notes?
2. What seating arrangement is appropriate when the audience will be viewing visuals?
3. Describe four considerations in preparing a meeting room for a presentation.
4. What risks are involved if a speaker dresses inappropriately?
5. Why is maintaining eye contact with listeners important during the presentation?
6. What are non-words? Why do many of us use them? What should you do instead of using non-words?
7. Describe appropriate posture and movement or gestures a speaker should use.
8. What is voice intonation, and why is appropriate use of intonation important for a speaker?
9. Describe two strategies for using visuals effectively when giving a presentation.
10. Why should you anticipate questions your listeners may ask during a presentation?
11. Why should you restate or rephrase a question before you answer it?
12. How can you discourage an individual who is beginning to dominate the question-and-answer session?

Interacting with Others

After you completed a presentation before a group of colleagues about how to operate a new copier, you asked for questions from the listeners. One individual in your audience is very knowledgeable about the topic and is dominating the question-and-answer session. During one of his questions, he implies that you are not correct in the information you have presented.

1. How would you respond to the implication that your information is not correct?
2. How can you regain control of the situation so that this person does not continue to dominate the session?

Reinforcing Math Skills

At a recent presentation, you asked your listeners to complete presentation evaluation forms. Listeners scored each item on a scale of 1 to 10. Evaluators are identified by letter because the evaluation was anonymous. Compile and average the ratings to determine an overall evaluation score.

1. Calculate the average score given by all evaluators for each item.
2. Calculate the average score given on all the items by each evaluator.
3. Find an overall evaluation score by averaging the average scores for the ten evaluators.

Evaluation Items	A	B	C	D	E	F	G	H	I	J
					Evaluators					
The coverage of the topic met my expectations.	8	9	7	9	10	10	9	7	8	9
The topic was of interest to me.	6	10	8	10	8	9	7	9	8	8
The length of the presentation was appropriate.	9	9	10	10	10	9	8	6	10	10
The presenter addressed the topic effectively.	8	9	8	9	8	9	9	7	10	10
The concepts were presented clearly.	8	9	8	9	8	9	9	7	10	10
The presenter related the information to my experiences.	6	8	9	9	7	7	7	5	8	8
The information presented will be useful to me.	6	8	8	8	8	7	8	6	7	9
The visuals used were helpful and appropriate.	9	10	9	9	8	9	8	7	10	10

COMPOSITION
TEAMWORK
WORD PROCESSING

Topic 5-3 ACTIVITY 1

Create Presentation Evaluation Form

In this activity, you will create a presentation evaluation form to use in evaluating presentations given by your classmates. Work with three or four classmates to complete this assignment.

1. Review the information from this chapter related to effective speaking and presentations. Think about the information that a listener might want to comment on. Also think about the information a speaker would find useful for judging the effectiveness of the current presentation and for improving future presentations. Then create a list of evaluation points or questions to be included on the evaluation form.

2. Key the form using a format that will be easy to use for both the evaluators and the speakers. A sample evaluation form is shown in Figure 5-3.9. Include an appropriate title for the form and blanks to record the speaker name, topic, and date of the presentation. Also include a place for the evaluator to make comments on the form.

3. Print copies of the form for use in Topic 5-3 Activity 2. You will need forms to evaluate all the other students in your group.

COMPOSITION
PRESENTATION
TEAMWORK
WORD PROCESSING

Topic 5-3 ACTIVITY 2

Deliver a Presentation and Evaluate Performance

In this activity, you will deliver the presentation created in Topic 5-2 Activity 2 to a group of your classmates. You will also evaluate your performance and that of your classmates.

1. Work in the same group as you did for Topic 5-3 Activity 1 to complete this assignment. Take turns with the other students in your group so that all students complete steps 2 and 3.

2. Deliver your five-minute presentation to the group. Include a question-and-answer session at the end of your presentation. Ask fellow students to evaluate your presentation using the form created in Topic 5-3 Activity 1.

3. Review the evaluations of your presentation prepared by your classmates. Then write a brief self-evaluation of your presentation. Comment on your overall performance, areas where you performed particularly well, and areas where you will try to improve for future presentations.

CHAPTER 5: COMMUNICATING ORALLY

Chapter Review

Summary

Whether you are talking with a coworker, addressing meeting participants, or giving a presentation, you will need to express yourself clearly in your oral communications at work. To prepare an effective presentation, you must profile your listeners and develop your presentation with them in mind. Practicing the delivery of a presentation is as important as planning and preparing the content of the presentation. The following key points will reinforce your learning from this chapter.

- When you listen effectively, you will be able to use the information you heard to complete your work correctly, make decisions, and manage your time productively.

- Listening involves a mental process as well as the physical aspects of hearing. Your prejudgments and attitudes can influence your listening.

- To listen effectively, focus your attention on what is being said, mentally summarize and review the information, and ask questions to clarify your understanding of the information.

- To speak effectively, show a sincere interest in what you are saying, express your ideas clearly, use an appropriate tone of voice, avoid using non-words, and use standard language.

- Consider what your listeners want to know, what they might already know, and how what you are saying can be related to their experiences. Be aware of how nonverbal behavior can add to or detract from your message.

- When preparing a presentation, begin by identifying the purpose of your presentation and the specific goals you wish to accomplish.

- Address the interests of your listeners as you plan the content of your presentation. Describe the advantages the listeners can gain from the information you will provide.

- Use a storyboard to help you organize and illustrate your ideas. Use a logical sequence for presenting your ideas that will help your listeners stay interested in what you have to say.

- Much of what we remember is in the form of pictures. Use visual elements to help you communicate your message.

- Handouts are effective for providing your listeners with a summary of the key points in your presentation or providing additional details.

- Practicing your presentation out loud is important. Videotaping your practice sessions can also be very helpful.

- Knowing how to communicate with your audience and keeping them involved is essential for a successful presentation.

- Question-and-answer sessions are important for both the speaker and the audience. Handling questions effectively helps you direct the focus of the session.

- Evaluations provide valuable feedback for improving your performance in future presentations.

Key Terms

audience	mental outline	review
comprehension	nonverbal commu-	speaking
enunciation	nication	standard language
eye contact	objections	storyboarding
handout	presentation	summarize
listener advantages	profile	tone of voice
and objections	purpose	visual aid
listening	question-and-	
media	answer session	

COMPOSITION
INTERNET
RESEARCH
WORD PROCESSING

Chapter 5   ACTIVITY 1

Research for a Presentation

When you must prepare a presentation, the topic may be a familiar one about which you are very knowledgeable. Often, however, you will need to do research to find the latest information or supporting details related to the topic. Practice your research skills in this activity.

1. In a later activity, you will create a presentation related to flextime. Use the Internet or other reference sources to find three articles or reports about flextime. Print or copy the articles, if possible.

2. For each article, key the name of the article and complete source information. Then compose and key a summary of the main points you learned from reading the article.

Team Presentation

You work in the accounting department for a large insurance company. Approximately 25 workers are in your department, and they have diverse ages and lifestyles. During the past year, you worked with several other employees in writing a proposed plan for employee flextime options. Recently, management decided to test the flextime schedule with a two-month pilot program for employees in your department only. If the pilot program is successful, management will offer the flextime options to most employees.

You and a team of coworkers have been asked to prepare and deliver a ten-minute presentation to motivate coworkers in your department to participate in the flextime pilot program.

1. Work with a team of three classmates to complete this assignment.

2. Open and print the data file **Flextime.pdf**, which contains specific details about the flextime program.

3. Plan the presentation. Create storyboard worksheets and develop an outline of the main points of the presentation.

4. Develop the detailed contents of the presentation. Use information found in articles from your research in Chapter 5 Activity 1 to provide supporting details. Develop the visual aids. Anticipate questions and plan sample answers.

5. Decide who will present each part of the presentation and practice with your team.

6. Deliver the presentation to your class or to another team as directed by your instructor. Include time for a question-and-answer session.

7. Ask your listeners to complete an evaluation form such as the one you developed in Topic 5-3 Activity 1. Review the evaluation forms and write a summary of how the listeners rated your presentation and what you need to improve in future presentations.

Processing and Understanding Financial Information

S ound financial information is very important to the success of a business. Many day-to-day business decisions are based on financial information: How much do we owe our suppliers? How much overtime will be needed to complete this order? Will this expense exceed our budget? Businesspeople need current and correct financial information to make informed decisions.

···

In this chapter, you will learn about concepts and procedures used in cash and banking activities and basic financial procedures and reports used in financial management.

Cash and Banking Procedures

OBJECTIVES

- Explain the value of internal control for cash handling
- Describe billing procedures and prepare an invoice
- Prepare a check voucher
- Prepare and post checks
- Prepare a bank deposit and a bank account reconciliation
- Prepare a petty cash fund report

A business must control cash receipts carefully to avoid losing money or recording customer payments incorrectly. A business must also make payments on time to avoid paying late charges, losing discounts, or endangering its credit rating. Most businesses have developed procedures to help ensure that the processing of receipts and payments is done securely, accurately, and efficiently.

In the business world, cash refers to currency (coins and bills), **checks**, money orders, and funds in checking accounts in banks. Some businesses accept only currency or money orders. Other companies, such as supermarkets and retail stores, handle large volumes of currency. In still other companies, almost all transactions are paid by check, credit card, **debit card**, or electronic funds transfer.

If you work in a small office, you are likely to have some responsibility for cash-related transactions. If you work in a large company, you may work in a department where many cash-related transactions are processed. In either case, you should understand the safeguards for cash and procedures for processing cash transactions used in your company.

Safeguarding Cash

Cash is a valuable **asset** of the business and must be safeguarded. Currency stolen from a business can be spent easily because currency is generally considered to be owned by the person in possession of it. Checks can be stolen and exchanged for currency with some ease because signatures and **endorsements** can be **forged**. Therefore, businesses must carefully monitor the handling of cash, regardless of its form. The overall method a business uses to safeguard assets is known as **internal control**. Internal control methods fall into three categories—preventive, detective, and corrective.

Preventive Internal Control

Preventive internal control attempts to stop loss of cash due to employee error, **fraud**, or theft. Procedures that divide the responsibilities for handling cash among two or more employees are usually a part of preventive internal control. In Figure 6-1.1, note the separation of tasks designed to ensure that all checks received by the company are properly deposited and recorded. Procedures for accuracy checks also help prevent error. Preventive internal control is the most important category because it is designed to prevent loss of cash.

Detective Internal Control

Detective internal control attempts to identify losses that have taken place. Losses may be detected by reviewing financial reports and customer accounts. A bank reconciliation is an example of detective internal control because it can help identify missing deposits or other errors.

checks: written orders to a bank to make payment against the depositor's funds in that bank

debit card: a kind of bank card that allows the cost of purchases to be automatically deducted from the cardholder's bank account

asset: cash and all other goods and property owned by a business

endorsement: a signature of a payee on the back of a check authorizing the bank to cash or deposit the check

forge: imitate or counterfeit for illegal purposes

internal control: methods used by a business to safeguard assets

fraud: intentional deception to cause a person or business to give up property (assets) or some lawful right

Processing Customer Payment Checks

Mail Clerk	Cashier	Accounting Clerk
1. Delivers checks to cashier	1. Makes a list of checks received 2. Prepares deposit slip and makes bank deposit 3. Forwards list of checks to an accounting clerk	1. Records the customers' payments 2. Verifies that the total customers' payments equals the total of checks listed

Figure 6-1.1

Separation of duties helps assure internal control of incoming checks.

audit: verify facts or procedures

In some companies, an internal **audit** department establishes and oversees the system for safeguarding assets. Audits are performed to determine if the procedures for internal control are being applied correctly. You may be expected to assist the employees responsible for internal audits.

WORKPLACE **CONNECTIONS**

verify: check for accuracy

Jill, a staff member in the internal audit department, was asked to determine whether the procedures for recording customer payments were being followed. Jill requested a list of the checks that were received on a particular day. She looked at the records for each customer from whom a payment was received on that date to **verify** that the payment was recorded correctly. Jill found no differences between the list of payments and the customers' records. All the procedures were followed correctly, so the audit revealed no problems.

Figure 6-1.2

Internal audits are performed regularly to determine whether procedures are being followed.

© KWAME ZIKOMO/SUPERSTOCK INTERNATIONAL

CHAPTER 6: PROCESSING AND UNDERSTANDING FINANCIAL INFORMATION

Corrective Internal Control

Corrective internal control is used to restore assets after a loss has occurred. For example, revising inadequate procedures that contributed to a loss is a form of corrective internal control. Using the proceeds from insurance policies to replace losses caused by employee fraud or theft is another type of corrective internal control.

One method used to protect cash is **bonding** employees. Bonding is insurance for financial loss due to employee theft or fraud. Bonding is effective because the company that insures bonded employees makes a search of the employee's work history and criminal record. They check with former employers and other references. This search, which is generally more thorough than that done by the company at the time employees are hired, is the major advantage of bonding.

Billing Customers

Customers may pay for goods or services at the time the goods are received, or they may establish **credit** with the seller. The seller then bills the customer periodically for the goods or services. The request for payment is commonly in the form of a sales invoice or a statement of account.

Sales Invoice

Sales invoices are usually created at the time a company ships products or performs services for a customer. An invoice can be sent with the products, left with the customer after a service is performed, or mailed separately to the customer. Although some invoices are handwritten or typed on a typewriter, many companies use invoices printed from a computer-based accounting system.

Verifying that the information on an invoice is correct is very important. A sales invoice documents a customer's legal obligation to pay for products or services received. If the information on an invoice does not agree with what a customer ordered or expected to receive, the customer has the right to delay payment until any **disputes** are resolved.

A sales invoice includes information such as the invoice date, the seller's name and address, the customer's name and address, quantities and prices of items purchased, shipping method and payment terms, and the invoice total. The invoice in Figure 6-1.3 shows payment terms of 2/10, net 30. This means that the customer may take a 2 percent discount from the merchandise total if payment is received by the seller within ten calendar days of the invoice date. If the discount is not taken, full payment is due within 30 days of the invoice date.

Statement of Account

A statement of account is a listing of unpaid invoices as of a certain date—usually the end of a month. Many businesses mail statements of account as a courtesy to their customers (to provide a gentle reminder of the amounts owed) and as a way to get feedback from customers if payments have not been recorded correctly. A business may prepare separate checks to pay for each invoice or one check to pay for several invoices from the same seller.

Professional Development Resources

- American Institute of Certified Public Accountants (AICPA) (A professional association for CPAs dedicated to serving the needs of its members and the accounting profession) American Institute of Certified Public Accountants 1211 Avenue of the Americas New York, NY 10036-8775 www.aicpa.org

- Beth Thomas Hertz. "To Stop Embezzlement, Be on Guard Right From the Start...." *Ophthalmology Times.* August 15, 2001.

- Joseph T. Wells. "And One for Me." *Journal of Accountancy.* January, 2002. Online. Available: http://www.aicpa.org/pubs/jofa/jan2002/wells.htm. January 22, 2002.

- Sarah Fister Gale. "How Three Companies Merged HR and Payroll." *Workforce.* January, 2002.

- Russ Banham. "Better Budgets." *Journal of Accountancy.* February, 2000. Online. Available: http://www.aicpa.org/pubs/jofa/feb2000/banham.htm. January 22, 2002.

- Search terms:
  - internal control
  - embezzlement
  - payroll
  - petty cash
  - strategic plan
  - financial statements
  - budgets

bonding: insurance for financial loss due to employee theft or fraud

credit: permission to pay later for goods or services

dispute: question or debate

229

Topic 6-1: Cash and Banking Procedures

Figure 6-1.3

Using correct information on a sales invoice is very important.

INVOICE

Shred-Rite Shredder Company
2200 New Prussia Road
Delray Beach, FL 33445-5688
(561) 555-9876

Date:	July 17, 20--
Invoice No.:	SR 107206
Customer No.:	5690
Ship Via:	UPS Ground
Terms:	2/10, net 30

Sold to:

MR HAROLD LEVITZ
LEVITZ OFFICE SUPPLY
1068 WABASHAW COURT
FERGUSON KY 42502-4664

Ship to:

Same

Item No.	Quantity	Description	Unit Price	Total
SR100	10	Personal shredder with waste receptacle	$89.00	$890.00
SR200	10	Medium duty console shredder	$399.00	$3,990.00

Subtotal	$4,880.00
Shipping & Handling	$130.00
Taxes	
Total	$5,010.00
Payment Received	$0.00
Amount Due	$5,010.00

WORKPLACE CONNECTIONS

Paducah Builders, a company that builds houses, has several workers who are authorized to pick up materials at a building supply store. When a worker picks up items at the store, the worker signs a form to show who picked up the items. He or she also receives an invoice for the items, which is forwarded to the company's business office. The building supply company sends a statement of account at the end of the month listing all the invoices. Paducah Builders pays all the invoices for the month with one check, which is more convenient than paying the invoices separately.

A statement of account includes information such as the statement date, the seller's name and address, the customer's name and address, invoices for the period, payment terms, and the total amount due (owed to the seller). The statement of account in Figure 6-1.4 shows four invoice amounts.

Receiving Payments

Specific procedures should be followed for processing customer payments. Three such procedures are handling the cash drawer, preparing bank deposits, and making bank deposits. In large companies, employees in the **accounts receivable** department process payments.

accounts receivable: short-term debts owed to a company by others, such as its customers

Figure 6-1.4

A statement of account lists invoice amounts for a period of time.

STATEMENT OF ACCOUNT

Shred-Rite Shredder Company
2200 New Prussia Road
Delray Beach, FL 33445-5688
(561) 555-9876

Date: July 31, 20--
Customer No.: 5690
Terms: 2/10, net 30

Customer:

MR HAROLD LEVITZ
LEVITZ OFFICE SUPPLY
1068 WABASHAW COURT
FERGUSON KY 42502-4664

Invoice No.	Invoice Date	Invoice Total
SR 107005	July 2, 20--	$849.32
SR 107006	July 2, 20--	$1,150.00
SR 107150	July 6, 20--	$3,090.49
SR 107206	July 17, 20--	$5,010.00
	Total Due	$10,099.81

Handling the Cash Drawer

A cash register drawer is assigned to an employee who deals with customers in person, receiving payments and making change. When the employee is assigned the cash drawer, it contains currency and coins to use in making change. As transactions are completed, currency, coins, checks, and credit card and debit card receipts from customer payments will be added to the drawer. Each sale is recorded in the cash register, either on a paper tape or electronically. The cash register will show the total sales made during the time the worker used the cash drawer.

An employee issued a cash drawer is required to verify the amount of cash in the cash drawer when he or she receives the drawer. When the drawer is turned in, the employee must verify that the proper amount of currency, checks, and bank card receipts are in the drawer. This procedure is known as **proving cash**. To prove cash, an employee would add total sales (as shown on the cash register for the employee's shift) to the beginning balance (the amount in the drawer when received). This total should match the amount in the cash drawer. In some businesses, employees may be required to list the contents of the drawer in detail by type of item (currency, coins, checks, bank card receipts).

proving cash: verifying that the proper amount of currency, checks, and bank card receipts are in a cash drawer

In some companies, the employee must pay his or her own money to make up shortages when his or her cash drawer does not balance. Even if employees do not have to make up shortages, frequent shortages in an employee's cash drawer may lead to a poor job evaluation, failure to receive a promotion, or even the employee being fired.

Topic 6-1: Cash and Banking Procedures

Preparing Deposits

Businesses commonly deposit cash in a bank shortly after it is received. In some organizations where many payments are received, deposits may be made several times a day. In other companies, deposits may be made only a few times a month because payments are received infrequently.

Employees responsible for preparing bank deposits should verify that all checks are properly endorsed. An endorsement is a signature or instructions stamped or written on the back of a check authorizing the bank to cash or deposit the check. An endorsement is required before a check is transferred from the company or person to whom the check is written to another person, company, or bank. In many companies, office workers who prepare deposits also endorse the checks using a stamp.

Endorsements vary. Some provide more protection or instructions than others. The most commonly used forms of endorsements are *blank*, *restrictive*, and *special*. Look closely at Figure 6-1.5 on page 233 as you read about each form of endorsement.

Many checks have an endorsement area printed on the back of the check. Be careful to write, print, or stamp the endorsement within the area provided. If no endorsement area is indicated or the back of the check is blank, place the check face up. Grasp the left edge of the check and turn it over, keeping the same edge at the left. Carefully stamp or write each endorsement on the left edge of the check or other marked endorsement area.

payee: person to whom the check is written

For a **blank endorsement**, the signature of the **payee** is written on the back of the check. The signature must be in ink. This endorsement provides little protection because anyone who gains access to the check can easily transfer it to another person or cash the check. Generally, use this endorsement only when you are at the bank ready to cash or deposit the check immediately.

In a **restrictive endorsement**, the purpose of the transfer of the check is indicated in the endorsement. For example, the check may be marked *For Deposit Only*. Restrictive endorsements are often made with a rubber stamp or a stamping machine.

In a **special endorsement**, the signature of the endorser is preceded by the name of the person or company to whom the check is being transferred. In some instances, a special endorsement is referred to as an endorsement in full.

A deposit slip is a form used to record currency, coins, and checks to be added to a bank account. On a deposit slip, *cash* refers to the total of currency and coins. When completing a deposit slip, do the following:

- Write the current date in the space provided.
- Write the amount of each item to be deposited. For each check, identify the bank on which the check is drawn. This is done by recording the bank's number, which is the upper portion of the fraction noted on each check.
- Write the amount of cash received from the deposit, if any, and sign the space to indicate that cash is received.
- Write the net deposit amount. This amount includes all checks listed on both the front and back of the deposit slip minus any cash received.

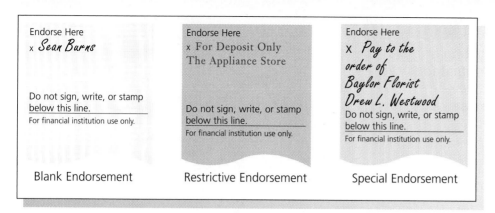

Blank Endorsement   Restrictive Endorsement   Special Endorsement

To verify the accuracy of the total deposit, add the checks and currency to be deposited. Verify that this total is exactly the same as the total listed on the deposit slip. If the totals match, you are assured that your list is correct and includes all items.

Making Deposits

Office workers may make deposits in local banks on a regular basis. If your tasks include going to the bank with deposits, be sure all checks, currency, coins, and deposit forms are in proper order and in an envelope before you leave the office.

WORKPLACE CONNECTIONS

One of Inez's daily tasks is preparing deposit slips for all items to be taken to a local bank. Inez works in a systematic fashion so that she makes no errors. She verifies that each deposit slip is correct by totaling the amounts carefully. Inez is proud that the bank has never sent the cashier a notice that an error had been made in a deposit she submitted.

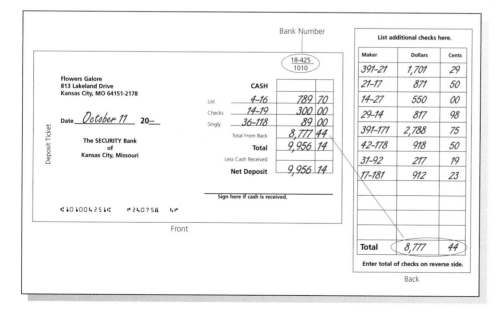

Topic 6-1: *Cash and Banking Procedures*

Figure 6-1.7

This worker is making a deposit at an automated teller machine conveniently located near the office.

© SUPERSTOCK INTERNATIONAL

Deposits can be made electronically at an automated teller machine (ATM) at a bank or at other convenient locations. If you make this type of deposit, follow instructions and get a receipt. Verify that the receipt shows the amount of your deposit.

A company may direct customers to send payments to a lockbox address at a bank. A worker in the bank's office typically processes the deposit and updates the company's bank balance. The bank may transfer updated information electronically to each company for which lockbox payments are received. Advantages to using a lockbox to collect payments include:

- Company employees do not have to spend as much time processing checks and preparing deposits.
- The checks received in a lockbox are processed each day by bank employees. Payments are immediately deposited in the company's bank account. Funds are usually available for use at least one day sooner than when checks are mailed to the company's office address and then deposited by company employees.
- Having the checks sent directly to the bank improves internal control by reducing the possibility of employee theft or errors.

Making Payments

In large firms, processing payments is the responsibility of employees in the **accounts payable** department. Accounts payable are the short-term debts your company owes to others. In a small business, however, one individual may be responsible for all aspects of financial transactions, including receiving and making payments.

accounts payable: short-term debts a company owes

Figure 6-1.8

Accounts payable workers review documents related to company purchases.

If it is your responsibility to make payments for your company, you will be involved in several related tasks: reviewing purchase-related documents, preparing vouchers, and preparing checks.

Review Documents

Companies want to be sure that payments are only made for **goods** or services purchased and received. The task of the accounts payable department or the individual responsible for making payments is to review all the documents related to each purchase.

goods: raw materials, merchandise

Several related documents may be generated with each purchase. The documents and their usefulness in making payments are as follows:

- A **purchase requisition** shows the items requested and an authorization to make the purchase.
- A **purchase order** shows exactly what was ordered and to what address it was to be shipped.
- A **receiving report** shows that goods were actually received by the company.
- An **invoice** from a **vendor** shows what is owed for the purchases.

vendor: organization that sells goods or services

- A **credit memorandum** shows any reduction in the amount owed due to return of goods or to **allowance** for goods not received or of poor quality.

allowance: credit given on account

The review of purchase-related documents is essentially a task of determining if all the appropriate documents are present for each purchase and that all the details on the documents are the same. You will not arrange for payment until all documents are accounted for and agree with each other or until there is a reasonable explanation for missing documents or differences in the information.

PURCHASE REQUISITION

The Lampshade Store
426 Monroe Street
Cedar Falls, IA 50613-3467

Date: October 17, 20--

Vendor of Choice	Description	Quantity	Unit Price	Total
Shred-Rite Shredder Co. 2200 New Prussia Road Delray Beach, FL 33445-5688	SR200 Medium duty console shredder	1	$399.00	$399.00
			Total	$399.00

Project No. _____

Account No. _____

Purchase Approved   Date

Harold Norton   *10/20/--*

Figure 6-1.9

A purchase requisition shows the items requested for purchase.

voucher: document that provides information and authorization to make a payment

tickler file: records or reminders arranged by date

Prepare Vouchers

In many offices a voucher system is used for payments. This system requires the preparation of a voucher before a check is written. A **voucher** is a document that shows the vendor name, invoice date, terms, and amount owed. The approved voucher serves as the authorization to make the payment. Figure 6-1.10 is an example of a voucher. If you have the responsibility for preparing vouchers, you should follow these general steps:

1. Check that all the documents related to the purchase are present. Often an envelope-type file folder is used to collect all the documents for a payment. A listing of collected documents is placed on the outside of the folder.

2. Prepare the voucher, checking every detail required on the form.

3. Obtain the authorized signature.

4. File the vouchers appropriately. Vouchers typically are filed by the dates on which they must be processed in order to meet the payment due dates. Filing vouchers in this way creates a **tickler file**. This file is reviewed daily for the purpose of taking action to clear the items from the file. In companies where the policy is to take all discounts allowed, the voucher is filed in the tickler file by the discount date.

The terms of the voucher in Figure 6-1.10 are 2/10, net 30. If the invoice is paid within ten days of the invoice date, a 2 percent discount can be taken from the invoice amount. If the invoice is paid after the 10th day and before the 30th day, the full amount of the invoice is paid. If payment is made after the 30th day, a penalty may be applied. Therefore, many businesses try to pay their bills in time to take advantage of the discount and to avoid being charged late fees.

CHAPTER 6: PROCESSING AND UNDERSTANDING FINANCIAL INFORMATION

VOUCHER

The Lampshade Store
426 Monroe Street
Cedar Falls, IA 50613-3467

Voucher No. 4379

Date: October 17, 20--

Pay To: Just Shades
135 Green Street
New York, NY 10003-4689

For the following: (All supporting documents are attached.)

Invoice Date	Terms	Invoice No.	Gross Amount	Discount	Net Payable
10/17/--	2/10, net 30	5479	$4,560.90	$91.22	$4,469.68

Payment Approved

Helen Northcut

Figure 6-1.10

Payment voucher

Preparing Checks

In some offices, especially small ones, a checkbook similar to one an individual uses for personal check writing is used for checks. If you are responsible for manually preparing checks, you should check your tickler file daily and retrieve all vouchers for which checks are to be prepared. If you are responsible for writing checks using a checkbook, these suggestions will be helpful:

1. Read carefully the name of the company or individual to whom payment is to be made as well as the amount of the check. If you are writing a check in time to take advantage of a discount, compute the discount using a calculator.

2. Fill in the checkbook stub or the check register. (See Figure 6-1.11 for the way in which an item is listed in a check register.)

3. Prepare the check. (See Figure 6-1.11.) Note that the amount is written in numbers as well as in words. Notice how the space between the name and the dollar sign and the space between the amount in words and the word *dollars* is filled in so that changes cannot be made easily. Notice that the purpose of the payment is shown on the face of the check on the memo line.

Some companies use voucher checks. Voucher checks are ordinary checks with an additional portion that gives a description of the payment. The two parts are perforated so they can be separated easily. The voucher is detached before the check is deposited. The procedures for preparing voucher checks are the same as those for ordinary checks, except that you also fill in the voucher portion rather than merely indicate the check's purpose.

Special Checks

From time to time, special checks that provide guarantee of payment are used by businesses.

Figure 6-1.11

Check register and
completed check

Check register and completed check

- A **certified check** is an ordinary check that the bank marks "certified" after establishing that the funds are in the account of the party drawing the check. The funds are immediately subtracted from the depositor's account.
- A **cashier's check** is a check written by a bank on its own funds. Such a check can be purchased with cash or with an ordinary check.
- A **bank draft** is an order drawn by one bank on its deposits in another bank to pay a third party. Such a draft can be purchased with cash or with an ordinary check.

Computer-Generated Checks

Many companies use computers to prepare checks. If you are authorized to prepare checks, you likely will be issued a password to access the company's accounts payable system. Security measures are taken to safeguard both the information used to prepare the checks and the printed checks.

You may need to refer to each vendor's file in the accounts payable system to obtain information needed to complete the checks, such as vendor name and address, amount to be paid, and the purpose of payment. In automated systems, you may need to enter only a vendor number or name and some information, such as the address, will be entered automatically by the system. Then, by selecting a menu option such as Print Checks, checks will be printed.

Electronic Funds Transfer

Payments, as well as deposits, can be made electronically. With electronic payments or deposits, there is no physical exchange of currency or checks. **Electronic funds transfer** (EFT) is the use of a computer and a telecommunications network to transfer funds from one party to another.

Some companies transfer funds electronically to the vendor's bank. The vendor's bank electronically processes the deposit and credits the vendor's

electronic funds transfer:
exchange of money by sending records from one bank's computer to another bank's computer

CHAPTER 6: PROCESSING AND UNDERSTANDING FINANCIAL INFORMATION

account. Also, many companies electronically deposit wage and salary payments to employees' designated banks where the funds are placed in the employees' accounts.

Reconciling a Bank Account

Companies need to be sure that receipts and payments shown in their records are reflected also in the bank's records. If you have the task of comparing these records, you will prepare a **bank reconciliation** using the **bank statement** as well as your own company's records.

Bank Statement and Company Records

A bank statement provided by the bank shows the activity in each account on a regular basis, usually monthly. As you will note in Figure 6-1.12 on page 240, a bank statement gives the following information:

- The balance as of the opening date of the statement
- Checks listed by number and amount that the bank has received and honored
- Automated teller machine transactions and miscellaneous charges
- Deposits
- The balance on the closing date of the statement

On the bank statement shown in Figure 6-1.12, the automated teller transactions are coded AW for ATM withdrawals, AC for ATM deposits and credits, and PD for preauthorized electronic deposits.

In addition to the bank statement, the bank may return canceled checks or photocopies of canceled checks and any notices reporting increases or decreases in the bank balance. Other banks may provide only the statement. Copies of checks that have been scanned may be provided on request.

The bank statement shown in Figure 6-1.12 shows that a check deposited was returned by the bank on which it was drawn. Because the person writing the check did not have sufficient funds to cover the amount of the check, the check was not honored. Such checks are referred to as NSF (not sufficient funds) checks. Figure 6-1.12 shows that Adler Knitting's balance was reduced by the amount of the check that was not honored.

Generally, there are no documents included that relate to automatic teller machine (ATM) transactions. These are deposits and withdrawals made at electronic machines. Keep the slips generated at the time these transactions are made. They provide your receipt of the transaction.

To complete the reconciliation, you will need the company's checkbook or check register, which records all checks written and all deposits made. You also will need last month's reconciliation.

Purposes for Reconciliation

Cash is a valuable resource for all business organizations. Knowing the exact status of the cash account, therefore, is important. A monthly reconciliation is completed to

- Determine that all deposits made have been recorded by the bank, as indicated on the bank statement.

bank reconciliation: report used to compare bank and company account records

bank statement: record of activity in a bank account

Figure 6-1.12

Bank statement for
Adler Knitting Manu-
facturing Co.

Neches Bank
Cincinnati, Ohio

ADLER KNITTING MANUFACTURING CO
658 TEAKWOOD AVENUE
CINCINNATI OH 45224-4578

Account No. 32921-6

Statement Date 08/31/--

Balance from Previous Statement	Number of Credits	Amount of Deposits and Credits	Number of Debits	Amount of Withdrawals and Debits	Total Activity Charge	Statement Balance
22,890.75	4	26,962.10	20	29,255.96	25.00	20,596.89

Date	Code	Transaction Description	Transaction Amount	Account Balance
22-Jul	AW	0248 634	200.00	22,690.75
23-Jul		Deposit	6,790.40	29,481.15
		Check 187	3,750.00	25,731.15
		Check 189	1,890.25	23,840.90
27-Jul	AW	0248 634	2,500.00	21,340.90
28-Jul		Check 190	6,590.70	14,750.20
29-Jul	PD	Rae's Sweater Corner Deposit	7,980.70	22,730.90
3-Aug		Check 191	3,875.00	18,855.90
4-Aug		Check 192	1,870.70	16,985.20
		Check 194	580.90	16,404.30
5-Aug		Check 193	450.00	15,954.30
6-Aug	AC	ATM Deposit	4,280.90	20,235.20
9-Aug	AW	0248 634	1,000.00	19,235.20
10-Aug		Check 197	2,975.25	16,259.95
		Check 195	1,800.00	14,459.95
11-Aug		Check 196	290.20	14,169.75
12-Aug	PD	Rae's Sweater Corner Deposit	7,910.10	22,079.85
		Check 198	378.28	21,701.57
16-Aug		Check 202	150.50	21,551.07
		Check 201	95.70	21,455.37
		Check 199	110.98	21,344.39
17-Aug		Check 206	525.00	20,819.39
18-Aug		NSF Check	197.50	20,621.89
19-Aug		Service Charge	25.00	20,596.89

- Verify that all the checks that cleared the bank were written by authorized persons in the company.
- Determine which checks have not yet cleared the bank.
- Identify additional bank charges, as indicated on the bank statement, that need to be recorded in the books of the company.
- Determine the cash balance as of the date of the bank statement.

Steps in Preparing a Reconciliation

The company in which you work will have an established procedure for preparing bank reconciliations. You will want to learn these specific procedures. Assume that you are working in an office where a bank statement is received monthly and a reconciliation is prepared at that time. The steps described here are likely to be similar to the ones you will learn on the job:

1. Compare the ending balance on last month's bank reconciliation with the beginning balance on this month's bank statement. Under normal circumstances, these two balances will be identical. If there is a difference, record the two figures on a sheet of paper. Investigate any differences before completing the reconciliation.

2. Record on your reconciliation worksheet the balance in your check register as of the last day of the month.

Adler Knitting Manufacturing Co.
Reconciliation of Bank Statement
August 31, 20--

Check register balance 8/31/--		$18,711.50	Bank statement balance 8/20/--	$20,596.89
Deduct:			Add:	
Service Charge	25.00		Deposit in transit 8/30	2,851.10
NSF	197.50			
		222.50	Deduct:	
			Outstanding Checks	
			No. 188	198.70
			No. 200	110.10
			No. 203	347.29
			No. 204	82.50
			No. 205	4,220.40
				4958.99
Adjusted check register balance 8/31/--		$18,489.00	Adjusted bank balance 8/31/--	$18,489.00

3. Record the ending balance as shown on the bank statement.

4. Compare each deposit shown on the bank statement with the deposits recorded on the check register. Put a small check mark in both places if the amount and date agree. Record on your worksheet any deposits shown in the check register that are not on the bank statement. Deposits made near the end of the month are not likely to have been processed by the bank by the date of the statement. Such deposits are referred to as deposits in transit.

5. Arrange in numeric order the checks returned with the bank statement. (Skip this step if it is not the bank's policy to return checks.)

6. Compare the amount of each check with that shown on the bank statement. Use small check marks by the items on the statement to show that there is agreement. Record any differences noted. Follow up on any differences before preparing your final reconciliation.

7. Compare each canceled check with related information in the check register. Place a small check mark in the register if there is agreement. (See Figure 6-1.14.)

Figure 6-1.13

Bank reconciliation for Adler Knitting Manufacturing Co.

Figure 6-1.14

One item on this check register does not have a check mark. What is the status of check #188?

Adler Knitting Manufacturing Co.
Check Register

Item No.	Date	Payment to or Deposit	Payment Amount	✓	Deposit Amount	Balance Forward
						28,681.15
187	7/17/--	Taylor Brothers	3,750.00	✓		24,931.15
188	7/16/---	Elman and Stone Co.	198.70			24,732.45
189	7/18/--	Marshall Gomez	1,890.25	✓		22,842.20
190	7/25/--	Leitz Mfg. Co.	6,590.70	✓		16,251.50
	7/29/--	Deposit		✓	7,980.70	24,232.20
191	8/1/--	Yarns, International	3,875.00	✓		20,357.20

8. Record on your worksheet the number, date, and amount for each check that was written but had not cleared as of the bank statement date. These checks are referred to as outstanding checks. The total of the outstanding checks will be subtracted from the bank statement balance.

9. Review last month's outstanding checks as listed on the bank reconciliation to determine which ones are still outstanding. List these on your worksheet also.

10. Record on your worksheet any charges shown on the statement that are not recorded in your company's records. For example, any checks returned for insufficient funds (NSF checks) must be subtracted from the balance in your check register. Bank charges, such as ATM fees, also must be subtracted.

11. Complete the calculations required on your worksheet. Note that the two balances are the same in the reconciliation shown in Figure 6-1.13. Having the same balances means that your cash account has been properly reconciled.

12. Prepare a clean, correct copy of the bank reconciliation. Print the reconciliation on plain paper or use the reconciliation form provided on the back of the bank statement.

When you have completed a bank reconciliation, obtain any required approval signatures. Once the reconciliation is approved, file it so that it can be readily retrieved. When you receive the next bank statement, you will refer back to this completed reconciliation to determine which checks were outstanding and should be in the next batch of canceled checks.

Record-keeping tasks in many large offices are computerized. Therefore, you may use a computer and software to prepare a bank reconciliation worksheet. The advantage of an electronic reconciliation is that the program automatically makes all calculations.

Maintaining a Petty Cash Fund

petty cash: money kept on hand for paying small expenses

In many offices, cash is needed occasionally to pay for small expenditures, such as delivery services, postage due, and taxi fares. To handle such payments, departments are given a small sum of money, which is called a **petty cash** fund. Amounts in such funds can range from $20 to as much as $1,000.

WORKPLACE CONNECTIONS

The sales office of a women's clothing manufacturing company has a petty cash fund of $500. The fund is used primarily to provide money for lunch ordered at a local coffee shop for visiting buyers and for late dinners when staff members must work or entertain major buyers from around the world. The fund is also used to pay for taxis and special delivery services. Wanda, the petty cashier, keeps careful records and requires receipts for all payments made from the fund.

Establishing the Fund

The department head establishes how much money is to be maintained in the petty cash fund. Once this amount is approved by the officer responsible for payments, a check is written payable to the **petty cashier**, the person in charge of the petty cash fund. The petty cashier will cash the check and keep the cash in a locked cash box. Only the petty cashier has access to the key.

In some organizations, petty cash funds are maintained in a separate checking account. However, the discussion here will be limited to a cash box system only.

Making Payments

The petty cashier keeps a complete and accurate record for every payment made from the petty cash fund. Petty cash receipt forms are filled out each time cash is given out. The following procedure is commonly followed in offices.

1. Ask each person who seeks payment from the petty cash fund to submit a sales slip, statement, or receipt that indicates the item purchased, the price, and that payment was made. Generally, payment should not be made without some kind of document. Occasionally, cash payments are made even though no sales slip, statement, or receipt is provided. On such occasions, the employee being **reimbursed** should present a brief memo giving the amount spent and describing the item or service purchased.

2. Prepare a petty cash receipt for each payment, and ask the person who will receive the cash to sign the receipt. Note the receipt shown in Figure 6-1.15. The receipt indicates the amount paid, to whom payment is made, and the purpose of the payment.

3. Attach the sales slip or other document to the receipt and place these papers in the cash box.

PETTY CASH RECEIPT
Hardesty Security Systems

No. _42_   Date _November 17, 20--_

                            Amount $ _10.75_

Ten and 75/100 _____ Dollars

For _Postage_ _____

                            Received by _Wanda T. Davis_

Figure 6-1.15

What is the value of a petty cash receipt issued for each payment from the petty cash fund?

Topic 6-1: *Cash and Banking Procedures*

Keeping a Record

In offices where many transactions require petty cash, an organized record is justified. In some departments, a petty cash record is maintained for receipts and payments. Such a record is shown in Figure 6-1.16. Note the headings of the columns under which the payments are recorded. In each office, the same types of payments are likely to occur again and again. However, the column headings for your office may be different from the ones shown here. By recording payments as they are made, the task of preparing a report at the end of the month or when you need to **replenish** the fund will be simplified.

replenish: restore to original level

You may work in an office where petty cash records are kept manually or one where spreadsheet or financial software is used to record petty cash transactions. In either case, attention to detail and entering all data accurately are critical when maintaining petty cash records.

PETTY CASH RECORD
November, 30--

Date	Receipt No.	Balance	Books	Taxi	Office Supplies	Postage	Art Supplies	Misc.
1-Nov	Beg. Balance	250.00						
6-Nov	39	237.05	12.95					
8-Nov	40	228.55		8.50				
8-Nov	41	220.85			7.70			
11-Nov	42	210.10				10.75		
17-Nov	43	203.65						6.45
19-Nov	44	184.90	18.75					
21-Nov	45	161.90		23.00				
22-Nov	46	150.40		11.50				
24-Nov	47	120.25					30.15	
25-Nov	48	108.80				11.45		
26-Nov	49	90.30			18.50			
29-Nov	50	78.20						12.10
30-Nov	End. Balance	78.20						
	Item Totals		31.70	43.00	26.20	22.20	30.15	18.55

Figure 6-1.16

Petty cash report

Replenishing the Fund

You will need to note the amount of cash in your cash box and to replenish your fund according to established company procedures. In some offices, the fund is replenished when a certain balance is reached. In others, the fund is restored to its original amount at the end of each month regardless of the level of funds. This procedure is commonly used in offices:

1. Count the money in the cash box and total the receipts in the petty cash box.

2. Compare the petty cash box total to the petty cash receipts total. They should be the same. If they are not, determine why there is a difference. Did you fail to include a receipt in your total? Did someone fail to turn in a receipt?

3. Add the amount of the petty cash receipts to the amount of petty cash remaining in the cash box. The total should equal the amount of petty cash you had when you last balanced and/or replenished the petty cash fund.

4. Investigate any **discrepancy**. Careful attention to managing the petty cash fund will result in few, if any, discrepancies. If, after your investigation, you find that you are over or short by a few pennies, note this difference on your petty cash record. For example, if in step 2 you found only $78.00 in cash, you would indicate on your petty cash record that the fund is short $.20.

discrepancy: lack of agreement

5. Prepare a voucher for a check for the amount needed to replenish the fund. Submit your petty cash record report, the accompanying receipts, and your check voucher for approval to your department head or other designated person.

6. Once approved, follow up by sending a copy of the report to the accounting department and by sending the voucher to the proper office.

7. Cash the check and immediately place the cash in the cash box.

Reviewing the Topic

1. What is included in the general category referred to as cash?
2. Why do companies use internal controls to protect cash? Describe three types of internal controls.
3. Explain why a company might bond an employee.
4. How does a blank endorsement differ from a restrictive endorsement?
5. What is the function of a voucher?
6. List and briefly describe three types of special checks.
7. Why is a deposit slip prepared?
8. What information is included on a bank statement?
9. Why is a bank account reconciliation completed?
10. Why are departments given petty cash funds?

Making Decisions

Assume that you are the cashier for the petty cash fund in your department. The fund is maintained at $1,000 because of the many small payments that must be made during the month. One Wednesday, shortly after the fund had been replenished, one of your friends in the department says to you: "I certainly didn't budget my money very well this week; I'm down to my last $5. You know that I'm dependable. Would you let me borrow $25 from the petty cash fund? You have almost $1,000 just lying there! And if I had only $25, I'd be able to take care of my expenses until Friday, which is payday."

1. Would you lend your friend money from the petty cash fund? Why or why not?
2. What might be the consequences of making an unauthorized payment from the fund?

Reinforcing Math Skills

Your tasks as an office assistant at Vine Associates include preparing bank deposits. The list of checks the company has received is shown below. These checks will be deposited in one of two banks. The checks from L. T. Mills, Olsen Corp., Yaroff Bros., Susi & Karlin, Rice Corp., Caputa & Zinn, and Prevetti Co. will be deposited at the Penn Avenue Bank; the remaining checks will be deposited at the Smithfield Bank.

1. Open and print the data file **Deposit.pdf**, which contains deposit slips for the two accounts.
2. Prepare a deposit slip for checks to be deposited at the Penn Avenue Bank.

3. Prepare a deposit slip for checks to be deposited at the Smithfield Bank.

4. Endorse the back of one check (shown on your data file printout) to show how you would endorse all checks for the two deposits. Use the company name in a restrictive endorsement to indicate that the checks are for being submitted for deposit only.

Checks Received 10/15/--

From	Bank No.	Amount	From	Bank No.	Amount
L. T. Mills	18-419	4,200.50	Rice Corp.	12-407	81.18
Olsen Corp.	18-426	6,592.60	Rabinowitz & Sons	07-190	2,668.61
Mars, Linwood & Co.	73-258	2,540.15	Caputa & Zinn	26-317	848.88
Gomes & Co.	18-403	985.40	Beilens, Lutz & Co	12-508	129.50
Yaroff Bros.	73-259	1,965.95	Prevetti Co.	18-403	8,912.50
O'Brien & Wickes	18-419	3,691.21	Jay F. Sterling	73-286	819.19
Susi & Karlin	18-419	6,296.45	W. N. Neeley	26-317	6,819.12

SPREADSHEET

Topic 6-1   ACTIVITY 1

Reconcile Bank Statement

You work at Harcourt View Company in the accounting department. One of your duties is to reconcile the bank statement each month. On October 30, you received a bank statement dated October 25. Follow the steps below to prepare a bank statement reconciliation.

1. Use your spreadsheet software to prepare a bank reconciliation. Format the document and enter appropriate headings as shown in Figure 6-1.13 on page 241. Use October 31 of the current year as the date.

2. The bank statement dated October 25 shows an ending balance of $4,452.03. The statement also shows a service charge of $15 for checks you ordered and received. Enter these amounts in the appropriate places on your spreadsheet.

3. You have checked all the deposits and all the checks shown on the statement. You also have compared the returned canceled checks with your check register. Enter the following information from your worksheet in the appropriate places on your spreadsheet:

- The check register balance on October 31, before adjustment, is $3,560.58.
- One deposit dated October 27 is in transit for $1,256.50.
- The following checks are outstanding: #457 for $356.76, #481 for $125.00, #482 for $890.65, and #483 for $790.54.

4. Enter formulas to calculate the adjusted check register balance and the adjusted bank balance. These two amounts should be the same. If they are not, check to see that the numbers and formulas have been entered correctly.

SPREADSHEET
WORD PROCESSING

Topic 6-1   ACTIVITY 2

Manage Petty Cash Fund

You work at Lawrence Industries, a small manufacturing company. You are responsible for handling the petty cash fund, along with other duties. The fund is replenished each month to the amount of $250. This is May 1 and you are ready to complete your petty cash report, prepare a check voucher, and prepare a check to replenish the fund.

1. Use your spreadsheet software to prepare a petty cash record similar to the one shown in Figure 6-1.16 on page 244. Use column heads that are appropriate for your company.

2. The fund beginning balance on April 1 was $250. Enter the data from the petty cash receipts in your cash box as shown below. Enter formulas to keep a running balance of the money remaining in the fund.

Receipt No.	Date	Amount	Item
156	April 2	14.90	Office Supplies
157	April 5	25.00	Food
158	April 5	13.00	Taxi
159	April 15	18.50	Office Supplies
160	April 18	42.67	Food
161	April 20	3.45	Miscellaneous
162	April 22	33.68	Food
163	April 25	11.30	Postage
164	April 26	7.42	Miscellaneous
165	April 28	12.98	Postage

3. Total the items columns of your petty cash record. Which item has the highest total for April?

4. Using the ending balance on your petty cash record, determine the amount needed to replenish the fund to $250.

5. Open the data file **Voucher**, which contains a check voucher form. Prepare check voucher no. 4926 using *May 1* as the date. Enter *Petty Cashier* after Pay To. Enter *5/1/--* in the Invoice Date column. Enter *Petty Cash Fund* in the Invoice No. column. Enter the amount for the check in the Net Payable column. Attach the petty cash record to the voucher as a supporting document.

6. Assume you submitted the voucher and petty cash record to the person authorized to approve payments. The voucher has been signed to approve payment, and the records have been returned to you.

7. Prepare a check for payment of the voucher. Open and print the data file **Check.pdf**, which contains a blank check form. Write the check using *May 1* as the check date. Make the check payable to *Petty Cashier* for the amount shown on the voucher. Enter *Voucher 4926* on the Memo line. Leave the signature line blank for signing by an authorized person.

8. Open the data file **Register**, which contains a section of the company's check register. Post the check information to the check register. Copy down the formula in the last column to update the balance forward amount. Print the updated check register page.

9. Once the check is signed, you would cash the check and place the money in the cash box. Submit the petty cash record, the check voucher, the check register, and the check to your instructor.

SPREADSHEET

Topic 6-1   ACTIVITY 3

Sales Invoice

At many companies, invoices for products sold are created automatically by the billing software program when products are shipped using data that was input at the time the product was ordered. Occasionally, companies need to create an invoice for a sale that falls outside of the normal billing process. For example, old computers or manufacturing equipment that is no longer used may be sold.

You work in the accounting department of Mica Associates. The accounting department is in the process of upgrading its printers to faster inkjet printers. All the old printers are in good working order. After determining that no other departments have use for the old printers, your supervisor has decided to sell the old printers to employees.

To determine the selling price, the asset records for the four printers were reviewed. These records show information such as the original cost, depreciation (the amount by which the value of an item is reduced each year for wear), and the remaining value.

Asset Number	Description	Purchase Date	Original Cost	Accumulated Depreciation	Remaining Value
2021	HP Laser Printer	02/21/1999	$2,500.00	$2,450.00	$ 50.00
2027	Okidata Printer	03/05/1999	799.00	774.00	25.00
2035	IBM Wheel Printer	06/24/1999	1,200.00	1,170.00	30.00
2040	Panasonic Printer	11/12/1999	3,450.00	3,325.00	125.00

Henry Vega, an employee in the marketing department, has decided to buy all four printers for his wife to use in her craft store. Your supervisor has asked you to prepare an invoice for the sale.

1. Open the data file **Mica Invoice**, which contains an invoice form.
2. Prepare an invoice for the four printers sold to Henry Vega, 160 Oak Canyon Drive, Loveland, OH 44150-1160. Refer to Figure 6-1.3 for an example invoice.
3. Use the current date. Use *MA 102103* for the invoice number. Use *VEGA* for the customer number and *Customer Pickup* for shipping. The terms are *Net 30*.
4. List each computer separately. Enter the asset number in the Item No. column. Enter appropriate data in the Quantity and Description columns. Enter the Remaining Value amount from the asset record for each computer in the Unit Price column. No shipping or handling cost or taxes are associated with this sale.
5. Amounts in the Total column will be calculated automatically by the formulas in the spreadsheet.
6. Proofread the invoice and correct any errors. Print the invoice.

Financial Reports and Payroll

OBJECTIVES

- Explain the purpose of a budget, income statement, and balance sheet
- Prepare a budget and income statement
- Explain concepts and procedures related to payroll payments
- Prepare a payroll register
- Create and update a supplies inventory

Many companies develop strategic plans to outline the overall direction in which the company wants to move. Strategic plans are long term in nature (from three to five years) and usually are developed by top management. Examples of strategic planning decisions include introducing or discontinuing products or expanding into new markets (overseas or ecommerce).

The success a business has in carrying out its strategic plan rests largely on how well the **resources** of the business are managed. Businesses use budgets and financial reports to aid in the management process. A **budget** is a plan detailing how the business intends to **allocate** its resources (money, equipment, personnel) and is typically prepared for a 12-month period. Businesses report their financial progress through financial statements such as the income statement and the balance sheet. Investors and lenders use these reports to make judgments about the financial health of the business.

In this topic, you will study common financial reports—budgets, income statements, and balance sheets. Additionally, you will learn about concepts and procedures related to payments for wages and salaries.

Financial Reports

Many reports relate to financial aspects of businesses. Some financial reports, such as budgets, are typically for internal use only. Others are provided to those outside the company, including shareholders in publicly owned corporations. Financial statements provide information about a company's financial status and results of operations. Publicly owned companies must provide financial statements to shareholders at the end of each quarter and at the end of the **fiscal year**.

In this section, you will examine commonly prepared financial reports— budgets, income statements, and balance sheets. You will also be given guidelines for preparing these important financial documents (also known as financial statements).

Budgets

A budget is a detailed portion of a financial plan for allocating business resources for the coming year or other period of time. Forecasts and budgets should be created with the goal of taking the steps needed in the current period to ensure that the company is moving in the direction outlined in the company's strategic plan. In a small business, much of the budget planning and control is handled directly by the owner or manager. In a large business, many people may provide information and suggestions about needs for resources in their departments. Preparing a budget for the coming year is a critical task. All employees are affected by the budget whether or not they actively participate in the budget process.

resources: property, goods, or other assets

budget: a plan for allocating resources

allocate: to set apart for a specific purpose

fiscal year: a 12-month period used for financial accounting purposes

251

© EYEWIRE COLLECTION

Figure 6-2.1

These managers are reviewing last year's data before preparing a new budget.

Preparing a Budget

Typically, the budget process begins with a review of last year's data to determine past expenses. Documents such as financial statements, tax returns, summary worksheets, and income and expense reports from previous years can provide information valuable for creating a new budget.

Procedures for preparing a budget will depend upon the size and nature of the business. In businesses large enough to have several units, many employees may be involved in planning a budget. Budget preparation often begins at the departmental level. Department heads and members may keep notes during the year about where they think additional funding will be needed or where funds could be reduced during the next budget period for their department.

In addition to the overall company budget, budgets may be created for completing specific projects, for the various departments in the company, or for a particular type of expenses such as supplies or travel. If you participate in the budget process, these suggestions will be helpful to you:

1. Learn all you can about the company's budget process including the forms used, data needed, terminology, documentation needed for requests, and deadlines.

2. Begin the preparation of your preliminary budget as soon as the budget information and instructions are received. You will often receive some

guidelines. For example, you might be told that every department budget must reflect an overall 10 percent decrease in expenses from the previous year. Use your financial records to help you determine what effect such guidelines will have on your department.

3. Consider the department's needs in relation to the company priorities for the coming year. What new projects will your department handle that may require additional expenses? What improvements have been made that may lower expenses?

4. Collect data to support your requests such as costs for new equipment or a recommended salary for a new employee that is to be hired for the department.

5. Be prepared to answer questions related to the portion of the budget you helped prepare as it is reviewed by company executives at various levels. The company's overall goals and limited resources are considered in making the final budget decisions.

Once final budget figures have been approved, highlight or prepare a summary of the portions of the budget that relate to your department or areas for which you are responsible. Be aware that the budget may be revised at some point during the budget period. A budget is a plan for how resources will be allocated. You or your department may have approval to spend for certain expenses merely based on a budgeted amount. In many companies, however, some or all expenses must be preapproved by an authorized person even if they are included on a budget.

Monitoring a Budget

A budget is generally developed for a particular period of time such as a fiscal year. Budgets for shorter periods are developed from the annual budget. As the year progresses, budget reports are prepared that compare the money spent in each category to the budgeted amount. Budget reports are typically prepared monthly or **quarterly**. If expenses in any category are too high, steps are taken to limit spending.

quarterly: four times per year

WORKPLACE **CONNECTIONS**

Pitzer Corporation budgeted $15,000 for staff training and development for the year. More training than anticipated was needed to prepare employees to use the new order entry and inventory software. By August 1, $12,650 of the $15,000 budgeted had been spent. As a means of controlling this budget item, Greg Tapier, vice president of the human resources department, issued a memo stating that all staff training for the remainder of the year must receive his prior approval as well as the usual approval from the department head.

A periodic (monthly or quarterly) budget report is often combined with a year-to-date budget report. The year-to-date report shows the amount spent in each category from the beginning date for the budget to the date the report was prepared.

Topic 6-2: *Financial Reports and Payroll*

DANDY'S DELIGHTS
OPERATING EXPENSES BUDGET REPORT
For the Month Ending June 30, 20--

June Actual	June Budget	Variance Fav. (Unfav.)	Variance Percent	Item	Year-to-Date Actual	Year-to-Date Budget	Year-to-Date Variance Fav. (Unfav.)	Variance Percent
$4,850	$4,850	0	0.0%	Salaries	$29,100	$29,100	0	0.0%
1,125	375	(750)	-200.0%	Payroll Taxes	2,250	2,250	0	0.0%
45	42	(3)	-7.1%	Advertising	245	250	5	2.0%
210	42	(168)	-400.0%	Delivery	610	250	(360)	-144.0%
60	67	7	10.4%	Office Supplies	395	400	5	1.3%
280	333	53	15.9%	Utilities	1,400	2,000	600	30.0%
35	42	7	16.7%	Miscellaneous	255	250	(5)	-2.0%
$6,605	$5,751	($854)	-14.8%	Total Expenses	$34,255	$34,500	$245	0.7%

Figure 6-2.2

This monthly budget report shows budgeted amounts and actual expenses.

Combining both a periodic and a year-to-date report provides a better view of expenses as they relate to the entire budget time period. Some expenses, such as insurance or taxes, for example, may be paid quarterly. When the payment is made, the amount of the payment may be larger than the monthly or quarterly budgeted amount. Yet the payment may be within the total amount allotted annually. An example of a budget report for Dandy's Delights is shown in Figure 6-2.2.

Income Statements

As you learned in Chapter 1, an income statement is a financial report that details the results of operations for a certain period of time. In this report you will find revenues, expenses, and the income or loss of a business for the reporting period. A projected income statement is part of a company's overall financial plan. The projected income statement lists the amounts and sources of revenues, as well as expenses, the company expects for the reporting period. A net income results if revenues are greater than expenses. A net loss results if expenses are greater than revenues. A projected income statement for Dandy's Delights (a single proprietorship) is shown in Figure 6-2.3.

WORKPLACE **CONNECTIONS**

Samantha is the office assistant to Dan Burls, the owner of Dandy's Delights. Mr. Burls's cookies and baked goods are sold in most local supermarkets, and he is planning to expand soon into nearby towns. One of Samantha's duties is to prepare both actual and projected financial statements. These statements will be used to help secure funds for expansion.

DANDY'S DELIGHTS
PROJECTED INCOME STATEMENT
For the Year Ended December 31, 20--

			% of Sales
Sales		$250,000	
Cost of Goods Sold	125,000		
Gross Profit on Sales		$125,000	50%
Operating Expenses			
Advertising Expense	1,000		
Delivery Expense	1,500		
Office Supplies Expense	1,000		
Payroll Taxes Expense	4,500		
Salaries Expense	58,200		
Utilities Expense	3,800		
Miscellaneous Expense	500		
Total Operating Expense		70,500	
Net Income from Operations		$54,500	22%
Other Income and Expenses			
Interest Expense		3,000	
Net Income Before Income Tax		$51,500	21%
Less Income Tax		14,600	
Net Income After Tax		$36,900	15%

Figure 6-2.3

This income statement shows projected income and expenses.

Balance Sheets

As you learned in Chapter 1, a balance sheet is a report that presents the financial condition of a company as of a specific date. A projected balance sheet is part of a company's overall financial plan. The balance sheet reports the assets, **liabilities**, and **owner's equity** or capital projected for the end of the plan period. The assets of a company include all the goods and property owned by the firm as well as the amounts due to the company from others. Liabilities are the debts of the company—what the company owes. The owner's equity or capital is the owner's share or the worth of the firm—the difference between assets and liabilities. A projected balance sheet for Dandy's Delights (a single proprietorship) is shown in Figure 6-2.4.

liabilities: debts owed by the company

owner's equity: owner's share of the worth of a firm; capital

Formatting Financial Documents

When you are responsible for keying and formatting financial documents such as budgets, income statements, and balance sheets, study earlier copies of these documents. If possible, use the same formats as in the previous documents. Continuing to use the same formats allows easier comparison of data from year to year. Such guidelines may be included in a company's procedures manual.

Although the financial statement formats may vary, the following format guidelines represent the generally accepted style of presenting financial statements in the absence of any company standards:

- Leave at least a one-inch margin at the top and bottom and on both sides.
- Center the lines in the statement heading—company name, statement name, and the date(s) covered by the statement.
- Double-space after headings in the body of the statement.
- Use a single line (extending the width of the longest item in the column) keyed underneath the last figure to indicate addition or subtraction.
- Use double lines underneath a final column total.
- Use the dollar sign with the first figure of each new column of figures to be added or subtracted or with every sum or difference if the figure is keyed directly underneath a single line.

Proofread the documents carefully, even if you have used a computer to prepare the statements. Give attention to detail. If another worker is available to help you, proofreading can be made easier with one person reading aloud from the original document while the other person proofreads the prepared

DANDY'S DELIGHTS
PROJECTED BALANCE SHEET
As of December 31, 20--

Assets

Current Assets		
Cash	$43,400	
Accounts Receivable	5,000	
Baking Supplies Inventory	4,000	
Office Supplies	500	
Total Current Assets		$64,900
Fixed Assets		
Delivery Van	$7,000	
Baking Equipment	5,000	
Building and Land	95,000	
Total Fixed Assets		107,000
Total Assets		$159,900

Liabilities

Current Liabilities		
Notes Payable	$5,000	
Accounts Payable	1,500	
Salary and Wages Payable	200	
Total Current Liabilities		$6,700
Fixed Liabilities		
Long-term Note Payable	$7,000	
Mortgage Payable	32,000	
Total Fixed Liabilities		39,000
Total Liabilities		$45,700

Owner's Equity

Dan Burts, Capital			
Beginning Balance		$82,300	
Net Income for 20--	$36,900		
Less Withdrawals	5,000	31,900	
Dan Burts, Capital			
Ending Balance		114,200	
Total Liabilities and Owner's Equity		$159,900	

Figure 6-2.5

All financial documents must be proofread carefully.

© DAVID YOUNG-WOLFF/PHOTOEDIT

copy. In addition to the words and figures, the person reading aloud should indicate details such as capitalization, punctuation, underscores, vertical spacing, indentions, and dollar signs. Be particularly alert to transposing figures (for example, keying $1,245,385 for $1,254,385). As a final proof, recalculate or prove all totals and compare them with the original. If you are using a computer software program to prepare the statement, check the accuracy of any formulas used in the statement.

Payments for Wages and Salaries

Typically, paying wages and salaries is the responsibility of the payroll department. A **payroll** is a list of the amount of salary or wages or other payments for work due to employees. The procedures used within the payroll department will vary depending on the size of the workforce and the degree to which the process is automated. However, common tasks completed by the payroll department include:

payroll: list of employees and amount of salary or wages due to each

- Ensuring that employee payroll records are kept up to date
- Calculating **deductions** and changes in salary, commissions, or overtime

deductions: items that reduce gross pay

- Updating attendance, vacation, and sick leave data
- Processing, printing, and distributing paychecks
- Creating tax reports related to payroll that must be submitted to local, state, and federal agencies

Some companies use time and attendance recording systems where employees register their attendance at a computer terminal. Attendance data goes directly into the company's computerized payroll system.

CHAPTER 6: PROCESSING AND UNDERSTANDING FINANCIAL INFORMATION

Ecommerce and Planning Strategies

"They can have any color they want, as long as it's black."
Attributed to pioneer automaker
Henry Ford

Ecommerce is changing the way businesses operate and creating a need for new planning strategies. Before ecommerce became established, most manufacturers operated according to one of two basic business models—mass production or customized production.

At the height of the Industrial Revolution, mass production allowed companies to lower costs by making large numbers of the same product. The lower costs were passed on to customers in the form of lower prices. Using a customized product business model, a product is made according to a customer's specifications. In the past, customized products were often expensive to make, and few people could afford customized products of good quality. Strategies for planning and budgeting for both these business models have been well established and practiced for many years.

Today the Industrial Revolution has given way to the Technology Revolution. Many companies participate in ecommerce by selling directly to customers and buying directly from suppliers on the Web. Ecommerce has made a third business model, mass customization, more widely used. Mass customization means making many products to many customers' specifications. Dell Computer Corporation is an example of a company that uses mass customization. Customers enter their product order on a company's Web site. Although the company makes thousands of computers each year, each one can be customized for a particular customer's needs.

Companies can now offer the best of both worlds—customized products at mass produced prices. This business model requires creative strategies for planning and budgeting. Planning for mass customization is difficult because of the large number of alternatives customers have to choose from when ordering products. The planning process is also much more complex. Companies who use this business model rely heavily on market research to help them create forecasts for future sales and supply needs.

Payroll information must be accurate and should be kept confidential. By following standard procedures, carefully verifying their work, and maintaining orderly records, payroll employees help ensure accurate employee records.

Compensation Plans

In some companies, all employees are **compensated** in the same way. In other companies, however, several different plans may be used for different groups of workers. The typical ones include salary, hourly, commission, and combination plans.

compensated: paid

gross salary: money earned before any deductions are made

Under a salary plan, the employee is paid an amount that is quoted on a weekly, monthly, or yearly basis. The **gross salary**, which is the salary before any deductions, is the figure quoted. A salary quoted on a yearly basis is subdivided into the number of pay periods per year. Thus, a person who earns $22,000 yearly and is paid twice each month will have a gross salary of $916.66 each pay period.

In some jobs, employees are paid on the basis of a wage rate per hour. The hourly rate applies to the hours considered standard. The standard workweek may be 35, 37.5, or 40 hours. When workers paid on an hourly basis work more hours than those specified as their standard workweek, they generally earn a higher rate for the **overtime** hours. Overtime rates are commonly 1.5 to 2 times the standard hourly rate. Many workers are paid on the basis of an hourly rate.

overtime: hours worked beyond the standard number in a workweek

commission: payment based on the price of items sold

Some workers' earnings are based on a **commission** or a percentage of the value of what they sell or process. The percentage may vary by volume of sales or amount of production. This method is commonly used for the payment of sales representatives. For example, sales representatives of a computer supplies company are assigned sales territories. Because their earnings depend on the sales they generate, they are motivated to please customers and secure new orders. For example, if the sales person earns a 10 percent commission on each sale, a $1,000 order would result in a $100 commission.

In some jobs, a combination compensation plan is used. For example, a commission, referred to as a bonus, may be given to employees who are successful beyond some established standard. Such a bonus is often a percentage of additional sales or production.

Figure 6-2.6

This sales person is paid a commission in addition to a base salary.

© CORBIS

Lauren works as a sales person for a furniture store. She is paid according to a combination plan. She earns a weekly salary of $500 plus a 5 percent commission on weekly sales exceeding $5,000. Last week Lauren's sales were $8,000. She earned $500 in salary plus $150 ($3,000 x 5%) in commission for a total of $650. Lauren likes the combination pay plan because the weekly salary assures her of a steady, basic income. At the same time, the bonus portion of the plan rewards her for using her sales skills to make higher sales for the company.

Deductions from Earnings

As you have learned, salaries and wages are quoted at their gross figures, which is before any deductions are considered. The earnings actually received will be less than the gross wages or salaries. Some payroll deductions are required by law; others are voluntary as requested by the employee.

Deductions Required by Law

Deductions required by law include the following:

- Federal income tax
- Federal Insurance Contributions Act tax (referred to as FICA or Social Security tax)
- State income tax (where applicable)
- City income tax (where applicable)

Federal income tax deductions vary depending on gross amount of wages or salary, the employee's marital status, and the number of **exemptions** claimed. Each employee must complete an Employee's Withholding Allowance Certificate (known as a W-4 form), which is kept on file by the employing company. The employee is responsible for notifying the human resources department of any changes in the number of exemptions. Figure 6-2.7 is an example of a W-4 form.

exemptions: withholding allowances

FICA deductions are a percentage of gross wages or salary, up to the maximum amount of wages or salary taxed. The employee's contribution to social security is matched by the employer. Each year the rates are reviewed by Congress, which has the authority to change the rate as well as the maximum amount taxed. The payroll office in your company can provide you with the up-to-date percentages for deductions and the amount of earnings subject to FICA tax. This information also is available from your local office of the Social Security Administration.

State and local government units that tax the earnings of citizens issue instructions regarding the taxes to be withheld. Your payroll office will have this information on file for your reference.

Form W-4
Department of the Treasury
Internal Revenue Service

Employee's Withholding Allowance Certificate

▶ For Privacy Act and Paperwork Reduction Act Notice, see page 2.

OMB No. 1545-0010

2001

1	Type or print your first name and middle initial	Last name		2	Your social security number

Jeffrey C. | *Hunter*   321 : 22 : 4697

Home address (number and street or rural route)

45 Newland Place

3 ☐ Single ☑ Married ☐ Married, but withhold at higher Single rate.

Note: *If married, but legally separated, or spouse is a nonresident alien, check the Single box.*

City or town, state, and ZIP code

Matawan, NJ 07747-6321

4 If your last name differs from that on your social security card, check here. You must call 1-800-772-1213 for a new card. ▶ ☐

5 Total number of allowances you are claiming (from line **H** above **or** from the applicable worksheet on page 2) ... **5** *1*

6 Additional amount, if any, you want withheld from each paycheck . . . . **6** $ —

7 I claim exemption from withholding for 2001, and I certify that I meet **both** of the following conditions for exemption:
- Last year I had a right to a refund of **all** Federal income tax withheld because I had **no** tax liability **and**
- This year I expect a refund of **all** Federal income tax withheld because I expect to have **no** tax liability.

If you meet both conditions, write "Exempt" here . . . . ▶ **7**

Under penalties of perjury, I certify that I am entitled to the number of withholding allowances claimed on this certificate, or I am entitled to claim exempt status.

Employee's signature
(Form is not valid
unless you sign it.) ▶ *Jeffrey C. Hunter*

Date ▶ *July 5, 20--*

8	Employer's name and address (Employer: Complete lines 8 and 10 only if sending to the IRS.)	9 Office code (optional)	10 Employer identification number

Cat. No. 10220Q

Figure 6-2.7

How many deductions does Jeffrey Hunter claim?

voluntary deductions: amount taken from pay at an employee's request

net pay: final earnings amount after all deductions

Voluntary Deductions

Voluntary deductions vary considerably. In some companies, employees may choose voluntary deductions for health insurance, savings plans, retirement plans, and other purposes. Employees who work in the payroll office have the responsibility of keeping the records up to date for employees' individual deductions.

Records for Payroll

Companies maintain careful records of all payments made to employees. Employee earnings records are prepared for each pay period and for the year to date. The earnings records show earnings, deductions, and **net pay**. Many companies issue payroll checks that have an attached voucher showing similar information.

At the end of the year, the company is responsible for issuing to each employee a Wage and Tax Statement (commonly called a W-2 form) for the calendar year. The information needed to prepare the W-2 form is found on the payroll register, which records all the earnings and deductions for the payroll period. Additionally, the company makes weekly, monthly, or quarterly reports to government agencies of taxes withheld and taxes the employer must pay. Periodically, the company makes deposits of the amounts withheld and the taxes owed.

EMPLOYEE EARNINGS RECORD

Employee: Jeffrey Hunter
Employee No.: 3415

SS No.: 321-22-4697
Marital Status: M
No. Allowances: 1

Year Ending: December 31, 20--
Position: Data Entry Clerk
Pay per Year: $19,200

Pay Period	Ended	Regular	Total	Income Tax	FICA	State Tax	Total Tax	Health Ins.	Net Pay	Gross Acc. Earnings
1	31-Jan	$1,600.00	$1,600.00	$242.00	$122.40	$37.59	$401.99	$123.00	$1,075.01	$1,600.00
2	28-Feb	1,600.00	1,600.00	242.00	122.40	37.59	401.99	123.00	1,075.01	3,200.00
3	31-Mar	1,600.00	1,600.00	242.00	122.40	37.59	401.99	123.00	1,075.01	4,800.00
4	30-Apr	1,600.00	1,600.00	242.00	122.40	37.59	401.99	123.00	1,075.01	6,400.00
5	31-May	1,600.00	1,600.00	242.00	122.40	37.59	401.99	123.00	1,075.01	8,000.00
6	30-Jun	1,600.00	1,600.00	242.00	122.40	37.59	401.99	123.00	1,075.01	9,600.00
7	31-Jul	1,600.00	1,600.00	242.00	122.40	37.59	401.99	123.00	1,075.01	11,200.00
8	31-Aug	1,600.00	1,600.00	242.00	122.40	37.59	401.99	123.00	1,075.01	12,800.00
9	30-Sep	1,600.00	1,600.00	242.00	122.40	37.59	401.99	123.00	1,075.01	14,400.00
10	31-Oct	1,600.00	1,600.00	242.00	122.40	37.59	401.99	123.00	1,075.01	16,000.00
11	30-Nov	1,600.00	1,600.00	242.00	122.40	37.59	401.99	123.00	1,075.01	17,600.00
12	31-Dec	1,600.00	1,600.00	242.00	122.40	37.59	401.99	123.00	1,075.01	19,200.00
		$19,200.00	$19,200.00	$2,904.00	$1,468.80	$451.08	$4,823.88	$1,476.00	$12,900.12	

MODERN SOFTWARE, INC.
PAYROLL REGISTER
January 31, 20--

Employee No.	Employee Name	Regular	Overtime	Total	Income Tax	FICA	State Tax	Total Tax	Health Ins.	Net Pay
4568	Acota, B.	$2,150.00		$2,150.00	$236.00	$164.48	$58.98	$459.46	$123.00	$1,567.54
4321	Beres, W.	1,088.00		1,088.00	131.00	83.23	19.64	233.87	123.00	731.13
3257	Cantrell, T.	2,840.00		2,840.00	635.00	217.26	103.97	956.23	76.00	1,807.77
3921	Evans, T.	2,010.00		2,010.00	249.00	153.77	55.32	458.09	76.00	1,475.91
3415	Hunter, J.	1,600.00		1,600.00	242.00	122.40	37.59	401.99	123.00	1,075.01
3401	Hutchins, W.	3,445.00		3,445.00	854.00	263.54	135.83	1,253.37	76.00	2,115.63
4563	Jacobs, S. L.	1,810.00		1,810.00	193.00	138.47	43.30	374.77	76.00	1,359.23

Figure 6-2.8

What are Jeffrey Hunter's net earnings for the year?

Topic 6-2: *Financial Reports and Payroll*

Payroll Check Distribution

Procedures for distributing paychecks will vary from company to company. A company may distribute checks in person or mail them to employees. Other companies use **direct deposit**. That is, they electronically deposit wage and salary payments to employees' designated banks where the funds are placed in the employees' accounts. The company provides the employee with a document that details the deposit. In some companies, employees may choose their payment method.

direct deposit: placing the amount of net pay in an employee's bank account

Figure 6-2.9

In this company, payroll checks are delivered in person.

© TOM ROSENTHAL/SUPERSTOCK INTERNATIONAL

1. What is the purpose of a budget?
2. What suggestions will be helpful if you participate in the budget process?
3. What information does a report used to monitor a budget typically include?
4. What is an income statement? What information does it typically include?
5. What is a balance sheet? What information does it typically include?
6. What tasks do employees in the payroll department perform in processing the payroll?
7. How does the hourly method of payroll payment differ from the salary method?
8. How does the salary method of payroll payment differ from the commission method?
9. Name two deductions from earnings that are required by law.
10. Describe the information recorded in a payroll register.

Making Decisions

Valerie's job responsibilities include filing all vendor invoices and purchase orders in the accounts payable department. Janie's job responsibilities include checking the accuracy of vendor invoices against purchase orders. From time to time, Janie must retrieve these documents from the files. Recently, Janie has had difficulty in locating specific documents. Often she must search through practically an entire file drawer to find what she needs. Janie noted that others seem to be spending too much time looking through the files also.

Janie has no authority to supervise Valerie. The supervisor has said nothing to Valerie about the matter as far as Janie knows. "Because the supervisor doesn't use the files, the supervisor may not be aware of this problem," thinks Janie. She believes the work of the department would be far more efficient if the filing were done carefully.

1. If you were in Janie's position, would you discuss this situation with Valerie's supervisor? Why or why not?
2. What might be an alternative action you could take to help remedy this problem?

Reinforcing English Skills

Reports and letters prepared by office workers often contain numbers. Review the following number rules. Then write or key the sentences expressing the numbers in correct form.

Number Usage Rules

- Spell numbers one through ten; use figures for numbers above ten.
- Spell a number that begins a sentence.
- Use the same style for related numbers in a sentence. If any of the numbers are above ten, use figures for all the numbers.
- Use figures and a dollar sign to express amounts of money. For money in round amounts of a million or more, the words *million* or *billion* may be used to replace the zeros ($4 million). For amounts under a dollar, use figures and the word *cents*.
- Use numbers to express measurements.

1. 15 people attended the meeting.

2. The report identifies 5 departments that are over budget.

3. The package weighs two pounds 11 ounces.

4. The sales forecast for next year is 3,000,000 dollars.

5. Of the 15 companies, 7 sent executives to the training session.

6. 4 managers reported expenses totaling one thousand dollars.

7. You have been asked to purchase eighty reams of paper for use by three departments.

8. The new printer is ten inches tall and 17 inches wide.

9. The pens with red ink cost fifty cents each.

10. Last year we sold five hundred and twenty-five different types of products.

Topic 6-2 ACTIVITY 1

Payroll Register

You are an office employee in Furniture Galore, a retail store in a suburban mall. You have been given a schedule of salaries to use in preparing a payroll register for the pay period November 1–15.

1. Open and print the data file **Salaries.pdf**, which contains salary and other information for employees.

2. Use your spreadsheet software to create a payroll register similar to the one shown in Figure 6-2.8 on page 263. Enter the appropriate headings for the register. The register is being prepared two weeks after the pay period end and should be dated November 31 of the current year. Use the heading Bonus rather than Overtime. Enter the employee numbers and names.

3. Enter formulas to calculate the regular pay for the employees for the pay period November 1–15. The regular pay is the monthly salary divided by two.

4. Enter formulas to calculate the bonus amount for employees who receive a commission. Multiply the commission amount by the net sales for the period. Enter a formula to add the regular pay to the bonus amount, if any, to find the total gross pay.

5. Enter formulas in the spreadsheet to calculate the income tax, FICA, and state tax amounts. Use the tax rates on the printout. To find a tax amount, multiply the total gross pay by the tax percentage. Enter a formula to find the total tax for each person.

6. Enter a formula to calculate the appropriate amount for the health care deduction for each person.

7. Enter a formula to calculate the net pay for each person. To find the net pay, subtract the total tax and the health insurance amount from the total gross pay.

8. Sort the data in alphabetic order by the employee name. Print the payroll register.

Create Supplies Inventory and Budget

You are an office employee in the accounting department at Mica Associates. You have been asked to create an inventory record of your department's office supplies and office equipment such as paper cutters and electric pencil sharpeners. You have also been asked to plan a budget for office supplies for your department for the coming year.

1. Your first step is to determine the supplies that were purchased by the department during the previous year and the supplies that remain on hand. You reviewed the purchase orders from the previous year, noting quantities and prices of items purchased. You also counted items remaining in the supply closet. Open and print the data file **Supplies.pdf**, which contains your notes on supplies purchased last year and those remaining on hand.

2. Use your spreadsheet software to create an inventory for the items on hand. Also include items purchased last year, even if none of the items currently remain on hand. Title the spreadsheet with the company name, *Office Supplies Inventory*, and the date *January 3, 20--*.

3. Include the following column headings in the inventory spreadsheet: *Item, Unit of Measure, Price*, and *Quantity on Hand*. Enter information from your notes for each item. In the Unit of Measure column, enter *Each, Box, Ream*, etc., as appropriate for the item. Enter only the price number in the price column, not "per ream," for example. Copy the Item, Unit of Measure, and Price columns of data to another sheet of the spreadsheet for use later in preparing a budget.

4. On the inventory sheet, add a column at the right with the column head, *Total*. Enter a formula to multiply the price times the quantity on hand to find the total cost. Enter a formula to sum the Total column to find the total value of the current office supplies inventory.

5. Sort the records alphabetically by the Item column. Format the sheet to print the column headings on the top of each page. Create a footer to print the page number on each page. Make other adjustments in formatting as needed for an attractive, easy-to-read report. Print the inventory report. Keep this inventory report file for use in a later activity.

6. Go to the sheet where data was copied for use in creating a budget. Add a column to the right of the spreadsheet, *Quantity Purchased*. Using your notes, record the quantity of each item that was purchased last year.

7. Add a column, *Total Amount*, at the right of the spreadsheet. Enter a formula to multiply the price times the quantity purchased to find the total amount. Enter a formula to sum the Total Amount column to find the total amount spent for office supplies last year.

8. In planning your budget, consider which items will need to be purchased again. For consumable items, such as file folders or pens, assume you need to purchase about the same as for the previous year. For nonconsumable items, such as staplers or paper cutters, use your judgment about how many may need to be purchased next year.

9. Add a column, *Adjustments*, at the right of the spreadsheet. In this column, enter amounts for items you do not plan to include in the budget this year. Enter a formula to sum the Adjustments column. Enter a formula to subtract the total of the Adjustments column from the total of the Total Amount column. Place the formula a couple of rows below the total of the Adjustments column. Label this answer *Total After Adjustments* to the left of the answer.

10. Prices may increase for some items during the coming year. Place the amount .05 under the cell that contains the Total After Adjustments answer. Label this amount *Allowance for Price Increases* to the left of the amount. In the cell below this amount, enter a formula to multiply the Total After Adjustments by 105 percent. Label this answer *Yearly Budget Total*.

11. In the cell below the Yearly Budget Total amount, enter a formula to divide the Yearly Budget Total by 4. Label this answer *Quarterly Budget Amount*.

12. Title the spreadsheet with the company name, *Office Supplies Budget*, and the date *January 3, 20--*. Format the sheet to print the column headings on the top of each page. Create a footer to print the page number on each page. Make other adjustments in formatting as needed for an attractive, easy-to-read report. Print the budget report. Keep this budget report file for use in a later activity.

Summary

In Chapter 6, you were introduced to concepts and procedures for processing financial information. Although procedures may vary from company to company, employees have responsibility for maintaining accurate, up-to-date financial records at all times. From your study of this chapter, you should be able to discuss the following key points.

- The overall method a business uses to safeguard assets is known as internal control. Internal control methods fall into three categories—preventive, detective, and corrective.

- Companies generally separate responsibility for tasks in processing cash, and they may also bond employees in order to have good internal control.

- Companies bill their customers periodically for the goods or services purchased on credit. The request for payment is commonly in the form of a sales invoice or a statement of account.

- Employees assist in the processing of cash by seeing that checks are endorsed properly, filling in deposit slips, preparing bank reconciliations, and maintaining petty cash funds.

- In larger firms, processing cash payments is often the responsibility of employees in the accounts payable department. Employees who make cash payments review purchase-related documents, prepare vouchers, and prepare checks.

- Bank accounts are reconciled to be sure that receipts and payments shown in company records match the bank's records.

- The petty cash fund is used in many offices to pay for small expenditures such as postage or delivery services.

- Sound financial management includes planning, analyzing, and reporting financial information.

- A budget is a detailed portion of a financial plan for allocation of the resources of the business. Budgets are used for planning and monitoring expenditures.

- Companies design payroll procedures to ensure that employees are paid accurately and on time.

- Financial statements provide information about a company's economic resources and the results of the company's operations.

Key Terms

accounts payable	commission	gross salary
accounts receivable	credit	internal control
allowance	debit card	liabilities
asset	deductions	net pay
audit	direct deposit	overtime
bank reconciliation	electronic funds	owner's equity
bank statement	transfer	payroll
bonding	endorsement	petty cash
budget	exemptions	proving cash
checks	fiscal year	voucher

COMPOSITION
INTEGRATED DOCUMENT
SPREADSHEET
WORD PROCESSING

Chapter 6   ACTIVITY 1

Monitor Budget, Update Inventory, Purchasing Schedule

For this activity you will need to refer to the supplies inventory and budget information you prepared in Topic 6-2 Activity 2. The budget you prepared was based on last year's purchases and divided to calculate the quarterly budget. In this activity, you will create a purchasing schedule for office supplies for each quarter. You will update your office supplies inventory when items are purchased and monitor your office supplies budget. You will also prepare a purchase requisition for supplies.

Purchasing Schedule

1. Create a purchasing schedule to identify the office supplies you plan to purchase at the beginning of each quarter. Your goal is to have items on hand when needed and to spread the purchase cost across the four quarters as evenly as possible.

2. Consider each item on your supplies inventory. How many of the items were purchased last year, and how many do we have on hand? Decide how to spread purchase of the items over the year. Assume most items will be used evenly over the year. If you plan to purchase only one or two of particular items, you may want to put them in your purchasing schedule in the first or second quarter even though they will be used throughout the year.

3. Use your spreadsheet software to create a purchasing schedule showing which items you plan to purchase each quarter. Use the company name, *Mica Associates*, *Office Supplies Purchasing Schedule*, and the current date

as the heading for the spreadsheet. Include column headings for *Item*, *Unit of Measure*, and *Price* (assume that there will be no price increases). Copy the data from these same columns on the office supplies budget you created earlier to these columns on your purchasing schedule.

4. Enter column headings *Qty. Qtr. 1* and *Cost Qtr. 1*. Enter the quantity of each item you plan to purchase in quarter 1. Enter a formula in the Cost Qtr. 1 column to multiply the price times the quantity to be purchased. Sum the Cost Qtr. 1 column. Repeat this step for quarters 2, 3, and 4.

5. Enter column headings for *Total Qty.* (for the year) and *Total Cost* (for the year). Enter formulas to calculate the total cost for the year. Sum the Total Cost column.

6. Format the spreadsheet attractively. Set the column headings to print on each page. Enter a footer to print the page number. Print a copy of your purchasing schedule in landscape orientation.

Update Inventory

7. Assume this is the end of the first quarter. You have purchased and received the items you ordered for the first quarter. You noted items removed from the supply cabinet by employees as they were removed. Now you are ready to update the office supplies inventory (created in Topic 6-2 Activity 2). Open the data file `Supply Usage.pdf`, which contains your notes regarding supplies used.

8. Open the supplies inventory file you created earlier. Copy the Item, Unit of Measure, Price, and Quantity on Hand columns to a new sheet in your purchasing schedule spreadsheet. Change the heading of column D to *Qtr. 1 Beg. Inv.* Add a column heading to the right of the spreadsheet, *Qtr. 1 Purchases*. Copy the data from the Qtr. 1 Qty. column on the purchasing schedule into the Qtr. 1 Purchases column.

9. Add a column at the right of the spreadsheet, *Qtr. 1 Usage*. Enter the amount of each item used as shown in your notes on the original inventory.

10. Add a column to the right of the spreadsheet, *Qtr. 1 End. Inv.* Enter a formula to add the quarter 1 purchases to and subtract the quarter 1 usage from the beginning inventory to find the ending inventory.

11. Add a column at the right of the spreadsheet, *Total*. Enter a formula to multiply the ending inventory by the price to find the total inventory amount. Sum the Total column. By what amount did the inventory of office supplies increase or decrease from the beginning of quarter 1 to the end of quarter 1?

12. Enter the company name, *Mica Associates, Office Supplies Inventory*, and *March 31, 20--* as the heading for the spreadsheet. Enter a footer to print the page number. Set the column headings to print at the top of each page. Print the updated inventory. You may need to use landscape orientation.

Monitor the Budget

13. Assume this is the end of the second quarter. You need to compare the amount you have spent for office supplies to your first- and second-quarter budgeted amounts. Assume you purchased all the items as

planned on your purchasing schedule for quarters 1 and 2. You did not purchase any other items. Determine the amount you spent for office supplies in quarters 1 and 2. Compare this amount to the amounts budgeted for quarters 1 and 2 on the office supplies budget you created in Topic 6-2 Activity 2. Are you over or under budget and by how much? If you are over budget, what changes might you be able to make in the last two quarters to get back on budget?

14. Create a memo form for Mica Associates to include the company name and the appropriate headings. Write a memo to the department head, Freda Amosa. Use the date *July 3, 20--* and an appropriate subject line. Give Freda an update on the amount you had budgeted for office supplies for quarters 1 and 2 and the amounts you have actually spent. If you are under budget, explain why, mentioning some of the items or a strategy you used to save money. If you are over budget, explain the steps you will take in quarters 3 and 4 to stay within the yearly budget.

15. Create a bar graph to compare budgeted and actual costs for office supplies for quarters 1 and 2. Copy the graph into your memo to illustrate the data. Proofread carefully and correct all errors before printing the memo.

Purchase Requisition

16. Even though you make purchases according to the purchasing schedule, occasionally a special need for office supplies arises. The department head will conduct meetings with all employees to discuss changes in the company health insurance plan. She has asked you to purchase 80 binders. Each employee will receive a binder containing information about the new plan.

17. Open the data file **Mica Requisition**, which contains a purchase requisition form. Create a purchase requisition for the binders. Refer to Figure 6-1.9 for an example purchase requisition.

18. Use *September 22, 20--* as the date. You will need 3-ring vinyl binders, 1-inch size, in green with the company name printed on the front cover. Because of the special printing, you will purchase these binders from Print-Quick Custom Printers, 126 Irwin Simpson Road, Mason, OH 44050-0126 for $3.50 each. Print the completed purchase requisition.

Projected Income Statement

You are an office worker for Duncan's Auto Detailing. The owner, Mr. Duncan, has asked you to create two projected income statements for next year based on two different levels of potential business.

1. Open the data file **Duncan Income Statement**, which contains last year's income statement for Duncan's Auto Detailing.

2. Copy the income statement to the next two empty sheets in your spreadsheet. Name the sheets *Last Year*, *Best Case*, and *Worst Case*.

Change the second line of the title of the Best Case and Worst Case sheets to *Projected Income Statement*. On the Best Case and Worst Case sheets, insert a row above the date and add the heading *Best Case* or *Worst Case*.

3. Make the changes Mr. Duncan projects for the best case as listed below.
   - Sales will increase 25 percent compared to last year.
   - Detailing labor will increase $20,000.
   - Supplies will increase 25 percent.
   - Advertising will increase $400.
   - Payroll taxes will increase $1,500.
   - Utilities will increase 25 percent.
   - Income tax expense will be at the same rate as last year. To find last year's rate, divide the income tax by the net income before tax on last year's sheet.

4. Make the changes Mr. Duncan projects for the worst case as listed below.
   - Sales will decrease 20 percent compared to last year.
   - Detailing labor will decrease $20,000.
   - Supplies will decrease 20 percent.
   - Payroll taxes will decrease $1,500.
   - Utilities will decrease 20 percent.
   - Income tax expense will be at the same rate as last year. To find last year's rate, divide the income tax by the net income before tax on last year's sheet.

5. Format the Best Case and Worst Case sheets to print attractively on the page. Print copies of the sheets for the best-case and worst-case projections. What were the gross profit on sales percentages for the two alternatives? How much profit or loss will Mr. Duncan have under each alternative?

— After completing all the chapters in Part 2, complete the Part 2 simulation, *At Work at Maple Valley Chamber of Commerce.* The simulation is found in the *Student Activities and Projects workbook.*

Part 3

Managing Time, Tasks, and Records

As an office worker, you need to effectively use the resources that support your work activities: time, workstation, reference sources, office supplies and equipment, and paper and electronic records. You need to participate in meetings with coworkers and make travel arrangements for yourself and others. You also need to be acquainted with the critical concerns for your office health, safety, and security that are the responsibility of all employees. You will build skill in these important areas as you study *Managing Time, Tasks, and Records*.

OBJECTIVES

- Manage your time; workstation; and office health, safety, and security effectively
- Plan and participate in meetings
- Make travel arrangements
- Manage paper, magnetic, and optical records and media

PHOTO © PHOTODISC, INC.

275

Time and Workstation Management

The concept of time management is actually misleading—none of us can manage time. How we manage ourselves in relation to time is important, however. Effectively arranging and managing the furniture, equipment, files, supplies, and other resources used in your work is as critical as managing your time wisely. Arranging furniture and equipment in your work area properly can enhance your overall productivity and make your workplace safer.

....

In this chapter, you will learn time management techniques and tools that will help you work productively. You will learn about the critical concerns for safety and security that affect office workers. You also will learn about ergonomic factors, such as lighting, color, sound, office equipment, and furniture, that affect how you feel and how productive you are in the office environment.

and Reminder Systems

OBJECTIVES

- Identify common time-wasters
- Analyze how you spend your time
- Plan your work activities
- Use common reminder systems
- Compare and contrast manual and electronic reminder systems

Time management is a major factor in your productivity and effectiveness as an office worker. Managing your time at the office is a process of choosing the most effective way to do your job. The creative use of techniques to manage time will enrich your work life.

Calendar and other reminder systems are helpful in bringing to mind events, tasks, and other office-related activities. These reminder systems assist you in scheduling activities for the most efficient use of time and resources.

Manage Your Time

Time management is the process of planning your activities to gain better control over how you spend your time. Managing your time effectively is critical to your success on the job. You will want to learn how to eliminate time-wasters and handle time **obligations** efficiently. Analyzing how you spend your time will increase your effectiveness in managing your work. One of the first steps in learning how to use your time is to recognize how it can be wasted.

time management: planning to gain control over how time is spent

obligations: commitments, duties, responsibilities

Common Time-Wasters

All time spent at work is not productive. You can waste time without realizing it. Some common time-wasters, along with suggestions for overcoming them, are discussed in the following paragraphs.

Unnecessary Telephone Conversations

The telephone can be either a time-saver or a time-waster, depending on how you use it. Often, a telephone call that could save time wastes time instead. For example, if an office worker takes ten minutes to verify price information and five minutes to discuss the latest episode of a favorite television program, a conversation that began productively ends by wasting time. If this happens two or three times a day, the time wasted can add up rapidly.

Frequent Interruptions

Interruptions in your work can come from many sources—unplanned visits or questions from coworkers or customers, phone calls, and delays in receiving work or material from others are common ones. On the surface, each of these interruptions may appear to be a time-waster. Remember, however, that working with coworkers and customers is an important element of most jobs. Evaluate the interruptions by determining whether they contribute to better relations with coworkers and customers or whether they are actually causing a delay in meeting established deadlines or producing a quality product.

Excessive Socializing

Although some socializing will help you maintain good working relations with your coworkers, too much socializing is misuse of company time. Some

Topic 7-1: *Time Management and Reminder Systems*

Figure 7-1.1

Socialize with coworkers at appropriate times such as lunch or during breaks.

© JACK HOLLINGSWORTH/PHOTODISC

workers may socialize excessively, and you will be wise to avoid engaging in long conversations with them. When a coworker tries to involve you in idle conversation, offer a simple response such as: "I really must get back to work. Maybe we could discuss this at lunch." You will maintain good working relations while excusing yourself to continue your work. If you are consistent in your responses, the coworker will soon learn that you are not easily distracted from your work. Be careful to limit your lunch and breaks to the planned or approved times.

Ineffective Communication

As an office worker, you will receive information in both written and oral form from customers and coworkers. You also will give information in written and oral form to others. If the information that is given or received by you is inaccurate or incomplete, lost time and money can be the result of the poor communication. Be certain the information you give others is specific and accurate. Ask for feedback from those to whom you give information to be sure you have communicated the information clearly and completely. Likewise, be sure that you understand any instructions or information you receive. Ask questions to clear up any misunderstandings and to gain all the needed information.

Disorganization

Being disorganized can be a major time-waster. Searching for the paper you just had in your hands, forgetting important deadlines, and shifting unnecessarily from one project to another are all signs of a disorganized person. Take the time to organize your work area and prepare a daily plan for your work. Think through and plan complicated jobs before starting them. Group similar tasks together and avoid jumping from one project to another before finishing the first one. Do not **procrastinate**. If unpleasant or difficult tasks are needlessly delayed, they can become problems later.

procrastinate: delay intentionally, put off

Time Analysis Procedures

Time is a valuable resource that should be used wisely; it cannot be replaced. You have learned about common ways time can be wasted. One of the smartest things you can do is to analyze how you spend your time on the job. Time analysis aids you in determining how effectively your time is used. By keeping a written account of what you do, you can determine whether you are using your time effectively. With this information, you can then develop a plan of action to correct or redirect the use of your time.

Keep a Time Log

Start a time analysis by keeping a written record of what you do and how much time is used. Record all activities in a time-use log: tasks accepted and completed, telephone calls, meetings, discussions, receiving and responding to e-mail messages or other correspondence, and so forth.

You may choose to keep a time-use log for a day, for several days, or even a week. The longer you keep the log, the more representative it will be of how your time is spent. A partial time-use log is shown in Figure 7-1.2.

Analyze How You Spend Your Time

When you have completed your time-use log, you are ready to analyze the results. By studying your time-use patterns, you will be able to spot problem areas quickly. Be alert to the following points as you review the log:

- During what time of the day was I most productive? least productive? Why?
- How did I lose (or waste) my time? Was it because of unnecessary interruptions, visitors/socializing, crises, telephone? Who and what was involved in each case?

Figure 7-1.2

A time-use log will aid in determining how effectively your time is used.

Time-Use Log

Name _Michele Fitch_

Time	Monday	Tuesday	Wednesday	Thursday	Friday
8:45 a.m.	Arrived early Opened office	Arrived early Opened office	Arrived early Opened office	Arrived early Opened office	Arrived early Opened office
9:00 a.m.	Checked calendar and task list	Checked calendar and task list	Checked calendar and task list	Checked calendar and task list	Checked calendar and task list
9:15 a.m.	Meet with supervisor	Meet with supervisor	Keyed meeting notes and report	Meet with supervisor	Meet with supervisor
9:30 a.m.	Wrote report	Composed letter		Organized trip folder	Wrote e-mail to staff
9:45 a.m.		Took notes at meeting		Keyed new expense report form	Made copies
10:00 a.m.					
10:15 a.m.			Coffee break	Phone calls	Coffee break
10:30 a.m.	Coffee break		Keyed supplies requisition form	Coffee break	Meeting with Nancy
10:45 a.m.	Phone calls	Sorted and opened mail	Sorted and opened mail	Sorted and opened mail	Filing
11:00 a.m.	Sorted and opened mail	Filing	Filing	Filing	Sorted and opened mail

Topic 7-1: *Time Management and Reminder Systems*

- Does a pattern emerge that might show the times when most interruptions occur? Does a pattern indicate that more time is needed to handle crises or emergency tasks that may arise? Do I need more time to complete specific tasks?
- Do I think that I have used my time wisely?

Develop a Plan of Action

After you have analyzed how you spend your time, determine how well the tasks you complete contribute to meeting your work goals. For each activity you have listed in your time-use log, ask yourself if that activity contributed to the satisfactory completion of your work. If not, develop a **systematic** approach to your work that will increase the effective use of your time.

Manage Your Work

Using time efficiently requires developing an organized approach to your work. Calendars and time-management systems can help you identify **peak** and **slack** work periods. Once you know when to expect such periods, you can plan your work to allow for more productive use of your time and for a more even workload. To accommodate a peak period, think ahead to determine what jobs could be completed in advance. Then the peak period will not place undue pressure on you. Planning for the slack periods is equally important. During these times, you can catch up on those tasks that do not have deadlines but nevertheless must be done.

Plan Your Work Activities

Planning your daily work activities will help you avoid forgetting tasks that need to be completed. Take five or ten minutes either at the beginning or the close of the workday to plan the coming day's work. Prepare a task list or update an ongoing list and complete the tasks according to their order of importance or to meet deadlines. Keep the list at hand as you work. Check it frequently. This list should guide you through your daily activities. When a task is completed, indicate this on the list. Tasks not completed can be carried over to the next day's list. Be alert, however, to any item that seems to

systematic: methodical, well organized, orderly, efficient

peak: a period of increased work activity

slack: a period of decreased work activity

Figure 7-1.3

A task list details work or meetings for the day.

🔘 Tasks - Microsoft Outlook
File Edit View Favorites Tools Actions Help

| Tasks ▾ |

🗋	❗	📎	Subject	Due Date	% Complete
			Click here to add a new Task		
⊟ Categories : A (2 items)					
☑	❗		Prepare minutes from the sales meeting and distribute	Fri 1/4/2002	0%
☑	❗		Send an e-mail announcing a staff meeting for next Monday	Fri 1/4/2002	0%
⊟ Categories : B (3 items)					
☑			Call Karen to get data for Perez conference	Fri 1/4/2002	0%
☑			Prepare draft of Section A of the Roberts year-long project	Fri 1/4/2002	0%
☑			Call McPhetter to coordinate travel dates to sales meeting	Fri 1/4/2002	0%
⊟ Categories : C (2 items)					
☑	↓		Research purchase options for PDAs for sales force	None	0%
☑	↓		Delete backup copies of old vendor agreement files	None	0%

CHAPTER 7: TIME AND WORKSTATION MANAGEMENT

be carried over too many times. Perhaps it should be broken down into smaller segments, or perhaps you are procrastinating in completing the task. Your task list can be a simple handwritten or keyed list. If you have the software available, your list may be created using a calendar program or personal information management software that allows you to manage appointments and schedule tasks as well as other functions.

Set Priorities

Once you have identified tasks for the day, rank them on your task list and complete the most important ones first. To determine the priority of the tasks, ask yourself these questions:

- How much time will the task require?
- By what date (time) should the task be completed?
- Are others involved in completing the task?
- What will happen if this task is not completed on time?
- Do I have all of the information (or materials) I need to complete the task?

At times you may need to discuss your priorities with coworkers or a supervisor to be certain that you agree on the order for doing tasks. Once you set your priorities, finish the tasks in their priority order. Remain **flexible**, however, about revising your priorities as circumstances change.

flexible: able to adapt or change as necessary

Ana Maria's task list for tomorrow is shown in Figure 7-1.3. Notice that she has identified the tasks as Category A, B, or C. The A-level tasks need immediate attention or completion. B-level tasks can be done once the A-level tasks have been completed. C-level tasks have no specific deadline, but can be done when the A and B tasks have been completed. If the item is a long-term project, the portion of the task that should be finished that day is listed.

WORKPLACE **CONNECTIONS**

Before Ana Maria left work, she jotted down the tasks she needed to complete the next day at work. She checked her task list for any unfinished items to be carried over to the current list. She also checked her calendar and her supervisor's calendar for any **pertinent** notes. Her calendar contained a reminder notation that the national sales meeting would be held three weeks from tomorrow. Jim McPhetter, a regional sales manager, is to accompany her to the meeting.

pertinent: to the point, relevant

Control Large Projects

Sometimes, getting started on a large project is difficult even though it may be very important. Smaller tasks can be checked off your task list with ease; a large task may seem overwhelming. Do not let the size of a project keep you

Topic 7-1: *Time Management and Reminder Systems*

from getting organized and moving toward satisfactory completion of the task. Follow these suggestions for handling a large project:

- Break the large project into smaller tasks.
- Determine the steps to be taken in each of the smaller tasks.
- Establish deadlines for each section or smaller task and meet those deadlines.
- Look for ways to improve your procedures and simplify the completion of the project.
- If the large project is one that will be repeated periodically, record your procedures and suggestions you want to follow in the future for improvements.

Simplify Your Work

work simplification: process of improving the procedures for doing work

Work simplification is the process of improving the procedures for getting work done. The process often involves simplifying some steps and eliminating others. Your goal is to use the most efficient procedure for completing a task. As you complete a task, be aware of the steps you are completing. Eliminate any unnecessary steps and/or details. Consider alternative methods for completing the task. Are those methods more efficient than those you are using? Look at the task and your procedures objectively to find ways to improve your productivity.

WORKPLACE **CONNECTIONS**

Yoshi uses the address book feature of his personal information management software to store names; addresses; work, fax, and home telephone numbers; e-mail addresses; and specific notes about the clients and coworkers he contacts on a regular basis. Yoshi's e-mail, word processing, and database programs can access information from the address book—reducing the time needed to rekey the information. For example, when Yoshi wants to key a letter to send to all his clients, he can use his address book as the data source for names and addresses for a form letter.

Analyze the Workflow

Consider the information and work assignments you receive and those you forward to others. Ask yourself these questions:

- Does the flow of work to my desk make good use of my time and effort? of everyone's time and effort?
- Does the flow of work provide the right information to customers or others outside the company in a timely fashion?
- Are the materials and equipment needed to complete my work readily at hand or nearby?
- Am I using the capabilities of my office equipment and software to their fullest extent?

CHAPTER 7: TIME AND WORKSTATION MANAGEMENT

Your answers to these questions should provide clues to simplifying your work. Incorporate these suggestions into your workflow analysis:

- Group and complete similar tasks together. For example, if you need photocopies of the letters you are preparing, make them all at once rather than making several trips to the copier. If you have several related phone calls to make, try to make them in sequence.

- Combine tasks if doing so will increase your efficiency. For example, if you plan to leave a request at the records center for a series of files you need to complete a report and the records center is near the company cafeteria, stop by the records center on your way to lunch.

- Determine how to best organize and arrange the equipment and supplies you use to complete a task. For example, if you cross a room every few minutes to retrieve pages from a printer, perhaps you can reorganize the placement of the equipment to provide a smoother flow of work.

- Enlist the help of others when you have an important deadline to meet and the workload is overwhelming. Be sure to **reciprocate** when the roles are reversed.

reciprocate: repay in kind

Handle Information Overload

When the amount of information you receive on a daily basis becomes overwhelming, you are experiencing information overload. Being able to provide timely information to the right person at the right time means that you will be responsible for effectively handling many types of records and documents you encounter. You will save time (yours and others') by trying to handle each file or piece of paper just once. Take any needed action immediately if that is appropriate, or note the task on your task list for completion at the proper time. In this way, the amount of information you receive will not become overwhelming. A good rule of thumb is to make a decision about how to handle every message, piece of paper, or file the first time you view it.

Reminder Systems

As an office worker, you must keep track of appointments, meetings, travel dates, and deadlines. Perhaps the most widely used device for keeping track of such items is a calendar. A reminder file, arranged **chronologically**, also can be helpful by providing a convenient place to keep notations of tasks to be performed on specific dates.

chronologically: arranged in order of time

Calendars

Calendars, time-management systems, and electronic organizers are useful tools for recording deadlines, appointments, telephone numbers and addresses, and daily or monthly reminders.

Manual Systems

A well-maintained desk calendar can assist you in keeping track of the many tasks and deadlines in your job, as well as being helpful to others who may have access to it. Figure 7-1.4 shows commonly used manual calendars on which appointments, deadlines, meetings, or other important data can be written.

Topic 7-1: *Time Management and Reminder Systems*

Figure 7-1.4

Manual time-management systems can help you plan and organize tasks.

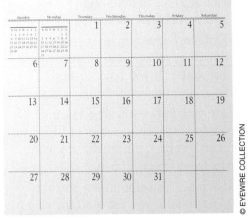 

Personal planners, also called day planners or organizers, are small notebooks that contain a calendar and space for recording appointments, listing tasks, writing notes, and keeping a contacts list. Many businesspeople find these manual aids very helpful in organizing tasks and schedules.

Wall calendars also are useful when large projects or those involving a number of people are broken into various small tasks with many deadlines. By displaying the wall calendar, you and others can keep track of deadlines.

Electronic Systems

Electronic organizers may be used in the same way as paper-based systems to keep track of project deadlines, appointments, and work schedules. Rather than recording information on paper, the information is entered into a computer program.

minimal: smallest or least possible

Calendar and personal information management (PIM) programs have various features. Some programs allow only **minimal** information to be entered. Others include task lists, additional notes regarding appointments or projects, deadlines, and completion dates. Some programs sound an alarm to remind users of specific engagements or deadlines. PIM programs usually include an electronic address book where you can record contact information for coworkers, clients, and other people or companies. Programs that include more advanced features for planning large or long-term projects are sometimes called scheduling or **project management programs**.

project management programs: software with advanced features for planning large or long-term tasks

WORKPLACE **CONNECTIONS**

Donna uses a program to track her weekly schedule. The calendar shows an 8:30 a.m. staff meeting that the supervisor has scheduled for Monday of this week as well as several other appointments. She can print the information, make a note regarding the meeting, or forward the message electronically to a coworker as a reminder.

CHAPTER 7: TIME AND WORKSTATION MANAGEMENT

Personal Digital Organizers

Personal digital organizers fall under a variety of names: electronic calendars or schedulers, personal information managers (PIMs), personal data managers, and personal digital assistants (PDAs). Basic features of personal digital organizers include storing telephone numbers and addresses, e-mail addresses, appointments, task lists, and **recurring** events. The more sophisticated electronic organizers can:

- Recognize handwriting
- Automatically track telephone calls
- Access and send e-mail messages
- Work with other programs such as word processors or spreadsheet software
- Do currency conversion calculations
- Upload data to or download data from desktop or laptop computers
- Record notes of telephone calls
- Recognize schedule conflicts
- Sound alarms as reminders of meetings or deadlines
- Provide space for writing memos

Some personal digital assistants can share data with calendar or personal information management computer programs, allowing the user to coordinate schedules easily.

personal digital organizer: electronic device for storing contact information and scheduling appointments and tasks

recurring: repetitive, ongoing, regular

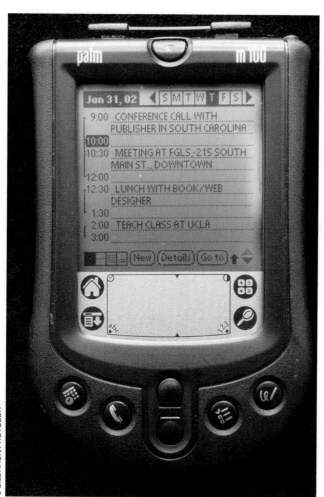

© BILL ARON/PHOTOEDIT

Figure 7-1.5

Personal digital assistants provide a variety of calendar features.

Topic 7-1: *Time Management and Reminder Systems*

Scheduling Appointments

Typically, you will have your own calendar to maintain. You also may make appointments and schedule meetings for coworkers. People request appointments in different ways: in person, by telephone, by letter or memo, or by e-mail. Although the manner in which you respond to these requests may vary, the basic information you need will be the same:

Who: Name, e-mail address, and telephone number of the individual requesting the appointment

When: Date, time, and approximate length of appointment

Where: Location of the appointment

Why: Purpose of meeting

Responding to Appointment Requests

When you receive a request for an appointment, check the calendar to determine whether the date and time requested are available. If not, you may suggest alternative appointment dates and times. By knowing the purpose of the meeting, you can determine and provide all supporting materials needed. To maintain a calendar properly, clarify the following points:

- To what extent do you have authority to make appointments for others?
- When should you check with others before making appointments?
- At what regular times are appointments not to be made, such as the first half-hour of the day?
- To what extent will the manager or coworkers make appointments without checking with you?
- Does the person for whom the appointment is made want to know the purpose of each appointment you schedule?

Figure 7-1.6

This executive is checking for schedule conflicts with her office assistant before recording an appointment.

The authority you have to make appointments will depend in great part on the nature of your business. For example, if you work in a doctor's office, most of the appointment requests would be from patients. You would be expected to schedule appointments without having to verify each one with the doctor. On the other hand, you may work in a general office where both you and your coworkers make appointments. You must agree on procedures that will allow you to operate effectively. Follow these guidelines when making appointments:

- Do not schedule overlapping appointments. Try to determine the amount of time needed for each one. Leave some time unscheduled between appointments to allow for meetings that run longer than planned, to return telephone calls, or to prepare for the next appointment.

- Keep a complete calendar. Record names, telephone numbers, e-mail addresses, and other pertinent information.

- Use legible handwriting to record entries on handwritten calendars. Avoid crossing out and rescheduling over scratched-off entries. To make changes easily, write appointment information in pencil.

- If you make appointments for a manager or coworker, you may need to set a tentative time for the appointment and then confirm that time with the individual. Determine a symbol to designate confirmed appointments. As appointments are confirmed, record the symbol. Commonly used symbols include a check mark, an asterisk, or an underscore of the individual's name.

- If you are responsible for keeping a calendar for others, provide a daily listing of appointments and reminders at the beginning of the workday. Show the appointments for the day in chronological order.

- Keep the previous year's appointment calendar. You may find it necessary to refer back to a calendar to find needed information. If you use an electronic calendar, print a copy of the calendar before deleting the data or save the information in an electronic file.

Entering Recurring Items

Some meetings and tasks are performed weekly, monthly, quarterly, or annually. As you set up your calendar at the beginning of the year, enter the recurring meetings and tasks on both your calendar and your coworkers' or work group's calendar as appropriate. If you block out the times for these recurring items, both you and others will know what time is available for scheduling other appointments.

Coordinating Calendars

If both you and your coworkers schedule appointments using desk calendars, you need to coordinate appointment calendars so that they are consistent and up to date. Adjustments to schedules are usually made at the beginning or the end of the workday. They include confirming tentative appointments, rescheduling appointments, deleting canceled appointments, changing time allotments, and preparing materials for the appointments.

You may use an electronic calendar program for your individual schedule or to set up group activities. An electronic calendar that resides on the computer network often can be updated by everyone using the calendar. Changes made are reflected instantly and may be viewed by anyone accessing the calendar.

Donna needs to schedule a meeting with six other people. She can access a program on the company's computer network to check the schedules of the six people for times available for the meeting. She can either check all of the schedules herself or she can enter the names of the people she wants to attend the meeting and a general time frame. The program then will look at everyone's schedule and the other **parameters** she entered to find a meeting time. Depending on the program available to her, she also might be able to schedule a meeting room.

parameters: guidelines, criteria

Tickler Files

A **tickler file** is a chronological system for keeping track of future actions. A paper-based tickler file is divided into 12 monthly divisions with 31 daily parts for each day of the month. Tickler files can be set up using index cards or file folders.

tickler file: a chronological system for keeping track of future actions

Reminders similar to those used in a tickler file also can be recorded on a computer using a calendar or **desktop organizer program**. You enter data into the program related to a task for a particular date. On that date, a reminder for that task appears on your screen. A reminder for a task entered using Microsoft Outlook is shown in Figure 7-1.7.

desktop organizer program: computer software used to schedule appointments and tasks and manage contact information

Store or record in a tickler file items requiring future action. Assume your employer says to you, "Please call the Morgan Company on Monday and make an appointment for us to discuss our purchasing contract with them." You would prepare a reminder to make the phone call and record it under next Monday's date.

As soon as you become aware of a deadline or a detail that needs to be checked in the future, place a notation in your tickler file or software program under the relevant day. Check your file each morning and note those items requiring attention for the current day. Complete the appropriate action for each item. Using this procedure will help your work flow smoothly.

Figure 7-1.7

Reminders help ensure that tasks are completed on time.

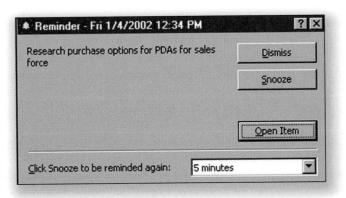

CHAPTER 7: TIME AND WORKSTATION MANAGEMENT

1. Define time management. Why is time management important to office workers?

2. Identify and describe common time-wasters in the office.

3. Describe the procedures you can use to handle your time obligations effectively.

4. Define workflow analysis. What steps can you take to complete an analysis of your workflow?

5. What are reminder systems?

6. What steps can you complete to analyze how you spend your time?

7. What is a personal digital organizer? Name some common features of a digital organizer.

8. What does work simplification involve?

9. What guidelines should you follow in scheduling appointments?

10. To maintain calendars effectively and efficiently, what points should be discussed and clarified with your manager or coworkers?

11. What is the purpose of a tickler file? What types of software can be used to enter reminders electronically?

Making Decisions

Ana Maria arrived at the office a few minutes early to review the items on her task list for the day. Just as she was about to begin, her supervisor arrived and told Ana Maria she had received a call at home last night. The national sales meeting scheduled for three weeks from today had been moved to one week from today because of an emergency. Ana Maria said to Ms. Baldwin: "This definitely changes the priorities for today." The items that Ana Maria had on her task list for today are shown below. She had not prioritized them.

- Revise sales contract for national sales meeting in three weeks.
- Complete weekly sales report due in three days.
- Start planning monthly sales meeting two weeks from today.
- Call Tom about the Patterson report for the monthly sales meeting.
- Call Lisa for lunch.
- Look in tickler file.
- Check e-mail messages.
- Schedule room for monthly sales meeting in two weeks.
- Make airline and hotel reservations for national sales meeting.
- Verify travel expense vouchers.
- Replenish desk supplies.

1. Think about the changes Ana Maria needs to make in her task list. List the items that will be affected by the supervisor's news. Will other items be added to her task list? If yes, list them.

2. Prioritize the items to reflect the change in the date and time of the national sales meeting. Key a revised task list.

Reinforcing English Skills

You work in the human resources department of Raleigh Corporation, a manufacturer of modular business furniture. Your supervisor, Florita Langford, has prepared a punctuation test to be administered to job applicants. She asks you to complete the punctuation test to be sure that the instructions are clear before she has large quantities of the test printed.

1. Open and print the data file **Test.pdf**, which contains the test.
2. Follow the instructions to complete the test.

COMPOSITION
INTEGRATED DOCUMENT
SPREADSHEET
WORD PROCESSING

Topic 7-1   ACTIVITY 1

Analyzing a Time Log

As you have learned in this topic, managing your time and developing an orderly approach to your work are important for your success on the job. In this activity, you will complete a daily time log. After you have charted your activities, you will use your chart to help you determine your most and least productive time periods.

1. Prepare a time-use log similar to the one shown in Figure 7-1.2 on page 279 using your spreadsheet software. Use 15-minute time intervals. Prepare the chart to cover your entire waking day; for example, 6:30 a.m. until 11:00 p.m. for one week. Print seven copies of the log, one for each day.

2. Complete your time-use log. Record your activities every 15 minutes as you progress through each day and evening. Record all your activities: studying, attending class or going to work, watching TV, talking on the telephone, eating, and so on.

3. Enter the data from your handwritten logs into your spreadsheet. Summarize your time spent by hours into categories: for example, school, work, leisure, sleep, hobbies, and so on. Use an *Other* category to group activities that occurred only once or twice for very short periods. Create a pie chart showing the percentages of time spent in each different category as part of your total time.

4. Analyze your time log. Identify the hours where you used your time most productively as well as those hours where you wasted your time. During what hours do you get the most accomplished? During what hours do you tend to waste your time?

5. Write a short report titled *TIME USE ANALYSIS* discussing the analysis of your time-use log. Include the pie chart in your written summary. Format the report in unbound report style. Describe what you intend to do differently as a result of your time analysis.

COMPOSITION
SPREADSHEET
WORD PROCESSING

Topic 7-1   ACTIVITY 2

Long-Term Portfolio Project

As an office worker, you will need to prioritize work to fulfill responsibilities and meet deadlines. Office work often involves planning and completing long-term projects. In this activity, you will plan, schedule, and complete a long-term project: a portfolio to display your work.

The general purpose of a portfolio is to demonstrate your skills and abilities related to work. A portfolio can contain samples of your work, awards or other recognitions, certificates or degrees related to training or education, a description of assignments or projects that have been successfully completed, and letters or recommendations related to your work abilities. A good portfolio can be helpful in finding a job.

1. This project should be completed four to six weeks from now. You and your instructor should agree on the specific timeline for this activity. Consult with your instructor to determine the deadline for completing the project.

2. List the steps to complete the portfolio. For example, define clearly the purpose for your portfolio, research portfolio layouts, schedule time to work on the portfolio, collect materials (classroom and other), create a tentative layout, and plan initial documents to go into the portfolio.

3. List the materials and resources you will need to complete the portfolio, such as folders, time, money, paper, dividers, notebooks, classroom projects, and so forth.

4. List the people you need to contact to complete the project: instructors, administrators, students, parents, businesspeople, etc.

5. Construct a tentative long-range schedule, using spreadsheet software to list the dates and tasks to be completed by specific dates. (Hint: Enter your ending date or deadline first.) Enter a title and beginning date on your schedule to make it uniquely yours. Print a copy of your schedule to use as you complete your portfolio project.

6. Follow your plan to prepare the portfolio. Make a note of the changes that have to be made to your original schedule as you complete your project. Were your deadlines realistic? Were the people available at the times you listed? Did you find the materials and resources available when you needed them? Did you follow your schedule? If no, why not?

7. Write a short report in unbound style summarizing your experiences as you created the portfolio. Discuss the factors listed above and your own observations. Include in your summary a copy of your beginning and ending schedule for comparison purposes.

8. Display or share your portfolio with other class members. Update your portfolio periodically as you gain new skills, complete training, or produce documents that will demonstrate your skills effectively.

Management and Office Safety

OBJECTIVES

- Explain the importance of an organized workstation
- Identify factors related to ergonomics and their importance to the office worker
- Discuss the importance of routine maintenance and care of office equipment
- Describe significant safety and security procedures for the office
- Create a presentation about office safety

As an office worker, you must be able to manage your work effectively to be productive. Proper lighting, the arrangement of your materials, and the design of your workstation contribute to your productivity. Most companies make efforts to provide physically comfortable and safe environments for their office employees. Your responsibility is to keep your work area well organized and to be aware of safety and security issues that affect you in the office environment.

Workstation Management

Your workstation is a key component of your work environment. A **workstation** is the physical area in which a worker performs his or her job. A typical workstation provides a work surface and space for equipment and supplies.

Manage Your Workstation

Arrange your workstation so that you have easy access to the items used frequently, such as the computer keyboard, telephone, supplies, and reference materials. Many companies use **modular** workstations made up of interchangeable components, such as sound-absorbing wall panels, storage areas, and a desktop surface. Interchangeable components permit the workstation to be arranged to meet the company's and the worker's individual needs.

workstation: physical area in which a worker performs a job

modular: made up of interchangeable components

Figure 7-2.1

Many companies provide flexible workstations that can be arranged to meet specific user needs.

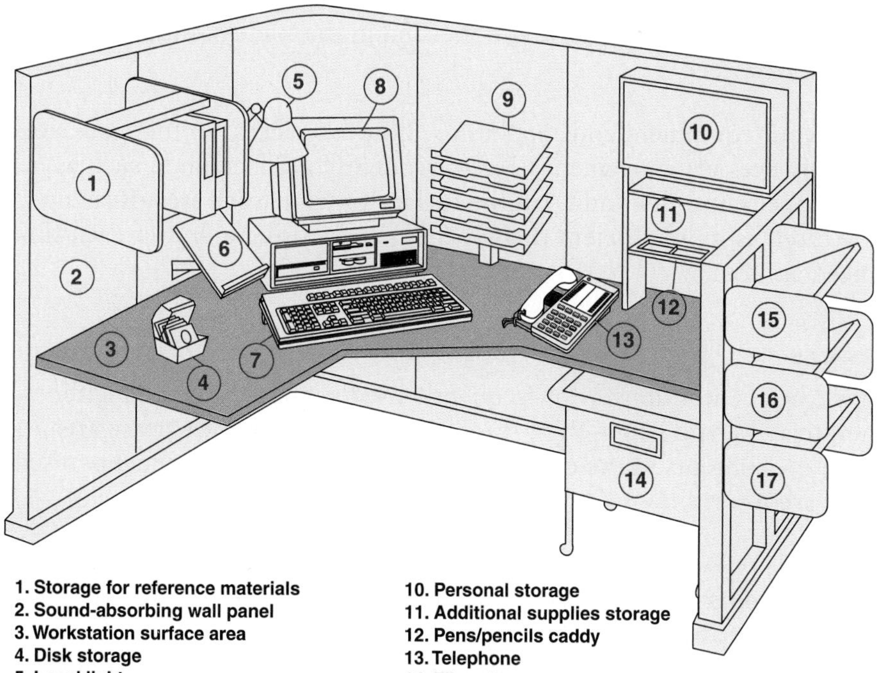

1. Storage for reference materials
2. Sound-absorbing wall panel
3. Workstation surface area
4. Disk storage
5. Local light
6. Document holder
7. Keyboard
8. Computer monitor
9. Forms caddy
10. Personal storage
11. Additional supplies storage
12. Pens/pencils caddy
13. Telephone
14. Files storage
15. In-basket
16. Out-basket
17. Additional basket

Figure 7-2.2

An organized desktop area will enhance productivity.

© CORBIS/STOCK MARKET

The effective organization of your workstation increases your efficiency. A functional work area is one that is well maintained, well equipped, well organized, and efficiently managed. Figure 7-2.2 displays a work area that is arranged for productivity and efficiency. Give specific attention to managing the desktop area; your desk drawers; reference materials; and office equipment, supplies, and accessories.

Desktop Area

Keep your workstation's surface clear. Clutter on the desktop can cause unnecessary delays as you search for papers or objects. Remove materials that do not relate to your current project. Put descriptive labels on file folders and place documents that are not needed in the folders. Place the folders in your file drawer.

Arrange your equipment and supplies to allow easy access so that you avoid making unnecessary movements. Keep frequently used supplies, such as pencils and paper clips, in a caddy on the surface of your work area. Reaching for the caddy is more efficient than opening and closing a drawer each time you need an item.

Drawers

Reserve your center drawer for frequently used supplies, such as a letter opener, scissors, and paper clips, that are not needed on the surface area. Arrange the contents of the center drawer so that the most frequently used supplies are toward the front where you can reach them easily.

The top side drawer may be used to store stationery supplies or to lay file folders containing current work so that they are at hand when you need them. You avoid cluttering the desktop by putting the file folders in a specific location in your desk. In this way, you also can protect any confidential items.

A desk also may contain either a file drawer or additional side drawers. A file drawer can be used to store files that are referred to often but are not in current use. Other drawers can be used to store supplies.

CHAPTER 7: TIME AND WORKSTATION MANAGEMENT

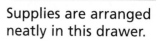

Figure 7-2.3

Supplies are arranged neatly in this drawer.

Reference Materials

The nature of your job will determine which references you will use most often. Some items may be in print form, while others may be accessed via your computer. Reference materials that should be accessible at your workstation may include a dictionary, a **thesaurus**, telephone directories, company and office reference manuals, safety handbooks, and equipment and software manuals. Other reference items used less often may include an almanac, atlas, and vendor supply catalogues.

thesaurus: book of words with synonyms

Supplies and Accessories

Office employees use a variety of supplies and accessories to do their jobs. In fact, the right resources help you perform your job more efficiently. What you need at your workstation will depend on your particular job. An adequately stocked workstation is essential to your productivity. If you run out of supplies in the middle of a critical task, you could lose valuable work time by stopping to gather needed supplies. Also, you run the risk of not completing the task on time. Use supplies properly for best results and to save money. Follow these guidelines:

- Select the quality of the supply according to the nature and importance of the task. For example, if you are preparing a rough draft of an important letter, don't use expensive letterhead paper. Use a lower-quality paper for the rough draft and the letterhead paper for the final copy.

- Learn to read product labels for the correct use of a product. For example, paper designed for use in a laser printer may not work well in an inkjet printer.

- Look for ways to conserve supplies. For example, reuse file folders by placing new file folder labels over the old ones. To save paper, preview documents carefully onscreen before printing.

- Do not **hoard** supplies in your workstation. Check your workstation periodically. If you have not used a supply item in several weeks, perhaps it should be returned to the supply cabinet.

hoard: collect in great numbers

Topic 7-2: *Workstation Management and Office Safety*

Office Equipment

preventive maintenance: servicing equipment and replacing parts to prevent failure

Because the condition of your equipment affects the quality of your work, you will want to keep your equipment in top working order. To get dependable service from your equipment, you will need to practice **preventive maintenance** and give your equipment routine care. This involves servicing equipment and replacing parts while the equipment is functioning properly in order to prevent failure. Fewer repairs are necessary when equipment is cared for properly on a regular basis. By practicing preventive maintenance, you can extend the life of your equipment over a longer period of time. Follow these maintenance guidelines:

troubleshooting: finding and solving minor problems

- Learn how to use and care for the equipment properly. Read and understand the manufacturer's operating instructions. Follow the **troubleshooting** guidelines so that you are able to recognize and correct minor problems.

- Inspect and clean equipment regularly. Know the basic care routines your equipment requires. Establish a regular inspection schedule. Perform the preventive measures (such as cleaning and replacements) recommended by the manufacturer.

- Report problems immediately. When you spot a potential problem, take steps to prevent it from occurring or report it to the appropriate person. Many minor problems can be corrected before they become serious and require costly repair.

Manage Ergonomic Factors

ergonomics: study of the effects of the work environment on the health and well-being of employees

Ergonomics is the study of the effects of the work environment on the health and well-being of employees. How well a workstation and its components—chairs, desks, lighting, and computer equipment—are designed can influence your productivity, efficiency, and physical well-being. Figure 7-2.5 focuses on the height and angle dimensions of an ergonomically sound workstation. This workstation allows the user to adjust the chair, desk, lighting, and computer equipment.

Figure 7-2.4

By practicing preventive maintenance, you can extend the life of office equipment.

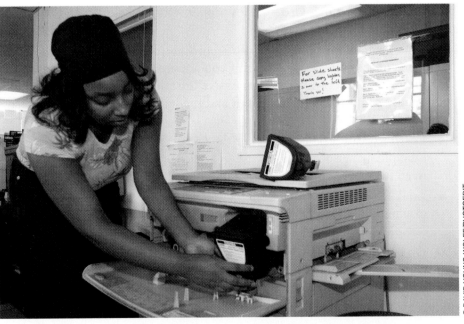

© DAVID YOUNG-WOLFF/PHOTOEDIT

CHAPTER 7: TIME AND WORKSTATION MANAGEMENT

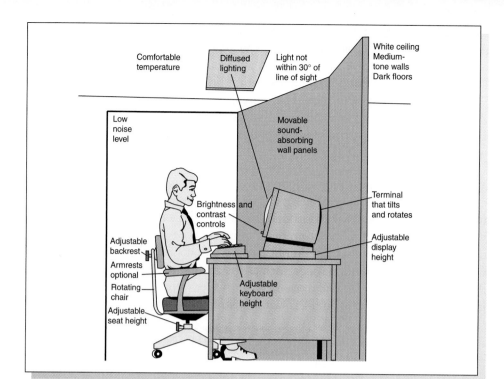

Figure 7-2.5

Ergonomic factors affect productivity.

A well-designed chair is essential because many office workers spend much of their time sitting. However, ergonomic seating involves more than just quality. An ergonomic chair must be adjustable, like the one shown in Figure 7-2.6. Office workers should be able to adjust their chairs to fit individual physical requirements for comfort and good posture.

The height of the desktop should allow your elbows to be parallel to the computer keyboard and floor as shown in Figure 7-2.5. This arrangement prevents unnecessary strain on the arms and wrists. Keep the desktop clear of materials not related to the current task.

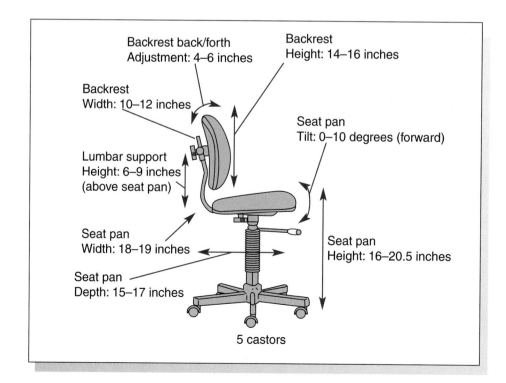

Figure 7-2.6

Some experts believe a chair is the most vital component of a workstation.

Topic 7-2: *Workstation Management and Office Safety*

ambient: surrounding, on all sides

Two kinds of lighting are often found in workstations: **ambient** and task. Ambient lighting is provided by overhead light fixtures for the entire work area. Although you may not be able to adjust the overhead lighting, you can adjust the arrangement of your workstation. Task lighting focuses on the immediate work area and should be adjustable for your specific needs. Adjust the task lighting to prevent glare on your computer monitor or the desktop. Eliminate dark or dimly lit areas where you may have to retrieve files or work away from your desktop.

Your computer monitor should be placed at eye level, as shown in Figure 7-2.5, to help reduce eyestrain and neck pain. Glare on the monitor often contributes to eyestrain. Common symptoms of eyestrain are teary or burning eyes, blurred vision, and headaches. Glare from outside light can be prevented by placing the computer monitor so that you do not face a window or have your back to a window. Peripheral input devices, such as the mouse, should be located next to the computer keyboard. The movement of the arm from the keyboard to the input device should be natural and without strain.

FOCUS ON . . .

Workplace Wellness

Wellness in the workplace is now an important focus in business. Wellness includes issues such as stress management, nutrition and weight management, exercise, and balancing work and family life. Employers know that when these lifestyle factors are controlled, everyone benefits. This is why companies are consulting with wellness experts to help keep employees healthy and happy. As a result, medical expenses can decrease and productivity can increase.

With the workforce increasing and Americans spending more hours at work, the office has become an important place for employees to understand health and wellness. The Wellness Councils of America (WELCOA) give tips and strategies for health and well-being.* For example, find ways to avoid interruptions throughout the workday. Interruptions waste valuable time and cause stress as deadlines approach. Find time to recharge during the day with a nutritional snack. An apple or raisins can provide an energy boost.

Get an adequate amount of rest and sleep. Good sleep habits will help avoid unnecessary stress to the body.

Nutrition and weight management are important parts of wellness. Many Americans with busy work schedules find making time for exercise and preparing healthy meals difficult. Some of the ways employers can promote nutrition and weight management include:

- Providing purified water or juice as an alternative to soft drinks
- Posting the calories and fat grams of foods served in the company dining room
- Encouraging employees to use the stairs instead of the elevators as a way to include physical exercise in the workday

When wellness is addressed in the workplace, the cost of absenteeism and lost productivity decreases while employee morale and well-being increases. For more information on wellness, visit the WELCOA Web site at www.welcoa.org.

* The Wellness Councils of America. Online. Available: http://www.welcoa.org. February, 2002.

298

Manage Your Office Health

Being aware of the physical responses your body has to your work procedures and habits will enhance your job satisfaction, comfort, and productivity. The following guidelines may help you complete your work without feelings of strain, fatigue, or other physical discomforts:

- Learn to adjust the workstation components for the best fit to your work habits and procedures. Follow the manufacturer's recommended work postures and practices even if at first they feel unnatural.

- Take rest breaks often—at least 15 minutes every two hours. Do not sit in front of your computer monitor or at your desk for long uninterrupted periods of time. Arrange your work so that you have to get out of your chair and walk to the copier or to the supply cabinet. If you feel yourself becoming bored, stop working and do simple breathing or relaxation exercises.

- Learn stretching exercises for your hands, wrists, arms, and fingers to relieve pressure on them. **Carpal tunnel syndrome** is a repetitive strain injury that occurs when stress is placed on the hands, wrists, or arms while working at the computer keyboard or using computer input devices for prolonged periods of time.

- Focus your eyes away from your computer monitor often. Remember to blink your eyes. If possible, face your computer monitor against a wall to avoid looking directly out of a window or into glare from other bright light sources. Place antiglare filters similar to the one shown in Figure 7-2.7 over the monitor screen. Filters reduce glare, static electricity, and dirt and smudge buildup on the screen. Adjust the screen brightness to a contrast level that is comfortable for you. Adjust the screen angle so that it is at eye level or slightly lower.

- Learn and use good posture: back straight against the back of your chair and feet flat on the floor. To enhance your posture, adjust your chair so that your feet do not dangle off the floor. Use a footrest if your feet don't touch the floor. Use a back pad to keep your back in a straight line and adjust your computer monitor to the right height and angle for you.

carpal tunnel syndrome: a repetitive strain injury that occurs when stress is placed on the hands, wrists, or arms

Figure 7-2.7

Antiglare screens reduce glare and reflection from computer monitors.

© DAVID YOUNG-WOLFF/PHOTOEDIT

Topic 7-2: *Workstation Management and Office Safety*

- Arrange your work materials so that you do not have to overreach for the telephone or supplies, lift heavy binders or boxes, bend or stretch to reach files, or strain to use staplers or paper punches. Avoid repetitive motions for extended periods of time without taking a break.
- Report any prolonged physical discomfort that affects your work performance to your supervisor.

Marletta works long hours at her desk and computer. In the past, she often experienced sore wrists and eyestrain. After hearing a presentation about ergonomics at a workshop, Marletta realized she could take some simple steps to help prevent these problems. Now she takes breaks from the computer keyboard frequently to give her hands, wrists, and arms a chance to relax. She drops her arms to her side and dangles them to relieve tension. She also squeezes a handgripper to strengthen and relieve tension in her hands and wrists.

Marletta rearranged her workstation to reduce glare on the monitor from a nearby window. The addition of an antiglare screen eliminated the remaining glare problem. These measures resulted in reduced eyestrain. These small changes in Marletta's routine and the arrangement of her workstation can make a big difference in the long run.

Office Safety

Most of us think of the office as a safe place to work. Office workers are not required to use heavy equipment or power tools. They are seldom exposed to poisonous chemicals or dangerous working conditions. Yet, thousands of office workers have disabling accidents each year. Falling, tripping, or slipping account for many office accidents. Common causes of falls include drawers partially open, slippery floors, torn or loose carpeting, obstructions on stairs or in walkways, and dangling telephone or electrical cords.

Other causes of office accidents include faulty or poorly maintained equipment, collisions and obstructions, falling objects, fire and electrical hazards, and human carelessness. Potential safety problems can exist in any office. With knowledge of correct safety procedures, however, you can learn how to correct and report potential safety problems and prevent injury to yourself and your coworkers.

Accident Prevention

To many people, the office seems to hold little danger. Becoming aware of the potential safety hazards in an office is the first step to gaining control over unsafe procedures and conditions. Unfortunately, accident control often is imposed only after an accident occurs. An accident prevention approach should be used to decrease the chances that an undesirable incident will occur. Workers who develop positive safety attitudes are able to detect potential safety problems and take steps to eliminate them.

Molly came around the corner with her arms full of supplies for the supply cabinet. She could not see where she was going very well because her arms were so loaded down. She should not have been trying to carry so much, but she was trying to save a few steps to prevent having to make a second trip.

Laverne looked up from the phone to see Molly just a few feet from her open file drawer. When Laverne realized that Molly could not see where she was walking, she called, "Watch out!" Too late—Molly fell with a loud crash over the bottom file drawer. X-rays showed that Molly had broken her wrist while trying to catch herself in the fall. She was unable to resume her full duties for eight weeks.

This accident could have been prevented if Molly and Laverne had acted responsibly. Laverne should have closed the file drawer, and Molly should have carried the supplies in two trips rather than in one.

Workstation Safety

Most office employees spend the majority of their working time at their workstations. The wise safety practices you use at your own workstation will repay you in personal safety benefits. Remember the following safety pointers.

Desktop Area

As you work, you will occasionally use scissors and other sharp objects. Place them away from the edge of your workstation so they will not be knocked off easily. Pencils stored on the top of your desk with the sharp points up are dangerous; they are best stored flat or with points down. Use a staple remover, rather than your fingernail, to remove staples. Never examine a jammed stapler by holding it near your eyes or testing it over your finger.

Drawers

Keep your workstation drawers neat. Do not allow papers to collect to the point of clutter. If the drawers are cluttered, your hands could easily be punctured by hidden scissors, pins, or pencils. Sharp objects such as pins and thumbtacks should be placed in closed containers.

Even with these precautions, never reach blindly into a desk drawer or file drawer. Take time to look where you are placing your hands, even if you are rushed or are talking to someone. Close workstation and file drawers by the handle. Don't push a drawer shut by placing your hand at the top or side of the drawer. You may lose a fingernail or suffer a crushed finger or hand.

Chairs/Mats/Static Control

Most office chairs have casters, which are small wheels that provide ease of movement for the worker. This same ease of movement can

---

Professional Development Resources

- Human Factors and Ergonomics Society
  P.O. Box 1369
  Santa Monica, CA 90406-1369
  www.hfes.org

- Ted Pollock. "RX for Procrastination" (Time management). *Electric Light and Power.* August, 2001.

- William Van Winkle. "The Healthy Home Office" (Ergonomics). *Home Office Computing.* October, 2000.

- Timothy S. Mustard. "Telecommuting Safely" (Safety issues for workers who telecommute from home offices). *Occupational Hazards.* April, 2001.

- Ken Habeeb. "Avoiding Workplace Violence." *InfoWorld.* February 5, 2001.

- Search terms:
  time management
  work simplification
  personal digital organizer
  ergonomics
  office health and safety
  workplace violence

produce painful injury unless you look at the chair and hold onto its arms or seat as you sit down. When seated, be careful not to lean too far forward or backward to prevent falling out of the chair.

A chair mat is a vinyl pad placed underneath the chair to eliminate wear on the carpet from rolling the chair. Static control mats are designed for use on floors underneath workstations and computers. The static control mat safeguards valuable computer data and electronic equipment from possible harm from a charge of static electricity.

Chair mats and static control mats can cause you to trip, particularly if the edges are beginning to curl. Replace worn mats when they become a hazard.

Work Area Safety

In addition to your workstation, other objects in your immediate work area can either add to your comfort and work productivity or become a source of injury.

Office Furnishings

Learn how to use small furnishings, such as a step stool and paper cutter. In using a step stool with casters, step firmly in the middle of the stool. Never step to the side because this can cause the stool to slide out from under you. When using the paper cutter, keep your fingers away from the blade and never leave the blade up. Furniture with rough or sharp edges should be sanded or taped to prevent injury to employees and to prevent clothing from being torn. Report tears in carpets, burned-out lights, broken handles or mechanisms on equipment, and other potential hazards related to office furnishings to the appropriate person.

File drawers should be filled beginning with the bottom drawer of the cabinet and moving to the top drawer. They should be emptied from the top drawer down. When working with file cabinets, pull out only one drawer at a time so that you do not change the cabinet's center of gravity and cause it to tip over. Avoid placing objects that have the potential to harm you or your coworkers on top of filing cabinets. Coffeemakers or heavy plants can slip off the cabinet and cause serious injuries.

Electrical Equipment

Office equipment, such as electric staplers, electric pencil sharpeners, electric hole punchers, desk-side paper shredders, computers and related peripherals, adds to the convenience of office workers. With the increase in electrical and computer equipment in the office, many cords and cables become a safety hazard. Cables and cords should never extend into traffic areas. Do not overload electrical outlets. If necessary, purchase a power strip or **surge suppressor** made specifically for multiple appliances. An extension cord should be used only to extend the position of the electrical appliance, not to increase the power load.

surge suppressor: electrical outlet that controls unexpected sharp increases in electricity

Electrical cords or power strips, surge suppressors, and extension cords should be placed behind equipment or within the walls of the workstation. If cords must be placed where people walk and they present a tripping hazard, tape them down or cover them with materials made specifically for this purpose.

CHAPTER 7: TIME AND WORKSTATION MANAGEMENT

Figure 7-2.8

Extension cords often present a tripping hazard.

© DAVID YOUNG-WOLFF/PHOTOEDIT

General Office Equipment

You will want to keep the following safety procedures in mind when you use office equipment:

- When operating office equipment, follow the manufacturer's directions for safe and efficient equipment use.

- When you are operating equipment, avoid other activities that will distract you from the operation of the equipment.

- If you feel a tingling sensation, notice smoke, or smell something burning while you are operating the equipment, turn it off and investigate the problem or report it to the appropriate person immediately.

- Know where the power switches are located on the equipment in your general area. In the event of an emergency, power surge, or power outage, you may need to turn off the equipment.

Emergency Procedures

Learn **emergency procedures** immediately on beginning a new job. If your office does not have established procedures, do what you can to help initiate practices such as those described in the following paragraphs.

emergency procedures: steps to follow in time of trouble or danger

Topic 7-2: *Workstation Management and Office Safety*

Emergency Telephone Numbers

Emergency telephone numbers are used to seek help for an immediately dangerous situation. The most important are those of the company medical and security personnel, police and fire departments, paramedics, and the general emergency number for your area, such as 911.

Emergency numbers should be posted beside each telephone or, ideally, stored in each telephone's memory. The memory feature saves valuable time in an emergency. You press only one or two buttons, and the number is automatically dialed.

First Aid Procedures

First aid kits should be located conveniently within the office. They should be inspected frequently and restocked whenever supplies are used from the kit. Some firms will send an employee from each floor or work group for first aid training and/or CPR (cardiopulmonary resuscitation) classes. These courses are given periodically by the American Red Cross and other organizations. Each employee should know who has completed first aid training and who is qualified to help in the critical first minutes of an emergency. First aid posters can be placed where they can easily be seen to further assist employees.

Fires

Some companies prohibit the use of appliances, such as cup warmers and space heaters, because of their potential fire hazard. If appliances are allowed in your office, always unplug them when they are not in use and before leaving the office. Know the location of the nearest fire exit, fire alarm box, and fire extinguisher. Large office buildings generally have the fire alarm boxes and fire extinguishers in the same location patterns on each floor. Learn how to use the fire extinguisher and what type of fire it is intended to put out. Never attempt to fight a fire alone. Always have someone report it to the proper agency.

Figure 7-2.9

First aid kits should be easily accessible in office areas.

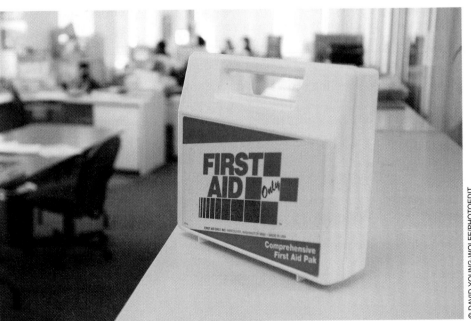

© DAVID YOUNG-WOLFF/PHOTOEDIT

Building Evacuation Plans

Learn the established escape routes and **evacuation** procedures for your building. Emergency exit routes should be posted in noticeable places throughout the building. Employees should know their individual responsibilities during a drill or evacuation. Who, for example, is responsible for checking conference rooms, restrooms, and other areas where the alarm may not be heard?

evacuation: leaving, clearing an area

WORKPLACE CONNECTIONS

Jacob, a new employee at Park Company, was impressed when he learned during his orientation that the owners were very concerned about employee safety. Jacob learned that established fire evacuation routes and routes to tornado shelters are posted in visible locations. The company holds fire and tornado safety drills on a monthly basis. He was also impressed to learn that the company sponsors classes held by the local fire department on the use of fire extinguishers, general fire safety, first aid, and CPR.

With the company-wide emphasis on safety, Jacob is confident he will be able to concentrate on his work without worrying about his personal safety.

Personal Security on the Job

Protection for yourself and your property requires continuous attention on your part. Most businesses strive to provide a safe and secure work environment for their employees. To support the company's effort in providing for your safety and security on the job, always use good common sense.

Protecting Personal Property

A purse left at a workstation, a jacket slung over the back of a chair or left in an unoccupied office, cash left out in plain sight—all are invitations to a would-be thief. Keep personal belongings out of sight and locked in a drawer, file cabinet, or employee locker or closet. The key to this drawer or other container should be issued only to the employee who is assigned its use.

Working Alone

Sometimes you may find it necessary to stay late at the office or to come in early. If your company has established security measures, follow the company procedures for being in the building during non-working hours. If no after-hours procedures exist, establish your own security routine and follow it. Follow these security procedures when you work alone:

- Always work near a phone and keep emergency telephone numbers handy.
- Lock all doors to your work area. Do not open the door to anyone you are not expecting or cannot identify.
- Get to know the cleaning staff and when to expect them.
- If you use the elevator to leave the building, do not enter the elevator if anyone is in it whom you find suspicious.

Topic 7-2: *Workstation Management and Office Safety*

- Avoid using a restroom that is located away from your work area.
- When working late, phone home before leaving the office to let someone know what time to expect you. If you live alone, call a friend before leaving the office and again when you get home to let her or him know you've arrived safely.
- Park your car near the building entrance and/or in a lighted parking lot. Check the parking lot visually before leaving the building. Have your car keys in your hand and ready to use. If security personnel are available, ask to be escorted to your car.

Building and Office Security

Building and office security measures are necessary safeguards. Many businesses take a serious approach to planning and analyzing security needs. Discontented workers, theft, sabotage, and fire are major security concerns of a business.

Many companies today have established security procedures to guard against employees who have been fired or who are experiencing pressures from work. Sometimes discontented or upset workers can pose a hazard to themselves and to their fellow workers. Be alert to changes in your coworkers' behavior and to statements they may make that sound like threats against employees or the company. Know the procedures for protecting yourself from these workers:

- Do not get involved in a verbal exchange.
- Leave the work area if you are feeling threatened and proceed to an area designated as safe.
- Report any unusual behavior to your supervisor and/or company security personnel.

The protection of computer-generated information and records is an issue in many companies. Entrance to secure areas is carefully controlled. In addition, privacy and protection for employees while on company property are important concerns.

Figure 7-2.10

Office security guards provide protection for workers and office property.

© RYAN MCVAY/PHOTODISC

Controlling Outsider Access

Although many businesses cannot operate without being open to the public, the public does not need uncontrolled access to all parts of most office buildings. Businesses use varied security means to safeguard their personnel and assets. In some areas, for example, the presence of a highly visible, centrally located security station with personnel in the lobby has proved effective.

Some companies have security personnel who make sure each visitor signs a log and gives his or her name, address, and the name of the person or office being visited. Other companies find it more convenient to send an employee to the lobby to escort the visitor back to the office. In smaller offices, the receptionist may be the controlling agent simply by being present in the front office.

Controlling Employee Access

Many medium- and large-sized businesses require positive identification of those employees who should have access to the buildings and grounds through the use of identification (ID) cards or badges. Photo ID cards, like the one shown in Figure 7-2.11, are issued by many companies. Your cooperation in wearing your ID helps ensure your personal safety and security on the job.

Figure 7-2.11

Some companies issue photo IDs or magnetically coded access cards to their employees.

Vikki
Foxx

© BILL ARON/PHOTOEDIT

Topic 7-2: *Workstation Management and Office Safety*

Businesses that must restrict employee entry to selected areas of a building often use a magnetically coded card as a substitute for keys. This card can be inserted by the employee into a magnetic card reader to gain access. If the card is authorized for entrance, the door opens.

Some companies use magnetically coded badges that can be sensed by electronic readers, referred to as proximity readers. As the wearer approaches a controlled access point, the electronic reader reads the code on the badge and transmits the information to a computer. This information provides a record of who enters and leaves designated areas, the time of entry, and in some instances, the time of exit—all valuable security information.

WORKPLACE CONNECTIONS

Olivia looked up to see a repairman coming through the doorway. "I'm here to check your computer. Apparently, you had a large electrical surge last night. Here's the order," he said, as he flashed a copy of a repair order in front of Olivia. "This will take a few minutes—why don't you just take a short break?"

Olivia got up from her terminal, but she was puzzled. She hadn't heard that an electrical surge had occurred. "Besides," she thought, "we have surge suppressors for the equipment." Olivia felt she should check this with her supervisor, Ms. Calibre.

Ms. Calibre was not aware of an electrical surge occurring either. "Let me check on this before we do anything," she said. Olivia stepped back into her office to see the repairman disconnecting the computer.

Repairman: *"Looks like I'll have to take your computer back to the shop for repairs."*

Olivia: *"You'll have to wait until my supervisor authorizes you to take the computer."*

Repairman: *"Well, I have several other computers to check. Why don't I come back after I've checked them and pick this one up."*

The repairman left hurriedly, and a minute or so later Olivia's supervisor appeared at the door: "No one authorized a computer repair check. We had better report this."

Ms. Calibre called the police immediately to report the incident. The police sergeant told her that several businesses had recently lost computers and other electronic equipment in this manner. "You're lucky to have an alert employee," the sergeant told Ms. Calibre. "None of the others questioned an unexpected repair check. When the employees returned from their 'short breaks,' their equipment was gone."

Detection Systems and Alarms

Companies often choose to use a combination of security systems and procedures. Detection systems and alarms reinforce other security measures. A detection system consists of **monitoring** devices and alarms that sense and signal a change in the condition of an area being protected. Some detection systems detect entry into the area while others are designed to detect movement in the area.

monitoring: warning, watching

Detection systems and alarms are designed to reduce a firm's reliance on an on-site security guard. Even if a firm has security officers, they cannot be at all stations at once. Closed-circuit television, as shown in Figure 7-2.12, can be used to provide continuous monitoring of corridors, entrances, or other sensitive areas. When used with a videotape recorder, closed-circuit television provides the firm with a record of significant events for review.

© G.D.T./STONE

Figure 7-2.12

Closed-circuit television provides continuous monitoring of the building and grounds.

Topic 7-2: *Workstation Management and Office Safety*

Reviewing the Topic

1. What is the guiding principle you should follow in planning the arrangement of any workstation?

2. Describe how you can organize your workstation (both desktop areas and drawers) to increase your productivity.

3. Discuss the guidelines an office worker should follow when using office equipment, supplies, and accessories.

4. Why is routine maintenance and care of office equipment important?

5. What are the safety practices you should follow in maintaining your own workstation?

6. What are the safety practices you should follow with regard to office furnishings and electrical and electronic equipment?

7. What are the safety practices you should follow with regard to general office equipment?

8. Describe the emergency office procedures you should learn immediately on starting a new job.

9. Describe some of the precautions you may take as an office worker to protect yourself and your personal property on the job.

10. How can you help ensure your personal security when you are working alone?

11. Explain the procedures businesses use to control access to their property and employees by other employees and by outsiders.

Thinking Critically

At a department meeting your manager, Mr. Joe Petersen, discusses a memo regarding company security. He shakes his head and says: "This is the second memo the managers have received about security leaks. One of our competitors has just introduced a new product, and it's identical to a product we have been working on. Apparently they discovered our plans. The president wants our thoughts on how to improve our product security. In addition to the main shredder in the reprographics center, he is suggesting a shredder for each office. Well, I'm just glad everyone in our department can be trusted."

As you hear this, you remember several situations you have observed in the office:

- You have seen poor photocopies—even photocopies of confidential material—discarded in the wastebasket.

- Computer printouts with product-testing results are left stacked next to the filing cabinets rather than being locked inside them.

- Workers often talk about current projects during their breaks.

- Workers have a habit of using the offices of other workers who are out of town or on vacation.

- Workers too freely give out unnecessary information to callers, such as telling a caller exactly where the individual is.

"Tell me," Mr. Petersen says, "do you think we need a shredder? What other measures can we take to tighten security? Please give this matter some thought and send me your ideas." How do you respond to him? What suggestions can you make for tightening office security?

1. Prepare a response to the questions to Mr. Petersen asks in the form of an e-mail message. Address the message to Jpeterson@trophe.com. (Save and print the message. Do not actually send the message to this address.) Prepare a memo instead if you do not have access to e-mail.

2. In the e-mail message, include suggestions for correcting the problems discussed as well as other security measures that you think would be effective.

Reinforcing English Skills

In this exercise, you will practice your writing and editing skills by preparing a letter from a rough draft.

1. Open and print the data file **Petty.pdf**, which contains the rough draft letter.

2. Key the letter. Correct all grammatical, spelling, number/word usage, capitalization, and punctuation errors in the letter. Insert paragraphs and reword the letter to correct errors where appropriate. Evaluate the letter with the five Cs of effective communication in mind.

3. Assume the letter will be printed on letterhead paper. Arrange the letter in an acceptable format and add any missing letter parts. Use your name in the signature block. Print one copy and sign the letter.

SPREADSHEET
WORD PROCESSING

Topic 7-2   ACTIVITY 1

Needs Assessment for Equipment

You are the administrative assistant for the information systems department of Wayne Electronics. Your department is responsible for purchasing all computer equipment for the company. The department head has received requests from several departments asking that he consider purchasing one or more multimedia projectors. Currently, employees rent a projector when it is needed.

You have been asked to do a needs assessment to determine whether renting or buying a projector is more cost effective for the company. A needs assessment involves gathering data about the proposed need, analyzing the data, and making a recommendation or decision about how to proceed.

1. Complete the data-gathering phase of the needs assessment. Prepare a memo form for Wayne Electronics using the appropriate headings. Compose a memo addressed to *Department Heads* to send to the manager of each department asking about the use of multimedia projectors by the department. Ask specific questions about how often a projector is used, the purpose of the presentation, the number of people attending the presentations, and the length of time the projector is rented for each presentation. Include any other questions you think are relevant. Ask the managers to include any other pertinent information they may have in their replies.

2. Analyze the information received from the other departments. Open and print the data file **Projector.pdf**, which contains replies from five departments. Use your spreadsheet software to record and summarize the information in the replies. Find the estimated total spent by all departments for renting multimedia projectors for a year.

3. Analyze the usage patterns for the projectors. Are they used regularly throughout the year or do several department members need a projector at the same time? Are different departments likely to need the projector at the same time?

4. Consider the sizes of the audiences for the various presentations. Will one projector be appropriate for most of the presentations? What is the maximum audience size the projector should be appropriate for?

5. Review the types of projectors available for purchase and their features by accessing office equipment Web sites or office equipment catalogs. Determine the type of projector that would be appropriate for most presentations given by employees. What is the cost of this projector and a spare bulb? How does this cost compare to the estimated annual rental cost for projectors?

6. Write a memo to your supervisor, Shawn Valdez, giving your recommendation for buying or continuing to rent projectors. Discuss how your data was collected. Summarize the information that led to your recommendation.

Topic 7-2   ACTIVITY 2

Preventive Maintenance and Care for Office Equipment

You work in the marketing department of Robert's Distributors. One of your duties is to make sure that all preventive maintenance is done on the office equipment in your department. Preventive maintenance is usually done by a qualified repair technician to prevent equipment breakdowns and prolong the life of the equipment.

PREVENTIVE MAINTENANCE SCHEDULE

Equipment	Month Purchased	Maintenance Period
Copier, high volume	February	Every 3 months
Copier, small convenience	January	Every 6 months
Fax machine with laser printer	October	Every 4 months
Laser printer, desktop	April	Every 12 months
Laser printer, high volume	October	Every 6 months

1. Each piece of equipment was purchased last year in the month shown in the preventive maintenance schedule. Based on the preventive maintenance schedule, which equipment will need preventive maintenance in April? Begin counting time until maintenance is needed with the month after purchase.

2. Will any pieces of equipment need preventive maintenance in May? If yes, which ones?

3. Assume January is the current month. How many times will the fax machine need preventive maintenance during the remainder of this year?

4. Assume March is the current month. In what month will the small convenience copier be scheduled for its next maintenance?

5. You are also responsible for routine care of all of the equipment. Because you are getting ready to leave on a two-week vacation, your supervisor has asked you to develop a set of procedures for routine care that your coworkers can follow in your absence. Open and print the data file **Care.pdf**, which contains notes you have been jotting down this week about equipment care.

6. Using your notes, key a schedule for routine equipment care activities for each piece of equipment. Your notes are in rough form and incomplete sentences. Edit, correct errors, and compose as needed to create procedures that are well written and easy to understand.

313

Summary

In this chapter, you learned the importance of managing your time and workstation effectively. The roles of both employee and employer in establishing and following office safety and security procedures also were discussed. Consider the points listed below as you reinforce your understanding of the topics in this chapter.

- Task management is vital to your success on the job. Although what you actually do in your job will depend on the nature of your company, you will need to plan and organize your work activities, whatever they may be.

- You will need to manage effectively the resources that support your work activities. The basic resources for this are your workstation and your time. Your workstation provides the physical space for you to do your job. By correctly organizing the equipment and supplies at your workstation, you can increase your productivity.

- Your time on the job must be channeled to ensure that time obligations are handled effectively and that time-wasters are eliminated.

- The typical office employee uses a variety of office supplies and equipment. Correctly selecting, using, and caring for office supplies are important cost reduction factors in an office. Office workers are expected to learn how to use office equipment properly and to do their part in properly maintaining it.

- Ergonomic factors related to the office contribute to your physical comfort and well-being, as well as to enhancing your productivity and efficiency.

- Organizations strive to maintain a safe and secure environment for all their employees. As an office worker, you should follow safe practices at your workstation. You should understand and follow all security measures established by your company.

Key Terms

accident prevention
analyze workflow
carpal tunnel syn-
drome
desktop organizer
program
ergonomics
evacuation plan
functional work
area
information
overload

modular
workstation
monitoring devices
office health and
safety
personal digital
organizer
preventive
maintenance
reminder systems
schedule appoint-
ments

task list
tickler file
time analysis
time log
time management
time-wasters
work simplification

SPREADSHEET

WORD PROCESSING

Chapter 7 ACTIVITY 1

Prioritize and Schedule Tasks

Your manager has asked you to plan and submit a tentative schedule for advertising a sale of office equipment to begin two months from today. She hands you a rough draft of the inventory list of the products that will be included in the sale. Items marked with an asterisk (*) will have to be ordered from the suppliers so that they arrive in time for the sale.

1. Create a task list for the sale. Open and print the data file **Tasks.pdf**, which contains a partial list.

2. Create a form that includes these columns: *Priority*, *Task*, and *Completed*. Place the items on the form in the Task column. Next, prioritize the items by ranking them in order of importance:

   A Most Important

   B Medium Importance

   C Least Important

3. Key the rank in the Priority column. If an item is listed as a C item, does it need to be completed at all? If not, delete the item. Are there other items that need to be added to this list? If yes, add these items.

4. Create a schedule for preparing for the office equipment sale. Use spreadsheet software to create the schedule.

   • List tasks to be completed from your task list in order by date using the dates when a task should be begun. Start with your ending deadline and work backward to create your schedule. For example, if a task should be completed one week before the sale and the task takes two weeks to complete, then list the task on the date three weeks prior to the sale.

   • Show dates when each task should be completed.

   • Include a column to check off tasks and confirm that they have been completed on time.

COMPOSITION
PRESENTATION
RESEARCH
TEAMWORK
WORD PROCESSING

Chapter 7 **ACTIVITY 2**

Office Safety Presentation

Your supervisor, Ms. Perez, is concerned that each employee takes an active interest in good safety practices. She would like you and the other members of the safety committee to develop a list of office safety guidelines for employees. Ms. Perez has also asked your committee to present a short presentation about office safety. The presentation will be made to your coworkers to promote office safety during the company Safety Month. Work with three other students to complete this activity.

1. Use your textbook, magazine articles, Web sites, or other resources to research safety as it relates to an office environment. Compose a list of 10 to 15 office safety guidelines. Arrange the items on the safety guidelines list in order of importance, with Item 1 being the most important and Item 15 being the least important. Key your guidelines in an attractive format that can be posted or distributed to office employees.

2. Plan the content and create visuals for a short presentation on office safety. Your committee may choose to include all 15 items in the safety presentation or choose to focus on the 5 most important items according to your list. Your presentation should include the major points about safety as well as art, tables, graphs, or other elements to support and enhance the presentation.

3. Decide what content each person will present and practice your presentation.

4. Deliver the presentation to another work group or to the entire class.

Meetings and Travel

The purposes of business meetings range from getting acquainted to exchanging information to solving complex issues. Formats for meetings can be informal or formal, with many participants or only a few. Employees often travel to attend meetings. Travel arrangements might include setting up air travel, hotel accommodations, and car rental; confirming appointments; preparing an itinerary and gathering supporting items; and handling work while away from the office.

....

In this chapter, you will learn about planning and participating in meetings, about making travel arrangements, and about supporting activities related to business travel.

OBJECTIVES

- Plan business meetings
- Prepare documents related to business meetings
- Participate effectively in meetings

Business meetings bring people together to communicate or receive information, make decisions, and solve problems. Because businesspeople work together and many tasks are related, meetings are an important means of communication. Without meetings, keeping up to date on company matters, changing business conditions, and procedures would be difficult for employees.

Meetings may range from an informal chat in a manager's office to a formal gathering of the board of directors in the company boardroom. Although many meetings are held in person, technology allows people in different locations to conduct and attend meetings without leaving their offices. Well-organized meetings, whether held face-to-face or by electronic means, are necessary for businesses to run smoothly. Your role in assisting with these meetings will vary, depending on the degree of formality, purpose, size, and location of the meeting. In this topic, you will learn how to plan and participate in meetings efficiently and effectively.

Types of Business Meetings

The nature of the organization, the duties of your department, and the purpose of the meeting will determine the size and formality of the meeting. You will want to understand the differences in the nature of the meetings and your role in planning and participating in them.

Informal and Small Group Meetings

Many of the meetings in which office workers are involved will be informal discussions and small group meetings. Many times small, informal meetings are set up as committee meetings that address specific topics or ongoing concerns and issues, such as safety and security.

Working with customers or clients may also take the form of small group meetings. These meeting may be more formal than small group meetings with coworkers, especially if the meeting is your initial contact with the client. Follow the steps described in the following sections to plan and conduct the meeting.

Formal Business Meetings

A formal meeting follows a definite order of business, involves a specific audience, and requires some preparation. Many organizations set up formal staff meetings at a specific time on a weekly or monthly basis. Other formal business meetings, such as conferences or quarterly sales meetings, may be planned for longer periods of time. You may be asked to help to ensure that the meeting is planned properly, materials are available, and follow-up actions are noted and carried through.

This example shows how one office worker carried out her responsibilities for setting up and participating in a small, informal meeting.

Carla's manager sent her an e-mail as follows: "Carla, see if you can get the other four Pikesville project engineers together tomorrow at three o'clock for about an hour to discuss the status of the Pikesville project, and see if the conference room is available." As she read through the message, Carla noted the materials she needed to bring to the meeting, as well as the arrangements she needed to make for special equipment. Immediately after reading all the instructions, Carla inquired about the availability of the other engineers through the company's electronic calendaring system. She noted that all four of the other engineers were free at that time and added the meeting to their calendars.

Next Carla arranged for the conference room by electronically accessing the schedule for the room. Finding it free at the hour requested, she added her name as the person requesting the meeting and her telephone number as a reference. She sent an e-mail message to each of the engineers, noting the time, place, and approximate length of the meeting and telling them she had added the meeting to their electronic calendars. She then arranged for the necessary equipment and photocopied her materials for the meeting. To follow up the request, she sent an e-mail message to the manager to confirm her arrangements. She noted the meeting on her own calendar. The next day, Carla checked the conference room before the meeting to see that everything was in order.

Figure 8-1.1

Informal, small group meetings are held frequently in businesses.

© CORBIS/STOCK MARKET

Topic 8-1: *Planning and Participating in Meetings*

Multinational Meetings

Many companies conduct meetings in which all participants do not speak the same language or may not be in the same physical location. Multinational meetings for large groups are likely to be very formal, requiring detailed long-range planning and preparation. Knowledge of international and business etiquette, time differences, technology troubleshooting (if an electronic conference room is used), and your role as **coordinator** will be critical. Your role may include working with hotel personnel (if the meeting is held away from company offices), equipment providers, and the participants themselves.

coordinator: one who places things in proper order or arranges details

Planning the Meeting

Regardless of the size of the meeting, documents prepared for meetings require organization and planning. Typical documents may include:

- An agenda, which lists the topics to be discussed during the meeting
- Minutes, which are the written, historical record of the official business of a meeting
- A list of follow-up items or reminders to participants of tasks to do following the meeting

You may have responsibilities before, during, and after a formal meeting for preparing the agenda, taking the minutes, writing and distributing the minutes, and noting the follow-up items from the minutes.

Before the Meeting

The following suggestions will be helpful to you in your planning. You may not use all the suggestions for each meeting. However, these guidelines will be helpful as you plan for most business meetings.

- **Establish a meeting folder.** Once you are aware that a meeting will take place, set up a folder for it. Use this folder to collect items related to the meeting, such as the list of attendees, the agenda, notes, and copies of materials to be distributed.

- **Determine a meeting time.** You may be told the time at which a meeting is to take place, or you may be responsible for scheduling a time when all needed participants can attend. Contact each participant with a couple of suggested meeting times and ask if one of the times is convenient. This is especially important when the meeting involves clients or others from outside your organization. If the participants are all from within your organization and use calendaring software, you may be able to simply check each person's calendar for a time when he or she is available.

- **Reserve a meeting room.** When you know the date, time, and location of the meeting, check immediately to see if the desired meeting room and time are available.

- **Arrange for needed equipment**. Many times the purpose of the meeting will determine the kind of equipment that will be needed. Rooms may be equipped with overhead projectors, but more sophisticated projection systems may be required—especially if sharing sales or production figures is involved or if the information will be sent to an off-site location.

- **Notify the meeting participants.** Notify the participants as soon as possible of the time, place, approximate length, and purpose of the meeting. Identify any materials or supporting documents they should bring.

- **Use reminder systems.** Mark your and others' calendars with the meeting time and place. Use a tickler file or other reminder system to help you schedule the details. For example, if you must prepare 20 copies of a report to present at the meeting, create a reminder to do so.

- **Key an agenda.** All participants and the recording secretary should receive a copy of the **agenda** prior to the meeting. Topics should be stated concisely and listed in the order they will be discussed. The starting time for each agenda item may be listed, along with breaks in the program. Only the starting time for the meeting is listed if the meeting will be brief. The person who will lead the discussion or training for each topic may be listed to the right of the topic. Other relevant information, such as meeting rooms or materials required, may also be included. An agenda typically contains many of the items shown in Figure 8-1.2 on page 322.

> **agenda:** document that contains the information for a meeting such as the participants and topics to be discussed

- **Organize meeting materials.** You may be expected to gather certain materials such as extra notepads, pencils, file folders, and courtesy identification badges and parking stickers. Also, organize any materials and handouts such as reports, letters, and statistical data that will be distributed at the meeting. Review any material to be presented at the meeting on the equipment that is available in the meeting room.

- **Prepare the meeting room.** The room temperature should be comfortable, and the seating arranged to fit the meeting style. A room arrangement in which all participants can be seen and heard will make discussion easier. Any presentation aids should be positioned so that they are near the leader and can be seen by everyone in the room. Check to be sure that requested equipment is present and working properly.

During the Meeting

The degree to which you participate during the meeting will depend on the purpose of the meeting, where it is held, and the preplanning to be done. You may be responsible for the minutes or for leading part of the discussion.

The **minutes** describe the action taken by the group, and they provide the reader with a concise record of what took place at the meeting. See Figure 8-1.3 on page 323 for an example of minutes. The minutes should not be a **verbatim** transcript of the meeting. However, the recorder must make note of all important information. The minutes must give a clear, accurate, and complete accounting of the happenings of the meeting. Although various reporting formats are acceptable for recording minutes, the following information appears in most of them:

> **minutes:** written record of meeting proceedings and decisions

> **verbatim:** word for word

- Name of group, committee, organization, or business holding the meeting
- Time, date, place, and type of meeting (for example, weekly, monthly, annual, called, special)
- Name of presiding officer

Topic 8-1: *Planning and Participating in Meetings*

2-inch top margin

Bold and ALL CAPS ⟶ **AGENDA**

Pikesville Improvement Council

Center heading lines

June 30, 20--

1-inch side margins

The meeting will begin at 9:30 a.m in Conference Room C.

1. Call to Order — Nancy Hollingshead, Pikesville Improvement Council Chair ⟵ **DS between items**

2. Roll Call — Troy Jones, Secretary

3. Reading of the Minutes — Troy Jones, Secretary

4. Treasurer's Report — Sean Petersen, Treasurer

5. Committee Report
    Recognitions Committee — Briana King, Chairperson

6. Unfinished Business
    Telecommunications Improvement Project

7. New Business
    East Pikesville Drive Improvement Project

8. Date of Next Meeting

9. Adjournment

Figure 8-1.2

An agenda is a list of topics to discuss during a meeting.

2-inch top margin

Center heading lines

PIKESVILLE IMPROVEMENT COUNCIL

Meeting Minutes

June 30, 20--

1-inch

side margins

1. The regular weekly meeting of the Pikesville Improvement Council was held on June 30, 20--, in Conference Room C at City Hall. The meeting was called to order by President Nancy Hollingshead at 9:30 a.m. **← SS items**

   DS between items

2. Present were members Elizabeth Larkin, Rodger Aycock, Douglas Ivey, Laura Johnson, Steven Minnhausen, Briana King, Sean Petersen, Troy Jones, and Nancy Hollingshead and a guest, John Byrd. Council member Kelly Pearce was absent.

3. The minutes of the June 23, 20--, meeting were read and approved.

4. Treasurer Sean Petersen reported that the Improvement Projects Fund has a balance of $359,450.

5. Briana King gave the Recognition Committee report, recommending Jane Ann Adamson be submitted for employee of the month. Laura Johnson moved that Jane Ann Adamson be submitted to the city council as employee of the month. Steven Minnhausen seconded the motion, and the motion was approved by the Council. President Hollingshead directed the secretary to prepare the resolution for submission (attached to the minutes).

6. The Council addressed unfinished business. President Hollingshead reported that the three recorded bids for the Telecommunications Improvement Project have been forwarded to the City Engineering Department for evaluation.

7. The Council addressed new business. Douglas Ivey reported that a community meeting will be held on July 6, 20--, to discuss the project with residents.

8. President Hollingshead announced that the next meeting will be held on July 7, 20--, at 9:30 a.m., in Conference Room C at City Hall.

Pikesville Improvement Council
Meeting Minutes for June 30, 20--
Page 2 **← Second-page heading**

9. Douglas Ivey moved and Rodger Aycock seconded that the meeting be adjourned. The motion was approved and the meeting was adjourned at 10:30 a.m.

_____   _____
Troy Jones, Secretary   Nancy Hollingshead, President

Attachment: Resolution of Recognition

Figure 8-1.3

Minutes are the official record of a meeting.

Topic 8-1: *Planning and Participating in Meetings*

quorum: minimum number of members that must be present to conduct business

adjournment: ending or closure

parliamentary procedures: guide for conducting meetings

motion: a proposal formally made in a meeting

second: to indicate formally one's support of a motion

- Members present and absent (In a large organization, only the number of members present must be recorded to verify that a **quorum** was present.)
- Reading and approval of the minutes from the previous meeting
- Committee or individual reports (for example, treasurer's report, standing committees, special committees)
- Unfinished business (includes discussion and action taken)
- New business (includes discussion and action taken)
- Time, date, and place of next meeting
- Time of **adjournment**
- Signature of the individual responsible for the minutes

The following suggestions will be helpful to you when it is your responsibility to prepare the minutes of a meeting.

1. Bring to the meeting copies of the agenda, the minutes of the previous meeting, and any report or document that might be referred to during the meeting.

2. If you record and transcribe minutes frequently, a **parliamentary procedures** reference source (such as *Robert's Rules of Order Newly Revised*) will help you to better understand the meeting proceedings and the correct terms to use when taking and preparing minutes.

3. Record the important points of discussion and the action taken or the conclusion reached.

4. Record the names of the persons making a **motion** or **seconding** a motion. Motions should be recorded verbatim, and a statement should be made in the minutes as to whether or not the motion was passed.

5. Correct minutes of the previous meeting. Sometimes at the following meeting, corrections must be made to the minutes before they can be approved. If only a few words are affected, lines may be drawn through the incorrect words and the proper insertions made above them. If more than a few words are affected, lines may be drawn through the sentences or paragraphs to be corrected and the changes written on a new page. The page number of each correction should be indicated on the original minutes. The minutes should not be rewritten after they have been read and approved at the meeting.

After the Meeting

Once the meeting is over, you may need to complete follow-up activities. Make calendar or reminder notations for any item from the meeting that will require future attention. Prepare the minutes as soon as possible. Preparing the minutes will be easier when the details of the meeting are fresh in your mind. Use examples of previous minutes for appropriate format or follow the sample shown in Figure 8-1.3. Ask the chairperson of the meeting to review the minutes be-fore they are distributed to be sure there are no omissions or errors.

Complete any correspondence associated with the meeting, such as thank-you letters to speakers or resource persons or letters requesting information. Items to be added to the agenda for the next meeting also should be noted.

Participating in Meetings

Meetings are an important part of business operations. Individuals, departments, and divisions need to communicate with one another on a daily basis to complete the work of the organization. Whether they are called staff, marketing, committee, ad hoc, client, or sales meetings, they are designed to allow the participants to discover problems, exchange information, and make decisions. As an office worker, you should be prepared to lead, participate in, contribute to, and feel a part of any meeting you attend.

Leading

All employees lead in their jobs: that is, they lead by knowing the elements of their jobs, meeting deadlines, improving how the tasks are completed, and working with people to get their jobs done. These same leadership skills are important in meetings. A good meeting leader conducts the meeting in an **assertive** way that accomplishes the goals of the meeting. At the same time, he or she also uses a nonaggressive communication style that makes everyone feel comfortable. Follow the guidelines below to develop a nonaggressive, yet assertive communication style when leading a meeting.

assertive: positive or confident in a persistent way

- Make the objectives of the meeting clear to all participants.
- Be familiar with the background material and have relevant documents at hand.
- Offer suggestions and ask questions during the meeting.
- Always be willing to listen to others' suggestions.
- Keep the meeting on topic and moving toward a solution or a **consensus**.
- Ensure that all participants have an opportunity to take part in the discussion.
- Remain open to new and creative approaches.
- Summarize the decisions or plans that have been made during the meeting.
- Identify clearly the responsibilities or tasks assigned to each group member in following up or completing plans.

consensus: common agreement or mutual understanding

Brainstorming

Brainstorming is a group technique used to facilitate and generate ideas that lead to making decisions or solving problems. The objective is to come up with as many ideas as possible to solve a problem. During the brainstorming process, the following rules are usually observed:

brainstorm: offer ideas or solutions

- All ideas are recorded, no matter how unrealistic they may appear.
- Criticism of ideas is not allowed until all ideas have been expressed. Comments such as "that will never work" or "we tried that once already" may block the flow of ideas—the main purpose of brainstorming.
- Explanations and combinations of ideas are encouraged. The value of brainstorming is that one idea may build on another.

To encourage brainstorming, a meeting leader must be willing to give time to the process and encourage everyone to participate.

Figure 8-1.4

Brainstroming in a
meeting generates ideas.

© CORBIS/STOCK MARKET

WORKPLACE **CONNECTIONS**

The members of the Marketing Department at Bell Industries, a small manufacturing company, travel often to meet with clients and exhibit the company's products at trade shows. Currently, each department member books his or her own travel, and few rules or restrictions related to travel are in place. The department's travel expenses are over budget for the first half of the year. The department manager, Penny Flag, has called a meeting of department members to discuss the problem and brainstorm ideas for how to lower travel costs for the remainder of the year.

Penny: *"As you are aware, we must take steps to lower our travel costs. Starting today, I will look at each situation more closely than in the past before I authorize travel for anyone in our department. Before you request travel, please consider whether you really need to make the trip. For example, can the meeting be held as a teleconference rather than in person? Now, I need suggestions from all of you. Who has an idea on how to lower travel costs?"*

Ralph: *"Making airline reservations at least seven days in advance will usually result in lower fares. Because we often know the dates for trade shows months in advance, we could book some flights 30 days in advance. That should save a lot money. Of course, all air travel should be booked business class or coach—no first class fares. I think we all do that already, though."*

Kim: *"Do we sometimes fly when driving would be almost as quick? I suggest that for any destination within five hours driving time, we drive rather than fly. Driving is almost always cheaper than flying."*

Penny:	"Good suggestions, Ralph and Kim. Anyone else? What do you think, Florence?"
Florence:	"Well, I know many companies set maximum amounts for certain expenses. Maybe we could do that also. For example, the maximum for hotel rooms might be $100 per day. The maximum for food might be $50 per day. The maximum for entertaining clients might be $40 per client per day. If we know ahead of time that more funds will be needed, such as for hotels in an expensive area, that expense could be approved ahead of time by Penny."
Ilena:	"Speaking of expensive hotels, would anyone want to share a hotel room at trade shows? If you feel comfortable doing so, this would make the travel budget go farther."
Jordan:	"What about rental cars? Let's always rent a subcompact or compact car for lower fees and use a car only when it's really necessary."
Penny:	"Thanks, everyone. I have recorded all these good ideas. Think about the issue for a couple of days and let me know if you have any more suggestions. I'll create a document containing our new travel guidelines to distribute at our meeting next week."

Group Dynamics

Group dynamics refers to how people interact and communicate, as in a meeting. Within the meeting environment, group dynamics can play an important part in reaching group consensus and decisions. The following sections focus on the three critical components of group dynamics.

group dynamics: the way people interact and communicate within a group

Interactions

Interactions among group members will depend on the purpose of the meeting. In almost all meetings, communications will be enhanced when group members can see one another, when eye contact can be used to gain attention or control a participant, and when all participants can see the leader and the visual aids. The purpose of the meeting should determine the seating arrangement.

The round table or circle may be used when the leader is seeking a true cooperative form of decision making. This format also reduces the appearance of **status** differences between the participants.

status: rank or position relative to others

The U-shaped arrangement can be used for larger meetings—those that include 10 or 12 participants. In this arrangement, the leader may sit in the middle of the U to maintain eye contact with all participants. At the same time, all participants can see each other and are less like to engage in side conversations.

Topic 8-1: *Planning and Participating in Meetings*

Figure 8-1.5

An appropriate seating arrangement can help accomplish the goal of the meeting.

The center table layout, with the leader at one end of the table, allows the leader to control the discussion and communications of the meeting. In this arrangement, all communication tends to flow toward the head of the table (where the leader is seated).

Exchange of Information

Exchange of information can be improved by the seating arrangement and the willingness of the leader to encourage open communication. Planning by the leader before the meeting can set up the open exchange of information among group members by:

- Providing in advance materials that will be discussed
- Arranging the room and seating to meet the needs of the meeting
- Preparing visual aids that guide the discussion
- Using an appropriate leadership style

Relationships

Relationships among the group's members will affect the meeting. A good leader listens, asks questions, accepts criticism, keeps the meeting on topic, and resolves conflicts. Conflicts arise when participants have strong opinions or hidden agendas (their own private objectives). Leaders and participants should follow these guidelines to help develop mutual trust and cooperation in meetings:

- Use neutral language in the discussion.
- Avoid placing blame.
- Ask open-ended questions.
- Use terms that all participants understand or define those that are unfamiliar.
- Allow all participants to speak without interruptions.
- Maintain a pleasant facial expression.
- Be open to new methods and ideas.

Involving Everyone

Questions or statements, such as those listed below, may encourage group participation and give each person at the meeting the opportunity to express his or her opinion:

- What do you think about…?
- What approach can we use to solve this problem?
- Jane, what do you think about Jim's idea?
- Ron, we haven't heard your ideas about….
- That's an interesting question, Mary. What would be a good answer?
- Are we ready to make a decision or is there still more discussion?
- Let me summarize what we have discussed so far.

Developing an Action Plan

For many meetings, developing a concrete, specific **action plan** to solve a problem or accomplish tasks is appropriate. A written plan of action can replace the traditional minutes of a meeting, because it focuses on the actions to be taken after the meeting rather than simply recording the proceedings (see Figure 8-1.6 on page 330). The following basic information about the meeting should be included in an action plan:

action plan: description of tasks to be accomplished

- Topic of the meeting, meeting date, the chairperson's name, and the recorder's name
- Specific actions to be taken and the person(s) responsible
- Deadlines for the actions and completion dates
- Key issues discussed and the participants
- The meeting length
- Announcement of the next meeting

To arrive at a plan of action, the meeting leader should ensure that all meeting participants:

- Understand the plan
- Have input into plans and decisions
- Have clear assignments to put the plan into action
- Complete their assignments so the plans are fulfilled

Teleconferences

A **teleconference** is a meeting of people in different locations connected by a telecommunications system. Teleconferences can be used to deliver training, exchange information, or solve problems and make decisions, just as face-to-face meetings can.

teleconference: a meeting of two or more people in different locations conducted using telecommunications equipment

Types of Conferences

The conference may involve only audio exchanges among the participants, as in a telephone conference. An audio conference room is equipped with microphone-speakers, arranged on tables at certain intervals, so that all participants can talk to and hear from other participants. Audio-graphic conferences, using a microphone-speaker system, a computer terminal, and an electronic tablet, make it possible to hear the other participants and see

Topic 8-1: *Planning and Participating in Meetings*

PIKESVILLE IMPROVEMENT COUNCIL

Center heading lines

Action Plan

April 30, 20--

SS items
DS between
items

1-inch
side margins

1. The purpose of the Pikesville Improvement Council meeting held on April 30, 20--, was to discuss the downtown improvement project. President Hollingshead called the meeting to order at 7:30 p.m. and declared a quorum present. Ms. Hollingshead called the members' attention to the information that was delivered to them during the week prior to the meeting.

2. Present were members Elizabeth Larkin, Rodger Aycock, Kelly Pearce, Troy Jones, Douglas Ivey, Sean Petersen, and Nancy Hollingshead. Guests present were John Byrd and Sharon Young.

3. The Council discussed the plans to acquire an additional piece of property that joins the downtown area. The property will be used for a park with an amphitheater and petting zoo for children. Mr. Byrd and Ms. Young discussed details on each piece of property under consideration:

    East Pikesville Drive (owner, Martin Victor Wolfe)
    North River Drive (owner, Hancock Industries)
    West High Street (owner, The McFaddin Family Group)

4. President Hollingshead appointed Kelly Pearce, Elizabeth Larkin, and Rodger Aycock to study each piece of property and make recommendations to the Council on which piece of property to purchase. The recommendation should be ready to present at the meeting on May 14, 20--.

5. The next meeting will be held on May 14, 20--. The meeting was adjourned at 8:30 p.m.

Troy Jones, Secretary   Nancy Hollingshead, President

Figure 8-1.6

An action plan focuses on tasks to complete after a meeting.

Project team leaders of a South Carolina firm need to meet as often as six times a week to refine ideas and reach decisions on project questions. When the executive assistant is asked to set up a teleconference meeting, he first checks all team leaders' electronic calendars for an open time. He then notifies the leaders of the meeting date and time, lists a call-in telephone number and password, and provides the Web address.

On the day of the meeting, leaders dial the telephone number to be connected to the audio portion of the meeting through their speakerphones. They access a Web site via their computers to see documents. A small digital camera sits on top of each team leader's computer. The team leaders can see each other as they speak or ask questions. The company's executives feel that being able to meet and share information in this way helps them solve problems quickly and be more responsive to market changes.

written information at the same time. A speaker at one location can explain material on the speaker system and write on the electronic tablet. The information appears on the computer screen at the receiving end along with the audio explanation. Because the tablet is electronic, with the touch of a button the information can be printed for all participants.

Video conferencing permits people at two or more locations to hear and see each other almost as if they were in the same room. A video conference room is equipped with cameras, microphones, viewing monitors, and other equipment that allows the participants to see and hear one another.

© CHAD BAKER/RYAN MCVAY/PHOTODISC

Figure 8-1.7

Teleconferences can be conducted using computers.

Topic 8-1: *Planning and Participating in Meetings*

real time: as an event happens, without delay

In a computer conference, people communicate using private computer networks or the Internet, allowing them to have virtual meetings. The conference may involve only written messages keyed and received by the participants in **real time**. If the users' computers are equipped with microphones and the proper software, the participants can talk with one another rather than key messages. Video conferences may also be conducted by computer. The user's computers must have speakers, microphones, video cameras, and the appropriate software.

FOCUS ON . . .

Web Conferencing

Web conferencing uses technology that combines audio, video, and computer conferencing. By using Web conferencing, participants can hear and see each other and share documents. With recent improvements in telephone and computer technologies, meeting on the Web is an effective and cost-saving alternative to many face-to-face meetings.

Some Web conferences may involve only a small number of people, such as two people meeting to work on an analysis or report. Others may involve a large number of people, such as thousands of individuals meeting to see and hear a speaker. The Web conferencing equipment a business uses depends in large part on the purpose of the meeting and the number of participants.

Teleconferencing equipment has become less expensive and easier to operate within the past few years. A small business or home office user might choose a product such as ViaVideo, which sells for less than $500 and includes a video camera and software. The user can be ready to teleconference in minutes by simply plugging

the digital camera into the computer and loading the software.

Teleconferencing programs may provide features such as program sharing, file transfer, and text chat features. Microsoft's NetMeeting conferencing program, which is a part of some versions of the Windows operating system, offers these features in addition to video and audio.

Companies that wish to hold teleconferences with people in many locations or that need very high-quality video may use a teleconference service provider. This type of business specializes in providing teleconferencing service to others. Some companies choose to develop a dedicated conference system using high-end equipment and powerful software or to make conferencing features part of their Web site or intranet.

Web conferencing has opened new ways for people in different locations to meet and to work cooperatively. At a moment's notice, a business can have its brightest and most productive members working together to solve a problem or brainstorm for new ideas.

Preparing for a Teleconference

Technology allows flexibility in planning, setting up, preparing for, and participating in meetings. Teleconferencing can be expensive, so the meeting time should be used wisely. Your role in preparing for a teleconference may include the following responsibilities:

1. Reserve the conference room and necessary equipment, if a special room is to be used.

2. Notify the participants of the date, time, length, and purpose of the meeting. Include a telephone number and the name of a contact for participants in the event of technical difficulties.

3. Prepare and distribute any related materials well in advance of the meeting. If several documents are to be sent, use different paper colors to copy different reports. That way, it will be easy to identify reports during the teleconference.

4. Prepare and distribute an agenda to the participants well in advance of the teleconference.

5. If the teleconference room is equipped with a fax machine, telephone, electronic tablet, or other electronic systems for exchanging information during the meeting, be sure these systems are in operating condition and are available for use during the teleconference.

6. If the services of a telecommunications technician or coordinator are needed, arrange to have that person available or in the room during the conference in the event of technical difficulties. Take it on yourself to learn the less complicated technical characteristics of computer teleconferencing, so that you can expand your skills and knowledge in this area.

Reviewing the Topic

1. List three general reasons why meetings are held in business.
2. Give an example of an informal business meeting and of a formal business meeting.
3. List in brief the guidelines you should follow to prepare for a meeting.
4. What information generally appears on a meeting agenda?
5. What information generally appears in the minutes of a meeting?
6. What guidelines does a good leader follow during a meeting to exhibit an assertive, nonaggressive style?
7. Describe three types of seating arrangement that may be used for meetings and how each one affects the interaction of the meeting participants.
8. What are the similarities between an action plan and meeting minutes? What are the differences?
9. Describe a Web conference.
10. What preparations need to be made for a teleconference?

Thinking Critically

Ms. Burris has asked you to take charge of preparations for a meeting with union leaders and company officials on April 2. In addition, she has asked you to sit in during the meeting and take minutes. You know from the agenda that the meeting has been scheduled for her conference room.

1. Key a list of the preparations you may need to make for the conference room.
2. Key a list of questions you have for Ms. Burris regarding the meeting preparations. For example: Will there be breaks for refreshments? If yes, how many and when?
3. What items will you need to take to the meeting with you?
4. Key a list of tasks you may to do before, during, and after the meeting.

Reinforcing English Skills

Pronouns are words that serve as substitutes for nouns. Pronouns must agree with their antecedents (nouns for which they stand) in person, number, and gender. Write or key the following sentences selecting the proper pronouns.

1. The executive (that, who) directed the meeting is an effective business leader.
2. Neither Jack nor Jim thinks that (his, their) itinerary should be changed.
3. The executives said that (them, they), along with a group from another company, would attend the seminar in Paris.
4. Office workers who take the minutes of meetings need a parliamentary procedures resource available to (them, they).
5. The committee has promised to have (its, their) findings ready for review at the departmental meeting next week.
6. The executives traveling on business from that office often use (its, their) company's credit cards.
7. The executive and her associate were uncertain how (she, they) should reschedule the trip.
8. The members of the group attending the meeting wanted (its, their) opinions aired before a final vote was taken.
9. The oval table (that, who) was placed in the meeting room will be there only a short time.
10. Joy and Wendy reviewed the meeting agenda before (it, they) was sent to the participants.

WORD PROCESSING

Topic 8-1   ACTIVITY 1

Agenda for a Teleconference

You work in Atlanta for Ernest Fogg, director of the marketing department. Mr. Fogg is making arrangements for a teleconference with marketing vice presidents located in five different regional offices. The teleconference will originate in Atlanta. Mr. Fogg hands you an edited copy of the agenda for the teleconference and says, "Please key this agenda in final form. Make the changes I've indicated and list the participants in alphabetic order according to city. Proofread very carefully to ensure that all numbers are correct."

1. Open the data file **Agenda.pdf**, which contains the rough draft agenda.
2. Key the final agenda following Mr. Fogg's oral and written instructions.

335

Meeting and Action Plan

Work in a group with three or four classmates to apply the meeting and planning skills you learned in this topic.

1. Identify a group chairperson who will lead the meeting and a recorder who will make notes during the meeting.

2. Choose one of the problem scenarios following step 4 as the reason for your group meeting. Discuss the possible causes of the problem and related factors. Consider what you have learned about the scenario topic in previous chapters.

3. Brainstorm ideas for solving the problem. Follow the suggestions in the *Group Dynamics* section of this topic as you participate in the meeting. Your goal is to be an active participant with an assertive, yet nonaggressive communication style.

4. Create an action plan detailing the steps your group will take toward solving the problem. Assign one or more people to complete each task and set deadlines for completing the tasks. Key an action plan document using Figure 8-1.6 on page 330 as a guide. Submit the action plan and the notes your recorder made during the meeting.

Scenario 1	You are employed in a small company that has five other office workers. All the office workers need help in handling office tasks such as keying reports, preparing mailings, and responding to inquiries.
Scenario 2	Your company's petty cash fund does not balance with the fund records. Cash is missing. The same situation has occurred for each of the past three months. The petty cash is kept in a small metal box in the secretary's desk. The desk is locked at night, but it is usually not locked during the day. The secretary's duties often take her away from her desk.
Scenario 3	You work for a small company that uses a local area computer network. Users can connect to the Internet via the LAN. Employees are supposed to follow procedures to log on and log off when using the network. Over the past month, computer viruses have been detected frequently on the company's computer network.

Arranging Travel

OBJECTIVES

- Use appropriate procedures for planning business travel
- Explain procedures for obtaining a passport and visa
- Prepare appropriate travel documents, including an itinerary
- Describe the factors involved in travel etiquette and travel safety
- Complete follow-up travel activities

Businesspeople travel for various reasons: to supervise company operations, to meet with clients or company associates, or to attend meetings and conferences. Increasingly, large and small organizations conduct business on an international scale. Telecommunications technology and accessible air travel have combined to make business travel convenient and worthwhile.

Travel arrangements are made in accordance with company policy. Large firms may have a travel department for this purpose, or they may rely on the services of a travel agency. In smaller firms, however, an office worker or the traveling employee may make the travel arrangements. Some companies have special agreements with travel agencies, hotels, and transportation companies for travel-related services. Follow company procedures and instructions to complete any travel arrangements you must make.

Preparing for Business Travel

You may have an opportunity to choose the mode of travel, the time of departure or arrival, and the overnight accommodations for a business trip. When such choices are available, you will need to know your personal preferences or those of the person traveling if you are making the arrangements for that person.

When you travel on company business, you must be able to meet your business obligations scheduled away from your office. You must arrive at meetings on time and with the necessary supporting materials. Carefully planned travel arrangements are important to the success of a business trip.

A **travel folder** (or trip file) will help you organize the details of an upcoming trip. Use the folder to collect background information and details about the trip. Notes on reservations, tickets, accommodations, and meeting or appointment confirmations may be placed in the trip file. The information in the travel folder will help you prepare an **itinerary**, complete company travel documents, and serve as a reminder system for tasks related to the trip.

travel folder: storage container for items related to a trip such as tickets or an itinerary

itinerary: document giving detailed plans for a trip

As you plan the trip, set aside time to:

- Schedule meetings and appointments to be held during the trip. Shortly before the trip, contact each individual with whom you plan to meet to confirm the appointment date, time, and meeting place.
- Organize the names, titles, company names, addresses, and telephone numbers or e-mail addresses of the individuals with whom meetings are scheduled.
- Check for travel safety conditions in the destination area.
- Make reservations for transportation and overnight accommodations.
- Prepare an itinerary and gather supporting materials for the trip.

337

Commercial Air Travel

Time is money for the busy business traveler, and the popularity of air travel among businesspeople reflects this point. Often, the only way to manage a tight schedule is by air travel. An extensive network of airline routes is provided by national, regional, and commuter airlines. If you are a frequent flyer on one particular airline, an updated airline timetable provides a convenient way to determine travel information such as flight schedules, services offered (meals, snacks, movies), and toll-free reservation numbers. Airline schedules are available free of charge at ticket counters in airports, at airline offices in major cities, at large hotels, and from travel agents. Most airlines maintain Web sites that provide similar information and may have more current information than printed guides.

If you use several airlines, you will find the Official Airline Guide (OAG) a valuable source of flight information and schedules. Your company may have a copy of this publication for your reference. If not, you can access the OAG online at www.oag.com. You simply enter the departure and arrival cities and the date of travel. The flight number and airline, departure and arrival cities, times, total travel time, number of stops, and a code that indicates the type of aircraft will be displayed.

You may make flight reservations by calling a travel agent, by calling an airline directly using a toll-free number, or by accessing various Web sites. When you purchase airline tickets online, you may receive a **paper ticket** or an **electronic ticket** by mail if time allows. If not, you can pick up the ticket at the airport.

paper ticket: actual ticket as opposed to an electronic ticket

electronic ticket: document and receipt that contains ticket information

Figure 8-2.1

Air travel helps busy employees maintain schedules.

© EYEWIRE COLLECTION

If you use the services of a travel agent, your flight itinerary and an invoice may be received with the airline tickets. Each of these documents serves a specific purpose. The flight itinerary is checked against your records and used to create the traveler's itinerary. Many travelers attach a copy of the flight itinerary to the overall itinerary for the trip. The invoice is retained to attach to the travel expense report.

Plan to arrive at the airport well ahead of your flight departure time (one to two hours) to allow time for checking in at the airline desk to receive boarding passes, checking luggage, and moving through security checkpoints. When checking bags, verify that the luggage tag attached by the airline attendant has the correct destination code and wait until you see your bags placed on the conveyor belt before leaving the check-in area. Comply with all reasonable requests of security personnel. Be aware that your checked bags or carried bags, as well as your person, may be subject to search. Never leave your bags or other possessions unattended or in the care of a stranger. Never agree to carry a bag or other items from a stranger.

Other Forms of Business Travel

Rental cars and trains provide alternative forms of business travel. You may have occasion to make travel arrangements using one of these forms of transportation.

For short trips, particularly in a local area, many people prefer to rent cars. A rental car may also be suitable when you fly to a city and have appointments in outlying areas. Be sure to allow ample time to reach your destination. Rental cars are available at most airports and other convenient locations. Rental fees vary in price according to the size of the car, the length of time the car is needed, and the miles driven. Follow any established company guidelines for renting a car. Many rental car companies have Web sites where you may choose and reserve a rental car.

© PETER GRIDLEY/FPG INTERNATIONAL

Figure 8-2.2

Some business trips require the use of a rental car.

Kim Park rented a car on her arrival at the Kansas City International Airport. She left the car rental agency at 1 p.m. for a meeting near Kansas City scheduled for 2 p.m., giving herself ample travel time for the half-hour trip. Kim arrived at the office where the meeting was scheduled and introduced herself to the receptionist. "Oh, I'm glad you finally made it. We were concerned that something might have happened to you," the receptionist said. "I don't understand," said Kim. "The meeting is scheduled for 2 p.m. It's only 1:40." "Let's see," said the receptionist. "You traveled from Denver, right?" "Did you remember that Kansas City is in the Central time zone?" Kim was embarrassed about being late for the meeting and promised herself to check carefully all times, including the time zone, in the future.

Train travel is popular in some sections of the country, particularly in areas with high population concentrations. Train stations are located in the centers of cities and can provide an alternative to air travel on certain routes. Overnight trains have sleeping and dining accommodations on board. Check with a travel agent or look in the yellow pages of your telephone directory for information on the railway lines serving your area. Amtrak, a company that provides train services in many areas of the United States, provides a Web site at www.amtrak.com where customers may make reservations online.

Hotel/Motel Accommodations

Many business travelers must stay overnight at their destinations and will need hotel or motel accommodations. You may specify a particular hotel or motel, especially if you are familiar with the city or if a convention or meeting is being held at a specific hotel. In other cases, you may rely on a travel agent or administrative assistant to select the lodging.

When you make reservations by telephone, use toll-free telephone numbers whenever possible. Write down the names of the persons who make and confirm reservations. Always make a note of the rates you are quoted. Record the **confirmation number** and repeat it to the reservation agent to ensure the accuracy of the number. The confirmation number should be included on the itinerary. A written confirmation from the hotel or motel is helpful. Many hotels have Web sites where reservations may be made. A confirmation number is usually provided, and the reservation may also be confirmed by e-mail.

confirmation number: series of characters (often text and numbers) associated with a reservation

directory: listing of items with related information

Many printed, electronic, and online **directories** of hotels are available. The *World Hotel Directory (year): The Essential Guide for Business Travelers* is an example of a printed guide that contains hotel information. The *OAG Travel Information* system is a comprehensive travel planning tool that provides

Figure 8-2.3

Business travelers should choose hotels that are safe and convenient to their travel destinations.

information on airline flights and thousands of hotels worldwide. Travelers can search for hotels by name, location, quality rating, room rate, or amenities. Maps and nearby points of interest can be printed for use on the road. The software may be installed from CD-ROM on a personal computer. Versions for a company LAN, intranet, or extranet are also available. Web sites such as USAHotelGuide.com provide information and reservation service for over 50,000 hotels worldwide.

Itinerary and Supporting Materials

Once the travel plans are set, prepare an itinerary and assemble travel documents and related materials for meetings or appointments. If the plans for the trip change, alternative arrangements may need to be made. Changes can generally be made at the time you cancel the original plans. Have your confirmation numbers and other reservation details available when you call to change reservations or appointments.

Prepare an Itinerary

An itinerary is a detailed plan of a trip that serves as a guide for the business traveler away from the office. The itinerary includes travel arrangements, appointments, hotel or motel reservations, and reminders or special instructions. When planning an itinerary, allow enough travel time between appointments to avoid having to rush to make the next appointment.

You may need several copies of the itinerary: one to carry, another to be carried in the baggage, one to leave with a contact person at the office, and possibly one for family members. The itinerary should be in an easy-to-read format that gives the day-by-day schedule for the complete trip, as shown in Figure 8-2.4 on page 343.

Gather Supporting Items

Before the trip, gather the travel documents, supplies, and supporting materials, such as those listed below, that are needed for the trip.

Ali Strong is away from the office on a trip when an important client, Mr. Jobel, calls. Mr. Jobel plans to be in town on Thursday and requests a meeting with Ali. As Ali's administrative assistant, you know that Ali has been hoping to meet with Mr. Jobel, but he is not scheduled to be back in the office until Friday. You tell Mr. Jobel that Ali is out of the office right now, but you will try to arrange the meeting and call him back. Consulting Ali's detailed itinerary, you find that he is scheduled to meet with Mrs. Bridge at this time, and the itinerary includes a phone number for Mrs. Bridge's office. You hesitate to interrupt Ali's meeting with Mrs. Bridge, but decide to call her office and ask to speak to Mr. Strong. Ali seems annoyed at first when he answers your call but soon thanks you for calling. "Tell Mr. Jobel I can meet with him at any time Thursday," said Ali. "I'll reschedule my other meetings and fly home on Wednesday." You are pleased that preparing a detailed itinerary for Ali's trip has proved to be so useful.

- Itinerary
- Travel tickets
- Travel funds
- Passport, visa, health documents
- Hotel/motel and car rental confirmations
- Maps of cities or states as appropriate
- Directions to offices or other meeting locations
- Speeches, supporting correspondence, reports, or files for each appointment/meeting
- Forms for recording expenses
- Extra notepaper, pens, and business cards
- Equipment, such as a laptop computer, portable phone, or presentation projection system

If the supporting materials, such as a large number of handouts, will be too heavy or bulky to carry with you, arrange to have them shipped to your hotel or meeting location. Arrange for special packaging for equipment, such as computers and projection panels, to prevent damage to these items while en route. Confirm the safe arrival of supporting materials prior to or immediately on arrival and have a backup plan to follow in case items are lost or damaged. For example, you might carry one set of handouts with you so that copies can be made at your destination if necessary.

Travel Etiquette

The behavior of a business traveler reflects on more than the traveler alone. Your behavior also reflects on your company and your home area. Proper dress and travel **etiquette** will contribute to a successful business trip.

etiquette: standards for proper behavior

U.S. companies of all sizes have extended their operations internationally. This global perspective is handled differently in each company. Many companies have international divisions to deal with their branch offices in other

1-inch side margins

1-inch top margin or center on the page

ITINERARY FOR CHARLENE STANFORD

May 17 to May 19, 20--

Bold and ALL CAPS for column heads

SS items
DS between items

DATE AND TIME	ACTIVITY
Wednesday, May 17	**Atlanta to Dallas**
9:43 a.m.	Leave Hartsfield Atlanta International airport on Delta Flight 17.
10:50 a.m.	Arrive Dallas/Ft. Worth International Airport. Pick up rental car keys at Sun Rentals counter, confirmation number 388075.
	Hotel reservations at Fairmont Hotel, 1717 W. Akard Street. Phone: 214-555-0102. Confirmation number 7K4995F.
2:30 p.m.	Meeting with George Thatcher, Vice President of Marketing, Fabric Wholesalers, 1314 Gaston Avenue (Phone: 214-555-0196) to discuss purchase agreement.
7:00 p.m.	Dinner with staff at hotel to review plans for Apparel Fair.
Thursday, May 18	**Dallas to San Diego**
12:02 p.m.	Leave Dallas/Ft. Worth International Airport on Delta Flight 444. Drop rental car keys at Sun Rentals and take shuttle to airport.
12:55 p.m.	Arrive at Lindbergh Field International Airport and meet Richard Stanley (Phone: 619-555-0152) at baggage claim. Travel to Naples plant with Richard, take tour, and return to hotel.
	Hotel reservations at the Seven Seas Lodge, 411 Hotel Circle South (Phone: 619-555-1300). Confirmation number 4478S84.
Friday, May 19	**San Diego to Atlanta**
7:55 a.m.	Leave San Diego Lindbergh Field International Airport on Delta Flight 880. Richard will meet me at my hotel at 6:45 a.m. and drive me to the airport.
3:52 p.m.	Arrive Hartsfield Atlanta International Airport.

Figure 8-2.4

Travel itinerary

countries. The personnel in these departments can provide valuable advice about dress, etiquette, travel documents, health considerations, and other information for the business traveler while abroad.

Dress

Remember that you represent your organization when you travel. Your dress will contribute to that most important first impression you make on others. Follow these guidelines for appropriate travel attire:

- Dress appropriately for the type of meeting or function you are attending. Many companies send employees to training sessions in which the attire is less formal than while on the job. If the meeting is to take place at another company's site, the attire may be more formal.

- Dress for travel. Many times, employees need a day to travel to a business destination. Dress in this case will be less formal on the airplane or in a car. When a short plane or car ride is all that is necessary to reach your destination, however, dress more formally to be ready to conduct business on arrival.

- Dress to impress. Consider the persons with whom you will be doing business and the impression you want to leave about your organization. Many companies may permit less formal dress while on the job; however, while on business in another city or country, more formal business dress is expected. Proper dress is especially important when traveling in foreign countries or meeting with persons from a culture different from your own. Be aware of the dress customs for the country in which you will do business and dress accordingly.

Figure 8-2.5

Dressing appropriately for a meeting will contribute to a successful business trip.

© JACK HOLLINGSWORTH/CORBIS

Jagu Patel looked forward to attending a conference at a popular golf resort in Florida. He carefully packed his business suits as well as casual clothes for playing golf and sight-seeing. On Monday morning, Jagu ate breakfast early and arrived on time for the first meeting session. As other participants began to enter the room, he noticed that he was the only person wearing a business suit. Jagu quietly left the meeting area and went back to his room. Reviewing the conference agenda booklet again, he found that it did, indeed, indicate that business casual or resort wear would be the appropriate dress for the conference. Jagu was glad that he had packed plenty of casual clothes as he changed outfits and returned to the meeting.

Customs

Proper etiquette plays an important role in conducting business successfully, both in the United States and in foreign countries. The etiquette will vary from country to country. Various print and electronic resources are available to provide in-depth information about business and travel etiquette. For information about a specific country, consult a travel agent or someone who has lived or done business there. Consider the following customs and protocols related to business travel:

- Be on time for appointments. Arrange your schedule to allow time for unexpected delays in travel.

- Take an ample supply of business cards. Business cards are always presented by a caller and serve the purposes of introducing the person who is visiting and providing an easy future reference. Business cards should include your name, your company's name, your position, and your title. Avoid using abbreviations on the card. For international travel, have the same information printed in the local language on the reverse side of the card.

- If and when appropriate, provide a gift that is company associated, such as a pen or sweatshirt with a company logo. Flowers are generally a safe and appreciated gift in almost every country.

- Paying for meals and tipping for clients is generally accepted as the role of the host—the person who initiated the meeting.

- The universal business greeting in the United States is the handshake. When you offer your hand or reach out to take another's hand, be sure your grasp is firm but not painful. Establish eye contact with the person at the same time.

- Know the body language and gestures that may be offensive or have different meanings in other cultures. The universal form of communication that all people recognize and appreciate is the smile. Use it often to break the ice and ease tense situations that may arise.

- Know how to pronounce the name of the person you are visiting, as well as how to address the person. Use academic or honorary titles when appropriate.

Figure 8-2.6

A handshake is an accepted business greeting in the United States.

© STEVE MASON/PHOTODISC

- Taste any food that is offered by the host. Many hosts will proudly present the best delicacy the area has to offer.
- Speak standard English. Avoid using slang terms. This is especially important when meeting with people for whom English is a second language.

Documents for Foreign Travel

Two documents are required for foreign travel in most countries: a passport and a visa. Other documents, such as work permits, tourist cards, prescriptions for medicine carried, and health records may also be needed.

Passport

passport: official U.S. government document that grants permission to travel outside the United States

A **passport** is an official document granting permission to travel. Issued by the United States Department of State, it authenticates a person's right to protection in the foreign country. A passport is needed for travel in most foreign countries.

To secure a passport, application forms may be obtained from designated government offices and many travel agencies. Passport forms can also be downloaded from the Internet at http://travel.state.gov or obtained by calling the National Passport Information Center. Look in the white pages telephone directory (under "Government Agencies") to find the passport office nearest you. The U.S. Department of State provides a page on its Web site (www.state.gov) designed to help you locate a passport facility near you.

The requirements to obtain a passport for the first time are listed on the passport application and on the U.S. Department of State Web site. Because processing the application normally takes up to six weeks, you should allow

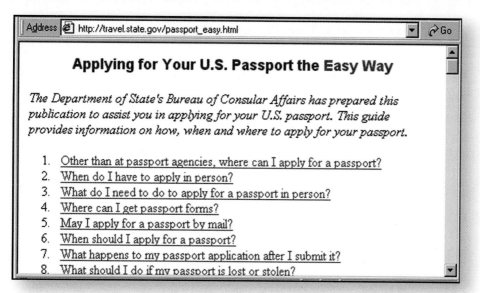

Source: U.S. Department of State. Online. Available: http://travel.state.gov/passport_easy.html. December 15, 2001.

enough lead time to avoid having to delay travel plans. Requesting *expedited* service and paying an extra fee can speed the process to as little as two weeks. After the passport is received, it should be signed, and the information requested on the inside cover should be completed. A passport for a person who was 16 years or older when the passport was issued is valid for 10 years from the date it was issued. To replace an expired passport, obtain a renewal application. Submit the renewal application well in advance of the expiration date for the current passport to avoid being without a current passport.

A passport should be carried or kept in a hotel security box or safe and never left in a hotel room. Make a photocopy of the identification page so the passport can be replaced if it is lost. Report the loss of a passport immediately to the nearest passport office or, if traveling abroad, to the U.S. Embassy.

Visa

A **visa** is a permit granted by a foreign government for a person to enter its country. The visa usually appears as a stamped notation in a passport, indicating that the person may enter the country for a certain purpose and for a specific period of time. Be sure to note the effective dates of a visa.

visa: a permit granted by a foreign government for a person to enter its country

If you are unsure whether it is necessary to obtain a visa for the country in which travel is planned, contact the **consulate** or **embassy** of the country or a travel agent before leaving the United States. Addresses and telephone numbers of consulates of most foreign countries in the United States can be obtained through an online search, using the term "embassy," or by looking in the yellow pages of telephone directories in major cities under "Consulates." Addresses and telephone numbers for many consulates are provided on the U.S. Department of State Web site. Again, allow lead time to obtain the visa stamp from the appropriate consulate prior to traveling to that country.

consulate: person appointed by a government to serve its citizens and business interests in another country

embassy: the offices of an ambassador in a foreign country

Health Documents

When traveling to some countries, certain **vaccinations** may be required to protect against a variety of diseases. A country may require individuals

vaccination: injection given to produce immunity to a disease

Topic 8-2: *Arranging Travel*

Figure 8-2.8

The U.S. Department of State Web site provides contact information for many foreign consulates.

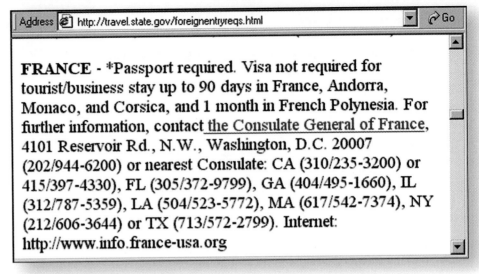

Address http://travel.state.gov/foreignentryreqs.html   Go

FRANCE - *Passport required. Visa not required for tourist/business stay up to 90 days in France, Andorra, Monaco, and Corsica, and 1 month in French Polynesia. For further information, contact the Consulate General of France, 4101 Reservoir Rd., N.W., Washington, D.C. 20007 (202/944-6200) or nearest Consulate: CA (310/235-3200) or 415/397-4330), FL (305/372-9799), GA (404/495-1660), IL (312/787-5359), LA (504/523-5772), MA (617/542-7374), NY (212/606-3644) or TX (713/572-2799). Internet: http://www.info.france-usa.org

Source: U.S. Department of State. Online. Available: http://travel.state.gov/foreignentryreqs.html. December 15, 2001.

HIV: retroviruses that infect human T cells and cause AIDS

entering the country to have health tests, such as a test for **HIV**. A travel agency or the consulate of the country to be visited can supply information about required vaccinations or tests. Records of the vaccinations and tests must be signed by a physician and validated by the local or state health officer on a specific form that may be obtained from a travel agent, the passport office, the local health department, or some physicians. Even if the country to be visited does not require vaccinations, the traveler is well advised to carry a written record of childhood vaccinations and booster shots.

Other health considerations for international flights and travel may include medicine for air sickness, documents from a physician verifying special prescription medicines that must be taken by the traveler, and permission to carry over-the-counter medicines that might not be available in the country to be visited. Check with a travel agent or the country's consulate to see what arrangements must be made for these medicines.

Other Travel Documents

work permit: registers the presence of the person as a visitor on specific business

The foreign consulate of the country to be visited can tell you whether other travel documents, such as a work permit, are required. A **work permit** registers the presence of the person as a visitor on specific business. Several destinations—Mexico, Canada, Bermuda, the West Indies, or Central America—do not require a U.S. citizen to have a passport, but it is a good idea for a visitor to these countries to have a tourist card and to carry proof of citizenship. A **tourist card** authorizes a person to travel throughout the country. Proof of American citizenship can be provided with a passport or birth certificate.

tourist card: authorizes a person to travel throughout the country

Travel Safety

Many airlines, hotels and motels, and travel agencies provide tips for travelers to ensure personal safety. Follow these safety suggestions as you travel or make travel preparations:

- Access the U.S. Department of State Web site (www.state.gov) for travel warnings, consular information sheets, and public announcements regarding travel.

- Do not leave your luggage or other items unattended in hotel lobbies or in waiting areas in airports. Unattended luggage may be stolen or have illegal or unsafe items placed in it.
- Keep your passport and travel funds in a safe, secure place.
- Do not display cash or expensive jewelry or other items when traveling.
- Do not agree to carry items in your luggage for another person.
- Use all locking devices on doors and windows in your hotel room.
- Do not leave valuables in your car, and be sure to lock your vehicle.
- Be aware of your surroundings, and look around before entering parking lots late at night. Always return to your hotel through the main entrance after dark.
- Protect your credit card and telephone calling card numbers at all times.

Many motels and hotels place safety guidelines on specially printed cards in rooms. Read and follow their guidelines for your personal safety.

Handling Work While Away from the Office

Business travelers may depend on an office assistant to handle routine tasks and communications while away from the office on business. Before the traveler leaves for the business trip, the office assistant should understand how to deal with routine matters, **crisis** situations, and out-of-the-ordinary situations.

crisis: a time of trouble or danger

Figure 8-2.9

Never leave your luggage unattended.

© CORBISIMAGES.COM

During the Trip

Answers to the following questions may be helpful to the traveler in keeping work flowing and situations under control during the trip:

- Who will handle crises that may arise while you are out of the office? What kinds of emergencies or crises have occurred in the past that you need to be prepared for?
- Who will be making routine decisions for you while you are out of the office?
- What kinds of messages or documents should be forwarded to you?
- When will you be in touch with the office during the trip?
- What kinds of documents will be forwarded to the office prior to returning to the office?

To keep the office running smoothly, the following suggestions may be helpful to the office assistant:

- Keep an itemized list of incoming mail for the traveler.
- Answer routine mail or e-mail for the traveler if authorized to do so.
- Keep a log of faxes, telephone calls, and office visitors for the traveler.
- If possible, avoid making appointments for the traveler for the first day he or she will be back in the office.
- Keep notes of matters you want to discuss with the traveler on his or her return.

Staying in Touch

Technology makes it possible to take the office anywhere. Business information can be sent and received easily with the appropriate equipment. Using laptop computers with modems and cell phones, business travelers can easily stay in touch with the office or clients. Some hotels provide office support services and fully equipped business centers for travelers. Many hotels offer rooms with special data access phone lines designed for modem use. Airlines provide in-flight telephones and conference rooms in airports. Having access to telecommunications technology allows the traveler to complete tasks such as:

- Send and receive business data by fax
- Access messages (voice or electronic mail)
- Participate in teleconferences
- Access the Internet for travel information
- Transfer travel expense records to an office assistant
- Check availability of products for clients
- Place orders and receive confirmation of orders placed by clients
- Access a company intranet for policy or procedural changes that occur while the traveler is out of the office

Technology will continue to play an increasingly important role in how work is handled while workers are traveling on business.

Business Travel Follow-up Activities

Certain follow-up activities should be completed as soon as possible after a trip. These activities include completing a travel expense report, generating a variety of reports, and writing letters.

Figure 8-2.10

Today's technology allows travelers to complete work away from the office.

Expense Reports

A complete record of travel expenses incurred while on company business is usually reported on a specific form provided by the company. The expenses listed on a **travel expense report** may include charges for hotel or motel rooms, meals and tips, ground and air transportation, entertainment, and other approved business expenses. If company funds were advanced to the business traveler, they are accounted for on the travel expense report. Receipts may be required for travel expenses. Follow company procedures to prepare expense reports, obtain the necessary signatures, and submit the completed forms.

travel expense report: lists expenses to be reimbursed such as hotel, meals, and airfare

Meeting Reports

Examples of meeting reports include sales summaries, client visit logs, project progress updates, or other communications that present the results of the business trip. The completed reports provide a written record of decisions that were made, goals that were set, complaints or suggestions from customers, or ideas that needed to be discussed. Reports are forwarded to persons who will be affected by the decisions, goals, complaints, or ideas.

Letters

Thank-you letters may be sent to people with whom you meet during the trip. The need for thank-you letters will depend on the purpose of the travel and business etiquette guidelines.

Other follow-up letters may provide a written record of agreements made during the visit, give details that where not available during the meeting, or discuss tasks related to the meeting that should be accomplished. When writing follow-up letters, remember to use the five Cs of effective communications to evaluate your documents.

351

Topic 8-2: *Arranging Travel*

Reviewing the Topic

1. In planning a business trip, what activities should you set aside time to complete?
2. What procedures should you follow in making hotel reservations by phone?
3. What items might be collected in a travel folder?
4. List five important travel safety tips.
5. Identify and describe three common forms of business travel.
6. Where can airline schedules be obtained?
7. What items generally appear in a travel itinerary?
8. Define travel etiquette. List five etiquette tips related to business travel.
9. Where can you obtain forms to apply for a passport? How much time should you allow for processing the passport application?
10. Describe three follow-up activities a traveler may need to complete after returning from a trip.

Thinking Critically

You are a department manager for Ellis Tools, Inc. An employee in your department has submitted an expense travel form for your approval before it is forwarded to the accounting department. Your company reimburses employees 30 cents per mile for travel by car. The maximum amounts allowed per day for meals are: breakfast, $10; lunch, $15; and dinner, $25. Employees must submit a receipt for any expense item greater than $25. The purpose of the business trip should be clearly explained on the form including the destination, people with whom the employee met, and the purpose of the meeting.

1. Open and print the data file **Expenses.pdf**, which contains a travel expense form and related receipt.
2. Verify the numbers on the form and note any needed corrections. Circle any other items on the form that are incorrect or require more information.
3. Create a memo form for Ellis Tools, Inc., to include the company name and appropriate memo headings. Write a memo to the employee indicating the changes that should be made to the form and indicate that the form is attached.

Writing thank-you letters is an important follow-up activity for business travelers. In this exercise, you will revise, edit, and key a thank-you letter.

1. Open and print the data file **Thanks.pdf**, which contains a rough draft of a thank-you letter.

2. Key the letter, correcting the grammar and punctuation mistakes. Rewrite and revise as needed to make the letter clear and concise. Use an appropriate letter style and the current date. Assume the letter will be printed on company letterhead.

COMPOSITION
RESEARCH
TEAMWORK
WORD PROCESSING

Topic 8-2 ACTIVITY 1

Travel Reservations and Itinerary

Your manager, Miss Patti Walker, has sent you some notes for a conference she plans to attend in Orlando, Florida. She asks you to research and make reservations and then key an itinerary for her trip. Work with a classmate to complete this assignment.

1. Open the data file **Conference.pdf**, which contains an e-mail from your manager with notes about the trip.

2. Using a printed airline guide or an airline Web site (such as www.delta.com), research airline flights for Miss Walker's trip. You could also telephone airlines for flight information and costs. Miss Walker prefers coach nonstop flights if available. Choose the flights you think are most appropriate, considering the costs and the schedule. Pretend that you have reserved these flights for Miss Walker. Make a note of the flight information for her itinerary or print the information from the Web site if possible.

3. Miss Walker would like to stay at a hotel near the Orange County Convention Center (www.orlandoconvention.com). Use a printed hotel guide or a Web site (such as www.Marriott.com) to find a hotel near the convention center and to find rooms available and rates. You could also telephone hotel reservations numbers (many are toll free) for information. Choose the room and rates you think are most appropriate. Pretend that you have reserved a room for Miss Walker. Make a note of the information for her itinerary or print the information from the Web site if possible. Use the confirmation number *MH2933X2*.

4. Miss Walker will need a rental car while she is in Orlando. Use a rental car Web site (such as www.alamo.com) or call a rental car company to

find the costs of a mid-size car. Pretend that you have reserved a car for Miss Walker. Make a note of the information for her itinerary or print the information from the Web site if possible. Use the confirmation number *C835LX1*.

5. Create an itinerary for Miss Walker. Use the itinerary in Figure 8-2.4 on page 343 as an example. Attach any reservation information you have printed from Web sites for the airline, hotel, or car rental. If you did not print information, key notes about each reservation and attach the notes to the itinerary.

COMPOSITION
DESKTOP PUBLISHING
INTERNET
RESEARCH
TEAMWORK

Topic 8-2   ACTIVITY 2

Travel Etiquette and Safety Brochure

Your manager has asked your work group to create a brochure about travel etiquette and safety tips for business travelers in your company. Many managers are traveling to domestic and international destinations. The brochure would be helpful to them and their office assistants. Work in a group with two classmates to complete this assignment.

1. Create a list of travel etiquette and safety tips that both domestic and international travelers need to know. Supplement the information found in the textbook with information you can find from magazines or from an online search. Use search terms such as *travel etiquette, business etiquette, travel tips,* or *travel safety tips.*

2. Plan the format for your brochure. Lay out your brochure on paper before you create it on the computer. The answers to the following questions may be helpful to your group: What is the name of your brochure? What are the most important points you should emphasize? What supporting information can you provide? What kind of clipart will you need? What clipart is available to you in your classroom? What software is available to you to create your brochure?

3. Use word processing or desktop publishing software to complete your brochure. Review the information on desktop publishing in Chapter 4, pages 145–147. Your finished brochure should include bulleted items and clipart or other graphics to support and enhance the brochure.

Chapter Review

Summary

In this chapter, you learned about the important role office workers play in planning and conducting meetings, participating in meetings, arranging travel, and conducting business away from the office. You also learned about travel etiquette and travel safety. Key points in this chapter include:

- Office workers spend a significant portion of their time in meetings and traveling on business. Your ability to complete meeting and travel arrangements efficiently and accurately adds to your effectiveness. Such arrangements typically involve procedures that must be completed before, during, and after the event.

- Office workers are involved with informal discussions and small group meetings as well as formal business meetings. Office workers may be asked to help to ensure that the meeting is planned properly, materials are available, and follow-up actions are noted and carried through.

- Regardless of the size of the meeting, documents prepared for meetings require organization and planning. Typical documents include an agenda, minutes, and a list of follow-up or action items.

- Meetings are designed to allow the participants to discover problems, exchange information, and make decisions. As an office worker, you should be prepared to lead or participate in any meeting you attend.

- For many meetings, developing a concrete, specific action plan to solve a problem or accomplish tasks is appropriate. A written plan of action can replace the traditional minutes of a meeting.

- A teleconference is a meeting of people in different locations connected by a telecommunications system. Teleconferences can be used to deliver training, exchange information, or solve problems and make decisions.

- Carefully planned travel arrangements are important to the success of a business trip. A travel folder (or trip file) will help you organize the details of an upcoming trip.

- Business trips may involve travel by airplane, train, or car and staying at hotels or motels. Reservations can be made by calling the appropriate hotel or airline, train, or car rental company. Many companies also allow travelers to check schedules and make reservations online at company Web sites.

- An itinerary is a detailed plan of a trip that serves as a guide for the business traveler away from the office. The itinerary includes travel arrangements, appointments, hotel or motel reservations, and reminders or special instructions.

- Travel etiquette and safety guidelines for domestic and international travel are becoming increasingly important to the business traveler. The U.S. Department of State provides travel warnings, consular information sheets, and public announcements regarding travel.

- A passport and a visa are required for foreign travel in most countries. Other documents, such as work permits, tourist cards, prescriptions for medicine carried, and health records may also be needed.

- The office assistant plays a critical role in the office while coworkers travel on business trips. The scope of the activities the assistant will handle must be agreed to by both the assistant and the business traveler.

- Telecommunications technology has made it easier for the business traveler to stay in touch with the office.

- After returning to the office from a business trip, certain follow-up activities must be completed. Thank-you notes, reports, travel expense forms, and other travel-related documents will provide a record of the business that has been completed during the business trip or that needs to be completed after the trip.

Key Terms

action plan	embassy	teleconference
adjournment	etiquette	tourist card
agenda	group dynamics	travel documents
brainstorm	itinerary	travel expense
business card	minutes	report
confirmation	motion	travel folder
number	paper ticket	vaccination
consensus	parliamentary	verbatim
consulate	procedures	visa
coordinator	passport	work permit
directory	quorum	
electronic ticket	second	

COMPOSITION
DESKTOP PUBLISHING
TEAMWORK
WORD PROCESSING

Chapter 8 **ACTIVITY 1**

Teleconference on Travel Etiquette and Safety

Your manager has asked your work group to plan an interactive teleconference that will focus on international travel etiquette and safety. She indicates that the teleconference should be planned for three weeks from today in the company's interactive teleconference room. Those who will attend the teleconference include office workers in various positions who will travel to a new company site abroad and office assistants who will help make travel arrangements. Work with two classmates to complete this assignment.

1. Decide on the date and time for the teleconference. Key a paragraph or list describing the procedures and information you would use to prepare before the meeting.

2. Choose a city and country where the company has the new branch office. Obtain the address of the U.S. consulate for the country you have chosen. You can find this information by completing an online search. For example, if the country you have chosen is Japan, you might search using the term *U.S. consulate Japan*. Write a letter to the consulate asking for information about traveling and doing business in the country.

3. Because it may take some time for your request to the consulate to be processed, also search for information from other sources. Complete an online search for customs, business etiquette, and travel safety tips for the country you have chosen. Revise the brochure on travel etiquette and safety that you created earlier to include customs and etiquette guidelines and safety tips for a traveler to that country.

4. Research the travel documents needed to travel in that country. Key a list and description of travel documents a traveler needs for the country. Obtain samples of or applications for the documents if possible.

5. Plan the topics to be discussed during the teleconference based on the information you have collected. Key an agenda for the meeting. Review the contents and format of an agenda in Figure 8-1.2 on page 322.

6. Submit the following items to your instructor:
   - List describing meeting preparations
   - Letter you have written to the consulate
   - Revised brochure describing customs, etiquette guidelines, and travel tips
   - Samples or applications for travel documents
   - Teleconference agenda

COMPOSITION
INTERNET
RESEARCH
WORD PROCESSING

Chapter 8   **ACTIVITY 2**

International Travel Arrangements

You are one of the office workers who participated in the teleconference on international travel etiquette and safety described in Chapter 8 Activity 1. You need to make travel arrangements for a trip next month to the company's new branch office.

1. You will travel from your home city to the city and country your group chose for the company's new branch office in Activity 1. Your travel date to that city is one month from today. Your return travel date is one week later.

2. Using a printed airline guide or an airline Web site, research airline flights to that city. You could also telephone airlines for flight information and costs. (If you chose a small city for the company branch office, you may need to fly to a larger city that is nearby.) Choose the flights you think are most appropriate, considering the costs and the schedule. Pretend that you have reserved these flights. Make a note of the flight information for your itinerary or print the information from the Web site if possible.

3. Use a printed hotel guide or search the Web to find a hotel in that city. You could also telephone hotel reservations numbers (many are toll free) for information. Choose the room and rates you think are most appropriate. Pretend that you have reserved a room. Make a note of the information for your itinerary or print the information from the Web site if possible. Use the confirmation number *V1379XA*.

4. A company representative, Ms. Kitty How, will meet you at the airport and provide transportation during your stay. She will take you to the airport for your return flight.

5. Create an itinerary for your trip to include travel details and the scheduled activities shown below. See Figure 8-2.4 on page 343 for an example itinerary. Attach any reservation information you have printed from Web sites for the airline and hotel. If you did not print information, key notes about each reservation and attach the notes to the itinerary.

Day 1	Travel to destination city
Day 2	9:30 a.m. – 11:30 a.m. Tour of new office
	12 noon – 2:00 p.m. Lunch with branch manager, Mr. Lou
	2:30 p.m. – 4:30 p.m. Prepare meeting room and materials
Days 3, 4, and 5	9:30 a.m. – 4:30 p.m. Provide training to employees at the branch office
	(1-hour lunch break starting around noon)
Day 6	9:30 a.m. – 11:30 a.m. Meeting with department managers to discuss additional training needs
Day 7	Travel to home city

Records Management Systems

Information is important to the operation of an organization. A system is needed for organizing, storing, and retrieving records and for removing outdated records. As an office worker, you will need to follow records management procedures carefully. These procedures include how to organize, store, retrieve, remove, and dispose of records. This series of steps is known as the record life cycle.

···

You will learn in this chapter that organizations keep records on a variety of media. They use paper, magnetic tapes and disks, optical discs, and micrographics. You will also learn that there are advantages and disadvantages to each. You should know about these media so that you can maintain records properly. This chapter will give you the latest information about the various media and the skills to use the most common filing systems.

OBJECTIVES

- Explain the purposes of records management
- Identify the benefits of records management
- Describe types of media on which information is kept
- Identify the cost factors involved in a records management system
- Describe the phases of the record life cycle
- Describe the process for the removal and archiving of records
- Describe disaster recovery

record: information kept for future reference

records management system: a set of procedures used to organize, store, retrieve, and dispose of records

An office cannot operate without records. For example, each time an item or service is purchased or sold by an organization, a record of the transaction is made and kept in the files. When you work in an office, you will keep a copy of correspondence you mail or transmit. You will also keep items that you receive from other individuals or companies, such as letters, memos, reports, and advertisements. You may even keep a written record of important telephone conversations.

Records are kept so that you and others in the office can refer to the information later or use it to complete another task. A records management system will help you store and retrieve records efficiently and keep the files current.

Overview of a Records Management System

A **record** is any information—text, data, image, or voice—kept for future reference. A **records management system** is a set of procedures used to organize, store, retrieve, remove, and dispose of records.

The main purpose of a records management system is to make sure records are available when needed so that the organization can operate efficiently. Such a system fulfills this purpose in several ways by:

- Using storage media
- Providing proper storage equipment and supplies
- Outlining procedures for filing
- Developing an efficient retrieval procedure
- Setting up a schedule for when records should be kept or discarded

An effective records management system benefits the organization in two ways. First, workers are more productive. Second, customer goodwill is maintained.

To make an intelligent decision or complete a task well, you need accurate, current information. For example, to prepare a monthly sales report, you need to have the sales figures for each sales representative. Before you pay an invoice, you should check your records to be sure the charges are correct. Before you can mail a package, you need to know the recipient's complete address.

You must be able to access needed records easily and quickly. An effective records management system will enable you to be more productive because you will not waste valuable time searching for information that should be easily available.

Customers and business associates may not fully appreciate efficient records management in your organization, even though they like the results of such

Figure 9-1.1

This medical assistant can quickly access patient records.

© MARK ADAMS/SUPERSTOCK INTERNATIONAL

management. They are pleased when you retrieve pertinent information quickly. Yet, they may take the smooth operation of the records management system for granted.

Storage Media

An organization may keep records on a variety of **media**: paper, **magnetic media** such as computer disks or tape, and **micrographics** (documents reduced and placed on film). A good records management system includes a program for analyzing the needs of the company to determine which storage **medium** or combination of media is best. As an office worker, you may be expected to work with all these media. Each medium has particular advantages and disadvantages, and you will learn more about these in this topic.

Storage Equipment and Supplies

Storage equipment, such as filing cabinets, should be chosen with specific storage media in mind. For example, if your records are on paper, you might use a filing cabinet or open shelf files. You may use supplies such as file folders to hold paper records, but you would not use them for storing computer tapes. Chapter 10 discusses the various equipment and supplies appropriate for each type of storage medium.

medium or media: material(s) or form(s) on or in which information may be stored

magnetic media: disks or tapes used to store documents electronically

micrographics: photographically reducing documents to file on microfilm

361

Topic 9-1: *Maintaining Office Records*

Figure 9-1.2

Open shelf files are used for storing paper records in some offices.

You should keep certain especially valuable records in fireproof cabinets or vaults. A good records management system includes policies that help you determine which records require special protection. For example, you may be instructed to protect original copies of contracts by storing them in a fireproof vault.

Filing Procedures

filing: the process of storing records in an orderly manner within an organized system

Filing is the process of storing office records in an orderly manner within an organized system. The procedure you follow to file records will vary according to the storage media used and the manner in which the files are organized. Topic 9-2 explains the various paper filing systems. Chapter 10 presents specific filing procedures for managing hard copy and electronic media files.

charging out: removing a record from the file and recording pertinent information

Employees need an orderly way to retrieve records. Efficient retrieval procedures include specific instructions for removing or charging out records. **Charging out** a record usually means that the following information is recorded when the record is removed from the file: the name and department of the worker who took the record, the date the record was retrieved, and the date it was returned. This information is kept in case someone else must locate the record. A retrieval procedure also should indicate whether all workers or only designated staff members have free access to the records. Chapter 10 explains retrieval procedures in more detail.

Records Retention and Disposition

retention schedule: list of how long each type of record should be kept

A records management system should include information on how long records are kept and how they are to be disposed of. Most companies use a **retention schedule**, which lists how long each type of record should be

CHAPTER 9: RECORDS MANAGEMENT SYSTEMS

kept. You should follow this schedule to be certain that the files are free of outdated or unnecessary records so that you can work efficiently. Proper **records disposition** can be equally important. Later in this topic, you will learn more about this aspect of records management.

records disposition: transferring records to permanent storage or destroying records

Storage Media for Records

Businesses and other organizations typically store records on a variety of media. The most common storage medium continues to be paper. Although paper records will remain a major part of filing systems for years, businesses are recording more and more information on magnetic media and micrographics. These systems require less space to store the records and allow them to be accessed more quickly.

Paper

Each time you print a copy of a letter, record an address on an index card, complete a telephone message form, or print a statistical report or complicated graph from the computer, you are recording information on paper. These paper records are referred to as **hard copy**.

hard copy: documents printed on paper

The advantage of keeping paper records is that you can immediately read the information recorded. With magnetic media records, such as a word processing file stored on your computer, however, you need a display screen or printer to access the information. Two disadvantages of storing records on paper are that such records take up a great deal of space and they can be easily misfiled.

Minimizing Paper Records

The best records management system is one in which a mixture of paper and other storage media are used. You may keep those records that are vitally important in more than one medium. You might keep records that must be seen all at once or are signed, legal documents in paper form. Records that are no longer needed daily but, perhaps, occasionally may be kept in electronic form. Whatever the needs of your office, you should consider keeping paper records to a minimum. Follow these rules:

- Do not be a pack rat. Know what paper to save and what to throw away.
- Do not wait until you are afloat in a sea of paper or have a large number of electronic files to store or organize. Set aside time for records management each day.
- Keep a file directory. Maintain a written directory for files.

Accessibility Is Key

When paper records are maintained, they must be accessible. Topic 9-2 offers an explanation of the various filing systems used for paper records. Chapter 10 covers the equipment you will need for filing. A good office designer and a manager can coordinate the most efficient combination of systems and equipment so that you will know where to go to find records easily. For instance, moveable filing racks are great for quick access; an alphabetic filing system may be just right for an office with lots of files of patient names.

Magnetic Media

hard disk: magnetic medium used to store large amounts of information

floppy disk: portable magnetic medium used to store small amounts of information

magnetic tape: magnetically coated material used to store information

Magnetic media are reusable and contain information that is stored electronically. The most frequently used forms of magnetic media are hard computer disks (hard drives), flexible (floppy) disks, and tapes. **Hard disks** are metal disks that are specially magnetized to hold the information put onto them and are usually internal to a computer. These disks vary in storage capacity, and, with advances in technology, their storage capacity continues to increase. **Floppy disks** are bendable disks placed inside a hard casing to protect them. They work in the same way as hard disks but hold less information and are less durable. Their main use is portability. Information can be placed on a floppy disk in one computer and transported by that disk to be read or used in another computer. These disks hold from 1.44 megabytes to 120 megabytes of information. **Magnetic tape** is used primarily for backing up (making a copy of the files on) hard drives and for holding large amounts of information that is not used on a regular basis. Because tape may be of great length, it has a large storage capacity.

Advantages and Disadvantages of Using Magnetic Media

Four major advantages to the use of magnetic media are:

- Records can be retrieved quickly and easily.
- The storage space required for housing records on magnetic media is much less than that required for paper media.
- Records stay in the same sequence on the magnetic media even after being retrieved several times.
- Records can be organized and updated easily.

Three disadvantages to using magnetic media to store records are:

- An output device such as a monitor or printer is needed to read the information recorded on the magnetic media.
- Electrical power surges and failures can erase or change the information recorded on magnetic media.
- Magnetic media require special protection from extreme heat and cold and should be kept away from magnetic fields.

Compact Discs (CDs)

CD: compact disc, an optical information storage medium

The **CD**, or compact disc, is an optical storage form. Information is put on the disc by laser and read by a CD drive in the computer. These discs are in many ways better than most magnetic media, such as floppies, because they can hold more information than any but a hard disk. The biggest advantage of CDs over magnetic media is their ability to hold large files needed for graphic information, including moving pictures with stereo sound. The disadvantage is that most older computers only have a drive to read CDs and cannot write (or save) information to these discs. New computers and stand-alone drives are available that write to CDs.

CDs should be handled carefully and kept in a protective jacket or case to prevent the surface from being scratched or getting dirty. Scratches or dirt on the surface and warping, which can be caused by exposure to extreme heat, may make a CD unreadable.

Figure 9-1.3

Many records are stored on optical media.

© GOODSHOOT/SUPERSTOCK INTERNATIONAL

WORKPLACE CONNECTIONS

When Joyce walked by Ken's workstation, she noticed that several floppy disks and a CD out of its protective jacket were lying on top of the monitor. Ken was working at the computer and seemed unconcerned about the situation.

Joyce: "Ken, did you know you could be destroying all your hard work right now?"

Ken: "What do you mean?"

Joyce: "Floppy disks are sensitive to magnetic forces such as those found in the computer and even the telephone. You should never place them on top of the monitor! And, by leaving the CD out of its jacket you risk scratching it or dropping something on it that will mar the surface and make it unreadable."

Ken: "I guess you're right. (He removes the floppy disks from the top of the monitor and places the CD in its jacket.) I'd hate to lose everything I just worked on."

Micrographics

Microimaging systems, also called micrographics, photographically reduce documents to a fraction of their original size to fit on film or **microfiche**. The following steps are involved in the process:

microfiche: a small rectangular sheet of microfilm that contains a series of records arranged in rows and columns

1. Records are gathered so they can be imaged to film. (Chapter 10, Topic 10-2, describes methods of organizing records for micrographic storage.)

2. A special camera is used to take pictures of the hard copies.

3. The film is developed. Each record then appears as a tiny picture—a microimage—on the film or fiche, as shown in Figure 9-1.4.

4. A device called a reader is used to display the microimage for reading. Some readers, referred to as **reader/printers**, will also print a hard copy of the microimage.

reader/printer: displays and prints images from microfilm

Computer output microfilm (COM) is the process of transferring computer files directly to microfilm or fiche. The computer reads information recorded on magnetic media and outputs it as microimages on film rather than as paper printouts. Computer input microfilm (CIM) is the process of converting data to electrical impulses stored on magnetic media and using the data as input to the computer to create files. Microimages take less space to store than paper and will not, if properly stored, **deteriorate** after long periods of time.

deteriorate: become lower in quality or value

Micrographics are used when paper or computer files would be inappropriate or less practical. For instance, an automobile dealer usually will keep parts lists for past-year vehicles on microfiche. Because the list is unchanging, keeping the data on magnetic media that can be updated is not necessary. Because the fiche is less bulky, it is easier to store and retrieve than paper records. Libraries often keep back issues of magazines and newspapers on microfilm because storing rolls of film is much easier and less costly than storing huge stacks of periodicals.

Microforms

You may use micrographics in different forms, collectively called microforms. The most frequently used microforms are described in Figure 9-1.5 along with details about each type of microform.

Figure 9-1.4

Microfilm and microfiche are used to store records that would be bulky in paper form.

CHAPTER 9: RECORDS MANAGEMENT SYSTEMS

Roll Microfilm	Available in different widths
	Usually a roll of 16mm or 35mm film that contains a series of images
	The most inexpensive microform
	Used to store records that are not used frequently or do not require changes
Aperture Card	Paper card that holds a piece of microfilm visible through an opening in the card
	Usually contains one microimage from 16mm or 35mm film
	Often used for large-format drawings
	Identifying information can be printed on the card
Microfiche	Small rectangular sheet of microfilm that contains a series of records arranged in rows and columns
	The 6" x 4" size is the most commonly used
	Identifying information appears at the top
	Individual records are more easily located on microfiche than on roll microfilm
Microfilm Jacket	A plastic holder for strips of 16mm or 35mm microfilm
	Strips or single microimages are inserted into sleeves or pockets
	Can be easily updated
	Space at the top of the jacket shows the contents

© Photo courtesy of Bell & Howell Imaging/South-Western/Thomson Learning

Figure 9-1.6

A microfilm jacket holds strips of microfilm or single microimages.

Advantages and Disadvantages of Using Microfilm

Storing records on microfilm has several advantages. These advantages include:

- A microimage takes up less space than a record stored on paper.
- In a microimaging system, the image is viewed but not removed from the film. The microimages are always in the same sequence on the same microform, regardless of how often the microform is retrieved and filed.
- Hard copies of microimages can be produced on reader/printers when needed.
- Microimaging is an inexpensive way to **archive** important records. Microimages are usually accepted in courts as legal evidence just as paper records are.
- Retrieval devices available for use with microfilm make it easy to access needed records.
- Microfilm can be easily duplicated and stored in a separate, protected location.

archive: keep permanently in inactive files

WORKPLACE **CONNECTIONS**

During their break, Mario and Carolyn began discussing the new microimaging system their company had recently implemented.

Mario: *"At first, I wasn't sure that microimaging would be helpful. But now, I'm glad we have the system."*

Carolyn: *"I was looking forward to having our records on microfilm! Our file cabinets were so crowded that I had difficulty just filing and retrieving records."*

Mario: *"What I've enjoyed is being able to refer to a record without cluttering my workstation with more paper. But if I need a hard copy, I can make one by using the microfilm reader/printer."*

Three disadvantages of storing records on microfilm are:

- The initial cost may seem high because a camera, reader/printer(s), and microfilm must be purchased to record information on film.
- Office workers must be given special training so they can operate the microimaging equipment.
- Records stored on microfilm cannot be updated or altered.

Imaging Systems

imaging system: converts documents to electronic form

digitized: converted to a form that can be read by a computer

Imaging is a common method of handling information and the media on which it is kept. An **imaging system** converts all types of documents to **digitized** electronic data that can be stored on CD-ROM or rewritable CDs and retrieved immediately. Electronic image systems include:

- A scanner to convert the paper documents to a digitized electronic form
- A processor that compresses the image
- A storage medium to retain the image
- A retrieval mechanism to convert the image for viewing on a monitor
- An output device that processes the image to hard copy format

Imaging systems reduce paper processing, speed up workflow, and make files instantly accessible. The best use of imaging is in organizations that have a high volume of documents, have high activity in files, and require a high level of security for documents.

Cost Factors

Costs are involved with any records management system. The cost factors involve buying equipment and supplies, leasing storage space, and paying office workers to file and retrieve records.

Equipment, Supplies, and Storage

Major equipment purchases such as filing cabinets and shelves, as well as periodic purchases of filing supplies, contribute to the cost of using a records management system. Proper care of equipment and careful use of supplies by employees will help control costs.

When businesses lease office space, they lease by the square foot. The company pays for the space occupied by records every time it writes a rent check. By keeping that space to a minimum, the room available for work is increased. Using microfilm or magnetic media to store records is one way to reduce the amount of space required to house records.

Human Resources

Workers are a key element in an effective records management system. Efficient procedures are worthless unless they are put into practice. Thus, the salaries a company must pay its human resources (workers) to handle records are a cost factor of records management.

Large companies often have an entire staff of records management personnel. A manager may be in charge of the records management department. The staff may include an analyst, a records center supervisor, and several clerks. Because records management is a field growing in importance, many businesses are looking for workers who specialize in this area. Records management is a major career opportunity.

Destruction Costs

Several costs are associated with destroying records. Paper must be shredded, removed from the business in bulk, and placed in a landfill in an ecologically sound manner. Some paper records may need to be placed on micrographic or optical media first, and storage of those resulting records will be an additional expense. Some of the costs can be reduced. Small businesses may take advantage of commercial records centers for destruction of records and of micrographics services if imaging is needed. Large businesses may find it more cost-effective to complete these steps in-house.

Topic 9-1: *Maintaining Office Records*

Figure 9-1.7

Human resources are a cost factor of records management.

© KEITH BROFSKY/PHOTODISC

Record Life Cycle

Records come from many sources. Some records, such as letters from clients, come from outside the organization. Others are created within the organization. Examples of these records include interoffice memos, records of sales and purchases, reports, and copies of outgoing correspondence. Records are categorized according to their usefulness and importance.

- **Vital records** are essential to the company. These records are often not replaceable. Examples include original copies of deeds, copyrights, and mortgages.
- **Important records** are needed for the business to operate smoothly and would be expensive to replace. Examples include tax returns, personnel files, and cancelled checks.
- **Useful records** are convenient to have but are replaceable. Examples include correspondence, purchase orders, and the names and addresses of suppliers.
- **Nonessential records** have one-time or very limited usefulness. Examples include meeting announcements and advertisements.

The usefulness of each record has a beginning and an end. Therefore, each record has a life cycle. The phases of the record life cycle are the same regardless of whether the records are kept on paper, magnetic or optical media, or micrographics. Sometimes, however, records will be stored on different types of media at different stages in their life cycle. A paper record might be converted to microfilm before being placed in inactive storage. A

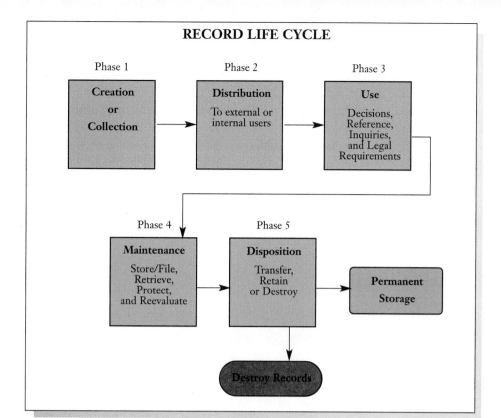

Figure 9-1.8

These phases make up the life cycle of a record.

record life cycle is shown in Figure 9-1.8. Refer to this figure as you read the following brief description of each phase.

1. **Creation or collection.** The cycle begins when you create or collect the records.

2. **Distribution.** During this phase, records are sent to the persons responsible for their use.

3. **Use.** Records are commonly used in decision making, for documentation or reference, in answering inquiries, or in satisfying legal requirements.

4. **Maintenance.** When records are kept for later use, they must be **categorized** and stored, retrieved as needed, and protected from damage or loss. The exact procedure you use in this phase will vary depending on whether the record is on paper, magnetic media, optical media, or micrographics. You also need to know whether the record should be filed alphabetically, numerically, or chronologically. Each record's value should be reevaluated regularly. Some records may remain in active storage while others are placed in inactive storage.

   categorize: assign to a group of similar items, arrange by type

5. **Disposition.** Records are disposed of either by destroying the records or by transferring them to permanent storage, often at less expensive storage sites.

Removing Records from Active Storage

When records are outdated, or needed only infrequently, you should remove them from the active storage area. An effective records management system will include a policy for such removal.

Topic 9-1: *Maintaining Office Records*

Retention Schedule

A retention schedule, shown in Figure 9-1.9, is a valuable records management tool that identifies how long particular types of records should be kept. The retention schedule includes a description of the type of record and the retention period (how long the record should be kept). The retention period may be shown in total years only or it may be divided into active and inactive storage periods. The authority who decides how long the record should be kept may also be included. Government authority dictates how long you should keep certain records, such as tax returns. Company executives may establish policies for how long to keep other records such as bank statements, expense reports, budgets, and correspondence. Therefore, retention schedules will vary from company to company.

Can you determine from this retention schedule how long bank statements must be kept?

Records Retention Schedule

Record Description	Active Storage Years	Inactive Storage Years	Total Years
ACCOUNTING RECORDS			
Accounts Payable Ledger	3	3	6
Accounts Receivable Ledger	3	3	6
Balance Sheets	3	P	P
Bank Statements	3	3	6
General Ledger Reports	3	P	P
P = Permanent			

Inactive Storage and Commercial Records Centers

inactive records: documents referred to infrequently

Inactive records are those that are needed by the organization but are not used often. Inactive records should be stored separately from active ones. For example, assume you are required to keep company bank statements for three years. Because you likely do not refer often to the past years' statements, you should remove them from active storage. You do not want inactive records to occupy valuable active storage space. Retrieving and filing active records is easier when inactive records are stored in a separate location because you have fewer records to deal with on a regular basis.

Carla Nagai works in the accounts payable department in a manufacturing company. Accounts payable personnel often refer to vendor invoices from the current or the previous year. Therefore, the company keeps invoices in active storage for two years. A new calendar year has just started, so Carla collected the invoices from the year before last for transfer to inactive storage. According to the company's retention schedule, vendor invoices are kept for a total of seven years. When the invoices Carla collected are placed in inactive storage, any invoices in inactive storage that are more than seven years old will be collected and destroyed.

The most cost-effective way for many businesses, particularly small ones, to store inactive records is to use commercial records centers. Most of these centers offer a number of services and charge on a unit-cost basis per month. These centers base the unit on a standard-sized box that fits their shelving and that customers are required to use—thus maximizing storage space. Other costs may include pickup and delivery, receiving and handling at initial storage, and destruction costs at the end of the record's life cycle.

Special records of historical value are stored apart from active records. An archive is a storage area that is dedicated to organizing and preserving such historical records. These archived records may be in the form of paper, optical media, or microimages.

Disaster Recovery

A disaster is an event that causes serious harm or damage. A disaster recovery plan provides procedures to be followed in the case of an event, such as an earthquake, fire, flood, power outage, sabotage by an employee, or other situation that results in a partial or total loss of records and other business resources. Plans will vary depending on the needs of the organization. The disaster recovery plan should be reviewed periodically and updated as needed.

Many companies provide services designed to aid in disaster recovery. Trained consultants to help create a recovery plan, secure off-site storage areas, methods for backing up data in various formats, and backup locations for the business to use during recovery are examples of these services. At some facilities, special below-ground vaults are used to store irreplaceable records.

Disaster Recovery Plans

The terrorist attacks on the federal office building in Oklahoma City, the World Trade Center in New York City, and the Pentagon are extreme examples of the need organizations have for disaster recovery plans. Hundreds of offices and records were destroyed in these disasters, and losses have been estimated in billions of dollars.

Although every business may not be involved in a major national crisis, every business does need a disaster recovery plan. A disaster may be caused by natural events such as a hurricane, tornado, or earthquake, or by accidental or intentional acts of man, such as fires, computer viruses, sabotage, bombs, or even human error. Disaster recovery planning, part of a broader concept called business continuity planning, can help prepare a business to deal with a crisis situation and to resume normal business operations as soon as possible.

With the growth of ecommerce and business practices such as just-in-time inventory, businesses must be concerned about the disaster recovery plans of partners and suppliers as well as their own. A disruption of normal operations for partners or suppliers can have a serious effect on a company. Businesses that work closely together may coordinate their disaster recovery plans.

A disaster recovery plan should include steps for prevention, readiness, reaction, and recovery.

- **Prevention** involves taking action to avoid a disaster. A disaster recovery plan should include procedures that are applied on a regular basis. For example, surge protectors and antivirus programs can prevent damage to computers and data. Buildings can be inspected regularly for fire hazards. Important data files can be backed up to secure locations to prevent loss. Many companies use climate controlled off-site records storage buildings to limit data loss.

- **Readiness** is being prepared for a disaster. Companies must try to judge the damage that disruptions may cause to the business and plan to minimize the damage. The plan should be reviewed and updated regularly. Testing the plan and providing training for employees on putting the plan into action is an important part of readiness.

- **Reaction** is setting your disaster plan in motion. Companies may move operations to backup sites; use alternate means of communication such as home e-mail addresses, pagers, and cell phones; and make preparations for beginning recovery. Reaction also involves taking steps to prevent further damage.

- **Recovery** means restoring the business to normal operations. As it pertains to records management, recovery involves replacing data lost in a disaster. Computer data may be restored from backup copies. Computers and other office equipment may be repaired or replaced.

Many organizations and companies promote awareness and education about disaster recovery and business continuity planning. The Disaster Recovery Institute International (www.drii.org) has a professional certification program for business continuity/disaster recovery planners.

Reviewing the Topic

1. Why is an effective records management system vital to the smooth operation of an organization?

2. How does an effective records management system result in greater productivity by office workers?

3. List one advantage and two disadvantages of using paper to store information.

4. What are three frequently used forms of magnetic media?

5. Identify four types of microforms.

6. List four advantages of storing records on microfilm.

7. What are four cost factors that affect the efficiency of a records management system?

8. List the phases of the record life cycle and describe the activities in each phase.

9. What is a retention schedule?

10. What is a disaster recovery plan, and why is it important?

Interacting with Others

An important folder is missing from the central files. You discover that someone in your department has signed it out. You go to this person, who is above your level in the company, and he says that he does not have it. The folder is essential for your work. What should you do?

1. Should you confront the higher-ranking person and insist that he give you the file? Why or why not?

2. Should you go to your supervisor and ask her to help resolve the situation? Why or why not?

3. Should you attempt to do your work without the folder and make mistakes because you do not have the information you need? Why or why not?

Reinforcing Math Skills

1. A single file drawer contains 75 folders. Documents from 15 of these folders were converted to micrographic form. The microforms were transferred to inactive storage. Of the remaining active folders, six had their contents divided into two folders each. How many active folders are now in the file drawer? What is the percentage of decrease in the number of folders in the active file?

2. Eight departments have requested additional file folders. Folders are ordered from the supply company in boxes, each containing 25 folders. The number of folders each department needs is shown below. How many folders are required to meet the needs of all the departments? How many boxes of folders should be ordered? How many folders will be left after each department has received the number of folders it requested?

Accounting	21	Production	175
Finance	48	Public Relations	100
Human Resources	99	Marketing	260
Information Systems	125	Customer Service	32

DATABASE
RECORDS MANAGEMENT

Topic 9-1   ACTIVITY 1

Retention Schedule

Each company creates its own records retention schedule. Your manager has written some notes that you will use to create a records retention schedule for your company. In determining the retention times for each record, she considered how long the records will be used, how frequently the records will be used, and the form in which the records will be kept, and laws that pertain to records retention.

1. Create a new database file to include the following six fields: *Records Series, Record, Years Active, Years Inactive,* and *Total Years.*

2. Open and print the data file `Retention.pdf`, which contains your manager's handwritten notes.

3. Create a record in your database for each type of record listed in your manager's notes. For each record, enter the series name in the Record Series field and the record description in the Record field. Enter numbers in the Years Active, Years Inactive, and Total Years fields or enter *P* for Permanent.

4. Sort the records by the Records Series field and then by the Record field in ascending order.

5. Create and print a report to show the records retention schedule. Group the records by records series. Title the report *Records Retention Schedule*.

6. Create a query to show all records with a *P* in the Years Total field. Print the query results.

Topic 9-1   ACTIVITY 2

Records Management Job Descriptions

Your supervisor, Ms. Suzuki, asks you to update the records management section of the office manual. She approaches your workstation and says: "Here is my edited draft of the updated material for the office manual. Please prepare a final copy, making the changes I've indicated on the draft. Correct any errors I may have overlooked."

1. Open and print the data file **RMJobs.pdf**, which contains the rough draft.

2. Prepare a final copy of the document and print it on plain paper.

OBJECTIVES

■ Identify the components of a paper filing system

■ Describe alphabetic filing systems

■ Explain how a numeric filing system is organized

■ Arrange records for terminal-digit and middle-digit filing systems

■ Explain how a chronologic filing system is organized

In Topic 9-1, you learned that each record has a life cycle. In this topic, you will become acquainted with systems for organizing paper files while the records are in the storage phase of the life cycle.

Although many companies use computerized filing systems, paper filing systems are still common. Many companies use both systems. Procedures for organizing magnetic and optical media and micrographic files are presented in detail in Chapter 10.

In a paper filing system, individual records are stored in folders. These folders are labeled and organized alphabetically according to names of individuals, organizations, businesses, subjects, or geographic locations. Files may also be organized numerically and by date. As an office worker, you will be expected to understand your organization's filing system so that you can file and retrieve records efficiently. You may even have an opportunity to suggest ways to improve the system.

Components of a Paper Filing System

A filing system requires equipment, procedures, and supplies. You need to understand the various types of each. You also need to understand the use of guides that apply to all of the systems.

Equipment

Various types of equipment—cabinets and shelves—are used to store paper records. Lateral file cabinets like those shown in Figure 9-2.1 are used in many offices. In this topic, we will assume that all records in your organization are stored in lateral file cabinets. Chapter 10 describes other equipment used in a paper filing system.

Procedures

Before placing records in folders, you should index and code each record. **Indexing** is the process of deciding how to identify each record to be filed—either by name, subject, geographic location, number, or date. **Coding** is the process of marking a record to indicate how it was indexed. As you learned in Topic 9-1, you may retrieve and refile a record many times while it is in active storage. By coding a record, you help ensure that it will be filed correctly each time it is returned to the files. Chapter 10 explains in detail the procedures for indexing and coding.

indexing: deciding how to identify each record to be filed

coding: marking a record to indicate how it was indexed

Supplies

Each drawer in a file contains two different kinds of filing supplies: guides and file folders. The guides divide the drawer into sections and serve as signposts for quick reference. They also provide support for the folders and their

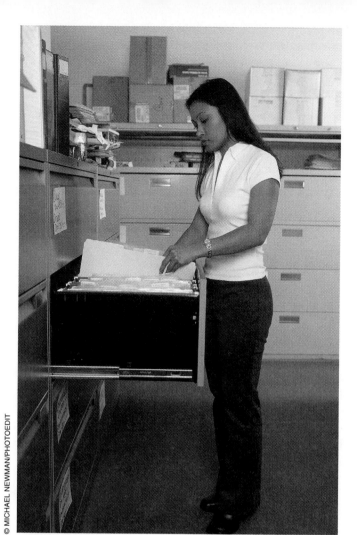

Figure 9-2.1

Lateral files are frequently used to store records in offices.

© MICHAEL NEWMAN/PHOTOEDIT

contents. File folders hold the papers in an upright position in the drawer and serve as containers to keep the papers together. Labels are attached to file folders to identify the contents of each folder. Labels are also attached to file cabinet drawers to identify the contents of each drawer.

Guides

Guides are heavy cardboard sheets that are the same size as the file folders. A tab extends over the top of each guide, and a notation is marked or printed on the tab. This notation is called a **caption**. By reading the captions, you can quickly identify divisions within the file. For example, a guide may carry the caption "A," which tells you that only records starting with the letter *A* are found between that guide and the next one.

guide: heavy cardboard sheet that creates divisions in a file

caption: notation on a guide, folder, or drawer that indicates the contents

Guides are classified as primary or special. Primary guides indicate the major divisions, such as letters of the alphabet, into which the filing system is separated. Special guides indicate subdivisions within these major divisions. Figure 9-2.5 on page 383 shows how primary and special guides are arranged in an alphabetic filing system. Behind primary guide "C" you may have a special guide such as "COOPER TEMPORARIES." For quick retrieval of files, place no more than ten folders behind a guide, and place only about 15 to 25 guides in a file drawer.

Figure 9-2.2

Drawer label

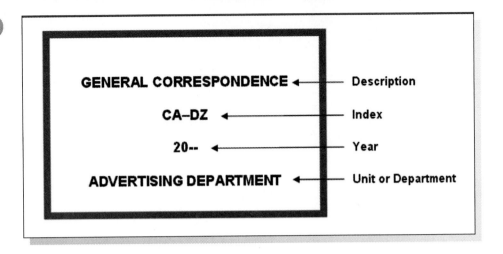

Labels

labels: strips of paper attached to file drawers or folders with captions identifying the contents

Labels are strips of paper, usually self-adhesive, that are attached to file drawers or folders and contain captions identifying the contents. You need labels on file drawers so that you can identify the contents of each drawer without opening it. The information on the drawer label should be specific, easy to read, and current. When the contents of a cabinet are changed in any way, the drawer label should be corrected immediately.

Folder labels are attached to the folder tabs. The caption on the label identifies the contents of the folder. The captions should be placed in a consistent manner, usually at the top, left-hand corner of the label. Labels come in standard sizes to match various tab sizes for folders. Some word processing programs have templates or other special features to format a document for these standard label sizes. Using these special software features makes creating and printing labels easy. Many companies use color-coded labels to improve filing efficiency. For example, a different color might be used for each alphabetic or numeric section of the files.

Folders

folder: container used to hold papers in a file

A **folder** is a container made of strong, durable paper called manila and used to hold papers in a file. Each folder is larger than the papers it contains so that it will protect the contents. Standard folder sizes are designed for papers that are 8½" × 11", 8½" × 13", or 8½" × 14".

Folder cuts are made in the back of a folder, which is higher than the front, to create a tab. You attach labels with captions to the tabs to identify the contents. Folder tabs vary in width and position, as shown in Figure 9-2.4 on page 382. Sometimes the tab is the full width of the folder. This is called a full-cut or straight-cut folder. Half-cut tabs are half the width of the folder and have two possible positions. Third-cut folders have three positions, each tab occupying a third of the width of the folder. Another standard tab has five positions and is called a fifth-cut folder. Some folders hang from metal frames

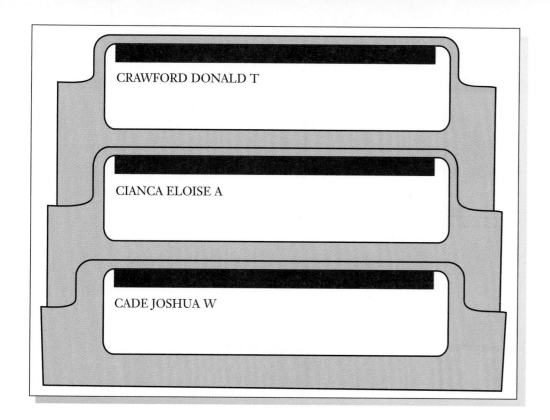

Figure 9-2.3

Folder labels

placed inside the file drawer. Removable tabs can be attached to these folders at appropriate positions.

Costs

The costs associated with paper filing include paper, folders, labels, organizers, indexing products, printing supplies for labels, equipment maintenance and upgrades, and other essentials. The largest budget item for records management systems is often for active files. The cost is ongoing because new files are added to the system regularly. New paper supplies and equipment such as storage cabinets must be purchased periodically.

Position of Guides and Folders

A variety of filing systems are used in offices today. The positioning of guides and folders within filing systems will vary from office to office. Regardless of the system used, the guides and folders should be arranged so they are easy to see and in a logical order. You can see that the arrangement in Figure 9-2.5 on page 383 allows your eye to move easily from left to right.

Guides

When you open a file drawer to store or retrieve a document, you look first for the appropriate primary guide. Because you read from left to right, the tab on the primary guide should be at the far left, where it will be easy to locate.

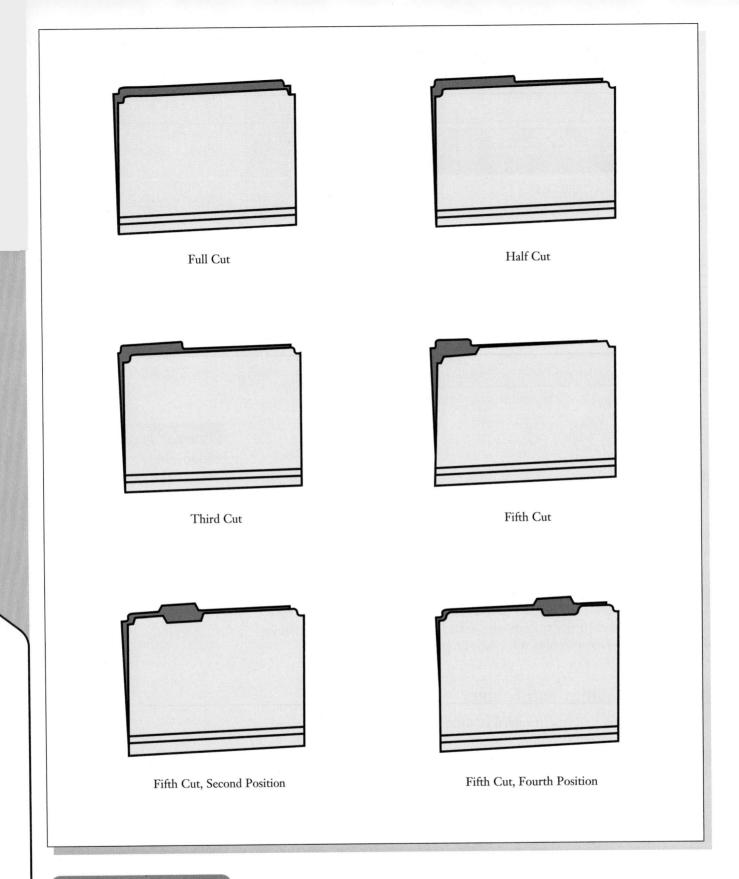

Full Cut

Half Cut

Third Cut

Fifth Cut

Fifth Cut, Second Position

Fifth Cut, Fourth Position

Figure 9-2.4

Folder tabs vary in width
and position.

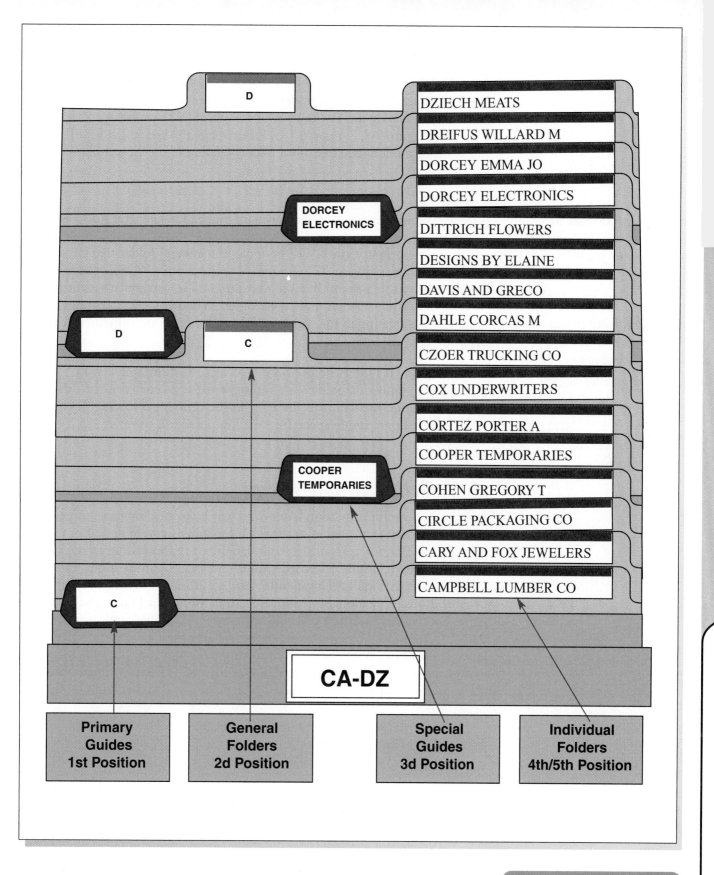

D

DZIECH MEATS

DREIFUS WILLARD M

DORCEY EMMA JO

DORCEY ELECTRONICS

DORCEY ELECTRONICS

DITTRICH FLOWERS

DESIGNS BY ELAINE

DAVIS AND GRECO

DAHLE CORCAS M

D   **C**

CZOER TRUCKING CO

COX UNDERWRITERS

CORTEZ PORTER A

COOPER TEMPORARIES

COOPER TEMPORARIES

COHEN GREGORY T

CIRCLE PACKAGING CO

CARY AND FOX JEWELERS

C

CAMPBELL LUMBER CO

CA-DZ

| Primary Guides 1st Position | General Folders 2d Position | Special Guides 3d Position | Individual Folders 4th/5th Position |

Figure 9-2.5

Note the position of guides and folders in this portion of a name file.

Topic 9-2: *Paper Records Systems*

Special guides are used to pinpoint the location of a specific fourth/fifth position individual folder. In Figure 9-2.5, special guides are located in the third position. For example, the special guide "DORCEY ELECTRONICS" was added because of frequent requests for the Dorcey Electronics folder. Using the special guide, this folder can easily be located. Sometimes a special guide is used to pinpoint the location of a series of folders relating to a specific subject. In Figure 9-2.7, on page 388, for example, the special guide "FILM" marks the location of two individual folders relating to the subject film.

Folders

general folder: used to hold records for which no individual folder has been created

A **general folder** is used for each primary guide. This general folder is placed in the second position folder and bears the same caption as the one shown on the primary guide. For example, the general folder that goes behind the primary guide "C" also will bear the caption "C." These folders are given the name general because they are used to accumulate records that do not justify the use of an individual folder. When you accumulate five or more records relating to one name or subject, prepare an **individual folder** for those records.

individual folder: used to hold five or more records for an individual, company, or subject

Using individual folders helps you locate records more quickly. In Figure 9-2.5, individual folders are shown in the combined fourth/fifth position. Notice the width of the tabs on the individual folders. This extra width allows ample space for labeling personal, company, or subject names.

Alphabetic Filing Systems

In an alphabetic filing system, letters and words (names, subjects, or geographic locations) are used as captions on the guides and folders. Both guides and folders are arranged in alphabetic order according to the captions. The Association of Records Managers and Administrators, Inc. (ARMA International) recommends standard filing rules for use of all organizations. The alphabetic indexing rules shown in Figure 9-2.6 on pages 386–387 are written to agree with the ARMA International standards. Common alphabetic filing systems use names, subjects, or geographic locations. Many offices do not have enough file space for separate name and subject files. When this is true for your office, you may file name and subject folders together.

Filing by Name

name file: records arranged according to the name of an individual or organization

If a **name file** is used, records are indexed according to the name of an individual or organization. The folders are arranged in alphabetic order within the file drawer.

Figure 9-2.5 shows how alphabetic primary and special guides are used in a name file to help you file and retrieve records efficiently. If you were looking for a folder labeled "EMMA JO DORCEY," you would find the primary guide

"D" and search for the individual folder for Emma Jo Dorcey. By using the guides, you should be able to locate the folder quickly without having to thumb through all the folders. If you do not find an individual folder for the record, file the record in the appropriate general folder.

WORKPLACE CONNECTIONS

Employees must understand proper filing procedures in order to store records in the correct folders and ensure that the records can be found later.

Carrie: *"Roy, there is no folder labeled* Dalton Real Estate *in the file. Where do I file this letter?"*

Roy: *"If there is no individual folder for Dalton Real Estate, file it in the general folder behind the D guide. When we have several more letters to or from Dalton Real Estate, we'll set up an individual folder for those records."*

Filing by Subject

When a subject filing system is used, you index records according to particular subjects—such as marketing, office machines, and public relations. A **subject file** is used when you request records by their contents more often than by the names of individuals or companies. Use subject titles as captions for primary guides. In Figure 9-2.7 on page 388, you can see that the primary guides are "ADVERTISERS," "APPLICATIONS," and "AUDIOVISUAL EQUIPMENT."

subject file: records arranged by topic

You may use special guides to identify subdivisions within the main subjects. In Figure 9-2.7, the main subject "AUDIOVISUAL EQUIPMENT" is divided by special guides into subdivisions of "FILM" and "OVERHEAD PROJECTORS." You may use names, geographic locations, numbers, or subjects as captions for special guides.

As you can see in Figure 9-2.7, the label for an individual folder behind a primary guide includes the primary guide caption ("ADVERTISERS," for example) and the caption for the folder ("GEBHART GLASSWARE," for example). The label for an individual folder behind a special guide should include:

- The primary guide caption ("AV EQUIPMENT," for example, and note that you may abbreviate "AUDIOVISUAL" as "AV")
- The special guide caption ("FILM," for example)
- The caption for the folder ("ROLLINS CATALOGS," for example)

Figure 9-2.6

Alphabetic indexing rules

Rule 1 Indexing Order of Names
In a personal name, the surname (last name) is the first unit, the given name (first name) or initial is the second unit, and the middle name or initial is the third unit. Business names are indexed as written using letterheads or trademarks as guides. Each word in a business name is considered a separate indexing unit.

Rule 2 Minor Words and Symbols in Business Names
Articles, prepositions, conjunctions, and symbols are considered separate indexing units. Symbols are considered spelled in full. When the word *the* appears as the first word of a business name, it is considered the last indexing unit.

Rule 3 Punctuation and Possessives
All punctuation is disregarded when indexing personal and business names.

Rule 4 Single Letters and Abbreviations
Initials in personal names are separate indexing units. Abbreviations of personal names and nicknames are indexed as they are written. Single letters in business and organization names are indexed as written. If single letters are separated by spaces, index each letter as a separate unit. An acronym (such as ARMA) is indexed as one unit regardless of spacing. Abbreviated words (Corp., Inc.) and names are indexed as one unit. Radio and television station call letters are indexed as one unit.

Rule 5 Titles and Suffixes
In personal names, a title before a name (Mrs., Dr.), a seniority suffix (II, III, Jr., Sr.) or a professional suffix (M.D., Mayor) after a name is the last indexing unit. Numeric suffixes are filed before alphabetic suffixes. If a name contains both a title and a suffix, the title is the last unit. Royal and religious titles followed by either a given name only or a surname only (Father Leo, Princess Anne) are indexed as written. Titles in business names are indexed as written.

Rule 6 Prefixes—Articles and Particles
A foreign article or particle (Mac, St., San, De, Von der) in a personal or business name is combined with

the part of the name following it to form a single indexing unit. Spaces in the prefix or between the prefix and the name are disregarded.

Rule 7 Numbers in Business Names

Numbers spelled out (Seven Acres Inn) in business names are filed alphabetically. Numbers written in digits are filed in ascending order before alphabetic letters or words (7 Acres Inn comes before Seven Acres Inn). Arabic numerals (2, 3) are filed before Roman numerals (II, IV). Names with inclusive numbers (33-37 Apartments) are filed by the first digits only (33 Apartments). For numbers containing *st*, *d*, and *th* (1st, 2d, 4th), ignore the letter endings and consider only the digits.

Rule 8 Organizations and Institutions

Banks and other financial institutions, clubs, colleges, hospitals, hotels, magazines, motels, museums, newspapers, religious institutions, schools, unions, universities, and other organizations are indexed and filed according to the names written on their letterheads.

Rule 9 Identical Names

When personal names or names of businesses or organizations are identical, filing order is determined by the address. Compare the addresses in this order: city names, state or province names, street names (including Avenue, Boulevard, Drive, Road, or Street), house or building numbers.

Rule 10 Government Names

Government names are indexed first by the name of the governmental unit—country, state, county, or city. For example, the first three indexing units of a United States government agency name are *UNITED STATES GOVERNMENT*. Next, index the name of the department, bureau, office, or board. Rearrange the units, if necessary, so the more distinctive parts come first. For example, the name *Dept. of Public Safety, Baltimore, Maryland* would be indexed in five units: *MARYLAND, PUBLIC, SAFETY, DEPT, OF.*

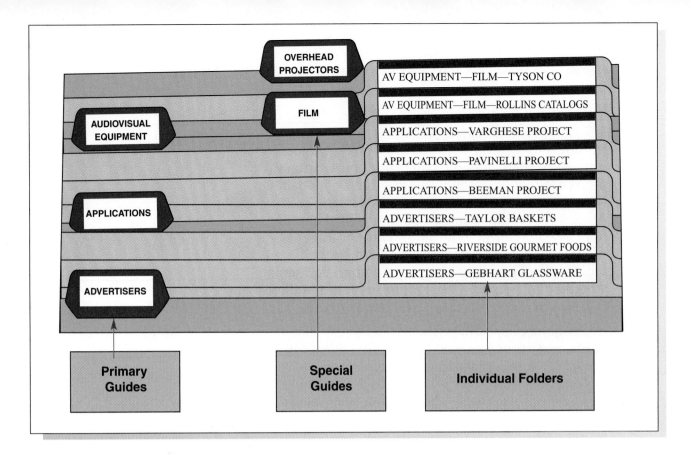

Figure 9-2.7

In subject files, the special guides identify subdivisions of the main subjects.

geographic file: records arranged according to locations

Filing by Geographic Location

When using a **geographic file**, you index records according to geographic location. You may base a geographic file on sales territories, states, or cities in a single state, for instance.

Typical users of geographic filing are publishing houses, mail-order houses, radio and television advertisers, real estate firms, and organizations dealing with a large number of small businesses scattered over a wide area. The human resources in these small businesses may change frequently. Therefore, the name of each individual owner or manager is often less important for filing purposes than the location of the business. Refer to Figure 9-2.8 as you read about the components of a geographic filing system.

Guides and Folders

The main geographic divisions used in a geographic file, such as states or countries, are placed on location name guides in the front of the file drawer. These divisions are sometimes called the *key units*. The primary guides in a geographic file are named for the largest geographic divisions below the level of the key units. For example, in Figure 9-2.8, the primary guides are based on cities. The key unit ("ALABAMA") appears on a location name guide positioned in the center front of the file. The special guide ("CAPITOL") is used to pinpoint the location of certain individual folders.

A general folder is placed behind each location name guide. In the figure, the general folder and the location name guide bear the same caption ("ALABAMA"). When you prepare labels for individual folders, give the geographic location on the first line ("AL BIRMINGHAM," for example). On the second line, indicate the caption for the individual folder ("CARTER MANUFACTURING CO," for example). These complete labels tell you behind which primary and special guide to refile the folder.

WORKPLACE **CONNECTIONS**

The firm where Carlota works uses a geographic filing system based on states. This morning, her supervisor needed a record pertaining to Wonderland Toy Company. To retrieve the record, Carlota first checked the alphabetic index file. She learned the toy company was located in Richmond, Virginia. She scanned the drawer labels and opened the drawer labeled *Virginia*. She then searched through the primary guides until she came to the city of Richmond. Then locating the individual folder for Wonderland Toy Company was easy. Carlota's supervisor appreciated her ability to locate the record so quickly.

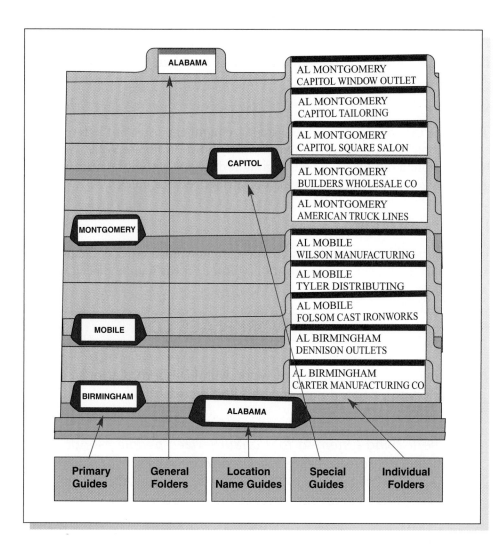

Figure 9-2.8

In a geographic file, the primary guides identify the largest geographic location within each key unit.

Topic 9-2: Paper Records Systems

numeric file: records arranged by numbers

Alphabetic Index

To retrieve a specific record in a geographic file, you must know the geographic location of each person or organization. Because you may not remember all this information, you will need an alphabetic index. This index can be in a computer database, a printed list, or an index card file. The index is arranged according to the names of organizations and individuals in the file. The record for each organization or individual shows the geographic location under which records are filed.

Numeric Filing Systems

In a **numeric file**, records are indexed by number. Files arranged in simple numeric order use a consecutive numbering method. Other numbering methods, such as terminal-digit or middle-digit, are discussed later in this topic.

The numeric method of filing is frequently used when records are already arranged in numeric order. For example, insurance companies may arrange their records according to policy number. Utility companies often index customers' records by account number. Some companies index records numerically even though they are not already numbered before the filing process. For example, a number may be assigned to each name or subject in a file. The caption on the individual folder would then be a number (for example, "3877" for "Global Security Systems" or "8551" for "West Coast Development Project") rather than a name or a subject.

Guides

The guide captions in a numeric system are numbers instead of letters or words. Look at the consecutive numeric file shown in Figure 9-2.9. Notice how the numbered special guides highlight divisions within the primary guide category. Special guides help you retrieve records quickly.

Individual Folders

In a numeric filing system, the caption on an individual folder is the number assigned to the person or organization whose records will be placed in the

WORKPLACE CONNECTIONS

Today is Carlos's first day of work. Mimi Dibbern, Carlos's supervisor, briefed him on the filing system they use:

Carlos, the records in our department are confidential. We use a numeric filing system so that unauthorized people cannot locate specific records easily. To keep these files secure, we have a policy that allows only workers in our department to have access to the control file and the accession file.

folder. An advantage to a numeric system is that it helps you keep records confidential. Scanning the numeric captions on folders will not tell a casual observer much about the contents.

Accession Log

To set up an individual folder, you first refer to an **accession log**, also called an accession file, book, or record. An accession log lists in numeric order the numbers already assigned and the name or subject related to each number. In Figure 9-2.10 on page 392, you can see that the last number, 3877, was assigned to Global Security Systems. The next number you assign will be 3878. By keeping an accession log, you avoid assigning the same number to more than one

accession log: list of numbers assigned in a numeric filing system

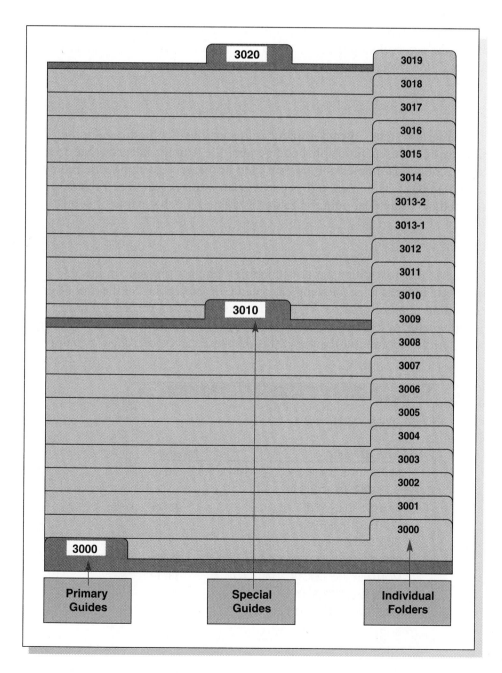

Primary Guides

Special Guides

Individual Folders

Figure 9-2.9

Insurance companies often arrange records by policy number using a numeric file.

Topic 9-2: *Paper Records Systems*

Figure 9-2.10

This database accession log shows the number assigned to each name or subject in the file.

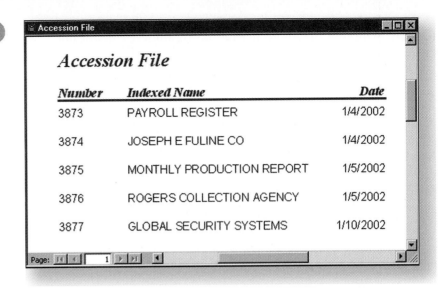

name or subject. Such a log might be written by hand in some offices. In other offices, the accession log is kept using a computer database. Using a computer database allows you to search for entries easily, either by number or by name.

General Alphabetic File

In a numeric system, a general folder is not included behind each numeric guide. Instead, a separate alphabetic general file is used. Records that do not have an individual numeric folder are filed in the general alphabetic file by name or subject. When enough records related to one name or subject are collected, an individual numeric folder is created for that name or subject.

Alphabetic Index

A numeric records system cannot function with an alphabetic index. An alphabetic index is a list showing each name or subject in the file and its corresponding number or code. When you must retrieve a record, you refer to the alphabetic index to learn the correct file folder number. If the accession log is kept in a computer database, this database can be searched by name,

Figure 9-2.11

A *G* indicates that a record is stored in the general alphabetic file.

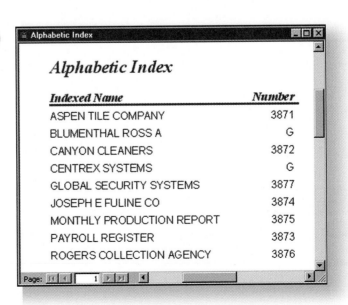

CHAPTER 9: RECORDS MANAGEMENT SYSTEMS

eliminating the need for a separate alphabetic index file. For records filed in the general alphabetic file, a *G* is entered in the number field to indicate that the record is in the general alphabetic file. Fields can be included in the database for information such as mailing address and telephone number.

Terminal-Digit and Middle-Digit Filing Systems

Sometimes in a numeric filing system numbers can be quite long. A social security number, for instance, is nine digits. Some insurance policy numbers might be fifteen or more digits. To improve the accuracy of numeric filing systems, terminal-digit or middle-digit numbering methods are often used.

Terminal-Digit Filing

Terminal-digit filing is a kind of numeric filing in which the last two or three digits of each record number serve as the primary division under which a record is filed. Numbers are assigned consecutively, just as in numeric filing; however, they are read from *right to left* in small groups beginning with the terminal (final) group of numbers.

Record numbers are divided into three groups of two or three digits each. If numbers have too few digits for three equal groups, zeros are added to the *left* of each number. These groups of digits are called primary, secondary, and tertiary (third). The right (terminal) group of digits is primary, the middle group is secondary, and the left group is tertiary. The primary number (right group) is used as the number of the file section, drawer, or shelf. The secondary number (middle group) is used for the guide. The tertiary number (left group) is the folder/record number. Just as in regular numeric filing, an alphabetic index file is used.

Middle-Digit Filing

Middle-digit filing is a method of numeric filing in which the middle two or three digits of each record number are used as the primary division under which each record is filed. Numbers are assigned consecutively; however, for filing, numbers are read from *middle to left to right*.

Just as in terminal-digit filing, groups of digits are identified as primary, secondary, or tertiary. In this system, the middle group is primary, the left group is secondary, and the right group is tertiary. Drawer, file, or shelf numbers are from the primary (middle) group. Guide numbers are from the secondary (left) group. Folder numbers are from the tertiary (right) group. As in other types of numeric filing, an alphabetic index file is used.

Chronologic Filing Systems

In a **chronologic file**, records are filed according to date. Chronologic files primarily help you keep track of tasks you need to complete each day. A desk calendar and a tickler file are two kinds of chronologic files used for this purpose.

chronologic file: records arranged according to date

You may also use chronologic filing in combination with name, subject, geographic, or numeric systems. In these situations, individual folders are all coded in the normal way of that system. However, records within the individual folder are organized by date, usually with the most recent document placed at the front of the folder.

Reviewing the Topic

1. What are the three components of a filing system?
2. What is the difference between indexing a record and coding a record?
3. Why are guides used in a filing system?
4. Describe an advantage of using color-coded labels.
5. Where should the tabs on primary guides be located? Why?
6. Name three frequently used alphabetic filing systems.
7. Why do you need an alphabetic index file in a geographic or numeric filing system?
8. What is an accession log or file? Why is it necessary to use an accession log?
9. In what direction are the numbers read in a terminal-digit filing system? in a middle-digit filing system?
10. When would you most often use a chronologic file?

Thinking Critically

For three months you have worked in the office of Davis Rider, Inc., a company with 12 employees. When you began the job, your supervisor, Mr. Davis, told you that you would be generally in charge of the files as well as having other duties. Although everyone has access to the files, he explained that you need to make sure the files are neat and that materials do not stack up.

Although the task seemed simple when Mr. Davis explained it to you, it has become a source of frustration. Some employees remove records and do not return them for several weeks. Other employees open file drawers and place folders on top of the other folders instead of inserting them in their proper places. Needless to say, the files are not being managed well. Because you are generally in charge of the files, you are being held accountable for the situation.

1. What steps could you take regarding your own work habits to help correct this problem?
2. What steps could you ask others to take to help correct this problem?

Reinforcing English Skills

Using *it's* and *its* incorrectly are common writing mistakes. *It's* is a contraction of *it* and *is* or *has*. *Its* is a possessive pronoun. To help you know which term to use, ask yourself: "Could I substitute the words 'it is' or 'it has' in the sentence and have it make sense?" If you can, use *it's*; if not, use *its*. Rewrite the following eight sentences, inserting either *it's* or *its*, whichever is appropriate.

1. You need to put the folder back in ____ place.
2. ____ time to remove the inactive files from active storage.
3. He replied, " ___ necessary to charge out each record."
4. This folder has lost ____ label.
5. ____ been returned to the files.
6. Please let me know when ____ ready.
7. The company improved ____ image.
8. ____ on the top shelf of the bookcase.

Topic 9-2 ACTIVITY 1

Accession Log and Alphabetic Index

You work for Philips Associates, a company in Miami, Florida. To help keep the records confidential, a numeric filing system is used. You have been asked to create a database file to serve as both an accession log and an alphabetic index.

1. Open and print the data file **Philips.pdf**, which contains information you will need to create records in the database.

2. Create a new database file with the following text fields: *Number*, *Indexed Name*, *Name*, *Street*, *City*, *State*, *ZIP*, and *Telephone*.

3. Create a record in the database for each person or company. In the Indexed Name field, enter the name in all capitals in the order it would be indexed for filing. (Review the alphabetic indexing rules in Figure 9-2.6 on pages 386–387.) Enter the name as written in the Name field. Enter a number or the letter *G* in the Number field. Enter data in the other fields as written.

4. Create a report titled *Accession Log* to include only the Number and Indexed Name fields. Sort the data in the report by the Number field. Adjust the format as needed for an attractive report and print the report. What number will be assigned to the next company or business for which an individual numeric folder is created? Write the number on the bottom of your report.

5. Create a report titled *Alphabetic Index* to include only the Indexed Name and Number fields. Sort the data in the report by the Indexed Name field. Adjust the format as needed for an attractive report and print the report.

6. Create a query to find the Indexed Name for all the people or companies whose records should be stored in the general alphabetic file. Sort the names in alphabetic order. Print the query results.

7. Keep this database for use in a later activity.

RECORDS MANAGEMENT

Topic 9-2   ACTIVITY 2

Numeric Filing

Numeric filing systems are widely used in businesses. Practice your numeric filing skills in this activity.

1. List the 16 numbers below, arranging them in order for a consecutive numeric filing system. Ignore the spaces in the numbers for this step.

2. List the 16 numbers below, arranging them in order for a terminal-digit numeric filing system. Spaces in the numbers indicate the number groups.

3. List the 16 numbers below, arranging them in order for a middle-digit numeric filing system. Spaces in the numbers indicate the number groups.

786	67	1258	231	55	2187
303	99	2891	189	40	2891
947	28	6314	287	29	6314
502	64	9284	502	64	9485
786	67	1269	287	40	2756
303	89	2977	647	28	6325
502	63	8922	287	29	2341
946	40	2891	303	52	2977

Chapter Review

Summary

An effective records management system improves efficiency in storing, retrieving, and managing records. In this chapter, you learned about the equipment, procedures, and supplies used in paper filing systems. As an office worker, you will probably be involved in some aspect of records management. You should be knowledgeable about the following key points:

- A records management system is the manner in which an organization chooses to organize, store, retrieve, remove, and dispose of its records.

- You may be called on to manage records on various media such as paper, magnetic or optical media, and micrographics. Storage equipment and supplies should be chosen with specific storage media in mind.

- Efficient retrieval procedures include specific instructions for removing or charging out records.

- Microimaging systems, also called micrographics, photographically reduce documents to a fraction of their original size to fit on film or microfiche.

- An imaging system converts all types of documents to digitized electronic data.

- Costs are involved with any records management system and include buying equipment and supplies, leasing storage space, and paying office workers to file and retrieve records.

- Records are categorized as vital, important, useful, or nonessential.

- The phases of the record life cycle include creation or collection, distribution, use, maintenance, and disposition.

- A retention schedule identifies how long particular types of records should be kept.

- A disaster recovery plan provides procedures to be followed in case of an event, such as an earthquake, fire, flood, power outage, sabotage by an employee, or other situation that results in a partial or total loss of records and other business resources.

- In a paper filing system, individual records are stored in folders. These folders are labeled and organized according to a records management system.

- Records can be organized alphabetically by name, by subject, by a combination of name and subject, or by geographic location. Records can also be organized numerically using a consecutive, terminal-digit, middle-digit, or chronologic system.

- An accession log lists in numeric order the numbers already assigned and the name or subject related to each number.

- An alphabetic index is a list showing each name or subject in the file and its corresponding number, code, or geographic designation used for filing.

Key Terms

accession log	guide	numeric file
archive	imaging system	optical media
caption	inactive records	reader/printer
charging out	indexing	record
chronologic file	individual folder	records disposition
coding	label	records manage-
filing	magnetic media	ment system
general folder	micrographics	retention schedule
geographic file	name file	subject file

Chapter 9   ACTIVITY 1

Tickler File

You work in the accounts payable department in a small company. One of your responsibilities is to determine payment dates for invoices to take advantage of discounts offered by vendors. You then file the invoices chronologically by payment date in a tickler file. You check the tickler file each day to see what invoices should be paid in the next couple of days. This ensures that payments are made within the discount periods and saves money for the company.

1. Determine the payment dates for each invoice shown below according to terms given. For example, terms *2/10, net 30* mean that a 2 percent discount may be taken if the invoice is paid within 10 calendar days of the invoice date. If the invoice is dated June 1, the payment date would be June 11. Terms *net 30* mean no discount is available, and the invoice should be paid in 30 days.

2. Determine the filing order of the invoices arranging the invoices chronologically by payment date. If more than one invoice has the same payment date, arrange them alphabetically by company name. Refer to the alphabetic indexing rules in Figure 9-2.6 on pages 386–387.

3. For checking purposes, indicate the order of the invoices by listing their item numbers.

ITEM	COMPANY NAME	INVOICE DATE	TERMS
1.	Centrex Systems	May 18	2/10, net 30
2.	James Office Supply	June 6	1/10, net 30
3.	Frank Brothers, Inc.	May 22	1/10, net 30
4.	Caldwell Industries	July 2	2/10, net 30
5.	Baker and Sons	June 9	1/10, net 30
6.	Rodriguez and Parker	June 9	net 30
7.	Ralston, Inc.	July 2	1/10, net 30
8.	Ace Plumbing	May 18	2/10, net 30
9.	5 Star Producers	July 2	1/10, net 30
10.	Paragon Cable	June 6	2/10, net 30
11.	All State Products	May 18	net 30
12.	Freedom Motors	May 2	net 30
13.	Franklin Associates	May 22	1/10, net 30
14.	Rodgers Design	June 30	1/10, net 30
15.	Bakersfield Market	May 20	net 30

Chapter 9   ACTIVITY 2

Filing Records Geographically

Businesses such as publishers, mail-order houses, radio and television advertisers, and real estate agencies often file records geographically. Practice your geographic filing skills in this activity.

1. Open and print the data file **Philips.pdf**, which contains the records you will need for this activity or use your printout from Topic 9-2 Activity 1.

2. Determine the filing order for the records. First, arrange the records alphabetically by city. Then arrange the records for each city alphabetically by the company or person's name. Refer to the alphabetic indexing rules in Figure 9-2.6 on pages 386–387. Number the records on your printout to indicate the correct filing order.

3. Open the database you created in Topic 9-2 Activity 1, which contains records for Philips Associates. Sort the records first by city, then by company name in ascending order.

4. Compare the order of records in the sorted database table with the order you indicated on your printout. Is the order the same on both? If not, why not? Which order is correct?

Chapter Review

Managing Records

O ffice records are stored on a variety of media. These storage media have different storage requirements. Special storage equipment and supplies are available for magnetic, optical, and micrographic files as well as for paper records. All records that relate to a particular topic, regardless of the storage media used, are often stored together. For example, a floppy disk containing a project proposal and the paper correspondence relating to the project are placed in a folder together.

· ·

This chapter describes the principles, procedures, equipment, supplies, and technology available to help you manage various forms of records efficiently. This includes reprographics and its use in the modern office. The second topic is devoted to the expanding field of managing magnetic and microimaging records and media.

Managing Paper Records

OBJECTIVES

- Explain how to prepare records for filing
- Apply efficient filing procedures
- Describe the use of requisition cards, OUT guides, and OUT folders in charge-out procedures
- Describe how inactive files are transferred and stored
- Describe storage plans for vital records protection
- Identify copier features and operating procedures

Wherever you work—whether in a small company or a large one—you probably will store some records on paper. Even in offices where magnetic media and micrographics are used extensively, certain paper (hard copy) records are needed.

Because paper is a major medium for storing records, you should understand how to maintain paper files. Once you have a clear understanding of the principles and procedures for managing these files, you can easily adapt this knowledge to maintaining records stored on other media.

In this topic, you will learn about preparing individual records for storage. You will study methods for locating and removing individual records as well as entire folders. You also will become acquainted with the equipment used to copy and store paper records.

Preparing Records for Storage

Before filing a record for the first time, you need to prepare it properly for storage. By doing so, you speed up the filing process and ensure that the record is filed correctly. Follow these five steps to prepare paper records for storage:

1. Collect the records.
2. Inspect the records.
3. Index/code the records.
4. Cross-reference the records, if needed.
5. Sort the records.

Figure 10-1.1

Office workers must be familiar with the procedures for managing paper files.

© BILL ARON/PHOTOEDIT

401

Topic 10-1: *Managing Paper Records*

Collect Records

accumulate: gather, collect

Throughout the workday, you will **accumulate** records that need to be filed. Instead of preparing and filing each record as you are finished with it, collect the records in a designated place such as a tray labeled *TO BE FILED*. Then at scheduled times, such as after lunch or at the end of the day, prepare a batch of records for storage at one time. You will not need to index, code, or cross-reference records that have been filed before. You will still need to inspect and sort them, however, before they can be refiled.

Inspect Records

After you collect a batch of records to prepare for storage, inspect each record by following these procedures:

release mark: official authorization to file a record

- When you are preparing a record for the first time, look for a **release mark**. The initials of someone authorized to release the record, written on the record, often serve as the release mark.
- Remove all paper clips or rubber bands from the records.
- Staple all related materials together.
- Repair any torn records with transparent tape.
- Attach small records to a full sheet of paper so that they will not be lost or crumpled in the file. Alternatively, you may copy the small record onto a full page—unless the original must be kept.

Index/Code Records

index: decide how to identify a record for filing purposes

You **index** a record by deciding how to identify it for filing purposes. The name, subject, geographic location, or number used to identify a record is called the filing segment. The name or subject most likely to be used in asking for the record is the one to be used for storage. On outgoing letters, the name of the recipient (company or person if no company is shown) is usually the most important. On incoming letters, the name of the sender (company or person if no company is shown) is the usually the most important.

code: mark the units of a filing segment for a record

You should **code** the record by the filing segment so you can quickly tell how to file a record by glancing at it. You will file the record the same way each time it must be refiled. Records may be coded by hand, the conventional method, or by bar coding.

Conventional Coding

Some companies prefer that you code records with a blue, nonreproducing pencil. If you must copy the record, the code markings will not copy. To code a record indexed by subject, geographic location, or number, write the filing segment in the upper-right corner of the record. Coding a record indexed by individual or company name involves three steps:

1. Identify the filing segment. Underline or circle the name the first time it appears on the record. If the name is not contained in the record, write it in the upper-right corner.

2. Identify the indexing units of a name, which include each word, initial, or abbreviation within a name. For example, there are three indexing

units in the name "Grady P. Hill." Use slash marks to divide the filing segment into separate indexing units:

Grady / P. / Hill

3. Number the units in the proper indexing order, which is the order in which units are considered when a record is filed alphabetically. For example, individual names are filed alphabetically by last names, not by first names. Therefore, in the case of Grady P. Hill, you would number the indexing units this way:

```
   2        3      1
Grady /   P. /   Hill
```

Figure 9-2.6 on pages 386–387 presents standard rules for identifying indexing units and for alphabetizing names. Refer to these rules as needed when indexing records. Figure 10-1.2 shows a record properly indexed and coded.

Bar Coding

A **bar code** is printed on a label, usually self-adhesive, and attached to an item to identify it electronically. The advantage of using preprinted labels is that an office worker will not accidentally assign the same bar code number to two files. When a bar-coding system is used, card indexes and manual logs, discussed in Chapter 9, are replaced by automated indexing and tracking systems. Bar codes can be used for filing and refiling records and for tracking files, documents, and correspondence.

In a bar-code system, a code on a record is scanned into an electronic tracking system, much as grocery prices are scanned at the register of a supermarket. The computer will add the date and time the record is filed or retrieved. When an item is refiled, the computer identifies the date and time of the

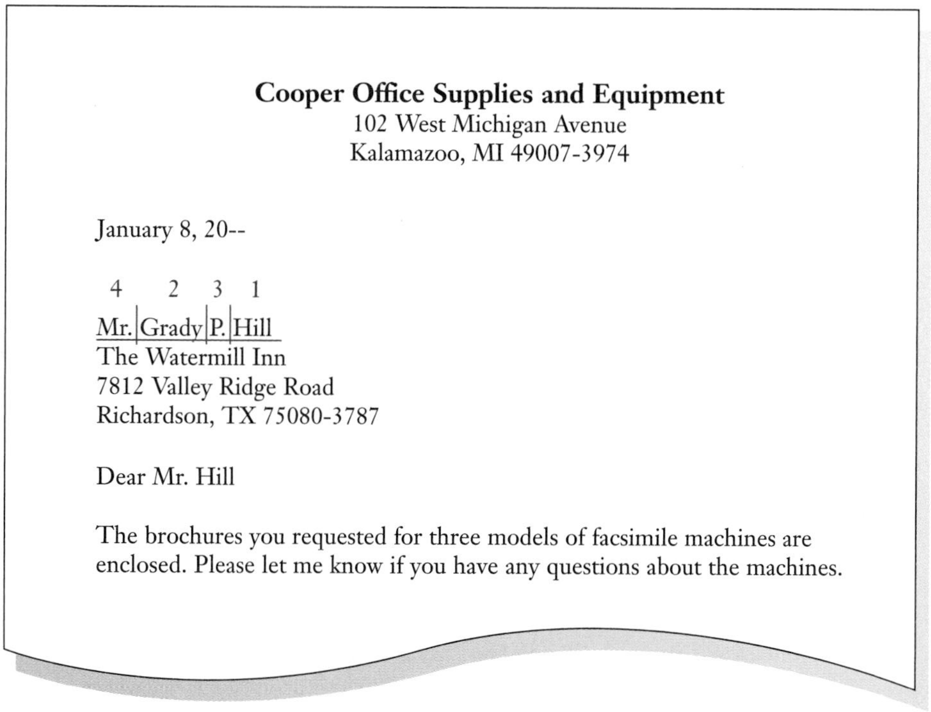

bar code: pattern of vertical lines of varying widths containing coded information that can be read by a computerized scanner

Cooper Office Supplies and Equipment
102 West Michigan Avenue
Kalamazoo, MI 49007-3974

January 8, 20--

```
 4    2   3  1
Mr. |Grady|P.|Hill
```
The Watermill Inn
7812 Valley Ridge Road
Richardson, TX 75080-3787

Dear Mr. Hill

The brochures you requested for three models of facsimile machines are enclosed. Please let me know if you have any questions about the machines.

Figure 10-1.2

This copy of an outgoing letter has been indexed and coded for filing.

return. A bar-coding system allows less margin for human error, and fewer files are lost.

Cross-Reference Records

cross-reference: document that gives the alternate name or subject by which a record may be requested and the name or subject by which the record is filed

A **cross-reference** is prepared when a record may be requested by more than one name or subject. For example, in Figure 10-1.3, the record may be indexed by the name of the company sending the letter or by the subject of the letter. In this case, you would first index and code the record by the name or subject of primary importance, which is Star Wholesale Groceries (the name of the company sending the letter). Then you would code the name or subject of secondary importance, which is SPRING BONANZA OF VALUES (the subject of the letter). Note that you code the subject by underlining it, numbering the indexing units if appropriate, and placing an X in the margin. The X is a signal that the record is cross-referenced under that particular subject.

A record may be requested by a variation of the name under which it is filed. For example, a letter filed under the name Bird and Casey Associates might be requested as Casey and Bird Associates. In this case, you would write the cross-reference caption on the document followed by an X. You would then index and code the cross-reference name on the letter and prepare a cross-reference sheet.

Cross-Reference Sheet

A cross-reference sheet includes information about the record and is filed in the cross-referenced folder. The following information is recorded on the cross-reference sheet as shown in Figure 10-1.4.

- The name or subject under which the record was cross-referenced
- The date the record was originated

Figure 10-1.3

This incoming letter has been coded by name and marked for a cross-reference.

                    1   2   3
          ★ Star│Wholesale│Groceries ★
             56096 Mount Vernon Highway
               Alexandria, VA 22309-1746

April 9, 20--

Mr. Arnold J. Amonti
Arnold's Delicatessen
489 King Street
Alexandria, VA 22314-4920

Dear Mr. Amonti

Take advantage of special savings at our SPRING BONANZA OF VALUES. X
Star Wholesale Groceries will hold this special promotion from April 20
through April 26. Be sure to mark those dates on your calendar.

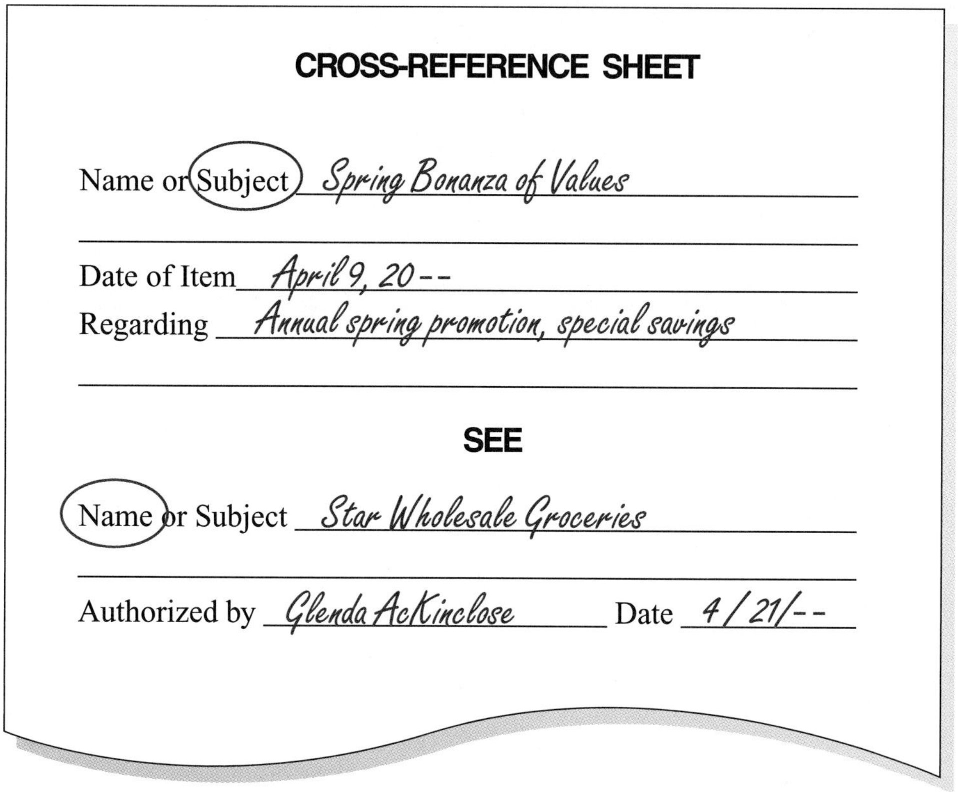

Figure 10-1.4

This is a cross-reference sheet for the letter in Figure 10-1.3.

CROSS-REFERENCE SHEET

Name or (Subject) *Spring Bonanza of Values*
_____

Date of Item *April 9, 20--*
Regarding *Annual spring promotion, special savings*
_____

SEE

(Name) or Subject *Star Wholesale Groceries*
_____

Authorized by *Glenda AcKinclose* Date *4/21/--*

- A brief description of the record
- The location of the record in the files
- The name of the authorized person who released the record and the date it was released

File the cross-reference sheet in the SPRING BONANZA OF VALUES folder and the record in the STAR WHOLESALE GROCERIES folder.

Copies of Records

Some companies do not use cross-reference sheets. Instead, they copy the original record and place the copy in the cross-referenced folder. This speeds retrieval because a complete copy of the record is available at each file point. The process does not often slow filing because making a copy may take the same or less time than completing a cross-reference sheet. If you are instructed to use this method, be sure to code the copy for cross-referencing so you will file it in the proper folder. Procedures for copying records and information about copying equipment are presented later in this topic.

Cross-Reference Guides

If a permanent cross-reference is desired, you will need to prepare a cross-reference guide using a stiff board the same size as a file folder. A typical situation requiring a permanent cross-reference guide might occur when a company with which you do a great deal of business changes its name. You would label a fresh folder using the new company name and place in it all materials from the old folder. Then you would replace the old folder with a permanent cross-reference guide showing the necessary retrieval information on the tab. The cross-reference guide remains in the file as long as the name or subject is still active.

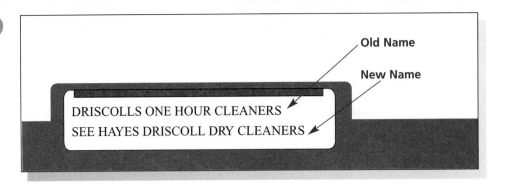

Figure 10-1.5

Prepare a permanent cross-reference guide for a company that changes its name.

Old Name
New Name

DRISCOLLS ONE HOUR CLEANERS
SEE HAYES DRISCOLL DRY CLEANERS

When to Cross-Reference

As a general rule, you should cross-reference a record if doing so will save you time when you need to retrieve the item later. Too much cross-referencing, however, will hinder your ability to retrieve records quickly. An effective records management program will include guidelines to help you know when to cross-reference.

You will usually cross-reference only records filed in name or subject filing systems. Geographic and numeric filing systems have alphabetic indexes that lead you directly to the item you need.

Sort Records

sorting: process of arranging the records alphabetically or numerically

After you have coded the records and cross-referenced them, if necessary, you are ready to sort them. **Sorting** is the process of arranging the records alphabetically or numerically before placing them in the folders.

Sorting serves two important purposes. First, it saves you filing time. Because records are in the proper sequence, you are able to move quickly from file drawer to file drawer as you place the records in folders. Second, if records are requested before you file them, you can find them quickly.

Filing Paper Records

You need to set aside time each day to file. Many other tasks may often seem more important than filing. If the rest of your work is to go smoothly, however, the records management system cannot become clogged with stacks of unfiled records. If you have followed the five steps for preparing records for storage, you can file the records easily and quickly by following these points:

1. Locate the proper file drawer by reading the drawer labels.

2. Search through the guides in the drawer to locate the desired alphabetic or numeric section.

3. If an individual folder has been prepared for the record, place the record in the folder with the front of the record facing the front of the folder and the top of the record at the left side. You should arrange records in an individual folder according to date, with the most recent in front.

4. If no individual folder is available, file the record in the general folder for that section. You should arrange records in a general folder alpha-

Charlotte Running-Bear is training Henry Davis, a new office worker. This afternoon they are preparing the records collected that day for storage. They have already indexed, coded, and cross-referenced the records that had never been filed before. Henry thinks they are ready to place the records in the folders. But Charlotte explains they have one more step to complete first.

Charlotte: *"Henry, we need to sort these records alphabetically before we file them."*

Henry: *"It will take forever to sort this stack of records. Let's just file them in the order they are in, now."*

Charlotte: *"Sorting doesn't take that long. First, we'll rough sort."*

Henry: *"What does that mean?"*

Charlotte: *"It means we'll group all the A records together, all the B records together, and so forth. Then we'll fine sort. That means we'll place all the A records in alphabetic order, then all the B records, and so on."*

Charlotte and Henry quickly sort the records and begin to file. Their supervisor, Ms. DeRosa, approaches them and asks a question.

Ms. DeRosa: *"Charlotte, I placed the Norris letter in the TO BE FILED tray, but I need it again. Have you filed it yet?"*

Charlotte: *"No, Ms. DeRosa. We've only filed up to the Cs."*

Charlotte flips through the records, which are in alphabetic order, and quickly retrieves the Norris letter. Ms. DeRosa takes the letter and leaves.

Charlotte: *"Well, Henry, now you see why I believe sorting is worth the time it takes?"*

betically by name or subject. If there are two or more records for the same name or subject, they are arranged according to date with the most recent in front.

Using Special Folders

Some companies use special folders as well as general and individual folders. A **special folder** is a type of general folder that is used for a variety of purposes. For example, you may remove all the records coded Smith from the general folder and place them in a special folder. This procedure permits material filed under Smith to be found more quickly. You also may prepare special folders to collect miscellaneous information about a particular subject or project, such as ARMA Convention Travel Plans. You arrange records alphabetically in a special folder. Within each group of names or subjects, arrange the records by date.

special folder: folder used to store records for a name or subject for which records are requested frequently

Figure 10-1.6

Set aside time each day to file paper records.

Professional Development Resources

- Institute of Certified Records Managers
  4318 Oak Street
  Syracuse, NY 13203
  www.icrm.org

- Noelle Tarabulski. "Where the Heck Is It?" (File management). *Professional Builder.* July, 2001.

- Jennifer Lee. "And the Password Is...Waterloo." *The New York Times.* Online. Available: www.nytimes.com. December 27, 2001.

- J. Wesley Cochran. "Using Copyrighted Works for Meetings, Seminars, and Conferences." *Information Outlook.* July, 1999.

- Philip Hunter. "Archiving for the Digital Age." *Computer Weekly.* November 30, 2000.

- "Cylinder, Disc, and Tape Care in a Nutshell." The Library of Congress Web site. Online. Available: http://lcweb.loc.gov/preserv/care/record.html. January 14, 2002.

- Search terms:
  - records management
  - records retention
  - storage media
  - micrographics
  - imaging systems
  - reprographics
  - copyright law

Avoiding Overcrowded Files

Never allow folders to become overcrowded. Usually, a folder has score lines at the bottom. Creasing the score lines widens the folder and increases its capacity. A folder should not contain more than an inch of filed material. When a folder becomes too full, subdivide the records into two or more folders. The labels of each should accurately reflect the contents of the new folders. For example, they could be labeled by date or subject.

Be sure to examine general folders often so that you can prepare individual and special folders when necessary. Do not fill a file drawer completely. You should have enough room in the drawer to move the folders easily.

Storage Equipment

Because paper is the oldest and most commonly used storage medium, equipment and supplies for filing paper records are plentiful. Each business must decide what system works best to fit its particular filing needs. Each office must balance the costs of replacing their current system of filing cabinets against the advantages of using the optimal one. The following descriptions will give you a general idea of the equipment that is available to help you maintain paper files and the best uses of each.

Vertical file cabinets contain one to five drawers. Of this kind of system, five-drawer cabinets use storage space most economically and provide the most filing space for the amount of floor space used. Vertical file cabinets must be arranged so there is space in front of each one to allow drawers to be opened fully.

Lateral file cabinets are common storage equipment. Lateral files are manufactured in a variety of drawer heights, widths, and depths

Figure 10-1.7

Both vertical file cabinets and shelf files are used in some offices.

to fit different office needs. Fully opened drawers in such a cabinet do not open as far out into the room as drawers in a vertical file cabinet.

Horizontal (flat) files are used in offices that store large-format documents. Examples of such documents include architectural plans, advertising layouts, engineering drawings, and geographic surveys.

Storage drawers are interconnected, stackable file drawers that work like traditional vertical files. They may be put together in any configuration needed. These drawers come in a variety of heights, widths, and depths. Some storage drawers, often used for temporary storage, are made of cardboard; others are made of metal.

Shelf files store records on open shelves instead of in drawers. They come in a wide variety of configurations. Records on open shelves are immediately accessible. Shelf filing is most appropriate for filing and retrieving entire folders and is ideally suited for numeric filing systems. Because folders on open shelves are readily visible, many companies use color-coded folder labels to improve filing efficiency. Bar coding may be used with shelf filing systems. Shelf files are generally the most efficient and modern system.

Figure 10-1.8

Open shelf files provide easy access for office workers.

Figure 10-1.9

Card files are used in many offices.

© C SQUARED STUDIOS/PHOTODISC

Mobile files are shelf files that have many shelves but only one aisle. The shelves are arranged next to each other on a track. To form the aisle in front of the desired shelf, the shelves are moved along the track manually or electronically. Mobile files take up less floor space than either fixed shelf files or cabinets holding the same number of records.

Card files are still used in many offices even though many businesses are moving to computer databases for storing information. The devices for housing card files are varied. Cards can be stored vertically in plastic or metal boxes. They can also be stored in vertical file cabinets designed to house cards. When information on cards is referred to often, an open card file is used. In this system, the cards are on special trays or wheels that make it easy to locate specific cards quickly.

Storage boxes are fiberboard cartons that are often used to hold files temporarily while moving them. These boxes are also used by some companies for the storage of inactive files.

Retrieving Paper Records

Once records are in active storage, you may retrieve and refile them many times. An effective records management program includes charge-out procedures that help you keep track of records when workers remove them from the files.

Requisition Cards

requisition card: form that has space for charge-out information for a record

Many companies that use central files have a staff of trained records management personnel to file and retrieve records. In companies using this arrangement, other office workers do not have direct access to the files. To retrieve records, you must submit a requisition card. A **requisition card** is a form that has space for all the charge-out information needed, such as:

- A description or file number of the record
- The name and contact information of the person taking the record
- The current date
- The date the record is to be returned

If you work in the central files, you will keep a copy of each requisition card in a tickler file. When a record has not been returned by the expected date, you need to take appropriate follow-up action. This is an important part of

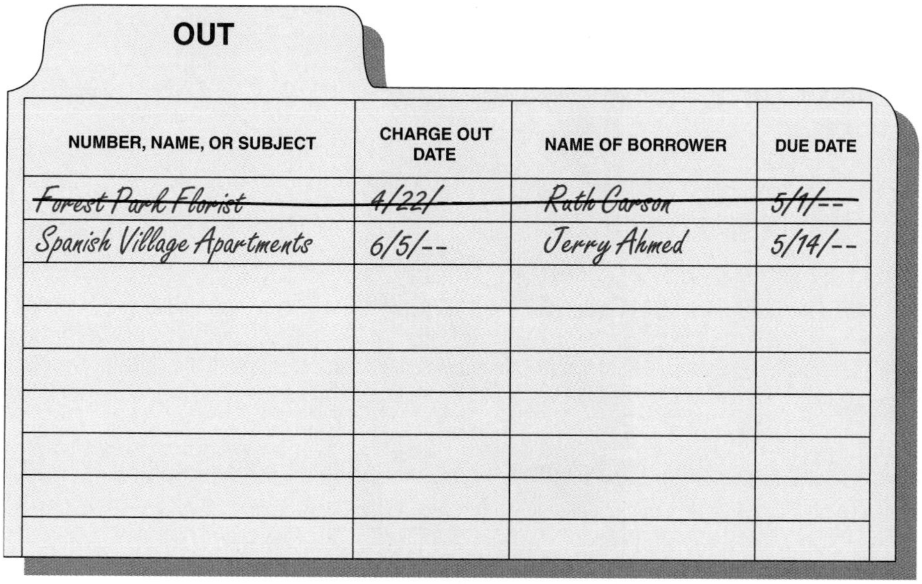

OUT

NUMBER, NAME, OR SUBJECT	CHARGE OUT DATE	NAME OF BORROWER	DUE DATE
~~Forest Park Florist~~	~~4/22/~~	~~Ruth Carson~~	~~5/1/--~~
Spanish Village Apartments	6/5/--	Jerry Ahmed	5/14/--

Figure 10-1.10

An OUT guide may replace a folder that has been removed from the file.

an effective records management program. A records manager also may use requisition cards to analyze how often the files are used and which records are most active.

OUT Guides

When you remove a record from the files, you must replace it with a record of the charge-out information. This can be accomplished by using an OUT guide, which is a sheet of thick cardboard that has the word *OUT* printed on the tab. On some OUT guides, you write the charge-out information on ruled lines. On other OUT guides, there is a pocket where you insert the completed requisition card. You usually use OUT guides when individual records within a folder are removed.

OUT Folders

An OUT folder is used when an entire folder is removed from the file. When an OUT folder is used, you may temporarily file additional records in the OUT folder until the regular folder is returned.

WORKPLACE **CONNECTIONS**

When Lakisha removed the Brandon-Mills folder from the files, she provided the charge-out information on the printed lines of an OUT folder. Later, when Chin Lu was filing, he placed two letters in the Brandon-Mills OUT folder. If Lakisha had not provided the OUT folder, Chin Lu would not have been able to file the two letters. This way, Chin Lu could file the records. Lakisha then would insert those records into the Brandon-Mills folder when she returned it to the files.

Figure 10-1.11

Inactive records may be stored in cardboard or fiberboard boxes.

© C SQUARED STUDIOS/PHOTODISC

Removing Records from Active Storage

retention schedule: list of how long each type of record should be kept

An efficient records management system will have a **retention schedule** that identifies which records should be removed from active storage and on which dates. Whether they are sent out to a storage facility or kept in-house, records that are placed in inactive storage usually are put into cardboard or fiberboard storage files like the ones shown in Figure 10-1.11 rather than in metal cabinets. The boxes are sturdy and provide a place to identify the contents. Some storage boxes can be stacked, saving storage space. Color-coded storage boxes can help you locate inactive records quickly. As discussed in Chapter 9, some companies store inactive records in off-site locations, which range from rented storage space to underground vaults.

Protecting Vital Records

Vital records are those of significant importance to maintaining the operations or fulfilling the legal obligations of an organization. There are numerous methods of storage that can be used to protect vital records:

- **Multisite storage.** If a company has two or more locations, it may choose to keep duplicates of vital records at each of its locations.
- **Planned dispersing.** Some companies use a secure vital records storage center and have a plan to disperse records there on a regular basis.
- **Duplication.** A number of organizations place vital records in micrographic media that is placed in a disaster-proof facility.
- **Vaulting.** Some businesses have special fire-resistant vaults, safes, or filing cabinets in which they store vital records. Other companies use an off-site facility with such protection.

Any combination of these methods may be used. Because the cost involved in storing vital records can be significant, records should be reviewed regularly. Those that are no longer of use should be removed and destroyed. The subject of vital records and disaster recovery is also discussed in Chapter 9.

Copying Paper Records

Reprographics is the process of making copies of graphic images, such as printed documents, and also includes other image processing such as scanning images into computer files. Reprographics plays an important role in the records management system. Although technology is bringing changes to records management systems, paper is still the most common medium for storing documents and for sharing information with others. Copies of paper records are often needed at both the use and maintenance phases of the record life cycle.

Businesses have different needs for reprographic services, depending on the size of the organization and the types of documents to be reproduced. Large businesses frequently have a reprographics center. In this setting, you would prepare the original from which the copies are made. You would use special forms to give detailed copying instructions to reprographics personnel. Organizations often have a minimum number of copies that will be made by the reprographics center. Smaller copying jobs are handled by individual employees using convenience copiers located throughout the business.

Small organizations do not usually have a reprographics center. In this setting, you would be responsible for preparing the original and making the copies. Even many larger organizations have done away with their reprographics centers. Instead, copiers are placed throughout the offices.

Office Photocopiers

Photocopiers, often simply called copiers, produce copies directly from an original document. The original can be handwritten, printed, or drawn. The quality of the copy is excellent if the machine is in good condition and the original is of high quality. Many copiers reproduce onto one or both sides of a sheet of paper and can copy onto letterhead paper, mailing labels, bond paper, and colored paper. Some machines copy in color as well.

reprographics: process of making copies of graphic images, such as printed documents

Figure 10-1.12

Many businesses have convenience copiers located throughout the offices for employee use.

Topic 10-1: *Managing Paper Records*

Figure 10-1.13

Files can be transmitted electronically to a copier/printer.

© CORBISIMAGES.COM

Electronic Copiers/Printers

Electronic copier/printers, sometimes called intelligent copiers, can receive, transmit, store, print, and copy data. Microprocessor technology enables these copier/printers to produce copies from sources such as a computer file, graphic scanners, or even pictures. For example, you may key material at your computer, proofread the copy, and then transmit it electronically to the copier/printer in a reprographics center or at a nearby location, where the copies will be printed.

Electronic copier/printers can easily be commanded to use specific print fonts, justify lines, number pages, or insert graphics within the text material. These machines can merge data from various electronic sources. They can also communicate with other intelligent copier/printers.

WORKPLACE CONNECTIONS

Daisuke is a new employee at Textron, Inc. His supervisor, Lakisha, is explaining the features and capacities of each copier available for Daisuke's use. Lakisha emphasizes that choosing the most appropriate copier for each copying job is an important step. She hands Daisuke two copying jobs. One is a ten-page proposal requiring one photocopy. The other is a 55-page report requiring six photocopies. Lakisha asks Daisuke to choose the copiers that will complete each job most efficiently. On the basis of what Daisuke has learned about the company's copiers, he knows it is most efficient to copy the ten-page proposal on the low-capacity copier and the 55-page report on the high-capacity copier.

Copier Classifications and Features

Copiers can be classified according to their capacity: low, mid, high, and duplicating. Copier capacity is usually determined by two factors: speed (copies produced per minute) and volume (copies produced per month). As an office worker, you should know the capacities of your company's copiers so that you can select the best copier for the task at hand when more than one machine is available to you.

Special features designed to meet specific copying needs and to increase the user's productivity are available on many copiers. Most of the copiers you will use will offer several of the features listed in Figure 10-1.14, which are only a few of those available.

Common Copier Features

Automatic duplexing	Allows you to copy on both sides of the paper, saving paper and postage costs.
Automatic image shift	Creates a margin on one or both sides of the copy paper to allow space for three-hole punching or for binding the copies.
Book copy mode	Allows you to copy both pages of an open book or magazine onto the front and back of a single sheet of copy paper.
Image enlargement and reduction	Allows you to make a photocopy larger or smaller than the original document.
Sorter	Automatically collates the copies, arranging the copies in order or sets.
Automatic document feed	Automatically feeds the originals into the machine.
Self-diagnosis feature	Detects common problems (a paper jam, for example) and displays words or symbols to alert the user.
Automatic exposure control	Adjusts the darkness or lightness of copies after sensing the density of the original.
Copy counter	Allows the user to select the number of copies to be made.
Roll feeding	A roll of continuous-feed paper allows copies of varying sizes to be made at one time. The paper is cut by the machine to match the sizes needed.
Job recovery	Allows an interrupted print job to be begun again at the place where the user stopped the job.
Color	Color images on the original are reproduced on the copies.

Figure 10-1.14

You will want to be familiar with the common features of copiers found in your office.

Topic 10-1: *Managing Paper Records*

Operating Procedures

When employees do not follow proper procedures, copying costs can rise dramatically. If a company has convenience copiers located throughout the building, copier misuse may be more frequent than if copying is done by only a few employees in a copying center. Employees who do not know how to operate the equipment properly may damage the copier or misuse supplies.

WORKPLACE **CONNECTIONS**

When Larry found that there was no paper in the copier, he added two reams to the paper bin. Before he had run three copies, the machine was jammed. He was upset and sought help from Robin, a coworker. When Robin checked the paper bin, she said, "You haven't inserted the paper under the guides correctly." Larry responded, "Oh, is there a special way to place the paper in the bin?" Robin then showed Larry how the paper should be placed in the bin so that it will be guided into the copier correctly.

Office employees need to be knowledgeable about the proper use and selection of reprographic supplies. You will find that the selection of paper, toner, and other materials can significantly affect the cost of making copies and the operation of the machines. All employees are expected to follow closely the recommendations of the vendor or manufacturer and company guidelines when using copier supplies in order to control costs.

Management often takes steps to help control copying costs and procedures. Companies with large copying needs may use a central copying center to control the number of copies made and to make the best use

Figure 10-1.15

An occasional paper jam is easily cleared by an employee familiar with the equipment.

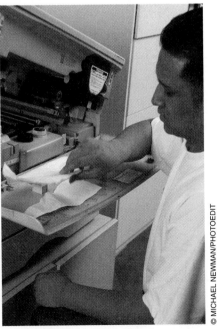

© MICHAEL NEWMAN/PHOTOEDIT

of the equipment. Companies often use a **chargeback procedure** to allocate copying costs to the individual or department requesting the copying from the copy center. Devices that monitor copier use may be placed on the convenience copiers located throughout the offices. A common copier control procedure is a copier log book or, more commonly, a computerized log based upon a code or card used by each employee or department. When a copier log book is used, employees record information pertaining to each copy job such as the employee name or department and the number of copies made. This function is done automatically when a code or card is used.

chargeback procedure: assigns costs, such as for copying, to an individual or department

Many companies post guidelines for employees who use copiers near each copier. As a responsible employee, you should adhere to these general guidelines:

- Follow company policy regarding the maximum number of copies to be made at convenience copiers. Large copier needs are best handled through the central copying center, when available.

- Be cost conscious when planning to use the copier. Use the copier's economy features, such as duplexing, and do not make more copies than you need.

- Comply with **copyright laws**. Copyright laws describe those documents that cannot be legally copied. Documents that should not be copied at their original size and with the intent to represent the original include money, postage stamps, United States securities, birth certificates, passports, draft cards, drivers' licenses, automobile registrations, and certificates of title. Many books and other documents may also be copyrighted and should not be reproduced.

copyright laws: regulate what documents or other information can be legally copied

- Do not use company resources to make copies for personal use.

- Follow good housekeeping rules. Always clean up the area after you have completed your copying project. Deal with any copier problems, such as a paper jam, or notify the appropriate person of the problem.

- Practice common courtesy when using the copier. If you have a long copy job and another worker needs a priority copy, stop at a convenient point and let the other person have access to the machine. If you need a few copies and someone else is near the end of a long copying job, wait until the other person is finished to make your copies.

Reviewing the Topic

1. List the five steps involved in preparing paper records for storage.
2. What is the purpose of a release mark?
3. Describe the process for coding a record indexed by name.
4. Why is it necessary to cross-reference some records?
5. Give two reasons for sorting records before filing them.
6. How should you arrange records in an individual folder?
7. What is a special folder, and how might it be used?
8. Why are shelf files the overall optimal filing equipment?
9. Under what circumstances might a requisition card be used?
10. What is the difference between an OUT guide and an OUT folder?
11. In what phases of the record life cycle are paper documents often reproduced?
12. Name and describe four common copier features.
13. Name three ways management may attempt to control copying costs.
14. What information is typically recorded on a copier log?
15. List three general guidelines for copier use.

Thinking Critically

Professional Support Services, Inc. is a small personnel agency that places workers in both permanent and temporary jobs. The office is staffed by two placement officers and one office support worker, Eileen. Although Eileen is considered a competent office worker, she sometimes gets behind in her filing. This morning, one of the placement officers says to her, "I can't even see the top of the filing cabinet because it's so cluttered with file folders. Don't you think you should take time to file them?" Eileen thought to herself, "I don't even have time to take a coffee break during the day. When am I going to find time to file all these folders?"

1. Why do you think Eileen puts filing so low on her priority list of things to do?
2. How might she find time to file and fulfill her other responsibilities as well?

Reinforcing English Skills

For written communication to be clear to the reader, you must use commas correctly. Test your skill in using commas in the sentences below. Prepare a copy of each sentence, inserting commas in the correct positions.

1. Records can be organized alphabetically numerically and chronologically.
2. You will however be responsible for preparing paper records for storage.
3. As a general rule you should cross-reference a record if doing so will save you time when you need to retrieve it later.
4. Before filing a record for the first time you need to prepare it properly for storage.
5. Records may be coded by hand or bar coding may be used to code records.

RECORDS MANAGEMENT

Topic 10-1   ACTIVITY 1

Code and Cross-reference Letters

Paper records, such as letters, must be indexed and coded properly before filing. A cross-reference should be prepared when a record may be requested under a different name than the one it is filed under. Practice coding letters and preparing cross-reference sheets in this activity.

1. Open and print the data file **Letters.pdf**, which contains six letters to be coded and two blank cross-reference sheets.
2. Index and code each letter for filing. You work at Star Satellite Systems, so the letters with this company name in the letterhead are outgoing letters. The other letters are incoming letters. See Figure 10-1.3 on page 404 for an example of a coded letter.
3. The letter to Anne Ashby and the letter from William Abbott require cross-references. Code cross-reference captions and prepare cross-reference sheets for these letters. See Figure 10-1.4 on page 405 for an example of a cross-reference sheet. Which of these letters might require a permanent cross-reference guide?

Topic 10-1 ACTIVITY 2

Reprographics Equipment Presentation

Schools, companies, libraries, government offices, and other organizations have reprographics equipment to help employees complete tasks efficiently. In this activity, you will research how reprographics equipment is used at a local organization and report your findings to the class.

1. Work in a team with three or four other students to complete this activity.

2. With the members of your team, visit one of these local organizations as assigned by your instructor: school, library, business, government office, or copy center (any business that provides copying services for a fee).

3. Ask to see the various types of reprographics equipment used at the organization. Take note of the location and features of the equipment, the types of supplies used, and the procedures or controls established by the organization related to reprographics.

4. Prepare a presentation about the reprographics equipment available at the organization. In the presentation, give the name and a brief description of the organization your team visited. For each piece of equipment, give the brand name, location, and features. Discuss the intended use of the machine—for convenience copies, moderate-size copying jobs, or large jobs. Describe the types of supplies you saw in use or readiness. Discuss any controls or other procedures used (such as monitoring devices and copy logs).

5. Prepare appropriate visuals for use in your presentation. Identify the content each team member will present. Practice your presentation as a team.

6. Deliver your presentation to the class.

7. Write a thank-you letter from your team to the organization you visited. Thank the organization for allowing you to visit and mention some information that you found particularly interesting or helpful in creating your presentation.

Optical, and Microimaging Media

OBJECTIVES

- Explain how to store individual records on magnetic media
- Describe supplies used to store and organize magnetic and optical media
- Explain why databases are useful in businesses
- Describe ways to organize microforms
- Explain how computer-assisted retrieval systems are used to speed the record retrieval process

Advancements in technology affect almost every aspect of office work, including records management. As an office worker, you will need to know how to store and access information recorded on magnetic media such as tapes, floppy disks, and hard disks and on optical discs.

Unlike paper records, records stored on magnetic and optical media are not readable by simply looking at the storage medium. These records must be accessed via a computer. For this reason, organizing and managing these media with great care is especially important. The procedures presented in this topic are used to store and access information recorded on magnetic and optical media.

Organizations that keep many records for an extended period of time frequently use microforms to store records conveniently and safely. Many companies use this medium for active records as well. As an office worker, you should know how micrographic records are created and maintained and how to use computer-assisted retrieval systems.

Stored information is useful only if it can be accessed when needed. A carefully designed and implemented records management system is essential for the efficient operation of an organization. This topic provides an overview of the technology, procedures, and supplies used to manage magnetic and optical media and micrographic files.

Figure 10-2.1

Records stored on magnetic or optical media must be accessed using a computer.

© LISETTE LE BON/SUPERSTOCK INTERNATIONAL

Topic 10-2: *Managing Magnetic, Optical, and Microimaging Media*

Records Management Software

records management software: computer program that allows electronic tracking and control of records

Records management software is a computer program that allows electronic management and control of records from receipt or creation, through processing, storage, and retrieval, to disposal. The advantage of such a system is that it allows records management tasks to be performed with limited personnel. Records management software is a tool that allows companies to manage records efficiently.

When records management software is used with a network of computers, the entire organization has access to inventory, record research, and retrieval. Thus, a reduced number of records management clerks is required. Some software can also perform the library-like function of retrieving records, avoiding the need for human management of requisition records. Records management software performs the functions such as:

- Tracking records from creation/reception to destruction
- Tracking stored records, whether on-site or off-site
- Creating and maintaining a retention schedule
- Archiving and managing record archives
- Identifying and managing vital records as part of a disaster recovery program

Storing Files on Magnetic or Optical Media

secondary storage: storage media or devices outside the internal memory of a computer system

compact disc: optical storage medium for electronic data

Storage media used for information stored outside the internal memory of a computer system is referred to as auxiliary or **secondary storage**. Each collection of related information treated as a unit is called a file. Common auxiliary media used for storing files include magnetic tape, magnetic floppy disks, hard disks, and optical media such as **compact discs** (CDs). Because CDs can hold many more records than a floppy disk or magnetic tape, this

---

Figure 10-2.2

Training employees is an important step in updating a records management system.

© CORBIS/STOCK MARKET

medium is a good choice for archiving records or for records that do not need to be updated frequently.

Converting to Electronic Media

For many large businesses, the need to automate their systems has become very important because the totally paper-based system has become unmanageable. However, decisions beyond which records management software will be used have to be made. What computer system will be used? What files will be on individual hard drives or network drives? What records will be stored on secondary media, and which media will be used?

Converting to electronic media or updating the current electronic records management system involves several stages as shown in Figure 10-2.3.

The Importance of Secondary Storage

The internal storage medium for most computer systems is a hard disk. The hard disk is used to store programs that run the system and data files as they are being created and processed. Many companies use secondary storage to **back up** files or for freeing hard disk space of files that are not used regularly.

back up: make a copy of

Electronic Records Management System		Figure 10-2.3

Evaluation	Make a careful study of the current system.
	Determine the number of workers employed to operate it and the equipment used.
	Evaluate the efficiency of the system.
Development	Examine the records management software available.
	Determine the kinds of computer equipment that would work best and be most cost-efficient.
	Determine the types of storage media best suited to the software, the equipment, and the organization.
	Determine the number of employees to implement the system and the training required.
Implementation	Install the equipment and software.
	Train the employees.
	Institute evaluation procedures.
Evaluation	Evaluate the system on an ongoing basis.
	Alter the system as necessary so that it will continue to meet the organization's needs over time.

Topic 10-2: *Managing Magnetic, Optical, and Microimaging Media*

If an electronic records management system is to be efficient, the files stored on the system should be examined periodically. Inactive files should be saved onto a secondary storage medium and then deleted from the internal memory of the system.

Storing Electronic Files

One company stores its mailing list for the city of Austin, Texas, on a floppy disk. This mailing list is stored in a single file, and it must be assigned to a folder or directory and given a name so that it can be identified and accessed when needed. While some operating systems limit the length of a filename to eight characters, other systems allow longer, more descriptive names to be used. Some systems allow you to add a three-character extension (such as "doc" for document) to further identify your file. Many application programs automatically add the three-character extension. Naturally, you will want to assign a name that reflects the type of information stored in the file. For example, the name assigned to the Austin mailing list file could be "AustinMl.doc" or "Austin TX Mailing List."

The following guidelines may be used in storing electronic files:

- Create folders or subdirectories to group related files. When a large number of files accumulate in the folder or directory, reorganize files into two or more new folders or directories.
- Give each file a unique name even if it is stored in a different folder or directory than a file with a similar name.
- Use abbreviations that are commonly recognized, for example, "Dept" for department or "Proj" for project.
- If your system allows the use of long file names, use as many characters as needed to make the filename readable and the file easily identifiable.
- Use numbers to label versions of a file. For example, your fourth letter to the accounting department might be labeled "AcctDpt4.doc" or "Acct Dept Letter 4.doc." Or use numbers to date such a file. For example, the letter to the accounting department might be the one of April 7, and the file might be named "ActDp407.doc" or "Acct Dept Letter 4-07.doc."
- Use the default file extension assigned by the program. For example, all word processing documents created with Microsoft Word might use the file extension "doc."

file path: the complete location designation (directory and subdirectories) for an electronic file

You must understand the system of drives and folders or subdirectories on your computer system or network to store and retrieve files efficiently. The filename alone may not be enough information to retrieve the file quickly. You need to know the drive designation and folder or directory name where the file is stored. This information is sometimes called the **file path**. Figure 10-2.4 shows a list of files and subdirectories in the Abbott Project folder on the C: drive (hard drive) of a computer. The Abbott Project folder contains subfolders for project bid documents, correspondence, invoices, and meeting summaries. Individual files are shown for a schedule, a project summary, and a press release.

Businesses must develop policies and procedures for storing files on secondary storage media. For example, will all letters be stored in one folder or directory? all mailing lists in another? all business forms in another? Will

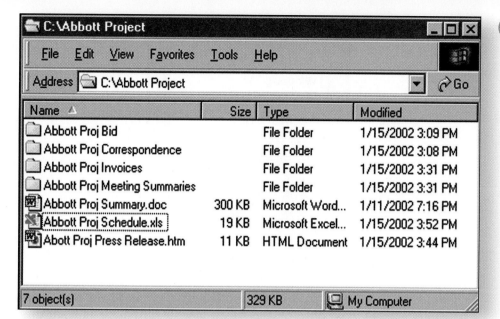

Figure 10-2.4

This directory shows folders or subdirectories and individual files.

various files related to one project be stored in the same folder? Will documents be stored in chronological order? by the name of the **originator**? by the name of the department? The type of records management system a company uses will determine how and where files will be stored.

originator: creator

Identifying Individual Disks and Tapes

Magnetic media can be organized alphabetically or numerically. Each disk, tape, or CD should be labeled so that it can be located quickly. Captions should be as descriptive as possible, just as folder label captions are descriptive of the folder's contents. Often, the labels are color coded to indicate how long the data on the disk or tape should be kept.

WORKPLACE **CONNECTIONS**

The Petro-Davis Company has classified all information placed on its floppy disks as permanent, semipermanent, or temporary in nature. To aid in identifying the disks by their retention category, disk labels are color coded. Permanent storage disks have labels with a red bar; semipermanent, a blue bar; and temporary, a green bar. The label identifies the type of information on the disk, the operating system, and computer programs used to create the files. The retention category is also included on the label.

Making Backup Copies

Data files can be expensive to create again or replace if they become damaged and are no longer useable. Loss of important data files, such as customer, payroll, and personnel records, can cause serious problems for the

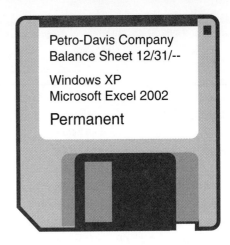

Figure 10-2.5

This 3.5" floppy disk is labeled for storage.

Petro-Davis Company
Balance Sheet 12/31/--

Windows XP
Microsoft Excel 2002

Permanent

organization. Make a backup copy of each file, disk, or tape if the loss of the data would have serious consequences. Backing up a hard drive, tape, or disk means making a copy of all the data onto another tape, floppy disk, or CD. Backing up a file means making a copy of an individual file onto a different tape, disk, CD, or drive.

Applications software, such as records management, spreadsheet, and word processing programs, can be expensive to replace if damaged. Store the original disks or CDs in a safe location after the programs have been loaded onto the computer. If the programs come preloaded on the computer, original disks may not be included. Make backup copies of the programs for use in restoring the software if the programs on the computer should become damaged.

In many companies, each office worker has a computer for his or her sole use. Often these computers are linked together in a local area network or via

Figure 10-2.6

Make a backup copy of important data files.

© DICK LURIA/FPG INTERNATIONAL

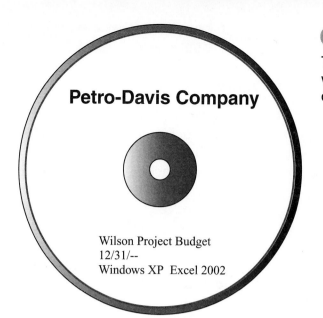

Figure 10-2.7

This CD is properly labeled with the contents and date.

Petro-Davis Company

Wilson Project Budget
12/31/--
Windows XP Excel 2002

a modem to a wide area network of computers. In some cases, files may be backed up automatically or by command to a network location before the user exits the network. In other cases, each employee is responsible for backing up her or his own files. High-capacity external disks, such as ZIP or SyQuest cartridges, are popular choices for backups from individual computers.

Most computer operating systems provide easy-to-follow procedures for making backup copies on tapes and disks. Research and practice the backup or copy commands for your particular system if you are not familiar with them. Backup disks should be labeled in the same manner as their original, perhaps with the word *Backup* added to the label. Backup copies of tapes and disks should be stored in a separate, safe location.

Controlling File Security

The security of confidential files stored on magnetic media is a concern to you as an office worker. You would not want a competitor to have access to a customer mailing list or a sales report that you keyed. Some companies use security measures such as access logs and **passwords**, which allow only authorized employees to access certain files. Employees in some companies are required to change passwords frequently. Choose passwords carefully so others cannot easily guess your password. For example, do not use variations of family members' names or birthdates or a favorite sport or hobby as a password. Choose a series of meaningless letters and numbers instead. Do not leave your password in a location where others can access it easily such as taped to your monitor or under your keyboard. Store your password in a safe place.

password: series of letters, numbers, or symbols used to identify a user and gain access to a computer system

Take steps to safeguard files when in use. For example, clear a document from the computer screen when you take a break or leave your computer for other reasons. Log off the computer network before leaving your computer

Topic 10-2: *Managing Magnetic, Optical, and Microimaging Media*

Protecting Online Records

Online records are records stored in electronic format on a single computer or a computer network. Records are stored online so they may be accessed quickly by authorized users. Security procedures are needed to protect online records from destruction, damage, theft, or misuse.

Destruction or damage to online records can result from human error, such as when an employee accidentally deletes the wrong file or updates a database record with incorrect information. Employee training and restricting access to only certain users are strategies companies use to combat this type of threat to online records.

Online records can be destroyed, stolen, or misused by intentional acts of employees or persons outside the company who gain access to the records. Dishonest employees may access

records to steal information, such as product designs or customers' credit card numbers. Unauthorized users, called hackers, may access a computer network to steal information or to introduce computer viruses that can destroy records. A virus can also be loaded accidentally by an employee using an infected file. A virus is dangerous because it can replicate itself and quickly use all of your computer's memory, increase system crashes, and delete important data. Some viruses can transmit across networks and avoid security systems.

To protect online records against unauthorized access and computer viruses, companies use data backup procedures, password access procedures, firewalls, and antivirus software. Online records can be backed up regularly so the data will not be lost if online records are damaged or destroyed. Backup copies

so others cannot use your computer to access files. Do not send files containing confidential information as e-mail attachments. Store disks in a concealed location rather than on the surface of your workstation. Store disks with highly confidential information in a locked cabinet or drawer.

Many companies have a policy manual that outlines the procedures for handling files. In addition to security and backup procedures, such a manual often includes policies regarding:

- E-mail
- Downloaded files
- Internal audits for proper use and storage of files
- Retention schedules
- Accessing or storing files at home or other off-site locations

Storing Magnetic and Optical Media

Magnetic and optical media require special care to protect the valuable information they contain. Magnetic media, such as floppy disks, must be

of records are often saved on magnetic or optical media and stored in a safe location. Companies commonly issue passwords to employees that must be used to access the company's computer network. Passwords should be chosen carefully to decrease chances of unauthorized users being able to guess the passwords. Passwords should be stored in a secure location.

Companies use software and equipment called firewalls in an effort to prevent unauthorized users from gaining access to a computer network. All messages entering or leaving the network pass through the firewall. The firewall examines each message and blocks those that do not meet specified security. Another method of protection is an intrusion detection system (IDS). An IDS will detect attempts at unauthorized access or other attacks on the computer system. Most of these programs are affordable for personal computer users and small business owners.

Antivirus software is designed to detect computer viruses and can destroy many viruses as well. Antivirus software can be set up to scan automatically each file loaded on the computer or network to check for viruses. Antivirus software must be updated regularly to be effective because new viruses are created on an ongoing basis.

As an office worker, you have an important role to play in protecting online records. Security procedures are effective only if used correctly by employees. Regularly back up online records for which you are responsible. Choose passwords carefully and store your password in a secure location where others cannot accidentally or intentionally read it. Use antivirus software to scan all files loaded onto your computer and update the software regularly. If your company uses firewalls or other security systems, follow the procedures you are given for using those systems to protect online records.

protected from extreme heat or cold, moisture, dust, and magnetic fields. Optical media, such as a CD, should be protected from dust, moisture, and rough surfaces that may scratch the CD. By becoming familiar with the wide variety of equipment and supplies available, you can adequately protect the media that you handle and organize.

Floppy Disk and CD Storage

Floppy disks and CDs can be organized and stored in a variety of ways. The way selected will depend on the number of items you need to store, the frequency with which you use the disks or CDs, and the storage space available. Many companies color code the labels to expedite the storage and retrieval process. Floppy disks with the hard protective covering in various colors are also available.

Floppy disks and CD cases are often filed in plastic boxes, cases, or trays designed to protect the disks. Within the cases are guides in which to slide the disks; these guides also make storage and retrieval simpler.

Topic 10-2: *Managing Magnetic, Optical, and Microimaging Media*

Figure 10-2.8

Colored labels on jewel cases can be used to help organize CDs.

© PHOTOLINK/PHOTODISC

CDs and floppy disks may be stored in plastic pockets designed to fit a ring binder or folder. Each disk is protected by the pocket into which it slides. Some plastic pockets can hold hard copy as well as disks; others are designed to allow disks to be placed in a standard paper file.

Reel Tape Storage

Reels of tape are stored in round, protective cases. These cases are usually hung for easy access or stored on wire racks. Sometimes the cases have handles or hooks that allow the reels to be attached to frames or cabinets. Other times the cases rest on a backward-slanting shelf. Labels on the protective cases can be color coded for easy reference.

Database Management Systems

electronic database: a collection of records accessible by computer

A database is any collection of related records. An **electronic database** is a collection of records accessible by computer. Electronic databases are useful to businesses because thousands of records can be searched in only a few seconds to locate the specific information needed. If you had to go through the same number of records stored on paper, the search would be overwhelming. Electronic databases are often accessible to many employees via a computer network. Accessibility to a central electronic database helps decrease the need to have information stored in several different departments within the organization. Electronic databases can be very flexible and may be designed especially to meet the needs of a particular organization.

The more efficiently you can retrieve records from a database, the more productive you will be. A database management system (DBMS) organizes and manipulates large numbers of records in a database. A major advantage of a DBMS is that information can be compared and shared among the tables in the database. For example, the Internal Revenue Service uses a DBMS to compare information on a person's current income tax return with information on past tax returns.

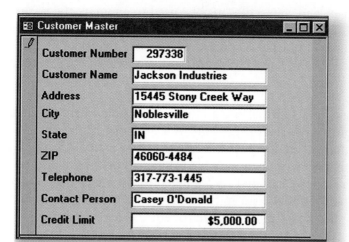

Figure 10-2.9

Master customer record
from a DBMS

A DBMS helps you keep database records up to date. Suppose you work in a company that uses a DBMS to manage its personnel and payroll records. If an employee's last name changes, you need to make the change only in the personnel record, and the system will automatically update the payroll record.

A DBMS eliminates repetition in the database. Because the system can automatically locate information requested, the information needs to be stored only once. Another advantage of a DBMS is data security. Access to parts of the database can be limited to authorized employees who have been issued passwords.

WORKPLACE **CONNECTIONS**

Lao Ji works for The Supply Closet, a distributor of office supplies. The company's database management system contains a master record for each customer. When Lao Ji inputs data for a customer order, he simply enters the customer name in the customer order form screen. The appropriate customer information, such as the customer number, address, and available credit amount are completed automatically by the DBMS using the data from the customer master record. Lao Ji can create the customer order quickly and accurately because he does not need to key the customer number and address. He can also see immediately whether the customer has enough available credit to cover the order.

Image Processing Systems

Image processing is an effective way to store documents that must be seen in their original form to verify information. An **image processing system** uses software and special equipment, including scanners and optical discs (CDs), to store an exact reproduction of a paper document. The images may be

image processing system: software and special equipment used to create and store a graphic reproduction of a paper document

431

Topic 10-2: *Managing Magnetic, Optical, and Microimaging Media*

very complex, and sound files may be used to annotate the images. These systems are like enormous electronic filing cabinets linked together that allow the user to quickly access and review the images of original documents. A computer is used to display a document on the screen or to print a hard copy of it.

Optical discs (CDs), which are an important component of image processing systems, offer large storage capacity. A 4 3/4" optical disc can store about the same number of documents as two file drawers, a 14" disc about the same number as six four-drawer file cabinets. For ease of access, discs can be stored in a retrieval system called a jukebox. An image processing jukebox contains many optical discs and allows records to be retrieved quickly. Image processing jukeboxes can be linked together electronically, which further increases storage capacity and speed of record retrieval.

An imaging system may use various platforms: an imaging computer system, stand-alone computers, or networked computers. In choosing a system, the organization must consider:

- The organization's imaging needs
- The number of employees that will use the system
- Employee training
- Cost to implement and maintain the system

A large business with training funds and a significant budget for equipment would likely choose an entire imaging computer system. A small company with limited employees and budget might pick a stand-alone computer. A medium-sized company would likely decide to use networked computers. Regardless of the system chosen, certain basic components are required—the imaging software, the scanning device, and the reading device. If cost makes buying the scanner impossible, an organization may choose to purchase document scanning services.

WORKPLACE CONNECTIONS

Sharmane is a customer service supervisor at a savings and loan company. All questions and comments from customers regarding their mortgage accounts are directed to her. The company stores all its customer accounts on optical discs. Sharmane is describing the features of the image processing system to Dewey, a new employee.

Sharmane: *"Our new image processing system lets me retrieve documents quickly. When customers call with questions about a mortgage payment, I just key the customer's name at my computer. The system almost instantaneously locates the account and displays it on my screen. I can even get a printout if I want."*

Dewey: *"That's certainly efficient."*

Sharmane: *"Right! Before, locating document files took so long that I'd have to tell customers that I'd call them later after I'd pulled the folder."*

Organizing Microforms

In a paper system, you file individual records in folders. You label each folder so that you can identify the contents and file the folder alphabetically, numerically, or chronologically with other folders. A microform is similar to a folder because it contains many records.

Microforms should be labeled and organized alphabetically, numerically, or chronologically so that they can be retrieved easily. How you label and organize the microforms will depend on the particular filing system used in your organization.

A microfiche is a transparent sheet of film containing several rows of microimages. At the top of each microfiche (or fiche) is space to label the contents of that particular microform. The caption on a microfiche is similar to the caption used on a folder in a paper filing system. Microfiche labels are frequently color coded for easy retrieval.

Microfiche is the microform commonly used for active (frequently used) storage. Fiche can be stored efficiently in panels, which are pages of paper or vinyl that have several slots into which you insert the microfiche. The slots are deep enough to protect the fiche, yet shallow enough to allow the caption to be read easily. Microfiche can also be stored in trays or file cabinets where guides and color-coded labels are used to organize the media.

Roll microfilm is kept in protective cases or boxes. A label is attached to the case or box to identify that particular roll of microfilm. The roll is filed alphabetically, numerically, or chronologically with other rolls in a drawer or cabinet.

The most commonly used aperture card contains only one record or image. Because identifying information can be printed along the top edge of the card, you may file and retrieve aperture cards much as you would file and retrieve paper records. Aperture cards are often housed in trays.

Figure 10-2.10

The identifying information printed on an aperture card is used in storage and retrieval.

Topic 10-2: *Managing Magnetic, Optical, and Microimaging Media*

Retrieving Records on Microfilm

When you find it necessary to refer to a record on microfilm, you must know on which roll, fiche, or aperture card the record is stored. If the record is on roll microfilm or microfiche, you also must know the specific location of the record on the film. An index provides you with the information you need by listing an address for each microfilm record. The first step in retrieving a specific record is to consult the index to determine the exact location of that record. Next, a reader is used to view the record. A full-sized hard copy of the record can be printed if needed.

computer-assisted retrieval: the process of locating records on film by using computer-stored indexes

Computer-assisted retrieval (CAR) is the process of locating records on film by using computer-stored indexes. A CAR system may be very simple or very sophisticated. A simple CAR system uses a computer and a reader/printer. When you need to refer to the index, you use the computer to print or display the index. Then you consult the index and manually locate and load the proper microform into the reader.

Advanced CAR systems use computer software to maintain an index that is similar to an electronic database. An advantage of a database index is that you can search for a record by name, subject, or date. The address of the needed record will be displayed on the screen. Then you place the microform into the reader/printer and view the record.

film autoloader: equipment that houses, loads, and scans microfilm records

Some CAR systems automatically locate the correct image and display it on the reader screen by using a film autoloader. A **film autoloader** is a piece of equipment that not only loads and scans the film but also houses the microfilm rolls until they are needed. These systems allow microform records to be viewed from remote locations via a computer network or modem.

Figure 10-2.11

A microform reader can be used to view and print records.

© Photo courtesy of Bell & Howell Imaging/South-Western/Thomson Learning

Reviewing the Topic

1. What is the advantage of using records management software?
2. What functions does records management software perform?
3. List three guidelines to follow when naming files for electronic storage.
4. When labeling individual disks or tapes, what descriptive information should appear on the label(s)?
5. Why should you make backup copies of disks and tapes?
6. Why are databases useful to businesses?
7. What is one major advantage of using optical disc (CD) storage?
8. Describe how microforms may be stored.
9. What are the components of a simple CAR system?
10. List an advantage of using a film autoloader.

Interacting with Others

You and two of your coworkers, Tom and Paula, are working late one evening. All the other employees have gone for the day. During a brief break, Tom says to you: "I hear the company is about to close some pretty big real estate deals. Because you know the access code for the financial database, let's look and see what's going on." Paula agrees, saying, "Sure! No one else is here. What difference will it make? We won't tell anyone you let us see the information."

1. How would you react in this situation? What would you say to your coworkers?
2. What might be the consequences of accessing and sharing this confidential information with coworkers?

Reinforcing Math Skills

1. Your company estimates that it takes you 20 minutes less to file each day using folders with color-coded file labels than when using folders without them. Calculate how many hours the use of color-coded file labels saves you each week (5 working days), each month (4 weeks), and each year (50 weeks). Show your calculations.

2. Eight file folders have captions with *Randolph* as the first indexing unit, six folders have *Reynolds* as the first unit, and two folders have *Rogers* as the first unit. One hundred and thirty folders are filed under the letter *R*. Of the total *R* folders, calculate what percentage are *Randolph* folders, what percentage are *Reynolds* folders, and what percentage are *Rogers* folders. Round your answers to the nearest whole percentages. Show your calculations.

Organizing Electronic Files

Electronic files must be named and organized properly to make them easy to retrieve when needed. You have recently begun a new job as administrative assistant to three executives in the accounting firm, Carson Associates. Several files that were created by the person who previously had this job are stored on your computer. However, no clear organization or consistent file names have been used. You must organize the existing files and create a plan for naming and organizing the files you will store in the future. The plan should be simple and clear so that someone unfamiliar with your files, such as one of the executives or a temporary worker, could easily find a particular file.

1. You have quickly scanned the contents of the files on your computer and made notes about what each file contains. Open and print the data file **Files.pdf**, which contains the information you noted about the files.

2. Review the guidelines for naming electronic files found in this topic. Then create a plan that includes folders and subfolders that will let you quickly find files about a particular topic for any of the three executives. Outline your plan showing the structure and names of main folders and subfolders so that it would be easy for someone else to understand.

3. Create a plan for naming files that will be consistent and simple. Write a brief description of your plan. For each file currently on your computer (as listed on the printout), key the current file name. Then key the file path (main folder and any subfolders in which the file will be stored) and the new name you will give the file.

    Example: Star bid 1.doc   C:/Stone/Bids/Stardust Bid 6-30.doc

4. Show the structure of your new file system. Arrange the folder names and new file names in groups to show each main folder, each subfolder within each main folder, and each new file name within a main folder or subfolder.

5. Keep all your notes and a copy of your file structure and file names for use in a later activity.

	COMPOSITION
	DATABASE
	INTEGRATED DOCUMENT
	RECORDS MANAGEMENT
	SPREADSHEET
	WORD PROCESSING

Topic 10-2   ACTIVITY 2

Copier Log

A copier log is used to determine which persons or departments use the copier and to help identify ways to improve efficiency of copier use. In this activity, you will use database software to create a copier log and answer questions about copier use.

1. Create a database to include the following fields: *Date*, *Department*, *Document*, *Originals*, and *Total Copies*.

2. Open and print the data file **Log.pdf**, which contains a copy log employees used to record information about copy jobs. Create a database record for each entry on the log.

3. Sort the records in ascending order first by the Department field and then by the Total Copies field.

4. Which department made the most copies during the two-day period? Which other departments made extensive use of the copier? Which departments made a small number of copies?

5. Export the data table to your spreadsheet software. Create subtotals of the total copies for each department.

6. Create a pie chart showing the percentage of copies made by each department.

7. Create a memo form to include the company name and appropriate headings. The company name is Keystone Distributors.

8. Write a memo report to your supervisor, Amy Blackwell, from you. Use the current date. In the memo, discuss which departments routinely make many photocopies and which ones require only a moderate or small number of copies. (Assume the log for the two days shows typical use.) Copy the pie chart into the memo to show a comparison of copier use by departments.

9. Recommend which departments might benefit from having convenience copiers in their department. Identify departments that might benefit from having a centralized copying center in the company or from outsourcing some copy jobs.

10. Proofread carefully and correct all errors. Print the memo report.

Summary

In this chapter, you learned about the procedures, equipment, supplies, and technologies available to help you manage records stored on paper, magnetic, optical, and microimaging media, and about reprographics. You should be knowledgeable about the following key points:

- Five steps are involved in preparing paper records for storage: collecting, inspecting, indexing/coding, cross-referencing (if necessary), and sorting the records.

- Although vertical and lateral file cabinets are still used most frequently in offices to house folders, shelf files are overall the optimal choice. Other equipment includes horizontal (flat) files, mobile files, and card files.

- Supplies such as requisition cards, OUT guides, and OUT folders are used to manage records efficiently.

- An efficient records management system has a retention schedule that identifies which records should be removed from active storage and on which dates.

- Methods of storage that can be used to protect vital records include multisite storage, planned dispersing, duplication, and vaulting.

- Reprographics is the process of making copies of graphic images such as documents. Photocopiers are found extensively in business offices and are used by almost all employees.

- Large businesses frequently have a reprographics center to handle large copying jobs and convenience copiers for use with small copying jobs.

- Electronic copier/printers, sometimes called intelligent copiers, can receive, transmit, store, print, and copy data.

- Copiers can be classified according to their capacity and have many different features, such as duplexing and image enlargement or reduction.

- Measures used to control copier use include monitoring devices, copy logs, user guidelines, and centralized copying centers.

- Many businesses store records on magnetic disks, optical discs, and tapes. These media must be identified appropriately and organized carefully.

- A company that has many records to maintain may use a database. A database management system simplifies and speeds up the retrieval process by organizing and manipulating large numbers of records.

- Image processing systems allow users to quickly access and review images of original documents. The documents are stored on optical discs. Advantages of optical disc storage are high-storage capacity and speedy record retrieval.

- Electronic files should be organized and named consistently for easy retrieval. Many companies use secondary storage to back up electronic files and free hard disk space.

- Companies use measures such as data backup procedures, password access procedures, firewalls, and antivirus software to protect online records against unauthorized access and damage or destruction.

- Many companies use computers to retrieve microimages. A computer-assisted retrieval (CAR) system can be very simple or very sophisticated.

Key Terms

back up	file cabinet	records manage-
bar code	file path	ment software
card file	file security	release mark
code records	image processing	reprographics
computer-assisted	system	requisition card
retrieval	index records	retention schedule
copyright laws	inspect records	secondary storage
cross-reference	mobile file	shelf file
database manage-	OUT folder or	sort records
ment system	guide	
electronic database	password	

Chapter 10   ACTIVITY 1

Alphabetic Filing

Applying standard alphabetic filing rules correctly is essential for effective records management. In this activity, you will index and code names of individuals and organizations, applying rules for alphabetic indexing. You will also arrange the records in filing order for an alphabetic card file.

1. Open and print the data file **Cards.pdf**, which contains the records you will code and arrange. Cut the sheets along the lines to create 60 records for a card index file.

2. Review the alphabetic indexing rules in Figure 9-2.6 on pages 386–387 or in Reference Section F in your *Student Activities and Projects* workbook.

3. On each record, write the name at the upper-left corner of the card, placing the units in correct indexing order. Place slash marks between the units. Number the indexing units above the name.

1   2   3

Example: Sweeney / Albert / P

4. Arrange the cards alphabetically. Prepare a list of the card numbers as they are arranged in alphabetic order to submit to your instructor.

DATABASE
RECORDS MANAGEMENT
WORD PROCESSING

Chapter 10   ACTIVITY 2

Electronic Files Index and Backup

In this activity, you will continue your work as an administrative assistant at Carson Associates. You created a file organization and naming plan in Topic 10-2 Activity 1. Now you will create a computer index to track the electronic records and their retention dates. You will use the index to locate files and to identify files to be transferred to secondary storage. You will also determine the filing order for the backup disks.

1. Create a new database to include the following fields: *File Name, File Path, Date, Originator, Key Content, Category, Active Storage,* and *Inactive Storage.*

2. Use the list of new file names and paths you created in Topic 10-2 Activity 2. Create a record in your database for each file.
   - Enter the file name in the File Name field, for example: Stardust Bid 6-30.doc.
   - Enter the path for the file in the File Path field, for example: C:/Stone/Bids.
   - Enter the date of the file in the Date field.
   - Enter the name of the executive for whom the file was created in the Originator field.
   - Enter a few words that indicate what the record relates to in the Key Content field, for example: cover letter for bid.
   - Enter the type of record, such as letter, report, spreadsheet, presentation, or database, in the Category field.
   - Enter the retention period for which the document will be kept in active online storage on your computer in the Active Storage field. See the list below to determine retention periods.
   - Enter the retention period for which the document will be kept in inactive storage (on a disk or CD) in the Inactive Storage field.

3. Sort the records in ascending order, first by the Originator field, then by the File Name field. Print a table of the records.

4. Assume six months have gone by since you created your electronic records index. You would have created many more files during this time. Mr. Stone asks you to find any records related to taxes for Beal Tires. Create a query to find this information. Display the File Name, File Path, Date, Originator, and Key Content fields in the query results. Print the query results.

RETENTION PERIODS

Category	Active Storage	Inactive Storage
Bank reconciliations	3 years	Permanent
Bids and related correspondence	1 year	4 years
Client database	Permanent	
Correspondence	1 year	4 years
Financial statements (balance sheets and income statements)	3 years	Permanent
Invoices	2 years	7 years
Presentations	1 year	2 years

5. Assume you created your records index on August 10 of the current year. Now assume that 13 months have gone by since that date when the index was created. Create a query to find all records that have been in active storage longer than the active storage retention time indicated on the retention schedule. Sort the query results by the Originator field. Display all fields in the query results. Print the query results.

6. Decide how to group these records for transfer to inactive storage on floppy disks. How many disks will be used? Which files will be placed on each disk?

7. Key a label to place on each disk after the files have been backed up on the disks. Each label should indicate the content of the disk, the date the backup disk is created, and how long the files should be retained. Also indicate the operating system and software used to create the records. See your original notes about the files for this information. Print the labels. (Print on plain paper if disk labels are not available.)

> Stone
> Presentations
>
> Backup Created: 9/10/--
> Retention: 2 years
>
> Windows ME
> Microsoft PowerPoint 2002

8. You will store your floppy disks containing backup files in a plastic storage container. You have decided to arrange the disks alphabetically first by originator and then by subject. Arrange the disk labels in the order in which the floppy disks would be arranged according to your plan.

9. Give your instructor your database printouts from steps 3, 4, and 5 and your disk labels arranged in filing order.

> *After completing all the chapters in Part 3, complete the Part 3 simulation, At Work at Maple Valley Chamber of Commerce. The simulation is found in the* Student Activities and Projects *workbook.*

Part 4

Mail and Telecommunication Systems

Fast, efficient, and effective communications are critical for the success of most businesses. Whether you communicate with coworkers and customers around the corner or around the world by mail, telephone, fax, e-mail, or other electronic means, your ability to handle communciations effectively is a valuable skill. You will build your communication skills as you study *Mail and Telecommunication Systems*.

OBJECTIVES

- Apply procedures for handling incoming and outgoing mail
- Respond to incoming calls and place outgoing calls effectively
- Describe the equipment, technology, and procedures for commons forms of telecommunications

Processing Mail

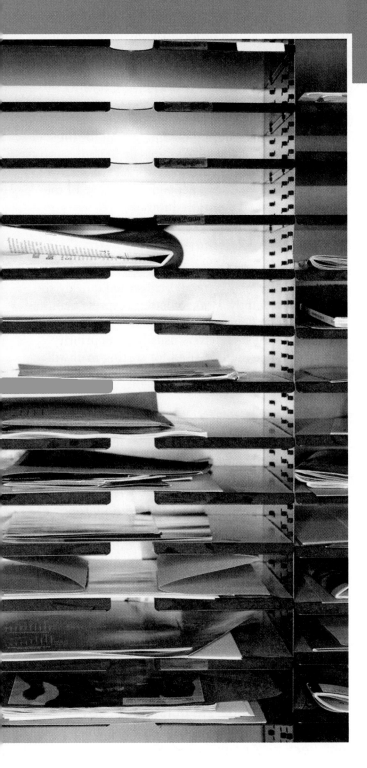

Workers frequently use written messages to communicate with coworkers as well as individuals outside the company. Mail must be processed as efficiently as possible so that communication is not delayed. The size of a company and the amount of automated equipment available affect the procedures used for processing incoming and outgoing mail. In a small company, one worker may handle incoming and outgoing mail (as well as perform other office tasks) using limited automated equipment. In a large company, a full-time mailroom staff often uses specialized equipment to process mail. Even in large companies, workers outside the mailroom may have certain mail-handling responsibilities.

In this chapter, you will learn procedures for processing incoming and outgoing mail in both small and large companies. You also will learn about the equipment available to process mail with maximum efficiency.

OBJECTIVES

- Sort and distribute incoming mail
- Open, separate, and annotate incoming mail
- Document the receipt of mail
- Refer, route, and prioritize mail

Office workers often need to act promptly in response to items received in the mail. They may need to deposit checks, fill orders, pay invoices, read literature, review reports, and answer correspondence. Mail must be accurately sorted and promptly distributed to the appropriate people so necessary actions can be taken without delay. In this chapter, you will learn how to handle incoming mail from outside the company, as well as interoffice mail.

You may be responsible for sorting and distributing incoming mail for the entire company or just for handling your own mail. You may help your supervisors or coworkers process their mail after another worker has distributed it. Your role in processing incoming mail will depend on the size of the company, the volume of incoming mail, and your job duties.

Sorting and Distributing Mail

Mail for various individuals and departments is all mixed together when it is delivered to an organization. Most companies want all mail sorted quickly so that it can be delivered and handled promptly. Priority letters, express mail, registered mail, and insured mail may be delivered to the addressee immediately upon receipt. In fact, the delivery of such letters usually takes priority over the processing of ordinary mail. The method used for sorting mail will vary depending on the size of the company and how it is organized.

In Small Companies

In a small company, you can easily sort the mail at your workstation by making a stack of mail for each employee or department. In a small company, one person may process incoming mail as well as perform other office tasks.

To distribute the mail, you hand deliver each stack of mail to the appropriate person or department. If you have several stacks or bundles of mail to deliver, you may need to carry them in a pouch, alphabetized expanding folder, lightweight mail basket, or mail cart as you make your rounds through the office. You should arrange the bundles according to the route you will take.

WORKPLACE CONNECTIONS

When Ted finishes sorting the mail, he places rubber bands around each stack, creating a separate bundle for each worker. Then he places the bundles in a mail cart in the order that he will deliver them. Because Angela Duncan's workstation is his first stop, Ted places her mail bundle at the front of the cart. Using this procedure, Ted distributes the mail quickly.

Figure 11-1.1

The mail clerk delivers mail at regularly scheduled times during the workday.

© TONY FREEMAN/PHOTOEDIT

In Large Companies

Many large companies have mailrooms. A mailroom is a designated area where large volumes of incoming mail are processed. Mailrooms are easily accessible to postal workers who deliver the mail to the company. You are likely to find specialized equipment to aid mailroom workers in opening, sorting, and delivering the mail. Such equipment typically includes electric envelope openers, sorting units, and automated delivery systems.

Opening Envelopes and Packages

In some companies, mailroom workers open all the mail (except envelopes marked *Personal* or *Confidential*) before delivering it. An electric envelope opener often is used for opening envelopes. An electric envelope opener trims

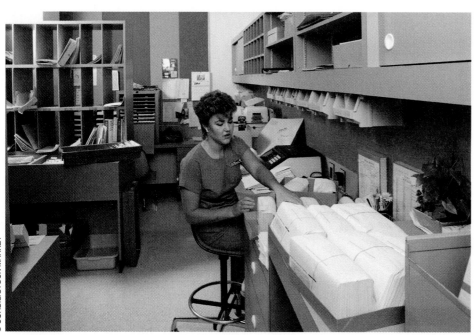

Figure 11-1.2

This mailroom worker is sorting incoming mail from the post office and from private mail services.

© CORBIS/STOCK MARKET

Topic 11-1: *Incoming Mail Procedures*

a narrow strip off one edge of each envelope. The amount trimmed off is very small so that there is little risk that the contents of the envelope will be damaged. To reduce the chances of cutting the contents, tap each envelope on the table before placing it in the opener, so the contents will fall away from the edge that you are trimming. Take care not to damage the contents when opening packages and boxes.

Safety Precautions

Office workers should take care to protect themselves against dangerous substances that might be present in envelopes or packages received via mail. Wearing gloves and a face mask can provide some protection from airborne substances that might be dangerous. When handling mail, avoid touching your face and mouth to help prevent the transfer of germs. Wash your hands with disinfectant soap after handling mail. The United States Postal Service recommends that you do not handle a piece of mail that you suspect is dangerous.

According to the Centers for Disease Control and Prevention (CDC), "Characteristics of suspicious packages and letters include inappropriate or unusual labeling, strange return address or no return address, postmarks from a city or state different from the return address, excessive packaging material, and others. If a package appears suspicious, it should not be opened. The package should be handled as little as possible. The room should be vacated and secured promptly, and appropriate security or law enforcement agencies should be promptly notified."* For more information, access the CDC Web site at www.cdc.gov.

Sorting Mail

A wide variety of sorting units are used to sort the mail. Each compartment is labeled with the name of an individual or department within the organization. To sort the mail, you place each piece of mail in the appropriate compartment.

Companies with a huge amount of incoming mail have found that they can save time and effort by using a rotary sorting unit. The unit turns easily, and the worker can remain in one place as he or she sorts the mail.

Distributing Mail

Once the mail has been sorted, it is ready for distribution. Procedures for delivering mail within the organization vary from company to company. For example:

- A worker from each department comes to the mailroom to pick up the department's mail.
- A mailroom employee carries the mail in a basket or cart from the mailroom to the departments.
- An **automated** delivery system transports mail to the various departments. This robot-like cart follows a chemical path on the floor and is programmed to stop at certain locations throughout the building. Employees can then pick up incoming mail and deposit outgoing mail.

automated: processed by machine

---

*"Update: Investigation of Bioterrorism-Related Anthrax and Interim Guidelines for Exposure Management and Antimicrobial Therapy, October 2001." Centers for Disease Control and Prevention. Online. Available: http://www.cdc.gov/mmwr/preview/mmwrhtml/mm5042a1.htm. December 8, 2001.

Figure 11-1.3

In some companies, an employee delivers mail to each department.

Handling Incoming Mail

Some office workers are asked to process the mail before giving it to their supervisors or coworkers. You may simply separate and open the mail, or you may be expected to annotate, route, or prioritize correspondence.

In handling your own mail or mail for others, you may have access to **confidential** information related to business plans or products, employee records, or customer profiles. You will be expected to take precautions to protect this confidential information, and you may be asked to sign a confidentiality agreement.

confidential: private or secret

WORKPLACE **CONNECTIONS**

Sarah is an administrative assistant in the Office of Housing at a state university. In that position, she has access to potentially sensitive and personal information about residents. Sarah has been directed not to disclose or abuse any of the information she has access to while employed by the university. If she fails to comply with the confidentiality agreement she signed when she was hired, she could be fired from her job.

Opening Mail

If the mail is not opened when it reaches you, use a letter opener to open all envelopes. (See *Safety Precautions* on page 446.) When you are opening mail for supervisors or coworkers, do not open envelopes marked *Personal* or

Confidential. If you mistakenly open such an envelope, write on it, "Sorry, opened by mistake," and add your initials. Check the outside of each envelope carefully before you open it to avoid making that error.

As you remove the contents from the envelopes, be sure to verify that all enclosures referred to in the correspondence are actually enclosed. If an enclosure is missing, you should note in the margin of the letter that it is missing. Notify the sender of the missing enclosure right away, especially if it is a check, money order, cash, or stamps.

Check each letter for the signature and the address of the sender before you discard the envelope. If either is missing on the letter, attach the envelope to the back of the letter, because the envelope usually has a return address on it. Sometimes the envelope is stapled to a document because the mailing date may be important.

Record the current date on each item received. In some cases, recording the time the item was received may also be helpful. This can be done with a pen or pencil, a rubber stamp, or a time-stamp machine.

Separating and Annotating Mail

As you inspect the mail, put the letters that you will answer or handle yourself in one stack and those that will be handled by a supervisor or coworkers in another stack. You may be able to handle communications that could be answered by a form letter, circular, or advertisement. Requests for catalogs or price lists can also be handled this way. However, your supervisor may wish to see all inquiries that are received.

annotate: write comments related to the content of a message

At your supervisor's request, or to help with answering your own mail, you may want to underline or **annotate** the correspondence. Using good judgment is necessary here, however, because too many marks on a letter can be distracting.

First, underline the key words and phrases in the correspondence that will aid in understanding the content quickly. Note the key phrases underlined in Figure 11-1.4 on page 450. Then determine the answers to questions in the correspondence. Where appropriate, make related comments on the letter. Write the clearly worded answers and/or comments in legible handwriting in the margin, on a note placed on the correspondence, or on a photocopy of the correspondence. Note the annotations on the letter shown in Figure 11-1.4.

Copies of previous correspondence, reports, and other related documents might help in responding to the mail. For example, you may attach the file copy of a letter written to Ms. McCoy to the reply you receive from her. Or you might retrieve a folder related to an inquiry from the files and place it with the incoming letter.

Documenting Receipt of Mail

You should keep a record of items you expect to receive under separate cover (in another envelope or package) to be sure that you receive them. You might create a spreadsheet or database table to record the current date, the item expected, the date you expect to receive the item, and the person or

Protecting Confidential Information

Confidential information is information that is private or secret. Intentional or accidental release of such information could cause harm to the business or its employees, clients, or customers. Businesses may have several types of confidential information. *Inside information* is information about the company that has not yet been released to the public, such as plans to open a new plant or merge with another company. *Proprietary information* is information about the company's products or services, such as the formula or design for a product. *Private information* about employees and customers, such as salaries or credit card numbers, is often stored in company files. Usually, only those employees who need the information to do their jobs are allowed to see confidential information.

As an office worker, you may come in contact with confidential information as you process the mail, prepare documents, or handle employee or customer records. The following guidelines will help you keep business information confidential.

- **Know your supervisor's preferences.** Know what information you should and should not give to visitors or callers. When your supervisor is not in the office, know who is to be allowed in your supervisor's office or who can use your supervisor's computer.

- **Follow your company's mail procedures.** Place confidential mail in a folder or in a secure location where it will be seen only by the intended recipient. Do not send confidential information by fax or e-mail. Use overnight mail services if speed is a consideration.

- **Secure your workstation.** Take precautions to keep others from reading confidential information from your computer screen. Turn over confidential mail or papers or place them in a drawer when you leave your desk—even for a few moments. At the end of the day, secure papers in a locked desk or file cabinet. Shred confidential documents rather than placing them in your wastebasket.

- **Protect written documents.** Use a folder or an envelope to conceal documents if you carry documents to another office. If you transport confidential documents outside the office, lock them in a briefcase or in the trunk of your car. If you use a briefcase, always keep it in your possession.

- **Reduce electronic information loss.** Use password sign-on and sign-off procedures and change your password frequently. Be alert to remove printouts from the printer when you finish the print job, particularly if the printer is shared with others. Make backup copies of confidential files and place them in a secure location.

company who will send the item. A field or column might be included to record the date the item is received. If you handle mail for several people, you would include the name of the person expecting the item. Check the table at least twice a week to see which items have not been received. Then take follow-up action on delayed mail.

Topic 11-1: Incoming Mail Procedures

Figure 11-1.4

The date-time stamp, underlined words and phrases, and annotations make a quick response easier.

Russell White and Brothers Lumber Company

Route 32
Linwood, KY 40455-0077

December 5, 20--

DEC 8, 20-- 11:30 a.m.

Ms. Michele R. Carrell
Ashland Computerland, Inc.
800 Cleveland Avenue
Ashland, KY 44550-0770

Copy sent to Mr. Edwards
in installation dept.

Dear Ms. Carrell

Our new <u>computer system was installed on November 26,</u> and we were impressed <u>with the efficiency of your installation team.</u> The hardware and software are installed and working well. Feedback from the end-users has been positive.

Ed Jones, your installation team director, advises that we need to add one more workstation to maximize the use of the computer network. <u>Please add another PC2-2020 workstation</u> to our order.

Prepared Inv. 22892 12/9

Mr. Jones also reminded us to make plans for our unit director, <u>Mary Ann McCoy,</u> to attend your <u>End-User Workshop on January 6-10.</u> Ms. McCoy is eager to attend, and we know this additional education will improve our utilization of the new computer system. Please send registration forms for the workshop to Ms. McCoy in the <u>information services department.</u> Our address is listed at the top of this letter.

Registration forms sent.

Sincerely

Harold G. White

Harold G. White
Chief Information Officer

de

Workers in the mailroom usually do not keep expected mail records because they do not read the contents of the mail. If you handle mail only for yourself, you might simply enter a reminder in your desktop utility software, such as Microsoft Outlook, to alert you on the date the mail is expected. Figure 11-1.5 shows such as entry.

Whether you process incoming mail in a small company or in the mailroom of a large company, you should **document** the receipt of mail sent by special postal services or private mail services. For example, you should record the receipt of certified, insured, registered, or express mail. You might use a printed form or record information in a database table as in Figure 11-1.6.

document: make a written record of

Figure 11-1.5

Keep a reminder of incoming mail you expect to receive.

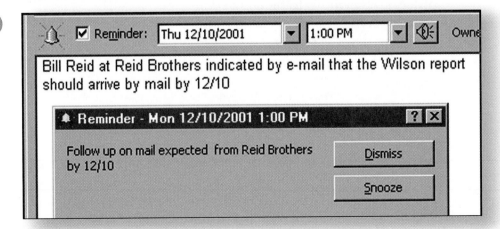

CHAPTER 11: PROCESSING MAIL

Item	For	From	City	State	Date	Time
Insured Package	B. Rudd	T. J. McIntosh	St. Louis	MO	4-5-02	3:20 p.m.
Special Delivery Package	S. Nowell	Bates Mfg. Co.	Memphis	TN	4-6-02	9:15 a.m.
Registered Letter	J. Jones	Ken Stewart	Des Moines	IA	4-9-02	10:45 a.m.
Express Mail Package	W. Yeager	Haskins Associates	Erie	PA	4-12-02	3:15 p.m.

Record: 5 of 5

Referring or Routing Mail

You or your supervisor may decide to refer certain items to an assistant or associate to handle. To help with this process, a *referral slip* is attached to the item. The referral slip shown in Figure 11-1.7 lists a series of instructions from which to choose. A check mark is used to indicate the specific instruction to be followed.

When action is requested of another individual, you should keep a record of the referral. You should note the date the item was referred, the name of the person to whom it was referred, the subject, the action to be taken, and a follow-up date if one is necessary.

Often more than one person in the company should read items, such as correspondence and important magazine articles. You may be asked to make a copy for each person who should read the item or to **route** the item through the office. To do so, attach a routing slip, which is similar to a referral slip. Indicate with check marks the individuals who should read the item.

Figure 11-1.6

Use a mail register to document the receipt of special mail.

route: send on a particular path

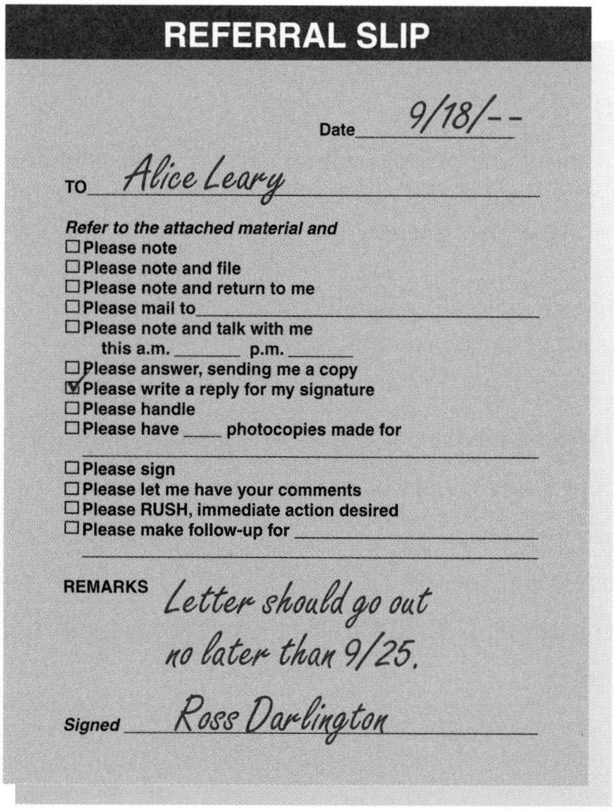

REFERRAL SLIP

Date _9/18/--_

TO _Alice Leary_

Refer to the attached material and
☐ Please note
☐ Please note and file
☐ Please note and return to me
☐ Please mail to_____
☐ Please note and talk with me
    this a.m. _____ p.m. _____
☐ Please answer, sending me a copy
☑ Please write a reply for my signature
☐ Please handle
☐ Please have ____ photocopies made for
_____

☐ Please sign
☐ Please let me have your comments
☐ Please RUSH, immediate action desired
☐ Please make follow-up for _____

REMARKS _Letter should go out no later than 9/25._

Signed _Ross Darlington_

Figure 11-1.7

Mail is often forwarded to an associate for action.

451

Topic 11-1: *Incoming Mail Procedures*

Figure 11-1.8

A routing slip is attached to mail to be distributed to others.

ROUTING SLIP

FROM:
Ryan Talbert
Information Services Department
DATE: *3/25*

TO:	**Date Forwarded**
___Everyone	_____
___R. Bernardin	_____
✓ R. Carlson	*3/25*
___M. Carrell	_____
___J. Fouch	_____
✓ J. Hensen	*3/25*
___C. Hickman	_____
___H. Iwuki	_____
✓ S. Lansing	*3/26*
___M. Lucky	_____
___C. Tesch	_____
✓ R. Williams	*3/27*

Please:
___Read and keep in your files
___Read and pass on
___Read and return to me
✓ Read, route, and return to me

Prioritizing Mail

prioritized: put in order of importance

Incoming mail should be **prioritized** for further processing. As a general rule, mail is categorized in the order of its importance. The following arrangement is usually satisfactory, moving from the top to the bottom of the stack:

1. Urgent messages, such as documents received by fax or overnight delivery, that require prompt attention

2. Personal and confidential letters

3. Business letters, memos, or other correspondence of special importance

4. Letters containing checks or money orders

5. Other business letters

6. Letters containing orders

7. Letters containing bills, invoices, or other requests for payment

8. Advertisements

9. Newspapers and magazines

10. Packages

Todd Gardner is the receptionist in a small real estate agency. Todd's duties include sorting and prioritizing mail for several coworkers. Todd noticed that 25 to 50 percent of the mail received by the agency each day was advertisements or other unsolicited or "junk" mail. He took the initiative to write to **Direct Marketing Association** and request that the company's name be removed from national mailing lists. Now Todd has many fewer advertisements to handle and can sort the mail more quickly each day.

Direct Marketing Association: a trade group of telephone and mail marketers

Handling Mail While Away from the Office

Technology makes it possible to receive and forward important mail and messages for immediate action while away from the office. In this way, business matters are not delayed and deadlines are not missed. You will need to decide which mail should be forwarded and which mail should be held for action after returning to the office. The following guidelines may be helpful in keeping track of incoming mail for your supervisors or coworkers who are away from the office.

- Maintain a mail register as described on page 451, Figure 11-1.6.
- Communicate with the traveler immediately if important, unexpected action seems required.
- Refer routine mail to others who can respond.
- Answer mail yourself if it is within your area of responsibility.
- Send a **synopsis** of received mail (or a copy of the mail log) if the traveler is on an extended business trip.
- After the mail has been prioritized, store it in an appropriate place.

synopsis: general overview or summary

Effective processing of the incoming mail helps keep the office running smoothly while the traveler is away and saves time for the traveler upon returning to the office.

453

Reviewing the Topic

1. What is interoffice mail?
2. What three factors affect your role in processing incoming mail?
3. Describe safety precautions office workers can take to protect themselves against dangerous substances that might be present in envelopes or packages received via mail.
4. What equipment is used in mailrooms to process incoming mail?
5. What should you do if you open a confidential letter by mistake?
6. When you remove the contents from an envelope, what should you verify?
7. How might your annotating a letter save your supervisor time?
8. What is the purpose of keeping a record of expected mail?
9. Give an example of when a routing slip might be used.
10. What is the generally accepted order for prioritizing incoming mail?

Thinking Critically

You work in the general office of Sperling Enterprises. Because your supervisor receives a large amount of mail of different types, she has asked you to prioritize it prior to delivering it to her.

1. Key the list of the mail items shown below.
2. Arrange the list of mail items in order of priority. (Begin the list with the most important and continue to the least important.)

- Personal letter from Michelle Jackson
- Overnight package from Hancock Associates
- Letter containing an order from Jackie Yung
- Advertisement for office furniture
- Newspaper
- Interoffice memo from coworker Paul Flynn
- Fax from Karl Shelton, at Shelton Brothers
- Business letter of special importance from Norman Steel of Steel, Inc.
- *PC Magazine*
- Letter containing a bill from Office Depot
- Letter containing a check from Howard Supply Company
- Fax from David Foster of Foster Insurance

- Business letter from Robert Potter of Quality Leasing
- Package from Anderson Office Supplies
- Advertisement from Media Plus
- *Business Week* magazine
- Letter containing a bill from Jackson Electric Company
- Letter containing a check from Susan Patrick
- Letter containing an order from Danny Wright
- Business letter from Creative Calendars, Inc.

Reinforcing Math Skills

1. Based on records kept by the mailroom supervisor, about 3,000 pieces of incoming mail are sorted and distributed each month in your company. Additionally, the volume of mail is expected to increase by 6 percent next year. How many pieces of mail will be processed this year? How many more pieces of mail will be processed next year than will be processed this year?

2. An envelope has been prepared for each address on a mailing list of 18,000 names. The mailing machine can feed, seal, meter stamp, count, and stack 200 envelopes a minute. Of the 18,000 envelopes being processed, 20 percent are being sent to Minnesota, 30 percent to Wyoming, 15 percent to Wisconsin, and 35 percent to Nebraska. How long it will take to process all the envelopes using the mailing machine? How many envelopes will be sent to each state?

COMPOSITION
INTEGRATED DOCUMENT
SPREADSHEET
WORD PROCESSING

Topic 11-1 ACTIVITY 1

Mail Report

Your work for Jackson Insurance, a small agency, where more than 6,000 pieces of incoming mail are processed each year. Your supervisor, Cecil Thompson, left this message on your voice mail.

Hi, this is Cecil. I need some summary information about the types of incoming mail that are processed in our mailroom. About how many pieces of incoming mail (including interoffice mail) do we process each year? What general types or categories of items are processed? Please create a pie chart showing the different types of items and the percentage each item represents of the total. I need this information in a short memo report by tomorrow afternoon. Thanks.

1. Create a memo form for Jackson Insurance to include the company name and appropriate memo headings.

2. Write a short memo report to your supervisor providing the information he requested. Use the categories of mail and the numbers shown below to create your report. Title the chart *INCOMING MAIL PROCESSED* and include a legend.

Number of Items	Category
1,000	Express mail packages or letters
1,500	Advertisements, newspapers, and magazines
1,250	Interoffice mail
2,200	Letters, checks, and invoices
300	Other

COMPOSITION
WORD PROCESSING

Topic 11-1   ACTIVITY 2

Annotate Letter and Compose Reply

You work for Shred-Rite Shedder Company, a retailer for office and personal paper shredders. Your supervisor, Ms. Wanda Albertson, is the customer service manager. You often annotate mail and compose replies for her signature.

1. Open and print the data file **Shred-Rite Letter.pdf**, which contains a letter from a customer. Read the letter and underline the important points.

2. Open and print the data file **Shred-Rite Invoice.pdf**, which contains a copy of the customer invoice. Review the invoice and then annotate the customer's letter with appropriate comments.

3. Compose a reply to the customer for your supervisor's signature. Assume the letter will be printed on company letterhead. Tell the customer how the problem will be corrected and express regret for the customer's inconvenience. Examine your letter for the five Cs of effective writing.

4. Submit the customer's letter with your annotations, the invoice, and your reply to your supervisor (instructor).

Outgoing Mail Procedures

OBJECTIVES

- Prepare outgoing mail
- Identify the classes of domestic mail
- Explain the various services provided by the USPS
- Identify address and packaging requirements
- Describe services provided by private mail delivery companies

Throughout a working day, many forms of communication are sent to those outside the company. For example, you may be asked to send purchase orders to customers, letters to business organizations, and advertisements to potential customers. Preparing outgoing mail properly is important for prompt delivery.

You probably have prepared letters for mailing and are acquainted with addressing envelopes, inserting documents, and affixing proper postage. You will find, however, that companies have developed specific procedures for completing these tasks in order to handle outgoing mail efficiently.

The way outgoing mail is processed will depend on the size of your company and the procedures designated by the company. If you work in a small office, you probably will be responsible for all the details involved with processing outgoing mail. If you work in the mailroom of a large company, however, you may weigh and seal mail, apply postage, and mail envelopes that have been prepared and stuffed by workers in other departments.

The United States Postal Service (USPS) processes over half a billion pieces of mail each day! Businesses all across the country use the varied services of the USPS to send such items as letters, financial reports, computer printouts, architectural drawings, invoices, manuscripts, newsletters, and merchandise to their intended destinations. In some cases, the items are destined for delivery in the same city; in other cases, they travel to an individual or an organization in a city halfway around the world.

Although most outgoing mail is sent through the USPS, local, national, and worldwide private mail delivery companies, sometimes called **courier** services, also deliver envelopes and packages. Most delivery services guarantee their delivery times. You also may send mail through an interoffice mail system. As an office worker, you need to be acquainted with the mailing options available to you. This topic will help you learn about procedures for processing outgoing mail efficiently.

courier: messenger

Processing Outgoing Mail

In a small organization you may be responsible for processing all the outgoing mail, as well as handling other office tasks. In a large company, however, these steps may be divided between mailroom workers and workers in other departments. If you are an office worker in a large company, the extent of your mail-handling duties will be determined by company policy and your specific job.

The USPS picks up and delivers mail to some organizations twice a day. In other organizations, a postal carrier may come to the office in the morning, and an office worker may take outgoing mail to a post office or a **drop box** in the afternoon. You need to know the scheduled times for pickup so you can have the mail ready on time. The USPS recommends mailing as early in the day as possible for the fastest service.

drop box: container for outgoing mail

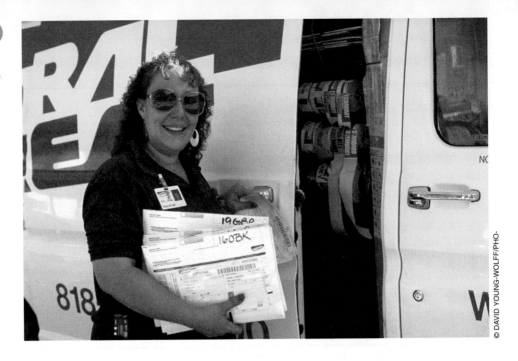

Figure 11-2.1

Many private mail carriers pick up and deliver mail to business locations.

© DAVID YOUNG-WOLFF/PHO-

Melynda is the receptionist in a small real estate office. On her workstation is an out basket where all the workers place their outgoing mail. A postal carrier usually picks up and delivers the mail about 10:30 a.m. At 10:00 a.m., Melynda prepares an envelope for each item in the out basket. Then she stuffs the envelopes, seals them, weighs them, and applies the appropriate postage. By 10:30 a.m., the mail is ready to be picked up by the postal carrier.

Brenner Industries is a large corporation with many departments. Office workers in each department address the envelopes and insert the correspondence into the envelopes. Each department has a central location for collecting outgoing mail. A mailroom worker picks up the mail and takes it to the company mailroom. The mailroom workers then seal, weigh, and place postage on the mail in time for scheduled pickups from the post office.

In a large company these steps for processing mail may be divided between mailroom workers and workers in other departments. If you are an office worker in a large company, the extent of your mail-handling duties will be determined by company policy and your specific job.

Folding and Inserting Mail

Once a document is ready to mail, it is a good idea to give it a final check before inserting it in the envelope. Be sure that:

- Copies have been made, if necessary.
- Letters have been signed.
- Your initials appear below your supervisor's signature on any letter you have signed for your supervisor.
- All enclosures noted at the bottom of a letter are actually enclosed in the envelope.
- The address on the envelope agrees with the address on the letter.
- The nine-digit ZIP code appears on the last line of both the envelope address and the return address.

You usually will insert documents into standard or window envelopes. Folding business documents correctly to fit into envelopes is a simple but important task. You should take care that the creases are straight and neat. A document should be inserted in an envelope so that it will be in a normal reading position when it is removed from the envelope and unfolded.

Standard Envelopes

The size for a standard envelope used for business letters is 9½" × 4⅛" (No. 10). Figure 11-2.2 shows how to fold a letter and insert it into a No. 10 envelope. The enclosures that accompany a document should be folded with the document or inserted so that they will come out of the envelope when the document is removed.

Window Envelopes

A window envelope has a see-through panel on the front of the envelope. A window envelope eliminates the need to address an envelope because the address on the letter or form is visible through the window. The address on the letter or form must be positioned so that it can be seen through the window after the letter is folded and inserted into the envelope. Figure 11-2.3 shows how to fold a letter and insert it into a No. 10 window envelope.

Business forms are available in a variety of custom sizes. Special size envelopes are used to match the forms. When using special size forms

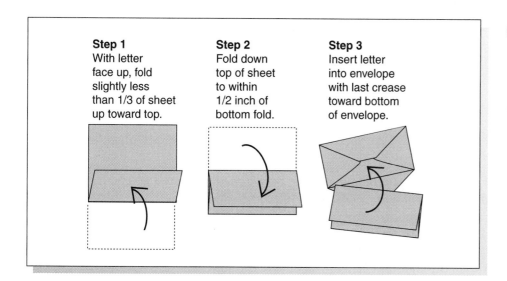

Step 1
With letter face up, fold slightly less than 1/3 of sheet up toward top.

Step 2
Fold down top of sheet to within 1/2 inch of bottom fold.

Step 3
Insert letter into envelope with last crease toward bottom of envelope.

Figure 11-2.2

Follow these steps to fold an 8 ½" × 11" sheet to insert into a No. 10 envelope.

Figure 11-2.3

Follow these steps to fold an 8 ½" × 11" sheet to insert into a No. 10 window envelope.

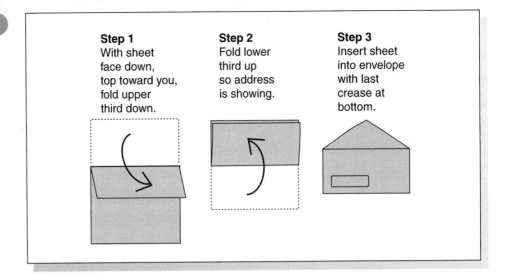

Step 1
With sheet face down, top toward you, fold upper third down.

Step 2
Fold lower third up so address is showing.

Step 3
Insert sheet into envelope with last crease at bottom.

and envelopes, make sure the mailing address shows properly in the envelope window.

Sealing and Weighing Envelopes

Envelopes must be sealed before they are mailed. When you need to seal more than one or two envelopes, you probably will want to use a moist sponge or moistener. Mail processing equipment that can insert letters into envelopes and seal the envelopes is available. If your office processes large mailings frequently, this equipment can save valuable time.

WORKPLACE **CONNECTIONS**

Alberta prepares several letters for mailing each morning. To quickly seal many envelopes at once, she spreads about ten envelopes on a table or desk. She places the letters address-side down, flap open, one on top of the other, with the gummed edges showing. Next, Alberta brushes over the gummed edges with a sponge or moistener. Starting with the top envelope, she quickly folds the flaps down one at a time until all the envelopes are sealed.

Each piece of outgoing mail must be weighed accurately so you can apply the proper amount of postage. Electronic scales are available that automatically calculate the correct amount of postage for each piece of mail. You simply place the item to be mailed on the scale and indicate which postal class you wish to use. The amount of the postage is displayed on a small screen. When postal rates change, you update the scale with the new rates.

Figure 11-2.4

© MICHAEL NEWMAN/PHOTOEDIT

Stamping Mail

Postage must be paid for all mail before it is delivered by the USPS. You may purchase postage stamps in sheet, booklet, or rolled form. Rolled stamps often are used in business because they can be placed quickly on envelopes and packages, and they are less likely than individual stamps to be lost or damaged.

The post office sells envelopes and cards that already have the correct postage printed on them. You can buy them one at a time or in quantity. First-class postcards may be purchased in single or double form. The double form is used when a reply is requested on the attached card.

Printing Postage for Mail

A **postage meter** is a machine that prints postage in the amount needed. The meter prints the postage either directly onto the envelope or onto a label that you apply to the envelope or package. You can use the numeric keys on the postage meter to set it to print postage for a letter weighing one ounce and easily reset it to print postage for a letter weighing three ounces. The postage meter prints the date as well as the postage amount. Always be sure the correct date is set on the meter. Some meters also print a business slogan or advertisement next to the postmark. Because metered mail is already dated and postmarked, it can be processed faster than stamped mail.

postage meter: a machine that prints postage in the amount needed

For some postage meters, you take the meter with you to the post office to buy postage. A postal worker will reset the meter for the amount of postage purchased. As you use the postage meter, the meter setting decreases, showing you how much postage remains. Do not let the postage get too low before buying more. The meter locks when the postage runs out.

volume mailing: sending the same items to many people at the same time

Several companies offer postage meters that allow you to purchase postage online. The user connects the meter, which contains a modem, to a standard phone line. Using a keypad, the user indicates the amount of postage to be purchased. The meter is updated, and the user is billed for the cost of the postage.

The USPS has authorized several companies to sell postage on the Internet. Users can access the Web site for one of these companies and subscribe to a postage service plan. The user receives computer software and, with some plans, a postage scale. The software allows the user to print a postmark and the appropriate amount of postage on an envelope or label using any computer printer.

Handling Volume Mailings

A **volume mailing** involves sending the same items to many people at the same time. For example, a marketing research company may send a questionnaire to all residents in a city asking about products, such as televisions or breakfast cereals. Companies doing volume mailings may qualify for reduced postage rates. To qualify for reduced postage rates, mailing must be prepared according to current USPS mailing regulations and standards.

Address labels may be used for volume mail items, or the items may be addressed individually. One method of preparing mailing labels is to type all the addresses on paper in a format that will allow you to photocopy the addresses onto sheets of labels. Each time you have a mailing, you simply photocopy the addresses, peel the labels off the backing sheets, and apply them to the envelopes.

Many companies use computer-generated mailing lists. Mailing lists for volume mail may contain addresses for customers, prospective customers,

Figure 11-2.5

An electronic postage meter prints the postmark and the postage.

© SPENCER GRANT/PHOTOEDIT

subscribers, or those who live in certain geographic areas. Mailing lists should always be current. Delete, correct, and add addresses as soon as you learn about changes. The post office recommends having the words *FOR-WARDING AND ADDRESS CORRECTION REQUESTED* printed on all envelopes. Then the post office will **forward** mail with an old address to the new address. For a small fee, the post office will send you a card giving the new address. Some of the advantages of using computer-generated mailing lists include the ability to:

forward: send on

- Quickly retrieve, change, or delete addresses
- Easily avoid duplicate addresses
- Select addresses from a master list to create a smaller list for a special mailing
- Print letter addresses and salutations on form letters as well as address labels

WORKPLACE **CONNECTIONS**

Willa Flag works in the human resources department of a small company. She prepares volume mailings to employees, such as sales representatives, who are not located at the company's home office. Benefits information, policy changes, and new procedures must be communicated to these employees on a timely basis. Until recently, Willa keyed the address and printed an envelope for each employee each time a mailing was prepared. Willa soon realized that she was repeating work needlessly.

After reviewing the features of her database and word processing programs, Willa created a database to include the name, address, and other relevant information for each employee. She also created an envelope document and a mailing label document with which she can merge information from the database. Now when Willa needs to prepare a mailing, she simply enters any updates in the database and completes the merge. Envelopes and labels are printed in a fraction of the time previously required.

Specialized mailing equipment is available to totally automate the process of preparing volume mailings. Some machines can print personalized letters and matching envelopes, fold the letters, insert the letters and any enclosures in the envelopes, and seal the envelopes. Postage can also be applied by machine.

Figure 11-2.6

Large companies may use equipment that can fold and insert documents, seal envelopes, weigh mail, and apply postage to speed mail processing.

© PITNEY BOWES, INC./SOUTH-WESTERN/THOMSON LEARNING

optical character reader:
electronic equipment that quickly scans the address on an envelope and prints a bar code at the bottom of the envelope

Address Requirements for Automated Handling

The USPS uses high-speed electronic mail-handling equipment in many of its postal centers to speed mail to its destination. This equipment includes optical character readers and bar code sorters. An **optical character reader** (OCR) is electronic equipment that quickly scans or "reads" the address on an envelope and prints a bar code at the bottom of the envelope.

During the sorting process, the bar codes are "read" by a bar code sorter, and the mail is quickly routed to its proper destination. Not all postal centers are equipped with OCR equipment and bar code sorters; therefore, not all mail you receive will have a printed bar code on the envelope.

If the optical character reader is unable to read an address, the envelope is routed to a manual letter-sorting machine. This, of course, increases the processing time. Some of the reasons why an OCR may be unable to read an address are listed below. Use care when preparing mail to avoid these problems that may slow delivery of the mail.

- The address is handwritten.
- The address is not printed or typed in the proper format.
- The envelope is too small or too large for the OCR equipment to handle. (To avoid this problem, use rectangular envelopes no smaller than $3\frac{1}{2}" \times 5"$ and no larger than $6\frac{1}{8}" \times 11\frac{1}{2}"$.)
- The address is not within the OCR read area.
- The complete address is not visible through the panel of a window envelope.

ZIP Codes

To assure prompt delivery of your mail, always use the nine-digit ZIP code, if known, to help with mail delivery. The first three digits of the

ZIP code indicate a major geographic area or post office, while the next two digits designate a local post office. A hyphen and the four digits that follow help the post office sort the mail more specifically. The first two digits after the hyphen indicate a delivery sector. A sector is several blocks within a city, a group of streets, several office buildings, or another small geographic area. The last two digits represent a delivery segment, which can indicate one side of a street, one floor in an office building, or specific departments in a firm.

ZIP code directories for both the five-digit and nine-digit codes can be purchased from the post office. If a directory is not available in the office where you work, you can call the post office to obtain a particular ZIP code. You can search for ZIP codes on the USPS Web site at www.usps.gov.

Address Format

The address should be printed on the envelope or label. The characters should be dark, even, and clear as shown in Figure 11-2.7 on page 466. The address should be printed according to the following guidelines.

- Block the left margin of the address.
- Use all capital letters and omit all marks of punctuation (except the hyphen in a nine-digit ZIP code).
- Use the standard two-letter abbreviation for the state for domestic mail. Leave one or two spaces between the state abbreviation and the ZIP code.
- Add the delivery point ZIP + 4 bar code on the envelope for domestic mail, if your software has this capability.
- For international addresses, place the foreign postal code, if known, on the same line as the city or town name. Place the city or town name and the province or state name on the next line after the street address information. Place the name of the foreign country in capital letters on the last line of the address. (On mail to Canada, the location of the country name and postal code are interchangeable.)

The post office has an approved list of abbreviations for states, cities, and other words commonly used in addresses. Always use the two-letter state abbreviations (as shown in Figure 11-2.8 on page 466) with the ZIP code in domestic addresses. Use other approved abbreviations if the address is too long to fit on a label.

Classes of Domestic Mail

Domestic mail is distributed by the USPS within the United States and its territories (such as Puerto Rico, the Virgin Islands, and Guam). Domestic mail is divided into various classes, which are described in the following paragraphs.

First-Class

First-class mail is commonly used for items such as letters, bills, **postcards** and **postal cards**, checks, money orders, and business reply mail. A minimum amount is charged for all first-class mail weighing up to one ounce. An additional charge is made for each additional ounce or fraction of an ounce. If you are sending material in an oversized envelope that does not bear a

postcard: privately purchased mailing card that requires postage

postal card: card sold by the U.S. Postal Service with postage imprinted on it

Topic 11-2: *Outgoing Mail Procedures*

Figure 11-2.7

Use the proper address format, abbreviations, and postal codes for addresses.

MS EMMA JO BERMAN
132 CANNON GREEN TOWERS APT 6A
SANTA BARBARA CA 93105-2233

MR ARTURO FUENTES
VICE PRESIDENT MARKETING
ROSSLYN WHOLESALE COMPANY
1815 N LYNN STREET
ARLINGTON VA 22209-6183

MS JOYCE BROWNING
2045 ROYAL ROAD
LONDON WIP 6HQ
ENGLAND

MS HELEN SAUNDERS
1010 CLEAR STREET
OTTAWA ON K1A0B1
CANADA

MR JACQUES MOLIERE
RUE DE CHAMPAIGN
06570 ST PAUL
FRANCE

Figure 11-2.8

USPS two-letter state and territory abbreviations

State and Territory Abbreviations

Alabama	AL	Illinois	IL	Nebraska	NE	South Carolina	SC
Alaska	AK	Indiana	IN	Nevada	NV	South Dakota	SD
Arizona	AZ	Iowa	IA	New Hampshire	NH	Tennessee	TN
Arkansas	AR	Kansas	KS	New Jersey	NJ	Texas	TX
California	CA	Kentucky	KY	New Mexico	NM	Utah	UT
Colorado	CO	Louisiana	LA	New York	NY	Vermont	VT
Connecticut	CT	Maine	ME	North Carolina	NC	Virgin Islands	VI
Delaware	DE	Maryland	MD	North Dakota	ND	Virginia	VA
District of Columbia	DC	Massachusetts	MA	Ohio	OH	Washington	WA
Florida	FL	Michigan	MI	Oklahoma	OK	West Virginia	WV
Georgia	GA	Minnesota	MN	Oregon	OR	Wisconsin	WI
Guam	GU	Mississippi	MS	Pennsylvania	PA	Wyoming	WY
Hawaii	HI	Missouri	MO	Puerto Rico	PR		
Idaho	ID	Montana	MT	Rhode Island	RI		

Figure 11-2.9

Various classes of domestic mail are sorted by postal workers each day.

© MARY KATE DENNY/PHOTOEDIT

preprinted FIRST CLASS notation, print or stamp *FIRST CLASS* on the envelope. Mail that weighs over 13 ounces must be sent as priority mail to receive handling comparable to first-class mail.

Priority Mail

Priority mail offers two- to three-day service to most domestic addresses. The maximum weight for priority mail is 70 pounds. Priority mail items must measure 108 inches or less in combined length and girth. Priority mail envelopes, boxes, and labels are available at no charge at post offices. If other envelopes or boxes are used, mark them *Priority Mail*.

The amount of postage for priority mail envelopes or packages of up to five pounds is set at flat rates. The rates for a priority mail weighing over five pounds are based on the weight of the item and its destination. A flat-rate envelope is also available. Any amount of material that fits in the flat-rate priority mail envelope provided by the USPS, regardless of weight, may be mailed for one price.

Figure 11-2.10

The United States Postal Service and many private companies offer express mail services.

Express Mail

Express mail is the fastest service offered by the USPS, with next day delivery by noon to most destinations. No extra fee is charged for Saturday, Sunday, or holiday delivery. All packages must use an *Express Mail* label. The maximum weight for express mail is 70 pounds. Express mail items must measure 108 inches or less in combined length and girth. Express mail envelopes, boxes, and labels are available at no charge at post offices.

The amount of postage for express mail envelopes of up to five pounds is set at flat rates. The rate varies for packages weighing over five pounds. A flat-rate envelope is also available. Any amount of material that fits in the flat-rate express mail envelope provided by the USPS, regardless of weight, may be mailed for one price. Insurance up to $500 is provided at no additional cost. Additional merchandise insurance is available up to $5,000. Pickup service is available for an additional fee.

Periodicals

Approved publishers and registered news agents may mail publications such as newspapers and periodicals at the periodicals rates of postage. To do so, you need authorization from the USPS, must pay a special fee, and must mail in bulk lots (volume mailings). Other rates, such as first-class or standard mail, must be used when periodicals are mailed by the general public.

Standard Mail

Standard mail (A) is used primarily to advertise products and services. Advertising brochures and catalogs often are sent standard class. Charitable organizations may use nonprofit standard mail rates for their large mailings. Mailings must contain at least 200 pieces or weigh 50 pounds to qualify for standard mail rates. Each item must weigh less than 16 ounces and be marked with a correct ZIP code. Sorting and postage restrictions apply.

Standard mail (B), also known as **parcel post**, may be used for packages, printed matter such as books, and other mailable items. The rates are based on the weight of the item and the distance it must travel to be delivered. Packages may weigh 1 to 70 pounds and measure up to 130 inches in combined length and girth. Pieces exceeding 108 inches but not more than 130 inches in combined length and girth are mailable at parcel post oversized rates.

parcel post: a class of standard mail used for packages

Follow these guidelines when preparing packages for mailing.

- Select a box that is strong enough to protect the contents.
- Leave space for cushioning inside the carton. Cushion package contents with shredded or rolled newspaper, bubble wrap, or other packing material. Pack tightly to avoid shifting.
- Always use tape that is designed for shipping, such as pressure-sensitive or reinforced tape. Do not use wrapping paper, string, masking tape, or cellophane tape.
- Put the delivery and return addresses on one side only of the package. Place a return address label inside the package.

Mixed Classes of Mail

Sometimes sending two pieces of mail of different classes together as a single mailing is desirable to make sure they both arrive at the same time. For example, you may attach a first-class invoice to the outside of a large package sent fourth class, or you may enclose a first-class letter in a large envelope or parcel. When a first-class letter is attached, the postage is affixed to each part separately. When a first-class letter is enclosed, its postage is added to the parcel postage on the outside of the package. You should write or stamp the words *FIRST-CLASS MAIL ENCLOSED* below the postage and above the mailing address. A piece of mixed mail is not treated as first-class mail. The class of mail that the larger piece falls into determines how the mixed mail is handled.

Special Postal Services

In addition to the regular delivery services, special postal services also are available. You must pay a fee for each of these special services. As a worker who processes outgoing mail, you need to know the different services that are available so you can choose the one best suited to your company's mailing needs.

Registered or Insured Mail

Registered mail provides the most secure service offered by the USPS. Mail can be registered to give protection to valuable items such as money, checks, jewelry, stock certificates, and bonds, as well as important papers including contracts, bills of sale, leases, mortgages, deeds, wills, and other vital business records. First-class and priority mail may be registered. Insurance is provided for items valued up to a maximum of $25,000. Additional handling charges apply for items valued at more than $25,000. You will be given a receipt showing that the post office has accepted your registered mail for transmittal and delivery. For an additional fee, you may obtain a return receipt to prove that the mail was delivered.

Insured mail provides insurance coverage of up to $5,000 for items lost or damaged in the mail. Insured mail is available for merchandise sent at first-class or priority mail rates. A receipt is issued to the sender of insured mail. You should keep the receipt on file until you know that the insured mail has arrived in satisfactory condition. If an insured parcel is lost or damaged, the post office will **reimburse** you for the lesser of the value of the merchandise or the amount for which it was insured.

reimburse: pay back

SENDER: *COMPLETE THIS SECTION*

- Complete items 1, 2, and 3. Also complete item 4 if Restricted Delivery is desired.
- Print your name and address on the reverse so that we can return the card to you.
- Attach this card to the back of the mailpiece, or on the front if space permits.

1. Article Addressed to:

MR ROLAND G FREED
FREED HOLLIS INC
101 WATERFORD PIKE
EVANSVILLE IN 47708-6711

COMPLETE THIS SECTION ON DELIVERY

A. Received by *(Please Print Clearly)*   B. Date of Delivery

Clyde Faulkner   8/22/--

C. Signature

X   *Clyde Faulkner*   ☐ Agent   ☐ Addressee

D. Is delivery address different from item 1?   ☐ Yes
If YES, enter delivery address below: ☐ No

3. Service Type
   ☒ Certified Mail   ☐ Express Mail
   ☐ Registered   ☐ Return Receipt for Merchandise
   ☐ Insured Mail   ☐ C.O.D.

4. Restricted Delivery? *(Extra Fee)*   ☐ Yes

2. Article Number *(Copy from service label)*

PS Form 3811, July 1999   Domestic Return Receipt   102595-99-M-1789

Figure 11-2.11

Certified mail receipt

Proof of Mailing or Delivery

An inexpensive way to obtain proof that an item was mailed is to purchase a certificate of mailing. The certificate is not proof of delivery; it serves only as proof that the item was mailed. If you want proof of mailing and delivery, send the item by certified mail. Certified mail provides a receipt for the sender and a record of delivery.

COD Mail

A company may send merchandise to a buyer and collect payment for the item when it is delivered. Mail sent in this manner is referred to as COD—collect on delivery. The seller may obtain COD service by paying a fee in addition to the regular postage. Because fees and postage must be **prepaid** by the seller, the seller often specifies that the total COD charges to be collected from the buyer include the postage and the collect-on-delivery fee. The maximum amount collectible on one package is $1,000. If the company you work for did not order an item that arrives COD, do not accept the package.

prepaid: paid in advance

International Mail

Many companies send mail to other countries. A company may have branch offices or customers in countries throughout the world. Postage for letters and postal cards mailed to other countries is higher than for domestic mail, and the mail weights are limited. For current rates and weight limitations, contact your local post office or access the USPS Web site at www.usps.gov.

Global express delivery for letters and packages is available to more than 200 countries from specified post offices. Rates vary by weight and destination country. Overseas packages must be packed very carefully to ensure safe delivery.

Customs forms are required when you send letter packages, small packets, and parcels that are subject to **duty** to international destinations. The specific customs form is governed by the type of mail, the weight of the item, and the regulations of the country to which the mail is sent. Individual countries may restrict or prohibit certain articles. Specific information about restrictions and prohibitions for individual countries and about the forms required for mailing is listed in the *International Mail Manual*, available at your local post office or online at pe.usps.gov. For customs information, contact the U.S. Customs Service.

customs: government tax or duty on imported items

duty: government tax on imported or exported items

Private Courier/Delivery Service

Many companies sometimes use a private courier/delivery service rather than the USPS, especially when a guaranteed delivery time is required. Most cities are served by several private mail delivery companies that deliver both locally and nationwide. Check under *Delivery Service* in the yellow pages of the telephone directory for a listing of companies in your area. You will want to ask about services and fees to identify the delivery company that best meets your needs.

471

Figure 11-2.12

DHL Worldwide Express is a popular private mail delivery company.

© MICHAEL NEWMAN/PHOTOEDIT

You must prepare a delivery form to accompany the package that includes information such as:

- Your name, address, and phone number
- The recipient's name, address, and phone number
- The class of delivery service
- The weight of the package
- The current date
- The payment method or account number

If you use the delivery company often, the company may provide you with forms that are preprinted with your name, address, and account number. Completing the entire delivery form accurately is essential for prompt delivery. Private courier/delivery services do not deliver to a post office box. Many delivery companies have Web sites that allow you to track packages that have been sent using the delivery company.

Figure 11-2.13

Interoffice mail envelope

© EYEWIRE COLLECTION

Interoffice Mail

In a small company, processing interoffice mail may involve hand delivering a memo from one worker to another. In a large company, however, interoffice mail is collected from the departments, sorted in the mailroom, and redistributed to the appropriate department or individuals. Interoffice mail envelopes usually differ in color and size from envelopes used for mail going outside the company. That way, interoffice mail will not be sent to the post office accidentally.

Telegrams

A **telegram** is a message transmitted by Western Union. Telegrams can be sent anywhere in the continental United States. You can send a telegram by calling Western Union or using the company's Web site at www.westernunion.com.

telegram: message delivered by Western Union

Messages will be delivered by courier service on the next business day if received by Western Union by 6 p.m. EST. Messages received after 6 p.m. EST will be delivered on the second business day. Charges for telegrams vary depending on the number of words in the message. For an additional charge, the messages will be delivered by phone within two to four hours. Also for an additional charge, the sender can receive a confirmation copy by mail or a report of the delivery time of the telegram.

Reviewing the Topic

1. How does the procedure for mailing an item in a window envelope differ from that for a standard envelope?

2. Give two examples of items that might be sent in a volume mailing.

3. What is the function of a postage meter? Describe two methods for adding more postage to the meter when it runs low.

4. What is an optical character reader (OCR)? List three reasons why an OCR might not be able to read the address on an envelope.

5. Describe the recommended address format for mail items.

6. Name and briefly describe three of the classes of domestic mail.

7. What kinds of items may be mailed using priority mail? What is the maximum weight allowed for a priority mail package? What is the maximum width and girth for a priority mail package?

8. What are two inexpensive USPS special services that can be used for proof of mailing?

9. Under what circumstances would you use COD mail? What is the maximum amount collectible on one COD package?

10. Why should interoffice mail be placed in envelopes distinctly different from those used to send mail by the postal service?

Interacting with Others

You work in an office where the mail is picked up by postal workers twice a day, at 10:30 a.m. and 2:45 p.m. Monday afternoon you receive a call from the regional vice president in a branch office. He needs six copies of the company's annual report by Wednesday. If the reports are in the 2:45 p.m. mail today, they will be delivered on Wednesday. You gather the annual reports, place them in a large envelope, and take them to the mailroom. You explain to Glenna, a mailroom worker, that the envelope must go with the 2:45 p.m. mail pickup. Glenna says she understands.

Later in the day, you call Glenna to verify that the annual reports were sent. Glenna sheepishly replies that she was on break at 2:45. When she returned, she noticed that the postal carrier had overlooked the envelope. The annual reports were not mailed.

1. You are very annoyed that the envelope was not mailed. Should you tell Glenna how you feel? If so, what should you tell her? Should you report this incident to Glenna's supervisor? How can you and Glenna work together to solve this problem?

2. The reports still need to be sent. How would you suggest that Glenna mail the reports so that they reach the vice president by Wednesday?

1. Key the text that describes the U.S. Postal Inspection Service shown below.
2. Correct all errors in spelling, grammar, and word usage.

The U.S. Postal Inspection Serviec is the law enforcment branch of the U.S. Postal Service. Postal inspectors investigate any crime in which the U.S. Mail is used to further a scheme, whether they originated in the mail, by telephone, or on the Internet. The use of the U.S. Mail is what makes it a mail fraud issue. Some important areas of jurisdition include:

- Assaults and threats that occurr while postal employees is performing official duties

- Distribution of child pornography and other crimes exploiting childs through the mail

- Distributing narcotics or other controlled substances thru the mail

- Forgged, altered, or counterfieted postage stamps or postal money orders

- Delay of delivery or destructin are theft of mail

- Mail that contains threats of kidnapping, physical injury, or injury too the property or reputations of others

- Money laundering—attempts to conceal the proceeds of ilegal acts through monetary transactions

---

INTERNET
RESEARCH
WORD PROCESSING

Topic 11-2   ACTIVITY 1

Calculating Postage

You work in a small office. You need to determine the correct postage for various items you have been given to mail.

1. Determine the amount of postage needed to mail each item listed at the top of page 476 using the USPS. Use your town as the origination point in figuring the postage. Consult current USPS rate charts available in print from your local post office or online at the USPS Web site at www.usps.gov.

2. Create a document that lists the items to be mailed and the correct postage for each item.

- A package weighing 4¾ pounds to be sent parcel post to Ann Arbor, Michigan

- A letter weighing three ounces to be sent by express mail (post office to addressee) to Camden, Maine

- A 12-ounce package containing a printed report to be sent by first-class mail to Santa Barbara, California

- A two-ounce letter to be sent by first-class certified mail to Denver, Colorado

- A ten-ounce letter to be sent to a local bank

INTEGRATED DOCUMENT
RESEARCH
SPREADSHEET
TEAMWORK
WORD PROCESSING

Topic 11-2   ACTIVITY 2

Delivery Services Comparison

You have been asked to compare rates for the USPS and two private mail delivery services for mailing several types of items. Work with a classmate to complete this activity.

1. Identify two private mail delivery companies that serve your area.

2. Research the cost of mailing the items listed below step 4 using the USPS and the two private mail delivery services. Create a bar graph that compares the cost of mailing the six-ounce envelope to Tampa, Florida, using next-day delivery for two private mail delivery services. Adjust the scale of the graph, if necessary, to show the data clearly.

3. Create a memo form to include your company's name, Parnell Products, Inc., and the appropriate headings. Write a short memo report to your supervisor, Jeremy Waters, to report your findings.

   - Recommend the mail service that should be used for routine mailings and the service that should be used for items that must have guaranteed overnight or second-day delivery.

   - Introduce and include the graph you created in your report.

   - Determine whether each service has a system available for customers to track packages that have been mailed. Research mailing time deadlines, any special packaging requirements, and drop-off or pickup locations for each service. Consider these factors when making your decisions.

   - Give reasons to support your recommendations.

4. Attach a table to your report that gives the mailing cost for each item below for each of the three services.

> **Items to be mailed:**
>
> - A package weighing ten pounds to be sent to Chicago, Illinois, which you would like to arrive within about ten days (Delivery time is not critical.)
>
> - A letter weighing six ounces sent to Tampa, Florida, which must arrive the next business day (Delivery time is critical.)
>
> - A 12-ounce envelope to Santa Barbara, California, which must arrive within two working days (Delivery time is critical.)
>
> - A four-ounce letter to Denver, Colorado, which you would like to arrive within seven working days (Delivery time is not critical.)
>
> - A ten-ounce letter to be sent to a local business, which you would like to arrive within three or four days (Delivery time is not critical.)

Summary

In this chapter, you learned the procedures for processing both incoming and outgoing mail. You should be knowledgeable about the following key points.

- The extent of your mail-related tasks will depend on the size of the company, the volume of mail handled, and your job duties.

- To speed the processing of incoming mail, some companies use electric envelope openers, rotary units to help sort mail, and automated delivery systems.

- Classes of domestic mail include first-class, priority, express, periodicals, and standard. Special postal services are available such as registered mail, insured mail, and certified mail.

- To expedite the processing of outgoing mail, some companies use electronic postage scales, postage meters, computer-generated mailing lists, and automated equipment for addressing, labeling, folding, and inserting mail.

- The USPS uses electronic equipment such as optical character readers and bar code sorters to speed mail to its destination. You can help speed the process by following USPS address format guidelines and by using nine-digit ZIP codes.

- Special considerations for address formats, different postage rates, and customs regulations apply to international mail.

- Many companies sometimes use a private courier or mail delivery service rather than the USPS, especially when a guaranteed delivery time is required.

- Interoffice mail envelopes usually differ in color and size from envelopes used for mail going outside the company to avoid accidentally mixing in-house and outside mail.

Key Terms

annotate
certified mail
confidential
   information
courier
customs
express mail
first-class mail
mailing list

optical character
   reader (OCR)
parcel post
postage meter
priority mail
private mail delivery
   company
referral slip
registered mail

routing slip
standard envelope
standard mail
telegram
volume mailing
window envelope
ZIP code

DATABASE
DESKTOP PUBLISHING
WORD PROCESSING

Chapter 11   **ACTIVITY 1**

Mailing List and Flyer

You work as an office assistant at Chaparral Coffee Company. Your supervisor approaches your workstation with this request:

Please create a flyer to send to all our current customers with our next catalog mailing. The flyer will contain an introductory half-price offer for two new products—our Dessert Coffee Assortment gift box and our Classic Delight package. Our new customer referral program is getting off to a good start. We have received 14 referrals thus far. Use this list to create a database for these prospective customers. Print labels from the list and send each person our catalog and the new product flyer.

1. Open the data file **Chaparral.pdf**, which contains information about the new products and a list of prospective customers.

2. Use your desktop publishing skills to design a flyer to introduce the two new products. Explain that these two new products will be available at half their regular price for a limited time. Use the current date through two months from the current date as the time for the special offer.

3. Create a database to contain the names and addresses of the prospective customers. Use the all-caps, no punctuation format recommended by the USPS and the two-letter state abbreviations in the addresses. Print mailing labels of the addresses sorted by state. Include a postal bar code with each address if possible with your software. (Print the mailing list on plain paper if labels are not available.)

ZIP Code Update

Your company sends several volume mailings each quarter using standard mail. Periodically, an automated check for correct ZIP codes is performed. During the last check, the computer identified ten addresses that may have incorrect ZIP codes.

1. Find and record the correct ZIP code for each address on the list. Use a printed ZIP code directory or access the USPS Web site at www.usps.gov to find current ZIP code information.

2. Key a list of the addresses using the correct ZIP codes for each address.

1800 AUGUSTA CT
LEXINGTON KY 40555-2860

8701 TOWN PARK DR
HOUSTON TX 88036-2614

2006 CENTRAL AVE
ALBANY NY 17205-4500

8500 KELLER DR
LITTLE ROCK AR 72402-2356

174 MAIN ST
BANGOR ME 14401-6401

1133 N DEARBORN ST
CHICAGO IL 60690-2783

11115 N NEBRASKA AVE
TAMPA FL 36312-5748

8730 N HIMES AVE
TAMPA FL 33618-8355

7203 N FLORIDA AVE
TAMPA FL 33694-4835

2730 BRANDY DR
COLUMBUS OH 44232-5303

Telephone Systems and Procedures

Today's telephone technologies play a key role in worldwide communications. Telephone systems continue to be enhanced by computerization. Data, text, images, and video as well as voice can be transmitted across the country or around the world with new, state-of-the-art equipment.

· ·

You will use a variety of technologies as well as the telephone for your daily communications. As these technologies evolve, you must continue to educate yourself about communications advancements. In this chapter you will become familiar with telephone equipment and services, learn to use effective telephone procedures, and become aware of emerging telephone technology.

OBJECTIVES

- Identify methods of transmitting information (voice, data, text, video, and images) using telephone technology

- Describe equipment and features of image and voice communication systems

- Describe effective procedures for using image and voice transmission systems

- Discuss emerging telephone technologies

telecommunications:
electronic transfer of information over a distance

Advancements in the way we communicate information have made it easier and faster than ever before to send voice, text, or video messages to others. We can now transmit documents and exchange information with coworkers who are as close as an office across the hall or on another continent 10,000 or more miles away.

Telephone technology is a vital part of today's fast-growing communications industry. A company's communication needs determine what telephone technologies it chooses. As a worker in today's changing workplace, you will benefit from learning about the many features of telephone equipment, telephone services, and the integration of telephone technologies with computers.

Telecommunications is the electronic transfer of information over a distance. All forms of information (voice, video, data, text, and images such as photographs, drawings, and graphs) can be sent electronically. Office workers depend on their ability to access and transmit up-to-date information quickly and reliably.

Transmitting Information Using Telephone Technology

Methods of sending information across the country or around the world include telephone lines, communication satellites, microwave towers, and radio signals. Telephone lines and communication satellites will be discussed in this chapter.

Figure 12-1.1

Telecommunications technology enables us to communicate globally.

© CORBIS/STOCK MARKET

Telephone Lines

When you place a telephone call, use a facsimile machine, or transfer information from one computer to another, the information usually travels over telephone lines as either **analog** or **digital** signals. Most companies are replacing older analog lines with digital lines because digital signals can transmit larger quantities of information at faster speeds. This means your electronic message (a letter, a long report, or a chart) is received quickly and reliably. Business computer output is digital rather than analog.

Some communication systems continue to use only analog signals. They require a device called a **modem**, which is used to convert the digital output of a computer into analog signals that can be transmitted over telephone lines. A modem can be internal (installed inside the computer case) or external (a separate, attached device outside the computer case).

analog: transmitted by a signal that corresponds to a physical change such as sound

digital: stored or transmitted by a process using groups of electronic bits of data

modem: a conversion device for digital and analog data

Communication Satellites

Satellites play an important part in worldwide communication systems. A communication satellite is a transmitter/receiver relay station that orbits the earth. A satellite dish is a transmitter/receiver relay station that remains stationary, on earth. Satellite dishes receive microwave signals bounced to earth from an orbiting communications satellite. They also send voice, video, and data communications in the form of microwave signals to the space satellite.

WORKPLACE **CONNECTIONS**

Jeorge must send a price quote from his office in Miami to a customer in London. Using the company fax machine, he sends the price list to London in minutes via a worldwide satellite communication network. The customer reviews the quote and sends Jeorge an order by return fax. This time savings allows Jeorge to receive and fill the customer's order quickly.

Image Communication Systems

Telecommunications technology is used to transmit and receive images in many forms. Text, photographs, video, blueprints, drawings, diagrams, graphs, and statistical information are examples of images that are frequently sent from one location to another. Two common image communication systems, facsimile and videoconferencing, will be explained.

Facsimile Technology

Facsimile, often called fax, transfers images (text, photographs, drawings) electronically using telephone lines. Fax machines are an easy-to-use, convenient, relatively inexpensive, fast way to transmit and receive information.

Topic 12-1: *Telephone Technology and Services*

Facsimile technology is such an everyday part of communications that fax machines have become a necessity in offices. A company may have one or many facsimile machines. They may have desktop or portable models, which can be used to transmit and receive documents while workers are away from the office. Fax machines are also being purchased for personal use in homes. You can have a fax installed as an option in your car.

As long as the sending and receiving machines are compatible, facsimiles can communicate with each other to send and receive images. Scanning technology is combined with telephone technology. The sending facsimile machine scans a page and encodes (electronically "takes a picture of") the information to be sent. The information is transmitted over telephone lines to a receiving facsimile machine. Within seconds, the document is reproduced as an exact copy—or "facsimile."

Fax machine to fax machine is not the only method of transmitting documents as images. An image can also be sent over telephone lines from a computer directly to a fax machine or another computer. The computer must have a fax card and software to control the process.

WORKPLACE CONNECTIONS

Laticia works for an environmental waste firm in Phoenix that has branch offices in Denver, St. Louis, and Salt Lake City. This morning she receives a typical assignment. An engineer in her office needs to send a copy of project plan changes that are in a word processor document file as soon as possible to a supervisor with a portable fax machine at a customer's waste system construction site outside Denver. Using her computer equipped with a fax card, Laticia is able to send the document within minutes from her computer to the portable fax machine the supervisor is using.

Features

Facsimile machines offer many features. Among the more common features are:

- Laser or full-color printing
- Store-and-forward capability
- Automatic dialing and redialing if the receiving number is busy
- Automatic answering without a human attendant
- Automatic document feed
- Activity-reporting of date, time, and number of pages sent and received
- Small screens that display messages such as information about transmission and errors or problems with the system
- Security features

Figure 12-1.2

Facsimile machines speed the process of sending and receiving messages.

© SIEDE PREIS/PHOTODISC

The automatic answering feature makes fax systems almost self-operating. Many users leave their machines on 24 hours a day, unattended, for receiving messages.

Procedures

Procedures for using facsimile machines vary from office to office and from machine to machine. Many procedures depend on the sending and receiving equipment to be used. When you are sending information from one fax machine to another, follow these common procedures for successful transmission.

1. Prepare a facsimile transmission cover sheet or note with the following information: current date; total pages being sent including the transmission sheet; name, company name, and address of the recipient of the message; fax number of the recipient; your name, company name, address, telephone number, and fax number; subject of the document or message; and any special remarks you wish to include.

2. Check the accuracy of your count of the number of pages to be sent and the number of pages you recorded on the transmission sheet.

3. Confirm the number carefully before dialing the fax number of the recipient.

4. Enter your name, department, date, and number of pages transmitted or other required information on a fax log sheet if one is used in your office.

After all pages have been transmitted, your fax machine will let you know that the transmission has been completed. You may hear a series of beeps or a message may be displayed telling you that your message has been received at the location you dialed. If a report form is printed after each transmission, attach it to the fax cover sheet and return it with the original materials to the sender. In Figure 12-1.3, the transmission report includes date, start time of the message, fax number dialed, number of pages sent, and the time used to transmit pages. Note that the results are reported as "OK"—the transmission was successful.

Figure 12-1.3

Fax cover sheet and
transmission report

Nouveau Investment Company
800 Elm Avenue
Mt. Vernon, NY 10500-3113
Fax # 914-555-9626
Telephone # 914-555-9692

FAX

To:	John Mayfield	**From:**	Sherman Kuntz
Fax:	513-555-6956	**Pages:**	3
Phone:	513-555-6988	**Date:**	March 9, 20--
Re:	Quarterly Report	**Time:**	11:35 a.m.

Comments:

Please review this report and send me your comments.

FAX TRANSMISSION REPORT

DATE	START TIME	REMOTE TERMINAL	MODE	TIME	RESULTS	TOTAL PAGES
Mar 09	11:38	513-555-6956	G3ST	02 min 02 sec	OK	03

Videoconferencing

videoconferencing:

communication system that uses
two-way voice and video

Videoconferencing is an image communication system that allows people at two or more locations to have two-way voice and video communication. A special conference room equipped with microphones, television cameras, and screens is used to conduct meetings in which data, text, voice, and documents may be exchanged.

WORKPLACE **CONNECTIONS**

Will Flowers, Director of Sales, is located in Detroit. Will called a meeting with local managers, top management located in the corporate headquarters in San Francisco, and a third group of managers located at a branch in Hong Kong. Using videoconferencing technology, they could see and hear each other. Will wrote on an electronic whiteboard as he discussed sales projections. Will's notes from the board appeared on a video monitor at the remote locations. The information was transmitted and later printed for the managers at each location. This meeting was very cost effective when compared to the expense and time that would be required for all the managers to travel and meet in one location.

Figure 12-1.4

Video conferences allow people at different locations to see and hear each other and exchange information electronically.

© FISHER/THATCHER/STONE

Video conferences, sometimes called Web conferences, may also be conducted by computer. In a Web conference, people communicate using private computer networks or the Internet, allowing them to have virtual meetings. The users' computers must have speakers, microphones, video cameras, and the appropriate software. See Chapter 8, *Meetings and Travel*, for more information about Web conferencing. Also see *Integration of Telecommunications Technologies* on page 496 in this chapter.

Voice Communication Systems

You are very familiar with and have used the most popular voice communication device ever invented—the telephone. Today's telephones are becoming smarter and smarter with each new technological advance. New telephone systems are making voice communication more convenient and are being equipped with features to meet the ever-changing variety of user needs. Some widely used systems and equipment will be discussed here; however, technology is rapidly changing. You must be prepared to constantly become acquainted with new telephone features and equipment as they become available.

Many factors have led to changes in the way companies handle voice communications. Global mergers and the demand for faster, more efficient customer service are two reasons companies have had to consider better methods for handling voice communications. Telephone service and equipment providers are very competitive. This competitiveness can benefit telephone consumers in better service and lower prices. Companies are able to negotiate for their own customized list of equipment and services.

Centralized Systems

Centralized telephone systems route calls coming into and going out of an organization. All calls in a centralized system are handled by a single computer or operator switchboard that routes calls to the requested location.

Topic 12-1: *Telephone Technology and Services*

Older systems required the assistance of a switchboard operator to answer calls and transfer them to the appropriate department or individual. Many telephone systems in business today are answered by an **automated attendant**. An automated attendant is a computerized system for handling telephone calls.

When an incoming call is answered by an automated attendant, a recorded message is played. Messages vary depending on company needs. However, the message usually instructs the caller to dial the extension number of the person being sought and may provide the caller with various menu options. Callers make selections using the telephone number keypad. Some systems also enable users to select menu options by speaking the appropriate word or term into the receiver. A computer will identify the spoken command and perform the chosen action. This feature is called speech recognition. Additional messages may then instruct and direct the caller.

The option of speaking with a person is no longer always a choice for the caller. Many companies continue to offer an option to speak to a person to provide better service for customers. Some callers prefer to communicate with a person rather than with a computer. Other callers may not have a touch-tone phone, which is usually required for the automated system.

Many callers have adjusted to computerized systems; however, frustration with systems that seem to block human contact is understandable. Businesses must deal with these complaints and do their best to meet callers' needs, thereby preserving good customer relations.

Figure 12-1.5

Some callers become frustrated with computerized automated attendants.

© EYEWIRE COLLECTION

Figure 12-1.6

Common Features of Telephone Systems

Auto redial	Redials automatically the last number dialed by pressing a key
Call block	Restricts callers from making telephone toll calls or calls for which an extra charge is made
Caller ID	Records or displays the telephone number of the caller
Call queuing or camp on	Reestablishes the connection after a busy signal when both parties are free
Call return	Redials the number of the last call received for several minutes
Call waiting	Signals an incoming call is waiting while a call is in progress
Conferencing	Allows the user to set up conversations with three or more people at the same time
Memory	Allows the user to store numbers and then dial a number with one button
Speakerphone	Allows the user to speak into a microphone on the telephone rather than the handset

Common Features of Telephone Systems

Telephone technologies are designed to increase your efficiency in handling communications. Many features are available so that you can customize your telephone depending on your duties and responsibilities. The needs of your organization and the size of the system will determine the equipment and features chosen.

A users' manual is generally provided that details procedures for using your telephone keypad to activate and deactivate all features available. To activate **call forwarding**, for example, you may be instructed to lift the handset, push the * (asterisk, or "star") and four keys, listen for a tone, dial the extension number to which you want all incoming calls routed, and hang up. Your incoming calls will then be forwarded and will ring automatically at that extension. Figure 12-1.6 lists common features of telephone systems.

call forwarding: send a call automatically to another telephone number

Voice Mail Systems

Voice mail is a messaging system that uses computers and telephones to record, send, store, and retrieve voice messages. Voice messaging systems are popular because they eliminate the problems of time lost in playing "telephone tag" or trying to place calls to individuals in different time zones. Most voice mail systems operate 24 hours per day and provide important communication links in an organization.

voice mail: messaging system that uses computers and telephones to record, store, and retrieve voice messages

Topic 12-1: *Telephone Technology and Services*

Figure 12-1.7

Telephone push buttons are used to access the features of a voice mail system.

© EYEWIRE COLLECTION

Each user of a voice messaging system has a voice mailbox. A voice mailbox is a space reserved in a computer to hold recorded voice messages. A caller leaves a voice message that is recorded by the computer and held in storage until the recipient of the message chooses to access it. Unless a message is deleted, it remains in storage and can be accessed later for reference. Because of the ability to store and forward messages, voice mail is sometimes called a store-and-forward voice messaging system. Some of the voice mail features that may be used by companies include:

- Long-term incoming message storage capabilities
- Message prioritizing
- Ability to broadcast recorded messages to multiple or all users of the system
- Creation of multiple greetings for selection and deselection

Specialized Telephone Equipment

Telephone technology innovations have resulted in a wide choice of equipment for the consumer. Various types of mobile telephone equipment are available to help the traveler stay in touch with the office or home. Whether in an automobile, an airplane, or in a meeting with a client anywhere in the world, a telephone product can provide a communication link. Telephone equipment to meet the growing demands and special needs of consumers is making communications easier and more convenient for everyone.

Mobile Telephone Equipment

The nature of business communications today makes it necessary for business workers to have ready access to voice communications systems wherever they are. To enable traveling, out-of-the-office workers to remain

Voice Mail

Voice mail is a computerized voice messaging system with many features that can be modified to meet the individual needs of companies. A standard personal computer, a special voice processing card, and voice software are needed. The voice card helps the computer perform many tasks such as understanding and creating touch-tone signals, playing recorded messages, recording sounds, and transferring or retrieving calls. Both the sender and the receiver use the telephone push buttons to activate and use the features of voice mail.

Because of the convenience and efficiency of voice mail, its use has become widespread in business. Still, with all its advantages, voice mail does not replace human contact. Follow proper procedures to ensure that the negatives of voice mail are reduced and the full benefits are realized. When using your voice mail system:

- Prepare a message that presents you as a professional and delivers appropriate information and instructions to the caller. Include your name, department, and other necessary information. Give instructions as to how to get immediate assistance if the caller cannot wait for you to return the call.

- Record the message yourself. Speak clearly and distinctly. Pronounce words correctly and use correct grammar.

- If you are going to be out of the office for one or several days, refer callers to another worker who can provide help while you are away, if appropriate.

- Check your voice mail several times a day. Return all calls as soon as possible.

- Answer your telephone when you are at your desk unless you have visitors in your office or are involved in an important work project. Do not let voice mail answer your phone for you the majority of the time when you are at your desk.

Follow these procedures when leaving messages for others on their voice mail systems:

- Leave your name, telephone number, company, and a brief reason for your call. Make your message neither too lengthy nor too brief. You want the person you called to have enough information to return your call promptly and efficiently.

- Speak slowly and distinctly. Spell out any difficult names (your name, your company's name).

- Do not communicate bad news or negative statements in the voice message. Wait until you actually speak with the person to convey any negative information.

Figure 12-1.8

Mobile telephones allow workers to keep in touch with the office wherever they are.

productive, in touch, and accessible, wireless services are growing to meet demands. You will learn about two of these products.

cellular telephone: communications device that uses wireless, radio frequencies to transmit voice across geographic segments

Cellular telephones use wireless radio frequencies to transmit voice across geographic segments called cells. When you dial a mobile telephone number, the radio signal "switches" from cell to cell until the right number is reached. Mobile service providers furnish the user with the transmission.

Cellular phones have familiar telephone features such as call forwarding, call waiting, and automatic redial. They are designed to be portable, lightweight, and small. You may use them in your automobile or carry them in your briefcase to use wherever you are.

pager: electronic device that alerts the user of the need to respond by telephone

Pagers are very small devices that alert the user of the need to respond by telephone to whomever has sent the "page." Early pagers got the attention of the user with audio beeper signals. They became known as "beepers" because of the sounds they made. Today's pagers use a variety of signals such as vibrations, voice, and digital readout. The recipient of the signal should respond as soon as possible by finding the nearest telephone to call the number on the readout or to call the office.

Figure 12-1.9

Pagers alert the user to call a telephone number.

CHAPTER 12: TELEPHONE SYSTEMS AND PROCEDURES

Figure 12-1.10

Specialized equipment and services are available for telephone users with impairments.

The need for travelers to communicate with their offices or customers even while flying has resulted in airlines accommodating this need. Airplanes are now equipped with telephones that are available for use by passengers for placing calls. Telephones may be positioned at passenger seats or at a location made available by the flight staff. Because these telephones work while in flight, they are sometimes called airphones.

Features for Impairments

Special telephone equipment and services are available for the visually or hearing impaired. Features that enable the blind, deaf, hard of hearing, or speech disabled to communicate on the telephone with others include text telephone (TTY) and the telebraille telephone (TB). With these services a telephone company employee serves as an "interpreter" between the hearing person and the deaf or blind person. The messages are relayed by the telephone assistant by typing the spoken words, which are relayed to the TTY or TB user verbatim. The blind person reads the **Braille**; the deaf person reads the screen.

Other features for impaired callers include:

- Large-button phones
- Headsets or speakerphones for hands-free operation
- Speech amplifiers to make voices louder
- Loud bells and flashing light indicators

Braille: a system that enables the blind to read by feeling a pattern of raised dots

Conference Call Services

At times it may be necessary to place calls that will have three or more participants speaking at different locations with voice-only communication. These calls are known as conference calls. Decisions may require input from busy individuals who are in different locations. Staff meetings, sales conferences, problem-solving discussions, or any type of information sharing that

Topic 12-1: *Telephone Technology and Services*

Figure 12-1.11

A conference call involves several people at different locations.

must take place quickly can be arranged conveniently with a conference call. Conference calls may be handled in several ways: with the user's own equipment, operator-dialed service, or dial-in service.

You may use your own telephone equipment to set up a conference call within a centralized, in-house telephone system. No outside help is needed from a telephone company service provider.

With **operator-dialed service**, a long-distance operator handles the setup and connections. After you inform the operator of the date, time, time zone, and estimated length of the call, the operator does the following:

- Informs all participants of the time that the conference call will take place
- Makes all the necessary connections at the prescribed time
- Calls the roll to make sure all callers are connected
- Can provide specialized services such as a recording or written transcript of the conference, or a translator for those who do not understand the main language used

Dial-in service allows participants to call a special number at a prearranged time without operator assistance. They may call from any telephone rather than wait for an operator to call them at one specific number.

Successful conference calls require advance planning to ensure that all the necessary information and equipment are at hand. Follow these guidelines in planning a conference call.

- Inform all participants of the date, time, and proposed length of the call.
- Verify everyone's telephone number.
- Send any needed information or items for discussion to all participants in advance.

CHAPTER 12: TELEPHONE SYSTEMS AND PROCEDURES

- Identify the objectives and intended outcomes of the call.
- If using a service provider, call in advance and give accurate numbers, names, date, time, and expected duration of the call.

Participating in a conference call requires the use of your best communication skills. Think of the conference call as a type of meeting where you will both contribute to the conversation and listen to others. Follow these procedures during the call.

- Take roll. Call out the names of all participants.
- Lead the call by presenting the agenda and conference guidelines.
- Have participants identify themselves when speaking.
- Speak clearly, spelling out difficult or unusual names and terms. Repeat numbers.
- Avoid interrupting other speakers. Only one person should speak at a time.
- Take notes of important points and comments.
- Apply good listening skills.
- Encourage discussion and participation from everyone.

Telephone Service Providers

Telephone systems may be purchased from many independent vendors who offer a variety of equipment in all price ranges. Many of these providers will customize features, conduct training, and offer product support to purchasers.

Your local telephone company provides services to all users within a specified local area. You can choose your own long-distance carrier for services beyond your local calling area. Long-distance carriers such as MCI, Sprint, and AT&T are very competitive in their marketing and pricing. They offer many services and features for businesses and other consumers. Carefully compare prices and services before choosing a long-distance service provider.

Long Distance Rate Periods

Rates	Hours	Days
Weekday full rate	8 a.m. to 5 p.m.	Monday through Friday
Evening discount rate	5 p.m. to 11 p.m.	Monday through Friday and Sunday
Night and weekend discount rate	11 p.m. to 8 a.m. All day 8 a.m. to 5 p.m.	Every day Saturday Sunday

Figure 12-1.12

This figure shows a sample of one long-distance carrier's rate periods for direct-dial calls.

Figure 12-1.13

Telephony technology allows two-way video and audio communications.

© EYEWIRE COLLECTION

Integration of Telecommunications Technologies

Today's information technologies are integrated. This means that machines that once performed only a single function can now be linked with other machines to expand their use and speed the flow of information. For example, computers can electronically transmit information to printers, to photocopiers, to facsimile machines, and to other computers. They can transmit information to one or all of these almost instantly.

A digital revolution is taking place in the telecommunications industry that integrates previously separate technologies through a standardized, digital network. Integrated Services Digital Network (ISDN) is not an actual network, but rather a set of **interface** standards. These standards enable many types of computer or electronic devices to communicate with other computers and devices.

interface: connection

As telecommunications technology evolves, businesses are acquiring new equipment and using new procedures to improve communications. The integration of the computer and the telephone is known as CTI (computer telephony integration) or **telephony**. A new class of technology has been created that provides computer control and access of telephone functions along with telephone control and access of computer functions. New telephony technology equipment offers features such as:

telephony: integration of computer and telephone technologies

- Simultaneous two-way video, audio, and computer communications that let callers open, view, and edit the same computer files and send notes to each other as they talk
- Computer software that lets users manage all telephone activity at their personal computer
- Caller ID service that allows the user to see the number of the caller and enables incoming calls to be screened—whether from within or outside the company
- Conference calling that can be initiated by clicking on and dragging together names from within the user's personal computer phone directory
- Access to banking services that allow the customer to access account balances, transfer funds, pay bills, and print records of all banking transactions
- Support for accessing the Internet and the World Wide Web
- Built-in personal information management software that can be connected to other workers' computers
- Management of all voice, facsimile, or e-mail messages with either a touch-tone phone or a personal computer
- Multimedia tutorials that help users learn the features and procedures of using advanced voice technologies

Computer telephony is a fast-growing area. Developments in equipment and user services are rapidly changing the way people communicate through the telephone and computers.

Reviewing the Topic

1. Why are most companies replacing older analog telephone lines with digital lines?

2. Explain how facsimile is used to transmit information.

3. List four features that a facsimile machine may offer.

4. What information should be included in a facsimile transmission cover sheet?

5. When an incoming call is answered by an automated attendant, what information does the recorded message that is played usually contain?

6. How is a voice mail system different from an answering machine connected to a telephone?

7. What information should you include in the voice mail message you record on your telephone?

8. Describe two types of wireless telephone services available to keep traveling office workers in touch with their businesses.

9. What are three specialized features or equipment available to help those with physical impairments communicate on the telephone?

10. What are five features offered by new telephony equipment?

Interacting with Others

Your sales team member, Jeremy, is letting voice mail answer his phone the majority of the time, even when he is at his desk. You and Jeremy share sales and service responsibilities for several accounts. Your clients have complained to you that Jeremy seems never to be at his desk. Also, they complain that he takes several days to answer their voice mail messages. You realize that this is a problem situation. What should you do?

1. Should you inform your supervisor about Jeremy's voice mail procedures? Why or why not?

2. Should you apologize to clients for Jeremy's poor voice mail habits? Why or why not?

3. Should you tell clients to call you instead of Jeremy? Why or why not?

4. What could you say to Jeremy about the clients' complaints to encourage him to handle his voice mail messages following professional procedures?

Reinforcing English Skills

Your knowledge of punctuation rules will be an asset in your written communications on the job. Ten sentences follow that will reinforce your ability to use proper punctuation marks. Write or key each sentence, inserting the proper punctuation.

1. She faxed a report from Cheyenne Wyoming to Tucson Arizona

2. Our telephone bill was credited with two months interest

3. Did you place the call to Jeorge my friend from Mexico City

4. On Tuesday January 23 we began using our new computerized telephone system

5. To qualify for a position you must have a years experience using a computer telephony system

6. Showing you our new voice mail system was a pleasure we have a training session planned for all new users

7. We prefer using voice mail for recording messages not an answering machine

8. Conferencing lets you set up conversations with three four or more people at the same time

9. A speakerphone allows hands free speaking capabilities

10. Is the toll free number an 800 or an 888 number

COMPOSITION

WORD PROCESSING

Topic 12-1 ACTIVITY 1

Facsimile Procedures

You work at the headquarters of Prudent Development Corporation. Your supervisor, Janet Naisbitt, asks you to prepare a well-designed one-page list of common procedures to be followed for a successful facsimile transmission. The procedures list is to be faxed to the office manager at the Denver branch. She also wants you to compose a short memo to include with the procedures.

1. Compose and key a document that lists procedures for successful fax-to-fax transmission. Follow effective document design guidelines.

2. Create a memo form for the company using appropriate headings. Compose a memo to Ed Stoddard, Office Manager. In the memo, explain that this list is to be distributed to all fax users at the Denver location. Also ask him to write any additions or comments on the list and return it to you within three days.

499

Topic Review

3. Create a facsimile transmission cover sheet to send with the memo and the fax procedures document. Use the cover sheet in Figure 12-1.3 on page 486 as an example, or use a facsimile cover sheet template from your word processor software.

> **Your company's information:**
> Prudent Development Corporation, 8700 Martin Luther King Blvd., Austin, TX 78765-0800
> Fax number: 512-555-0139
> Telephone number: 512-555-0142
>
> **Mr. Stoddard's information:**
> Prudent Development Corporation in Denver, CO
> Fax number: 303-555-0102
> Telephone number: 303-555-1122

COMPOSITION
WORD PROCESSING

Topic 12-1 ACTIVITY 2

Voice Mail Messages

You are the manager for the accounting department at your company, Ryan Associates. While you were away from the office on a trip recently, you called several employees in your department. You noticed that the voice mail messages used by some department members were not very helpful and did not sound professional. You have decided to give department members suggestions for improving their messages and to provide sample messages.

1. Review the guidelines for effective voice mail messages found in this topic.
2. Compose a memo or an e-mail message to the *Accounting Department* from you. Use the current date and an appropriate subject line. (If you are using e-mail, save and print the message. Do not actually send the e-mail.)
3. In the memo or e-mail, mention tactfully that the voice mail messages used by some department members could be improved. Explain the reasons why department members should record an effective voice mail message to be heard by persons reaching their voice mail and why they should leave effective messages for others. Include guidelines for effective voice mail messages in the memo or e-mail. Include a sample message that you might record for persons reaching your voice mail. Also include a sample message you might leave when you reach another person's voice mail. Ask department members to prepare and record effective and professional voice mail messages.

Effective Telephone Communications

OBJECTIVES

- Describe and apply skills required to make a favorable first impression over the telephone
- Apply telephone techniques and procedures to handle incoming calls courteously and efficiently
- Plan calls efficiently using tools such as published and computerized directories
- Describe procedures to place local and long-distance domestic and international calls
- Describe techniques for controlling telephone costs

The most universal tool for voice communication is the telephone. Think of the many calls a company receives and places each day. Workers in the company receive and place calls to others both inside and outside the company to discuss common concerns, to place orders, or to request information. Messages must be taken and recorded either manually or electronically. Telephone calls are often less time consuming than a memo, a letter, or even an e-mail message.

Because the telephone is such an important communication tool, all office workers should be able to use proper telephone techniques when answering incoming calls and placing outgoing calls. When you place calls to businesses, your first impression of the organization is often based on how you are treated by the person answering your call. If the person is pleasant, courteous, and interested in helping you, you probably form a good impression of the company. If the person is abrupt, rude, or unwilling to help, you probably form a negative impression. When you answer the telephone or place an outgoing call, you may be making an initial customer contact. You will want to give callers a positive impression by what you say and how you say it.

As a consideration in controlling telephone costs, businesses must carefully compare the general services, equipment, and long-distance services available. To place and receive calls efficiently and economically, you should become aware of the services offered by the telephone companies that provide both local and long-distance service to your office. In this topic, you will learn to create a professional first impression, use directories, and use proper techniques and procedures when placing and receiving telephone calls.

Making a Favorable First Impression

When you handle telephone communications for an organization, you are representing that company. To the individual on the other end of the connection, you are the company, you are the department. To create a positive image for your organization, you should develop good communication skills. Your voice, pronunciation, grammar, and vocabulary, as well as your attitude, contribute to the impression you make when using the telephone. Although technology has changed communication, the need for good speaking skills remains.

Your Voice

When you communicate with others in person, you make them feel welcome by smiling and perhaps by shaking hands. You show interest and alertness by maintaining eye contact with them during the conversation. When you communicate by telephone, however, all you have to convey interest, alertness, and courtesy is your voice. Elements of your voice that you must pay attention to include tone, pace, and volume.

501

Figure 12-2.1

You represent your organization every time you place or answer a call.

© GOODSHOOT/SUPERSTOCK INTERNATIONAL

tone: changes in pitch in voice

The **tone** of your voice refers to the changes in pitch used to emphasize words and to get your meaning across to the listener. You have, no doubt, listened to speakers who talked in a monotone. Paying attention is difficult when someone is speaking in a monotonous voice. The listener may become bored or may perceive the speaker as indifferent or inattentive. Vary the tone of your voice to express feelings and emphasis of ideas but avoid using extremes. An animated voice reflects interest in the caller and helps you achieve successful communication. Avoid speaking in a very high-pitched voice, a very low-pitched voice, or with an up-and-down, "singsong" manner.

pace: rate, speed

Pace is the rate or speed of speech. The rate at which you talk to someone on the telephone can affect the ability of the listener to understand your message. If you speak too rapidly, the listener may not hear all the information, especially if the information is technical or detailed. On the other hand, if you speak too slowly, the listener may become bored, insulted, or inattentive.

Consider the listener when determining a proper pace for speech. You may be speaking with people from different parts of your nation and with people from countries all over the world. You may be conversing with people who, even though they speak the same language as you, have speech patterns and regional dialects that are different from your own. You must learn to adjust your pace to fit the needs of the listener.

Extremes in **volume** should be avoided when speaking on the telephone. Do not shout or speak so softly that the listener cannot hear what you are saying. Control the volume of your voice so that you are speaking neither too loudly nor too softly. Speak directly into the telephone receiver or mouthpiece.

volume: amount or level

Your Speaking Skills

Your voice and speaking skills are put to the test when you speak on the telephone. Speaking skills such as word pronunciation, grammar, and vocabulary usage affect the impression you project over the phone. Although you may have a pleasant tone, a good pace, and a well-modulated voice, communication is difficult if the person you are speaking with cannot understand your words.

Pronunciation

Correct pronunciation of words is essential for understanding. Proper enunciation is also important. When you **enunciate** effectively you pronounce words clearly and distinctly. For example, you should say "what do you" instead of "whaddaya," you should say "going to" instead of "gonna." Enunciate word endings such as "ing," "ed," possessives, and plurals.

enunciate: pronounce words clearly and distinctly

You will find that many people speak with a regional accent. An accent involves a certain rhythm, speed, **modulation**, and pronunciation of vowels that is native to a particular region. You probably have an accent even though you may not be aware of it. If you find that you must overcome barriers to effective communication as a result of dialects or accents, several strategies can help you succeed:

modulation: controlling the volume of speech

- Pronounce words correctly and enunciate clearly.
- Speak slowly, but not so slowly that you insult or annoy the caller.
- Avoid long words, complicated phrases, or long sentences.
- If you are unsure of any word's pronunciation, look it up in the dictionary.

Figure 12-2.2

Your voice and speaking skills help you create a positive impression over the phone.

Topic 12-2: *Effective Telephone Communications*

503

Grammar

Just as pronunciation can be a reflection of your professionalism and education, so can your grammar skills. Although some rules of grammar are relaxed for spoken communications, you should follow basic standards to project a favorable impression of yourself and your organization. Avoid the use of slang or regional expressions that may not be widely known or understood, especially if the call is an international one. Other people may use terms that you do not recognize. When you do not understand an expression or phrase, always ask for an explanation.

Vocabulary

You should constantly improve your professional and personal vocabulary. You can learn new terms that relate to your position or your organization and new words that will help you express your feelings, ideas, and needs. Remember that clear and courteous communication is always your goal. Avoid using trendy, slang expressions in formal business communications. State your ideas simply without using highly technical terms or lengthy words.

Many companies deal directly with clients, customers, or suppliers from other countries. Your organization may even be an international one whose owners or headquarters are located outside the United States. Learn some simple courtesy phrases to use when speaking with international callers. Your attempts at learning and using some simple, basic phrases will be appreciated by foreign callers and will help you establish a favorable impression. Keep a list of basic phrases along with their translations and pronunciations. Practice them and make sure that you are pronouncing them correctly.

Professional Development Resources

- Thomas B. Allen. "The Future Is Calling." *National Geographic.* December, 2001.

- Howard Feiertag. "Poor Voice-Mail Technique Can Hurt Sales Efforts." *Hotel and Motel Management.* September, 2000.

- Evan Rosen. "Videoconferencing Pays Off in Boondocks." *Workforce.* January, 2002.

- Search terms:
    telecommunications
    video conference
    facsimile
    ergonomics
    telephony
    online telephone directory

Your Attitude

When you speak to someone over the telephone, all you have is your voice to convey information and express your feelings. Even though you may not be seen by the person with whom you are speaking, your attitude is continually being transmitted to that person. Any boredom, anger, or indifference you are feeling is intensified as your message is sent to the person on the line. On the other hand, a smile and an upbeat, caring attitude are also clearly projected to the person with whom you are speaking.

Whether you are the caller or the listener, you must put all your personal feelings aside and take responsibility for responding to the communication with a sincere, positive attitude.

Incoming Telephone Communications

Handling incoming telephone calls requires skill in using proper telephone techniques and effective procedures. When answering the telephone, you usually do not know who is calling or what the caller wants. Your work may be interrupted, or you may have a visitor in your office. You should know how to handle a variety of situations and take care of caller requests, needs, and problems.

Proper Telephone Techniques

You now know that your voice, your speaking skills, and your attitude all affect a caller's impression of you, your department, and your company. Every organization wants employees to give a positive, professional impression when communicating over the telephone. Your call may be an initial customer contact—the first time the customer has spoken with someone at your company. How well you handle the call may determine, at least in part, whether the customer will do business with your company. Using proper telephone techniques will help you make a positive impression.

Answer Promptly

Answer all incoming calls promptly and pleasantly. If possible, answer the telephone after the first ring. When you reach for the receiver, also pick up a pen or pencil and a notepad or message form. You must be ready to take notes or a message.

Identify Yourself

Because many companies use automated telephone systems that answer the calls initially and route them to the requested department or person, you may not need to identify your company when you answer a call. However, if you are the person to whom all incoming calls are routed, you should identify first your company, then yourself.

A telephone conversation cannot begin until the caller knows that the correct number, department, or person has been reached. Following are examples of improper and proper telephone answering responses.

© CORBIS

Figure 12-2.3

When you reach for the receiver, have a pen and pad ready to take notes.

Topic 12-2: *Effective Telephone Communications*

Improper:	*"Hello" or "Yes?" (These greetings do not give any identification of the person or of the company.)*
Improper:	*"Hello, hold please." (This greeting does not give any company identification to the caller. Also, abruptly placing the caller on hold is rude and abrasive.)*
Improper:	*"Good morning. International Electronics. Our company is number one in the field of international electronics products sales and service. Pat Lopez speaking. May I be of help to you?" (This greeting is too long and distracting.)*
Proper:	*"Good morning. International Electronics, Pat Lopez." (Use this greeting when you are answering an outside call.)*
Proper:	*"Marketing department, Leon DiMarco." (Use this greeting when you are answering an inside or outside call in a company where all calls are routed through a switchboard operator or an automated attendant that has already identified the company.)*
Proper:	*"Ms. Yamaguchi's office, Lisa Stein." (Use this greeting when you are answering the telephone for a supervisor or if you are answering someone else's phone.)*

Assist the Caller

Your job is to help the caller as efficiently as you can. Never assume that you know what the caller wants. Instead, listen attentively to the caller's questions and comments. If you know that it will take several minutes to access the information needed for the call, do not keep the caller waiting. Explain the situation to the caller and offer the choice of being placed on hold or hanging up and receiving a return call. Follow through on any promise you make to return a call.

Make sure that you give accurate information to callers. If you do not know the answer to a question, admit it. Either tell the caller that you will obtain the information and call back, or offer to transfer the call to someone who can answer the question. Avoid passing off a caller to someone else if there is any way that you can be of help yourself.

Figure 12-2.4

Have reference materials handy to assist callers.

Conclude the Call

As a general rule, the person who places a call is the one who should end the call and hang up first. If you follow this rule, you avoid making the caller feel as if the conversation has been "cut off" before he or she was ready to hang up.

Use the caller's name as you end the conversation. For example: "Yes, Ms. O'Toole, I will be sure to mail you a copy of our latest catalog today" or "Thank you for calling, Mr. Haliz. I will be sure to give Ms. Schmidt the information." Such a practice personalizes the conversation.

Effective Telephone Procedures

As you answer incoming calls, you need to handle many tasks efficiently. You may be requested to screen calls, give information, or take messages. You may need to place a caller on hold, transfer calls, handle disconnected calls, and deal with difficult callers. Effective procedures make managing each of these situations easier.

Screening Calls

In some offices, you may be asked to **screen calls**. Screening incoming calls is a procedure used to determine who is calling and, at times, the purpose of the call. For example, your supervisor may instruct you to screen calls and take a message from all salespeople who call. You may inform the caller that you will relay the message; however, refrain from committing your supervisor to a return call. Your supervisor may be in an important meeting and ask you not to interrupt except for certain callers. Screening can save you and the caller time because you may be able to help the person yourself or transfer the call immediately to another person.

When screening calls, find out who is calling. Be tactful, yet direct. To learn the caller's name, ask questions such as "May I say who is calling?" or "May I tell Ms. Johnson who is calling?"

screen calls: determine who is calling and the purpose for each call

---

WORKPLACE **CONNECTIONS**

Jerry has been instructed not to transfer a call without first identifying the caller. Notice how Jerry is polite, yet firm, about this requirement when dealing with callers.

Jerry:	"Hannibal, Krohe, and Levy. Jerry Timms speaking."
Caller:	"I want to speak to Anna Yong."
Jerry:	"May I tell Ms. Yong who is calling?"
Caller:	"My name is not important. Just let me talk to Anna."
Jerry:	"I'm very sorry, sir, but I have been instructed not to transfer a call without first identifying the caller."
Caller:	"I understand. I'm Jim Evans, Anna's uncle."

Sometimes callers refuse to give their names. If your company requires you to identify each caller by name before transferring the call, you must be courteous, yet firm. Explaining the policy to the caller will usually encourage the caller to give you his or her name. Even if the caller becomes rude or still refuses to tell his or her name, you should at all times be courteous yet remain firm in upholding your supervisor's wishes.

Placing a Caller on Hold

At times, you must place a caller **on hold** while you answer another call. Ask the first caller if you may place him or her on hold. Then answer the second call. Ask permission to place the second caller on hold while you complete your conversation with the first caller.

Sometimes you will need to place a caller on hold while you look up information to answer a question. Politely inform the caller that you are placing him or her on hold. If you think several minutes will be needed to find the answer, ask if you should call back or if the caller would prefer to hold. In the latter case, check back frequently to reassure the caller that he or she has not been forgotten.

Transferring Calls

Calls are usually transferred when the caller has reached a wrong extension, wishes to speak with someone else, or has a request that can be handled more effectively by another person or department. The caller may request the transfer, or you may determine that the transfer is necessary. Always tell the caller why the transfer is necessary. For example, you may say:

> *"I'm going to transfer your call to Mr. Rosen. He will be able to provide you with the information you need."*

You may prefer to place the caller on hold while you speak with the person to whom you intend to transfer the call. This will allow you to confirm that this person can help the caller and to introduce the caller for screening purposes. Calls can sometimes become accidentally disconnected during a transfer. You may wish to give the caller the extension number or name of the person to which the call is being transferred. Then if the call is accidentally disconnected, the caller can reach the appropriate person or extension when he or she calls again.

Figure 12-2.5

Transfer a call carefully to avoid disconnecting the caller.

© ADAM SMITH/FPG INTERNATIONAL

Handling a Disconnected Call

Occasionally, you will be disconnected while you are talking on the telephone or while you are waiting on hold. In general, the person who placed the call should call back immediately after the disconnection. That person has the telephone number of the party being called and should, therefore, be able to redial the call quickly.

The caller should report a disconnected long-distance call to the telephone company. Depending on the telephone company used, an adjustment may be made in the long-distance charge.

Giving Information

You may take calls for a manager or coworkers who are out of the office for several days. In these situations, you must tactfully communicate to the caller that the person is not available and offer to take a message or assist the caller yourself. When coworkers are unavailable to receive calls, give the caller enough information to explain the person's absence without divulging unnecessary or sensitive details.

Improper	*"Ms. Fox has a hair appointment this afternoon."*
Improper	*"Ms. Fox had to pick up her son from school."*
Improper	*"Mr. Chandler is playing golf with a prospective client."*
Proper	*"Ms. Fox is out of the office until tomorrow morning. May I take a message or ask her to call you?"*
Proper	*"Mr. Chandler is in a meeting this afternoon and won't be available the rest of the day. May I take a message or ask him to return your call?"*

Taking Messages

Today's telephone and computer technologies have changed many of the procedures for recording telephone messages. Voice mail has reduced the errors caused by incorrect or incomplete written messages. Even with voice mail, it will be necessary for you to record information for yourself such as the caller's name, telephone number, and purpose of the call.

Printed message forms are usually available in offices for recording telephone messages. When you record a message, it is essential that it is accurate and complete. Verify names and telephone numbers by reading back the information to the caller. Ask for accurate spellings of names if you are in doubt. Write the message carefully, making sure that your handwriting is legible so you do not waste time rewriting it later or fail to be able to read it. Each message should include the following data:

- Date and time of the call
- Name of the caller with the caller's company (Check spellings of any names about which you are uncertain.)
- Caller's telephone number, including area code if it is a long-distance call (Remember to repeat the number for verification.)
- Details of the message
- Your name or initials

Your office may have software that can be used to complete an onscreen message form rather than a preprinted one to record telephone messages. Using a computer message offers these advantages:

Figure 12-2.6

Record information on message forms legibly and accurately.

To **Mr. Lesinski**

Date **8/21/--**   Time **1:30 p.m.**

WHILE YOU WERE OUT

Name **Ms. Rosanna Robbins**

Of **Advanced Realty**

Phone **606-555-3478   Ext. 248**

Telephoned	✓	Please Call	✓
Called to See You		Will Call Again	
Wants to See You		Returned Your Call	

Message

Wants to discuss your meeting scheduled for next week.

By **DR**

- Less time is needed to key a message than to write it.
- The number of lost messages is reduced because messages can be transferred immediately to the intended receiver.
- Printed message forms are not needed.

Each computer message you key should include the same basic information as a handwritten message. As you key the message, make sure that it is accurate and complete. Verify all names and numbers. The current date and time may be entered automatically by the system into the onscreen form or you may need to enter this information. The message may be transferred to the receiver's computer screen by keying in the correct extension number. A reminder or some form of electronic notation will appear on the receiver's screen showing that a message is waiting. In some offices, e-mail is used to record and forward telephone messages.

Handling Difficult Callers

On occasion you may receive calls from persons who are angry, unreasonable, rude, demanding, or highly emotional. These calls may be few, but they can be very stressful. You must control yourself and remain professional

Answering the telephone in an appropriate manner and taking accurate messages is important for effective telephone communications. Notice how the office worker answering this call gives enough information to satisfy the caller but does not give inappropriate information.

Office Worker: *"Hello. Mr. Lesinski's office. Jan House speaking."*

Caller: *"May I please speak with Mr. Lesinski? This is Rosanna Robbins from Advanced Realty."*

Office Worker: *"I'm sorry, Ms. Robbins, but Mr. Lesinski is out of the office until Thursday. I'm Mr. Lesinski's assistant. Could I help you, or may I ask him to call you when he returns?"*

Caller: *"Yes. Please ask him to call me at 606-555-3478, extension 248, regarding our meeting scheduled for next week."*

Office Worker: *"Thank you, Ms. Robbins. To confirm, your number is 606-555-3478, extension 248. I will give Mr. Lesinski the message."*

when dealing with difficult callers. Your goal is to diffuse the situation and to maintain goodwill with the caller, if possible. Follow these guidelines when dealing with difficult telephone callers.

- Try to resolve the matter if possible. Usually the caller just wants the company to solve a problem or rectify a mistake. Do not hesitate to apologize to the caller for any problems or inconveniences that have been experienced.

- Always present a helpful, positive, and sincere attitude, even in an adverse situation.

- If the caller is personally abusive to you or uses profanity, end the conversation quickly after identifying the caller and record relevant information about the call.

- Remain outwardly calm and do not display defensive behavior. Usually, the caller is not upset with you but with the company or its actions. Do not take the caller's anger personally.

With experience and reliance on good human relations and communication skills, you will be able to deal with callers who will put those skills to the test.

Handling Personal Telephone Calls

You must understand and follow your company's policy regarding making or receiving personal telephone calls at work. Most companies permit a limited number of personal calls; others discourage such calls or ask that a pay phone located on the premises be used. Generally, brief, urgent, or emergency calls are permitted. Long, frequent personal calls are never acceptable in any business. You should learn your company's policy and follow it.

Outgoing Telephone Communications

As with incoming telephone calls, outgoing telephone communications may be made to a person outside or inside the company. Calls may be interoffice, local, or long distance. You should understand the process and procedures for placing all outgoing calls. Your goal is efficiency and economy.

Planning Calls

Every call you make requires preparation and planning. Most calls may be simple; however, others may require detailed planning. When preparing for any call, confirm the name and number of the person you are calling. Identify clearly the main purpose of the call. Outline briefly the points you want to cover during the call. Gather other information or items you need to have available before making the call, such as:

- Dates and times of any meetings or planned events that relate to the call
- Documents that relate to the topic of your conversation
- Questions that you want to ask
- Pen and paper or your computer to take notes during the call

Figure 12-2.7

Outline the points you want to cover before placing a call.

© CORBIS/STOCK MARKET

CHAPTER 12: TELEPHONE SYSTEMS AND PROCEDURES

Time Zones

Be aware of time zone differences when placing long-distance calls to avoid calling before or after business hours or during lunch. The continental United States and parts of Canada are divided into five standard time zones: Atlantic, eastern, central, mountain, and Pacific. As you move west, each zone is one hour earlier. For example, when it is 1 p.m. in Washington, D.C. (eastern zone), it is noon in Dallas (central zone), 11 a.m. in Denver (mountain zone), and 10 a.m. in Los Angeles (Pacific zone). If you are in San Diego and need to speak to a coworker in the New York City office, you will need to place the call before 2 p.m. Pacific time. Otherwise, the New York office may be closed because it will be 5 p.m. (eastern time). A time zone map of the United States is included in most telephone directories. Web sites, such as Maps.com (www.maps.com), display the current time in all U.S. time zones as well as providing a time zone map.

When making international calls, being aware of the differences in time zones and certain customs is especially important. If a caller is located in a time zone in which it is impossible for you to call during your regular business hours, you may have to make the call after your normal work time. If you make frequent international calls or calls to distant parts of the country in other time zones, you may want to keep a copy of a world time zone map at hand.

WORKPLACE CONNECTIONS

Sula works for Castor Imports, a company that recently began doing business with a company in Mexico. Sula has tried to phone her contact at the company, Pedro Martinez, several times. Sula and Pedro cannot seem to find one another in the office. Sula usually calls Pedro between 1 p.m. and 2 p.m. when she returns from lunch. Pedro is always out. Pedro returns Sula's calls between 5 p.m. and 6 p.m. and finds that she is not in. Sula and Pedro need to learn about one another's customs and work schedules. For example, in Mexico during the hours of noon to 3 p.m., many offices are closed. Workers return at 3 p.m. and often remain in the office until 7 p.m. or 8 p.m. In the United States, the typical office work day ends at 5 p.m. Understanding these customs will help Sula and Pedro find a time to communicate that is convenient for both of them.

Today's technology makes it easy to place direct calls to over 150 countries all over the world. Twenty-four time zones are used throughout the world. To place a call to London, England, all you have to do to direct-dial is to dial the following sequence of numbers: 011 (international access code) + 44 (country code) + 71 (city code) + seven-digit phone number. Consult the International Calling or similar section of your local telephone directory for country codes.

Topic 12-2: *Effective Telephone Communications*

Using Directories

Many resources are available for you to use when planning a call. Your local telephone company publishes a yearly directory. Local as well as national organizations publish a variety of business and professional directories. National telephone directories are available on CD, and directory information is available on the Internet. You should become familiar with the wide range of information contained in these resources.

Local Directories

Local telephone companies usually provide directories to their customers free of charge. You may want to find the telephone number of a business or individual in your local area. You can usually find the number in the white pages of the local directory. If you are searching for a particular service or product rather than a company, you may find the number in the yellow pages section of the directory. You should become familiar with all sections of your local telephone directory. Typical directories contain the sections discussed in the following paragraphs.

Telephone directories with names of persons, businesses, and organizations arranged alphabetically are referred to as the *white pages*. The front section of most directories is actually a user's guide for the directory itself and a "how-to" guide for the telephone services consumer. Some of the information you will find here includes types of telephone services provided by the company, local emergency numbers, and directions for making many types of calls. You should read and become very familiar with this section.

Figure 12-2.8

Telephone numbers for local businesses can be found in the local telephone directory.

© CORBISIMAGES.COM

The next section of the local telephone directory contains names, addresses, and telephone numbers of businesses, government agencies, and individuals in your city. In some locations, the white pages may be divided into two sections. The first section lists personal names and numbers only, while the second section lists only business names and numbers. Sometimes these sections are each contained in separate books. When personal and business numbers are divided, another section called the *blue pages* also may be included. The blue pages serve as an easy reference for locating telephone numbers of government offices and other helpful numbers, such as those of the chamber of commerce, consumer protection agencies, and weather service.

A type of directory called the *yellow pages* contains an alphabetic listing of businesses arranged according to the services they provide or the products they sell. For example, if you want to find names and telephone numbers of businesses in the area that might cater your company's 50th anniversary dinner, you would look under *caterers* in the yellow pages.

Personal and Company Directories

You should make a list of all numbers that you call often. You may be able to program a limited number of frequently dialed numbers into your telephone. Your company may provide you with a directory of employees working at a particular location. The directory may also include procedures for using features of the telephone system including the management of your voice mailbox. Tips for proper telephone techniques as well as how the company wants you to identify yourself and your department may also be included.

Computerized Directories

Integration of computer and telephone technology is changing how we access all types of data. The types of information contained in the paper directories can also be accessed using a personal computer. National telephone directories can be purchased on CD. Web sites, such as Switchboard.com or SuperPages.com, provide access to a variety of data including telephone numbers and services of businesses.

Figure 12-2.9

Create a directory for telephone numbers you call frequently.

TELEPHONE DIRECTORY

Andersen Realty	606-555-8841
Burnett, Conley	606-555-3487
Captain J's Boat Shop	606-555-5698
Cash, Susan E.	513-555-8339
Century One Realtors	606-555-7722
Dautrich, Ela	606-555-7489
Estes, Sandra	513-555-4985
Guzzeta, Freia	270-555-3934
Habeeb, Mo	606-555-3519
Park, Kim	606-555-5681
Perez, Juan	606-555-2248

Topic 12-2: *Effective Telephone Communications*

Directory Assistance

If you are unable to locate a telephone number, call the directory assistance operator for help. Dial 411 for a local directory assistance operator. For long-distance directory assistance, dial 1, the area code, and 555-1212. A directory assistance operator will ask you what city you are calling. Be prepared to supply the operator with as much information as possible about the person or business for which you need the number. Be prepared to give the correct spelling and street address if known. After giving the information, there will be a pause; then you will hear the number repeated twice. Make a note of the number for future reference.

Long-Distance Service

Long-distance calls are made to numbers outside the service area of your local telephone company. Several factors may determine the cost of long-distance service: time of day the call is placed, type of call, length of call, and type of long-distance call. Long-distance carriers provide a variety of pricing plans. The consumer chooses a long-distance provider. You may want to find out about the varied long-distance programs and prices available before selecting a carrier. Your local telephone directory usually may list several long-distance carriers (MCI, Sprint, AT&T, etc.) and their numbers for you to contact. You may also visit these companies' Web sites to learn of pricing and special offers and regulations. To place calls efficiently and economically, you must become familiar with the various long-distance services available.

Direct-Dial Calls

Direct-dial calls, also called station-to-station calls, are those placed without assistance from an operator. To make a direct-dial call, first dial 1, which gives you access to a long-distance line. Then dial the area code and the number you are trying to reach. Charges for these calls begin as soon as the telephone is answered. If you make a direct-dial call and the person you need to speak with is unavailable, your company still will be charged for the call.

Figure 12-2.10

Direct-dial calls are placed without assistance from an operator.

CHAPTER 12: TELEPHONE SYSTEMS AND PROCEDURES

Specialized Long-Distance Calls

Specialized long-distance calls are more expensive than those you dial direct. Person-to-person, collect, credit card, and conference calls are all types of special long-distance calls.

Person-to-person calls are an expensive type of operator-assisted calls. To place a person-to-person call, dial 0 (zero), the area code, and the telephone number of the individual or business you are calling. When you have finished dialing, you will be asked what type of call you wish to place, such as a person-to-person or collect call. You will say "person-to-person call" and will then be asked to supply the name of the person you are calling. Pronounce the name clearly and accurately. You may have to spell it for clarity.

Charges for the call begin only after the person you have requested is on the line. If that person is not available, you will not be charged for the call. If you must call repeatedly before reaching the person, or if it takes the person several minutes to get to the phone, this type of call may be less expensive than a direct-dialed call. You do not pay until you begin speaking with the person you have indicated.

The charges for a **collect call** are billed to the telephone number being called, not to the number from which the call was placed. To place a collect call, dial 0 (zero), the area code, and the telephone number. You will be asked what type of call you are placing. Speak clearly into the phone, answering "collect." You will then be asked to give your name. Once again, speak very clearly and distinctly into the phone. The call will be completed, and the recipient will be asked whether or not the call and the charges will be accepted.

People who travel for a business may find it necessary to make collect calls to their offices. Customers or clients may be invited to call collect.

A **conference call** is placed when it is necessary to talk with persons at several different locations at the same time. With some telephone systems, you can use special features to arrange these calls yourself. In many cases, conference calls are set up in advance with a conference operator. To place a conference call with this type of assistance, dial the number of this specialized service. You can obtain this number from your long-distance service provider or dial the operator and request a conference call. Be prepared to give the names, telephone numbers, and locations (cities and states) of the participants as well as the exact time the call is to be placed. At the designated time, the operator will call you and indicate that the other parties are on the line. Review the tips for planning and carrying out conference calls that were presented in Topic 12-1 in this chapter.

For people who travel frequently for business or pleasure, **telephone credit cards** can be very practical. The user is able to charge telephone calls to the credit card. A special PIN (personal identification number) is issued to the cardholder for security. The PIN number is entered using the telephone keypad. Some telephones, such as those found in airports, are specially equipped to read a magnetic card number when the credit card is slid through a slot.

Another type of phone card that is often used by travelers is a **prepaid phone card**. This card is purchased in advance and used to pay for a certain number of minutes of phone use. The user receives a PIN number and a

prepaid phone card: card purchased in advance and used to pay for a certain number of minutes of phone use

Topic 12-2: *Effective Telephone Communications*

Figure 12-2.11

Prepaid phone cards are convenient for business travelers.

© LISETTE LE BON/SUPERSTOCK INTERNATIONAL

toll-free access number. The phone system will inform you of the amount of calling time remaining for the card. Prepaid phone cards may be purchased in many locations such as airports and convenience stores and from your long-distance carrier.

Toll-Free Service

As a convenience to customers who call long-distance, a company may subscribe to toll-free service for callers. This discounted service applies to incoming calls only, and no charge is made to the caller. For toll-free numbers, users dial 800 or 888 rather than an area code. To determine whether a company in the United States has a toll-free number, dial 1-800-555-1212 and give the company name. Some telephone service providers, such as AT&T, provide a lookup service for toll-free numbers on the company's Web site (www.att.com).

As with other telephone services, rate plans and regulations for toll-free service plans vary widely. Compare price plans and features from several telephone companies to find the plan that will be most cost-effective for your company.

Controlling Telephone Costs

As an office worker, you will be expected to help control telephone costs. Some guidelines to follow for controlling telephone costs and improving efficiency are listed below.

- Use direct dialing most of the time. Make more specialized, expensive types of calls that require extra assistance only when necessary.
- Plan your calls so the time spent during a long-distance or any other call is used efficiently.
- If possible, call when long-distance rates are least expensive.
- Notify the operator immediately after reaching a wrong number so you can receive credit for the call.
- Be an informed consumer of telephone services. Compare rate plans and promotional offerings.
- Learn how to use the equipment and features of your telephone system.

1. What factors influence the first impression you make when you respond to a telephone call?

2. Why should you use the caller's name as the conversation ends?

3. What information should you record when taking a telephone message or retrieving telephone messages from your voice mailbox?

4. What should you do if you have placed a caller on hold and you think several minutes will be needed for you to locate the requested information?

5. What questions might you ask to learn a caller's name?

6. Give three suggestions for handling difficult telephone callers.

7. Describe information found in the white pages. How are organizations listed in the yellow pages? For what purposes are the blue pages used?

8. Name the five time zones into which the continental United States and parts of Canada are divided.

9. List five examples of information that may be needed before making a call.

10. Describe the procedure for dialing a domestic, long-distance direct-dial call.

11. Describe the procedure for dialing an international, long-distance direct-dial call.

12. List three guidelines for controlling telephone costs.

Thinking Critically

You are employed in a growing computer sales and service business, Hooser's Computer Corner. Numerous calls are received daily for the fifteen sales associates, seven service technicians, and four administrative services employees. The owner is considering the purchase of an automated attendant telephone system. The office manager, Lin Wong, would like to hear your suggestions before deciding whether to purchase a system. You are aware of both advantages and disadvantages of using these systems. What do you recommend?

1. Make a list of the pros and cons of using an automated attendant at Hooser's Computer Corner.

2. Prepare a memo or e-mail message to Lin Wong. Include your list of pros and cons. Give your recommendation as to whether or not you think the company should install an automated attendant. Give reasons for your recommendation.

Reinforcing Math Skills

You work for Carrlson-Greer, which has offices in Seattle, Houston, and St. Louis. You are responsible for monitoring the costs of the various forms of telecommunications used by the company. As part of your analysis, prepare a table showing the monthly long-distance telephone charges for each regional office for a period of six months.

1. Prepare a spreadsheet to record and calculate the telephone charges. Enter the company name as the main title of the spreadsheet. Enter *Long-Distance Charges for Regional Carriers* under the company name.
2. Enter *Months*, *Seattle*, *Houston*, *St. Louis*, and *Totals* as the column heads. Enter the data for each office for each month as shown below step 4.
3. Enter formulas to calculate:
   - Total charges for the three offices for each month
   - Total charges for each regional office for the six-month period
   - Total charges for the six-month period for all regional offices
   - The average monthly charges for each regional office
   - The average monthly charges for all offices
4. Format the spreadsheet so it is attractive and easy to read. Print the spreadsheet.

Months	Seattle	Houston	St. Louis
January	$201.56	$58.67	$250.78
February	190.45	75.34	277.56
March	175.66	68.90	265.19
April	188.34	92.51	281.40
May	205.22	61.61	275.37
June	199.29	74.27	259.39

Topic 12-2 **ACTIVITY 1**

Company Telephone Directory

As a special project, you will create a directory of employees for your office at the Home and Hearth Insurance Agency. The information will be contained in a database that can be accessed and updated easily.

1. Open and print the data file **Directory.pdf**, which contains the information for the directory.
2. Prepare a database containing the names, titles, departments, and extensions of all the workers at your location.
3. Sort the records in alphabetical order by last name and print the directory showing all fields.
4. Sort the records in alphabetical order, first by department and then by last name. Print the directory showing all fields.

Topic 12-2 **ACTIVITY 2**

Directory Research

Telephone directories provide a wealth of information for your use in planning telephone communications and locating people and services. Use your local telephone directory or online directories to find the information requested. Key and print your answers.

1. Number of the nearest Federal Bureau of Investigation office
2. Number to call to report telephone problems on your line
3. Number to call if you have questions about your telephone bill
4. List of the first three digits of the telephone numbers in your local calling area
5. List of all area codes for Illinois, Colorado, and Washington, D.C.
6. The time zones for Nashville, TN; Prince Edward Island, Canada; Seattle, WA; and Wichita, KS

7. The country codes for dialing the following countries: Japan, Mexico, Kenya, and Greece

8. Number for your state's motor vehicle department

9. Number for the local public schools

10. Subject in the yellow pages where you would find:
   - Agencies that supply temporary office workers
   - A vision center that sells eyeglasses
   - A service station that will change your car's oil
   - A company that will repair your computer
   - A company that sells voice mail equipment
   - A doctor who specializes in eye surgery

Chapter Review

Summary

Telecommunications play a vital role in the way we conduct business as well as in our personal lives. Innovations in the methods we use to transmit voice, text, graphics, and video make it faster and easier to communicate with others all over the world. Because the technology changes rapidly, you should be prepared to learn how new, improved techniques and equipment can help you access, use, and share all forms of information. After studying this chapter, you should be knowledgeable about the following key points.

- Office workers rely on telecommunications technology to access and transmit information quickly and reliably, both locally and globally.

- A variety of image and voice transmission equipment is available, such as facsimile, videoconferencing, centralized telephone systems, voice mail systems, mobile telephone equipment, and speakerphones.

- Specialized equipment and services available to the telephone consumer include features for individuals with impairments, conference call services, toll-free number service, and prepaid long-distance phone cards.

- When you answer or place a call for your organization, you immediately make an impression on the other person. Workers should use proper techniques and procedures so that all incoming and outgoing calls are handled professionally and efficiently.

- Plan an outgoing call before placing the outgoing call to make sure all the points you want to discuss are included.

- Information needed for placing calls is contained in a variety of print and electronic directories.

- You can help control telephone costs by using direct-dial calls, planning outgoing calls, and placing calls when rates are least expensive.

Key Terms

analog	directory	telephony
automated atten-	facsimile	time zone
dant	modem	toll-free call
call forwarding	on hold	tone
cellular telephone	pace	videoconferencing
collect call	pager	voice mail
country code	prepaid phone card	volume
digital	screen calls	
direct-dial call	telecommunications	

COMPOSITION
TEAMWORK
WORD PROCESSING

Telephone Conversations

Role-playing telephone conversations will help you develop your telephone skills. For the role-playing activities, work with another member of your class. Rotate in each situation between being the caller and being the person answering the telephone.

1. Open and print the data file **Phone.pdf**, which describes several dramatic situations that you will role play.

2. After you have read each dramatic situation, work with your teammate to prepare a script. Compose the dialog that each person might say in this situation and print a copy for each of you.

3. Practice the telephone conversations. If you have a tape recorder available, record the call. Evaluate yourself and your teammate using the form provided in the data file.

4. Present your dramatization to the class or another team. Have classmates complete an evaluation form for each presentation. Your classmates will also be acting out the situations and you will complete forms to evaluate them.

COMPOSITION
INTEGRATED DOCUMENT
INTERNET
RESEARCH
SPREADSHEET
WORD PROCESSING

Chapter 12 ACTIVITY 2

New Long-Distance Carrier

Your company, Dee-Lite's Chocolates, is dissatisfied with its current long-distance service provider. Prices have risen dramatically on domestic calls over the last six months. The company remains open 24 hours a day, seven days a week to meet the demands of a growing market for its gourmet chocolates. Long-distance telephone calls are being placed all during the seven-day work period.

Timothy has researched several plans and recorded the domestic rates per minute for long distance calls. You will complete the research by finding rate plans for two additional long distance carriers. You will use your spreadsheet software to find the average rates for each plan and then integrate the spreadsheet table into a document with your recommendation for which plan to choose.

1. Create a spreadsheet titled *TELEPHONE RATES COMPARISON*. Enter Timothy's data.

Provider	Plan Name	Day Rate	Evening Rate	Weekend Rate
E-CON-O-ME	All-4-U	$ 0.10	$ 0.10	$ 0.10
VARI-PLAN	Ten Plan	0.10	0.10	0.10
EAGLE LINE	Wings	0.11	0.09	0.08
VALU-COM	Circle	0.12	0.08	0.08
BL&T	Makes Cents	0.14	0.08	0.07

2. Complete the research for this project. Use the Internet or other resources to find the rates charged by at least two telephone service providers for long-distance calls within the United States. Record rate amounts for the same times as shown for the companies Timothy researched. Enter the data into your spreadsheet.

3. Enter the column heading *Average* at the right of the spreadsheet. Enter formulas to find the average per minute rate for each company. For the plans listed above, the day rate applies for 10 hours each day, Monday–Friday. The evening rate applies for 14 hours each day, Monday–Friday. The weekend rate applies for 24 hours each day, Saturday–Sunday.

4. Create a memo to Murray Washford. Give your recommendation for which telephone service provider the company should choose. Point out the reasons for your choice and include the rate comparison table in the message to support your position.

5. Check the document for format and content. Print the integrated document.

— *After completing all the chapters in Part 4, complete the Part 4 simulation, At Work at Buckhorn Mountain Outfitters. The simulation is found in the* Student Activities and Projects *workbook.*

Part 5

Personal and Career Development

Success at work is based on a combination of technical competencies and personal qualities. Both will prove important in finding a job and advancing your career. You will want to understand how to search for a job, how to present your credentials and yourself, and what the expectations are as you begin work. Companies seek employees at all levels who are good team players—cooperative, willing to assume responsibility, focused on meeting organizational goals, and able to work with others effectively. *Personal and Career Development* focuses on you as a worker and how you interact with others to secure a position and perform satisfactorily.

OBJECTIVES

- Plan for entry into the workplace and for career development
- Describe and develop personal characteristics valuable at work
- Discuss and develop the basic attitudes that support organizational goals
- Interact effectively with others at work

Planning and Advancing Your Career

You have had many opportunities to consider the types of tasks common to many jobs. You may have made a firm decision about your choice for an initial job or career. On the other hand, you may be planning full-time study for a while and postponing a decision about your first full-time job. Regardless of your present plans, you will find it valuable to understand what is generally involved in getting a job.

You will become acquainted with various ways of learning about jobs and how to respond to these career opportunities. Use your study of this material to become aware of your own interests and begin developing career goals. You can feel confident about finding a job and advancing your career when you have learned about effective job search and career planning strategies.

OBJECTIVES

- Identify the factors to consider when planning a career strategy
- Discuss the role of a career goal in your planning
- Describe the steps in planning a job search
- Prepare a resume
- Prepare for an interview
- Explain what generally is expected of an interviewee

While studying this textbook, you have had an opportunity to learn what many jobs require, especially in office-related careers. You can see to what extent positions in today's workplace require information-related competencies. At this point, you may be planning to:

- Begin work full time
- Begin work full time while pursuing further education on a part-time basis
- Begin work part time and become a full-time student in college or some other training or educational program
- Be a full-time college student with no plans for present full-time employment

Regardless of your present plans, you will find the information provided in this topic helpful for understanding how to enter the job market.

career goals: desired achievements related to work such as jobs, education, or work experience

career strategy: plans to meet career goals

interview: meeting to question or evaluate, as for a job applicant

Thinking Ahead About Careers and Jobs

Whatever your present plans for employment or further education, you should consider your long-term **career goals**. You might wonder why someone who is considering a first job should be thinking beyond that job. Thinking ahead may help you choose a first job that is closely related to long-term interests. Thinking ahead to what you see as a career goal and planning realistic steps to meet that goal is known as a **career strategy**. With a career goal in mind, you can evaluate beginning job offers in relation to that goal.

WORKPLACE **CONNECTIONS**

© Bluestone Productions/SuperStock International

Christine works part-time in a large company in downtown Denver during her senior year in high school. She would like to be a secondary school teacher and plans to work full time for at least two years while she studies education at a local college. Then she plans to become a full-time student. The manager where she works has suggested that because she wants to be a teacher, she might like to work full time in their human resources department and help the director of their extensive training programs. After an **interview** in the human resources department, Christine was offered a position. She is looking forward to beginning her new full-time position in late July.

Career planning is not a once-in-a-lifetime task. As you gain experience, you will become better acquainted with jobs that match your interests and talents. As you learn more about various jobs and professions, your career goals may change.

Planning with a Career Goal Established

Perhaps you and some of your classmates have clear ideas for your future work goals. If this is true for you, you may have thought about what you can do well, what the opportunities are for your chosen field, and in general what will be required to achieve your career goals. When thinking about careers, consider the following questions:

- What specific kinds of jobs are available to a person who has chosen the career goals I have?
- What job opportunities in this career field are projected for the next five to ten years?
- What are the educational qualifications for entry-level jobs in this career?
- What educational and/or experience qualifications are needed to advance in this career?

Planning Without a Career Goal

Even if you do not yet know what career you wish to choose, you can still enter the workplace and perform successfully. When seeking a job, you can highlight a willingness to:

- Perform every task assigned according to instructions
- Strive always to improve performance
- Learn more about the company and make a valuable contribution to its goals

When you begin working, you will learn about a wide variety of positions through your dealings with other workers. Such knowledge will be helpful in exploring career options.

© SPENCER GRANT/PHOTOEDIT

Figure 13-1.1

A person who is still considering career goals can be successful on a first job.

Planning a Job Search

Whether you have specific career goals or not, you can effectively plan your search for a full-time job. Your success in meeting job requirements need not be related to whether or not you have a career goal. Common steps in a job search include:

1. Become acquainted with the types of jobs you wish to consider.

2. Explore job opportunities related to these jobs.

3. Prepare a **resume**.

4. Prepare a **letter of application** when you have identified a specific job opening appropriate for your education and experience.

5. Send resumes and letters of application to companies considering candidates for jobs.

6. Accept interviews with companies that wish to talk with you about available jobs.

7. Follow up all job interviews.

8. Accept a job.

resume: document that presents job qualifications such as training, skills, and work experience

letter of application: letter expressing interest in a job and requesting an interview

Exploring Job Opportunities

A number of sources are available to help you locate specific jobs in which you may be interested and for which you are qualified. Friends, relatives, and former employers often know about good job opportunities for you. Other sources are discussed briefly in the following paragraphs.

School Placement and Counseling Services

Become familiar with the placement and counseling services available in your school. In schools without a placement counselor, prospective employers often inform school guidance counselors or business teachers about job opportunities in their organizations. Let your business teachers and your counselors know about your plans and your job interests. This will help

Figure 13-1.2

Discuss your plans and your job interests with your counselors and instructors.

© RHODA SIDNEY/PHOTOEDIT

Source: USAJOBS, U.S. Office of Personnel Management. Online. Available: http://www.usajobs.opm.gov/aboutus.htm. January 12, 2002.

Figure 13-1.3

This job board provides information about U.S. government jobs.

them identify you as a candidate when they learn about a job that may be right for you.

The World Wide Web

Many sites on the World Wide Web contain job listings. These sites are sometimes called **job boards**. Job boards allow job seekers to post a resume and to view job listings from many organizations. Job boards allow employers to post **job descriptions** and review resumes posted by job seekers. Most job boards are free to job seekers. Employers may be required to pay a fee to search for job candidates. Jobs boards may offer information on a wide variety of jobs, or they may be related to a particular career area or a particular geographic region. For example, the Admin Exchange Web site (www.adminexchange.com) provides information on jobs in the administrative support field. All services for job seekers at this site are free.

USAJobs (www.usajobs.opm.gov) is the official federal government job Web site. This site offers listings for entry-level professional, clerical, trade, labor, and summer jobs, among others. Many states and some cities have Web sites with information about their government jobs.

Many companies allow applicants to complete a job application online and post a resume electronically at the company's Web site. Other company Web sites provide information about jobs available at the company for which you may apply using a traditional hard copy letter and resume.

Newspapers

The classified advertisement sections of newspapers list many job openings. Some employers advertise directly, asking you to call or to fax your resume to them. Other employers use blind advertisements that do not identify the employer and request that applications be sent to a post office box. Magazines, newsletters, and other periodicals related to a particular industry also often have sections listing job openings.

job board: Web site that provides job listings and allows persons seeking employment to post resumes

job description: listing of the duties and responsibilities of a job and information about the work environment and the skills, experience, and education required for the job

Topic 13-1: *An Effective Job Search*

Figure 13-1.4

Want ad from a
newspaper

ADMINISTRATIVE ASSISTANT

Entry-level position to assist financial dept. and
business affairs, data entry and various office duties.
Requires good math skills. Send resume w/cover
letter to: P.O. BOX 274, NEW YORK, NY 10003.

Employment Agencies

Employers submit job openings to employment agencies, and counselors at
the agencies help match applicants' qualifications and goals with jobs available. Private employment agencies charge a fee for their services. Sometimes
the person seeking a job pays a fee. At other times, the employer pays a fee,
which is usually a percentage of the first year's salary. Government employment agencies provide services to citizens and employers free of charge.

Temporary employment agencies hire individuals to fill temporary jobs that
may last from a single day to many months. Many businesses use temporary
workers on a regular basis. By taking temporary jobs, young workers can
gain a variety of experiences and understand better which full-time, permanent jobs will be most appealing to them. In some instances, temporary
workers are asked to accept permanent positions.

WORKPLACE CONNECTIONS

Jan registered with a temporary employment agency when she
graduated from college with a degree in business administration. Because having a temporary job provided Jan with an
income, she felt less pressure to find a permanent job immediately. Jan worked at three different companies during a four-
month period after graduation. At each job, Jan's manager and
coworkers learned about her talents and job skills, and Jan
learned more about the business world. When an opening for
a management trainee became available at the first company
where Jan had worked, a former coworker at the company
called Jan about the position. Jan applied and was hired for the
job. Jan's new manager was pleased to hire Jan because he was
familiar with her talents and skills.

Government Announcements

Many different types of employees are required in government agencies at
the local, county, state, federal, and even international levels. You will be
able to get information from your state employment office about state and
federal job opportunities. As mentioned earlier, the federal government and
many state and city governments have Web sites that list job openings.
Candidates for state and federal jobs usually must satisfactorily complete
job-related examinations, which are given periodically with the dates
announced in advance.

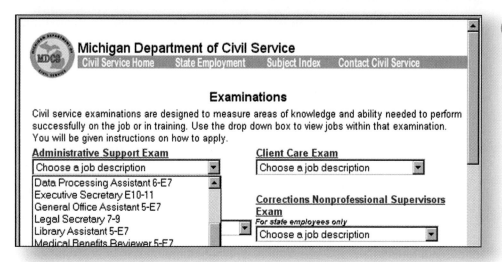

Source: Michigan Department of Civil Service. Online. Available: http://www.state.mi.us/mdcs/Employ/CareerFields/ExamAnnouncements/Exams.htm. December 26, 2001.

Figure 13-1.5

Many government employees must pass civil service examinations.

Personal Inquiry

If you have a special interest in working for a particular organization, you may want to write a carefully worded letter inquiring about job possibilities. In your letter, you should explain the reason for your interest in being an employee, describe the kind of job you want, and briefly outline your qualifications. You need not include a resume with your letter of inquiry, but you may want to state that you will be happy to forward a detailed resume.

Preparing A Resume

A resume, also called a data sheet or vita, is a concise, well-organized presentation of your qualifications for a job. The prospective employer usually will see your resume before interviewing you. Your resume should make a positive impression on the reader. A resume should be accurate in every detail.

A resume usually has several categories: personal information, job interest, education, work experience, and references (or a statement about availability of references). You may want to include additional categories, such as computer competencies, extracurricular activities, or scholastic honors when appropriate. As a general rule, list the most important information first. Refer to Figure 13-1.6 on page 535 as you read about common resume categories.

- **Personal Information.** List your contact information clearly at the beginning of your resume. This information should include your name, mailing address, and telephone number. If you have an e-mail address or fax number, list those also. You need not provide information such as age, date of birth, or marital status.

- **Job Interest.** Briefly state the job for which you are applying. A prospective employer will then be able to assess your qualifications in relation to specific job openings in the organization.

- **Education.** List the name and address of your high school and the graduation date or anticipated date. List the cousrses you completed that prepared you for the job market. You may also include any scholastic honors or awards you have earned. You may want to show any extracurricular activities in which you participated, such as membership in special interest clubs.

- **Work Experience.** List in chronological order the jobs you have had, beginning with the most recent one. For each job, include the name and address of the organization, your job title, a brief description of the tasks performed, and the beginning and ending dates of your employment. If your job experience is limited, include part-time positions as well as any volunteer work you performed. Be sure to indicate clearly the work you did as a volunteer.

- **References. References** are persons who know your academic ability and/or work skills and habits and are willing to recommend you to prospective employers. List references on your resume or include a note stating that references will be provided on request. When you list a reference, be sure to include a complete name, job title, address, and telephone number for each one. Generally, three references are considered sufficient. Ask permission before using a person as a reference on an application or in an interview with a prospective employer.

references: persons who know your work abilities, skills, and habits and are willing to recommend you to prospective employers

Because there is no standard resume format, a prospective employer may consider your resume to be an example of your ability to organize information in a useful and meaningful form. The form in which you submit your resume will influence the format, content, and organization of the information. You may need a traditional hard copy resume, a hard copy resume formatted for ease of scanning, and an electronic resume saved in a file format that can be successfully posted online or sent by e-mail.

A hard copy resume for traditional use should be attractive and easy to read. Limit a hard copy resume to one page, or use a second page only if needed to list complete work history. Do not crowd text on the page. Use bold to emphasize categories of information and a leave blank line between categories. Print your resume on a laser printer or have it photocopied on high-quality paper. Whichever method you use, be sure the copies are clean with clear, sharp print.

Many companies and employment agencies receive hundreds or thousands of resumes each year. These resumes are often scanned and converted to electronic files. When a company has a job opening, the resume database is searched for key words or terms that relate to the qualifications for that job. To improve the chances that your resume will be readable after it has been scanned, keep the format simple. Do not use fancy fonts, bold type, bullets, rule lines, or a complicated layout with tables or columns of text. An attractively formatted hard copy resume that may make a good first impression on a person may be difficult for a computer to read. Keep the language simple and use key terms that are likely to match the description for the job you seek. For example, an accountant might use terms such as "month-end close" or "general ledger entries" in a list of duties at a previous job. Key terms are often nouns or noun phrases, so use terms such as "project supervisor" instead of "supervised projects." If you do not know whether your hard copy resume will be scanned, call the company to which you are sending the resume and ask for this information.

You may decide to prepare several variations of your basic resume. For example, when submitting a resume for a particular job, use the title of that

CHAPTER 13: PLANNING AND ADVANCING YOUR CAREER

Valerie Gomez
3467 Mandelin Drive
Albuquerque, NM 87112-0341
(505) 555-0130

Job Interest

An administrative assistant position in an historical museum or college.

Education

Will graduate from Southwest High School, May, 20--
Grade Point Average: 3.57
Class Standing: 34th in class of 329

Related courses:

American History
Keyboarding
Computer Skills
Office Procedures

Special skills:

Keyboarding: 65 words per minute
Good command of Microsoft Office: Word, Excel, Access
Historical research experience in local libraries

School activities:

Vice President of American Historical Club
Member of Student Council

Work Experience

Assistant to the librarian of the historical archives in the Albuquerque Public Library. (Part-time during school year; full time during the past two summers.)

Student assistant to school librarian during first two years in high school.

References

Provided upon request.

Figure 13-1.6

A resume presents an applicant's job qualifications.

job in the job interest section of your resume. If you know the company scans hard copy resumes, use a simple format that will scan well. If the resume is to be posted online or submitted via e-mail, use the appropriate formatting and file format to ensure that the document will be readable on other computer systems. See the *Focus On... Online Job Search and Resume* (page 536) for more information about electronic resumes. Computer programs, such as Individual Software's ResumeMaker, are available to provide guidance and allow you to create a resume in an appropriate format for many different jobs and situations.

Online Job Search and Resume

When you conduct a job search online, you may chose to search only one or two job boards or many job boards and company Web sites. The wider your search, the better your chances are of finding the job you want. Because new jobs may be posted daily, you should search for jobs frequently. Many job boards provide **intelligent agents**, often called job scouts or job agents, that can aid in this process. Simply indicate your search criteria for jobs, such as job titles and geographic locations, and the search frequency you desire (daily, weekly). The job scout will search for jobs that meet your criteria.

When jobs are located by your job scout, you will receive an e-mail containing links to the job postings. You can review these job postings and apply for the jobs that interest you. For some jobs, you can apply online by posting your resume and completing a job application form. For other jobs, you can apply by sending a hard copy resume and letter of application.

Just as job seekers search online for jobs, employers search online for prospective employees. Employers may search resumes that have been posted online at job boards or submitted via e-mail or a company Web site using search terms that reflect the skills and qualifications they seek in job applicants. Preparing your electronic resume in a format that can be searched easily for key terms will increase your chances

of being selected as a job candidate by an employer. Follow these guidelines when preparing electronic resumes.

- Use default fonts and font sizes. Save the resume as a plain ASCII text file (also called Text Only by some programs). ASCII text is simply words without any special formatting and can be read by many programs. Keeping the format simple will increase the chances that your electronic resume will be readable at the many different sites where you may choose to post or send it.

- When submitting an electronic resume via e-mail, send the resume as an attachment only if you know the company's e-mail system can handle attachments. If you are not sure, place the resume in the body of the e-mail message instead.

- Keep the resume fairly short, although you do not need to limit it to a single printed page as is recommended for hard copy resumes. The computer can search two pages almost as quickly as one page.

- Include contact information and identify the type of job you seek as you would on a hard copy resume.

- Use concise, specific terms that describe your work experience, skills, and education or training. For example, say "Proficient with Microsoft

intelligent agent: computer program that works independently to accomplish a specific task such as retrieving and delivering information

Word" instead of "I have had training and work experience using word processing software."

- When posting a resume for a specific job, use the same terms for a particular skill or other requirement in your resume as are used in the job description or announcement. (Do not misrepresent your qualifications, however.)

- Use a professional, positive tone for the resume.

- Proofread carefully. Be sure all information is current and accurate.

Writing a Letter of Application

A letter of application introduces you to a prospective employer and requests an interview. Although your resume may be a high-quality photocopy, a hard copy letter of application that accompanies a resume should be an original.

The tone of the letter should appeal to the reader, and its content should be concise and informative. Remember, the reader is interested in you only in terms of your qualifications for a job in the company. These guidelines will aid you in composing a letter of application.

- When submitting a hard copy letter, address the letter to a person, not to a department or position. If you do not have the name of the person to whom your letter should be addressed, call the company to ask for the name and title. When submitting a letter of application online, you may not be able to address the letter to a specific person. Follow the directions on the Web site.

- Explain in the first paragraph the reason for the letter, stating specifically the position in which you are interested.

- Briefly indicate why you believe you are qualified for the position. Refer to specific classes, work experience, and/or interests you have that you believe are related to the position. Indicate that a resume is enclosed or is also being transmitted to provide more details about your qualifications.

- In a final paragraph, request an interview.

- Limit your letter to a single printed page (or about the equivalent of a printed page for online letters of application).

The Interview

Companies may interview several candidates before hiring someone for a position. Successful interviewing is a critical step in securing a job that meets your expectations.

Figure 13-1.7

A letter of application
requests a job interview.

3467 Mandelin Drive
Albuquerque, NM 87112-0341
May 10, 20--

Ms. Gretchen T. Wellington
Director, Hansen Historical Center
356 Front Street
Albuquerque, NM 87102-0356

Dear Ms. Wellington:

Your job opening for a library assistant came to my attention through
my school librarian, Ms. Eva Elison. Please consider me as an
applicant for the position. I am very interested in working in an
organization that is involved in historical research.

I am currently completing my senior year at Southwest High School.
I also work about ten hours each week at the Albuquerque Public
Library. My work there is in the historical archives under the direction
of Ms. Sarah Forman. A copy of my resume is enclosed to give you
more details about my education and experience.

Please consider granting me an interview to discuss employment
opportunities with your center. You may telephone me at 555-0130.
Because I am at school or work most of the day, please leave a message;
I will return your call as soon as possible.

Sincerely,

Valerie Gomez

Valerie Gomez

Enclosure: Resume

Prepare for an Interview

Prepare carefully for each interview you accept. Consider how you will present your qualifications and interests to the interviewer. Anticipate questions and think about how you will respond to them. Learn about the company. What are the company's primary products or services? Does the company have branch offices? Is the company owned publicly or privately? What do your family and friends know about the firm? If the company has a Web site, review the site to learn about the company. If you prepare well, you will approach the interview with confidence, increasing your chances of making a favorable impression on the interviewer.

Make a Good First Impression

At an interview, you are usually approaching a stranger—someone who has had no prior experience with you. Your appearance and manner will influence the interviewer's first impression of you. A day or two before the interview, plan what you will wear, considering what is appropriate and at the same time comfortable. Generally, you should choose conservative, businesslike attire, even though you may know that employees in the organization dress casually at most times. Your manner should be polite and professional. Be friendly, but not overly familiar with people you meet at the company.

WORKPLACE **CONNECTIONS**

Marion was excited about his interview at a local garden design and landscape company. He arrived for the interview on time, answered all the questions clearly, and expressed his interest in working for the company. When a letter arrived thanking Marion for his interest and telling him that another candidate had been hired, he was very disappointed. A few days later Marion had lunch with Jean, a friend who works at the company. "Do you know why someone else was chosen for the job instead of me?" he asked. "If I did something wrong in the interview, I would really like to know so I can improve before my next interview." "Well," said Jean, "I did hear the manager comment once that he thinks everyone should dress in professional business attire for an interview." "Oh," said Marion. "Then I definitely made a poor decision when I showed up in khakis and a polo shirt. I thought I should dress like the workers I have seen at the company." Marion learned the hard way that appearance can influence an interviewer's impression of a candidate.

Anticipate Questions

You will be asked a number of questions during the interview. Some are likely to be ones that are commonly asked in such a situation. Others may be unique to the interview. Some common questions include these:

- Tell me about yourself.
- Why does this job interest you?
- What courses did you study that you found most interesting? Why?
- What do you believe are your strongest qualifications for this job?
- What school activities or previous work experience required you to work in groups? on your own?
- How do you evaluate your participation in group activities?
- Why do you think you would enjoy working in our company?
- What are your career goals at this time?
- What new skills or knowledge do you want to acquire?
- What is your greatest weakness?
- What salary do you expect for this job?

In the United States, laws have been established to safeguard your right to an equal opportunity for employment. Questions regarding age, marital status, ethnic background, religious beliefs, and physical and emotional disabilities (unless job related) are not considered appropriate and may be illegal for many jobs. If you are asked questions on these matters, you may wish to respond simply: "I prefer not to answer that question." You can, of course, answer such a question if you wish. You might also respond with a question such as "Why do you ask?" This response may cause the interviewer to explain the work-related issue that prompted the question.

Prepare Questions

Interviewers sometimes ask: "Do you have any questions about the company or the position?" While you are preparing for the interview, you may want to list any questions that come to mind. Some would naturally pertain to the job for which you are applying: "How much orientation is provided for the job?" "How often are employees evaluated?" "Are there promotional opportunities for which employees may apply?" "Has the company established benchmarks for the tasks related to the job in which I am interested?"

Other questions cover a broad range of subjects, such as the company's mission statement, product lines, and employee benefits. Do not make salary and benefits the main focus of your questions. Ask questions that will help the interviewer focus on the contributions you can make to the company.

Arrive on Time

Arrive at the interview shortly before the scheduled time so that you can be calm and collected when you are called into the interviewer's office. If you are not familiar with the location of the interview, you may want to visit the site in advance, noting how much time you should allow to arrive on schedule. Consider the traffic conditions or possible delays that are likely during the time of day you will be traveling to the interview. Once you arrive, use a visitor parking space in the company parking lot if available. You may need to give your name and the purpose of your visit to a security guard to be admitted to the parking lot or building. Parking lots and garages in downtown or other business areas are often crowded during business hours. Allow ample time to find a parking space and walk to the company location if necessary.

Complete an Application Form

A receptionist may greet you and ask you to fill out an **employment application** form. Complete the form carefully in neat, legible handwriting. Glance over the entire application to see what information is requested in each section before you begin writing. Read each question carefully and completely before answering.

employment application: form that provides information about a job applicant

Note every item included and do not leave blanks on an application. You should indicate with a N/A ("not applicable") any item that does not apply to you such as military service, for example. The interviewer then knows that you have read the question. Take a copy of your resume with you as a source for details as you complete the application. Often the interviewer will read the application form before turning to your resume.

Participate Attentively

A common procedure is for the receptionist to introduce you to the interviewer. You should extend your hand for a firm handshake and look directly at the interviewer in a friendly, calm manner.

Being a little nervous at a job interview is natural, especially at your first interview. Instead of dwelling on your uneasiness, concentrate on what the interviewer asks and tells you. Remember that the interview is a two-way communication process. The interviewer is learning about you, and you are learning about the job and the company.

When you attend an interview, do the following:
- Dress appropriately.
- Greet the interviewer with a smile and a firm handshake.
- Remain standing until you are asked to have a seat.
- Use good posture when sitting or standing.
- Listen attentively and answer questions honestly and clearly.
- Use correct grammar.
- Exhibit a positive attitude.
- Ask questions about the company and its products or services.
- Make eye contact with the interviewer frequently.

When you attend an interview, do not do the following:
- Bring a friend or relative with you.
- Display nervousness by tapping a pencil, twirling your hair, or other annoying habits.
- Use poor posture or chew gum.
- Answer questions with "yeah," "nope," or "uh-huh."
- Misrepresent your strengths or accomplishments.
- Criticize past employers or teachers.
- Ask questions only about salary and benefits.
- Stand at the door after the interview is over and continue to talk.

Figure 13-1.8

Greet the interviewer with a smile and a firm hand-shake.

© EYEWIRE COLLECTION

The interviewer will write an evaluation of the interview in which judgments are recorded about key factors such as:

- Appearance
- Voice and language usage
- Knowledge and skills
- Effectiveness in working with others
- Attitude toward work and learning
- Self-confidence
- Flexibility
- Job interest

Follow Up

Review the interview in your mind and jot down notes to yourself about its good points and its weak points. Think of questions that you do not believe you answered well, or that you failed to understand. Review this information later before your next interview.

Write a brief follow-up letter in which you thank the interviewer for talking with you. Indicate again your interest in the job and how you believe your qualifications fit the position. A follow-up letter is perceived favorably as proof of your willingness to follow through after a meeting. If the interviewer does not communicate with you within the time period mentioned at the interview, you should call and express your continued interest in the position.

If you receive a job offer and decide to take the job, you should accept in writing. If you have determined that you are not interested in the job, you should write a brief letter stating your decision and expressing thanks for the offer.

Documenting Your Job Search

A job search may be completed in a relatively short time if there are many opportunities in your field of interest in the community where you seek employment. Job searches sometimes require a considerable amount of time, however, and you may have to make changes in your strategy and in your job expectations before you find a job.

Keeping a complete record of what you do and the outcome of each effort is a valuable practice during a job search. Maintain a **job search diary** of your activity, indicating clearly the date, time, name of the company, and complete names of all persons with whom you talked. Indicate in your diary the communication you receive after each interaction with someone related to getting a job. This information will be helpful if you are called for a second interview or interview for another job with the same company at a later time.

job search diary: document that lists activities and contacts related to looking for employment

Job Title:	Order Entry Clerk
Company Name:	MBA Manufacturing
Address:	P.O. Box 235
	Somerset, KY 42501
Phone:	(606) 555-0127
Contact Person:	Robin McCrae, Office Manager

Date	Contact	Comments
6/2	Mailed letter and resume	See attached job ad and copies of letter and resume
6/15	Phone message from Robin McCrae	
6/16	Returned phone call	Interview scheduled for 6/20 at 9 a.m. at company offices in Governor's Hill Office Park
6/20	Interview	Interview went well. Training provided for order entry system. Flexible hours. Expect to hear from Robin within two weeks.
6/21	Sent follow-up letter	Expressed continued interest. See attached copy of letter.

Figure 13-1.9

A job search diary

Reviewing the Topic

1. How might thinking ahead to a career goal help an individual think about a first full-time job?
2. Why is career planning unlikely to be a once-in-a-lifetime task?
3. Identify some questions that a person with a career goal is likely to be able to answer.
4. What are some attitudes employers will find appealing when considering applicants who have not yet established career goals?
5. Where can you learn of job opportunities?
6. What information should an interviewer see on your resume?
7. What is the purpose of a letter of application?
8. Describe appropriate planning for a job interview.
9. What are some factors that an interviewer will probably evaluate about an interviewee?
10. What content should be included in a follow-up letter written after an interview?

Thinking Critically

1. Assume that you are ready to begin full-time employment. Identify the type of job you will seek. Choose a job you are qualified for. Describe these factors related to the job:
   - Typical titles for this job
   - Typical tasks or activities associated with this job
   - Typical wages or salary for this job in your area
   - Education, skills, and experience required for the job
2. Describe how your education, skills, or experience qualify you for this job. Describe an experience that shows your ability to work successfully in a team.
3. Open the data file **Application.pdf**, which contains a sample job application. Complete the form assuming you are applying for the job identified in step 1.

4. Prepare written responses for the sample interview questions below.

a) Tell me about yourself.

b) What is your greatest strength? weakness?

c) Where you do want to be in your career five years from now?

d) What is your greatest accomplishment?

e) Why should I hire you rather than another applicant with comparable skills?

f) How would your current employer or teacher describe your job performance and attitude?

Reinforcing Math Skills

You have been offered two jobs—one as an appliance salesperson and one as an office assistant. Use your math skills to help you evaluate the jobs and make a decision about which one to accept.

1. Read the information about each job below. What can you expect your gross pay less the deduction for health insurance coverage to be per year for each job?

2. Which job would you choose and why? Consider your job interests and the locations of the jobs in addition to salary and health insurance costs.

Sales Position in an Appliance Store

Your base salary will be $960 per pay period (one month). You will also receive a 5 percent commission on the price of items you sell during the pay period. The store manager says you can expect to sell around $4,000 in merchandise in an average month. This amount can vary widely, however, and will depend on your selling skills. The deduction from your paycheck for health insurance will be $125 per pay period. The job is close to your home, and you can ride the public bus to work.

Office Assistant

As an office assistant, you will work 80 hours per pay period (two weeks) and receive $8 per hour. Your deduction for health insurance will be $50 per pay period. The company is located 20 miles from your home and is not accessible by bus.

Topic 13-1   ACTIVITY 1

Application Letter and Resume

In this activity, you will prepare a letter of application for a job and a resume.

1. Identify a job for which you are qualified. Identify at least one organization where a position is open for the job you have chosen or there is some possibility that such a job might become available.

2. Prepare a letter of application to an organization where the job you seek exists. If a job opening currently exists, apply for that particular job. If not, express your interest in working for the company in the position you have chosen. Ask to be considered when an opening becomes available.

3. Prepare a resume to include with your letter. See Figure 13-1.6 on page 535 for an example resume. Include complete information for three references on a separate page attached to the resume.

Topic 13-1   ACTIVITY 2

Follow-up Letter and Job Search Diary

Writing a follow-up letter after an interview and preparing a job search diary are important steps in a job search. Practice these skills in this activity.

1. Assume that you have completed an interview for a job. You may use the job you chose in Topic 13-1 Activity 1 or a different job. Write a follow-up letter to thank the interviewer and to express your continued interest in the job.

2. Begin documenting your job search. Create a table similar to the one shown in Figure 13-1.9 on page 543. Record information related to this job and the one from the previous activity if a different job was used.

The First Job and Beyond

OBJECTIVES

- Describe typical ways organizations provide orientation for new employees
- Explain the responsibility for self-evaluation of performance
- Identify resources for continuous improvement of an employee's knowledge and skills
- Explain effective ways of facing job changes

When you begin a new job, you will have a great deal to learn about the company and how it operates. As you think ahead about your first full-time job, you may have questions such as the following:

- What will they expect me to be able to do immediately?
- Will I be able to learn everything I should know about this job?
- Will my coworkers be willing to help me?

Employers expect to provide new employees with an introduction to the company and to new jobs. Company leaders realize that employees who understand their jobs and the total company are likely to enjoy their work and contribute a great deal to the goals established by its leaders. In some instances, the introduction is provided in a formal, organized manner. In other instances, the introduction is done informally by the employee's supervisor or manager.

Introduction to a New Job

Initial introduction to a new company and job is called **orientation**. Orientation programs may be formal or informal. Formal orientation programs are scheduled for a particular time and include a series of presentations or meetings. Formal orientation programs are common in large organizations, where a number of new employees may begin their jobs at the same time.

orientation: introduction

WORKPLACE **CONNECTIONS**

A large bank in downtown Charlotte, North Carolina, provided an all-day orientation on the first day of employment for 25 new employees. At the morning sessions, new employees learned about the company's mission and the activities of the total organization. After lunch, the 25 new employees had small group meetings with managers in the departments where they would be working.

Informal orientation programs are common in smaller organizations where fewer employees are likely to begin their new jobs at the same time. Generally, an informal program is directed by the new employee's immediate supervisor or by an experienced coworker, who often has a checklist to guide the explanations during the orientation. Some of these topics and activities are likely to be included:

W-4 form: document that provides information needed by an employer to withhold the correct federal tax from an employee's pay

I-9 form: document that an employer must keep on file to show verification of employment eligibility and list identity documents presented by the employee

- Goals and policies of the organization
- The company's organization chart and key personnel
- Employment forms such as a **W-4 form** and an **I-9 form**
- Employee benefits provided
- Completion of forms related to benefits such as health care or retirement plans
- Company policies related to ethics, safety, and security
- Personnel policies, including performance evaluations
- Policies and procedures that guide the new employee's responsibilities

Orientation does not always end with the program offered on the initial day or days of work. Sometimes additional orientation meetings are scheduled after employees have had several weeks of experience in their new positions.

Learning on the Job

As a new employee, realize that your supervisor is aware that you do not know everything that the job may require. Learning on the job is expected and is considered a normal part of your total orientation. Some of the learning is guided by an experienced person, and some is done on your own.

As a new worker, you can expect to be given specific information about the tasks for which you will have responsibility. The company may have a clearly stated job description of what you are to do, or you may be in a newly created

---

------- Cut here and give Form W-4 to your employer. Keep the top part for your records. -------

Form **W-4** Department of the Treasury Internal Revenue Service	**Employee's Withholding Allowance Certificate** ▶ For Privacy Act and Paperwork Reduction Act Notice, see page 2.	OMB No. 1545-0010 **2001**

1 Type or print your first name and middle initial Last name	2 Your social security number
Jeffrey C. |Hunter*	321 : 22 : 4697

Home address (number and street or rural route) *45 Newland Place*	3 ☐ Single ☑ Married ☐ Married, but withhold at higher Single rate. **Note:** If married, but legally separated, or spouse is a nonresident alien, check the Single box.
City or town, state, and ZIP code *Matawan, NJ 07747-6321*	4 If your last name differs from that on your social security card, check here. You must call 1-800-772-1213 for a new card. ▶ ☐

5 Total number of allowances you are claiming (from line **H** above **or** from the applicable worksheet on page 2) — **5** *1*

6 Additional amount, if any, you want withheld from each paycheck . . . . **6** $ —

7 I claim exemption from withholding for 2001, and I certify that I meet **both** of the following conditions for exemption:
- Last year I had a right to a refund of **all** Federal income tax withheld because I had **no** tax liability **and**
- This year I expect a refund of **all** Federal income tax withheld because I expect to have **no** tax liability.

If you meet both conditions, write "Exempt" here . . . . ▶ **7**

Under penalties of perjury, I certify that I am entitled to the number of withholding allowances claimed on this certificate, or I am entitled to claim exempt status.

Employee's signature
(Form is not valid unless you sign it.) ▶ *Jeffrey C. Hunter* Date ▶ *July 5, 20--*

8 Employer's name and address (Employer: Complete lines 8 and 10 only if sending to the IRS.)	9 Office code (optional)	10 Employer identification number

Cat. No. 10220Q

Figure 13-2.1

Form W-4 documents tax withholding information.

V anessa was hired as an assistant to the director of a new laboratory in a growing biotechnology company. Her background in sciences and her work as a lab assistant while in college were considered appropriate background for a person filling a position not yet fully defined. Vanessa likes having an unstructured job. As she said, "I have to be alert to see where I can be helpful; that's a challenge I'll enjoy."

position. In the latter case, just a general description of your duties may exist. An employee's actual work responsibilities may differ from the job description because the job has changed but the description has not yet been updated.

A new employee will generally find coworkers who are generous in helping the new worker understand what is being done. They understand that a knowledgeable coworker is going to be a valuable asset to the unit or department. You will quickly realize which of your coworkers are most likely to respond positively to questions you might have.

References and Resources

During your orientation, you will become acquainted with basic references available to you. Some of these may be accessed using your computer, while some may be in print:

- A company manual or **employee handbook** of policies and procedures
- A complete organization chart
- A calendar of events and a company newsletter
- An annual report, if the company is publicly owned
- A directory of all personnel with phone numbers and possibly e-mail addresses

employee handbook: printed or online manual containing company policies and procedures

Companies have developed a wide range of materials to aid employees. You will want to learn what company databases and network or intranet resources are available for your use. If your company has a library or resource center, spend some time, possibly during lunch time, getting acquainted with the range of information that you can access. Your department may subscribe to magazines, newspapers, or databases that are useful to you in your job.

Evaluation of Employee Performance

Many organizations have a plan for evaluating employee performance and discussing the results with the employee at least once a year. An organization may have several reasons for conducting performance evaluations, also called **performance reviews** or appraisals. Information from performance reviews may be used in determining pay increases, promotions, employee disciplinary actions, or dismissals. Evaluations help identify employee strengths and areas for improvement. Setting goals for the employee to accomplish in the coming evaluation period and beyond is often a part of the evaluation process.

performance review: evaluation of an employee's work

Figure 13-2.2

Some companies provide an employee handbook on the company intranet.

Employee Handbook

This Employee Handbook is an outline of your privileges and obligations as an employee and should be your primary reference. When you have questions about policies or procedures outlined in this manual, refer them to your manager or contact the Human Resources Department. Choose a link to learn more about the company's policies and procedures.

- Attendance
- At-Will Employment
- Company Overview and Mission
- Compensation and Employee Benefits
- Confidentiality Policy
- Drug and Alcohol Policy

Although a formal evaluation may be completed only once a year, effective managers provide feedback about employee performance, both good and bad, throughout the year. In a work situation where managers and employees communicate regularly and effectively about job performance, the performance review will bring no big surprises for the employee.

Companies expect workers to be competent and perform their jobs satisfactorily. Some factors commonly considered in employee evaluations include:

- Job knowledge and skills
- Quality of performance
- Quantity of work completed
- Initiative and judgment
- Cooperation and teamwork
- Flexibility and adaptability
- Adherence to schedules and deadlines
- Accomplishment of goals set previously

New workers are given a period of time for learning their jobs. The trial or probation period typically lasts three to six months. The length of the trial period is determined by the complexity of the job and the level of skills possessed by the employee. Employees often receive their first formal evaluation at the end of the probation period. Future evaluations follow the company's normal evaluation schedule.

Ways of Evaluating Employees

Companies use varying methods for evaluating workers. In some companies, evaluation practices may be informal, and little, if any, information may be recorded in the personnel file of the employee. In such companies, the manager is usually responsible for writing a performance appraisal

Forced Distribution Scoring Method

Figure 13-2.3

Excellent	10 percent of employees
Good	20 percent of employees
Satisfactory	40 percent of employees
Poor	20 percent of employees
Unacceptable	10 percent of employees

of each employee at designated times. Generally, the employee signs the appraisal to indicate that it was read and may add comments to the appraisal document.

Other companies use clearly stated employee evaluation procedures with carefully developed appraisal forms. In a traditional approach, employees are evaluated by a manager or supervisor. In a multiple-evaluator approach, a manager, coworkers, and the employee may all contribute to the evaluation. This approach, also called a 360-degree evaluation, is becoming more popular because some people think getting feedback from several people in different positions (the employee's circle of contacts) gives a better picture of an employee's overall performance.

Performance evaluations are rated or scored in a variety of ways. Using a checklist, where skills and characteristics are listed and points are awarded for each area, is a popular evaluation method. Using this method, the employee's performance is compared to reasonable standards. Ideally, all employees in a unit or department could receive high scores using this method. Ranking employees in a unit or department from highest to lowest is an evaluation method used by some companies. Using this method, the evaluator compares employees to one another, and all employees cannot receive high scores. With a forced distribution method, employees are assigned scores that fall into preselected categories. For example, the evaluation procedures might state that a certain percent of employees will receive scores that fall in a particular category as shown in Figure 13-2.3. As with the ranking method, all employees cannot receive acceptable scores with this method.

Whatever the scoring method used for a formal evaluation, employee performance is usually compared to standards that have been established for acceptable performance. For example, standards based on keystrokes, lines, or pages may be the basis for determining the productivity of an employee doing word processing. Often, standards are specified per hour or per day. Devices that keep track of such factors as keystrokes and lines may allow for detailed monitoring of output of many employees, especially those who work in factories and in offices where there are repetitive tasks. Standards for some evaluation categories, such as teamwork or responsibility, may be more subjective. Manager or coworker observations of employee behavior may be used to judge performance for these categories.

A major insurance company interested in increasing productivity of all employees began a study of key tasks. As a part of this project, the work of employees in the largest departments was measured so that performance standards could be determined. With the standards established, the company introduced training courses to aid employees in achieving the new standards, called **benchmarks**.

benchmarks: standards for comparison

Professional Development Resources

- "Don't Forget to Say Thank You" (After a job interview). *Career World.* September, 2000.

- Bill Leonard. "The Early Bird Gets the Job Interview." *HR Magazine.* January, 2001.

- Tom Bonigut. "Getting That Resume on the Internet." *Los Angeles Business Journal.* August 21, 2000.

- Gail Dutton. "Making Reviews More Efficient and Fair." *Workforce.* April, 2001.

- Search terms:
    interview tips
    resume writing
    electronic resume
    job board
    performance review
    employee evaluation
    job promotion

Evaluating Your Own Performance

To progress in your job, you will want to ask yourself: "How well am I doing my job?" Such an evaluation might be scheduled to be completed approximately a month before the evaluation by your manager. The following steps should be helpful in your evaluation.

1. List the competencies, tasks, and goals that relate to your position. For this step, a copy of the performance appraisal form used or your job description will be useful.

2. Think carefully about your work behavior, either daily for one week or one day each week for four or five weeks.

3. Record any instances of exceptionally effective or disappointing performance, indicating the date of each entry.

4. Assess what you have written at the end of your review period, noting especially instances of disappointing performance. Consider what you might change to improve your performance.

5. Compare your own evaluation with the one given you by your manager or supervisor. Reconsider your own evaluation in relation to that given by your manager or supervisor and make appropriate changes in how you assess yourself.

Continuous Improvement

You may realize that a plan for self-evaluation and the performance evaluation made by your manager are closely related to the concept of continuous improvement. The evaluations, if followed up in a thoughtful, realistic manner, should help you be more productive and may lead to promotional opportunities. Consider these points as you strive for continuous improvement in your job.

- Simplify; eliminate needless steps in doing tasks.

- Follow an organized approach to completing each task. Do not think of "getting organized" as a separate activity.

- Consider the overall **scope** of a new project and set realistic estimates of the time and work required to meet deadlines.

- Think critically about the information you receive in various forms such as reports, letters, and e-mail messages. Keep what has value and discard that which does not.

- Document steps or other information related to tasks and activities such as meetings or projects for later reference.

- Prioritize tasks and complete them in order of importance, keeping deadlines in mind.

scope: range or extent of an activity or concept

WORKPLACE **CONNECTIONS**

Tonya, an administrative assistant, commented about her program of continuous improvement:

Instead of simply performing my normal tasks as I have always done them, I am now carefully thinking about how I do my work. What a revelation! For example, I never realized why my desk, which is clean at the beginning of each day, becomes a mess by midday. By observing my behavior, however, I know exactly what causes this problem—my failure to return material to its proper place when I no longer need it. I am now making an effort to modify my behavior so I can be more productive.

© EYEWIRE COLLECTON

Figure 13-2.4

Evaluate documents you receive carefully to determine which ones to save.

Promotional Possibilities

promotion: advancement in rank, grade, or position

Although you may be content with your present job, remember to consider the future. While focusing primarily on your current job, also consider what you can do to prepare for future jobs, some of which may be **promotions**.

Your knowledge of your organization's structure will help you understand the promotional opportunities that may be available in your company. The job openings listed by your company internally, in local newspapers, or on the company Web site may provide information about higher-level jobs. You will also deal with people at varying levels of the company and learn, in informal ways, what qualifications are required for various jobs. Your observations of what higher-level positions require can help you determine if you wish to strive for such positions.

Beginning workers may find limited opportunities to move into jobs at higher levels or with broader responsibilities within their organizations. If you find yourself in such a situation, you may need to look elsewhere for opportunities to move to higher-level jobs. Do some investigation of what types of positions relate to your interests and build on the experience you have begun to accumulate. Learn the educational and experience requirements for the jobs in which you are interested. Then you can create a plan for acquiring the education, skills, and work experience you need for the job you want. Professional and trade organizations and their publications can help you build your qualifications for jobs in your career area. Programs offered by local schools, colleges, or community organizations can also help you improve your job skills.

Professional and Trade Associations

People with common work interests often belong to associations that provide programs and activities that may enhance their work skills and knowledge. Thousands of professional organizations related to the various kinds of work provide training and information related to careers. Internet resources and local libraries will help you become acquainted with those available.

Figure 13-2.5

Review your company's job openings to learn about promotional possibilities.

Human Resources

Current Job Openings

Choose a department below to view current job openings for that department.

Corporate Communications
Finance & Accounting
Legal Services
Human Resources
Information Technology
Manufacturing, Warehousing, & Shipping
Marketing, Sales, & Support

Figure 13-2.6

The International Association of Administrative Professionals (IAAP) is the world's largest association for administrative support staff, with nearly 700 chapters and 40,000 members and affiliates worldwide. For over 59 years, we have provided up-to-date research on office trends, cutting-edge publications, outstanding seminars and conferences, and top-notch resources to help administrative professionals enhance their skills and become more effective contributors to their employers.

Source: International Association of Administrative Professionals. Online. Available: http://www.iaap-hq.org/. February 22, 2002.

Your company's human resources department may have information about organizations that you may wish to join.

The organization in which you work may subscribe to magazines and newspapers related to the organization's business. Check the resources of your local libraries and search the Web to become acquainted with what is available in print and electronic format.

Educational Resources

Think about skills you would like to acquire or improve to become a more effective worker, such as using new software programs, more effective public speaking, handling meetings, or problem solving. You can probably find educational resources to help you develop these skills. Consider local educational programs offered by a local public school system through adult education or by a local college or university. Many courses are also offered via the Internet.

Changing Jobs

A typical worker changes jobs several times during his or her career. A job change may be the worker's choice, or it may be caused by events beyond the worker's control. Organizations sometimes change their structures as they strive to grow and accomplish their goals. Companies are bought and sold, merged with other companies, relocated to other geographic areas, or **downsized**. A company may also fail or go out of business. Changes in organizations may mean that workers are promoted or transferred to different jobs, asked to move to another city, laid off temporarily, or dismissed from their jobs.

downsize: reduce, as in decreasing the number of workers in an organization

Job Termination

Being dismissed from a job can be an emotionally upsetting and stressful experience, even when you are dismissed through no fault of your own. You may have some prior warning that the dismissal may happen, or you may have no warning at all. Try to remain calm and professional during the **job termination** process.

job termination: ending of employment

Topic 13-2: *The First Job and Beyond*

termination meeting: meeting to discuss termination reasons, status of benefits, or other issues related to ending employment; also called an exit interview

Depending on the size and policies of the company, dismissal procedures may vary widely. Typically, you will be given a written notice or letter stating that you are dismissed from the company's employ and the reason for the dismissal. You may be asked to attend a **termination meeting** with your supervisor or someone from the human resources department. In this meeting, the reasons for your dismissal and the status of any continuing benefits will be discussed. You should receive a final paycheck as well as pay for items such as unused vacation or sick days on or shortly after your dismissal. You will be expected to return items such as company keys, credit cards, security badges, or access cards. Your manager or a coworker may escort you to your desk or work area to collect personal items and then out of the building. If the company's dismissal procedures are less formal, you may be allowed to leave on your own and take time to say good-bye to coworkers.

If your job is terminated, remember that while one company no longer needs your services, others are likely to. You may wish to ask your supervisor to give you a letter of recommendation or allow you to list him or her as a reference when you look for a new job. When employees' jobs are terminated for reasons such as downsizing or a move to a new location, the company may provide assistance in helping workers find other positions. Some companies use outplacement services, which are organizations that provide counseling and other services to aid displaced employees in finding new jobs.

severance pay: payment made to an employee being dismissed from a company

Companies typically provide **severance pay** to workers whose jobs are terminated through no fault of the employees. One or two weeks pay for each year a worker has been employed at the company is a typical severance payment. Workers who are dismissed because of poor job performance or a serious violation of company policies, such as theft or harming or threatening a coworker, usually do not receive severance pay.

Job termination will not always be the company's decision. You may decide to terminate your employment at a company for a variety of reasons. You might move to a different city, complete training or education that qualifies you for a higher-level job, or find better pay or more opportunity for

Figure 13-2.7

The reason for dismissal is discussed at a job termination meeting.

© IMAGE 100/ROYALTY-FREE/CORBIS

CHAPTER 13: PLANNING AND ADVANCING YOUR CAREER

advancement at a different company. Although you will want to take advantage of good opportunities, be aware that a record of changing jobs too often (sometimes called job hopping) may make a negative impression on prospective employers. As a general rule, plan to stay in any full-time job you accept for at least one year. If you have changed jobs frequently, have an explanation for the frequent changes prepared to discuss in interviews.

When possible, give the company at least two weeks' notice when quitting a job. Always submit a formal **resignation letter**. The letter should be written to your immediate supervisor and should use a polite, professional tone. Keep the letter short and simple. In the first paragraph, ask your manager to accept your resignation from your job (state the job title) as of a particular date. Indicate that you are willing to do whatever you can to organize material or document procedures to help another worker assume your duties. In the second paragraph, thank the manager for the opportunity to work for the company and wish the company continued success. You need not give a reason for your resignation.

resignation letter: letter stating intention to end employment as of a certain date

Depending on the size and policies of the company, the dismissal procedures when you quit a job will probably be similar to those discussed earlier. You would typically have your termination meeting, also called an exit interview, on your last day of work.

When you leave a company's employ, you may retain some of the benefits of having worked for the company. For example, if you were employed by the company for several years and **vested** in the company's pension plan, you may draw benefits from the pension on retirement even though you are no longer employed by the company. Retaining health insurance coverage when changing jobs is a serious concern for many workers. COBRA (Consolidated Omnibus Budget Reconciliation Act) is a law that gives employees the right to elect to continue health insurance coverage for a minimum of 18 months after leaving the company if covered before job termination. Although you must pay the cost of the insurance coverage, this cost will be at the company's group rate, which is usually lower than the cost you would pay for purchasing insurance individually.

vested: having fixed rights or participation in something, as in a pension plan

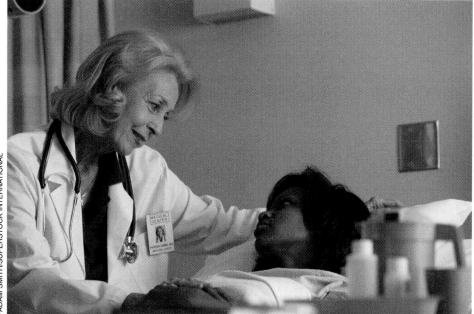

Figure 13-2.8

COBRA makes keeping health insurance coverage easier when changing jobs.

Job Portfolio

To be prepared to consider other jobs when it seems appropriate or is necessary, you should maintain a **job portfolio** or career portfolio file. Keep items such as the following in your job portfolio:

job portfolio: file containing documents and information related to employment

- Copies of your resume in hard copy and electronic formats
- Sample letters of application and thank-you letters
- Your job search diary that includes job search activities and contact persons
- Copies of any awards or honors you have received
- Letters, notes, and other items related to your work
- Programs and newsletters that report your participation in school or community activities
- School transcript of courses completed
- Diplomas and certificates of completion of courses
- A detailed work history (job descriptions, evaluations, and related information about earlier full-time positions and about your current position)

As you begin full-time employment or pursue further education, continue to broaden your awareness of the career possibilities. Consider your potential as a contributor in the workplace and view career opportunities with confidence and optimism.

1. Why is orientation provided for new employees?
2. What general references will aid a new employee in learning about the company?
3. List five of the factors generally considered in an employee evaluation.
4. Describe the steps employees might follow in evaluating their own performance.
5. How can an employee learn about promotional opportunities in the company?
6. What types of changes in an organization may lead to a worker changing jobs?
7. What topics are usually discussed at an exit interview?
8. What services are provided by out placement firms?
9. What is a typical amount for a severance payment?
10. What is job hopping, and what impression may it give a prospective employer?
11. What does COBRA provide employees?
12. What types of information or documents should be included in a job or career portfolio?

Making Decisions

Nancy and Ellie both accepted full-time jobs in a local company where they had worked during the summers for the last two years. They received information about when they should report for their first day of work and about the first day's schedule of orientation sessions. Nancy called Ellie and said, "Ellie, did you see the schedule for orientation on Monday, our first day at work? Don't you think we can skip most of the day? I'd say we should plan to arrive at three o'clock when we will learn from our managers what exactly they want us to do on our jobs. Why should we waste our time hearing about things we already know? What do you think?"

1. What types of important information are likely to be presented at the orientation session?
2. What impression will the employer have of Nancy and Ellie if they do not attend the orientation session?
3. The orientation is being held during regular working hours. Do Nancy and Ellie have a right to decide not to attend this work activity? What might be the result of not reporting for work?

Thinking Critically

When you begin a job, you will be asked to complete employment-related forms. Critical thinking will be required as you make decisions about issues related to federal tax withholding allowances.

1. Open and print the data file **W4 Form.pdf**, which contains an Employee's Withholding Allowance Certificate, commonly called a W-4 Form. (This form is current for 2001. Your instructor may give you a form for the current year or instruct you to download a current form from the Internal Revenue Service Web site at www.irs.gov.)

2. Assume that you are single and have no children or other dependents. Read the instructions on the form and complete the Personal Allowance Worksheet section of the form. Then complete the Employee's Withholding Allowance Certificate portion of the form, which you would give to your employer for use in withholding federal taxes from your pay. See Figure 13-2.1 on page 548 for a sample of a completed certificate.

3. Read the Privacy and Paperwork Reduction Notice on the second page of the form. What will failure to provide a properly completed form result in?

COMPOSITION

WORD PROCESSING

Topic 13-2 ACTIVITY 1

Letter of Resignation

You have worked for Hinkle Trucking as an administrative assistant for four years. You have accepted a new job, and you must resign from your current position.

1. Write a letter of resignation to your manager, Mr. Juan Alverez. Use the current date for your letter and make the date of your resignation two weeks from today. The company address is 24 Motor Way, Ferguson, KY 42502-0024.

2. Because this is a personal business letter, print the letter on plain paper. Include your return address on the two lines above the letter date. Assume your address is 34 Apple Street, Ferguson, KY 42502-8834. Format the letter in block style with open punctuation.

3. Review your letter for the five Cs of effective correspondence. Remember to use the *you* approach. Proofread carefully and correct all errors.

Topic 13-2   ACTIVITY 2

Research Resources for Training or Education

When you enter the workforce, you may not have the skills or education needed for the job you have chosen as your career goal. In many careers, a worker may hold an entry-level job while gaining further education or experience to prepare for a higher-level job. In this activity, you will research resources available for career training and education.

1. Identify a job in a career area that interests you, but for which you are not currently qualified.

2. List the qualifications for this job. You may find the required skills, education, and work experience for the job by reading job advertisements or job descriptions found in newspapers, on job boards, or in job postings on company Web sites. The *Occupational Outlook Handbook*, available online at the Bureau of Labor Statistics Web site (www.bls.gov), gives information about training, other qualifications, and advancement for many job titles.

3. Identify resources for the education or skills needed for this job. Consider colleges, universities, vocational/technical schools, adult education programs, professional associations, and private training companies. Many schools have Web sites that provide a list of courses available. Remember that many colleges offer courses via the Internet, so do not limit the resources to those available in your local area. List each school or organization you identify and the program or course available that relates to this job.

Summary

Conducting an effective job search is critical in securing a job that matches your interests and skills. Proper orientation to a new job and continuous efforts to improve your performance can aid in your success and lead to opportunities for promotion. Realistic self-evaluation and planning to secure needed education, training, and experience are important in carrying through your long-term career strategy. The following points related to these concepts were highlighted in the chapter.

- A career strategy is thinking ahead to a career goal and considering your first job in relation to that goal.

- Even if you do not yet know what career you wish to choose, you can still enter the workplace and perform successfully at a first job.

- A number of sources are available that may help you locate jobs. These sources include friends, relatives, former employers, school placement and counseling services, sites on the World Wide Web, newspapers, employment agencies, and government job announcements.

- A carefully prepared resume and a letter of application will aid in communicating your qualifications for a job.

- An interview is a critical step in getting a job. It is your opportunity to convince the interviewer that you have the education, skills, experience, and attitudes to be successful in the job. You may be asked to complete a job application when you arrive for an interview.

- A follow-up letter should be sent after an interview to thank the interviewer and to express continued interest in the job.

- Maintaining a diary of what you do and the outcome of each effort is a valuable practice during a job search. This information will be helpful if you are called for a second interview or interview for another job with the same company at a later time.

- Organizations plan orientation for new employees to introduce them to the company and to the new jobs. Learning on the job is expected and is considered a normal part of your total orientation. Some of the learning is guided by an experienced person, and some is done on your own.

- Many organizations have a plan for evaluating employee performance and discussing the results with the employee. Information from performance reviews may be used in determining pay increases, promotions, employee disciplinary actions, or dismissals and in setting goals for the employee.

- Evaluating your own performance is important to your effectiveness on the job.

- Striving for continuous improvement can help you be more productive in your present position and may lead to promotional opportunities. While focusing primarily on your current job, also consider what you can do to prepare for future jobs, some of which may be promotions.

- Professional and trade associations, colleges, universities, and other educational organizations provide many opportunities for individuals to enhance their work skills and knowledge.

- Job changes, both voluntary and involuntary, are common in today's business world. A job change may be the worker's choice, or it may be caused by events beyond the worker's control.

- Depending on the size and policies of the company, job termination procedures may vary widely. Typically, you will be given a written notice stating that you are dismissed from the company's employ and the reason for the dismissal. You may be asked to attend a termination meeting.

- You may decide to terminate your employment at a company for a variety of reasons. When possible, give the company at least two weeks' notice when quitting a job. Always submit a formal resignation letter.

- To be prepared to consider other jobs when it seems appropriate or is necessary, maintain a job portfolio file. Keep items such as your resume, job search diary, work history, diplomas, and other related information in your job portfolio.

Key Terms

career goals	job board	promotion
career strategy	job description	references
downsize	job portfolio	resignation letter
employee handbook	job scout	resume
employment application	job search diary	severance pay
I-9 form	job termination	termination meeting
intelligent agent	letter of application	W-4 form
interview	orientation	
	performance review	

Changing Jobs Interview

You can learn a great deal from talking with people about their experiences with a job search and beginning a new job. In this activity, you will interview someone who has changed jobs recently.

1. Identify someone who began a new job within the past year, preferably in a field in which you are interested.

2. Interview this person asking the answers questions below. Prepare a written report to summarize your findings. Include the name of the person you interviewed in your report.
   - What is the organization's name, and what is the nature of the organization's business?
   - What is your job title?
   - How did you learn about the job?
   - What were the key questions you were asked during your interview for the job?
   - What did you find appealing about the job offer?
   - Has the job turned out to be what you anticipated it would be?
   - How were you introduced to your job responsibilities? Was any type of training provided?
   - What challenges have you faced in adjusting to the new job?

3. Write a thank-you letter to the person you interviewed. Thank the person for helping you and mention a couple of points from the interview that you found particularly interesting or unexpected. Mail one copy of the letter and give another copy to your instructor.

Role Playing Job Interviews

The interview is a critical step in a job search. In this activity, you will simulate the experiences of being the applicant interviewed and of interviewing someone else.

1. As a class, select four or five different beginning positions for which students will apply. Choose positions based on the job interests and abilities of the class.

2. In teams of two, identify one person to play the interviewer and the other to play the applicant. For the interview, choose one of the positions identified earlier.

3. As the interviewer, develop a list of questions related to this particular job and questions that will reflect attitudes related to responsibility, initiative, creative thinking, and ethics.

4. As the applicant, develop a resume to show your qualifications and interests related to this job. Develop a list of questions you plan to ask the interviewer about the job. Anticipate questions that you expect to be asked during the interview and plan your answers.

5. Conduct (role play) the interview. As the interviewer, complete an evaluation form for the applicant. (Open and print the data file `Interview.pdf`, which contains the evaluation form.) As the applicant, respond to the questions asked as though you were actually participating in a real interview. Review the evaluation completed by the interviewer to learn about areas for improvement.

6. Working in the same team or another as assigned by your instructor, switch roles so that you are now the interviewer if you were the applicant or the applicant if you were the interviewer. Repeat the interview preparation and role playing.

Chapter Review

Working with Others

The workplace is different today from what it was even a decade ago because of new technology, organizational structures, and procedures. However, one aspect remains the same—the way people interact. The personal qualities considered essential for work have not changed. They continue to reflect respect for oneself and others.

In this chapter, you will consider yourself as an individual at work interacting with other workers. You will be introduced to personal qualities critical for success in the workplace. You will learn about common interactions at work and the importance of participating effectively with others.

Personal Qualities at Work

OBJECTIVES

- Describe aspects of personality that are critical for effective performance at work
- Explain the attitudes that contribute to the success of organizations
- Describe expectations related to your appearance and manners at work

To work is to interact with other people. Even those who work at home interact with others. The character of each person in a group influences how effectively the group will work together. In fact, an employee identified as having "good character" is one who has a deep commitment to behaving appropriately.

Employers expect office workers to be reliable, productive, and cooperative. They also expect employees to be independent learners who can determine what new skills or knowledge are needed for success on the job and who can follow through in acquiring those skills or knowledge. This chapter focuses on underlying personal attitudes and behaviors that help employees meet these employer expectations.

In the business world, people are expected to behave in ways that others think are honorable and fair. Even though individuals may be acting on behalf of a company, they have personal responsibility for their actions. Individuals are expected to respect the rights of others. Employees should remember that they influence the nature and quality of their own work environment by their actions.

Your Personality at Work

Each individual is unique. The combination of characteristics that distinguishes one person from another is called **personality**. Your personal characteristics influence how you think, what you say, and how you respond to demands in your daily life. What is remarkable about your personality is that, to a far greater extent than many realize, you have control of who you are and what you believe. This means that you can make changes in your personality.

personality: patterns and qualities of behavior and attitudes of an individual

Character

The basic values and principles that are reflected in the way you live your life are referred to as **character**. Your parents, relatives, friends, or teachers have probably talked with you about issues such as character and **ethics**. This discussion, therefore, is not a new topic for you. You may want to use this opportunity, though, to review or reconsider some basic concepts related to character.

character: reputation, values or principles as shown by behavior

ethics: a system of moral standards or values

At the core of your character is what you believe about **integrity**. Honesty and trustworthiness are synonyms for integrity. Individuals with integrity are valuable at work because they can be trusted to use the resources of the company only for company purposes.

integrity: honesty, sincerity, being of sound moral principle

567

Consider what might happen when a person lacks integrity. An executive, Linda Ostrowski, confessed to embezzling funds. She and a vendor agreed on a scheme to take money from the company. The vendor issued invoices that overbilled the company. Linda processed the invoices as if they were legitimate. Then the vendor shared the money resulting from the overbilling with Linda. In a period of five years, the two had taken $6 million from the company. After the scheme was uncovered, Linda was sentenced to prison time.

Think what would happen in an organization if many people acted dishonestly. Such behavior could bankrupt a company in a short time. Fortunately, most employees are honest and would not steal funds that belong to their companies. In its annual report, one major U. S. company described the importance of integrity as follows:

> **Highest Standards of Integrity:** *We are honest and ethical in all our business dealings, starting with how we treat each other. We keep our promises and admit our mistakes. Our personal conduct ensures that our company's name is always worthy of trust.*

reliability: being dependable or trustworthy

Another critical component of character is **reliability**. Reliability means that you will do what you agreed to do or what you can reasonably be expected to do in your job. You will not ignore your responsibilities or dismiss them as unimportant. Company managers and supervisors cannot constantly watch over employees to see that they perform assigned tasks. Companies depend on the reliability of their employees.

Figure 14-1.1

Companies rely on employees to stay on task, even when unsupervised.

© RYAN MCVAY/PHOTODISC

CHAPTER 14: WORKING WITH OTHERS

Walt and Rick work from midnight to 8 a.m. in a 24-hour photocopying center. A supervisor rarely comes by to check on what they are doing. However, neither would ever think of closing the office for an hour and going off to an all-night diner. As Walt said: "I chose to work this late shift because I love the freedom and independence I have. I would never take my responsibilities lightly. I want my employer to know I can be counted on to complete my work without supervision."

Self-Acceptance

At the core of your personality is your attitude toward yourself. Experts in the field of mental health stress the value of accepting yourself. They have shown that you cannot change your personality without self-acceptance, which requires a realistic and honest view of who you are. To help bring about change in areas of your personality:

- Be honest with yourself. Do not deceive yourself about your behavior and beliefs. Admit your weaknesses and acknowledge your strengths.

- Understand that although you are a unique individual, you also share many of the same wants, needs, and fears of others. Remember that although others may not appear to have the problems you face, they usually have problems of their own.

- Believe in your own worthiness, while respecting the uniqueness of others. Regardless of your failings, you are worthy. Every human being is. Self-acceptance means that you are willing to accept your faults, but still have a feeling of confidence and a sense of security. For example, you are not shattered by constructive criticism.

WORKPLACE **CONNECTIONS**

Kimberly admired a classmate, Susanne, who seemed carefree, yet earned the top grades in her classes. Kimberly was certain that Susanne did not study, but lived an easy life. One afternoon, Kimberly asked Susanne to join her in a game of tennis during the weekend. Kimberly was stunned when Susanne said to her: "I'd love to join you, but I spend most of my weekend studying. Would you ask me again when school ends?" An awareness of how others meet their obligations and how they make choices can help you to understand how much individuals are alike.

Maturity

maturity: being fully developed

Even though people have the potential for growth throughout life, a person in our society is expected to behave in a mature manner by the end of adolescence. Of course, many young people show **maturity** earlier. To be mature, as the dictionary states, is "to have or express the emotional and mental qualities that are considered normal to a socially adjusted adult human being." To be mature means that you see beyond the moment, that you understand the consequences of your choices, consider the rights of others, and make decisions based on such understanding.

You are mature when you are willing to:

- Accept criticism or disappointment tactfully
- Acknowledge that you do not know or understand something
- Admit that you made a mistake
- Learn from your mistakes
- Face your weaknesses and determine how to overcome them
- Be considerate of others
- Demonstrate respect for differences of individuals
- Be objective and honest in your relationships with others
- Value the worth of every person and do not act superior to another person

Figure 14-1.2

A mature person can accept criticism or disappointment tactfully.

© JAVIER PIERINI/PHOTODISC

CHAPTER 14: WORKING WITH OTHERS

Attitudes that Support Quality Performance

The attitudes that support quality performance at work include a strong belief in the work ethic, willingness to participate in achieving the goals of the organization, and a desire to learn. You will want to develop these attitudes to increase your chances for success on the job.

The Work Ethic

As you have learned, high productivity and effective use of resources are common goals of businesses. Productivity depends in part on the **work ethic** of employees. Work ethic is a general term that combines a deep belief in the value of work in one's life and a willingness to meet the demands of work. Persons with a strong work ethic value both **tangible** and **intangible** rewards of work. Tangible rewards, such as pay and benefits, are important to most workers. Persons without a strong work ethic may not place much value on intangible rewards, such as enjoyment of the work performed or pride in a job well done. Persons with a strong work ethic tend to define job satisfaction differently than those without a strong work ethic.

Workers in the United States have long been credited with a strong work ethic. A positive attitude toward work, low absenteeism, willingness to work overtime, and low error rates are just some of the factors that reflect a strong work ethic. Companies looking for new locations want to be assured that potential employees in the area are willing to work hard to meet company goals.

work ethic: a system of values in which purposeful activity is of central importance

tangible: material, having substance to which a value can be attached

intangible: having no substance or material being

Participation and Cooperation

At the heart of cooperativeness is the willingness to participate in what needs to be done to achieve a goal. You may have heard someone say, "We could never have achieved our deadline if everyone hadn't chipped in and helped."

Well-organized companies develop job descriptions for each position in the organization. Given the changing nature of business, however, workers often need to perform tasks not included in their job descriptions. A positive attitude and a willingness to be helpful are critical at such a time.

WORKPLACE **CONNECTIONS**

Sam is a manager in one of the finest jewelry stores in the United States. Managers are not salespersons. Yet, Sam is likely to be assisting customers through much of a very busy shopping day. Furthermore, he pays no attention to the typical end of his working day. He stays on the job through the closing time for the store. He realizes that at a busy time, the most important task is assisting customers.

Learning

Work procedures can change frequently. Some changes may be needed to adapt to new technology. Other changes may be needed to adapt to new management styles or for entry into new markets that requires new products or services be produced. As companies change, supervisors or human resources personnel cannot always determine each employee's learning needs. Companies expect workers to be independent learners. As an office worker, you are expected to show a willingness to learn—a desire to improve your understanding or your skills that relate to your job.

Become aware of new technology and methods that relate to your field by reading industry magazines or newsletters and participating in professional organizations. Bring to your employer's attention opportunities for training that will improve your job performance. The company may be willing to pay the cost of such training or provide similar training for you and other workers.

Impressions Influence Others

Your appearance influences how you are thought of by others. People often form judgments on limited evidence such as a first impression. Appropriate dress and proper personal hygiene are important for making a good impression on others. Annoying habits and speaking in a manner that is not appropriate can create a poor impression.

Dress

If you are dressed appropriately for work, others are likely to think that you are giving proper attention to your job responsibilities. If your appearance is sloppy, others may think that your work is also sloppy and that you are probably not an efficient employee.

Dress considered appropriate for work varies somewhat from company to company. Some companies are specific about what they consider proper attire for work. Others expect new employees to determine appropriate dress

Figure 14-1.3

Your appearance should convey responsibility and good taste.

© EYEWIRE COLLECTION

from noting how the majority of workers dress on a regular basis. If you work in an organization that does not state its dress code, the safest course is to dress attractively in a businesslike manner. You want your appearance to convey responsibility, good taste, and wise judgment.

Annoying Habits

Annoying habits, such as throwing back your head to get your hair out of your eyes or drumming your fingers on a desk, can create a poor impression and have a negative effect on your interactions with coworkers. Over time, some people develop facial expressions that do not express how they feel. For example, an individual may appear to be frowning when frowning has nothing to do with how the person feels. Certain facial expressions seem to happen in an automatic fashion—they have become habits. Coworkers may think that you are unhappy or disagree with what they are saying or doing because of your expression.

Workers often must interact within a relatively small area. Many workers may share an open space, with only limited partitions to define workspaces for individuals. Conversations can be easily overheard in this type of office setting. When you are speaking by telephone or with a coworker, adjust the volume of your voice so that you speak to that person only. Do not speak so loudly that you disrupt or annoy others who are working near you.

Take an inventory of your behavior and identify what you believe might be annoying to others. Ask a trusted friend or coworker to help you identify any habits you have that others may find annoying. Make a decision to eliminate annoying habits and follow through with your decision.

Basic Work Manners

You have been learning about manners since you were a child. You may recall a parent saying to you, "Do not eat while you are talking; keep your elbows off the table" or "Shake hands with Mrs. Norris, who has come for a visit." What you know about good manners will be valuable when you interact with others at work. Only a limited number of points will be discussed here.

Introductions

In a meeting or other business situation, you may introduce individuals when you know both but they do not know each other. When you make an introduction, address the person of higher rank or age first. Then address the person of lower rank or age. For example, when introducing a new administrative assistant to the president of the company say: "Mrs. Carstairs, this is Miss Joy Pablo, our new office assistant. Miss Pablo, this is Mrs. Alma Carstairs, our company president." If the two people are from different companies or organizations, mention the affiliation. Use titles, such as Doctor, Major, or Reverend, if known. For example, say: "Dr. Tomas, this is Mr. Cary House of Ace Medical Supplies. Mr. House, this is Dr. Andy Tomas of Cumberland Area Hospital." When introducing a man and a woman of about the same age and rank, address the woman first. When introducing a customer to any member of your company, show courtesy for the customer by addressing the customer first.

In general, extending your hand to another person when being introduced is considered a gracious gesture. A handshake should be firm, yet not so strong it causes pain. A limp handshake is often considered a sign that someone does not want to interact with others.

Electronic Etiquette

New ways of interacting with people require an extension of the rules of good manners. Use of voice mail, cellular phones, speakerphones, fax

Figure 14-1.4

Introductions should be made in a courteous manner.

© EYEWIRE COLLECTION

CHAPTER 14: WORKING WITH OTHERS

machines, and conference calls all offer opportunities to improve or detract from your relationship with others through the use of good manners.

Voice Mail

The manners that are considered appropriate when talking with someone in person should be extended to leaving a message by voice mail. The caller should be courteous and remember to leave a complete message.

- Speak slowly.
- Keep the message as brief as possible.
- Include your complete name and telephone number.
- Explain why a return call is essential, if that is the case.

Cellular Phones

Cellular phones enable individuals to be "on the job" at all times. However, you should refrain from using your cellular phone during musical programs, lectures, films, in a crowded restaurant, or other areas where your conversation will disrupt activities or annoy others. If you are using a cellular phone at a conference, for example, you should move away from a place where others are conversing in person. Be careful not to discuss confidential business information when talking on your cell phone in a public area.

Speakerphones

When using a speakerphone, be sure the matter being discussed is not confidential if you or the caller is in an area where others can hear the conversation. If you place the call, you should establish that the other person does

Figure 14-1.5

Be careful not to disturb others when talking on a cell phone.

not mind the speakerphone. When using a speakerphone, give your full attention to the caller and do not attempt to do something else at the same time, even though your hands are free.

Fax Machines

In many offices, several individuals share the same fax machine. Reading another person's incoming messages is considered impolite. When you find a message that has not been distributed, you should read only to the point of identifying the recipient.

Conference Calls

Sensitivity to everyone participating in a conference call is critical for the call to proceed without problems. When you begin to speak, identify yourself. If you must step away from the call, do not put your line on hold if doing so will cause background music to play on the line. Good manners require that you not interrupt someone who is speaking.

General Courtesies at Work

Employees are expected to be aware of the responsibilities of their colleagues. Doing so means that you don't cause your coworkers to waste time. Conversations should generally be limited to matters of work during work time. Wait for breaks or lunchtime for personal talk. Employees often face deadlines, so when seeking assistance from a coworker, first inquire if the time is appropriate for an interruption.

monopolize: use or keep to the exclusion of others

Equipment is often shared with coworkers. Employees should not **monopolize** equipment to the point of keeping others from completing tasks. For example, suppose you and a coworker are both waiting to use the copier. You arrived first at the copier and have a large copying job to complete. Your coworker needs to make only two copies. Offer to let your coworker use the copier first so he or she does not waste time waiting for you to complete your job. Be alert to the needs of those around you.

1. What are three characteristics or attitudes employers expect of employees?
2. What is personality? How can you change your personality?
3. What is character?
4. Explain the meaning of integrity and give examples of how integrity relates to office workers.
5. What characteristics indicate that a person is reliable?
6. What are some basic attitudes important to self-acceptance?
7. What does it mean for a person to have a strong work ethic?
8. Why should an employee give attention to his or her appearance?
9. Why should annoying habits at work be eliminated?
10. Describe some general courtesies at work that should be extended to others.

Thinking Critically

You must take a realistic look at your personality before you can determine ways to improve it. In this activity you will describe what you believe reflects your personality.

1. Consider each of the factors listed below assuming that you are now a full-time employee and are making an assessment of yourself for your own benefit.
2. For each of the factors listed below, key a brief description that provides a realistic statement of how you see yourself relative to the factor. Are you satisfied with your personality in each of these areas? If not, what steps can you take to change or improve in this area?
   - Integrity
   - Maturity
   - Reliability
   - Work ethic
   - Self-acceptance
   - Willingness to learn
   - Willingness to participate in achieving goals

Reinforcing Math Skills

Employees in a large department were rated on the factors shown in the following table. The ratings were made on a scale from 1 to 5, with 5 being the best.

1. Compute the average score for each employee.
2. Compute the average score for the total group for each area.
3. Identify the areas where these employees as a group may need some further training.

Employee	Work Ethic	Participation	Willingness to Learn	Appearance	Manners
Abbot, Roy	2	1	3	1	2
Abrams, Peter	4	4	5	2	2
Bryant, Silvia	1	1	1	3	2
Cooper, Rachel	5	4	4	4	5
Cordero, Ana	2	2	2	1	1
Dones, Carole	4	4	4	4	2
Herbik, Sheri	4	3	2	5	5
Kulpa, Rudy	5	5	4	5	5
Merena, Samina	4	5	5	4	5
Nang, Li	5	5	5	4	3
Ramsey, Nilda	3	2	4	1	2

Topic 14-1 ACTIVITY 1

Business Dress Codes

Appropriate dress at work is important for making a good impression and projecting a professional image. The term "business attire" is generally understood to mean a conservative business suit or dress slacks and jacket for men or a conservative business suit or dress for women. The term "business casual attire," however, is not as clearly defined, although many companies use this term to describe appropriate dress for work. In this activity, you will research and write a report on this topic.

1. Use the Internet or other reference sources to find current articles that discuss business casual dress. Read the articles and make notes about the main points discussed. Record complete information for each source: author, title of article, magazine or periodical name, date of publication, and Web site address if the article is found online.

2. Compose a short report describing business casual dress. Give examples of what is and what is not considered business casual dress. Include other information you may find from reading the articles such as when companies allow business casual dress or when they require formal business attire. Discuss the effect that business casual dress has on issues such as employee morale or productivity.

3. Format the report in unbound report style and include a page to list references at the end of the report.

Topic 14-1 ACTIVITY 2

Tangible and Intangible Rewards of Work

Both tangible and intangible rewards of work will contribute to your job satisfaction. Which type of reward is most important to you? Identify and rank tangible and intangible rewards of work in this activity.

1. Create a list of ten or more tangible rewards of work such as salary, stock options, company-paid life insurance, and so on.

2. Create a list of ten intangible rewards of work such as a feeling of pride in work done well, the enjoyment of socializing with coworkers, or a feeling that your work contributes to the well-being of others.

3. Think about a job or career that interests you. Place the name of this job or career at the top of your two lists. Rank the tangible and intangible rewards you have listed in order of their importance to you.

4. Key a paragraph that explains how the job or career you identified in step 3 will allow you to experience the tangible and intangible rewards of work.

- interaction with others at work means
- Describe appropriate responses in handling conflicts at work
- Assess your ability to work with others
- Identify some of the basic laws and regulations that apply to the workplace

Working effectively with others requires an understanding of human behavior. Employees must be willing to participate with people in a cooperative, business-oriented manner. While you are able to choose your friends, you must accept those with whom you work. Employers expect office workers to show respect for others, be willing to listen to others, and be committed to helping meet the goals of the organization.

Interacting with Supervisors

Few people work totally alone or independently. Regardless of the position you hold, you will be reporting to someone. Even key executives report to a board of directors or to owners. In most organizations, employees have someone who supervises and guides their work.

What You Can Expect from Your Supervisor

What you can expect from your supervisor will depend in part on your job position and your rank within the organization. Assuming that you are an office worker who is not in a management position, you will probably report to someone in a middle management position. As you learned in Chapter 1, managers at this level direct the day-to-day activities of the organization.

Managers are responsible for communicating clearly the mission of the organization in relation to the work of the department or a particular job position. Managers provide general directions regarding the priorities of tasks or projects to be completed by the workgroup. In some situations, managers assign tasks or projects to various workers. In other situations, tasks are clearly associated with particular jobs. Informing employees of deadlines and quality standards for work are other tasks of managers.

Managers have varying ways of carrying through their tasks. Some managers have staff meetings frequently. Other managers seldom hold meetings, but instead they send e-mail messages or memos to employees on a regular basis. Some managers carefully plan schedules and projects well in advance and communicate the plans to all staff members. Others make decisions and communicate information on an as-needed basis.

Understanding your supervisor's management style will be helpful to you in meeting his or her expectations. The supervisor's personality, the nature of the work in the department, and the expectations of the person to whom the supervisor reports will all affect his or her management style. Some managers explain clearly how

Professional Development Resources

- Families and Work Institute (A non-profit center for research on the changing workplace, changing family, and changing community)
  Families and Work Institute
  267 Fifth Ave., Floor 2
  New York, NY 10016
  http://www.familiesandwork.org

- Tom Terez. "Things to Do: Learn from LaRue" (Work ethic). *Workforce.* October, 2001.

- Stephen Goode. "Clothes Do Make the Man, After All." *Insight on the News.* July 24, 2000.

- Gerald L. Maatman, Jr. "A Global View of Sexual Harassment." *HR Magazine.* July, 2000.

- Search terms:
    business dress code
    business etiquette
    confidentiality
    conflict resolution
    employment discrimination
    sexual harassment
    work ethic

Figure 14-2.1

© EYEWIRE COLLECTION

they will communicate and what they expect from employees. Others expect employees to determine from observations and comments what the manager expects.

Effective managers want employees to be successful. Everyone wins when employees are skillful and effective. The employee experiences a sense of accomplishment because of a job done properly, and the company is satisfied with the employee's performance.

What Your Manager Expects from You

Managers expect employees to focus on their tasks even though there is no direct, immediate supervision throughout the workday. Increasingly, workers are given authority to make decisions on the basis of general instructions without review by a manager. Managers expect to have work completed on schedule. They expect employees to keep them informed of unexpected work developments or about problems with meeting deadlines.

Managers expect employees to evaluate their own work and take needed steps to ensure a high quality of work. Employees are expected to continue to improve skills and gain knowledge as needed to be proficient in their jobs.

Managers expect employees to be willing to handle unplanned situations. At such times, regular assignments must be set aside to complete tasks that now have higher priority. Managers depend on the flexibility and willingness of staff to respond to new demands in a busy work environment.

Topic 14-2: *Human Relations at Work*

loyal: showing support or commitment

Managers expect employees to be **loyal** to the company and to their work group or department. Being loyal means making a commitment to support the efforts of the company and workgroup. A loyal employee does not make unfavorable remarks about the company or workgroup outside the group or take other actions that may harm the company. For example, several members of a department may have different ideas about plans for a new project. Each employee may offer suggestions and criticisms of the proposed plans. Once the manager or the group has made a decision about how to proceed, however, all members of the team are expected to do their best to make the plan successful.

Managers expect employees to be honest and behave in an ethical manner. Although employees are expected to be loyal to their companies, no employer should expect employees to engage in illegal or immoral behavior. Many companies publish a code of ethics that employees are expected to follow. When you begin a new job, ask if the company has a code of ethics that you are to follow. Become familiar with the rules of the company so that you do not unknowingly break the rules. Some activities that might seem harmless in a personal setting may not be appropriate at work. For example, employees may be forbidden to accept gifts from vendors or others related to work.

Interacting with Coworkers

The extent to which you must work with others will vary. If you are a member of a project team, you may perform many tasks as a group. If you serve as a research assistant, you may spend much time alone following through on the tasks that are your responsibility.

Even though much of your work may be done independently, at times you will need to interact with others. You will interact because you have common needs for information, tasks that overlap, or joint responsibility for some common task.

Figure 14-2.2

A project team performs many tasks as a group.

© ANDREW WAKEFORD/PHOTODISC

Cooperation

Employees in an organization must work together to achieve the goals of the organization. When a colleague from another department telephones, your natural response should be to want to provide the needed help or information (assuming the information is not confidential). When you work as part of a team, do your best to complete your part of the task and to contribute to the success of the team. For suggestions on how to work successfully on a team, refer to Chapter 2, page 52.

WORKPLACE CONNECTIONS

Sandra Hirsh works as a buyer of ingredients for a large candy manufacturing company. She communicates frequently with the company's laboratories where new products are being developed. She attends meetings to learn reactions to the ingredients being used and desired. She believes much of the success of her work depends on the cooperation she gets from the departments for which she buys ingredients.

Confidentiality

You will want to be sure you understand what aspects of your work require absolute **confidentiality**. Revealing confidential information may cause harm to the company or its employees or customers. Information about plans of the business might seem routine, but if the information reaches the company's competitors, the results could be disastrous. In some cases, information is confidential only for a period of time. Later, when decisions are firm, information that was earlier restricted may be widely distributed. For more information on protecting confidential information, refer to Chapter 11, page 449.

confidentiality: keeping private or secret

WORKPLACE CONNECTIONS

Valerie was a staff assistant in the human resources department. In her position, she knew all the candidates for key management positions. She reviewed resumes and assisted the director in making decisions. She knew which candidates were invited to headquarters for interviews. She saw the reports of the executives who interviewed candidates. She understood that all aspects of the recruiting process must be kept in absolute confidence. Valerie made a commitment to herself to never reveal any detail of what was happening. The director was grateful for Valerie's attitude.

Topic 14-2: *Human Relations at Work*

Figure 14-2.3

Gossiping is not appropriate in the workplace.

© ROB LEWINE/CORBIS/STOCK MARKET

Avoiding Gossip

Informal communications are common in an organization. The informal network by which employees communicate in an unofficial manner is sometimes called the "grapevine." All informal communication is not undesirable. Employees are naturally interested in the plans and events that affect the company and its employees.

Unfortunately, rumors and gossip, which are incomplete and/or false statements about individuals or situations, are also often spread by informal communications. Rumors and gossip may be harmful to the company or its employees. Use discretion in your informal communications with others. Avoid discussing company plans or events that you do not know are correct or that may be confidential at the present time. Do not discuss personal issues or affairs of fellow employees.

Accepting Responsibility for Mistakes

People are not perfect; they make mistakes. You may have a firm goal to be sure that the facts you communicate to others are accurate and to use good judgment in making decisions. Even with your best efforts, however, you will still make mistakes.

When you make a mistake, accept responsibility for the error as soon as you realize it was made. Take steps to correct the error immediately so that coworkers will not make decisions or plans based on incorrect information. Explain what led to the error if you think doing so will help resolve the problem. Do not, however, subject your coworkers to a long list of excuses about why you made the mistake. If possible, offer a solution to whatever problem the mistake may have caused when you alert others to the mistake or problem. Learn from your mistakes whenever possible to help avoid making a similar error in the future. Never blame others for your mistakes.

The assistant curator at the County Historical Society, Debra, realized that she had given a staff member the wrong dates for an exhibition. When the staff member called, Debra was very busy completing a report and failed to check the calendar. She merely gave the dates as she recalled them. Later in the day, she realized that she gave the staff member the wrong dates. She called the staff member and confessed: "Marian, I gave you the wrong dates! I am sorry. I hope it isn't too late to give you the correct information."

Facing Conflicts at Work

A **conflict** is a disagreement, quarrel, or controversy. Because human beings are not perfect, those with whom you work will have a variety of weaknesses and problems—just as you do. At times, problems may arise that hurt relations among coworkers. Responsible employees take steps to deal with conflicts in a mature and constructive way. These strategies can be helpful in resolving conflicts at work.

1. **Communicate.** Listen and talk with your coworkers to be sure you all have the same understanding of the situation. Consider everyone's concerns. Sometimes what seems like a problem can be merely a misunderstanding that is easily resolved by communicating openly.

2. **Analyze the situation.** Determine the real or underlying problems that may be leading to the conflict. Try to resolve a conflict at the earliest stage possible so that a small problem does not become a big problem.

3. **Be objective.** Focus on the issue—not the person. Do not let your personal feelings for the people involved stand in the way of resolving the problem.

4. **Look inward.** Objectively examine your role in the situation. Are you contributing to the problem or to a solution? Be willing to admit your mistakes and apologize when your behavior or comments hurt others.

5. **Look for solutions.** Brainstorm with coworkers to find ways to resolve the conflict.

6. **Be diplomatic.** Explain how resolving the conflict is of benefit to others. Be tactful when suggesting possible solutions. Focus on finding a solution rather than on placing blame.

7. **Compromise.** When appropriate, be willing to compromise to resolve a conflict.

Many employees spend 40 hours or more per week on the job. Making these hours as stress free as possible is to everyone's benefit. Remember that you do not have to be friends with your coworkers. You do, however, need to be able to work with them productively.

conflict: disagreement, quarrel, or controversy

diplomatic: tactful in dealing with people

compromise: give up demands or make adjustments to reach a settlement

585

Conflict with Your Manager

You hope to have what is commonly referred to as a "good working relationship" with the person to whom you report. However, there are times when the relationship may not be good. A misunderstanding about job assignments, insensitivity to seemingly unreasonable demands, and failure to communicate how one feels about performance can lead to conflicts.

Good managers are expected to be aware of what their staff members are doing and to assess the work assigned. However, when work demands are heavy, a manager may fail to think about your work. If you receive no feedback from your manager, you may assume the work is acceptable. Perhaps the manager, however, has simply been too busy to discuss the problems with you. This difference of opinion will be revealed at some point and may lead to conflict between the employee and manager. To avoid such a situation, actively seek feedback on your work from your manager regularly. Ask specific questions to determine whether the quality and quantity of your work meet your manager's expectations.

When given a new assignment or responsibility, ask questions to be sure you understand what is expected of you. If problems develop with your work that will cause missed deadlines or results different from what your manager expects, keep your manager informed as events happen. This will help avoid conflicts between you and your manager.

Conflict Related to Ethical Behavior

Sometimes values clash in the workplace. Increasingly, organizations have established codes of conduct or ethics for all employees at all levels of the company. Policy manuals, training sessions, or self-study materials are used to inform everyone of the rules. These rules are to be honored as employees work with each other, as well as with vendors and customers.

You will want to become fully acquainted with the ethical rules that guide the organization in which you work. You want to understand the rules clearly. You should not depend on the interpretations of your colleagues.

Figure 14-2.4

Discuss the quality of your work with your manager to avoid conflicts.

Violating the company's code of ethics can lead to disciplinary measures or even dismissal from your job.

As an individual, you also have a code of ethics—a system of moral values that help you decide what behavior is appropriate and what is not. At times, your sense of what is morally right may come into conflict with the behavior of coworkers or duties related to your job. For example, coworkers may make discriminatory remarks about other employees that you find offensive or your company may ask you to work on a religious holiday. You must use your own judgment to decide how to handle such a situation. Talking about the situation with your manager is a usually a good first step. Many companies have policies and procedures in place that employees can use to resolve conflicts or report unethical behavior.

FOCUS ON . . .

Work/Life Balance

The term *work/life balance* is commonly used to describe the need workers have to balance work with other aspects of life. In the last 20 years, the number of women in the workforce has increased significantly. This change has created more families with two working parents. Single-parent families are also on the rise. Many of the activities formerly handled by a nonworking parent must now be handled by a working parent.

When you think about a career, consider how your choice will affect all aspects of your life. Different careers make different demands on workers and their families. Some jobs may require much travel, overtime, or a long commute that will reduce time for family or participating in other activities. In many jobs, taking time off to care for a sick child or pursue a personal interest is very difficult.

When employees do not have enough time to take care of their personal matters, they bring stress to the workplace and are less productive. Many companies address this problem by creating a workplace that is supportive of workers' needs. For example, some companies have childcare facilities on-site or help pay for the cost of childcare. Other companies create positions with flexible work hours. Employees in these positions can choose to arrive and leave work earlier or later than the normal working hours to accommodate their schedules. Another alternative that might be offered is a compressed workweek. Employees might work ten hours a day for four days a week, then take the fifth day off. Some companies allow job sharing. This permits two part-time employees working different shifts to fulfill the duties of one full-time worker. More companies are also providing benefits for part-time workers. Telecommuting on a part-time or full-time basis is a helpful option for some employees.

Companies find that employee loyalty increases when the company makes accommodations for workers' personal needs. Employees find that these accommodations contribute to their job satisfaction. When choosing an employer, consider whether the company fits your needs, as well as whether you fit the needs of the company.

Understanding Relevant Laws and Regulations

Organizations in the United States must adhere to certain laws and regulations of federal, state, and local governments that relate to employment. Some of the laws and regulations that relate to employment and maintaining a safe work environment are discussed in this section.

If you have a problem related to an employment law or a regulation, you will find that generally the company has someone to whom you can direct your problem. If the problem is not resolved, report it to the closest office of the agency responsible for enforcing the particular law.

Fair Labor Standards

The Fair Labor Standards Act (FLSA) sets the minimum wages for employees covered by the law. Requirements related to overtime are also specified. The Equal Pay Act makes it unlawful to pay different wages to men and women where jobs are equal in skills required, effort, responsibility, and working conditions. The Equal Pay Act and other laws are enforced by the Equal Employment Opportunity Commission (EEOC).

Freedom from Discrimination

Title VII of the Civil Rights Act of 1964 makes it illegal to discriminate in employment on the basis of a person's race, color, religion, sex, or national origin. This is the principal federal employment discrimination law. Later acts outlaw discrimination against handicapped individuals; against women because of pregnancy, childbirth, or other related medical conditions; or against anyone 40 years or older on the basis of age.

Freedom from Sexual Harassment

Title VII of the Civil Rights Act of 1964 bans discrimination on the basis of gender. Sexual harassment is one form of gender discrimination. Sexual harassment is sexually directed, unsolicited, and unwanted actions or speech that create a difficult and hostile work environment or unreasonably interferes with an individual's work performance. Both men and women can be the victims of sexual harassment. The harasser can be of the opposite sex or the same sex as the victim. The harasser can be a superior, a coworker, a customer, or another person who is not an employee.

Many companies include policies on sexual harassment in their employee handbooks. Such a policy usually states that the company will not tolerate sexual harassment and describes the procedures for reporting an incident of sexual harassment.

Safe and Healthy Workplace

The Occupational Safety and Health Act of 1970 was enacted to assure safe and healthful working conditions for working men and women in the United States. The Occupational Safety and Health Administration (OSHA) is a

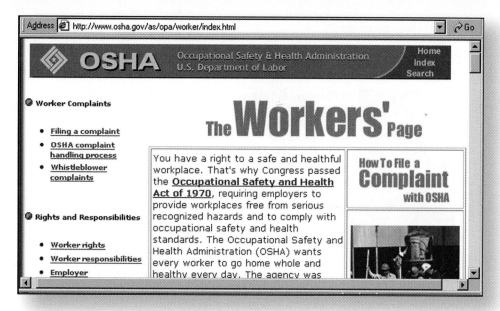

Source: Occupational Safety and Health Administration, U.S. Department of State. Online. Available: http://www.osha.gov/as/opa/worker/index.html. February 9, 2002.

Figure 14-2.5

OSHA has an extensive Web site to help employers and employees better understand how to comply with OSHA standards.

government agency responsible for enforcing this law. In addition to enforcement, OSHA provides research, information, education, and training in the field of occupational safety and health. Workplace consultations are available to businesses that want on-site help in establishing safety and health programs and identifying and correcting workplace **hazards**.

hazard: risk or danger

Unemployment Insurance

Unemployment insurance provides income for persons who have been dismissed from their jobs. To be eligible, individuals must have worked for a required time. The amount of unemployment benefit payments varies depending on the worker's wages paid during the previous year and the benefits of the particular state where the individual worked.

The provisions and restrictions of this benefit vary from state to state. In some states, workers may be denied unemployment payments for quitting a job without good reason, being fired because of misconduct while on the job, or refusing to take a job while unemployed.

Social Security Act Benefits

The Federal Social Security Act of 1935, also known as the Federal Insurance Contribution Act (FICA), provides eligible workers with:

- Retirement income
- Benefits for spouses of retired or disabled workers
- Survivor benefits
- Disability benefits
- Health insurance

Topic 14-2: *Human Relations at Work*

Figure 14-2.6

Information on full retirement age can be found on the Social Security Administration's Web site.

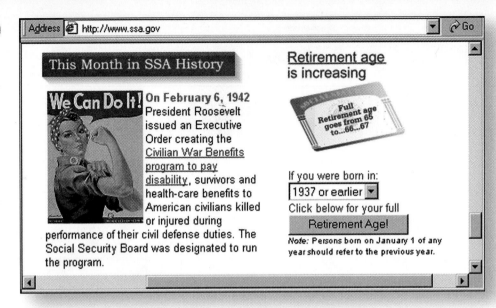

Source: Social Security. Online. Available: www.ssa.gov. February 9, 2002.

Eligible workers may start receiving reduced benefits at age 62. The age requirement for full benefits varies according to date of birth. The employee contributes to this fund, and the contributions are deducted from his or her paycheck. The employer is required to match the employee's contributions.

Reviewing the Topic

1. Identify and describe skills and characteristics required to work effectively with others.
2. List three tasks or duties that managers typically perform related to workers who report to them.
3. Why does a manager want the employees in her or his department to be successful?
4. Describe four behaviors or characteristics managers expect of office workers.
5. Why is employee loyalty important to a business?
6. Explain the meaning of confidentiality as it relates to office work.
7. Why should an employee avoid gossiping?
8. What steps can an employee take to resolve conflicts that arise at work?
9. What is the purpose of the Fair Labor Standards Act?
10. Why is freedom from discrimination important in the workplace?
11. Define sexual harassment in the workplace and give an example of speech or behavior that would likely be considered sexual harassment.
12. List three benefits provided to workers by the Social Security Act.

Interacting with Others

Peg, Jeff, and Mark were having lunch when the conversation turned to a fourth coworker, Sally, who was out ill that day. A week earlier, Sally had been told that she would not get the promotion she had expected. Sally was stunned by the news. She thought she was competent and handled all assignments she was given. When she told the unpleasant news to her three coworkers, she remarked: "How could they do this to me? Will you—my friends—tell me the truth?" Peg said: "Oh, Sally, don't make this a big deal. In a few months they will call you in to tell you that you have been promoted." Both Jeff and Mark agreed and the topic shifted.

Now, a week later, the three felt somewhat guilty about avoiding Sally's question. What they concluded was that Sally was "too loud" for the next level of responsibility. They liked Sally, but she apparently did not realize that she just didn't seem to know when she should talk quietly, when she should just keep silent, and when she should shorten her explanations! Her friends think that Sally's shortcomings resulted in her not being promoted.

1. As her friend, what would you say to Sally in this situation? Should you tell her why you think she did not get the promotion even if you think her feelings will be hurt? Why or why not?

2. Suppose that you and Sally's other friends are wrong about why Sally did not get the promotion. Who should Sally ask to be sure she learns the real reasons why she was not promoted?

Reinforcing English Skills

Companies have many different types of policies, which are often included in an employee handbook. Key the workplace monitoring policy shown below, correcting errors in spelling, punctuation, and word usage.

Workplace Monitoring Policy

Effective Date: 10/26/20--

Workplace montoring will be conducted bye the company to ensure quality control, employee safety; building security, and customer satisfoction. Because the company is sensitive to the legitimate privacy rights of employees; every effort will be made too guaranty that workplace monitoring is done inn an ethical and respectful manner. Employees should be aware of the following points related to this policy:

- Computers furnished two employes are the property of the company. As such, computer usage and files may be monitored or accesssed.

- The company may conduct video survaillance of non-private workplace areas. Video monitoring is used to identify safety concerns; maintain quality control, detect theft and misconduct, and discourage or prevent acts of harrassment and workplace violence.

- Employees can request access to information gathered throught workplace monitoring that may impakt employment decisions. Access will be granted unless their is a legitimate business reason to protect confidentiality or an ongoing investigation.

Topic 14-2   **ACTIVITY 1**

Encounter with a Manager

A staff assistant, Ana, had quietly taken on extra responsibilities when another assistant, Kay, was on an extended leave. By working extra hours and through lunch, she has just managed to do her regular work and the absent staff member's work, too. Near the end of Kay's leave, the manager stopped by Ana's desk and said: "Because you are handling both jobs so well, I'm going to recommend that Kay be assigned to another department. We really don't need her." At that point, the manager walked away.

Ana was stunned. Up to this time, she had not commented about what she was doing. She assumed that her manager was aware of the extraordinary efforts she had made to do both jobs. Ana has asked to meet with the manager to discuss the situation.

1. Assume you are Ana. Describe clearly in two or three sentences what you want the outcome of the meeting with your manager to be.
2. Compose a list of the main points you will make in the meeting with your manager in an effort to achieve the outcome you want.
3. What kinds of supporting materials might you take to the meeting to support your points?
4. Describe the attitude with which you will approach this meeting.
5. What might you (Ana) have done during the past few weeks to help avoid the conflict you now face with your manager?

Topic 14-2   **ACTIVITY 2**

Compare Policies and Procedures

To combat sexual harassment in the workplace, many companies adopt a sexual harassment policy. This policy usually defines sexual harassment, gives examples of inappropriate behavior and speech, and outlines a procedure for filing complaints. In this activity, you will compare the sexual harassment policies of three companies.

1. Open and print the data file **Harassment.pdf**, which contains the sexual harassment policies.
2. Read the three sexual harassment policies.
3. Write a short unbound report that gives a definition of sexual harassment. Describe how the three policies differ and how they are alike, especially in procedures for reporting cases of harassment.

Summary

The personal qualities that individuals bring with them to the workplace and the nature of working with others are the topics of this chapter. Among the key points you should understand from your study are these.

- Character, as reflected in a person's integrity and reliability, is a central component of an individual's personality.

- Self-acceptance is necessary if an individual wants to make personality changes.

- A positive yet realistic attitude toward yourself means that you can assess your own qualities honestly and that you understand that you share common wants, needs, and fears with others.

- Maturing is a long-term process that is critical to full development of a personality.

- Quality performance at work is a common, general goal in many organizations.

- Appearances influence impressions and therefore require attention on the part of individuals at work.

- Individuals are expected to behave in accordance with established business manners that promote pleasant interactions with each other.

- Employees need to become acquainted with the expectations and work style of their managers.

- Frequent interaction is common in organizations, and ways to ensure fair and honorable association with others need to be understood.

- Conflicts arise at work, but willingness to face them candidly can lead to resolutions.

- Laws and regulations related to work need to be understood by all employees.

Key Terms

business attire
character
confidentiality
conflict resolution
cooperation
employment
   discrimination

ethics
gossip
loyalty
personality
safe workplace
sexual harassment
Social Security Act

unemployment
   insurance
work ethic
work manners

COMPOSITION
INTERNET
RESEARCH
WORD PROCESSING

Chapter 14   ACTIVITY 1

Report on Unethical Behavior in Business

Companies expect employees to behave in an ethical manner, and the public expects companies to behave in an ethical manner. When ethics are disregarded, the company or the public often suffers. In this activity, you will do research to find examples of unethical behavior by businesspeople or by businesses and discuss the results of such behavior.

1. Use the Internet or other resources to find two articles that describe unethical behavior by a businessperson or a company. Copy or print the articles, if possible, or take notes of the important facts and points made in the articles. Record complete source information for each article.

2. Write a short report using your research. Begin by explaining what is meant by ethical behavior. Then describe the incidents of unethical behavior from the articles you found. Explain the consequences of the unethical behavior to the company or the public. Add your personal comments regarding the incidents. Include the reference information for the articles you read at the end of your report.

3. Format the report in unbound report style. Proofread and correct all errors before printing the report.

Compare Job Opportunities

Choosing a job that provides the tangible and intangible rewards of work that you desire will increase your job satisfaction. In this activity, you will evaluate two job opportunities and decide which one you would choose, considering both tangible and intangible benefits.

1. Open and print the data file **Jobs.pdf**, which contains information about two jobs. Read the description for each job. Identify tangible and intangible rewards for each job. Also identify any factors that you think are negative about each job.

2. Write a paragraph that identifies the job you would choose. Explain what tangible and intangible factors made you choose this job. Describe any factors that you think are negative about the job you chose.

Glossary

A

Accession log list of numbers assigned in a numeric filing system

Accounts payable short-term debts a company owes

Accounts receivable short-term debts owed to a company by others, such as its customers

Action plan description of tasks to be accomplished

Agenda document that contains the information for a meeting such as the participants and topics to be discussed

Analog transmitted by a signal that corresponds to a physical change such as sound

Annotate write comments related to the content of a message

Appendix section of a report that provides detailed or supplementary data

Aptitude a natural ability or talent

Archive keep permanently in inactive files

Assets cash or other goods or property owned by an organization or an individual

Automated processed by machine

Automated attendant computerized system for handling telephone calls

B

Bank reconciliation report used to compare bank and company account records

Bar code pattern of vertical lines of varying widths containing coded information that can be read by a computerized scanner

Bar graph chart used to show comparisons

Body language posture, body movements, gestures, and facial expressions that serve as nonverbal communication

Bonding insurance for financial loss due to employee theft or fraud

Budget a plan for allocating resources

C

Caption notation on a file guide, folder, or drawer that indicates the contents

Carpal tunnel syndrome a repetitive strain injury that occurs when stress is placed on the hands, wrists, or arms

Cellular telephone communications device that uses wireless, radio frequencies to transmit voice across geographic segments

Character reputation, values, or principles as shown by behavior

Charging out removing a record from the file and recording pertinent information

Checks written orders to a bank to make payment against the depositor's funds in that bank

Chronologic file records arranged according to date

Chronologically arranged in order of time

Code of ethics moral standards or values and related behavior; also called code of conduct

Coding marking a record to indicate how it is indexed

Colloquialism informal language used among a particular group

Commission payment based on the price of items sold

Compact disc optical storage medium for electronic data, CD

Comprehension ability to understand concepts or material that has been read

Compromise give up demands or make adjustments to reach a settlement

Computer virus destructive program loaded onto a computer and run without the user's knowledge

Computer-assisted retrieval the process of locating records on film by using computer-stored indexes

Confidential private or secret in nature

Consulate person appointed by a government to serve its citizens and business interests in another country

Continuous improvement being alert at all times to ways of working more productively

Copyright laws regulations covering what documents or other information can be legally copied

Corporation a business organized under the laws of a particular state for which a charter was secured

Cross-reference document that gives the alternate name or subject by which a record may be requested and the name or subject by which the record is filed

Custom government tax or duty on imported items; a usual practice, way of behaving, or social convention

D

Data mining process in which software program searches for significant patterns in data

Data processing collecting, organizing, analyzing, and summarizing of data

Debit card a kind of bank card that allows the cost of purchases to be automatically deducted from the cardholder's bank account

Demographic data statistics that describe a population such as age or race

Desktop organizer program computer software used to schedule appointments and tasks and manage contact information

Desktop publishing Using a computer and software to create high-quality and often complex printed documents

Digital stored or transmitted by a process using groups of electronic bits of data that can be read by a computer

Diplomatic tactful in dealing with people

Direct deposit electronically transferring an amount of money into a bank account

Diversity reflected in a workforce with people from a wide range of ethnic and cultural backgrounds

Downsize reduce, as in decreasing the number of workers in an organization

Draft a rough or preliminary version of a written message

E

Ecommerce business conducted electronically, as in making purchases or selling products via the World Wide Web

Electronic database a collection of records accessible by computer

Electronic imaging converting paper documents to pictures stored and displayed via computer

Electronic ticket document and receipt that contains ticket information as opposed to a paper ticket

E-mail the electronic transfer of messages using computers and software

Embassy the offices of an ambassador in a foreign country

Employee empowerment enabling employees to make decisions

Employee handbook printed or online manual containing company policies and procedures

Endorsement a signature of a payee on the back of a check authorizing the bank to cash or deposit the check

Enunciation pronouncing words clearly

Ergonomics study of the effects of the work environment on the health and well-being of employees

Ethics a system of moral standards or values

Etiquette standards for proper behavior

Extranet an information network like an intranet, but partially available to select outside users

Ezine electronic magazine available on the World Wide Web

F

File path the complete location designation (directory and subdirectories) for an electronic file

File transfer protocol (FTP) tool that allows files to be uploaded to or downloaded from a remote computer

Filing the process of storing records in an orderly manner within an organized system

Firewall software and hardware designed to prevent unauthorized users from gaining access to a computer or network

Fiscal year a 12-month period used for financial accounting purposes

Font style or design for a set of type characters

Footer information that appears below the body text at the bottom of document pages

Format arrangement or layout, as of text on a page

Freelancer independent contractors who work for others, usually on a project-by-project basis

G

Geographic file records arranged according to locations

Global marketplace buying and selling of goods or services throughout the world

Graph pictorial representation of data

Gross salary money earned before any deductions are made

H

Hard disk magnetic medium used to store large amounts of information

Hardware the physical parts of a computer or related equipment

Header information that appears above the body text on pages of a document

Hoteling assigning temporary office workspace to workers as needed

HTML hypertext markup language, authoring language used for World Wide Web and intranet documents

Hypertext highlighted, underlined, or contrast-colored words or images that, when clicked, take you to another location

I

Imaging system equipment and procedures used to convert documents to electronic form

Indexing deciding how to identify each record to be filed

Information data or facts that have been summarized or organized into a meaningful form

Information management organizing, maintaining, and accessing records or data

Information processing putting facts or numbers into a meaningful and useful form

Integrity honesty, sincerity, being of sound moral principle

Intelligent agent computer program that works independently to accomplish a specific task such as retrieving and delivering information

Interactive involving the user or receiver, exchanging information

Interactive voice response recorded messages accessed and directed by the user to provide or record information

Internal control methods used by a business to safeguard assets

Internet a public, worldwide computer network made up of smaller, interconnected networks that spans the globe

Internet service provider company that sells users access to the Internet

Intonation the rise and fall in voice pitch

Intranet communications network within an organization that is meant for the use of its employees or members

Itinerary document giving detailed plans for a trip

J

Job board Web site that provides job listings and allows persons seeking employment to post resumes

Job portfolio file containing documents and information related to employment

L

Liabilities debts owed by an organization or an individual

Line graph chart used to display trends that emerge over a period of time

Local area network group of connected computers that are close to each other

M

Macro a list of computer commands, actions, or keystrokes that can be executed with a single command

Magnetic media disks or tapes used to store documents electronically

Mailing list directory of Internet user addresses

Media materials or means used to communicate

Microfiche a small rectangular sheet of microfilm that contains a series of records arranged in rows and columns

Micrographics photographically reducing documents to file on microfilm

Minutes written record of meeting proceedings and decisions

Mission statement the goals, priorities, and beliefs of a company

Mobile office office temporarily located at a particular site or that can move from place to place

Modem device that allows computer data to be transmitted via the telephone system

Modular workstation work area made up of interchangeable components such as sound-absorbing wall panels, storage areas, and a desktop surface

Motion a proposal formally made in a meeting

Multimedia projector device that shows video images from a personal computer or videocassette recorder on a screen

N

Negligence failure to use a reasonable amount of care resulting in damage

Net pay final earnings amount after all deductions

Netiquette guidelines for proper behavior when communicating online, derived from *network* and *etiquette*

Newsgroup publication of online articles and messages related to a certain topic

Nonterritorial workspace area not assigned to a specific person or task

O

Online available in electronic format such as on the Internet or an intranet

Optical character reader electronic equipment that can scan or "read" text

Optical character recognition reading text printed on paper and translating the images into words that can be saved in a computer file and edited

Overhead business costs not directly related to a product or service sold

Overtime hours worked beyond the standard number in a workweek

Owner's equity owner's share of the worth of a firm, capital

P

Pager electronic device that alerts the user of the need to respond by telephone

Pagination the process of dividing a document into individual pages for printing

Parcel post a class of standard mail used for packages

Parliamentary procedures guide for conducting meetings

Partnership A business that is not incorporated and has two or more owners

Passive voice style of writing in which the subject is acted upon rather than performing the action

Passport official US government document that grants permission to travel outside the United States

Password series of letters, numbers, or symbols used to identify a user and gain access to a computer system

Payroll list of employees and amount of salary or wages due to each

Performance review evaluation of an employee's work, also called performance evaluation or performance appraisal

Personal digital organizer electronic device for storing contact information and scheduling appointments and tasks, may be able to share data with a computer

Personality patterns and qualities of behavior and attitudes of an individual

Petty cash money kept on hand for paying small expenses

Pie chart graph showing how a part contributes to the whole

Postage meter a machine that prints postage in the amount needed

Preventive maintenance servicing equipment and replacing parts to prevent failure

Prioritize put in order of importance

Proficiency ability to perform at a satisfactory level

Profile description, picture

Project management programs software with advanced features for planning large or long-term tasks

Proofreading checking a document carefully for errors or omissions

Proprietary information privately owned information, such as a design or formula, also called intellectual property

Q

Quorum minimum number of members that must be present at a meeting to conduct business

Quotation excerpt from a different source

R

Records disposition transferring records to permanent storage or destroying records

Records management software computer program that allows electronic tracking and control of records

Records management system a set of procedures used to organize, store, retrieve, and dispose of records

References sources of information, such as those used in preparing a report; persons who know your work abilities, skills, and habits and are willing to recommend you to prospective employers

Relational database software program that allows the user to link data from a number of database files or tables to find information or generate reports

Reprographics process of making copies of graphic images, such as printed documents

Requisition card form that has space for charge-out information for a record

Resume document that presents job qualifications such as training, skills, and work experience

Retention schedule list of how long various types of records should be kept

S

Sales channel method of marketing products, such as through retail stores or catalogs

Satellite man-made object placed in orbit around the Earth containing electronic devices for relaying communications data

Secondary storage storage media or devices outside the internal memory of a computer system

Severance pay payment made to an employee being dismissed from a company

Single proprietorship a business owned by one individual, also called sole proprietorship

Slang informal language

Software programs containing instructions for a computer

Spam electronic junk mail, advertisements, or other messages not requested by the recipient and often sent in a mass mailing

Speech recognition software computer programs that allow the user to input text and commands by speaking into a microphone

Storyboarding recording and organizing ideas, as for a presentation

Surge suppressor electrical outlet that controls unexpected sharp increases in electricity

Synopsis general overview or summary

T

Telecommunications electronic transfer of information over a distance

Telecommute the practice of working and communicating with others from a remote location

Teleconference a meeting of two or more people in different locations conducted using telecommunications equipment

Telegram message delivered by Western Union

Telephony integration of computer and telephone technologies

Tickler file a chronological system for keeping track of future actions

Time management planning to gain control over how time is spent

Tone style, manner of writing or speaking that shows a certain attitude

Total quality management establishing and maintaining high standards in how work is done

V

Vendor organization that sell goods or services

Videoconferencing communication system that uses two-way voice and video

Virtual office the capability to perform work activities away from a traditional office setting

Visa a permit granted by a foreign government for a person to enter its country

Visual aid picture, chart, graphic

Vocabulary collection of words

Voice mail messaging system that uses computers and telephones to record, store, and retrieve voice messages

Voice recognition software computer programs that allow voice input

W

Wide area network links computers that are separated by long distances

Word processing producing written documents such as letters or reports

Work ethic a system of values in which purposeful activity is of central importance

Work permit registers the presence of a person as a visitor to a country on specific business

Work simplification process of improving the procedures for doing work

World Wide Web computers on the Internet that use and transmit HTML documents

Index

Note: **Boldface** numbers indicate illustrations.

orientation programs for new jobs, 547, 562

professional and trade associations for, 554–555, 563

promotions, 554, 563

references and resources for, 549

references for resume, 534

resignation letters in, 557, 560, 563

resumes for, 530, 533–537, **535**, 546, 562

severance pay in, 556

sexual harassment in, 588

termination from job, 555–556, 563

vested benefits and, 557

W-4 form and, 548, **548**

point size, 147

portfolio, 291–292, 558, 563

positive messages, 133, 140–141, 174

postage meters, 461–462, 478

postcards and postal cards, 465

posters, presentation, 202–204, **204**

postsecondary schools, 44

posture and gestures, 214, 299

prejudgments, 182

preliminary pages for reports, 160, 187

prepaid, 471

prepaid phone cards, 517–518

presentation software, 76

presentations, 193–222

    advantages to listener in, 196

    appearance of speaker in, 211

    audience for, 212–215

    closing remarks for, 218

    color use in, 200

    continuity in, 205

    creating visual elements for, 198–199

    delivering, 209–222

    design strategies for, 200–201

    enthusiasm and convincing attitude in, 214

    evaluating, and evaluation forms for, 218–219, **219**, 222, 224

eye contact during, 212

flip charts in, 197, **197**

focusing the audience in, 215

graphics (pictures) vs. words in, 199

handouts and posters for, 202–204, **204**, 223

idea organization for, 194

intonation and inflection of voice in, 215

media selection for, 196–198

meeting room preparation for, 210–211

message development for, 194–196

motion in, 198, 201–202

multimedia, 198

non-words, avoiding use of, 212–213

notes for, 209

objections of listener in, 196

opening remarks for, 211

overhead transparencies in, 197–198, **198**, 200

planning and organizing, 207

posture and gestures of speaker in, 214

practicing and preparing for, 209–211

profiling listeners for, 193

purpose of, 193

question-and-answer period for, 216–218

researching for, 224

slides in, 200

sound (audio) in, 198, 202

speaking skills in, 212–215

storyboarding for, 194–195, **195**, 223

supporting details for, 196

team type, 204–205, 225

text in, 200

transitions in, 201

videotaping, 209, 223

visual aids for, 196–199, 208, 215–216, 223

white space in, 200

president, 23

press release, 176

preventive internal controls, 227–229

preventive maintenance, 296, 313

prioritizing, 42, 143, 281, 452

Priority Mail, 467

privacy of information, 83, 105, 110, 449

processing, 4, 5, 72, 109

procrastination, 278

product information systems, 91

production supervisors, 91

production workers, 25, 91

productivity, 10, 55–56

professional and trade associations, 554–555, 563

professional reading file, 61–62

professional service organizations, 16–17

proficiency, 38

profile, 193

profit, 15, 18, 19

profit and loss statement, 19

project management, 76, 281–282, 284, 291–292

projected income statements, 254, **255**, 273–274

projections, 34

promoting organizations on the Internet, 103–104, 110

promotions, 554, 563

pronouns, 191, 335

pronunciation, 503

proof of mailing or delivery, 471

proofreading, 132–133, **132**, 149

proportional fonts, 147

proprietary information, 84, 449

protecting vital records, 412

protocol, 135, 174

proving cash procedure, 231

Publication 587 (IRS), Business Use of Your Home, 13

punctuation, 87, 124, 137, 353

purchase orders, 235

purchase requisitions, 235, **236**, 273

purchasing schedules, 271–273

confirming reservations for, 340

consulates and embassies of U.S., 347

dress for, 344

etiquette for, 342–344, 354, 356–357

expense reports for, 351, 356

follow-up activities for, 350–351

foreign travel, customs, and protocols of, 345–348, 357–358

health documents for, 347–348, 356

hotel/motel accommodations for, 340–341

itinerary and travel folder for, 337, 341–342, **343**, 353–354, 355

meeting reports from, 351

passports, 346–347, 356

rental cars in, 339, 340, 353–354

reservations for, 353–354, 355

safety during, 348–349, 356–357

thank you and follow-up letters following, 351

tourist cards for foreign travel, 348, 356

trains for, 340

travel agencies and, 339

visas, 347, 356

work permits for foreign travel, 348, 356

working away from the office, 349–350

travel agencies, 339

travel expense reports, 351, 356

travel folder, 337

Trojan horses, 83

troubleshooting, 296

twisted-pair cable, 78

U

U.S. Census Bureau, 93, **93**

U.S. Department of Labor Web site, **101**

U.S. Department of State, 346, 348

unbound reports, 159, **161**

unemployment insurance, 589

Uniform Resource Locators (URLs), 100

United States Postal Service (USPS), 140, 457, 478

USAJobs Web site, 531

useful records, 370

Usenet, 103

utility software, 75, 76, 109

V

vaccination, 347

vaulting records, 412, 438

vendors, 4, 235

verbatim, 321

verify, 228

vertical file cabinets, 408, **409**, 438

vested benefits, 557

vice presidents, 23

videoconferencing, 331–332, 486–487

videotaping presentations, 209, 223

virtual offices, 7, 8

virus protection, 77, 83, 85

visas, 347, 356

visiting local offices, 12

visual aids in presentations, 196–199, 208, 215–216, 223

visual aids in reports, 164–168, 175

vital records, 370, 412, 438

vocabulary, 118, 504

voice communication systems, 487–495

voice information, 67, 109

voice mail systems, 489–490, 491, 500, 575

voice recognition systems, 156

volume mailings, 462–463

volume of voice, 503

voluntary deductions, 262

vouchers, 236, **237**

W

W-2 form, 262

W-4 form, 261, **262**, 548, **548**

Web browsers, 76, 99–100, 110

Web conferencing, 332

Web sites, 110

weighing envelopes, 460

Wellness Councils of America (WELCOA), 298

wellness in the workplace, 298

Western Union telegrams, 473

white space, 147, 200

wide area networks (WANs), 77, 79–81, 109

widow lines, 147, 169

window envelopes, 459

wireless communications, 78, 80

withholding allowance (See W-4 form)

wizards, 75

word processing, 37–39, 76

work activity planning, 280–281

work ethic, 571

work permits for foreign travel, 348, 356

work simplification, 282–283

workflow analysis, 282–283

working alone, safety considerations, 305

working with others, 566–596

attitudes supporting quality performance, 571–572

character and, 567

compromises in, 585

confidentiality in, 583

conflicts in, 585–587

cooperation in, 583

coworker interactions and, 582–584

diplomatic behavior in, 585

discrimination in, 588

dress, 572–573, 579

electronic etiquette in, 574–576

ethics and integrity in, 567, 586–587, 595

gossip, 584

habits and, 573

human relations at work, 580–596

impressions influence others in, 572–573